Android Studio 3.5 Development Essentials

Java Edition

Android Studio 3.5 Development Essentials – Java Edition

ISBN-13: 978-1-951442-01-9

Contents

Table of Contents

1. Introduction 1

    1.1 Downloading the Code Samples 1

    1.2 Feedback 2

    1.3 Errata 2

    1.4 Download the eBook 2

2. Setting up an Android Studio Development Environment 3

    2.1 System Requirements 3

    2.2 Downloading the Android Studio Package 3

    2.3 Installing Android Studio 4

        2.3.1 Installation on Windows 4

        2.3.2 Installation on macOS 4

        2.3.3 Installation on Linux 5

    2.4 The Android Studio Setup Wizard 5

    2.5 Installing Additional Android SDK Packages 6

    2.6 Making the Android SDK Tools Command-line Accessible 8

        2.6.1 Windows 7 8

        2.6.2 Windows 8.1 9

        2.6.3 Windows 10 9

        2.6.4 Linux 10

        2.6.5 macOS 10

    2.7 Android Studio Memory Management 10

    2.8 Updating Android Studio and the SDK 11

    2.9 Summary 11

3. Creating an Example Android App in Android Studio 13

    3.1 About the Project 13

    3.2 Creating a New Android Project 13

    3.3 Creating an Activity 14

    3.4 Defining the Project and SDK Settings 14

    3.5 Modifying the Example Application 15

    3.6 Reviewing the Layout and Resource Files 22

    3.7 Adding Interaction 25

    3.8 Summary 26

4. Creating an Android Virtual Device (AVD) in Android Studio 27

    4.1 About Android Virtual Devices 27

    4.2 Creating a New AVD 28

    4.3 Starting the Emulator 29

    4.4 Running the Application in the AVD 29

    4.5 Stopping a Running Application 31

    4.6 Supporting Dark Theme 31

    4.7 AVD Command-line Creation 33

    4.8 Android Virtual Device Configuration Files 34

4.9 Moving and Renaming an Android Virtual Device 34

4.10 Summary 35

5. Using and Configuring the Android Studio AVD Emulator 37

5.1 The Emulator Environment 37

5.2 The Emulator Toolbar Options... 37

5.3 Working in Zoom Mode 39

5.4 Resizing the Emulator Window... 39

5.5 Extended Control Options 39

5.5.1 Location 39

5.5.2 Cellular 40

5.5.3 Camera 40

5.5.4 Battery 40

5.5.5 Phone 40

5.5.6 Directional Pad.. 40

5.5.7 Microphone.. 40

5.5.8 Fingerprint 40

5.5.9 Virtual Sensors... 40

5.5.10 Snapshots... 40

5.5.11 Record and Playback 40

5.5.12 Google Play 41

5.5.13 Settings 41

5.5.14 Help 41

5.6 Working with Snapshots.. 41

5.7 Configuring Fingerprint Emulation 42

5.8 Summary 43

6. A Tour of the Android Studio User Interface 45

6.1 The Welcome Screen... 45

6.2 The Main Window 46

6.3 The Tool Windows 47

6.4 Android Studio Keyboard Shortcuts 50

6.5 Switcher and Recent Files Navigation 50

6.6 Changing the Android Studio Theme 51

6.7 Summary 51

7. Testing Android Studio Apps on a Physical Android Device... 53

7.1 An Overview of the Android Debug Bridge (ADB).. 53

7.2 Enabling ADB on Android based Devices... 53

7.2.1 macOS ADB Configuration 54

7.2.2 Windows ADB Configuration 55

7.2.3 Linux adb Configuration... 56

7.3 Testing the adb Connection.. 56

7.4 Summary 57

8. The Basics of the Android Studio Code Editor.. 59

8.1 The Android Studio Editor... 59

8.2 Splitting the Editor Window... 61

8.3 Code Completion 62

8.4 Statement Completion.. 63

8.5 Parameter Information 64

8.6 Parameter Name Hints 64
8.7 Code Generation 64
8.8 Code Folding... 65
8.9 Quick Documentation Lookup 67
8.10 Code Reformatting... 67
8.11 Finding Sample Code 68
8.12 Summary 68

9. An Overview of the Android Architecture **69**
9.1 The Android Software Stack 69
9.2 The Linux Kernel 70
9.3 Android Runtime – ART 70
9.4 Android Libraries 70
9.4.1 C/C++ Libraries 71
9.5 Application Framework... 71
9.6 Applications 72
9.7 Summary 72

10. The Anatomy of an Android Application **73**
10.1 Android Activities.. 73
10.2 Android Fragments 73
10.3 Android Intents 74
10.4 Broadcast Intents 74
10.5 Broadcast Receivers 74
10.6 Android Services 74
10.7 Content Providers 75
10.8 The Application Manifest 75
10.9 Application Resources 75
10.10 Application Context 75
10.11 Summary 75

11. Understanding Android Application and Activity Lifecycles **77**
11.1 Android Applications and Resource Management... 77
11.2 Android Process States 77
11.2.1 Foreground Process 78
11.2.2 Visible Process 78
11.2.3 Service Process 78
11.2.4 Background Process... 78
11.2.5 Empty Process 79
11.3 Inter-Process Dependencies 79
11.4 The Activity Lifecycle.. 79
11.5 The Activity Stack.. 79
11.6 Activity States 80
11.7 Configuration Changes 80
11.8 Handling State Change 81
11.9 Summary 81

12. Handling Android Activity State Changes.. **83**
12.1 New vs. Old Lifecycle Techniques... 83
12.2 The Activity and Fragment Classes... 83
12.3 Dynamic State vs. Persistent State... 86

12.4 The Android Lifecycle Methods 86
12.5 Lifetimes 88
12.6 Foldable Devices and Multi-Resume 89
12.7 Disabling Configuration Change Restarts 89
12.8 Lifecycle Method Limitations 89
12.9 Summary 90

13. Android Activity State Changes by Example **91**

13.1 Creating the State Change Example Project 91
13.2 Designing the User Interface 92
13.3 Overriding the Activity Lifecycle Methods 92
13.4 Filtering the Logcat Panel 96
13.5 Running the Application 97
13.6 Experimenting with the Activity 97
13.7 Summary 98

14. Saving and Restoring the State of an Android Activity **99**

14.1 Saving Dynamic State 99
14.2 Default Saving of User Interface State 99
14.3 The Bundle Class 100
14.4 Saving the State 101
14.5 Restoring the State 102
14.6 Testing the Application 103
14.7 Summary 103

15. Understanding Android Views, View Groups and Layouts **105**

15.1 Designing for Different Android Devices 105
15.2 Views and View Groups 105
15.3 Android Layout Managers 105
15.4 The View Hierarchy 107
15.5 Creating User Interfaces 108
15.6 Summary 108

16. A Guide to the Android Studio Layout Editor Tool **109**

16.1 Basic vs. Empty Activity Templates 109
16.2 The Android Studio Layout Editor 111
16.3 Design Mode 112
16.4 The Palette 113
16.5 Design and Layout Views 113
16.6 Text Mode 114
16.7 Setting Attributes 115
16.8 Converting Views 117
16.9 Displaying Sample Data 117
16.10 Creating a Custom Device Definition 118
16.11 Changing the Current Device 119
16.12 Summary 119

17. A Guide to the Android ConstraintLayout **121**

17.1 How ConstraintLayout Works 121
17.1.1 Constraints 121
17.1.2 Margins 122

17.1.3 Opposing Constraints 122

17.1.4 Constraint Bias 123

17.1.5 Chains 124

17.1.6 Chain Styles 124

17.2 Baseline Alignment 125

17.3 Working with Guidelines 126

17.4 Configuring Widget Dimensions 126

17.5 Working with Barriers 126

17.6 Ratios 128

17.7 ConstraintLayout Advantages 128

17.8 ConstraintLayout Availability 128

17.9 Summary 129

18. A Guide to using ConstraintLayout in Android Studio **131**

18.1 Design and Layout Views 131

18.2 Autoconnect Mode 132

18.3 Inference Mode 133

18.4 Manipulating Constraints Manually 133

18.5 Adding Constraints in the Inspector 135

18.6 Viewing Constraints in the Attributes Window 135

18.7 Deleting Constraints 136

18.8 Adjusting Constraint Bias 137

18.9 Understanding ConstraintLayout Margins 137

18.10 The Importance of Opposing Constraints and Bias 139

18.11 Configuring Widget Dimensions 141

18.12 Adding Guidelines 142

18.13 Adding Barriers 143

18.14 Widget Group Alignment and Distribution 145

18.15 Converting other Layouts to ConstraintLayout 146

18.16 Summary 146

19. Working with ConstraintLayout Chains and Ratios in Android Studio **147**

19.1 Creating a Chain 147

19.2 Changing the Chain Style 149

19.3 Spread Inside Chain Style 150

19.4 Packed Chain Style 150

19.5 Packed Chain Style with Bias 150

19.6 Weighted Chain 150

19.7 Working with Ratios 151

19.8 Summary 153

20. An Android Studio Layout Editor ConstraintLayout Tutorial **155**

20.1 An Android Studio Layout Editor Tool Example 155

20.2 Creating a New Activity 155

20.3 Preparing the Layout Editor Environment 157

20.4 Adding the Widgets to the User Interface 158

20.5 Adding the Constraints 161

20.6 Testing the Layout 162

20.7 Using the Layout Inspector 163

20.8 Summary 163

21. Manual XML Layout Design in Android Studio **165**

21.1 Manually Creating an XML Layout 165
21.2 Manual XML vs. Visual Layout Design 168
21.3 Summary 168

22. Managing Constraints using Constraint Sets **169**

22.1 Java Code vs. XML Layout Files 169
22.2 Creating Views 169
22.3 View Attributes 170
22.4 Constraint Sets 170
22.4.1 Establishing Connections 170
22.4.2 Applying Constraints to a Layout 170
22.4.3 Parent Constraint Connections 170
22.4.4 Sizing Constraints 171
22.4.5 Constraint Bias 171
22.4.6 Alignment Constraints 171
22.4.7 Copying and Applying Constraint Sets 171
22.4.8 ConstraintLayout Chains 171
22.4.9 Guidelines 172
22.4.10 Removing Constraints 172
22.4.11 Scaling 172
22.4.12 Rotation 173
22.5 Summary 173

23. An Android ConstraintSet Tutorial **175**

23.1 Creating the Example Project in Android Studio 175
23.2 Adding Views to an Activity 175
23.3 Setting View Attributes 176
23.4 Creating View IDs 177
23.5 Configuring the Constraint Set 178
23.6 Adding the EditText View 179
23.7 Converting Density Independent Pixels (dp) to Pixels (px) 180
23.8 Summary 181

24. A Guide to using Apply Changes in Android Studio **183**

24.1 Introducing Apply Changes 183
24.2 Understanding Apply Changes Options 183
24.3 Using Apply Changes 184
24.4 Configuring Apply Changes Fallback Settings 185
24.5 An Apply Changes Tutorial 185
24.6 Using Apply Code Changes 186
24.7 Using Apply Changes and Restart Activity 186
24.8 Using Run App 187
24.9 Summary 187

25. An Overview and Example of Android Event Handling **189**

25.1 Understanding Android Events 189
25.2 Using the android:onClick Resource 189
25.3 Event Listeners and Callback Methods 190
25.4 An Event Handling Example 190
25.5 Designing the User Interface 191

25.6 The Event Listener and Callback Method..192
25.7 Consuming Events 193
25.8 Summary 195

26. Android Touch and Multi-touch Event Handling **197**

26.1 Intercepting Touch Events 197
26.2 The MotionEvent Object 197
26.3 Understanding Touch Actions...198
26.4 Handling Multiple Touches 198
26.5 An Example Multi-Touch Application 198
26.6 Designing the Activity User Interface 199
26.7 Implementing the Touch Event Listener..199
26.8 Running the Example Application 202
26.9 Summary 203

27. Detecting Common Gestures using the Android Gesture Detector Class........................... **205**

27.1 Implementing Common Gesture Detection..205
27.2 Creating an Example Gesture Detection Project 206
27.3 Implementing the Listener Class..206
27.4 Creating the GestureDetectorCompat Instance 209
27.5 Implementing the onTouchEvent() Method 209
27.6 Testing the Application...210
27.7 Summary 210

28. Implementing Custom Gesture and Pinch Recognition on Android **211**

28.1 The Android Gesture Builder Application..211
28.2 The GestureOverlayView Class 211
28.3 Detecting Gestures..211
28.4 Identifying Specific Gestures 211
28.5 Installing and Running the Gesture Builder Application 212
28.6 Creating a Gestures File 212
28.7 Creating the Example Project...212
28.8 Extracting the Gestures File from the SD Card 213
28.9 Adding the Gestures File to the Project 213
28.10 Designing the User Interface 213
28.11 Loading the Gestures File 214
28.12 Registering the Event Listener..215
28.13 Implementing the onGesturePerformed Method..215
28.14 Testing the Application..216
28.15 Configuring the GestureOverlayView 217
28.16 Intercepting Gestures..217
28.17 Detecting Pinch Gestures..217
28.18 A Pinch Gesture Example Project..218
28.19 Summary 220

29. An Introduction to Android Fragments **221**

29.1 What is a Fragment? 221
29.2 Creating a Fragment 221
29.3 Adding a Fragment to an Activity using the Layout XML File...................................222
29.4 Adding and Managing Fragments in Code 224
29.5 Handling Fragment Events 225

29.6 Implementing Fragment Communication...225
29.7 Summary 227

30. Using Fragments in Android Studio - An Example..**229**

30.1 About the Example Fragment Application 229
30.2 Creating the Example Project 229
30.3 Creating the First Fragment Layout...229
30.4 Creating the First Fragment Class 231
30.5 Creating the Second Fragment Layout 232
30.6 Adding the Fragments to the Activity 234
30.7 Making the Toolbar Fragment Talk to the Activity 235
30.8 Making the Activity Talk to the Text Fragment 239
30.9 Testing the Application...240
30.10 Summary...240

31. Modern Android App Architecture with Jetpack..**241**

31.1 What is Android Jetpack? 241
31.2 The "Old" Architecture 241
31.3 Modern Android Architecture 241
31.4 The ViewModel Component 242
31.5 The LiveData Component 242
31.6 LiveData and Data Binding...243
31.7 Android Lifecycles 244
31.8 Repository Modules...244
31.9 Summary 245

32. An Android Jetpack ViewModel Tutorial..**247**

32.1 About the Project 247
32.2 Creating the ViewModel Example Project..247
32.3 Reviewing the Project 247
32.3.1 The Main Activity..248
32.3.2 The Content Fragment 248
32.3.3 The ViewModel 249
32.4 Designing the Fragment Layout 249
32.5 Implementing the View Model..250
32.6 Associating the Fragment with the View Model..251
32.7 Modifying the Fragment 251
32.8 Accessing the ViewModel Data 253
32.9 Testing the Project...253
32.10 Summary..254

33. An Android Jetpack LiveData Tutorial...**255**

33.1 LiveData - A Recap 255
33.2 Adding LiveData to the ViewModel..255
33.3 Implementing the Observer...257
33.4 Summary 259

34. An Overview of Android Jetpack Data Binding..**261**

34.1 An Overview of Data Binding...261
34.2 The Key Components of Data Binding 261
34.2.1 The Project Build Configuration..261

34.2.2 The Data Binding Layout File..262
34.2.3 The Layout File Data Element 263
34.2.4 The Binding Classes 264
34.2.5 Data Binding Variable Configuration 264
34.2.6 Binding Expressions (One-Way)...265
34.2.7 Binding Expressions (Two-Way)...266
34.2.8 Event and Listener Bindings 266
34.3 Summary 267

35. An Android Jetpack Data Binding Tutorial **269**
35.1 Removing the Redundant Code 269
35.2 Enabling Data Binding 271
35.3 Adding the Layout Element 272
35.4 Adding the Data Element to Layout File...273
35.5 Working with the Binding Class 273
35.6 Assigning the ViewModel Instance to the Data Binding Variable 274
35.7 Adding Binding Expressions 275
35.8 Adding the Conversion Method 276
35.9 Adding a Listener Binding 276
35.10 Testing the App...277
35.11 Summary 277

36. Working with Android Lifecycle-Aware Components **279**
36.1 Lifecycle Awareness 279
36.2 Lifecycle Owners 279
36.3 Lifecycle Observers 280
36.4 Lifecycle States and Events..281
36.5 Summary 282

37. An Android Jetpack Lifecycle Awareness Tutorial **283**
37.1 Creating the Example Lifecycle Project..283
37.2 Creating a Lifecycle Observer..283
37.3 Adding the Observer 285
37.4 Testing the Observer 285
37.5 Creating a Lifecycle Owner...286
37.6 Testing the Custom Lifecycle Owner...288
37.7 Summary 288

38. An Overview of the Navigation Architecture Component...**289**
38.1 Understanding Navigation...289
38.2 Declaring a Navigation Host...291
38.3 The Navigation Graph 292
38.4 Accessing the Navigation Controller 293
38.5 Triggering a Navigation Action 294
38.6 Passing Arguments...294
38.7 Summary 295

39. An Android Jetpack Navigation Component Tutorial **297**
39.1 Creating the NavigationDemo Project 297
39.2 Adding Navigation to the Build Configuration...297
39.3 Creating the Navigation Graph Resource File...298

39.4 Declaring a Navigation Host...299
39.5 Adding Navigation Destinations...301
39.6 Designing the Destination Fragment Layouts..303
39.7 Adding an Action to the Navigation Graph..304
39.8 Implement the OnFragmentInteractionListener..305
39.9 Triggering the Action 306
39.10 Passing Data Using Safeargs 307
39.11 Summary...310

40. Creating and Managing Overflow Menus on Android.. 311
40.1 The Overflow Menu 311
40.2 Creating an Overflow Menu...311
40.3 Displaying an Overflow Menu..312
40.4 Responding to Menu Item Selections...313
40.5 Creating Checkable Item Groups...313
40.6 Menus and the Android Studio Menu Editor...314
40.7 Creating the Example Project...315
40.8 Designing the Menu..315
40.9 Modifying the onOptionsItemSelected() Method..318
40.10 Testing the Application..319
40.11 Summary...319

41. Animating User Interfaces with the Android Transitions Framework............................ 321
41.1 Introducing Android Transitions and Scenes 321
41.2 Using Interpolators with Transitions..322
41.3 Working with Scene Transitions 322
41.4 Custom Transitions and TransitionSets in Code 324
41.5 Custom Transitions and TransitionSets in XML..324
41.6 Working with Interpolators 326
41.7 Creating a Custom Interpolator 327
41.8 Using the beginDelayedTransition Method..328
41.9 Summary...328

42. An Android Transition Tutorial using beginDelayedTransition 329
42.1 Creating the Android Studio TransitionDemo Project...329
42.2 Preparing the Project Files..329
42.3 Implementing beginDelayedTransition Animation 329
42.4 Customizing the Transition 332
42.5 Summary...333

43. Implementing Android Scene Transitions – A Tutorial... 335
43.1 An Overview of the Scene Transition Project 335
43.2 Creating the Android Studio SceneTransitions Project 335
43.3 Identifying and Preparing the Root Container 335
43.4 Designing the First Scene..335
43.5 Designing the Second Scene 336
43.6 Entering the First Scene 337
43.7 Loading Scene 2...338
43.8 Implementing the Transitions 339
43.9 Adding the Transition File...339
43.10 Loading and Using the Transition Set...340

43.11 Configuring Additional Transitions 341
43.12 Summary 342

44. Working with the Floating Action Button and Snackbar 343

44.1 The Material Design 343
44.2 The Design Library 343
44.3 The Floating Action Button (FAB) 343
44.4 The Snackbar 344
44.5 Creating the Example Project 345
44.6 Reviewing the Project 345
44.7 Changing the Floating Action Button 346
44.8 Adding the ListView to the Content Layout 347
44.9 Adding Items to the ListView 348
44.10 Adding an Action to the Snackbar 350
44.11 Summary 351

45. Creating a Tabbed Interface using the TabLayout Component 353

45.1 An Introduction to the ViewPager 353
45.2 An Overview of the TabLayout Component 353
45.3 Creating the TabLayoutDemo Project 354
45.4 Creating the First Fragment 354
45.5 Duplicating the Fragments 355
45.6 Adding the TabLayout and ViewPager 356
45.7 Creating the Pager Adapter 357
45.8 Performing the Initialization Tasks 358
45.9 Testing the Application 361
45.10 Customizing the TabLayout 362
45.11 Displaying Icon Tab Items 363
45.12 Summary 364

46. Working with the RecyclerView and CardView Widgets 365

46.1 An Overview of the RecyclerView 365
46.2 An Overview of the CardView 367
46.3 Summary 368

47. An Android RecyclerView and CardView Tutorial 369

47.1 Creating the CardDemo Project 369
47.2 Removing the Floating Action Button 369
47.3 Designing the CardView Layout 370
47.4 Adding the RecyclerView 371
47.5 Creating the RecyclerView Adapter 371
47.6 Adding the Image Files 373
47.7 Initializing the RecyclerView Component 374
47.8 Testing the Application 375
47.9 Responding to Card Selections 375
47.10 Summary 377

48. A Layout Editor Sample Data Tutorial 379

48.1 Adding Sample Data to a Project 379
48.2 Using Custom Sample Data 383
48.3 Summary 386

49. Working with the AppBar and Collapsing Toolbar Layouts **387**

49.1 The Anatomy of an AppBar 387
49.2 The Example Project 388
49.3 Coordinating the RecyclerView and Toolbar 388
49.4 Introducing the Collapsing Toolbar Layout 390
49.5 Changing the Title and Scrim Color 393
49.6 Summary 394

50. An Android Studio Master/Detail Flow Tutorial **395**

50.1 The Master/Detail Flow 395
50.2 Creating a Master/Detail Flow Activity.. 396
50.3 The Anatomy of the Master/Detail Flow Template 397
50.4 Modifying the Master/Detail Flow Template 398
50.5 Changing the Content Model... 398
50.6 Changing the Detail Pane 400
50.7 Modifying the WebsiteDetailFragment Class... 401
50.8 Modifying the WebsiteListActivity Class 402
50.9 Adding Manifest Permissions.. 403
50.10 Running the Application... 403
50.11 Summary 404

51. An Overview of Android Intents **405**

51.1 An Overview of Intents 405
51.2 Explicit Intents... 405
51.3 Returning Data from an Activity 406
51.4 Implicit Intents 407
51.5 Using Intent Filters.. 408
51.6 Checking Intent Availability 409
51.7 Summary 409

52. Android Explicit Intents – A Worked Example **411**

52.1 Creating the Explicit Intent Example Application.. 411
52.2 Designing the User Interface Layout for MainActivity.. 411
52.3 Creating the Second Activity Class.. 412
52.4 Designing the User Interface Layout for ActivityB.. 413
52.5 Reviewing the Application Manifest File 413
52.6 Creating the Intent... 414
52.7 Extracting Intent Data 415
52.8 Launching ActivityB as a Sub-Activity.. 416
52.9 Returning Data from a Sub-Activity... 417
52.10 Testing the Application... 417
52.11 Summary 417

53. Android Implicit Intents – A Worked Example **419**

53.1 Creating the Android Studio Implicit Intent Example Project 419
53.2 Designing the User Interface 419
53.3 Creating the Implicit Intent 420
53.4 Adding a Second Matching Activity 420
53.5 Adding the Web View to the UI... 421
53.6 Obtaining the Intent URL... 421
53.7 Modifying the MyWebView Project Manifest File 422

53.8 Installing the MyWebView Package on a Device 424

53.9 Testing the Application 424

53.10 Summary 425

54. Android Broadcast Intents and Broadcast Receivers 427

54.1 An Overview of Broadcast Intents 427

54.2 An Overview of Broadcast Receivers 428

54.3 Obtaining Results from a Broadcast 429

54.4 Sticky Broadcast Intents 429

54.5 The Broadcast Intent Example 430

54.6 Creating the Example Application 430

54.7 Creating and Sending the Broadcast Intent 430

54.8 Creating the Broadcast Receiver 431

54.9 Registering the Broadcast Receiver 432

54.10 Testing the Broadcast Example 433

54.11 Listening for System Broadcasts 433

54.12 Summary 434

55. A Basic Overview of Threads and AsyncTasks 435

55.1 An Overview of Threads 435

55.2 The Application Main Thread 435

55.3 Thread Handlers 435

55.4 A Basic AsyncTask Example 435

55.5 Subclassing AsyncTask 437

55.6 Testing the App 440

55.7 Canceling a Task 440

55.8 Summary 441

56. An Overview of Android Started and Bound Services 443

56.1 Started Services 443

56.2 Intent Service 443

56.3 Bound Service 444

56.4 The Anatomy of a Service 444

56.5 Controlling Destroyed Service Restart Options 445

56.6 Declaring a Service in the Manifest File 445

56.7 Starting a Service Running on System Startup 446

56.8 Summary 446

57. Implementing an Android Started Service – A Worked Example 447

57.1 Creating the Example Project 447

57.2 Creating the Service Class 447

57.3 Adding the Service to the Manifest File 449

57.4 Starting the Service 449

57.5 Testing the IntentService Example 450

57.6 Using the Service Class 450

57.7 Creating the New Service 450

57.8 Modifying the User Interface 452

57.9 Running the Application 453

57.10 Creating an AsyncTask for Service Tasks 453

57.11 Summary 455

58. Android Local Bound Services – A Worked Example 457

58.1 Understanding Bound Services...457
58.2 Bound Service Interaction Options..457
58.3 An Android Studio Local Bound Service Example 457
58.4 Adding a Bound Service to the Project 458
58.5 Implementing the Binder 458
58.6 Binding the Client to the Service 461
58.7 Completing the Example...462
58.8 Testing the Application...463
58.9 Summary 463

59. Android Remote Bound Services – A Worked Example **465**

59.1 Client to Remote Service Communication..465
59.2 Creating the Example Application..465
59.3 Designing the User Interface..465
59.4 Implementing the Remote Bound Service..466
59.5 Configuring a Remote Service in the Manifest File..467
59.6 Launching and Binding to the Remote Service...468
59.7 Sending a Message to the Remote Service 469
59.8 Summary 470

60. An Android Notifications Tutorial **471**

60.1 An Overview of Notifications...471
60.2 Creating the NotifyDemo Project 473
60.3 Designing the User Interface..473
60.4 Creating the Second Activity..473
60.5 Creating a Notification Channel 474
60.6 Creating and Issuing a Basic Notification..476
60.7 Launching an Activity from a Notification...479
60.8 Adding Actions to a Notification 480
60.9 Bundled Notifications...481
60.10 Summary 483

61. An Android Direct Reply Notification Tutorial **485**

61.1 Creating the DirectReply Project 485
61.2 Designing the User Interface..485
61.3 Creating the Notification Channel..486
61.4 Building the RemoteInput Object 487
61.5 Creating the PendingIntent...488
61.6 Creating the Reply Action..488
61.7 Receiving Direct Reply Input...491
61.8 Updating the Notification 492
61.9 Summary 493

62. Foldable Devices and Multi-Window Support **495**

62.1 Foldables and Multi-Window Support..495
62.2 Using a Foldable Emulator...496
62.3 Entering Multi-Window Mode 497
62.4 Enabling and using Freeform Support 498
62.5 Checking for Freeform Support 499
62.6 Enabling Multi-Window Support in an App..499
62.7 Specifying Multi-Window Attributes..499

62.8 Detecting Multi-Window Mode in an Activity..500

62.9 Receiving Multi-Window Notifications 500

62.10 Launching an Activity in Multi-Window Mode 501

62.11 Configuring Freeform Activity Size and Position...502

62.12 Summary 502

63. An Overview of Android SQLite Databases **505**

63.1 Understanding Database Tables...505

63.2 Introducing Database Schema 505

63.3 Columns and Data Types 505

63.4 Database Rows 506

63.5 Introducing Primary Keys 506

63.6 What is SQLite? 506

63.7 Structured Query Language (SQL)..506

63.8 Trying SQLite on an Android Virtual Device (AVD) 507

63.9 The Android Room Persistence Library...509

63.10 Summary 509

64. The Android Room Persistence Library **511**

64.1 Revisiting Modern App Architecture 511

64.2 Key Elements of Room Database Persistence...511

64.2.1 Repository...512

64.2.2 Room Database 512

64.2.3 Data Access Object (DAO) 512

64.2.4 Entities...512

64.2.5 SQLite Database 512

64.3 Understanding Entities..513

64.4 Data Access Objects 516

64.5 The Room Database 517

64.6 The Repository...518

64.7 In-Memory Databases 519

64.8 Summary 519

65. An Android TableLayout and TableRow Tutorial **521**

65.1 The TableLayout and TableRow Layout Views..521

65.2 Creating the Room Database Project 522

65.3 Converting to a LinearLayout..522

65.4 Adding the TableLayout to the User Interface..523

65.5 Configuring the TableRows 524

65.6 Adding the Button Bar to the Layout 525

65.7 Adding the RecyclerView...526

65.8 Adjusting the Layout Margins 527

65.9 Summary 527

66. An Android Room Database and Repository Tutorial..**529**

66.1 About the RoomDemo Project...529

66.2 Modifying the Build Configuration 529

66.3 Building the Entity 529

66.4 Creating the Data Access Object 531

66.5 Adding the Room Database 533

66.6 Adding the Repository 534

66.7 Modifying the ViewModel 538
66.8 Creating the Product Item Layout 539
66.9 Adding the RecyclerView Adapter 539
66.10 Preparing the Main Fragment 541
66.11 Adding the Button Listeners 542
66.12 Adding LiveData Observers 543
66.13 Initializing the RecyclerView 544
66.14 Testing the RoomDemo App 544
66.15 Summary 545

67. Accessing Cloud Storage using the Android Storage Access Framework 547

67.1 The Storage Access Framework 547
67.2 Working with the Storage Access Framework 548
67.3 Filtering Picker File Listings 548
67.4 Handling Intent Results 549
67.5 Reading the Content of a File 550
67.6 Writing Content to a File 550
67.7 Deleting a File 551
67.8 Gaining Persistent Access to a File 551
67.9 Summary 552

68. An Android Storage Access Framework Example 553

68.1 About the Storage Access Framework Example 553
68.2 Creating the Storage Access Framework Example 553
68.3 Designing the User Interface 553
68.4 Declaring Request Codes 554
68.5 Creating a New Storage File 555
68.6 The onActivityResult() Method 556
68.7 Saving to a Storage File 558
68.8 Opening and Reading a Storage File 560
68.9 Testing the Storage Access Application 562
68.10 Summary 563

69. Implementing Video Playback on Android using the VideoView and MediaController Classes 565

69.1 Introducing the Android VideoView Class 565
69.2 Introducing the Android MediaController Class 566
69.3 Creating the Video Playback Example 566
69.4 Designing the VideoPlayer Layout 566
69.5 Configuring the VideoView 567
69.6 Adding Internet Permission 568
69.7 Adding the MediaController to the Video View 569
69.8 Setting up the onPreparedListener 570
69.9 Summary 571

70. Android Picture-in-Picture Mode 573

70.1 Picture-in-Picture Features 573
70.2 Enabling Picture-in-Picture Mode 574
70.3 Configuring Picture-in-Picture Parameters 574
70.4 Entering Picture-in-Picture Mode 575
70.5 Detecting Picture-in-Picture Mode Changes 575
70.6 Adding Picture-in-Picture Actions 576

70.7 Summary 576

71. An Android Picture-in-Picture Tutorial **579**

71.1 Adding Picture-in-Picture Support to the Manifest 579
71.2 Adding a Picture-in-Picture Button 579
71.3 Entering Picture-in-Picture Mode 579
71.4 Detecting Picture-in-Picture Mode Changes 581
71.5 Adding a Broadcast Receiver 582
71.6 Adding the PiP Action 583
71.7 Testing the Picture-in-Picture Action 586
71.8 Summary 586

72. Making Runtime Permission Requests in Android **587**

72.1 Understanding Normal and Dangerous Permissions 587
72.2 Creating the Permissions Example Project 589
72.3 Checking for a Permission 589
72.4 Requesting Permission at Runtime 591
72.5 Providing a Rationale for the Permission Request 592
72.6 Testing the Permissions App 594
72.7 Summary 594

73. Android Audio Recording and Playback using MediaPlayer and MediaRecorder **595**

73.1 Playing Audio 595
73.2 Recording Audio and Video using the MediaRecorder Class 596
73.3 About the Example Project 597
73.4 Creating the AudioApp Project 597
73.5 Designing the User Interface 597
73.6 Checking for Microphone Availability 598
73.7 Performing the Activity Initialization 599
73.8 Implementing the recordAudio() Method 600
73.9 Implementing the stopAudio() Method 601
73.10 Implementing the playAudio() method 601
73.11 Configuring and Requesting Permissions 602
73.12 Testing the Application 605
73.13 Summary 605

74. Working with the Google Maps Android API in Android Studio **607**

74.1 The Elements of the Google Maps Android API 607
74.2 Creating the Google Maps Project 608
74.3 Obtaining Your Developer Signature 608
74.4 Adding the Apache HTTP Legacy Library Requirement 609
74.5 Testing the Application 609
74.6 Understanding Geocoding and Reverse Geocoding 610
74.7 Adding a Map to an Application 611
74.8 Requesting Current Location Permission 612
74.9 Displaying the User's Current Location 613
74.10 Changing the Map Type 614
74.11 Displaying Map Controls to the User 615
74.12 Handling Map Gesture Interaction 616
74.12.1 Map Zooming Gestures 616
74.12.2 Map Scrolling/Panning Gestures 616

74.12.3 Map Tilt Gestures...616
74.12.4 Map Rotation Gestures...617
74.13 Creating Map Markers...617
74.14 Controlling the Map Camera 618
74.15 Summary..619

75. Printing with the Android Printing Framework **621**
75.1 The Android Printing Architecture 621
75.2 The Print Service Plugins 621
75.3 Google Cloud Print..622
75.4 Printing to Google Drive...622
75.5 Save as PDF...623
75.6 Printing from Android Devices 623
75.7 Options for Building Print Support into Android Apps..........................624
75.7.1 Image Printing...624
75.7.2 Creating and Printing HTML Content...625
75.7.3 Printing a Web Page...626
75.7.4 Printing a Custom Document 627
75.8 Summary..627

76. An Android HTML and Web Content Printing Example **629**
76.1 Creating the HTML Printing Example Application.................................629
76.2 Printing Dynamic HTML Content...629
76.3 Creating the Web Page Printing Example...632
76.4 Removing the Floating Action Button 632
76.5 Designing the User Interface Layout...632
76.6 Loading the Web Page into the WebView...634
76.7 Adding the Print Menu Option...635
76.8 Summary..637

77. A Guide to Android Custom Document Printing...**639**
77.1 An Overview of Android Custom Document Printing...........................639
77.1.1 Custom Print Adapters..639
77.2 Preparing the Custom Document Printing Project..................................640
77.3 Creating the Custom Print Adapter...641
77.4 Implementing the onLayout() Callback Method.....................................642
77.5 Implementing the onWrite() Callback Method 645
77.6 Checking a Page is in Range 647
77.7 Drawing the Content on the Page Canvas 648
77.8 Starting the Print Job 650
77.9 Testing the Application...651
77.10 Summary..651

78. An Introduction to Android App Links..**653**
78.1 An Overview of Android App Links 653
78.2 App Link Intent Filters 653
78.3 Handling App Link Intents 654
78.4 Associating the App with a Website...654
78.5 Summary..655

79. An Android Studio App Links Tutorial **657**

79.1 About the Example App 657
79.2 The Database Schema 657
79.3 Loading and Running the Project 658
79.4 Adding the URL Mapping 659
79.5 Adding the Intent Filter 662
79.6 Adding Intent Handling Code 662
79.7 Testing the App Link 666
79.8 Associating an App Link with a Web Site 666
79.9 Summary 668

80. A Guide to the Android Studio Profiler **669**
80.1 Accessing the Android Profiler 669
80.2 Enabling Advanced Profiling 669
80.3 The Android Profiler Tool Window 670
80.4 The Sessions Panel 671
80.5 The CPU Profiler 672
80.6 Memory Profiler 675
80.7 Network Profiler 676
80.8 Energy Profiler 678
80.9 Summary 678

81. An Android Biometric Authentication Tutorial **679**
81.1 An Overview of Biometric Authentication 679
81.2 Creating the Biometric Authentication Project 679
81.3 Configuring Device Fingerprint Authentication 680
81.4 Adding the Biometric Permission to the Manifest File 680
81.5 Designing the User Interface 681
81.6 Adding a Toast Convenience Method 681
81.7 Checking the Security Settings 682
81.8 Configuring the Authentication Callbacks 683
81.9 Adding the CancellationSignal 684
81.10 Starting the Biometric Prompt 685
81.11 Testing the Project 685
81.12 Summary 687

82. Creating, Testing and Uploading an Android App Bundle **689**
82.1 The Release Preparation Process 689
82.2 Android App Bundles 689
82.3 Register for a Google Play Developer Console Account 690
82.4 Configuring the App in the Console 691
82.5 Enabling Google Play App Signing 691
82.6 Creating a Keystore File 692
82.7 Creating the Android App Bundle 694
82.8 Generating Test APK Files 695
82.9 Uploading the App Bundle to the Google Play Developer Console 696
82.10 Exploring the App Bundle 696
82.11 Managing Testers 698
82.12 Uploading New App Bundle Revisions 699
82.13 Analyzing the App Bundle File 700
82.14 Enabling Google Play Signing for an Existing App 701
82.15 Summary 702

Table of Contents

83. An Overview of Android Dynamic Feature Modules **703**

83.1 An Overview of Dynamic Feature Modules 703

83.2 Dynamic Feature Module Architecture 703

83.3 Creating a Dynamic Feature Module 704

83.4 Converting an Existing Module for Dynamic Delivery 706

83.5 Working with Dynamic Feature Modules 709

83.6 Handling Large Dynamic Feature Modules 711

83.7 Summary 712

84. An Android Studio Dynamic Feature Tutorial **713**

84.1 Creating the DynamicFeature Project 713

84.2 Adding Dynamic Feature Support to the Project 713

84.3 Designing the Base Activity User Interface 714

84.4 Adding the Dynamic Feature Module 715

84.5 Reviewing the Dynamic Feature Module 716

84.6 Adding the Dynamic Feature Activity 718

84.7 Implementing the launchIntent() Method 720

84.8 Uploading the App Bundle for Testing 721

84.9 Implementing the installFeature() Method 722

84.10 Adding the Update Listener 724

84.11 Handling Large Downloads 727

84.12 Using Deferred Installation 729

84.13 Removing a Dynamic Module 729

84.14 Summary 729

85. An Overview of Gradle in Android Studio **731**

85.1 An Overview of Gradle 731

85.2 Gradle and Android Studio 731

85.2.1 Sensible Defaults 731

85.2.2 Dependencies 731

85.2.3 Build Variants 732

85.2.4 Manifest Entries 732

85.2.5 APK Signing 732

85.2.6 ProGuard Support 732

85.3 The Top-level Gradle Build File 732

85.4 Module Level Gradle Build Files 734

85.5 Configuring Signing Settings in the Build File 736

85.6 Running Gradle Tasks from the Command-line 737

85.7 Summary 737

Index **739**

1. Introduction

In 2018 Google introduced Android Jetpack to the developer community. Designed to make it quicker and easier to develop modern and reliable Android apps, Jetpack consists of a set of tools, libraries and architectural guidelines. The main elements of Android Jetpack consist of the Android Studio Integrated Development Environment (IDE), the Android Architecture Components and the Modern App Architecture Guidelines, all of which are covered in this latest edition of Android Studio Development Essentials.

Fully updated for Android Studio 3.5 and Android 10 (Q), the goal of this book is to teach the skills necessary to develop Android based applications using the Java programming language.

Beginning with the basics, this book provides an outline of the steps necessary to set up an Android development and testing environment. An overview of Android Studio is included covering areas such as tool windows, the code editor and the Layout Editor tool. An introduction to the architecture of Android is followed by an in-depth look at the design of Android applications and user interfaces using the Android Studio environment.

Chapters are also included covering the Android Architecture Components including view models, lifecycle management, Room database access, app navigation, live data and data binding.

More advanced topics such as intents are also covered, as are touch screen handling, gesture recognition, and the recording and playback of audio. This edition of the book also covers printing, transitions, cloud-based file storage and foldable device support.

The concepts of material design are also covered in detail, including the use of floating action buttons, Snackbars, tabbed interfaces, card views, navigation drawers and collapsing toolbars.

In addition to covering general Android development techniques, the book also includes Google Play specific topics such as implementing maps using the Google Maps Android API, and submitting apps to the Google Play Developer Console.

Other key features of Android Studio 3.5 and Android 10 are also covered in detail including the Layout Editor, the ConstraintLayout and ConstraintSet classes, constraint chains and barriers, direct reply notifications and foldable device support.

Chapters also cover advanced features of Android Studio such as App Links, Dynamic Delivery, the Android Studio Profiler and Gradle build configuration.

Assuming you already have some Java programming experience, are ready to download Android Studio and the Android SDK, have access to a Windows, Mac or Linux system and ideas for some apps to develop, you are ready to get started.

1.1 Downloading the Code Samples

The source code and Android Studio project files for the examples contained in this book are available for download at:

https://www.ebookfrenzy.com/retail/androidstudio35/index.php

The steps to load a project from the code samples into Android Studio are as follows:

Introduction

1. From the Welcome to Android Studio dialog, select the Open an existing Android Studio project option.

2. In the project selection dialog, navigate to and select the folder containing the project to be imported and click on OK.

1.2 Feedback

We want you to be satisfied with your purchase of this book. If you find any errors in the book, or have any comments, questions or concerns please contact us at *feedback@ebookfrenzy.com*.

1.3 Errata

While we make every effort to ensure the accuracy of the content of this book, it is inevitable that a book covering a subject area of this size and complexity may include some errors and oversights. Any known issues with the book will be outlined, together with solutions, at the following URL:

https://www.ebookfrenzy.com/errata/androidstudio35.html

In the event that you find an error not listed in the errata, please let us know by emailing our technical support team at *feedback@ebookfrenzy.com*. They are there to help you and will work to resolve any problems you may encounter.

1.4 Download the eBook

Thank you for purchasing the print edition of this book. If you would like to download the PDF version of this book, please email proof of purchase (for example a receipt, delivery notice or photo of the physical book) to *feedback@ebookfrenzy.com* and we will provide you with a download link for the book in PDF format.

2. Setting up an Android Studio Development Environment

Before any work can begin on the development of an Android application, the first step is to configure a computer system to act as the development platform. This involves a number of steps consisting of installing the Android Studio Integrated Development Environment (IDE) which also includes the Android Software Development Kit (SDK) and OpenJDK Java development environment.

This chapter will cover the steps necessary to install the requisite components for Android application development on Windows, macOS and Linux based systems.

2.1 System Requirements

Android application development may be performed on any of the following system types:

- Windows 7/8/10 (32-bit or 64-bit though the Android emulator will only run on 64-bit systems)

- macOS 10.10 or later (Intel based systems only)

- ChromeOS device with Intel i5 or higher and minimum 8GB of RAM

- Linux systems with version 2.19 or later of GNU C Library (glibc)

- Minimum of 4GB of RAM (8GB is preferred)

- Approximately 4GB of available disk space

- 1280 x 800 minimum screen resolution

2.2 Downloading the Android Studio Package

Most of the work involved in developing applications for Android will be performed using the Android Studio environment. The content and examples in this book were created based on Android Studio version 3.5 using the Android 10.0 (Q) API 29 SDK which, at the time writing are the current versions.

Android Studio is, however, subject to frequent updates so a newer version may have been released since this book was published.

The latest release of Android Studio may be downloaded from the primary download page which can be found at the following URL:

https://developer.android.com/studio/index.html

If this page provides instructions for downloading a newer version of Android Studio it is important to note that there may be some minor differences between this book and the software. A web search for Android Studio 3.5 should provide the option to download the older version in the event that these differences become a problem. Alternatively, visit the following web page to find Android Studio 3.5 in the archives:

https://developer.android.com/studio/archive

2.3 Installing Android Studio

Once downloaded, the exact steps to install Android Studio differ depending on the operating system on which the installation is being performed.

2.3.1 Installation on Windows

Locate the downloaded Android Studio installation executable file (named *android-studio-ide-<version>-windows*.exe) in a Windows Explorer window and double-click on it to start the installation process, clicking the *Yes* button in the User Account Control dialog if it appears.

Once the Android Studio setup wizard appears, work through the various screens to configure the installation to meet your requirements in terms of the file system location into which Android Studio should be installed and whether or not it should be made available to other users of the system. When prompted to select the components to install, make sure that the *Android Studio* and *Android Virtual Device* options are all selected.

Although there are no strict rules on where Android Studio should be installed on the system, the remainder of this book will assume that the installation was performed into *C:\Program Files\Android\Android Studio* and that the Android SDK packages have been installed into the user's *AppData\Local\Android\sdk* sub-folder. Once the options have been configured, click on the *Install* button to begin the installation process.

On versions of Windows with a Start menu, the newly installed Android Studio can be launched from the entry added to that menu during the installation. The executable may be pinned to the task bar for easy access by navigating to the *Android Studio\bin* directory, right-clicking on the executable and selecting the *Pin to Taskbar* menu option. Note that the executable is provided in 32-bit (*studio*) and 64-bit (*studio64*) executable versions. If you are running a 32-bit system be sure to use the *studio* executable.

2.3.2 Installation on macOS

Android Studio for macOS is downloaded in the form of a disk image (.dmg) file. Once the *android-studio-ide-<version>-mac.dmg* file has been downloaded, locate it in a Finder window and double-click on it to open it as shown in Figure 2-1:

Figure 2-1

To install the package, simply drag the Android Studio icon and drop it onto the Applications folder. The Android Studio package will then be installed into the Applications folder of the system, a process which will typically take a few minutes to complete.

To launch Android Studio, locate the executable in the Applications folder using a Finder window and double-click on it.

For future easier access to the tool, drag the Android Studio icon from the Finder window and drop it onto the dock.

2.3.3 Installation on Linux

Having downloaded the Linux Android Studio package, open a terminal window, change directory to the location where Android Studio is to be installed and execute the following command:

```
unzip /<path to package>/android-studio-ide-<version>-linux.zip
```

Note that the Android Studio bundle will be installed into a sub-directory named *android-studio*. Assuming, therefore, that the above command was executed in */home/demo*, the software packages will be unpacked into */home/demo/android-studio*.

To launch Android Studio, open a terminal window, change directory to the *android-studio/bin* sub-directory and execute the following command:

```
./studio.sh
```

When running on a 64-bit Linux system, it will be necessary to install some 32-bit support libraries before Android Studio will run. On Ubuntu these libraries can be installed using the following command:

```
sudo apt-get install libc6:i386 libncurses5:i386 libstdc++6:i386 lib32z1 libbz2-
1.0:i386
```

On Red Hat and Fedora based 64-bit systems, use the following command:

```
sudo yum install zlib.i686 ncurses-libs.i686 bzip2-libs.i686
```

2.4 The Android Studio Setup Wizard

The first time that Android Studio is launched after being installed, a dialog will appear providing the option to import settings from a previous Android Studio version. If you have settings from a previous version and would like to import them into the latest installation, select the appropriate option and location. Alternatively, indicate that you do not need to import any previous settings and click on the OK button to proceed.

Next, the setup wizard may appear as shown in Figure 2-2 though this dialog does not appear on all platforms:

Figure 2-2

If the wizard appears, click on the Next button, choose the Standard installation option and click on Next once again.

Android Studio will proceed to download and configure the latest Android SDK and some additional components and packages. Once this process has completed, click on the *Finish* button in the *Downloading Components* dialog at which point the Welcome to Android Studio screen should then appear:

Figure 2-3

2.5 Installing Additional Android SDK Packages

The steps performed so far have installed Java, the Android Studio IDE and the current set of default Android SDK packages. Before proceeding, it is worth taking some time to verify which packages are installed and to install any missing or updated packages.

This task can be performed using the *Android SDK Settings* screen, which may be launched from within the Android Studio tool by selecting the *Configure -> SDK Manager* option from within the Android Studio welcome dialog. Once invoked, the *Android SDK* screen of the default settings dialog will appear as shown in Figure 2-4:

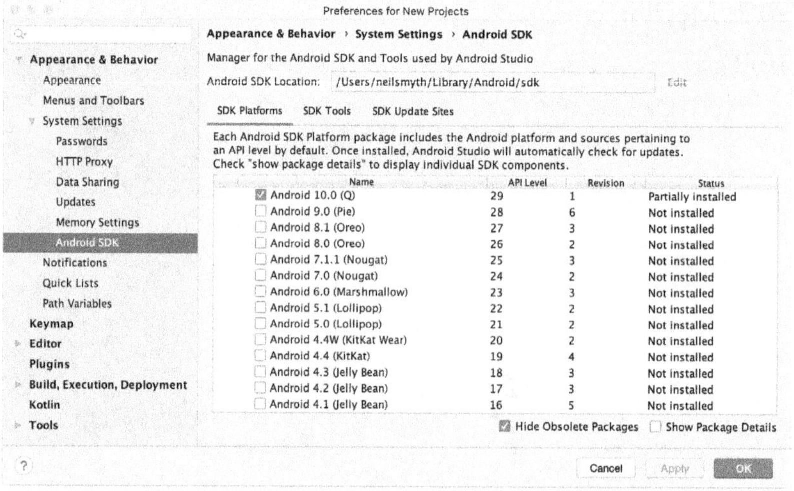

Figure 2-4

Immediately after installing Android Studio for the first time it is likely that only the latest released version of the Android SDK has been installed. To install older versions of the Android SDK simply select the checkboxes corresponding to the versions and click on the *Apply* button.

It is also possible that updates will be listed as being available for the latest SDK. To access detailed information about the packages that are available for update, enable the *Show Package Details* option located in the lower right-hand corner of the screen. This will display information similar to that shown in Figure 2-5:

Name	API Level	Revision	Status
Android TV Intel x86 Atom System Image	25	6	Not installed
Android Wear for China ARM EABI v7a System Image	25	3	Not installed
Android Wear for China Intel x86 Atom System Image	25	3	Not installed
Android Wear ARM EABI v7a System Image	25	3	Not installed
Android Wear Intel x86 Atom System Image	25	3	Not installed
Google APIs ARM 64 v8a System Image	25	8	Not installed
Google APIs ARM EABI v7a System Image	25	8	Not installed
Google APIs Intel x86 Atom System Image	25	8	Not installed
Google APIs Intel x86 Atom_64 System Image	25	6	Update Available: 8
Android 7.0 (Nougat)			
Google APIs	24	1	Not installed

Figure 2-5

The above figure highlights the availability of an update. To install the updates, enable the checkbox to the left of the item name and click on the *Apply* button.

In addition to the Android SDK packages, a number of tools are also installed for building Android applications. To view the currently installed packages and check for updates, remain within the SDK settings screen and select the SDK Tools tab as shown in Figure 2-6:

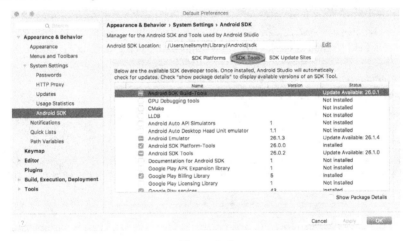

Figure 2-6

Within the Android SDK Tools screen, make sure that the following packages are listed as *Installed* in the Status column:

- Android SDK Build-tools

- Android Emulator

- Android SDK Platform-tools

- Android SDK Tools

- Google Play Services

- Intel x86 Emulator Accelerator (HAXM installer)

- Google USB Driver (Windows only)

In the event that any of the above packages are listed as *Not Installed* or requiring an update, simply select the checkboxes next to those packages and click on the *Apply* button to initiate the installation process.

Once the installation is complete, review the package list and make sure that the selected packages are now listed as *Installed* in the *Status* column. If any are listed as *Not installed,* make sure they are selected and click on the *Apply* button again.

2.6 Making the Android SDK Tools Command-line Accessible

Most of the time, the underlying tools of the Android SDK will be accessed from within the Android Studio environment. That being said, however, there will also be instances where it will be useful to be able to invoke those tools from a command prompt or terminal window. In order for the operating system on which you are developing to be able to find these tools, it will be necessary to add them to the system's *PATH* environment variable.

Regardless of operating system, the PATH variable needs to be configured to include the following paths (where *<path_to_android_sdk_installation>* represents the file system location into which the Android SDK was installed):

```
<path_to_android_sdk_installation>/sdk/tools
<path_to_android_sdk_installation>/sdk/tools/bin
<path_to_android_sdk_installation>/sdk/platform-tools
```

The location of the SDK on your system can be identified by launching the SDK Manager and referring to the *Android SDK Location:* field located at the top of the settings panel as highlighted in Figure 2-7:

Appearance & Behavior › System Settings › Android SDK

Manager for the Android SDK and Tools used by Android Studio

Android SDK Location: /Users/neilsmyth/Library/Android/sdk   Edit

SDK Platforms   SDK Tools   SDK Update Sites

Below are the available SDK developer tools. Once installed, Android Studio will automatically check for updates. Check "show package details" to display available versions of an SDK Tool.

Figure 2-7

Once the location of the SDK has been identified, the steps to add this to the PATH variable are operating system dependent:

2.6.1 Windows 7

1. Right-click on Computer in the desktop start menu and select Properties from the resulting menu.

2. In the properties panel, select the Advanced System Settings link and, in the resulting dialog, click on the Environment Variables… button.

3. In the Environment Variables dialog, locate the Path variable in the System variables list, select it and click on *Edit….* Locate the end of the current variable value string and append the path to the Android platform tools to the end, using a semicolon to separate the path from the preceding values. For example, assuming the Android SDK was installed into C:\Users\demo\AppData\Local\Android\sdk, the following would be appended to the end of the current Path value:

```
;C:\Users\demo\AppData\Local\Android\sdk\platform-tools; C:\Users\demo\AppData\
Local\Android\sdk\tools; C:\Users\demo\AppData\Local\Android\sdk\tools\bin
```

4. Click on OK in each dialog box and close the system properties control panel.

Once the above steps are complete, verify that the path is correctly set by opening a *Command Prompt* window (*Start -> All Programs -> Accessories -> Command Prompt*) and at the prompt enter:

```
echo %Path%
```

The returned path variable value should include the paths to the Android SDK platform tools folders. Verify that the *platform-tools* value is correct by attempting to run the *adb* tool as follows:

```
adb
```

The tool should output a list of command line options when executed.

Similarly, check the *tools* path setting by attempting to launch the AVD Manager command line tool (don't worry if the avdmanager tool reports a problem with Java - this will be addressed later):

```
avdmanager
```

In the event that a message similar to the following message appears for one or both of the commands, it is most likely that an incorrect path was appended to the Path environment variable:

```
'adb' is not recognized as an internal or external command,
operable program or batch file.
```

2.6.2 Windows 8.1

1. On the start screen, move the mouse to the bottom right-hand corner of the screen and select Search from the resulting menu. In the search box, enter Control Panel. When the Control Panel icon appears in the results area, click on it to launch the tool on the desktop.

2. Within the Control Panel, use the Category menu to change the display to Large Icons. From the list of icons select the one labeled System.

3. Follow the steps outlined for Windows 7 starting from step 2 through to step 4.

Open the command prompt window (move the mouse to the bottom right-hand corner of the screen, select the Search option and enter *cmd* into the search box). Select *Command Prompt* from the search results.

Within the Command Prompt window, enter:

```
echo %Path%
```

The returned path variable value should include the paths to the Android SDK platform tools folders. Verify that the *platform-tools* value is correct by attempting to run the *adb* tool as follows:

```
adb
```

The tool should output a list of command line options when executed.

Similarly, check the *tools* path setting by attempting to run the AVD Manager command line tool (don't worry if the avdmanager tool reports a problem with Java - this will be addressed later):

```
avdmanager
```

In the event that a message similar to the following message appears for one or both of the commands, it is most likely that an incorrect path was appended to the Path environment variable:

```
'adb' is not recognized as an internal or external command,
operable program or batch file.
```

2.6.3 Windows 10

Right-click on the Start menu, select Settings from the resulting menu and enter "Edit the system environment variables" into the Find a setting text field. In the System Properties dialog, click the *Environment Variables...*

button. Follow the steps outlined for Windows 7 starting from step 3.

2.6.4 Linux

On Linux, this configuration can typically be achieved by adding a command to the *.bashrc* file in your home directory (specifics may differ depending on the particular Linux distribution in use). Assuming that the Android SDK bundle package was installed into */home/demo/Android/sdk*, the export line in the *.bashrc* file would read as follows:

```
export PATH=/home/demo/Android/sdk/platform-tools:/home/demo/Android/sdk/tools:/
home/demo/Android/sdk/tools/bin:/home/demo/android-studio/bin:$PATH
```

Note also that the above command adds the *android-studio/bin* directory to the PATH variable. This will enable the *studio.sh* script to be executed regardless of the current directory within a terminal window.

2.6.5 macOS

A number of techniques may be employed to modify the $PATH environment variable on macOS. Arguably the cleanest method is to add a new file in the */etc/paths.d* directory containing the paths to be added to $PATH. Assuming an Android SDK installation location of */Users/demo/Library/Android/sdk*, the path may be configured by creating a new file named *android-sdk* in the */etc/paths.d* directory containing the following lines:

```
/Users/demo/Library/Android/sdk/tools
/Users/demo/Library/Android/sdk/tools/bin
/Users/demo/Library/Android/sdk/platform-tools
```

Note that since this is a system directory it will be necessary to use the *sudo* command when creating the file. For example:

```
sudo vi /etc/paths.d/android-sdk
```

2.7 Android Studio Memory Management

Android Studio is a large and complex software application that consists of many background processes. Although Android Studio has been criticized in the past for providing less than optimal performance, Google has made significant performance improvements in recent releases and continues to do so with each new version. Part of these improvements include allowing the user to configure the amount of memory used by both the Android Studio IDE and the background processes used to build and run apps. This allows the software to take advantage of systems with larger amounts of RAM.

If you are running Android Studio on a system with sufficient unused RAM to increase these values (this feature is only available on 64-bit systems with 5GB or more of RAM) and find that Android Studio performance appears to be degraded it may be worth experimenting with these memory settings. Android Studio may also notify you that performance can be increased via a dialog similar to the one shown below:

Figure 2-8

To view and modify the current memory configuration, select the *File -> Settings...* (*Android Studio -> Preferences...* on macOS) menu option and, in the resulting dialog, select the *Memory Settings* option listed under *System Settings* in the left-hand navigation panel as illustrated in Figure 2-9 below.

When changing the memory allocation, be sure not to allocate more memory than necessary or than your system can spare without slowing down other processes.

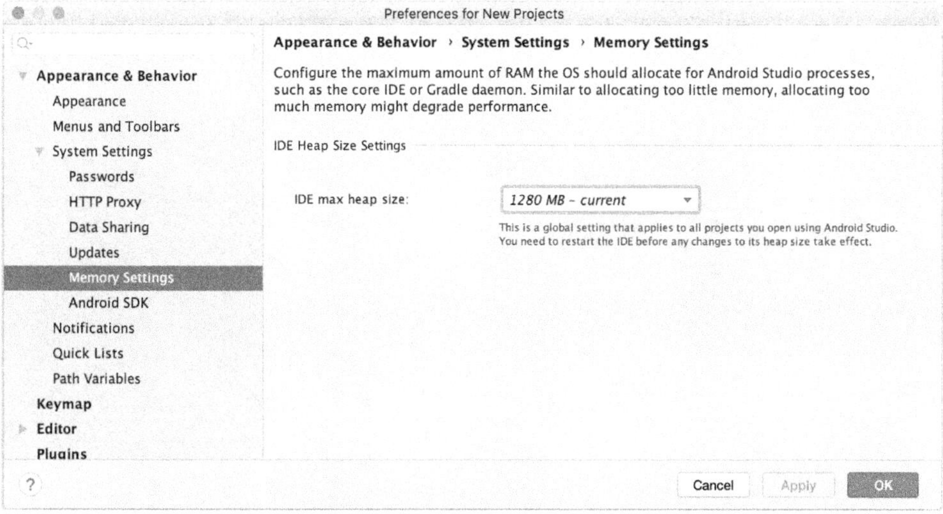

Figure 2-9

2.8 Updating Android Studio and the SDK

From time to time new versions of Android Studio and the Android SDK are released. New versions of the SDK are installed using the Android SDK Manager. Android Studio will typically notify you when an update is ready to be installed.

To manually check for Android Studio updates, click on the *Configure -> Check for Updates* menu option within the Android Studio welcome screen, or use the *Help -> Check for Updates...* (*Android Studio -> Check for Updates...* on macOS) menu option accessible from within the Android Studio main window.

2.9 Summary

Prior to beginning the development of Android based applications, the first step is to set up a suitable development environment. This consists of the Android SDKs and Android Studio IDE (which also includes the OpenJDK development environment). In this chapter, we have covered the steps necessary to install these packages on Windows, macOS and Linux.

3. Creating an Example Android App in Android Studio

The preceding chapters of this book have covered the steps necessary to configure an environment suitable for the development of Android applications using the Android Studio IDE. Before moving on to slightly more advanced topics, now is a good time to validate that all of the required development packages are installed and functioning correctly. The best way to achieve this goal is to create an Android application and compile and run it. This chapter will cover the creation of a simple Android application project using Android Studio. Once the project has been created, a later chapter will explore the use of the Android emulator environment to perform a test run of the application.

3.1 About the Project

The project created in this chapter takes the form of a very simple currency conversion calculator (so simple, in fact, that it only converts from dollars to euros and does so using an estimated conversion rate). The project will also make use of the most basic of Android Studio project templates. This simplicity allows us to introduce some of the key aspects of Android app development without overwhelming the beginner by trying to introduce too many concepts, such as the recommended app architecture and Android architecture components, at once. When following the tutorial in this chapter, rest assured that all of the techniques and code used in this initial example project will be covered in much greater detail in later chapters.

3.2 Creating a New Android Project

The first step in the application development process is to create a new project within the Android Studio environment. Begin, therefore, by launching Android Studio so that the "Welcome to Android Studio" screen appears as illustrated in Figure 3-1:

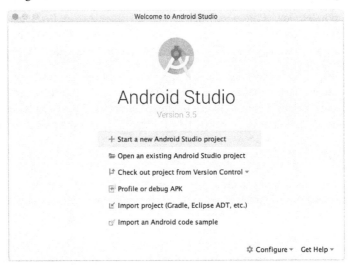

Figure 3-1

Once this window appears, Android Studio is ready for a new project to be created. To create the new project, simply click on the *Start a new Android Studio project* option to display the first screen of the *New Project* wizard.

3.3 Creating an Activity

The first step is to define the type of initial activity that is to be created for the application. Options are available to create projects for Phone and Tablet, Wear OS, TV, Android Audio or Android Things. A range of different activity types is available when developing Android applications, many of which will be covered extensively in later chapters. For the purposes of this example, however, simply select the option to create a *Basic Activity* on the Phone and Tablet screen. The Basic Activity option creates a template user interface consisting of an app bar, menu, content area and a single floating action button.

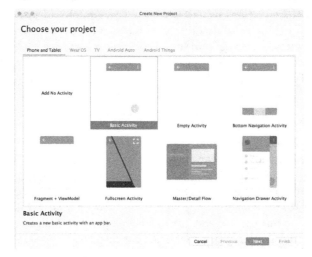

Figure 3-2

With the Basic Activity option selected, click *Next* to continue with the project configuration.

3.4 Defining the Project and SDK Settings

In the project configuration window (Figure 3-3), set the *Name* field to *AndroidSample*. The application name is the name by which the application will be referenced and identified within Android Studio and is also the name that would be used if the completed application were to go on sale in the Google Play store.

The *Package name* is used to uniquely identify the application within the Android application ecosystem. Although this can be set to any string that uniquely identifies your app, it is traditionally based on the reversed URL of your domain name followed by the name of the application. For example, if your domain is *www. mycompany.com*, and the application has been named *AndroidSample*, then the package name might be specified as follows:

```
com.mycompany.androidsample
```

If you do not have a domain name you can enter any other string into the Company Domain field, or you may use *example.com* for the purposes of testing, though this will need to be changed before an application can be published:

```
com.example.androidsample
```

The *Save location* setting will default to a location in the folder named *AndroidStudioProjects* located in your home directory and may be changed by clicking on the folder icon to the right of the text field containing the current path setting.

Set the minimum SDK setting to API 26: Android 8.0 (Oreo). This is the SDK that will be used in most of the projects created in this book unless a necessary feature is only available in a more recent version.

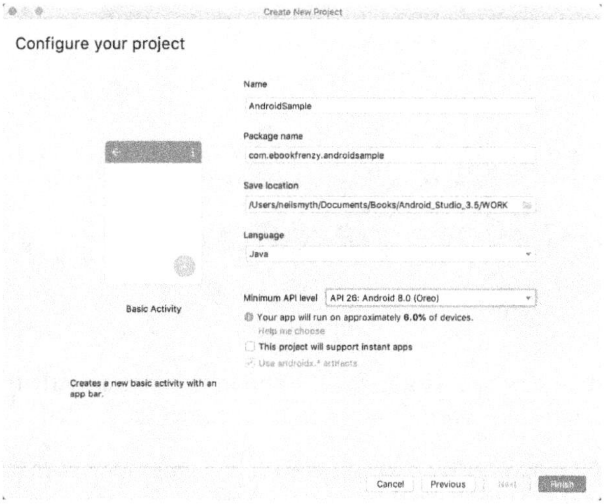

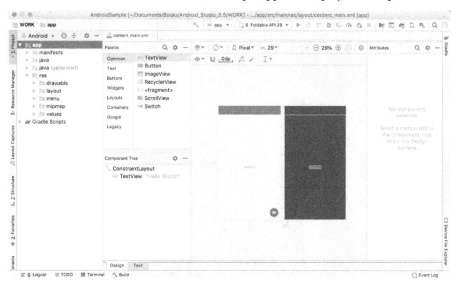

Figure 3-3

Finally, change the *Language* menu to *Java* and click on *Finish* to initiate the project creation process.

3.5 Modifying the Example Application

At this point, Android Studio has created a minimal example application project and opened the main window.

Figure 3-4

The newly created project and references to associated files are listed in the *Project* tool window located on the left-hand side of the main project window. The Project tool window has a number of modes in which information can be displayed. By default, this panel will be in *Android* mode. This setting is controlled by the menu at the top of the panel as highlighted in Figure 3-5. If the panel is not currently in Android mode, use the menu to switch mode:

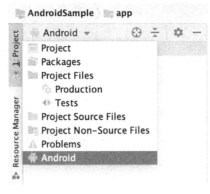

Figure 3-5

The example project created for us when we selected the option to create an activity consists of a user interface containing a label that will read "Hello World!" when the application is executed.

The next step in this tutorial is to modify the user interface of our application so that it displays a larger text view object with a different message to the one provided for us by Android Studio.

The user interface design for our activity is stored in a file named *activity_main.xml* which, in turn, is located under *app -> res -> layout* in the project file hierarchy. This layout file includes the app bar (also known as an action bar) that appears across the top of the device screen (marked A in Figure 3-6) and the floating action button (the email button marked B). In addition to these items, the *activity_main.xml* layout file contains a reference to a second file containing the content layout (marked C):

Figure 3-6

By default, the content layout is contained within a file named *content_main.xml* and it is within this file that changes to the layout of the activity are made. Using the Project tool window, locate this file as illustrated in Figure 3-7:

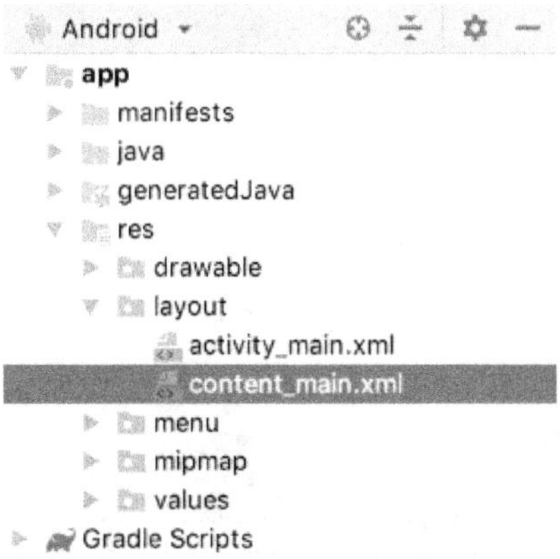

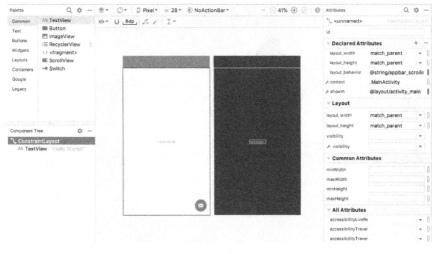

Figure 3-7

Once located, double-click on the file to load it into the user interface Layout Editor tool which will appear in the center panel of the Android Studio main window:

Figure 3-8

In the toolbar across the top of the Layout Editor window is a menu (currently set to *Pixel* in the above figure) which is reflected in the visual representation of the device within the Layout Editor panel. A wide range of other device options are available for selection by clicking on this menu.

To change the orientation of the device representation between landscape and portrait simply use the drop down menu immediately to the left of the device selection menu showing the ⬦ ▾ icon.

As can be seen in the device screen, the content layout already includes a label that displays a "Hello World!" message. Running down the left-hand side of the panel is a palette containing different categories of user interface components that may be used to construct a user interface, such as buttons, labels and text fields. It should be noted, however, that not all user interface components are obviously visible to the user. One such category consists of *layouts*. Android supports a variety of layouts that provide different levels of control over how visual user interface components are positioned and managed on the screen. Though it is difficult to tell from looking at the visual representation of the user interface, the current design has been created using a ConstraintLayout. This can be confirmed by reviewing the information in the *Component Tree* panel which, by default, is located

Creating an Example Android App in Android Studio

in the lower left-hand corner of the Layout Editor panel and is shown in Figure 3-9:

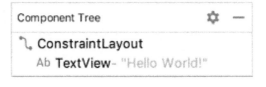

Figure 3-9

As we can see from the component tree hierarchy, the user interface layout consists of a ConstraintLayout parent with a single child in the form of a TextView object.

Before proceeding, check that the Layout Editor's Autoconnect mode is enabled. This means that as components are added to the layout, the Layout Editor will automatically add constraints to make sure the components are correctly positioned for different screen sizes and device orientations (a topic that will be covered in much greater detail in future chapters). The Autoconnect button appears in the Layout Editor toolbar and is represented by a magnet icon. When disabled the magnet appears with a diagonal line through it (Figure 3-10). If necessary, re-enable Autoconnect mode by clicking on this button.

Figure 3-10

The next step in modifying the application is to add some additional components to the layout, the first of which will be a Button for the user to press to initiate the currency conversion.

The Palette panel consists of two columns with the left-hand column containing a list of view component categories. The right-hand column lists the components contained within the currently selected category. In Figure 3-11, for example, the Button view is currently selected within the Buttons category:

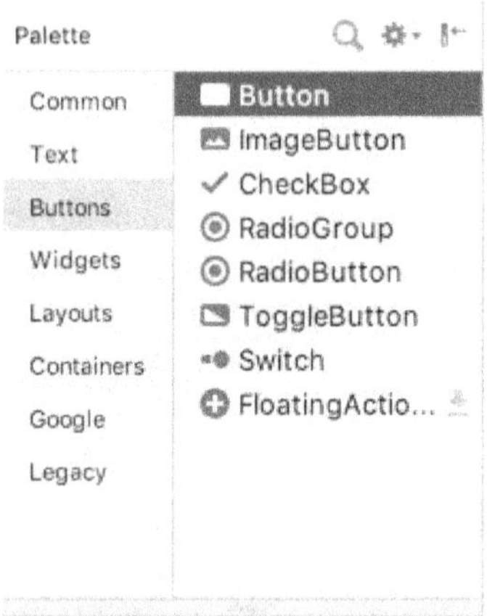

Palette

Common	◼ **Button**
Text	🖼 ImageButton
Buttons	✓ CheckBox
	◉ RadioGroup
Widgets	◉ RadioButton
Layouts	◳ ToggleButton
Containers	•◉ Switch
Google	⊕ FloatingActio... ⬆
Legacy	

Figure 3-11

Click and drag the *Button* object from the Buttons list and drop it in the horizontal center of the user interface design so that it is positioned beneath the existing TextView widget:

Figure 3-12

The next step is to change the text that is currently displayed by the Button component. The panel located to the right of the design area is the Attributes panel. This panel displays the attributes assigned to the currently selected component in the layout. Within this panel, locate the *text* property in the Common Attributes section and change the current value from "Button" to "Convert" as shown in Figure 3-13:

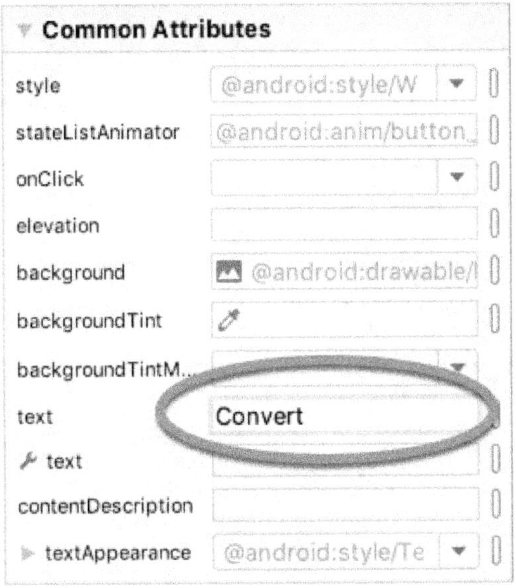

Common Attributes	
style	@android:style/W ▼
stateListAnimator	@android:anim/button
onClick	▼
elevation	
background	@android:drawable/
backgroundTint	
backgroundTintM...	▼
text	Convert
text	
contentDescription	
textAppearance	@android:style/Te ▼

Figure 3-13

The second text property with a wrench next to it allows a text property to be set which only appears within the Layout Editor tool but is not shown at runtime. This is useful for testing the way in which a visual component and the layout will behave with different settings without having to run the app repeatedly.

Just in case the Autoconnect system failed to set all of the layout connections, click on the Infer constraints button (Figure 3-14) to add any missing constraints to the layout:

Figure 3-14

At this point it is important to explain the warning button located in the top right-hand corner of the Layout Editor tool as indicated in Figure 3-15. Obviously, this is indicating potential problems with the layout. For details on any problems, click on the button:

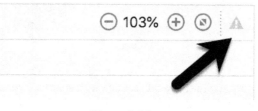

Figure 3-15

When clicked, a panel (Figure 3-16) will appear describing the nature of the problems and offering some possible corrective measures:

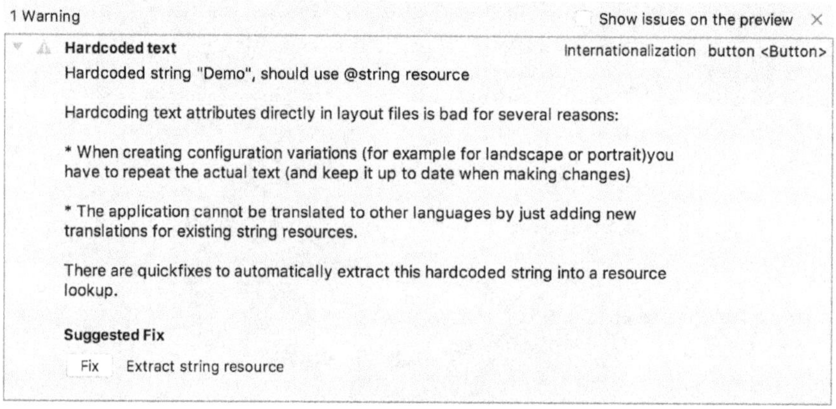

1 Warning	Show issues on the preview ✕

Hardcoded text   Internationalization button <Button>
Hardcoded string "Demo", should use @string resource

Hardcoding text attributes directly in layout files is bad for several reasons:

* When creating configuration variations (for example for landscape or portrait)you have to repeat the actual text (and keep it up to date when making changes)

* The application cannot be translated to other languages by just adding new translations for existing string resources.

There are quickfixes to automatically extract this hardcoded string into a resource lookup.

Suggested Fix

Fix   Extract string resource

Figure 3-16

Currently, the only warning listed reads as follows:

```
Hardcoded string "Convert", should use @string resource
```

This I18N message is informing us that a potential issue exists with regard to the future internationalization of the project ("I18N" comes from the fact that the word "internationalization" begins with an "I", ends with an "N" and has 18 letters in between). The warning is reminding us that when developing Android applications, attributes and values such as text strings should be stored in the form of *resources* wherever possible. Doing so enables changes to the appearance of the application to be made by modifying resource files instead of changing the application source code. This can be especially valuable when translating a user interface to a different spoken language. If all of the text in a user interface is contained in a single resource file, for example, that file can be given to a translator who will then perform the translation work and return the translated file for inclusion in the application. This enables multiple languages to be targeted without the necessity for any source code changes to be made. In this instance, we are going to create a new resource named *convert_string* and assign to it the string "Convert".

Click on the *Fix* button in the Issue Explanation panel to display the *Extract Resource* panel (Figure 3-17). Within this panel, change the resource name field to *convert_string* and leave the resource value set to *Convert* before clicking on the OK button.

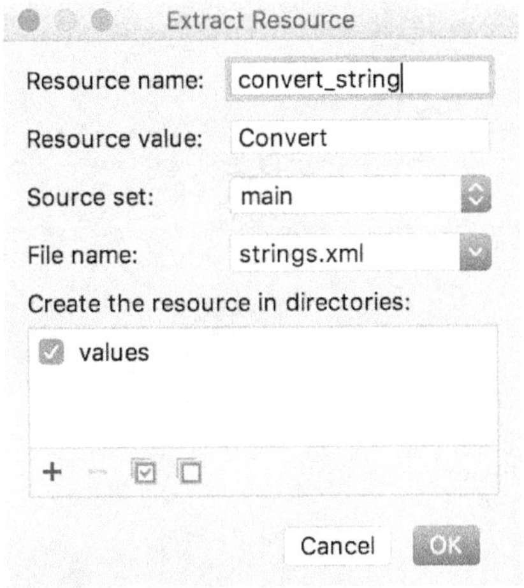

Figure 3-17

It is also worth noting that the string could also have been assigned to a resource when it was entered into the Attributes panel. This involves clicking on the narrow button to the right of the property field in the Attributes panel and selecting the *Add new resource -> New String Value...* menu option from the resulting Resources dialog. In practice, however, it is often quicker to simply set values directly into the Attributes panel fields for any widgets in the layout, then work sequentially through the list in the warnings dialog to extract any necessary resources when the layout is complete.

The next widget to be added is an EditText widget into which the user will enter the dollar amount to be converted. From the widget palette, select the Text category and click and drag a Number (Decimal) component onto the layout so that it is centered horizontally and positioned above the existing TextView widget. With the widget selected, use the Attributes tools window to set the *hint* property to "dollars". Click on the warning icon and extract the string to a resource named *dollars_hint*.

Add any missing layout constraints by clicking on the *Infer constraints* button. At this point the layout should resemble that shown in Figure 3-18:

Figure 3-18

The code written later in this chapter will need to access the dollar value entered by the user into the EditText field. It will do this by referencing the id assigned to the widget in the user interface layout. The default id assigned to the widget by Android Studio can be viewed and changed from within the Attributes tool window when the widget is selected in the layout as shown in Figure 3-19:

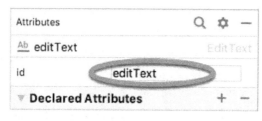

Figure 3-19

Change the id to *dollarText* before proceeding.

3.6 Reviewing the Layout and Resource Files

Before moving on to the next step, we are going to look at some of the internal aspects of user interface design and resource handling. In the previous section, we made some changes to the user interface by modifying the *content_main.xml* file using the Layout Editor tool. In fact, all that the Layout Editor was doing was providing a user-friendly way to edit the underlying XML content of the file. In practice, there is no reason why you cannot modify the XML directly in order to make user interface changes and, in some instances, this may actually be quicker than using the Layout Editor tool. At the bottom of the Layout Editor panel are two tabs labeled *Design* and *Text* respectively. To switch to the XML view simply select the *Text* tab as shown in Figure 3-20:

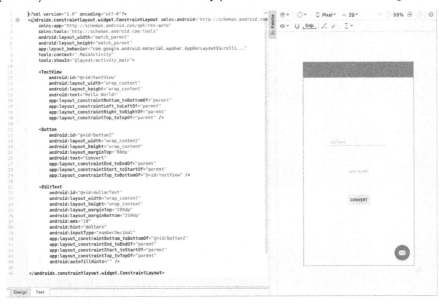

Figure 3-20

As can be seen from the structure of the XML file, the user interface consists of the ConstraintLayout component, which in turn, is the parent of the Button object. We can also see that the *text* property of the Button is set to our *convert_string* resource. Although varying in complexity and content, all user interface layouts are structured in this hierarchical, XML based way.

One of the more powerful features of Android Studio can be found to the right-hand side of the XML editing panel. If the panel is not visible, display it by selecting the *Preview* button located along the right-hand edge of the Android Studio window. This is the Preview panel and shows the current visual state of the layout. As changes are made to the XML layout, these will be reflected in the preview panel. The layout may also be modified visually from within the Preview panel with the changes appearing in the XML listing. To see this in action, modify the XML layout to change the background color of the ConstraintLayout to a shade of red as follows:

```
<?xml version="1.0" encoding="utf-8"?>
<androidx.constraintlayout.widget.ConstraintLayout
    xmlns:android="http://schemas.android.com/apk/res/android"
    xmlns:app="http://schemas.android.com/apk/res-auto"
    xmlns:tools="http://schemas.android.com/tools"
    android:layout_width="match_parent"
    android:layout_height="match_parent"
    app:layout_behavior="@string/appbar_scrolling_view_behavior"
    tools:context=".MainActivity"
    tools:showIn="@layout/activity_main"
    android:background="#ff2438" >
    .
    .
    .
</androidx.constraintlayout.widget.ConstraintLayout>
```

Note that the color of the preview changes in real-time to match the new setting in the XML file. Note also that a small red square appears in the left-hand margin (also referred to as the *gutter*) of the XML editor next to the line containing the color setting. This is a visual cue to the fact that the color red has been set on a property.

Before proceeding, delete the background property from the layout file so that the background returns to the default setting.

Finally, use the Project view to locate the *app -> res -> values -> strings.xml* file and double-click on it to load it into the editor. Currently the XML should read as follows:

```
<resources>
    <string name="app_name">AndroidSample</string>
    <string name="action_settings">Settings</string>
    <string name="convert_string">Convert</string>
    <string name="dollars_hint">dollars</string>
</resources>
```

As a demonstration of resources in action, change the string value currently assigned to the *convert_string* resource to "Convert to Euros" and then return to the Layout Editor tool by selecting the tab for the layout file in the editor panel. Note that the layout has picked up the new resource value for the string.

There is also a quick way to access the value of a resource referenced in an XML file. With the Layout Editor tool in Text mode, click on the "@string/convert_string" property setting so that it highlights and then press Ctrl-B on the keyboard (Cmd-B on macOS). Android Studio will subsequently open the *strings.xml* file and take you to the line in that file where this resource is declared. Use this opportunity to revert the string resource back to the original "Convert" text and to add the following additional entry for a string resource that will be referenced later in the app code:

```
<resources>
    <string name="app_name">AndroidSample</string>
    <string name="action_settings">Settings</string>
    <string name="convert_string">Convert</string>
    <string name="dollars_hint">dollars</string>
    <string name="no_value_string">No Value</string>
</resources>
```

Resource strings may also be edited using the Android Studio Translations Editor. To open this editor, right-click on the *app -> res -> values -> strings.xml* file and select the *Open editor* menu option. This will display the Translation Editor in the main panel of the Android Studio window:

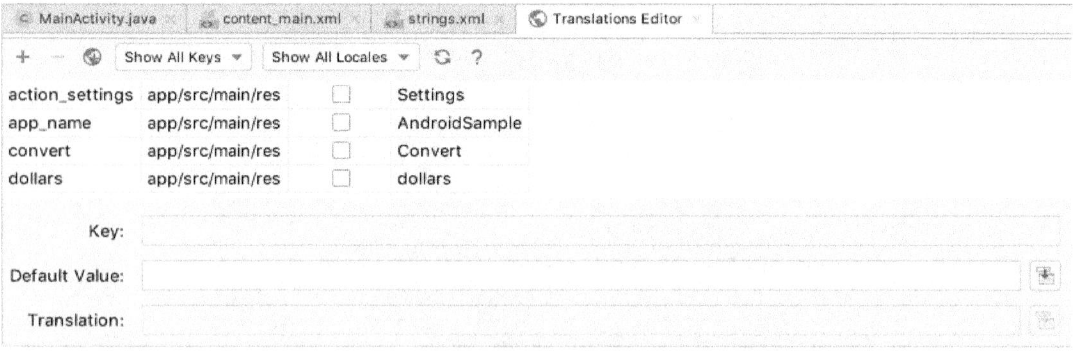

Figure 3-21

This editor allows the strings assigned to resource keys to be edited and for translations for multiple languages to be managed.

3.7 Adding Interaction

The final step in this example project is to make the app interactive so that when the user enters a dollar value into the EditText field and clicks the convert button the converted euro value appears on the TextView. This involves the implementation of some event handling on the Button widget. Specifically, the Button needs to be configured so that a method in the app code is called when an *onClick* event is triggered. Event handling can be implemented in a number of different ways and is covered in detail in a later chapter entitled *"An Overview and Example of Android Event Handling"*. Return the layout editor to Design mode, select the Button widget in the layout editor, refer to the Attributes tool window and specify a method named *convertCurrency* as shown below:

Figure 3-22

Note that the text field for the onClick property is now highlighted with a red border to warn us that the button has been configured to call a method which does not yet exist. To address this, double-click on the *MainActivity. java* file to load it into the code editor and add the code for the convertCurrency method to the class file so that it reads as follows, noting that it is also necessary to import some additional Android packages:

```
package com.ebookfrenzy.androidsample;

import android.os.Bundle;

import com.google.android.material.floatingactionbutton.FloatingActionButton;
import com.google.android.material.snackbar.Snackbar;

import androidx.appcompat.app.AppCompatActivity;
import androidx.appcompat.widget.Toolbar;

import android.view.View;
import android.view.Menu;
import android.view.MenuItem;
import android.widget.EditText;
import android.widget.TextView;

public class MainActivity extends AppCompatActivity {

    .

    .

    public void convertCurrency(View view) {
```

```
        EditText dollarText = findViewById(R.id.dollarText);
        TextView textView = findViewById(R.id.textView);

        if (!dollarText.getText().toString().equals("")) {

            float dollarValue = Float.valueOf(dollarText.getText().toString());
            float euroValue = dollarValue * 0.85F;
            textView.setText(euroValue.toString());
        } else {
            textView.setText(R.string.no_value_string);
        }
    }
    .
    .
    .
}
```

The method begins by obtaining references to the EditText and TextView objects by making a call to a method named *findViewById*, passing through the id assigned within the layout file. A check is then made to ensure that the user has entered a dollar value and if so, that value is extracted, converted from a String to a floating point value and converted to euros. Finally, the result is displayed on the TextView widget. If any of this is unclear, rest assured that these concepts will be covered in greater detail in later chapters.

The project is now complete and ready to run, a task that will be performed in the next chapter after an AVD emulator session as been created for testing purposes.

3.8 Summary

While not excessively complex, a number of steps are involved in setting up an Android development environment. Having performed those steps, it is worth working through a simple example to make sure the environment is correctly installed and configured. In this chapter, we have created a simple application and then used the Android Studio Layout Editor tool to modify the user interface layout. In doing so, we explored the importance of using resources wherever possible, particularly in the case of string values, and briefly touched on the topic of layouts. Next we looked at the underlying XML that is used to store the user interface designs of Android applications.

While it is useful to be able to preview a layout from within the Android Studio Layout Editor tool, there is no substitute for testing an application by compiling and running it.

Finally, an onClick event was added to a Button connected to a method that was implemented to extract the user input from the EditText component, convert from dollars to euros and then display the result on the TextView.

With the app ready for testing, the steps necessary to set up an emulator for testing purposes will be covered in detail in the next chapter.

4. Creating an Android Virtual Device (AVD) in Android Studio

In the course of developing Android apps in Android Studio it will be necessary to compile and run an application multiple times. An Android application may be tested by installing and running it either on a physical device or in an *Android Virtual Device (AVD)* emulator environment. Before an AVD can be used, it must first be created and configured to match the specifications of a particular device model. The goal of this chapter, therefore, is to work through the steps involved in creating such a virtual device using the Pixel 3 phone as a reference example.

4.1 About Android Virtual Devices

AVDs are essentially emulators that allow Android applications to be tested without the necessity to install the application on a physical Android based device. An AVD may be configured to emulate a variety of hardware features including options such as screen size, memory capacity and the presence or otherwise of features such as a camera, GPS navigation support or an accelerometer. As part of the standard Android Studio installation, a number of emulator templates are installed allowing AVDs to be configured for a range of different devices. Custom configurations may be created to match any physical Android device by specifying properties such as processor type, memory capacity and the size and pixel density of the screen.

When launched, an AVD will appear as a window containing an emulated Android device environment. Figure 4-1, for example, shows an AVD session configured to emulate the Google Pixel 3 model.

New AVDs are created and managed using the Android Virtual Device Manager, which may be used either in command-line mode or with a more user-friendly graphical user interface.

Figure 4-1

4.2 Creating a New AVD

In order to test the behavior of an application in the absence of a physical device, it will be necessary to create an AVD for a specific Android device configuration.

To create a new AVD, the first step is to launch the AVD Manager. This can be achieved from within the Android Studio environment by selecting the *Tools -> AVD Manager* menu option from within the main window.

Once launched, the tool will appear as outlined in Figure 4-2 if existing AVD instances have been created:

Figure 4-2

To add an additional AVD, begin by clicking on the *Create Virtual Device* button in order to invoke the *Virtual Device Configuration* dialog:

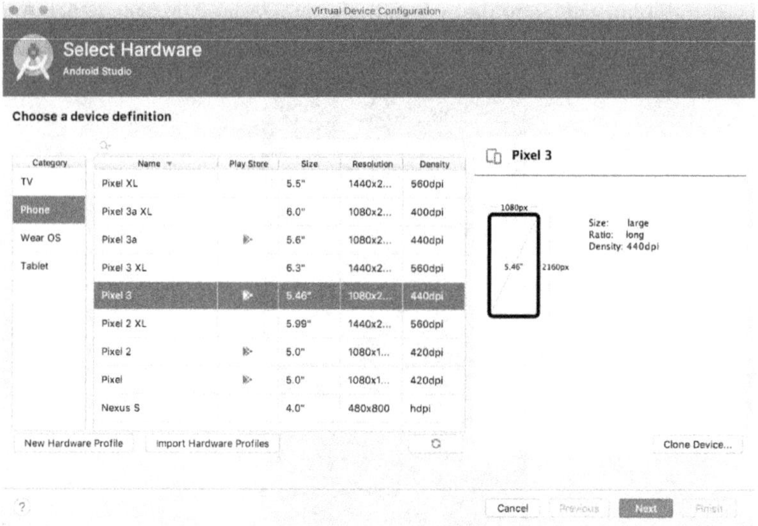

Figure 4-3

Within the dialog, perform the following steps to create a Nexus 5X compatible emulator:

1. From the *Category* panel, select the *Phone* option to display the list of available Android tablet AVD templates.

2. Select the *Pixel 3* device option and click *Next*.

3. On the System Image screen, select the latest version of Android for the *x86* ABI. Note that if the system image has not yet been installed a *Download* link will be provided next to the Release Name. Click this link to download and install the system image before selecting it. If the image you need is not listed, click on the *x86 images* and *Other images* tabs to view alternative lists.

4. Click *Next* to proceed and enter a descriptive name (for example *Pixel 3 API 29*) into the name field or simply accept the default name.

5. Click *Finish* to create the AVD.

6. With the AVD created, the AVD Manager may now be closed. If future modifications to the AVD are necessary, simply re-open the AVD Manager, select the AVD from the list and click on the pencil icon in the *Actions* column of the device row in the AVD Manager.

4.3 Starting the Emulator

To perform a test run of the newly created AVD emulator, simply select the emulator from the AVD Manager and click on the launch button (the green triangle in the Actions column). The emulator will appear in a new window and begin the startup process. The amount of time it takes for the emulator to start will depend on the configuration of both the AVD and the system on which it is running.

Although the emulator probably defaulted to appearing in portrait orientation, this and other default options can be changed. Within the AVD Manager, select the new Nexus 5X entry and click on the pencil icon in the *Actions* column of the device row. In the configuration screen locate the *Startup and orientation* section and change the orientation setting. Exit and restart the emulator session to see this change take effect. More details on the emulator are covered in the next chapter (*"Using and Configuring the Android Studio AVD Emulator"*).

To save time in the next section of this chapter, leave the emulator running before proceeding.

4.4 Running the Application in the AVD

With an AVD emulator configured, the example AndroidSample application created in the earlier chapter now can be compiled and run. With the AndroidSample project loaded into Android Studio, make sure that the newly created Pixel 3 AVD is displayed in the device menu (marked A in Figure 4-4 below), then either click on the run button represented by a green triangle (B), select the *Run -> Run 'app'* menu option or use the Ctrl-R keyboard shortcut:

Figure 4-4

The device menu (A) may be used to select a different AVD instance or physical device as the run target, and also to run the app on multiple devices. The menu also provides access to the AVD Manager and device connection trouble shooting options:

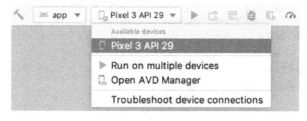

Figure 4-5

Once the application is installed and running, the user interface for the MainActivity class will appear within the emulator:

Figure 4-6

In the event that the activity does not automatically launch, check to see if the launch icon has appeared among the apps on the emulator. If it has, simply click on it to launch the application. Once the run process begins, the Run tool window will become available. The Run tool window will display diagnostic information as the application package is installed and launched. Figure 4-7 shows the Run tool window output from a successful application launch:

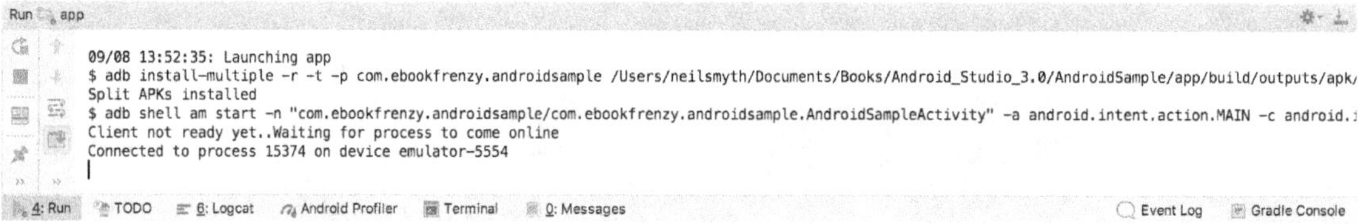

Figure 4-7

If problems are encountered during the launch process, the Run tool window will provide information that will hopefully help to isolate the cause of the problem.

Assuming that the application loads into the emulator and runs as expected, we have safely verified that the Android development environment is correctly installed and configured.

4.5 Stopping a Running Application

To stop a running application, simply click on the stop button located in the main toolbar as shown in Figure 4-8:

Figure 4-8

An app may also be terminated using the Run tool window. Begin by displaying the *Run* tool window using the window bar button that becomes available when the app is running. Once the Run tool window appears, click the stop button highlighted in Figure 4-9 below:

Figure 4-9

4.6 Supporting Dark Theme

Android 10 introduced the much awaited dark theme, support for which is not enabled by default in Android Studio app projects. To test dark theme in the AVD emulator, open the Settings app, choose the *Display* category and enable the *Dark Theme* option as shown in Figure 4-10 so that the screen background turns black:

Figure 4-10

With dark theme enabled, run the AndroidSample app and note that it appears as before and does not conform to the dark theme.

In order for an app to adopt dark theme, it must be derived from the Android DayNight theme. By default, new projects use the Light.DarkActionBar theme. To change this setting, navigate to the *res -> values -> styles.xml* file in the Project window as shown in Figure 4-11 and double-click on it to load it into the editor:

Figure 4-11

Once loaded, edit the AppTheme style entry so that it reads as follows:

```
<resources>

    <!-- Base application theme. -->
    <style name="AppTheme" parent="Theme.AppCompat.DayNight">
        <!-- Customize your theme here. -->
    .
    .
```

After making the change, re-run the app on the emulator and note that it now conforms to the dark theme as shown in Figure 4-12:

Figure 4-12

Open the Settings app, turn off dark theme and return to the AndroidSample app. The app should have automatically switched back to light mode.

4.7 AVD Command-line Creation

As previously discussed, in addition to the graphical user interface it is also possible to create a new AVD directly from the command-line. This is achieved using the *avdmanager* tool in conjunction with some command-line options. Once initiated, the tool will prompt for additional information before creating the new AVD.

The avdmanager tool requires access to the Java Runtime Environment (JRE) in order to run. If, when attempting run avdmanager, an error message appears indicating that the 'java' command cannot be found, the command prompt or terminal window within which you are running the command can be configured to use the OpenJDK environment bundled with Android Studio. Begin by identifying the location of the OpenJDK JRE as follows:

1. Launch Android Studio and open the AndroidSample project created earlier in the book.

2. Select the *File -> Project Structure...* menu option.

3. Copy the path contained within the *JDK location* field of the Project Structure dialog. This represents the location of the JRE bundled with Android Studio.

On Windows, execute the following command within the command prompt window from which avdmanager is to be run (where *<path to jre>* is replaced by the path copied from the Project Structure dialog above):

```
set JAVA_HOME=<path to jre>
```

On macOS or Linux, execute the following command:

```
export JAVA_HOME="<path to jre>"
```

If you expect to use the avdmanager tool frequently, follow the environment variable steps for your operating system outlined in the chapter entitled *"Setting up an Android Studio Development Environment"* to configure JAVA_HOME on a system-wide basis.

Assuming that the system has been configured such that the Android SDK *tools* directory is included in the PATH environment variable, a list of available targets for the new AVD may be obtained by issuing the following command in a terminal or command window:

```
avdmanager list targets
```

The resulting output from the above command will contain a list of Android SDK versions that are available on the system. For example:

```
Available Android targets:
----------
id: 1 or "android-29"
     Name: Android API 29
     Type: Platform
     API level: 29
     Revision: 1
----------
id: 2 or "android-26"
     Name: Android API 26
     Type: Platform
     API level: 26
     Revision: 1
```

The avdmanager tool also allows new AVD instances to be created from the command line. For example, to create a new AVD named *myAVD* using the target ID for the Android API level 29 device using the x86 ABI, the following command may be used:

```
avdmanager create avd -n myAVD -k "system-images;android-29;google_apis_
playstore;x86"
```

The android tool will create the new AVD to the specifications required for a basic Android 8 device, also providing the option to create a custom configuration to match the specification of a specific device if required. Once a new AVD has been created from the command line, it may not show up in the Android Device Manager tool until the *Refresh* button is clicked.

In addition to the creation of new AVDs, a number of other tasks may be performed from the command line. For example, a list of currently available AVDs may be obtained using the *list avd* command line arguments:

```
avdmanager list avd
```

```
Available Android Virtual Devices:
    Name: Pixel_XL_API_28_No_Play
  Device: pixel_xl (Google)
    Path: /Users/neilsmyth/.android/avd/Pixel_XL_API_28_No_Play.avd
  Target: Google APIs (Google Inc.)
          Based on: Android API 28 Tag/ABI: google_apis/x86
    Skin: pixel_xl_silver
  Sdcard: 512M
```

Similarly, to delete an existing AVD, simply use the *delete* option as follows:

```
avdmanager delete avd -n <avd name>
```

4.8 Android Virtual Device Configuration Files

By default, the files associated with an AVD are stored in the *.android/avd* sub-directory of the user's home directory, the structure of which is as follows (where *<avd name>* is replaced by the name assigned to the AVD):

```
<avd name>.avd/config.ini
<avd name>.avd/userdata.img
<avd name>.ini
```

The *config.ini* file contains the device configuration settings such as display dimensions and memory specified during the AVD creation process. These settings may be changed directly within the configuration file and will be adopted by the AVD when it is next invoked.

The *<avd name>.ini* file contains a reference to the target Android SDK and the path to the AVD files. Note that a change to the *image.sysdir* value in the *config.ini* file will also need to be reflected in the *target* value of this file.

4.9 Moving and Renaming an Android Virtual Device

The current name or the location of the AVD files may be altered from the command line using the *avdmanager* tool's *move avd* argument. For example, to rename an AVD named Nexus9 to Nexus9B, the following command may be executed:

```
avdmanager move avd -n Nexus9 -r Nexus9B
```

To physically relocate the files associated with the AVD, the following command syntax should be used:

```
avdmanager move avd -n <avd name> -p <path to new location>
```

For example, to move an AVD from its current file system location to /tmp/Nexus9Test:

```
avdmanager move avd -n Nexus9 -p /tmp/Nexus9Test
```

Note that the destination directory must not already exist prior to executing the command to move an AVD.

4.10 Summary

A typical application development process follows a cycle of coding, compiling and running in a test environment. Android applications may be tested on either a physical Android device or using an Android Virtual Device (AVD) emulator. AVDs are created and managed using the Android AVD Manager tool which may be used either as a command line tool or using a graphical user interface. When creating an AVD to simulate a specific Android device model it is important that the virtual device be configured with a hardware specification that matches that of the physical device.

5. Using and Configuring the Android Studio AVD Emulator

The Android Virtual Device (AVD) emulator environment bundled with Android Studio 1.x was an uncharacteristically weak point in an otherwise reputable application development environment. Regarded by many developers as slow, inflexible and unreliable, the emulator was long overdue for an overhaul. Fortunately, Android Studio 2 introduced an enhanced emulator environment providing significant improvements in terms of configuration flexibility and overall performance and further enhancements have been made in subsequent releases.

Before the next chapter explores testing on physical Android devices, this chapter will take some time to provide an overview of the Android Studio AVD emulator and highlight many of the configuration features that are available to customize the environment.

5.1 The Emulator Environment

When launched, the emulator displays an initial splash screen during the loading process. Once loaded, the main emulator window appears containing a representation of the chosen device type (in the case of Figure 5-1 this is a Nexus 5X device):

Figure 5-1

Positioned along the right-hand edge of the window is the toolbar providing quick access to the emulator controls and configuration options.

5.2 The Emulator Toolbar Options

The emulator toolbar (Figure 5-2) provides access to a range of options relating to the appearance and behavior of the emulator environment.

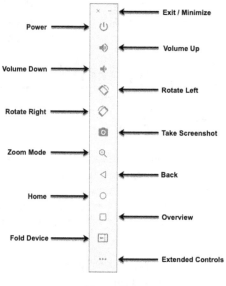

Figure 5-2

Each button in the toolbar has associated with it a keyboard accelerator which can be identified either by hovering the mouse pointer over the button and waiting for the tooltip to appear, or via the help option of the extended controls panel.

Though many of the options contained within the toolbar are self-explanatory, each option will be covered for the sake of completeness:

- **Exit / Minimize** – The uppermost 'x' button in the toolbar exits the emulator session when selected while the '-' option minimizes the entire window.

- **Power** – The Power button simulates the hardware power button on a physical Android device. Clicking and releasing this button will lock the device and turn off the screen. Clicking and holding this button will initiate the device "Power off" request sequence.

- **Volume Up / Down** – Two buttons that control the audio volume of playback within the simulator environment.

- **Rotate Left/Right** – Rotates the emulated device between portrait and landscape orientations.

- **Take Screenshot** – Takes a screenshot of the content currently displayed on the device screen. The captured image is stored at the location specified in the Settings screen of the extended controls panel as outlined later in this chapter.

- **Zoom Mode** – This button toggles in and out of zoom mode, details of which will be covered later in this chapter.

- **Back** – Simulates selection of the standard Android "Back" button. As with the Home and Overview buttons outlined below, the same results can be achieved by selecting the actual buttons on the emulator screen.

- **Home** – Simulates selection of the standard Android "Home" button.

- **Overview** – Simulates selection of the standard Android "Overview" button which displays the currently running apps on the device.

- **Fold Device** – Simulates the folding and unfolding of a foldable device. This option is only available if the emulator is running a foldable device system image.

- **Extended Controls** – Displays the extended controls panel, allowing for the configuration of options such as simulated location and telephony activity, battery strength, cellular network type and fingerprint identification.

5.3 Working in Zoom Mode

The zoom button located in the emulator toolbar switches in and out of zoom mode. When zoom mode is active the toolbar button is depressed and the mouse pointer appears as a magnifying glass when hovering over the device screen. Clicking the left mouse button will cause the display to zoom in relative to the selected point on the screen, with repeated clicking increasing the zoom level. Conversely, clicking the right mouse button decreases the zoom level. Toggling the zoom button off reverts the display to the default size.

Clicking and dragging while in zoom mode will define a rectangular area into which the view will zoom when the mouse button is released.

While in zoom mode the visible area of the screen may be panned using the horizontal and vertical scrollbars located within the emulator window.

5.4 Resizing the Emulator Window

The size of the emulator window (and the corresponding representation of the device) can be changed at any time by clicking and dragging on any of the corners or sides of the window.

5.5 Extended Control Options

The extended controls toolbar button displays the panel illustrated in Figure 5-3. By default, the location settings will be displayed. Selecting a different category from the left-hand panel will display the corresponding group of controls:

Figure 5-3

5.5.1 Location

The location controls allow simulated location information to be sent to the emulator in the form of decimal or sexigesimal coordinates. Location information can take the form of a single location, or a sequence of points representing movement of the device, the latter being provided via a file in either GPS Exchange (GPX) or Keyhole Markup Language (KML) format.

A single location is transmitted to the emulator when the *Send* button is clicked. The transmission of GPS data points begins once the "play" button located beneath the data table is selected. The speed at which the GPS data points are fed to the emulator can be controlled using the speed menu adjacent to the play button.

5.5.2 Cellular

The type of cellular connection being simulated can be changed within the cellular settings screen. Options are available to simulate different network types (CSM, EDGE, HSDPA etc) in addition to a range of voice and data scenarios such as roaming and denied access.

5.5.3 Camera

The emulator simulates a 3D scene when the camera is active. This takes the form of the interior of a virtual building through which you can navigate by holding down the Option key (Alt on Windows) while using the mouse pointer and keyboard keys when recording video or before taking a photo within the emulator. This extended configuration option allows different images to be uploaded for display within the virtual environment.

5.5.4 Battery

A variety of battery state and charging conditions can be simulated on this panel of the extended controls screen, including battery charge level, battery health and whether the AC charger is currently connected.

5.5.5 Phone

The phone extended controls provide two very simple but useful simulations within the emulator. The first option allows for the simulation of an incoming call from a designated phone number. This can be of particular use when testing the way in which an app handles high level interrupts of this nature.

The second option allows the receipt of text messages to be simulated within the emulator session. As in the real world, these messages appear within the Message app and trigger the standard notifications within the emulator.

5.5.6 Directional Pad

A directional pad (D-Pad) is an additional set of controls either built into an Android device or connected externally (such as a game controller) that provides directional controls (left, right, up, down). The directional pad settings allow D-Pad interaction to be simulated within the emulator.

5.5.7 Microphone

The microphone settings allow the microphone to be enabled and virtual headset and microphone connections to be simulated. A button is also provided to launch the Voice Assistant on the emulator.

5.5.8 Fingerprint

Many Android devices are now supplied with built-in fingerprint detection hardware. The AVD emulator makes it possible to test fingerprint authentication without the need to test apps on a physical device containing a fingerprint sensor. Details on how to configure fingerprint testing within the emulator will be covered in detail later in this chapter.

5.5.9 Virtual Sensors

The virtual sensors option allows the accelerometer and magnetometer to be simulated to emulate the effects of the physical motion of a device such as rotation, movement and tilting through yaw, pitch and roll settings.

5.5.10 Snapshots

Snapshots contain the state of the currently running AVD session to be saved and rapidly restored making it easy to return the emulator to an exact state. Snapshots are covered in detail later in this chapter.

5.5.11 Record and Playback

Allows the emulator screen and audio to be recorded and saved in either WebM or animated GIF format.

5.5.12 Google Play

If the emulator is running a version of Android with Google Play Services installed, this option displays the current Google Play version and provides the option to update the emulator to the latest version.

5.5.13 Settings

The settings panel provides a small group of configuration options. Use this panel to choose a darker theme for the toolbar and extended controls panel, specify a file system location into which screenshots are to be saved, configure OpenGL support levels, and to configure the emulator window to appear on top of other windows on the desktop.

5.5.14 Help

The Help screen contains three sub-panels containing a list of keyboard shortcuts, links to access the emulator online documentation, file bugs and send feedback, and emulator version information.

5.6 Working with Snapshots

When an emulator starts for the very first time it performs a *cold boot* much like a physical Android device when it is powered on. This cold boot process can take some time to complete as the operating system loads and all the background processes are started. To avoid the necessity of going through this process every time the emulator is started, the system is configured to automatically save a snapshot (referred to as a *quick-boot snapshot*) of the emulator's current state each time it exits. The next time the emulator is launched, the quick-boot snapshot is loaded into memory and execution resumes from where it left off previously, allowing the emulator to restart in a fraction of the time needed for a cold boot to complete.

The Snapshots screen of the extended controls panel can be used to store additional snapshots at any point during the execution of the emulator. This saves the exact state of the entire emulator allowing the emulator to be restored to the exact point in time that the snapshot was taken. From within the screen, snapshots can be taken using the *Take Snapshot* button (marked A in Figure 5-4). To restore an existing snapshot, select it from the list (B) and click the run button (C) located at the bottom of the screen. Options are also provided to edit (D) the snapshot name and description and to delete (E) the currently selected snapshot:

Figure 5-4

The Settings option (F) provides the option to configure the automatic saving of quick-boot snapshots (by default the emulator will ask whether to save the quick boot snapshot each time the emulator exits) and to reload the most recent snapshot. To force an emulator session to perform a cold boot instead of using a previous quick-boot snapshot, open the AVD Manager (*Tools -> AVD Manager*), click on the down arrow in the actions column for the emulator and select the Cold Boot Now menu option.

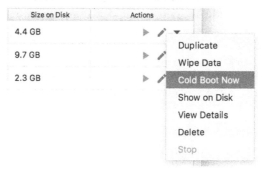

Figure 5-5

5.7 Configuring Fingerprint Emulation

The emulator allows up to 10 simulated fingerprints to be configured and used to test fingerprint authentication within Android apps. To configure simulated fingerprints begin by launching the emulator, opening the Settings app and selecting the *Security & Location* option.

Within the Security settings screen, select the *Use fingerprint* option. On the resulting information screen click on the *Next* button to proceed to the Fingerprint setup screen. Before fingerprint security can be enabled a backup screen unlocking method (such as a PIN number) must be configured. Click on the *Fingerprint + PIN* button and, when prompted, choose not to require the PIN on device startup. Enter and confirm a suitable PIN number and complete the PIN entry process by accepting the default notifications option.

Proceed through the remaining screens until the Settings app requests a fingerprint on the sensor. At this point display the extended controls dialog, select the *Fingerprint* category in the left-hand panel and make sure that *Finger 1* is selected in the main settings panel:

Figure 5-6

Click on the *Touch the Sensor* button to simulate Finger 1 touching the fingerprint sensor. The emulator will report the successful addition of the fingerprint:

Figure 5-7

To add additional fingerprints click on the *Add Another* button and select another finger from the extended controls panel menu before clicking on the *Touch the Sensor* button once again. The topic of building fingerprint authentication into an Android app is covered in detail in the chapter entitled *"An Android Biometric Authentication Tutorial"*.

5.8 Summary

Android Studio 3.5 contains a new and improved Android Virtual Device emulator environment designed to make it easier to test applications without the need to run on a physical Android device. This chapter has provided a brief tour of the emulator and highlighted key features that are available to configure and customize the environment to simulate different testing conditions

6. A Tour of the Android Studio User Interface

While it is tempting to plunge into running the example application created in the previous chapter, doing so involves using aspects of the Android Studio user interface which are best described in advance.

Android Studio is a powerful and feature rich development environment that is, to a large extent, intuitive to use. That being said, taking the time now to gain familiarity with the layout and organization of the Android Studio user interface will considerably shorten the learning curve in later chapters of the book. With this in mind, this chapter will provide an initial overview of the various areas and components that make up the Android Studio environment.

6.1 The Welcome Screen

The welcome screen (Figure 6-1) is displayed any time that Android Studio is running with no projects currently open (open projects can be closed at any time by selecting the *File -> Close Project* menu option). If Android Studio was previously exited while a project was still open, the tool will by-pass the welcome screen next time it is launched, automatically opening the previously active project.

Figure 6-1

In addition to a list of recent projects, the Quick Start menu provides a range of options for performing tasks such as opening, creating and importing projects along with access to projects currently under version control. In addition, the *Configure* menu at the bottom of the window provides access to the SDK Manager along with a vast array of settings and configuration options. A review of these options will quickly reveal that there is almost no aspect of Android Studio that cannot be configured and tailored to your specific needs.

The Configure menu also includes an option to check if updates to Android Studio are available for download.

6.2 The Main Window

When a new project is created, or an existing one opened, the Android Studio *main window* will appear. When multiple projects are open simultaneously, each will be assigned its own main window. The precise configuration of the window will vary depending on which tools and panels were displayed the last time the project was open, but will typically resemble that of Figure 6-2.

Figure 6-2

The various elements of the main window can be summarized as follows:

A – Menu Bar – Contains a range of menus for performing tasks within the Android Studio environment.

B – Toolbar – A selection of shortcuts to frequently performed actions. The toolbar buttons provide quicker access to a select group of menu bar actions. The toolbar can be customized by right-clicking on the bar and selecting the *Customize Menus and Toolbars...* menu option.

C – Navigation Bar – The navigation bar provides a convenient way to move around the files and folders that make up the project. Clicking on an element in the navigation bar will drop down a menu listing the subfolders and files at that location ready for selection. This provides an alternative to the Project tool window.

D – Editor Window – The editor window displays the content of the file on which the developer is currently working. What gets displayed in this location, however, is subject to context. When editing code, for example, the code editor will appear. When working on a user interface layout file, on the other hand, the user interface Layout Editor tool will appear. When multiple files are open, each file is represented by a tab located along the top edge of the editor as shown in Figure 6-3.

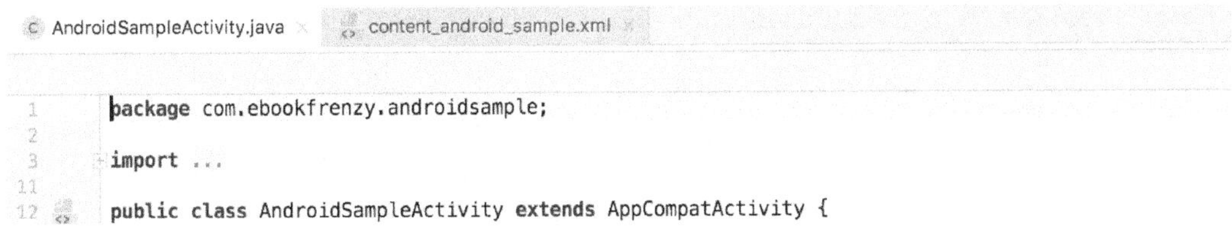

```
 C  AndroidSampleActivity.java  ×      content_android_sample.xml  ×

  1        package com.ebookfrenzy.androidsample;
  2
  3      ┌ import ...
 11
 12        public class AndroidSampleActivity extends AppCompatActivity {
```

Figure 6-3

E – Status Bar – The status bar displays informational messages about the project and the activities of Android Studio together with the tools menu button located in the far left corner. Hovering over items in the status bar will provide a description of that field. Many fields are interactive, allowing the user to click to perform tasks or obtain more detailed status information.

F – Project Tool Window – The project tool window provides a hierarchical overview of the project file structure allowing navigation to specific files and folders to be performed. The toolbar can be used to display the project in a number of different ways. The default setting is the *Android* view which is the mode primarily used in the remainder of this book.

The project tool window is just one of a number of tool windows available within the Android Studio environment.

6.3 The Tool Windows

In addition to the project view tool window, Android Studio also includes a number of other windows which, when enabled, are displayed along the bottom and sides of the main window. The tool window quick access menu can be accessed by hovering the mouse pointer over the button located in the far left-hand corner of the status bar (Figure 6-4) without clicking the mouse button.

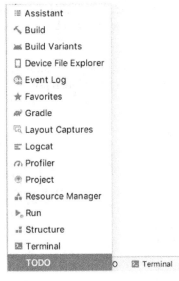

Figure 6-4

Selecting an item from the quick access menu will cause the corresponding tool window to appear within the main window.

Alternatively, a set of *tool window bars* can be displayed by clicking on the quick access menu icon in the status bar. These bars appear along the left, right and bottom edges of the main window (as indicated by the arrows in Figure 6-5) and contain buttons for showing and hiding each of the tool windows. When the tool window bars are displayed, a second click on the button in the status bar will hide them.

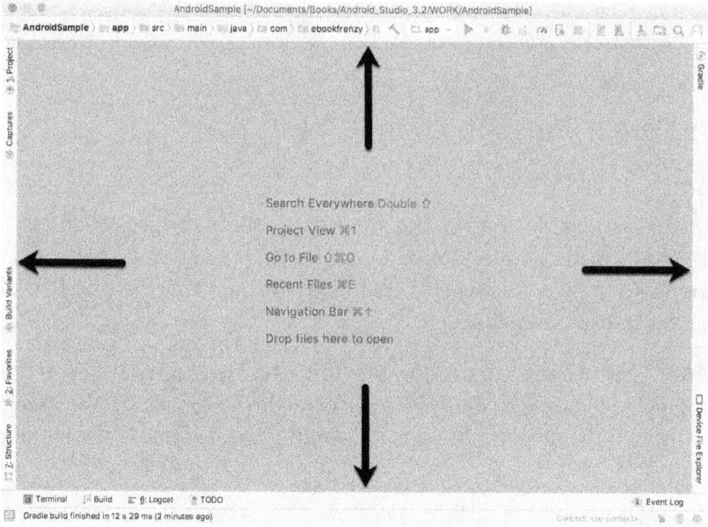

Figure 6-5

Clicking on a button will display the corresponding tool window while a second click will hide the window. Buttons prefixed with a number (for example 1: Project) indicate that the tool window may also be displayed by pressing the Alt key on the keyboard (or the Command key for macOS) together with the corresponding number.

The location of a button in a tool window bar indicates the side of the window against which the window will appear when displayed. These positions can be changed by clicking and dragging the buttons to different locations in other window tool bars.

Each tool window has its own toolbar along the top edge. The buttons within these toolbars vary from one tool to the next, though all tool windows contain a settings option, represented by the cog icon, which allows various aspects of the window to be changed. Figure 6-6 shows the settings menu for the project view tool window. Options are available, for example, to undock a window and to allow it to float outside of the boundaries of the Android Studio main window and to move and resize the tool panel.

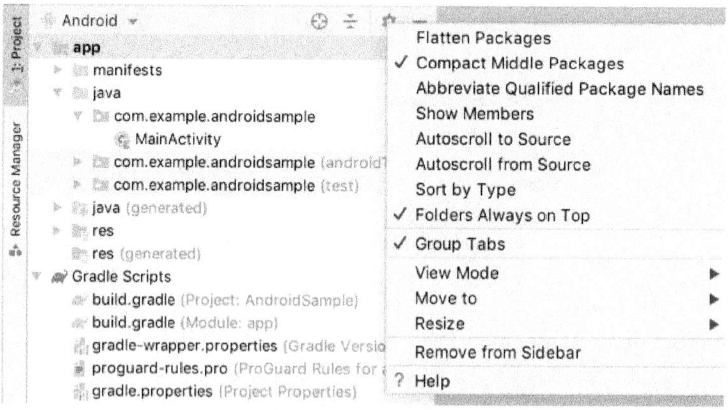

Figure 6-6

All of the windows also include a far right button on the toolbar providing an additional way to hide the tool window from view. A search of the items within a tool window can be performed simply by giving that window focus by clicking in it and then typing the search term (for example the name of a file in the Project tool window). A search box will appear in the window's tool bar and items matching the search highlighted.

Android Studio offers a wide range of tool windows, the most commonly used of which are as follows:

Project – The project view provides an overview of the file structure that makes up the project allowing for quick navigation between files. Generally, double-clicking on a file in the project view will cause that file to be loaded into the appropriate editing tool.

Structure – The structure tool provides a high level view of the structure of the source file currently displayed in the editor. This information includes a list of items such as classes, methods and variables in the file. Selecting an item from the structure list will take you to that location in the source file in the editor window.

Layout Captures – Provides access to all of the layout hierarchy snapshots previously captured using the Layout Inspector tool (*Tools -> Layout Inspector*).

Favorites – A variety of project items can be added to the favorites list. Right-clicking on a file in the project view, for example, provides access to an *Add to Favorites* menu option. Similarly, a method in a source file can be added as a favorite by right-clicking on it in the Structure tool window. Anything added to a Favorites list can be accessed through this Favorites tool window.

Build Variants – The build variants tool window provides a quick way to configure different build targets for the current application project (for example different builds for debugging and release versions of the application, or multiple builds to target different device categories).

TODO – As the name suggests, this tool provides a place to review items that have yet to be completed on the project. Android Studio compiles this list by scanning the source files that make up the project to look for comments that match specified TODO patterns. These patterns can be reviewed and changed by selecting the *File -> Settings...* menu option (*Android Studio -> Preferences...* on macOS) and navigating to the *TODO* page listed under *Editor*.

Logcat – The Logcat tool window provides access to the monitoring log output from a running application in addition to options for taking screenshots and videos of the application and stopping and restarting a process.

Terminal – Provides access to a terminal window on the system on which Android Studio is running. On Windows systems this is the Command Prompt interface, while on Linux and macOS systems this takes the form of a Terminal prompt.

Build - The build tool windows displays information about the build process while a project is being compiled and packaged and displays details of any errors encountered.

Run – The run tool window becomes available when an application is currently running and provides a view of the results of the run together with options to stop or restart a running process. If an application is failing to install and run on a device or emulator, this window will typically provide diagnostic information relating to the problem.

Event Log – The event log window displays messages relating to events and activities performed within Android Studio. The successful build of a project, for example, or the fact that an application is now running will be reported within this tool window.

Gradle – The Gradle tool window provides a view onto the Gradle tasks that make up the project build configuration. The window lists the tasks that are involved in compiling the various elements of the project into an executable application. Right-click on a top level Gradle task and select the *Open Gradle Config* menu option to load the Gradle build file for the current project into the editor. Gradle will be covered in greater detail later in this book.

Profiler – The Android Profiler tool window provides realtime monitoring and analysis tools for identifying performance issues within running apps, including CPU, memory and network usage. This option becomes available when an app is currently running.

Device File Explorer – The Device File Explorer tool window provides direct access to the filesystem of the currently connected Android device or emulator allowing the filesystem to be browsed and files copied to the local filesystem.

Resource Manager - A tool for adding and managing resources and assets such as images, colors and layout files contained with the project.

6.4 Android Studio Keyboard Shortcuts

Android Studio includes an abundance of keyboard shortcuts designed to save time when performing common tasks. A full keyboard shortcut keymap listing can be viewed and printed from within the Android Studio project window by selecting the *Help -> Keymap Reference* menu option.

6.5 Switcher and Recent Files Navigation

Another useful mechanism for navigating within the Android Studio main window involves the use of the *Switcher*. Accessed via the *Ctrl-Tab* keyboard shortcut, the switcher appears as a panel listing both the tool windows and currently open files (Figure 6-7).

Figure 6-7

Once displayed, the switcher will remain visible for as long as the Ctrl key remains depressed. Repeatedly tapping the Tab key while holding down the Ctrl key will cycle through the various selection options, while releasing the Ctrl key causes the currently highlighted item to be selected and displayed within the main window.

In addition to the switcher, navigation to recently opened files is provided by the Recent Files panel (Figure 6-8). This can be accessed using the Ctrl-E keyboard shortcut (Cmd-E on macOS). Once displayed, either the mouse pointer can be used to select an option or, alternatively, the keyboard arrow keys used to scroll through the file name and tool window options. Pressing the Enter key will select the currently highlighted item.

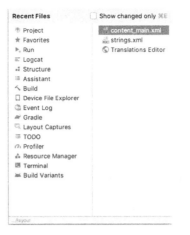

Figure 6-8

6.6 Changing the Android Studio Theme

The overall theme of the Android Studio environment may be changed either from the welcome screen using the *Configure -> Settings* option, or via the *File -> Settings...* menu option (*Android Studio -> Preferences...* on macOS) of the main window.

Once the settings dialog is displayed, select the *Appearance* option in the left-hand panel and then change the setting of the *Theme* menu before clicking on the *Apply* button. The themes available will depend on the platform but usually include options such as Light, IntelliJ, Windows, High Contrast and Darcula. Figure 6-9 shows an example of the main window with the Darcula theme selected:

Figure 6-9

6.7 Summary

The primary elements of the Android Studio environment consist of the welcome screen and main window. Each open project is assigned its own main window which, in turn, consists of a menu bar, toolbar, editing and design area, status bar and a collection of tool windows. Tool windows appear on the sides and bottom edges of the main window and can be accessed either using the quick access menu located in the status bar, or via the optional tool window bars.

There are very few actions within Android Studio which cannot be triggered via a keyboard shortcut. A keymap of default keyboard shortcuts can be accessed at any time from within the Android Studio main window.

7. Testing Android Studio Apps on a Physical Android Device

While much can be achieved by testing applications using an Android Virtual Device (AVD), there is no substitute for performing real world application testing on a physical Android device and there are a number of Android features that are only available on physical Android devices.

Communication with both AVD instances and connected Android devices is handled by the *Android Debug Bridge (ADB)*. In this chapter we will work through the steps to configure the adb environment to enable application testing on a physical Android device with macOS, Windows and Linux based systems.

7.1 An Overview of the Android Debug Bridge (ADB)

The primary purpose of the ADB is to facilitate interaction between a development system, in this case Android Studio, and both AVD emulators and physical Android devices for the purposes of running and debugging applications.

The ADB consists of a client, a server process running in the background on the development system and a daemon background process running in either AVDs or real Android devices such as phones and tablets.

The ADB client can take a variety of forms. For example, a client is provided in the form of a command-line tool named *adb* located in the Android SDK *platform-tools* sub-directory. Similarly, Android Studio also has a built-in client.

A variety of tasks may be performed using the *adb* command-line tool. For example, a listing of currently active virtual or physical devices may be obtained using the *devices* command-line argument. The following command output indicates the presence of an AVD on the system but no physical devices:

```
$ adb devices
List of devices attached
emulator-5554   device
```

7.2 Enabling ADB on Android based Devices

Before ADB can connect to an Android device, that device must first be configured to allow the connection. On phone and tablet devices running Android 6.0 or later, the steps to achieve this are as follows:

1. Open the Settings app on the device and select the *About tablet* or *About phone* option (on newer versions of Android this can be found on the *System* page of the Settings app).

2. On the *About* screen, scroll down to the *Build number* field (Figure 7-1) and tap on it seven times until a message appears indicating that developer mode has been enabled. If the build number is not displayed, unfold the Advanced section of the list.

Wi-Fi MAC address
02:00:00:44:55:66

Build number
PPP2.180412.012

Figure 7-1

3. Return to the main Settings screen and note the appearance of a new option titled Developer options. Select this option and locate the setting on the developer screen entitled USB debugging. Enable the switch next to this item as illustrated in Figure 7-2:

Debugging

USB debugging
Debug mode when USB is connected

Figure 7-2

4. Swipe downward from the top of the screen to display the notifications panel (Figure 7-3) and note that the device is currently connected for debugging.

USB debugging connected
Touch to disable USB debugging.

Figure 7-3

At this point, the device is now configured to accept debugging connections from adb on the development system. All that remains is to configure the development system to detect the device when it is attached. While this is a relatively straightforward process, the steps involved differ depending on whether the development system is running Windows, macOS or Linux. Note that the following steps assume that the Android SDK *platform-tools* directory is included in the operating system PATH environment variable as described in the chapter entitled *"Setting up an Android Studio Development Environment"*.

7.2.1 macOS ADB Configuration

In order to configure the ADB environment on a macOS system, connect the device to the computer system using a USB cable, open a terminal window and execute the following command to restart the adb server:

```
$ adb kill-server
$ adb start-server
* daemon not running. starting it now on port 5037 *
* daemon started successfully *
```

Once the server is successfully running, execute the following command to verify that the device has been detected:

```
$ adb devices
List of devices attached
74CE000600000001        offline
```

If the device is listed as *offline*, go to the Android device and check for the presence of the dialog shown in Figure

7-4 seeking permission to *Allow USB debugging*. Enable the checkbox next to the option that reads *Always allow from this computer*, before clicking on *OK*. Repeating the *adb devices* command should now list the device as being available:

```
List of devices attached
015d41d4454bf80c        device
```

In the event that the device is not listed, try logging out and then back in to the macOS desktop and, if the problem persists, rebooting the system.

7.2.2 Windows ADB Configuration

The first step in configuring a Windows based development system to connect to an Android device using ADB is to install the appropriate USB drivers on the system. The USB drivers to install will depend on the model of Android Device. If you have a Google Nexus device, then it will be necessary to install and configure the Google USB Driver package on your Windows system. Detailed steps to achieve this are outlined on the following web page:

https://developer.android.com/sdk/win-usb.html

For Android devices not supported by the Google USB driver, it will be necessary to download the drivers provided by the device manufacturer. A listing of drivers together with download and installation information can be obtained online at:

https://developer.android.com/tools/extras/oem-usb.html

With the drivers installed and the device now being recognized as the correct device type, open a Command Prompt window and execute the following command:

```
adb devices
```

This command should output information about the connected device similar to the following:

```
List of devices attached
HT4CTJT01906        offline
```

If the device is listed as *offline* or *unauthorized*, go to the device display and check for the dialog shown in Figure 7-4 seeking permission to *Allow USB debugging*.

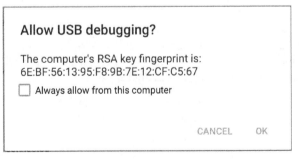

Figure 7-4

Enable the checkbox next to the option that reads *Always allow from this computer*, before clicking on *OK*. Repeating the *adb devices* command should now list the device as being ready:

```
List of devices attached
HT4CTJT01906    device
```

In the event that the device is not listed, execute the following commands to restart the ADB server:

```
adb kill-server
adb start-server
```

If the device is still not listed, try executing the following command:

```
android update adb
```

Note that it may also be necessary to reboot the system.

7.2.3 Linux adb Configuration

For the purposes of this chapter, we will once again use Ubuntu Linux as a reference example in terms of configuring adb on Linux to connect to a physical Android device for application testing.

Physical device testing on Ubuntu Linux requires the installation of a package named *android-tools-adb* which, in turn, requires that the Android Studio user be a member of the *plugdev* group. This is the default for user accounts on most Ubuntu versions and can be verified by running the *id* command. If the plugdev group is not listed, run the following command to add your account to the group:

```
sudo usermod -aG plugdev $LOGNAME
```

After the group membership requirement has been met, the *android-tools-adb* package can be installed by executing the following command:

```
sudo apt-get install android-tools-adb
```

Once the above changes have been made, reboot the Ubuntu system. Once the system has restarted, open a Terminal window, start the adb server and check the list of attached devices:

```
$ adb start-server
* daemon not running. starting it now on port 5037 *
* daemon started successfully *
$ adb devices
List of devices attached
015d41d4454bf80c        offline
```

If the device is listed as *offline* or *unauthorized*, go to the Android device and check for the dialog shown in Figure 7-4 seeking permission to *Allow USB debugging*.

7.3 Testing the adb Connection

Assuming that the adb configuration has been successful on your chosen development platform, the next step is to try running the test application created in the chapter entitled *"Creating an Example Android App in Android Studio"* on the device. Launch Android Studio, open the AndroidSample project and verify that the device appears in the device selection menu as highlighted in Figure 7-5:

Figure 7-5

Note that this menu also includes the option to test the app on multiple devices and emulators simultaneously.

When selected, this option displays the dialog shown in Figure 7-6 where multiple deployment targets may be selected.

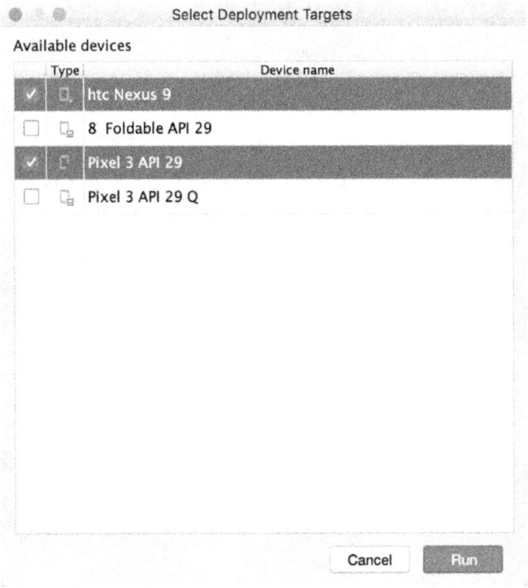

Figure 7-6

7.4 Summary

While the Android Virtual Device emulator provides an excellent testing environment, it is important to keep in mind that there is no real substitute for making sure an application functions correctly on a physical Android device. This, after all, is where the application will be used in the real world.

By default, however, the Android Studio environment is not configured to detect Android devices as a target testing device. It is necessary, therefore, to perform some steps in order to be able to load applications directly onto an Android device from within the Android Studio development environment. The exact steps to achieve this goal differ depending on the development platform being used. In this chapter, we have covered those steps for Linux, macOS and Windows based platforms.

8. The Basics of the Android Studio Code Editor

Developing applications for Android involves a considerable amount of programming work which, by definition, involves typing, reviewing and modifying lines of code. It should come as no surprise that the majority of a developer's time spent using Android Studio will typically involve editing code within the editor window.

The modern code editor needs to go far beyond the original basics of typing, deleting, cutting and pasting. Today the usefulness of a code editor is generally gauged by factors such as the amount by which it reduces the typing required by the programmer, ease of navigation through large source code files and the editor's ability to detect and highlight programming errors in real-time as the code is being written. As will become evident in this chapter, these are just a few of the areas in which the Android Studio editor excels.

While not an exhaustive overview of the features of the Android Studio editor, this chapter aims to provide a guide to the key features of the tool. Experienced programmers will find that some of these features are common to most code editors available today, while a number are unique to this particular editing environment.

8.1 The Android Studio Editor

The Android Studio editor appears in the center of the main window when a Java, Kotlin, XML or other text based file is selected for editing. Figure 8-1, for example, shows a typical editor session with a Java source code file loaded:

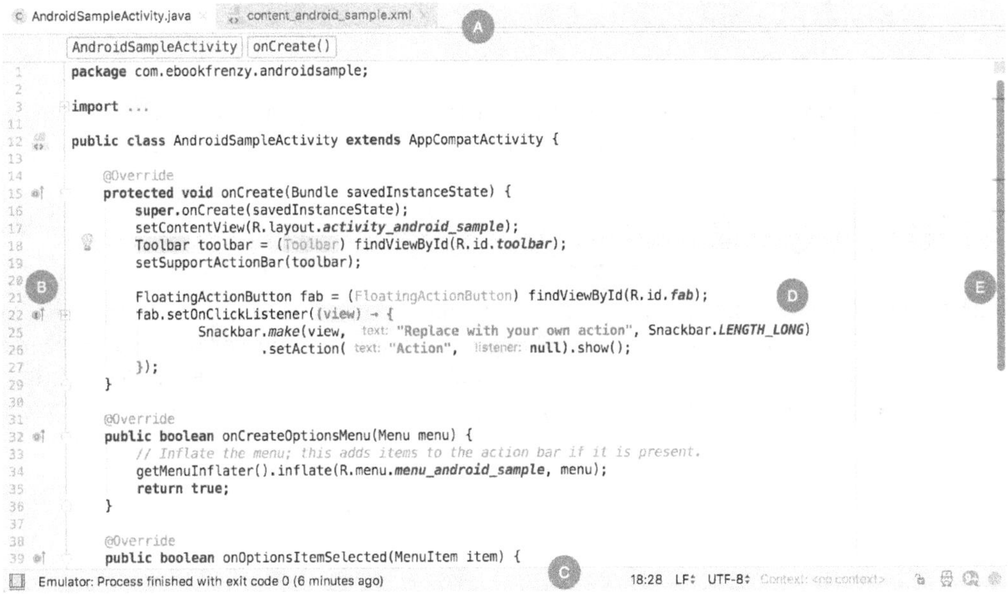

Figure 8-1

The elements that comprise the editor window can be summarized as follows:

A – Document Tabs – Android Studio is capable of holding multiple files open for editing at any one time. As each file is opened, it is assigned a document tab displaying the file name in the tab bar located along the top edge of the editor window. A small dropdown menu will appear in the far right-hand corner of the tab bar when there is insufficient room to display all of the tabs. Clicking on this menu will drop down a list of additional open files. A wavy red line underneath a file name in a tab indicates that the code in the file contains one or more errors that need to be addressed before the project can be compiled and run.

Switching between files is simply a matter of clicking on the corresponding tab or using the *Alt-Left* and *Alt-Right* keyboard shortcuts. Navigation between files may also be performed using the Switcher mechanism (accessible via the *Ctrl-Tab* keyboard shortcut).

To detach an editor panel from the Android Studio main window so that it appears in a separate window, click on the tab and drag it to an area on the desktop outside of the main window. To return the editor to the main window, click on the file tab in the separated editor window and drag and drop it onto the original editor tab bar in the main window.

B – The Editor Gutter Area - The gutter area is used by the editor to display informational icons and controls. Some typical items, among others, which appear in this gutter area are debugging breakpoint markers, controls to fold and unfold blocks of code, bookmarks, change markers and line numbers. Line numbers are switched on by default but may be disabled by right-clicking in the gutter and selecting the *Show Line Numbers* menu option.

C – Code Structure Location - This bar at the bottom of the editor displays the current position of the cursor as it relates to the overall structure of the code. In the following figure, for example, the bar indicates that a setOnClickListener method call is currently being edited, and that this line of code is contained within the onCreate method of the MainActivity class.

Figure 8-2

Selecting an element within the bar will move the cursor to the corresponding location within the code file. For example, selecting the onCreate() entry will move the cursor to the top of the onCreate method within the source code.

D – The Editor Area – This is the main area where the code is displayed, entered and edited by the user. Later sections of this chapter will cover the key features of the editing area in detail.

E – The Validation and Marker Sidebar – Android Studio incorporates a feature referred to as "on-the-fly code analysis". What this essentially means is that as you are typing code, the editor is analyzing the code to check for warnings and syntax errors. The indicator at the top of the validation sidebar will change from a green check mark (no warnings or errors detected) to a yellow square (warnings detected) or red alert icon (errors have been detected). Clicking on this indicator will display a popup containing a summary of the issues found with the code in the editor as illustrated in Figure 8-3:

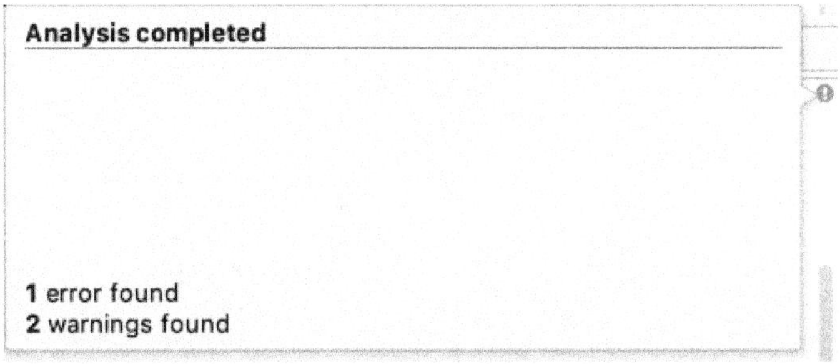

Analysis completed

1 error found
2 warnings found

Figure 8-3

The sidebar also displays markers at the locations where issues have been detected using the same color coding. Hovering the mouse pointer over a marker when the line of code is visible in the editor area will display a popup containing a description of the issue (Figure 8-4):

'infix' modifier is required on 'show' in 'com.google.android.material.snackbar.Snackbar'

Expecting an expression

Unresolved reference: nul

Figure 8-4

Hovering the mouse pointer over a marker for a line of code which is currently scrolled out of the viewing area of the editor will display a "lens" overlay containing the block of code where the problem is located (Figure 8-5) allowing it to be viewed without the necessity to scroll to that location in the editor:

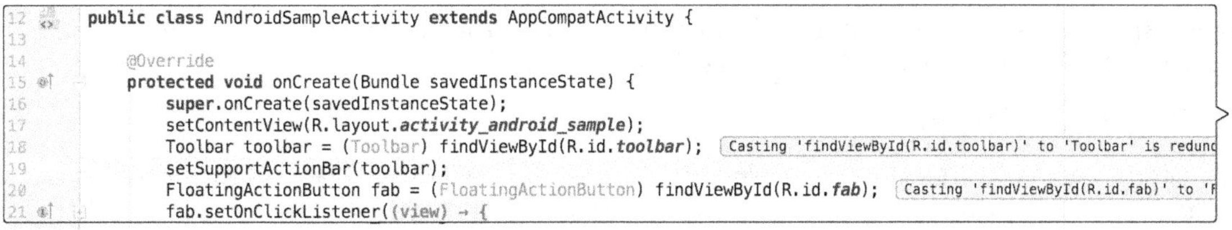

```
12    public class AndroidSampleActivity extends AppCompatActivity {
13
14        @Override
15        protected void onCreate(Bundle savedInstanceState) {
16            super.onCreate(savedInstanceState);
17            setContentView(R.layout.activity_android_sample);
18            Toolbar toolbar = (Toolbar) findViewById(R.id.toolbar);   Casting 'findViewById(R.id.toolbar)' to 'Toolbar' is redund
19            setSupportActionBar(toolbar);
20            FloatingActionButton fab = (FloatingActionButton) findViewById(R.id.fab);   Casting 'findViewById(R.id.fab)' to 'F
21            fab.setOnClickListener((view) → {
```

Figure 8-5

It is also worth noting that the lens overlay is not limited to warnings and errors in the sidebar. Hovering over any part of the sidebar will result in a lens appearing containing the code present at that location within the source file.

F – The Status Bar – Though the status bar is actually part of the main window, as opposed to the editor, it does contain some information about the currently active editing session. This information includes the current position of the cursor in terms of lines and characters and the encoding format of the file (UTF-8, ASCII etc.). Clicking on these values in the status bar allows the corresponding setting to be changed. Clicking on the line number, for example, displays the *Go to Line* dialog.

Having provided an overview of the elements that comprise the Android Studio editor, the remainder of this chapter will explore the key features of the editing environment in more detail.

8.2 Splitting the Editor Window

By default, the editor will display a single panel showing the content of the currently selected file. A particularly useful feature when working simultaneously with multiple source code files is the ability to split the editor into multiple panes. To split the editor, right-click on a file tab within the editor window and select either the *Split Vertically* or *Split Horizontally* menu option. Figure 8-6, for example, shows the splitter in action with the editor split into three panels:

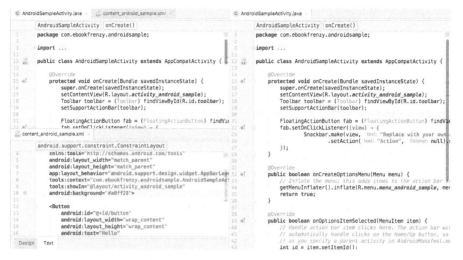

Figure 8-6

The orientation of a split panel may be changed at any time by right-clicking on the corresponding tab and selecting the *Change Splitter Orientation* menu option. Repeat these steps to unsplit a single panel, this time selecting the *Unsplit* option from the menu. All of the split panels may be removed by right-clicking on any tab and selecting the *Unsplit All* menu option.

Window splitting may be used to display different files, or to provide multiple windows onto the same file, allowing different areas of the same file to be viewed and edited concurrently.

8.3 Code Completion

The Android Studio editor has a considerable amount of built-in knowledge of Java programming syntax and the classes and methods that make up the Android SDK, as well as knowledge of your own code base. As code is typed, the editor scans what is being typed and, where appropriate, makes suggestions with regard to what might be needed to complete a statement or reference. When a completion suggestion is detected by the editor, a panel will appear containing a list of suggestions. In Figure 8-7, for example, the editor is suggesting possibilities for the beginning of a String declaration:

Figure 8-7

If none of the auto completion suggestions are correct, simply keep typing and the editor will continue to refine the suggestions where appropriate. To accept the top most suggestion, simply press the Enter or Tab key on the keyboard. To select a different suggestion, use the arrow keys to move up and down the list, once again using the Enter or Tab key to select the highlighted item.

Completion suggestions can be manually invoked using the *Ctrl-Space* keyboard sequence. This can be useful when changing a word or declaration in the editor. When the cursor is positioned over a word in the editor, that word will automatically highlight. Pressing *Ctrl-Space* will display a list of alternate suggestions. To replace the current word with the currently highlighted item in the suggestion list, simply press the Tab key.

In addition to the real-time auto completion feature, the Android Studio editor also offers a system referred to as *Smart Completion*. Smart completion is invoked using the *Shift-Ctrl-Space* keyboard sequence and, when selected, will provide more detailed suggestions based on the current context of the code. Pressing the *Shift-Ctrl-Space* shortcut sequence a second time will provide more suggestions from a wider range of possibilities.

Code completion can be a matter of personal preference for many programmers. In recognition of this fact, Android Studio provides a high level of control over the auto completion settings. These can be viewed and modified by selecting the *File -> Settings...* menu option (or *Android Studio -> Preferences...* on macOS) and choosing *Editor -> General -> Code Completion* from the settings panel as shown in Figure 8-8:

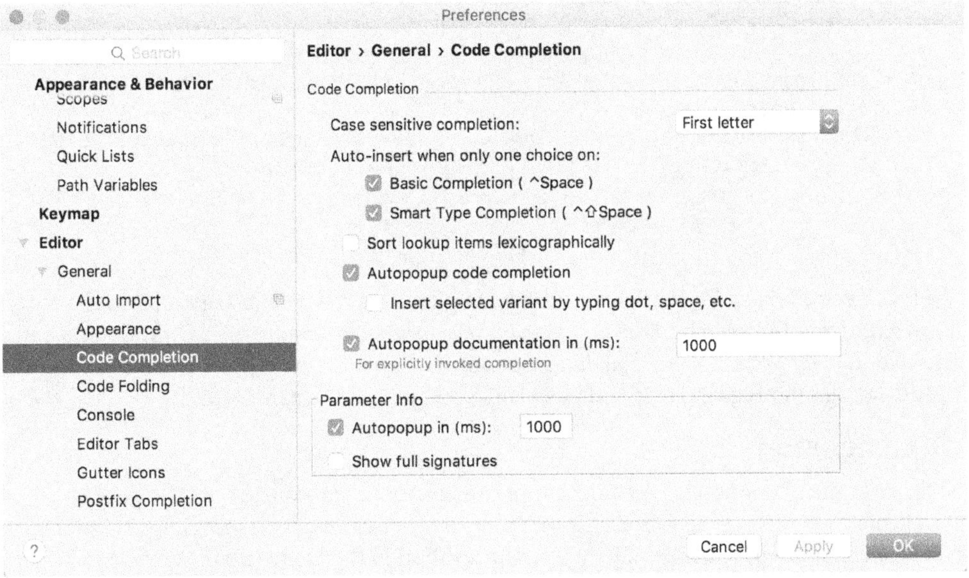

Figure 8-8

8.4 Statement Completion

Another form of auto completion provided by the Android Studio editor is statement completion. This can be used to automatically fill out the parentheses and braces for items such as methods and loop statements. Statement completion is invoked using the *Shift-Ctrl-Enter* (*Shift-Cmd-Enter* on macOS) keyboard sequence. Consider for example the following code:

```
myMethod()
```

Having typed this code into the editor, triggering statement completion will cause the editor to automatically add the braces to the method:

```
myMethod() {

}
```

8.5 Parameter Information

It is also possible to ask the editor to provide information about the argument parameters accepted by a method. With the cursor positioned between the brackets of a method call, the *Ctrl-P* (*Cmd-P* on macOS) keyboard sequence will display the parameters known to be accepted by that method, with the most likely suggestion highlighted in bold:

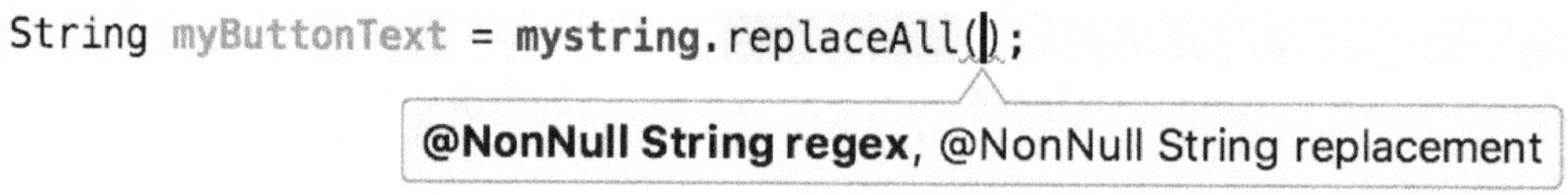

String myButtonText = mystring.replaceAll();
@NonNull String regex, @NonNull String replacement

Figure 8-9

8.6 Parameter Name Hints

The code editor may be configured to display parameter name hints within method calls. Figure 8-10, for example, highlights the parameter name hints within the calls to the *make()* and *setAction()* methods of the *Snackbar* class:

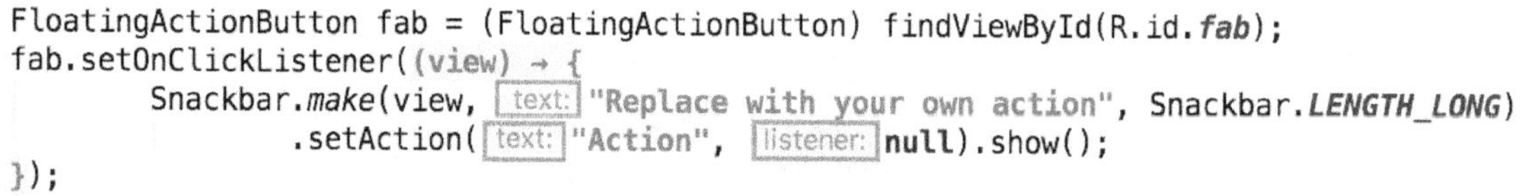

FloatingActionButton fab = (FloatingActionButton) findViewById(R.id.fab);
fab.setOnClickListener((view) → {
Snackbar.make(view, text: "Replace with your own action", Snackbar.LENGTH_LONG)
.setAction(text: "Action", listener: null).show();
});

Figure 8-10

The settings for this mode may be configured by selecting the *File -> Settings* (*Android Studio -> Preferences* on macOS) menu option followed by *Editor -> Appearance* in the left-hand panel. On the Appearance screen, enable or disable the *Show parameter name hints* option. To adjust the hint settings, click on the *Configure...* button, select the programming language and make any necessary adjustments.

8.7 Code Generation

In addition to completing code as it is typed the editor can, under certain conditions, also generate code for you. The list of available code generation options shown in Figure 8-11 can be accessed using the *Alt-Insert* (*Cmd-N* on macOS) keyboard shortcut when the cursor is at the location in the file where the code is to be generated.

Generate
Constructor
toString()
Override Methods... ^O
Implement Methods... ^I
Delegate Methods...
Test...
Copyright

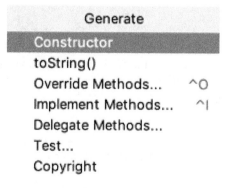

Figure 8-11

For the purposes of an example, consider a situation where we want to be notified when an Activity in our project is about to be destroyed by the operating system. As will be outlined in a later chapter of this book, this can be achieved by overriding the *onStop()* lifecycle method of the Activity superclass. To have Android Studio generate a stub method for this, simply select the *Override Methods...* option from the code generation list and select the *onStop()* method from the resulting list of available methods:

Figure 8-12

Having selected the method to override, clicking on *OK* will generate the stub method at the current cursor location in the Java source file as follows:

```
@Override
protected void onStop() {
    super.onStop();
}
```

8.8 Code Folding

Once a source code file reaches a certain size, even the most carefully formatted and well organized code can become overwhelming and difficult to navigate. Android Studio takes the view that it is not always necessary to have the content of every code block visible at all times. Code navigation can be made easier through the use of the *code folding* feature of the Android Studio editor. Code folding is controlled using markers appearing in the editor gutter at the beginning and end of each block of code in a source file. Figure 8-13, for example, highlights the start and end markers for a method declaration which is not currently folded:

Figure 8-13

Clicking on either of these markers will fold the statement such that only the signature line is visible as shown in Figure 8-14:

Figure 8-14

To unfold a collapsed section of code, simply click on the '+' marker in the editor gutter. To see the hidden code without unfolding it, hover the mouse pointer over the "{...}" indicator as shown in Figure 8-15. The editor will then display the lens overlay containing the folded code block:

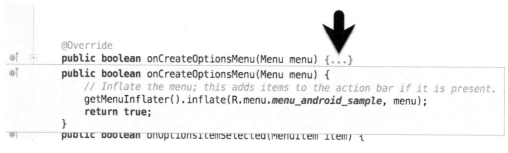

Figure 8-15

All of the code blocks in a file may be folded or unfolded using the *Ctrl-Shift-Plus* and *Ctrl-Shift-Minus* keyboard sequences.

By default, the Android Studio editor will automatically fold some code when a source file is opened. To configure the conditions under which this happens, select *File -> Settings...* (*Android Studio -> Preferences...* on macOS) and choose the *Editor -> General -> Code Folding* entry in the resulting settings panel (Figure 8-16):

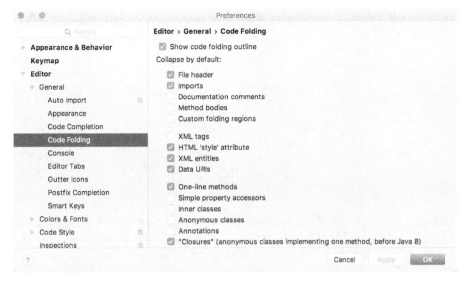

Figure 8-16

8.9 Quick Documentation Lookup

Context sensitive Java and Android documentation can be accessed by placing the cursor over the declaration for which documentation is required and pressing the *Ctrl-Q* keyboard shortcut (*Ctrl-J* on macOS). This will display a popup containing the relevant reference documentation for the item. Figure 8-17, for example, shows the documentation for the Android Snackbar class.

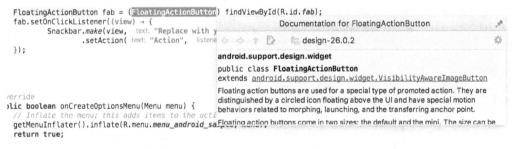

Figure 8-17

Once displayed, the documentation popup can be moved around the screen as needed. Clicking on the push pin icon located in the right-hand corner of the popup title bar will ensure that the popup remains visible once focus moves back to the editor, leaving the documentation visible as a reference while typing code.

8.10 Code Reformatting

In general, the Android Studio editor will automatically format code in terms of indenting, spacing and nesting of statements and code blocks as they are added. In situations where lines of code need to be reformatted (a common occurrence, for example, when cutting and pasting sample code from a web site), the editor provides a source code reformatting feature which, when selected, will automatically reformat code to match the prevailing code style.

To reformat source code, press the *Ctrl-Alt-L* (*Cmd-Opt-L* on macOS) keyboard shortcut sequence. To display the *Reformat Code* dialog (Figure 8-18) use the *Ctrl-Alt-Shift-L* (*Cmd-Opt-Shift-L* on macOS). This dialog provides the option to reformat only the currently selected code, the entire source file currently active in the editor or only code that has changed as the result of a source code control update.

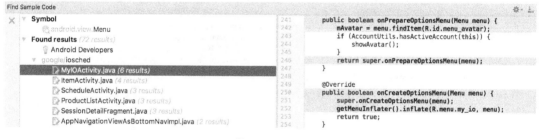

Figure 8-18

The full range of code style preferences can be changed from within the project settings dialog. Select the *File -> Settings* menu option (*Android Studio -> Preferences...* on macOS) and choose *Code Style* in the left-hand panel to access a list of supported programming and markup languages. Selecting a language will provide access to a vast array of formatting style options, all of which may be modified from the Android Studio default to match your preferred code style. To configure the settings for the *Rearrange code* option in the above dialog, for example, unfold the *Code Style* section, select Java and, from the Java settings, select the *Arrangement* tab.

8.11 Finding Sample Code

The Android Studio editor provides a way to access sample code relating to the currently highlighted entry within the code listing. This feature can be useful for learning how a particular Android class or method is used. To find sample code, highlight a method or class name in the editor, right-click on it and select the *Find Sample Code* menu option. The Find Sample Code panel (Figure 8-19) will appear beneath the editor with a list of matching samples. Selecting a sample from the list will load the corresponding code into the right-hand panel:

Figure 8-19

8.12 Summary

The Android Studio editor goes to great length to reduce the amount of typing needed to write code and to make that code easier to read and navigate. In this chapter we have covered a number of the key editor features including code completion, code generation, editor window splitting, code folding, reformatting and documentation lookup.

9. An Overview of the Android Architecture

So far in this book, steps have been taken to set up an environment suitable for the development of Android applications using Android Studio. An initial step has also been taken into the process of application development through the creation of a simple Android Studio application project.

Before delving further into the practical matters of Android application development, however, it is important to gain an understanding of some of the more abstract concepts of both the Android SDK and Android development in general. Gaining a clear understanding of these concepts now will provide a sound foundation on which to build further knowledge.

Starting with an overview of the Android architecture in this chapter, and continuing in the next few chapters of this book, the goal is to provide a detailed overview of the fundamentals of Android development.

9.1 The Android Software Stack

Android is structured in the form of a software stack comprising applications, an operating system, run-time environment, middleware, services and libraries. This architecture can, perhaps, best be represented visually as outlined in Figure 9-1. Each layer of the stack, and the corresponding elements within each layer, are tightly integrated and carefully tuned to provide the optimal application development and execution environment for mobile devices. The remainder of this chapter will work through the different layers of the Android stack, starting at the bottom with the Linux Kernel.

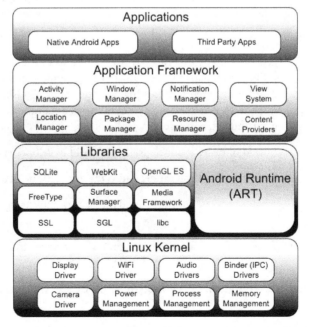

Figure 9-1

9.2 The Linux Kernel

Positioned at the bottom of the Android software stack, the Linux Kernel provides a level of abstraction between the device hardware and the upper layers of the Android software stack. Based on Linux version 2.6, the kernel provides preemptive multitasking, low-level core system services such as memory, process and power management in addition to providing a network stack and device drivers for hardware such as the device display, Wi-Fi and audio.

The original Linux kernel was developed in 1991 by Linus Torvalds and was combined with a set of tools, utilities and compilers developed by Richard Stallman at the Free Software Foundation to create a full operating system referred to as GNU/Linux. Various Linux distributions have been derived from these basic underpinnings such as Ubuntu and Red Hat Enterprise Linux.

It is important to note, however, that Android uses only the Linux kernel. That said, it is worth noting that the Linux kernel was originally developed for use in traditional computers in the form of desktops and servers. In fact, Linux is now most widely deployed in mission critical enterprise server environments. It is a testament to both the power of today's mobile devices and the efficiency and performance of the Linux kernel that we find this software at the heart of the Android software stack.

9.3 Android Runtime – ART

When an Android app is built within Android Studio it is compiled into an intermediate bytecode format (referred to as DEX format). When the application is subsequently loaded onto the device, the Android Runtime (ART) uses a process referred to as Ahead-of-Time (AOT) compilation to translate the bytecode down to the native instructions required by the device processor. This format is known as Executable and Linkable Format (ELF).

Each time the application is subsequently launched, the ELF executable version is run, resulting in faster application performance and improved battery life.

This contrasts with the Just-in-Time (JIT) compilation approach used in older Android implementations whereby the bytecode was translated within a virtual machine (VM) each time the application was launched.

9.4 Android Libraries

In addition to a set of standard Java development libraries (providing support for such general purpose tasks as string handling, networking and file manipulation), the Android development environment also includes the Android Libraries. These are a set of Java-based libraries that are specific to Android development. Examples of libraries in this category include the application framework libraries in addition to those that facilitate user interface building, graphics drawing and database access.

A summary of some key core Android libraries available to the Android developer is as follows:

- **android.app** – Provides access to the application model and is the cornerstone of all Android applications.

- **android.content** – Facilitates content access, publishing and messaging between applications and application components.

- **android.database** – Used to access data published by content providers and includes SQLite database management classes.

- **android.graphics** – A low-level 2D graphics drawing API including colors, points, filters, rectangles and canvases.

- **android.hardware** – Presents an API providing access to hardware such as the accelerometer and light sensor.

- **android.opengl** – A Java interface to the OpenGL ES 3D graphics rendering API.

- **android.os** – Provides applications with access to standard operating system services including messages, system services and inter-process communication.

- **android.media** – Provides classes to enable playback of audio and video.

- **android.net** – A set of APIs providing access to the network stack. Includes *android.net.wifi*, which provides access to the device's wireless stack.

- **android.print** – Includes a set of classes that enable content to be sent to configured printers from within Android applications.

- **android.provider** – A set of convenience classes that provide access to standard Android content provider databases such as those maintained by the calendar and contact applications.

- **android.text** – Used to render and manipulate text on a device display.

- **android.util** – A set of utility classes for performing tasks such as string and number conversion, XML handling and date and time manipulation.

- **android.view** – The fundamental building blocks of application user interfaces.

- **android.widget** - A rich collection of pre-built user interface components such as buttons, labels, list views, layout managers, radio buttons etc.

- **android.webkit** – A set of classes intended to allow web-browsing capabilities to be built into applications.

Having covered the Java-based libraries in the Android runtime, it is now time to turn our attention to the C/C++ based libraries contained in this layer of the Android software stack.

9.4.1 C/C++ Libraries

The Android runtime core libraries outlined in the preceding section are Java-based and provide the primary APIs for developers writing Android applications. It is important to note, however, that the core libraries do not perform much of the actual work and are, in fact, essentially Java "wrappers" around a set of C/C++ based libraries. When making calls, for example, to the *android.opengl* library to draw 3D graphics on the device display, the library actually ultimately makes calls to the *OpenGL ES* C++ library which, in turn, works with the underlying Linux kernel to perform the drawing tasks.

C/C++ libraries are included to fulfill a wide and diverse range of functions including 2D and 3D graphics drawing, Secure Sockets Layer (SSL) communication, SQLite database management, audio and video playback, bitmap and vector font rendering, display subsystem and graphic layer management and an implementation of the standard C system library (libc).

In practice, the typical Android application developer will access these libraries solely through the Java based Android core library APIs. In the event that direct access to these libraries is needed, this can be achieved using the Android Native Development Kit (NDK), the purpose of which is to call the native methods of non-Java or Kotlin programming languages (such as C and C++) from within Java code using the Java Native Interface (JNI).

9.5 Application Framework

The Application Framework is a set of services that collectively form the environment in which Android applications run and are managed. This framework implements the concept that Android applications are constructed from reusable, interchangeable and replaceable components. This concept is taken a step further in that an application is also able to *publish* its capabilities along with any corresponding data so that they can be found and reused by other applications.

The Android framework includes the following key services:

- **Activity Manager** – Controls all aspects of the application lifecycle and activity stack.

- **Content Providers** – Allows applications to publish and share data with other applications.

- **Resource Manager** – Provides access to non-code embedded resources such as strings, color settings and user interface layouts.

- **Notifications Manager** – Allows applications to display alerts and notifications to the user.

- **View System** – An extensible set of views used to create application user interfaces.

- **Package Manager** – The system by which applications are able to find out information about other applications currently installed on the device.

- **Telephony Manager** – Provides information to the application about the telephony services available on the device such as status and subscriber information.

- **Location Manager** – Provides access to the location services allowing an application to receive updates about location changes.

9.6 Applications

Located at the top of the Android software stack are the applications. These comprise both the native applications provided with the particular Android implementation (for example web browser and email applications) and the third party applications installed by the user after purchasing the device.

9.7 Summary

A good Android development knowledge foundation requires an understanding of the overall architecture of Android. Android is implemented in the form of a software stack architecture consisting of a Linux kernel, a runtime environment and corresponding libraries, an application framework and a set of applications. Applications are predominantly written in Java or Kotlin and compiled down to bytecode format within the Android Studio build environment. When the application is subsequently installed on a device, this bytecode is compiled down by the Android Runtime (ART) to the native format used by the CPU. The key goals of the Android architecture are performance and efficiency, both in application execution and in the implementation of reuse in application design.

10. The Anatomy of an Android Application

Regardless of your prior programming experiences, be it Windows, macOS, Linux or even iOS based, the chances are good that Android development is quite unlike anything you have encountered before.

The objective of this chapter, therefore, is to provide an understanding of the high-level concepts behind the architecture of Android applications. In doing so, we will explore in detail both the various components that can be used to construct an application and the mechanisms that allow these to work together to create a cohesive application.

10.1 Android Activities

Those familiar with object-oriented programming languages such as Java, Kotlin, C++ or C# will be familiar with the concept of encapsulating elements of application functionality into classes that are then instantiated as objects and manipulated to create an application. Since Android applications are written in Java and Kotlin, this is still very much the case. Android, however, also takes the concept of re-usable components to a higher level.

Android applications are created by bringing together one or more components known as *Activities*. An activity is a single, standalone module of application functionality that usually correlates directly to a single user interface screen and its corresponding functionality. An appointments application might, for example, have an activity screen that displays appointments set up for the current day. The application might also utilize a second activity consisting of a screen where new appointments may be entered by the user.

Activities are intended as fully reusable and interchangeable building blocks that can be shared amongst different applications. An existing email application, for example, might contain an activity specifically for composing and sending an email message. A developer might be writing an application that also has a requirement to send an email message. Rather than develop an email composition activity specifically for the new application, the developer can simply use the activity from the existing email application.

Activities are created as subclasses of the Android *Activity* class and must be implemented so as to be entirely independent of other activities in the application. In other words, a shared activity cannot rely on being called at a known point in a program flow (since other applications may make use of the activity in unanticipated ways) and one activity cannot directly call methods or access instance data of another activity. This, instead, is achieved using *Intents* and *Content Providers*.

By default, an activity cannot return results to the activity from which it was invoked. If this functionality is required, the activity must be specifically started as a *sub-activity* of the originating activity.

10.2 Android Fragments

An activity, as described above, typically represents a single user interface screen within an app. One option is to construct the activity using a single user interface layout and one corresponding activity class file. A better alternative, however, is to break the activity into different sections. Each of these sections is referred to as a fragment, each of which consists of part of the user interface layout and a matching class file (declared as a subclass of the Android *Fragment* class). In this scenario, an activity simply becomes a container into which one or more fragments are embedded.

In fact, fragments provide an efficient alternative to having each user interface screen represented by a separate activity. Instead, an app can consist of a single activity that switches between different fragments, each representing a different app screen.

10.3 Android Intents

Intents are the mechanism by which one activity is able to launch another and implement the flow through the activities that make up an application. Intents consist of a description of the operation to be performed and, optionally, the data on which it is to be performed.

Intents can be *explicit*, in that they request the launch of a specific activity by referencing the activity by class name, or *implicit* by stating either the type of action to be performed or providing data of a specific type on which the action is to be performed. In the case of implicit intents, the Android runtime will select the activity to launch that most closely matches the criteria specified by the Intent using a process referred to as *Intent Resolution*.

10.4 Broadcast Intents

Another type of Intent, the *Broadcast Intent*, is a system wide intent that is sent out to all applications that have registered an "interested" *Broadcast Receiver*. The Android system, for example, will typically send out Broadcast Intents to indicate changes in device status such as the completion of system start up, connection of an external power source to the device or the screen being turned on or off.

A Broadcast Intent can be *normal* (asynchronous) in that it is sent to all interested Broadcast Receivers at more or less the same time, or *ordered* in that it is sent to one receiver at a time where it can be processed and then either aborted or allowed to be passed to the next Broadcast Receiver.

10.5 Broadcast Receivers

Broadcast Receivers are the mechanism by which applications are able to respond to Broadcast Intents. A Broadcast Receiver must be registered by an application and configured with an *Intent Filter* to indicate the types of broadcast in which it is interested. When a matching intent is broadcast, the receiver will be invoked by the Android runtime regardless of whether the application that registered the receiver is currently running. The receiver then has 5 seconds in which to complete any tasks required of it (such as launching a Service, making data updates or issuing a notification to the user) before returning. Broadcast Receivers operate in the background and do not have a user interface.

10.6 Android Services

Android Services are processes that run in the background and do not have a user interface. They can be started and subsequently managed from activities, Broadcast Receivers or other Services. Android Services are ideal for situations where an application needs to continue performing tasks but does not necessarily need a user interface to be visible to the user. Although Services lack a user interface, they can still notify the user of events using notifications and *toasts* (small notification messages that appear on the screen without interrupting the currently visible activity) and are also able to issue Intents.

Services are given a higher priority by the Android runtime than many other processes and will only be terminated as a last resort by the system in order to free up resources. In the event that the runtime does need to kill a Service, however, it will be automatically restarted as soon as adequate resources once again become available. A Service can reduce the risk of termination by declaring itself as needing to run in the *foreground*. This is achieved by making a call to *startForeground()*. This is only recommended for situations where termination would be detrimental to the user experience (for example, if the user is listening to audio being streamed by the Service).

Example situations where a Service might be a practical solution include, as previously mentioned, the streaming of audio that should continue when the application is no longer active, or a stock market tracking application that needs to notify the user when a share hits a specified price.

10.7 Content Providers

Content Providers implement a mechanism for the sharing of data between applications. Any application can provide other applications with access to its underlying data through the implementation of a Content Provider including the ability to add, remove and query the data (subject to permissions). Access to the data is provided via a Universal Resource Identifier (URI) defined by the Content Provider. Data can be shared in the form of a file or an entire SQLite database.

The native Android applications include a number of standard Content Providers allowing applications to access data such as contacts and media files. The Content Providers currently available on an Android system may be located using a *Content Resolver*.

10.8 The Application Manifest

The glue that pulls together the various elements that comprise an application is the Application Manifest file. It is within this XML based file that the application outlines the activities, services, broadcast receivers, data providers and permissions that make up the complete application.

10.9 Application Resources

In addition to the manifest file and the Dex files that contain the byte code, an Android application package will also typically contain a collection of *resource files*. These files contain resources such as the strings, images, fonts and colors that appear in the user interface together with the XML representation of the user interface layouts. By default, these files are stored in the */res* sub-directory of the application project's hierarchy.

10.10 Application Context

When an application is compiled, a class named *R* is created that contains references to the application resources. The application manifest file and these resources combine to create what is known as the *Application Context*. This context, represented by the Android *Context* class, may be used in the application code to gain access to the application resources at runtime. In addition, a wide range of methods may be called on an application's context to gather information and make changes to the application's environment at runtime.

10.11 Summary

A number of different elements can be brought together in order to create an Android application. In this chapter, we have provided a high-level overview of Activities, Fragments, Services, Intents and Broadcast Receivers together with an overview of the manifest file and application resources.

Maximum reuse and interoperability are promoted through the creation of individual, standalone modules of functionality in the form of activities and intents, while data sharing between applications is achieved by the implementation of content providers.

While activities are focused on areas where the user interacts with the application (an activity essentially equating to a single user interface screen and often made up of one or more fragments), background processing is typically handled by Services and Broadcast Receivers.

The components that make up the application are outlined for the Android runtime system in a manifest file which, combined with the application's resources, represents the application's context.

Much has been covered in this chapter that is most likely new to the average developer. Rest assured, however, that extensive exploration and practical use of these concepts will be made in subsequent chapters to ensure a solid knowledge foundation on which to build your own applications.

11. Understanding Android Application and Activity Lifecycles

In earlier chapters we have learned that Android applications run within processes and that they are comprised of multiple components in the form of activities, services and broadcast receivers. The goal of this chapter is to expand on this knowledge by looking at the lifecycle of applications and activities within the Android runtime system.

Regardless of the fanfare about how much memory and computing power resides in the mobile devices of today compared to the desktop systems of yesterday, it is important to keep in mind that these devices are still considered to be "resource constrained" by the standards of modern desktop and laptop based systems, particularly in terms of memory. As such, a key responsibility of the Android system is to ensure that these limited resources are managed effectively and that both the operating system and the applications running on it remain responsive to the user at all times. In order to achieve this, Android is given full control over the lifecycle and state of both the processes in which the applications run, and the individual components that comprise those applications.

An important factor in developing Android applications, therefore, is to gain an understanding of both the application and activity lifecycle management models of Android, and the ways in which an application can react to the state changes that are likely to be imposed upon it during its execution lifetime.

11.1 Android Applications and Resource Management

Each running Android application is viewed by the operating system as a separate process. If the system identifies that resources on the device are reaching capacity it will take steps to terminate processes to free up memory.

When making a determination as to which process to terminate in order to free up memory, the system takes into consideration both the *priority* and *state* of all currently running processes, combining these factors to create what is referred to by Google as an *importance hierarchy*. Processes are then terminated starting with the lowest priority and working up the hierarchy until sufficient resources have been liberated for the system to function.

11.2 Android Process States

Processes host applications and applications are made up of components. Within an Android system, the current state of a process is defined by the highest-ranking active component within the application that it hosts. As outlined in Figure 11-1, a process can be in one of the following five states at any given time:

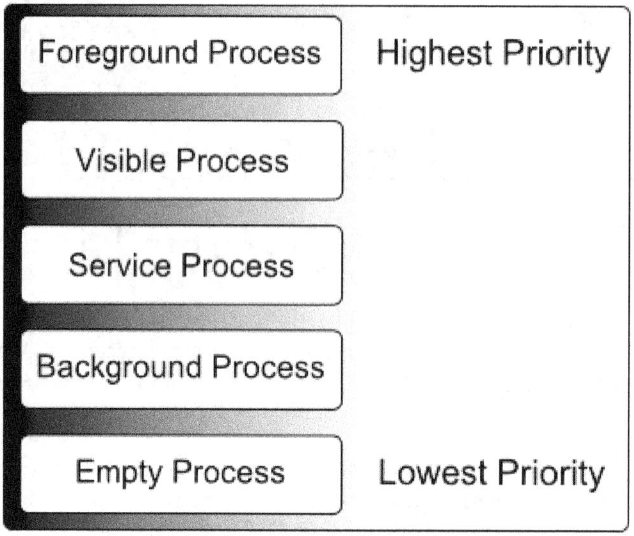

Figure 11-1

11.2.1 Foreground Process

These processes are assigned the highest level of priority. At any one time, there are unlikely to be more than one or two foreground processes active and these are usually the last to be terminated by the system. A process must meet one or more of the following criteria to qualify for foreground status:

- Hosts an activity with which the user is currently interacting.

- Hosts a Service connected to the activity with which the user is interacting.

- Hosts a Service that has indicated, via a call to *startForeground()*, that termination would be disruptive to the user experience.

- Hosts a Service executing either its *onCreate()*, *onResume()* or *onStart()* callbacks.

- Hosts a Broadcast Receiver that is currently executing its *onReceive()* method.

11.2.2 Visible Process

A process containing an activity that is visible to the user but is not the activity with which the user is interacting is classified as a "visible process". This is typically the case when an activity in the process is visible to the user, but another activity, such as a partial screen or dialog, is in the foreground. A process is also eligible for visible status if it hosts a Service that is, itself, bound to a visible or foreground activity.

11.2.3 Service Process

Processes that contain a Service that has already been started and is currently executing.

11.2.4 Background Process

A process that contains one or more activities that are not currently visible to the user, and does not host a Service that qualifies for *Service Process* status. Processes that fall into this category are at high risk of termination in the event that additional memory needs to be freed for higher priority processes. Android maintains a dynamic list of background processes, terminating processes in chronological order such that processes that were the least recently in the foreground are killed first.

11.2.5 Empty Process

Empty processes no longer contain any active applications and are held in memory ready to serve as hosts for newly launched applications. This is somewhat analogous to keeping the doors open and the engine running on a bus in anticipation of passengers arriving. Such processes are, obviously, considered the lowest priority and are the first to be killed to free up resources.

11.3 Inter-Process Dependencies

The situation with regard to determining the highest priority process is slightly more complex than outlined in the preceding section for the simple reason that processes can often be inter-dependent. As such, when making a determination as to the priority of a process, the Android system will also take into consideration whether the process is in some way serving another process of higher priority (for example, a service process acting as the content provider for a foreground process). As a basic rule, the Android documentation states that a process can never be ranked lower than another process that it is currently serving.

11.4 The Activity Lifecycle

As we have previously determined, the state of an Android process is determined largely by the status of the activities and components that make up the application that it hosts. It is important to understand, therefore, that these activities also transition through different states during the execution lifetime of an application. The current state of an activity is determined, in part, by its position in something called the *Activity Stack*.

11.5 The Activity Stack

For each application that is running on an Android device, the runtime system maintains an *Activity Stack*. When an application is launched, the first of the application's activities to be started is placed onto the stack. When a second activity is started, it is placed on the top of the stack and the previous activity is *pushed* down. The activity at the top of the stack is referred to as the *active (or running)* activity. When the active activity exits, it is *popped* off the stack by the runtime and the activity located immediately beneath it in the stack becomes the current active activity. The activity at the top of the stack might, for example, simply exit because the task for which it is responsible has been completed. Alternatively, the user may have selected a "Back" button on the screen to return to the previous activity, causing the current activity to be popped off the stack by the runtime system and therefore destroyed. A visual representation of the Android Activity Stack is illustrated in Figure 11-2.

As shown in the diagram, new activities are pushed on to the top of the stack when they are started. The current active activity is located at the top of the stack until it is either pushed down the stack by a new activity, or popped off the stack when it exits or the user navigates to the previous activity. In the event that resources become constrained, the runtime will kill activities, starting with those at the bottom of the stack.

The Activity Stack is what is referred to in programming terminology as a Last-In-First-Out (LIFO) stack in that the last item to be pushed onto the stack is the first to be popped off.

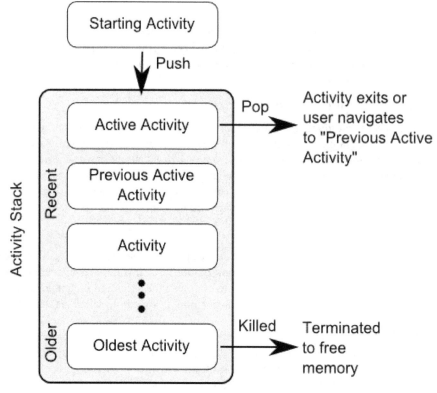

Figure 11-2

11.6 Activity States

An activity can be in one of a number of different states during the course of its execution within an application:

· **Active / Running** – The activity is at the top of the Activity Stack, is the foreground task visible on the device screen, has focus and is currently interacting with the user. This is the least likely activity to be terminated in the event of a resource shortage.

· **Paused** – The activity is visible to the user but does not currently have focus (typically because this activity is partially obscured by the current *active* activity). Paused activities are held in memory, remain attached to the window manager, retain all state information and can quickly be restored to active status when moved to the top of the Activity Stack.

· **Stopped** – The activity is currently not visible to the user (in other words it is totally obscured on the device display by other activities). As with paused activities, it retains all state and member information, but is at higher risk of termination in low memory situations.

· **Killed** – The activity has been terminated by the runtime system in order to free up memory and is no longer present on the Activity Stack. Such activities must be restarted if required by the application.

11.7 Configuration Changes

So far in this chapter, we have looked at two of the causes for the change in state of an Android activity, namely the movement of an activity between the foreground and background, and termination of an activity by the runtime system in order to free up memory. In fact, there is a third scenario in which the state of an activity can dramatically change and this involves a change to the device configuration.

By default, any configuration change that impacts the appearance of an activity (such as rotating the orientation of the device between portrait and landscape, or changing a system font setting) will cause the activity to be destroyed and recreated. The reasoning behind this is that such changes affect resources such as the layout of the user interface and simply destroying and recreating impacted activities is the quickest way for an activity to respond to the configuration change. It is, however, possible to configure an activity so that it is not restarted by the system in response to specific configuration changes.

11.8 Handling State Change

If nothing else, it should be clear from this chapter that an application and, by definition, the components contained therein will transition through many states during the course of its lifespan. Of particular importance is the fact that these state changes (up to and including complete termination) are imposed upon the application by the Android runtime subject to the actions of the user and the availability of resources on the device.

In practice, however, these state changes are not imposed entirely without notice and an application will, in most circumstances, be notified by the runtime system of the changes and given the opportunity to react accordingly. This will typically involve saving or restoring both internal data structures and user interface state, thereby allowing the user to switch seamlessly between applications and providing at least the appearance of multiple, concurrently running applications.

Android provides two ways to handle the changes to the lifecycle states of the objects within in app. One approach involves responding to state change method calls from the operating system and is covered in detail in the next chapter entitled *"Handling Android Activity State Changes"*.

A new approach, and one that is recommended by Google, involves the lifecycle classes included with the Jetpack Android Architecture components, introduced in *"Modern Android App Architecture with Jetpack"* and explained in more detail in the chapter entitled *"Working with Android Lifecycle-Aware Components"*.

11.9 Summary

Mobile devices are typically considered to be resource constrained, particularly in terms of on-board memory capacity. Consequently, a prime responsibility of the Android operating system is to ensure that applications, and the operating system in general, remain responsive to the user.

Applications are hosted on Android within processes. Each application, in turn, is made up of components in the form of activities and Services.

The Android runtime system has the power to terminate both processes and individual activities in order to free up memory. Process state is taken into consideration by the runtime system when deciding whether a process is a suitable candidate for termination. The state of a process is largely dependent upon the status of the activities hosted by that process.

The key message of this chapter is that an application moves through a variety of states during its execution lifespan and has very little control over its destiny within the Android runtime environment. Those processes and activities that are not directly interacting with the user run a higher risk of termination by the runtime system. An essential element of Android application development, therefore, involves the ability of an application to respond to state change notifications from the operating system.

12. Handling Android Activity State Changes

Based on the information outlined in the chapter entitled *"Understanding Android Application and Activity Lifecycles"* it is now evident that the activities and fragments that make up an application pass through a variety of different states during the course of the application's lifespan. The change from one state to the other is imposed by the Android runtime system and is, therefore, largely beyond the control of the activity itself. That does not, however, mean that the app cannot react to those changes and take appropriate actions.

The primary objective of this chapter is to provide a high-level overview of the ways in which an activity may be notified of a state change and to outline the areas where it is advisable to save or restore state information. Having covered this information, the chapter will then touch briefly on the subject of *activity lifetimes*.

12.1 New vs. Old Lifecycle Techniques

Up until recently, there was a standard way to build lifecycle awareness into an app. This is the approach covered in this chapter and involves implementing a set of methods (one for each lifecycle state) within an activity or fragment instance that get called by the operating system when the lifecycle status of that object changes. This approach has remained unchanged since the early years of the Android operating system and, while still a viable option today, it does have some limitations which will be explained later in this chapter.

With the introduction of the lifecycle classes with the Jetpack Android Architecture Components, a better approach to lifecycle handling is now available. This modern approach to lifecycle management (together with the Jetpack components and architecture guidelines) will be covered in detail in later chapters. It is still important, however, to understand the traditional lifecycle methods for a couple of reasons. First, as an Android developer you will not be completely insulated from the traditional lifecycle methods and will still make use of some of them. More importantly, understanding the older way of handling lifecycles will provide a good knowledge foundation on which to begin learning the new approach later in the book.

12.2 The Activity and Fragment Classes

With few exceptions, activities and fragments in an application are created as subclasses of the Android AppCompatActivity class and Fragment classes respectively.

Consider, for example, the simple *AndroidSample* project created in *"Creating an Example Android App in Android Studio"*. Load this project into the Android Studio environment and locate the *MainActivity.java* file (located in *app -> java -> com.<your domain>.androidsample*). Having located the file, double-click on it to load it into the editor where it should read as follows:

```
package com.ebookfrenzy.androidsample;

import android.os.Bundle;

import com.google.android.material.floatingactionbutton.FloatingActionButton;
import com.google.android.material.snackbar.Snackbar;
```

```java
import androidx.appcompat.app.AppCompatActivity;
import androidx.appcompat.widget.Toolbar;

import android.view.View;
import android.view.Menu;
import android.view.MenuItem;
import android.widget.EditText;
import android.widget.TextView;

public class MainActivity extends AppCompatActivity {

    @Override
    protected void onCreate(Bundle savedInstanceState) {
        super.onCreate(savedInstanceState);
        setContentView(R.layout.activity_android_sample);
        Toolbar toolbar = findViewById(R.id.toolbar);
        setSupportActionBar(toolbar);

        FloatingActionButton fab = findViewById(R.id.fab);
        fab.setOnClickListener(new View.OnClickListener() {
            @Override
            public void onClick(View view) {
                Snackbar.make(view, "Replace with your own action",
                        Snackbar.LENGTH_LONG)
                        .setAction("Action", null).show();
            }
        });
    }


    public void convertCurrency(View view) {

        EditText dollarText = findViewById(R.id.dollarText);
        TextView textView = findViewById(R.id.textView);

        if (!dollarText.getText().toString().equals("")) {

            Float dollarValue = Float.valueOf(dollarText.getText().toString());
            Float euroValue = dollarValue * 0.85F;
            textView.setText(euroValue.toString());
        } else {
            textView.setText(R.string.no_value_string);
        }
    }

    @Override
```

```
public boolean onCreateOptionsMenu(Menu menu) {
    // Inflate the menu; this adds items to the action bar if it is present.
    getMenuInflater().inflate(R.menu.menu_main, menu);
    return true;
}


@Override
public boolean onOptionsItemSelected(MenuItem item) {
    // Handle action bar item clicks here. The action bar will
    // automatically handle clicks on the Home/Up button, so long
    // as you specify a parent activity in AndroidManifest.xml.
    int id = item.getItemId();

    //noinspection SimplifiableIfStatement
    if (id == R.id.action_settings) {
        return true;
    }

    return super.onOptionsItemSelected(item);
}
}
```

When the project was created, we instructed Android Studio also to create an initial activity named *MainActivity*. As is evident from the above code, the MainActivity class is a subclass of the AppCompatActivity class.

A review of the reference documentation for the AppCompatActivity class would reveal that it is itself a subclass of the Activity class. This can be verified within the Android Studio editor using the *Hierarchy* tool window. With the *MainActivity.java* file loaded into the editor, click on AppCompatActivity in the *class* declaration line and press the *Ctrl-H* keyboard shortcut. The hierarchy tool window will subsequently appear displaying the class hierarchy for the selected class. As illustrated in Figure 12-1, AppCompatActivity is clearly subclassed from the FragmentActivity class which is itself ultimately a subclass of the Activity class:

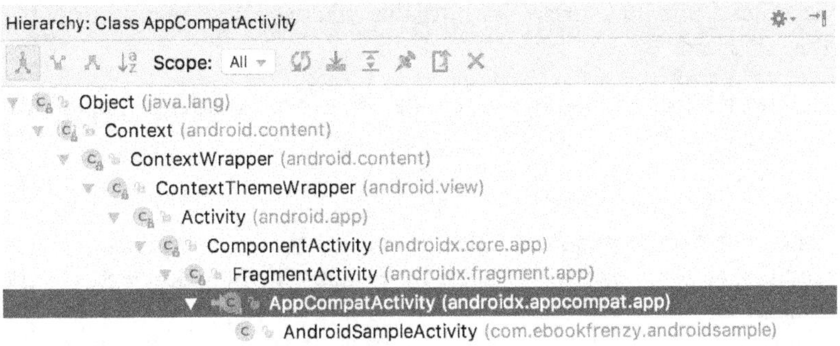

Figure 12-1

The Activity and Fragment classes contain a range of methods that are intended to be called by the Android runtime to notify the object when its state is changing. For the purposes of this chapter, we will refer to these as the *lifecycle methods*. An activity or fragment class simply needs to *override* these methods and implement the necessary functionality within them in order to react accordingly to state changes.

One such method is named *onCreate()* and, turning once again to the above code fragment, we can see that this method has already been overridden and implemented for us in the *MainActivity* class. In a later section we will explore in detail both *onCreate()* and the other relevant lifecycle methods of the Activity and Fragment classes.

12.3 Dynamic State vs. Persistent State

A key objective of lifecycle management is ensuring that the state of the activity is saved and restored at appropriate times. When talking about *state* in this context we mean the data that is currently being held within the activity and the appearance of the user interface. The activity might, for example, maintain a data model in memory that needs to be saved to a database, content provider or file. Such state information, because it persists from one invocation of the application to another, is referred to as the *persistent state*.

The appearance of the user interface (such as text entered into a text field but not yet committed to the application's internal data model) is referred to as the *dynamic state*, since it is typically only retained during a single invocation of the application (and also referred to as *user interface state* or *instance state*).

Understanding the differences between these two states is important because both the ways they are saved, and the reasons for doing so, differ.

The purpose of saving the persistent state is to avoid the loss of data that may result from an activity being killed by the runtime system while in the background. The dynamic state, on the other hand, is saved and restored for reasons that are slightly more complex.

Consider, for example, that an application contains an activity (which we will refer to as *Activity A*) containing a text field and some radio buttons. During the course of using the application, the user enters some text into the text field and makes a selection from the radio buttons. Before performing an action to save these changes, however, the user then switches to another activity causing *Activity A* to be pushed down the Activity Stack and placed into the background. After some time, the runtime system ascertains that memory is low and consequently kills *Activity A* to free up resources. As far as the user is concerned, however, *Activity A* was simply placed into the background and is ready to be moved to the foreground at any time. On returning *Activity A* to the foreground the user would, quite reasonably, expect the entered text and radio button selections to have been retained. In this scenario, however, a new instance of *Activity A* will have been created and, if the dynamic state was not saved and restored, the previous user input lost.

The main purpose of saving dynamic state, therefore, is to give the perception of seamless switching between foreground and background activities, regardless of the fact that activities may actually have been killed and restarted without the user's knowledge.

The mechanisms for saving persistent and dynamic state will become clearer in the following sections of this chapter.

12.4 The Android Lifecycle Methods

As previously explained, the Activity and Fragment classes contain a number of lifecycle methods which act as event handlers when the state of an instance changes. The primary methods supported by the Android Activity and Fragment class are as follows:

- **onCreate(Bundle savedInstanceState)** – The method that is called when the activity is first created and the ideal location for most initialization tasks to be performed. The method is passed an argument in the form of a *Bundle* object that may contain dynamic state information (typically relating to the state of the user interface) from a prior invocation of the activity.

- **onRestart()** – Called when the activity is about to restart after having previously been stopped by the runtime system.

- **onStart()** – Always called immediately after the call to the *onCreate()* or *onRestart()* methods, this method indicates to the activity that it is about to become visible to the user. This call will be followed by a call to *onResume()* if the activity moves to the top of the activity stack, or *onStop()* in the event that it is pushed down the stack by another activity.

- **onResume()** – Indicates that the activity is now at the top of the activity stack and is the activity with which the user is currently interacting.

- **onPause()** – Indicates that a previous activity is about to become the foreground activity. This call will be followed by a call to either the *onResume()* or *onStop()* method depending on whether the activity moves back to the foreground or becomes invisible to the user. Steps may be taken within this method to store *persistent state* information not yet saved by the app. To avoid delays in switching between activities, time consuming operations such as storing data to a database or performing network operations should be avoided within this method. This method should also ensure that any CPU intensive tasks such as animation are stopped.

- **onStop()** – The activity is now no longer visible to the user. The two possible scenarios that may follow this call are a call to *onRestart()* in the event that the activity moves to the foreground again, or *onDestroy()* if the activity is being terminated.

- **onDestroy()** – The activity is about to be destroyed, either voluntarily because the activity has completed its tasks and has called the *finish()* method or because the runtime is terminating it either to release memory or due to a configuration change (such as the orientation of the device changing). It is important to note that a call will not always be made to *onDestroy()* when an activity is terminated.

- **onConfigurationChanged()** – Called when a configuration change occurs for which the activity has indicated it is not to be restarted. The method is passed a Configuration object outlining the new device configuration and it is then the responsibility of the activity to react to the change.

The following lifecycle methods only apply to the Fragment class:

- **onAttach()** - Called when the fragment is assigned to an activity.

- **onCreateView()** - Called to create and return the fragment's user interface layout view hierarchy.

- **onActivityCreated()** - The *onCreate()* method of the activity with which the fragment is associated has completed execution.

- **onViewStatusRestored()** - The fragment's saved view hierarchy has been restored.

In addition to the lifecycle methods outlined above, there are two methods intended specifically for saving and restoring the *dynamic state* of an activity:

- **onRestoreInstanceState(Bundle savedInstanceState)** – This method is called immediately after a call to the *onStart()* method in the event that the activity is restarting from a previous invocation in which state was saved. As with *onCreate()*, this method is passed a Bundle object containing the previous state data. This method is typically used in situations where it makes more sense to restore a previous state after the initialization of the activity has been performed in *onCreate()* and *onStart()*.

- **onSaveInstanceState(Bundle outState)** – Called before an activity is destroyed so that the current *dynamic state* (usually relating to the user interface) can be saved. The method is passed the Bundle object into which the state should be saved and which is subsequently passed through to the *onCreate()* and *onRestoreInstanceState()* methods when the activity is restarted. Note that this method is only called in situations where the runtime ascertains that dynamic state needs to be saved.

When overriding the above methods, it is important to remember that, with the exception of *onRestoreInstanceState()* and *onSaveInstanceState()*, the method implementation must include a call to the corresponding method in the super class. For example, the following method overrides the *onRestart()* method but also includes a call to the super class instance of the method:

```
protected void onRestart() {
        super.onRestart();
        Log.i(TAG, "onRestart");
}
```

Failure to make this super class call in method overrides will result in the runtime throwing an exception during execution. While calls to the super class in the *onRestoreInstanceState()* and *onSaveInstanceState()* methods are optional (they can, for example, be omitted when implementing custom save and restoration behavior) there are considerable benefits to using them, a subject that will be covered in the chapter entitled *"Saving and Restoring the State of an Android Activity"*.

12.5 Lifetimes

The final topic to be covered involves an outline of the *entire*, *visible* and *foreground* lifetimes through which an activity or fragment will transition during execution:

- **Entire Lifetime** –The term "entire lifetime" is used to describe everything that takes place between the initial call to the *onCreate()* method and the call to *onDestroy()* prior to the object terminating.

- **Visible Lifetime** – Covers the periods of execution between the call to *onStart()* and *onStop()*. During this period the activity or fragment is visible to the user though may not be the object with which the user is currently interacting.

- **Foreground Lifetime** – Refers to the periods of execution between calls to the *onResume()* and *onPause()* methods.

It is important to note that an activity or fragment may pass through the *foreground* and *visible* lifetimes multiple times during the course of the *entire* lifetime.

The concepts of lifetimes and lifecycle methods are illustrated in Figure 12-2:

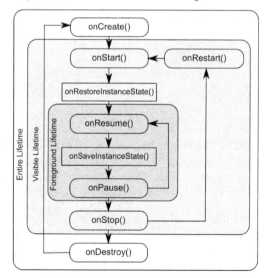

Figure 12-2

12.6 Foldable Devices and Multi-Resume

As discussed previously, an activity is considered to be in the resumed state when it has moved to the foreground and is the activity with which the user is currently interacting. On standard devices an app can have one activity in the resumed state at any one time and all other activities are likely to be in the paused or stopped state.

For some time now, Android has included multi-window support, allowing multiple activities to appear simultaneously in either split-screen or freeform configurations. Although originally used primarily on large screen tablet devices, this feature is likely to become more popular with the introduction of foldable devices.

On devices running Android 10 and on which multi-window support is enabled (as will be the case for most foldables), it will be possible for multiple app activities to be in the resumed state at the same time (a concept referred to as *multi-resume*) allowing those visible activities to continue functioning (for example streaming content or updating visual data) even when another activity currently has focus. Although multiple activities can be in the resumed state, only one of these activities will be considered to the *topmost resumed activity* (in other words, the activity with which the user most recently interacted).

An activity can receive notification that it has gained or lost the topmost resumed status by implementing the *onTopResumedActivityChanged()* callback method.

12.7 Disabling Configuration Change Restarts

As previously outlined, an activity may indicate that it is not to be restarted in the event of certain configuration changes. This is achieved by adding an *android:configChanges* directive to the activity element within the project manifest file. The following manifest file excerpt, for example, indicates that the activity should not be restarted in the event of configuration changes relating to orientation or device-wide font size:

```
<activity android:name=".MainActivity"
          android:configChanges="orientation|fontScale"
          android:label="@string/app_name">
```

12.8 Lifecycle Method Limitations

As discussed at the start of this chapter, lifecycle methods have been in use for many years and, until recently, were the only mechanism available for handling lifecycle state changes for activities and fragments. There are, however, shortcomings to this approach.

One issue with the lifecycle methods is that they do not provide an easy way for an activity or fragment to find out its current lifecycle state at any given point during app execution. Instead the object would need to track the state internally, or wait for the next lifecycle method call.

Also, the methods do not provide a simple way for one object to observe the lifecycle state changes of other objects within an app. This is a serious consideration since many other objects within an app can potentially be impacted by a lifecycle state change in a given activity or fragment.

The lifecycle methods are also only available on subclasses of the Fragment and Activity classes. It is not possible, therefore, to build custom classes that are truly lifecycle aware.

Finally, the lifecycle methods result in most of the lifecycle handling code being written within the activity or fragment which can lead to complex and error prone code. Ideally, much of this code should reside in the other classes that are impacted by the state change. An app that streams video, for example, might include a class designed specifically to manage the incoming stream. If the app needs to pause the stream when the main activity is stopped, the code to do so should reside in the streaming class, not the main activity.

All of these problems and more are resolved by using *lifecycle-aware* components, a topic which will be covered starting with the chapter entitled *"Modern Android App Architecture with Jetpack"*.

12.9 Summary

All activities are derived from the Android *Activity* class which, in turn, contains a number of lifecycle methods that are designed to be called by the runtime system when the state of an activity changes. Similarly, the Fragment class contains a number of comparable methods. By overriding these methods, activities and fragments can respond to state changes and, where necessary, take steps to save and restore the current state of both the activity and the application. Lifecycle state can be thought of as taking two forms. The persistent state refers to data that needs to be stored between application invocations (for example to a file or database). Dynamic state, on the other hand, relates instead to the current appearance of the user interface.

Although lifecycle methods have a number of limitations that can be avoided by making use of lifecycle-aware components, an understanding of these methods is important in order to fully understand the new approaches to lifecycle management covered later in this book.

In this chapter, we have highlighted the lifecycle methods available to activities and covered the concept of activity lifetimes. In the next chapter, entitled *"Android Activity State Changes by Example"*, we will implement an example application that puts much of this theory into practice.

13. Android Activity State Changes by Example

The previous chapters have discussed in some detail the different states and lifecycles of the activities that comprise an Android application. In this chapter, we will put the theory of handling activity state changes into practice through the creation of an example application. The purpose of this example application is to provide a real world demonstration of an activity as it passes through a variety of different states within the Android runtime. In the next chapter, entitled *"Saving and Restoring the State of an Android Activity"*, the example project constructed in this chapter will be extended to demonstrate the saving and restoration of dynamic activity state.

13.1 Creating the State Change Example Project

The first step in this exercise is to create the new project. Begin by launching Android Studio and, if necessary, closing any currently open projects using the *File -> Close Project* menu option so that the Welcome screen appears.

Select the *Start a new Android Studio project* quick start option from the welcome screen and, within the resulting new project dialog, choose the Basic Activity template before clicking on the Next button.

Enter StateChange into the Name field and specify com.ebookfrenzy.statechange as the package name. Before clicking on the Finish button, change the Minimum API level setting to API 26: Android 8.0 (Oreo) and the Language menu to Java. Upon completion of the project creation process, the *StateChange* project should be listed in the Project tool window located along the left-hand edge of the Android Studio main window.

The next action to take involves the design of the content area of the user interface for the activity. This is stored in a file named *content_main.xml* which should already be loaded into the Layout Editor tool. If it is not, navigate to it in the project tool window where it can be found in the *app -> res -> layout* folder. Once located, double-clicking on the file will load it into the Android Studio Layout Editor tool.

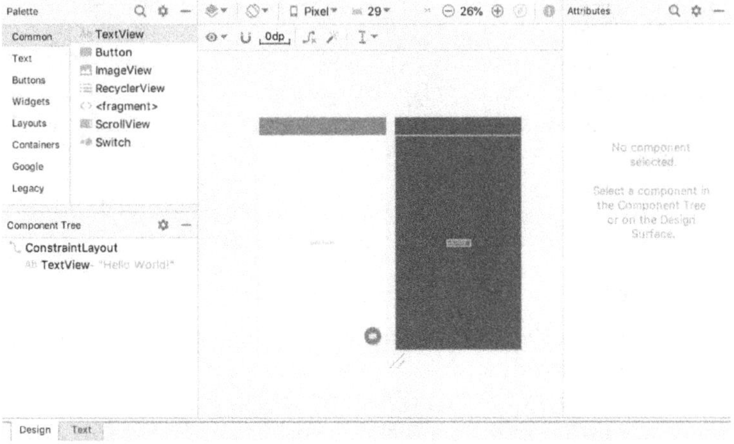

Figure 13-1

13.2 Designing the User Interface

With the user interface layout loaded into the Layout Editor tool, it is now time to design the user interface for the example application. Instead of the "Hello world!" TextView currently present in the user interface design, the activity actually requires an EditText view. Select the TextView object in the Layout Editor canvas and press the Delete key on the keyboard to remove it from the design.

From the Palette located on the left side of the Layout Editor, select the *Text* category and, from the list of text components, click and drag a *Plain Text* component over to the visual representation of the device screen. Move the component to the center of the display so that the center guidelines appear and drop it into place so that the layout resembles that of Figure 13-2.

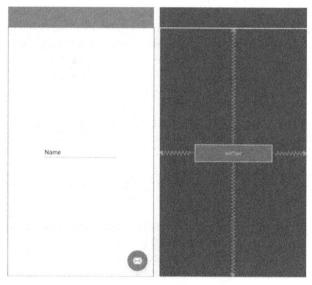

Figure 13-2

When using the EditText widget it is necessary to specify an *input type* for the view. This simply defines the type of text or data that will be entered by the user. For example, if the input type is set to *Phone*, the user will be restricted to entering numerical digits into the view. Alternatively, if the input type is set to *TextCapCharacters*, the input will default to upper case characters. Input type settings may also be combined.

For the purposes of this example, we will set the input type to support general text input. To do so, select the EditText widget in the layout and locate the *inputType* entry within the Attributes tool window. Click on the flag icon to the left of the current setting to open the list of options and, within the list, switch off *textPersonName* and enable *text* before clicking on the Apply button.

By default the EditText is displaying text which reads "Name". Remaining within the Attributes panel, delete this from the *text* property field so that the view is blank within the layout.

13.3 Overriding the Activity Lifecycle Methods

At this point, the project contains a single activity named *MainActivity*, which is derived from the Android *AppCompatActivity* class. The source code for this activity is contained within the *MainActivity.java* file which should already be open in an editor session and represented by a tab in the editor tab bar. In the event that the file is no longer open, navigate to it in the Project tool window panel (*app -> java -> com.ebookfrenzy.statechange -> MainActivity*) and double-click on it to load the file into the editor. Once loaded the code should read as follows:

```
package com.ebookfrenzy.statechange;
```

```java
import android.os.Bundle;

import com.google.android.material.floatingactionbutton.FloatingActionButton;
import com.google.android.material.snackbar.Snackbar;

import androidx.appcompat.app.AppCompatActivity;
import androidx.appcompat.widget.Toolbar;

import android.view.View;
import android.view.Menu;
import android.view.MenuItem;

public class MainActivity extends AppCompatActivity {

    @Override
    protected void onCreate(Bundle savedInstanceState) {
        super.onCreate(savedInstanceState);
        setContentView(R.layout.activity_main);
        Toolbar toolbar = findViewById(R.id.toolbar);
        setSupportActionBar(toolbar);

        FloatingActionButton fab = findViewById(R.id.fab);
        fab.setOnClickListener(new View.OnClickListener() {
            @Override
            public void onClick(View view) {
                Snackbar.make(view, "Replace with your own action", Snackbar.
LENGTH_LONG)
                        .setAction("Action", null).show();
            }
        });
    }

    @Override
    public boolean onCreateOptionsMenu(Menu menu) {
        // Inflate the menu; this adds items to the action bar if it is present.
        getMenuInflater().inflate(R.menu.menu_main, menu);
        return true;
    }

    @Override
    public boolean onOptionsItemSelected(MenuItem item) {
        // Handle action bar item clicks here. The action bar will
        // automatically handle clicks on the Home/Up button, so long
        // as you specify a parent activity in AndroidManifest.xml.
```

```
        int id = item.getItemId();

        //noinspection SimplifiableIfStatement
        if (id == R.id.action_settings) {
            return true;
        }

        return super.onOptionsItemSelected(item);
    }
}
```

So far the only lifecycle method overridden by the activity is the *onCreate()* method which has been implemented to call the super class instance of the method before setting up the user interface for the activity. We will now modify this method so that it outputs a diagnostic message in the Android Studio Logcat panel each time it executes. For this, we will use the *Log* class, which requires that we import *android.util.Log* and declare a tag that will enable us to filter these messages in the log output:

```
package com.ebookfrenzy.statechange;

.

.

import android.util.Log;

public class MainActivity extends AppCompatActivity {

    private static final String TAG = "StateChange";

    @Override
    protected void onCreate(Bundle savedInstanceState) {
        super.onCreate(savedInstanceState);
        setContentView(R.layout.activity_state_change);
        Toolbar toolbar = findViewById(R.id.toolbar);
        setSupportActionBar(toolbar);

        FloatingActionButton fab = findViewById(R.id.fab);
        fab.setOnClickListener(new View.OnClickListener() {
            @Override
            public void onClick(View view) {
                Snackbar.make(view, "Replace with your own action",
                    Snackbar.LENGTH_LONG)
                        .setAction("Action", null).show();
            }
        });

        Log.i(TAG, "onCreate");
    }
```

.

```
.
}
```

The next task is to override some more methods, with each one containing a corresponding log call. These override methods may be added manually or generated using the *Alt-Insert* keyboard shortcut as outlined in the chapter entitled *"The Basics of the Android Studio Code Editor"*. Note that the Log calls will still need to be added manually if the methods are being auto-generated:

```
@Override
protected void onStart() {
    super.onStart();
    Log.i(TAG, "onStart");
}

@Override
protected void onResume() {
    super.onResume();
    Log.i(TAG, "onResume");
}

@Override
protected void onPause() {
    super.onPause();
    Log.i(TAG, "onPause");
}

@Override
protected void onStop() {
    super.onStop();
    Log.i(TAG, "onStop");
}

@Override
protected void onRestart() {
    super.onRestart();
    Log.i(TAG, "onRestart");
}

@Override
protected void onDestroy() {
    super.onDestroy();
    Log.i(TAG, "onDestroy");
}

@Override
protected void onSaveInstanceState(Bundle outState) {
    super.onSaveInstanceState(outState);
```

```
    Log.i(TAG, "onSaveInstanceState");
}


@Override
protected void onRestoreInstanceState(Bundle savedInstanceState) {
    super.onRestoreInstanceState(savedInstanceState);
    Log.i(TAG, "onRestoreInstanceState");
}
```

13.4 Filtering the Logcat Panel

The purpose of the code added to the overridden methods in *MainActivity.java* is to output logging information to the *Logcat* tool window. This output can be configured to display all events relating to the device or emulator session, or restricted to those events that relate to the currently selected app. The output can also be further restricted to only those log events that match a specified filter.

Display the Logcat tool window and click on the filter menu (marked as B in Figure 13-3) to review the available options. When this menu is set to *Show only selected application*, only those messages relating to the app selected in the menu marked as A will be displayed in the Logcat panel. Choosing *No Filters*, on the other hand, will display all the messages generated by the device or emulator.

Figure 13-3

Before running the application, it is worth demonstrating the creation of a filter which, when selected, will further restrict the log output to ensure that only those log messages containing the tag declared in our activity are displayed.

From the filter menu (B), select the *Edit Filter Configuration* menu option. In the *Create New Logcat Filter* dialog (Figure 13-4), name the filter *Lifecycle* and, in the *Log Tag* field, enter the Tag value declared in *MainActivity.java* (in the above code example this was *StateChange*).

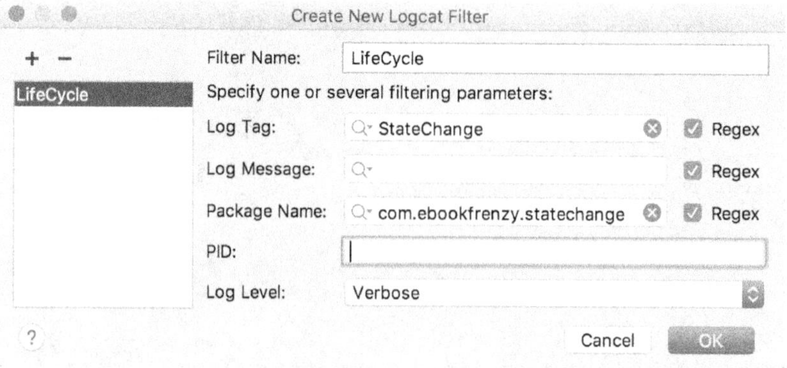

Figure 13-4

Enter the package identifier in the *Package Name* field and, when the changes are complete, click on the *OK* button to create the filter and dismiss the dialog. Instead of listing *No Filters,* the newly created filter should now be selected in the Logcat tool window.

13.5 Running the Application

For optimal results, the application should be run on a physical Android device or emulator. With the device configured and connected to the development computer, click on the run button represented by a green triangle located in the Android Studio toolbar as shown in Figure 13-5 below, select the *Run -> Run...* menu option or use the Shift+F10 keyboard shortcut:

Figure 13-5

Select the physical Android device from the *Choose Device* dialog if it appears (assuming that you have not already configured it to be the default target). After Android Studio has built the application and installed it on the device it should start up and be running in the foreground.

A review of the Logcat panel should indicate which methods have so far been triggered (taking care to ensure that the *Lifecycle* filter created in the preceding section is selected to filter out log events that are not currently of interest to us):

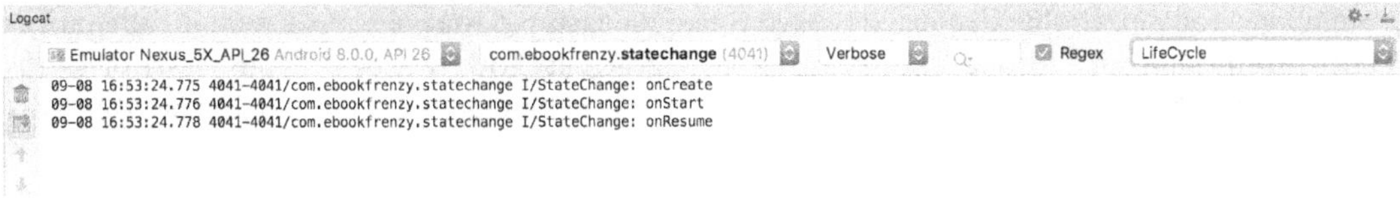

Figure 13-6

13.6 Experimenting with the Activity

With the diagnostics working, it is now time to exercise the application with a view to gaining an understanding of the activity lifecycle state changes. To begin with, consider the initial sequence of log events in the Logcat panel:

```
onCreate
onStart
onResume
```

Clearly, the initial state changes are exactly as outlined in *"Understanding Android Application and Activity Lifecycles"*. Note, however, that a call was not made to *onRestoreInstanceState()* since the Android runtime detected that there was no state to restore in this situation.

Tap on the Home icon in the bottom status bar on the device display and note the sequence of method calls reported in the log as follows:

```
onPause
onStop
onSaveInstanceState
```

In this case, the runtime has noticed that the activity is no longer in the foreground, is not visible to the user and has stopped the activity, but not without providing an opportunity for the activity to save the dynamic state.

Depending on whether the runtime ultimately destroyed the activity or simply restarted it, the activity will either be notified it has been restarted via a call to *onRestart()* or will go through the creation sequence again when the user returns to the activity.

As outlined in *"Understanding Android Application and Activity Lifecycles"*, the destruction and recreation of an activity can be triggered by making a configuration change to the device, such as rotating from portrait to landscape. To see this in action, simply rotate the device while the *StateChange* application is in the foreground. When using the emulator, device rotation may be simulated using the rotation button located in the emulator toolbar. The resulting sequence of method calls in the log should read as follows:

```
onPause
onStop
onSaveInstanceState
onDestroy
onCreate
onStart
onRestoreInstanceState
onResume
```

Clearly, the runtime system has given the activity an opportunity to save state before being destroyed and restarted.

13.7 Summary

The old adage that a picture is worth a thousand words holds just as true for examples when learning a new programming paradigm. In this chapter, we have created an example Android application for the purpose of demonstrating the different lifecycle states through which an activity is likely to pass. In the course of developing the project in this chapter, we also looked at a mechanism for generating diagnostic logging information from within an activity.

In the next chapter, we will extend the *StateChange* example project to demonstrate how to save and restore an activity's dynamic state.

14. Saving and Restoring the State of an Android Activity

If the previous few chapters have achieved their objective, it should now be a little clearer as to the importance of saving and restoring the state of a user interface at particular points in the lifetime of an activity.

In this chapter, we will extend the example application created in *"Android Activity State Changes by Example"* to demonstrate the steps involved in saving and restoring state when an activity is destroyed and recreated by the runtime system.

A key component of saving and restoring dynamic state involves the use of the Android SDK *Bundle* class, a topic that will also be covered in this chapter.

14.1 Saving Dynamic State

An activity, as we have already learned, is given the opportunity to save dynamic state information via a call from the runtime system to the activity's implementation of the *onSaveInstanceState()* method. Passed through as an argument to the method is a reference to a Bundle object into which the method will need to store any dynamic data that needs to be saved. The Bundle object is then stored by the runtime system on behalf of the activity and subsequently passed through as an argument to the activity's *onCreate()* and *onRestoreInstanceState()* methods if and when they are called. The data can then be retrieved from the Bundle object within these methods and used to restore the state of the activity.

14.2 Default Saving of User Interface State

In the previous chapter, the diagnostic output from the *StateChange* example application showed that an activity goes through a number of state changes when the device on which it is running is rotated sufficiently to trigger an orientation change.

Launch the *StateChange* application once again, this time entering some text into the EditText field prior to performing the device rotation (on devices or emulators running Android 9 it may be necessary to tap the rotation button in the located in the status bar to complete the rotation). Having rotated the device, the following state change sequence should appear in the Logcat window:

```
onPause
onStop
onSaveInstanceState
onDestroy
onCreate
onStart
onRestoreInstanceState
onResume
```

Clearly this has resulted in the activity being destroyed and re-created. A review of the user interface of the running application, however, should show that the text entered into the EditText field has been preserved. Given that the activity was destroyed and recreated, and that we did not add any specific code to make sure the text was saved and restored, this behavior requires some explanation.

Saving and Restoring the State of an Android Activity

In actual fact most of the view widgets included with the Android SDK already implement the behavior necessary to automatically save and restore state when an activity is restarted. The only requirement to enable this behavior is for the *onSaveInstanceState()* and *onRestoreInstanceState()* override methods in the activity to include calls to the equivalent methods of the super class:

```
@Override
protected void onSaveInstanceState(Bundle outState) {
    super.onSaveInstanceState(outState);
}


@Override
protected void onRestoreInstanceState(Bundle savedInstanceState) {
    super.onRestoreInstanceState(savedInstanceState);
}
```

The automatic saving of state for a user interface view can be disabled in the XML layout file by setting the *android:saveEnabled* property to *false*. For the purposes of an example, we will disable the automatic state saving mechanism for the EditText view in the user interface layout and then add code to the application to manually save and restore the state of the view.

To configure the EditText view such that state will not be saved and restored in the event that the activity is restarted, edit the *content_main.xml* file so that the entry for the view reads as follows (note that the XML can be edited directly by clicking on the *Text* tab on the bottom edge of the Layout Editor panel):

```
<EditText
    android:id="@+id/editText"
    android:layout_width="wrap_content"
    android:layout_height="wrap_content"
    android:ems="10"
    android:inputType="text"
    android:saveEnabled="false"
    app:layout_constraintBottom_toBottomOf="parent"
    app:layout_constraintEnd_toEndOf="parent"
    app:layout_constraintStart_toStartOf="parent"
    app:layout_constraintTop_toTopOf="parent" />
```

After making the change, run the application, enter text and rotate the device to verify that the text is no longer saved and restored before proceeding.

14.3 The Bundle Class

For situations where state needs to be saved beyond the default functionality provided by the user interface view components, the Bundle class provides a container for storing data using a *key-value pair* mechanism. The *keys* take the form of string values, while the *values* associated with those *keys* can be in the form of a primitive value or any object that implements the Android *Parcelable* interface. A wide range of classes already implements the Parcelable interface. Custom classes may be made "parcelable" by implementing the set of methods defined in the Parcelable interface, details of which can be found in the Android documentation at:

https://developer.android.com/reference/android/os/Parcelable.html

The Bundle class also contains a set of methods that can be used to get and set key-value pairs for a variety of data types including both primitive types (including Boolean, char, double and float values) and objects (such as Strings and CharSequences).

For the purposes of this example, and having disabled the automatic saving of text for the EditText view, we need to make sure that the text entered into the EditText field by the user is saved into the Bundle object and subsequently restored. This will serve as a demonstration of how to manually save and restore state within an Android application and will be achieved using the *putCharSequence()* and *getCharSequence()* methods of the Bundle class respectively.

14.4 Saving the State

The first step in extending the *StateChange* application is to make sure that the text entered by the user is extracted from the EditText component within the *onSaveInstanceState()* method of the *MainActivity* activity, and then saved as a key-value pair into the Bundle object.

In order to extract the text from the EditText object we first need to identify that object in the user interface. Clearly, this involves bridging the gap between the Java code for the activity (contained in the *MainActivity.java* source code file) and the XML representation of the user interface (contained within the *content_main.xml* resource file). In order to extract the text entered into the EditText component we need to gain access to that user interface object.

Each component within a user interface has associated with it a unique identifier. By default, the Layout Editor tool constructs the ID for a newly added component from the object type. If more than one view of the same type is contained in the layout the type name is followed by a sequential number (though this can, and should, be changed to something more meaningful by the developer). As can be seen by checking the *Component Tree* panel within the Android Studio main window when the *content_main.xml* file is selected and the Layout Editor tool displayed, the EditText component has been assigned the ID *editText*:

Figure 14-1

As outlined in the chapter entitled *"The Anatomy of an Android Application"*, all of the resources that make up an application are compiled into a class named *R*. Amongst those resources are those that define layouts, including the layout for our current activity. Within the R class is a subclass named *layout*, which contains the layout resources, and within that subclass is our *content_main* layout. With this knowledge, we can make a call to the *findViewById()* method of our activity object to get a reference to the editText object as follows:

```
final EditText editText = findViewById(R.id.editText);
```

Having obtained a reference to the EditText object and assigned it to a variable, we can now obtain the text that it contains via the object's *getText()* method, which, in turn, returns the current text:

```
CharSequence userText = editText.getText();
```

Finally, we can save the text using the Bundle object's *putCharSequence()* method, passing through the key (this can be any string value but in this instance, we will declare it as "savedText") and the *userText* object as arguments:

```
outState.putCharSequence("savedText", userText);
```

Bringing this all together gives us a modified *onSaveInstanceState()* method in the *MainActivity.java* file that reads as follows (noting also the additional import directive for *android.widget.EditText*):

```
package com.ebookfrenzy.statechange;
    .
    .
import android.widget.EditText;

public class MainActivity extends AppCompatActivity {
    .
    .
    .
        protected void onSaveInstanceState(Bundle outState) {
                super.onSaveInstanceState(outState);
                Log.i(TAG, "onSaveInstanceState");

                final EditText editText =
                        findViewById(R.id.editText);
                CharSequence userText = editText.getText();
                outState.putCharSequence("savedText", userText);
        }
    .
    .
```

Now that steps have been taken to save the state, the next phase is to ensure that it is restored when needed.

14.5 Restoring the State

The saved dynamic state can be restored in those lifecycle methods that are passed the Bundle object as an argument. This leaves the developer with the choice of using either *onCreate()* or *onRestoreInstanceState()*. The method to use will depend on the nature of the activity. In instances where state is best restored after the activity's initialization tasks have been performed, the *onRestoreInstanceState()* method is generally more suitable. For the purposes of this example we will add code to the *onRestoreInstanceState()* method to extract the saved state from the Bundle using the "savedText" key. We can then display the text on the editText component using the object's *setText()* method:

```
@Override
protected void onRestoreInstanceState(Bundle savedInstanceState) {
    super.onRestoreInstanceState(savedInstanceState);
    Log.i(TAG, "onRestoreInstanceState");

    final EditText editText =
        findViewById(R.id.editText);

    CharSequence userText =
                savedInstanceState.getCharSequence("savedText");

    editText.setText(userText);
}
```

14.6 Testing the Application

All that remains is once again to build and run the *StateChange* application. Once running and in the foreground, touch the EditText component and enter some text before rotating the device to another orientation. Whereas the text changes were previously lost, the new text is retained within the editText component thanks to the code we have added to the activity in this chapter.

Having verified that the code performs as expected, comment out the *super.onSaveInstanceState()* and *super. onRestoreInstanceState()* calls from the two methods, re-launch the app and note that the text is still preserved after a device rotation. The default save and restoration system has essentially been replaced by a custom implementation, thereby providing a way to dynamically and selectively save and restore state within an activity.

14.7 Summary

The saving and restoration of dynamic state in an Android application is simply a matter of implementing the appropriate code in the appropriate lifecycle methods. For most user interface views, this is handled automatically by the Activity super class. In other instances, this typically consists of extracting values and settings within the *onSaveInstanceState()* method and saving the data as key-value pairs within the Bundle object passed through to the activity by the runtime system.

State can be restored in either the *onCreate()* or the *onRestoreInstanceState()* methods of the activity by extracting values from the Bundle object and updating the activity based on the stored values.

In this chapter, we have used these techniques to update the *StateChange* project so that the Activity retains changes through the destruction and subsequent recreation of an activity.

15. Understanding Android Views, View Groups and Layouts

With the possible exception of listening to streaming audio, a user's interaction with an Android device is primarily visual and tactile in nature. All of this interaction takes place through the user interfaces of the applications installed on the device, including both the built-in applications and any third party applications installed by the user. It should come as no surprise, therefore, that a key element of developing Android applications involves the design and creation of user interfaces.

Within this chapter, the topic of Android user interface structure will be covered, together with an overview of the different elements that can be brought together to make up a user interface; namely Views, View Groups and Layouts.

15.1 Designing for Different Android Devices

The term "Android device" covers a vast array of tablet and smartphone products with different screen sizes and resolutions. As a result, application user interfaces must now be carefully designed to ensure correct presentation on as wide a range of display sizes as possible. A key part of this is ensuring that the user interface layouts resize correctly when run on different devices. This can largely be achieved through careful planning and the use of the layout managers outlined in this chapter.

It is also important to keep in mind that the majority of Android based smartphones and tablets can be held by the user in both portrait and landscape orientations. A well-designed user interface should be able to adapt to such changes and make sensible layout adjustments to utilize the available screen space in each orientation.

15.2 Views and View Groups

Every item in a user interface is a subclass of the Android *View* class (to be precise *android.view.View*). The Android SDK provides a set of pre-built views that can be used to construct a user interface. Typical examples include standard items such as the Button, CheckBox, ProgressBar and TextView classes. Such views are also referred to as *widgets* or *components*. For requirements that are not met by the widgets supplied with the SDK, new views may be created either by subclassing and extending an existing class, or creating an entirely new component by building directly on top of the View class.

A view can also be comprised of multiple other views (otherwise known as a *composite view*). Such views are subclassed from the Android *ViewGroup* class (*android.view.ViewGroup*) which is itself a subclass of *View*. An example of such a view is the RadioGroup, which is intended to contain multiple RadioButton objects such that only one can be in the "on" position at any one time. In terms of structure, composite views consist of a single parent view (derived from the ViewGroup class and otherwise known as a *container view* or *root element)* that is capable of containing other views (known as *child views*).

Another category of ViewGroup based container view is that of the layout manager.

15.3 Android Layout Managers

In addition to the widget style views discussed in the previous section, the SDK also includes a set of views referred to as *layouts*. Layouts are container views (and, therefore, subclassed from ViewGroup) designed for the sole purpose of controlling how child views are positioned on the screen.

The Android SDK includes the following layout views that may be used within an Android user interface design:

- **ConstraintLayout** – Introduced in Android 7, use of this layout manager is recommended for most layout requirements. ConstraintLayout allows the positioning and behavior of the views in a layout to be defined by simple constraint settings assigned to each child view. The flexibility of this layout allows complex layouts to be quickly and easily created without the necessity to nest other layout types inside each other, resulting in improved layout performance. ConstraintLayout is also tightly integrated into the Android Studio Layout Editor tool. Unless otherwise stated, this is the layout of choice for the majority of examples in this book.

- **LinearLayout** – Positions child views in a single row or column depending on the orientation selected. A *weight* value can be set on each child to specify how much of the layout space that child should occupy relative to other children.

- **TableLayout** – Arranges child views into a grid format of rows and columns. Each row within a table is represented by a *TableRow* object child, which, in turn, contains a view object for each cell.

- **FrameLayout** – The purpose of the FrameLayout is to allocate an area of screen, typically for the purposes of displaying a single view. If multiple child views are added they will, by default, appear on top of each other positioned in the top left-hand corner of the layout area. Alternate positioning of individual child views can be achieved by setting gravity values on each child. For example, setting a *center_vertical* gravity value on a child will cause it to be positioned in the vertical center of the containing FrameLayout view.

- **RelativeLayout** – The RelativeLayout allows child views to be positioned relative both to each other and the containing layout view through the specification of alignments and margins on child views. For example, child *View A* may be configured to be positioned in the vertical and horizontal center of the containing RelativeLayout view. *View B*, on the other hand, might also be configured to be centered horizontally within the layout view, but positioned 30 pixels above the top edge of *View A*, thereby making the vertical position *relative* to that of *View A*. The RelativeLayout manager can be of particular use when designing a user interface that must work on a variety of screen sizes and orientations.

- **AbsoluteLayout** – Allows child views to be positioned at specific X and Y coordinates within the containing layout view. Use of this layout is discouraged since it lacks the flexibility to respond to changes in screen size and orientation.

- **GridLayout** – A GridLayout instance is divided by invisible lines that form a grid containing rows and columns of cells. Child views are then placed in cells and may be configured to cover multiple cells both horizontally and vertically allowing a wide range of layout options to be quickly and easily implemented. Gaps between components in a GridLayout may be implemented by placing a special type of view called a *Space* view into adjacent cells, or by setting margin parameters.

- **CoordinatorLayout** – Introduced as part of the Android Design Support Library with Android 5.0, the CoordinatorLayout is designed specifically for coordinating the appearance and behavior of the app bar across the top of an application screen with other view elements. When creating a new activity using the Basic Activity template, the parent view in the main layout will be implemented using a CoordinatorLayout instance. This layout manager will be covered in greater detail starting with the chapter entitled *"Working with the Floating Action Button and Snackbar"*.

When considering the use of layouts in the user interface for an Android application it is worth keeping in mind that, as will be outlined in the next section, these can be nested within each other to create a user interface design of just about any necessary level of complexity.

15.4 The View Hierarchy

Each view in a user interface represents a rectangular area of the display. A view is responsible for what is drawn in that rectangle and for responding to events that occur within that part of the screen (such as a touch event).

A user interface screen is comprised of a view hierarchy with a *root view* positioned at the top of the tree and child views positioned on branches below. The child of a container view appears on top of its parent view and is constrained to appear within the bounds of the parent view's display area. Consider, for example, the user interface illustrated in Figure 15-1:

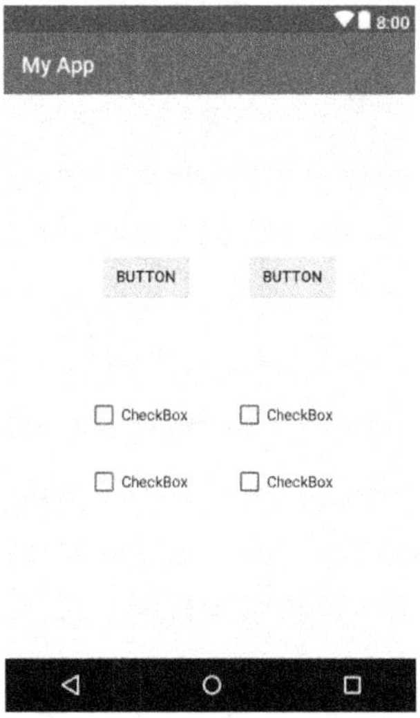

Figure 15-1

In addition to the visible button and checkbox views, the user interface actually includes a number of layout views that control how the visible views are positioned. Figure 15-2 shows an alternative view of the user interface, this time highlighting the presence of the layout views in relation to the child views:

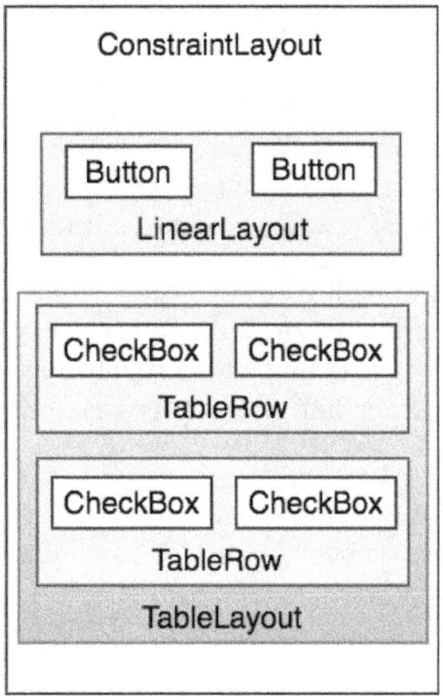

Figure 15-2

As was previously discussed, user interfaces are constructed in the form of a view hierarchy with a root view at the top. This being the case, we can also visualize the above user interface example in the form of the view tree illustrated in Figure 15-3:

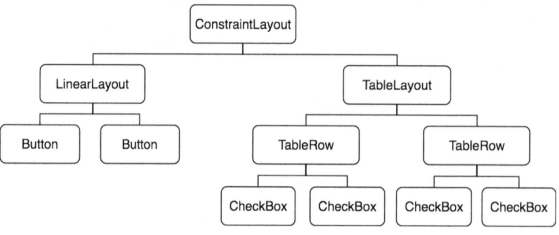

Figure 15-3

The view hierarchy diagram gives probably the clearest overview of the relationship between the various views that make up the user interface shown in Figure 15-1. When a user interface is displayed to the user, the Android runtime walks the view hierarchy, starting at the root view and working down the tree as it renders each view.

15.5 Creating User Interfaces

With a clearer understanding of the concepts of views, layouts and the view hierarchy, the following few chapters will focus on the steps involved in creating user interfaces for Android activities. In fact, there are three different approaches to user interface design: using the Android Studio Layout Editor tool, handwriting XML layout resource files or writing Java code, each of which will be covered.

15.6 Summary

Each element within a user interface screen of an Android application is a view that is ultimately subclassed from the *android.view.View* class. Each view represents a rectangular area of the device display and is responsible both for what appears in that rectangle and for handling events that take place within the view's bounds. Multiple views may be combined to create a single *composite view*. The views within a composite view are children of a *container view* which is generally a subclass of *android.view.ViewGroup* (which is itself a subclass of *android. view.View*). A user interface is comprised of views constructed in the form of a view hierarchy.

The Android SDK includes a range of pre-built views that can be used to create a user interface. These include basic components such as text fields and buttons, in addition to a range of layout managers that can be used to control the positioning of child views. In the event that the supplied views do not meet a specific requirement, custom views may be created, either by extending or combining existing views, or by subclassing *android.view. View* and creating an entirely new class of view.

User interfaces may be created using the Android Studio Layout Editor tool, handwriting XML layout resource files or by writing Java code. Each of these approaches will be covered in the chapters that follow.

16. A Guide to the Android Studio Layout Editor Tool

It is difficult to think of an Android application concept that does not require some form of user interface. Most Android devices come equipped with a touch screen and keyboard (either virtual or physical) and taps and swipes are the primary form of interaction between the user and application. Invariably these interactions take place through the application's user interface.

A well designed and implemented user interface, an important factor in creating a successful and popular Android application, can vary from simple to extremely complex, depending on the design requirements of the individual application. Regardless of the level of complexity, the Android Studio Layout Editor tool significantly simplifies the task of designing and implementing Android user interfaces.

16.1 Basic vs. Empty Activity Templates

As outlined in the chapter entitled *"The Anatomy of an Android Application"*, Android applications are made up of one or more activities. An activity is a standalone module of application functionality that usually correlates directly to a single user interface screen. As such, when working with the Android Studio Layout Editor we are invariably working on the layout for an activity.

When creating a new Android Studio project, a number of different templates are available to be used as the starting point for the user interface of the main activity. The most basic of these templates are the Basic Activity and Empty Activity templates. Although these seem similar at first glance, there are actually considerable differences between the two options. To see these differences within the layout editor, use the View Options menu to enable layout decorations as shown in Figure 16-1 below:

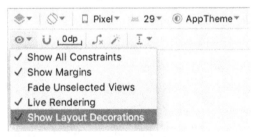

Figure 16-1

The Empty Activity template creates a single layout file consisting of a ConstraintLayout manager instance containing a TextView object as shown in Figure 16-2:

Figure 16-2

The Basic Activity, on the other hand, consists of two layout files. The top level layout file has a CoordinatorLayout as the root view, a configurable app bar, a menu preconfigured with a single menu item, a floating action button and a reference to the second layout file in which the layout for the content area of the activity user interface is declared:

Figure 16-3

Clearly the Empty Activity template is useful if you need neither a floating action button nor a menu in your activity and do not need the special app bar behavior provided by the CoordinatorLayout such as options to make the app bar and toolbar collapse from view during certain scrolling operations (a topic covered in the chapter entitled *"Working with the AppBar and Collapsing Toolbar Layouts"*). The Basic Activity is useful, however, in that it provides these elements by default. In fact, it is often quicker to create a new activity using the Basic Activity template and delete the elements you do not require than to use the Empty Activity template and manually implement behavior such as collapsing toolbars, a menu or floating action button.

Since not all of the examples in this book require the features of the Basic Activity template, however, most of the examples in this chapter will use the Empty Activity template unless the example requires one or other of the features provided by the Basic Activity template.

For future reference, if you need a menu but not a floating action button, use the Basic Activity and follow these steps to delete the floating action button:

1. Double-click on the main *activity* layout file located in the Project tool window under *app -> res -> layout* to load it into the Layout Editor. This will be the layout file prefixed with *activity_* and not the content file prefixed with *content_*.

2. With the layout loaded into the Layout Editor tool, select the floating action button and tap the keyboard *Delete* key to remove the object from the layout.

3. Locate and edit the Java code for the activity (located under *app -> java -> <package name> -> <activity class name>* and remove the floating action button code from the onCreate method as follows:

```
@Override
protected void onCreate(Bundle savedInstanceState) {
    super.onCreate(savedInstanceState);
    setContentView(R.layout.activity_main);
    Toolbar toolbar = findViewById(R.id.toolbar);
    setSupportActionBar(toolbar);

    FloatingActionButton fab =
        findViewById(R.id.fab);
    fab.setOnClickListener(new View.OnClickListener() {
        @Override
        public void onClick(View view) {
            Snackbar.make(view, "Replace with your own action",
                Snackbar.LENGTH_LONG)
                    .setAction("Action", null).show();
        }
    });
}
```

If you need a floating action button but no menu, use the Basic Activity template and follow these steps:

1. Edit the activity class file and delete the *onCreateOptionsMenu* and *onOptionsItemSelected* methods.

2. Select the *res -> menu* item in the Project tool window and tap the keyboard *Delete* key to remove the folder and corresponding menu resource files from the project.

16.2 The Android Studio Layout Editor

As has been demonstrated in previous chapters, the Layout Editor tool provides a "what you see is what you get" (WYSIWYG) environment in which views can be selected from a palette and then placed onto a canvas representing the display of an Android device. Once a view has been placed on the canvas, it can be moved, deleted and resized (subject to the constraints of the parent view). Further, a wide variety of properties relating to the selected view may be modified using the Attributes tool window.

Under the surface, the Layout Editor tool actually constructs an XML resource file containing the definition of the user interface that is being designed. As such, the Layout Editor tool operates in two distinct modes referred to as *Design mode* and *Text mode*.

16.3 Design Mode

In design mode, the user interface can be visually manipulated by directly working with the view palette and the graphical representation of the layout. Figure 16-4 highlights the key areas of the Android Studio Layout Editor tool in design mode:

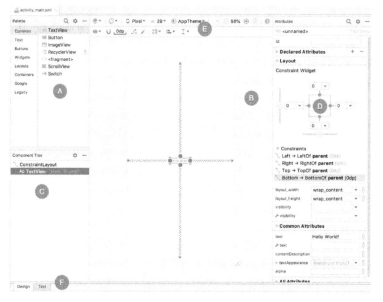

Figure 16-4

A – Palette – The palette provides access to the range of view components provided by the Android SDK. These are grouped into categories for easy navigation. Items may be added to the layout by dragging a view component from the palette and dropping it at the desired position on the layout.

B – Device Screen – The device screen provides a visual "what you see is what you get" representation of the user interface layout as it is being designed. This layout allows for direct manipulation of the design in terms of allowing views to be selected, deleted, moved and resized. The device model represented by the layout can be changed at any time using a menu located in the toolbar.

C – Component Tree – As outlined in the previous chapter (*"Understanding Android Views, View Groups and Layouts"*) user interfaces are constructed using a hierarchical structure. The component tree provides a visual overview of the hierarchy of the user interface design. Selecting an element from the component tree will cause the corresponding view in the layout to be selected. Similarly, selecting a view from the device screen layout will select that view in the component tree hierarchy.

D – Attributes – All of the component views listed in the palette have associated with them a set of attributes that can be used to adjust the behavior and appearance of that view. The Layout Editor's attributes panel provides access to the attributes of the currently selected view in the layout allowing changes to be made.

E – Toolbar – The Layout Editor toolbar provides quick access to a wide range of options including, amongst other options, the ability to zoom in and out of the device screen layout, change the device model currently displayed, rotate the layout between portrait and landscape and switch to a different Android SDK API level. The toolbar also has a set of context sensitive buttons which will appear when relevant view types are selected in the device screen layout.

F – Mode Switching Tabs – The tabs located along the lower edge of the Layout Editor provide a way to switch back and forth between the Layout Editor tool's text and design modes.

16.4 The Palette

The Layout Editor palette is organized into two panels designed to make it easy to locate and preview view components for addition to a layout design. The category panel (marked A in Figure 16-5) lists the different categories of view components supported by the Android SDK. When a category is selected from the list, the second panel (B) updates to display a list of the components that fall into that category:

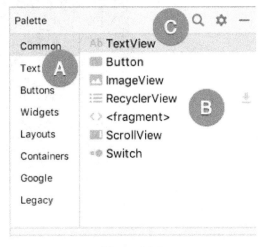

Figure 16-5

To add a component from the palette onto the layout canvas, simply select the item either from the component list or the preview panel, drag it to the desired location on the canvas and drop it into place.

A search for a specific component within the currently selected category may be initiated by clicking on the search button (marked C in Figure 16-5 above) in the palette toolbar and typing in the component name. As characters are typed, matching results will appear in real-time within the component list panel. If you are unsure of the category in which the component resides, simply select the All category either before or during the search operation.

16.5 Design and Layout Views

When the Layout Editor tool is in Design mode, the layout can be viewed in two different ways. The view shown in Figure 16-4 above is the Design view and shows the layout and widgets as they will appear in the running app. A second mode, referred to as Layout or Blueprint view can be shown either instead of, or concurrently with the Design view. The toolbar menu shown in Figure 16-6 provides options to display the Design, Blueprint, or both views. A fourth option, *Force Refresh Layout*, causes the layout to rebuild and redraw. This can be useful when the layout enters an unexpected state or is not accurately reflecting the current design settings:

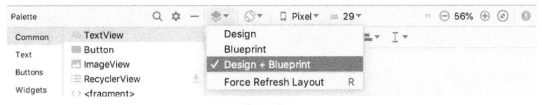

Figure 16-6

Whether to display the layout view, design view or both is a matter of personal preference. A good approach is to begin with both displayed as shown in Figure 16-7:

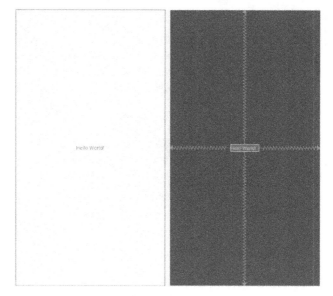

Figure 16-7

16.6 Text Mode

It is important to keep in mind when using the Android Studio Layout Editor tool that all it is really doing is providing a user friendly approach to creating XML layout resource files. At any time during the design process, the underlying XML can be viewed and directly edited simply by clicking on the *Text* tab located at the bottom of the Layout Editor tool panel. To return to design mode, simply click on the *Design* tab.

Figure 16-8 highlights the key areas of the Android Studio Layout Editor tool in text mode:

```
1    <?xml version="1.0" encoding="utf-8"?>
2    <androidx.constraintlayout.widget.ConstraintLayout xmlns:android="http://schemas.androi
3        xmlns:app="http://schemas.android.com/apk/res-auto"
4        xmlns:tools="http://schemas.android.com/tools"
5        android:layout_width="match_parent"
6        android:layout_height="match_parent"
7        tools:context=".MainActivity">
8
9        <TextView
10           android:layout_width="wrap_content"
11           android:layout_height="wrap_content"
12           android:text="Hello World!"
13           app:layout_constraintBottom_toBottomOf="parent"
14           app:layout_constraintLeft_toLeftOf="parent"
15           app:layout_constraintRight_toRightOf="parent"
16           app:layout_constraintTop_toTopOf="parent" />
17
18   </androidx.constraintlayout.widget.ConstraintLayout>
```

Figure 16-8

A – Editor – The editor panel displays the XML that makes up the current user interface layout design. This is the full Android Studio editor environment containing all of the features previously outlined in the *"The Basics of the Android Studio Code Editor"* chapter of this book.

B – Preview – As changes are made to the XML in the editor, these changes are visually reflected in the preview window. This provides instant visual feedback on the XML changes as they are made in the editor, thereby avoiding the need to switch back and forth between text and design mode to see changes. The preview also allows direct manipulation and design of the layout just as if the layout were in Design mode, with visual changes being reflected in the editor panel in real-time. As with Design mode, both the Design and Layout views may be displayed using the toolbar buttons highlighted in Figure 16-6 above.

C – Toolbar – The toolbar in text mode provides access to the same functions available in design mode.

D - Mode Switching Tabs – The tabs located along the lower edge of the Layout Editor provide a way to switch back and forth between the Layout Editor tool's Text and Design modes.

16.7 Setting Attributes

The Attributes panel provides access to all of the available settings for the currently selected component. Figure 16-9, for example, shows the attributes for the TextView widget:

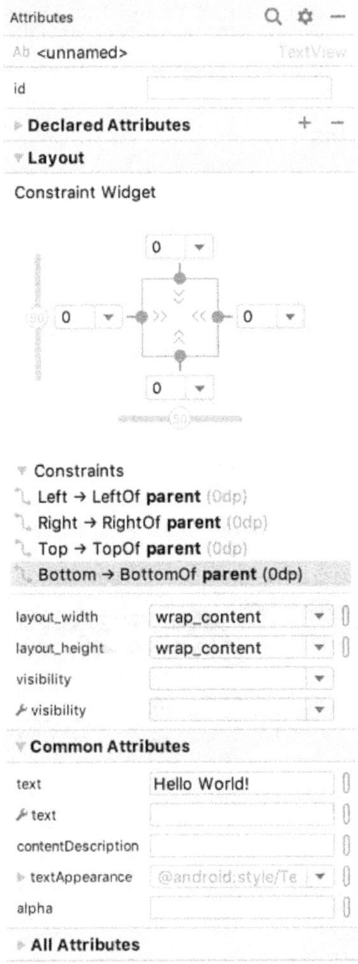

Figure 16-9

A Guide to the Android Studio Layout Editor Tool

The Attributes tool window is divided into the following different sections.

- **id** - Contains the id property which defines the name by which the currently selected object will be referenced in the source code of the app.

- **Declared Attributes** - Contains all of the properties which have already been assigned a value.

- **Layout** - The settings that define how the currently selected view object is positioned and sized in relation to the screen and other objects in the layout.

- **Common Attributes** - A list of attributes that commonly need to be changed for the class of view object currently selected.

- **All Attributes** - A complete list of all of the attributes available for the currently selected object.

A search for a specific attribute may also be performed by selecting the search button in the toolbar of the attributes tool window and typing in the attribute name.

Some attributes contain a narrow button to the right of the value field. This indicates that the Resources dialog is available to assist in selecting a suitable property value. To display the dialog, simply click on the button. The appearance of this button changes to reflect whether or not the corresponding property value is stored in a resource file or hardcoded. If the value is stored in a resource file, the button to the right of the text property field will be filled in to indicate that the value is not hard coded as highlighted in Figure 16-10 below:

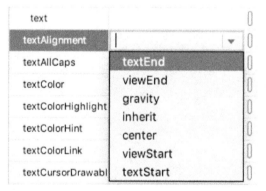

Figure 16-10

Attributes for which a finite number of valid options are available will present a drop down menu (Figure 16-11) from which a selection may be made.

Figure 16-11

A dropper icon (as shown in the backgroundTint field in Figure 16-10 above) can be clicked to display the color selection palette. Similarly, when a flag icon appears in this position it can clicked to display a list of options

116

available for the attribute, while an image icon opens the resource manager panel allowing images and other resource types to be selected for the attribute.

16.8 Converting Views

Changing a view in a layout from one type to another (such as converting a TextView to an EditText) can be performed easily within the Android Studio layout editor simply by right-clicking on the view either within the screen layout or Component tree window and selecting the *Convert view...* menu option (Figure 16-12):

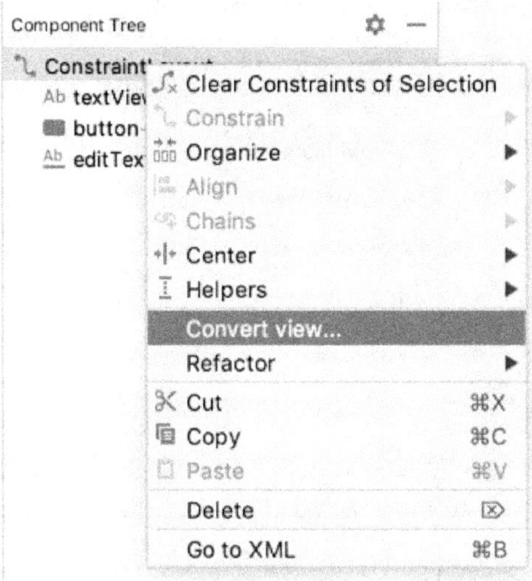

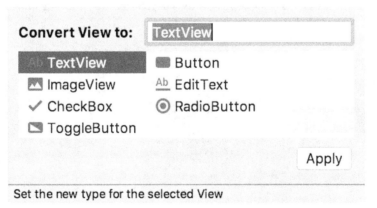

Figure 16-12

Once selected, a dialog will appear containing a list of compatible view types to which the selected object is eligible for conversion. Figure 16-13, for example shows the types to which an existing TextView view may be converted:

Figure 16-13

This technique is also useful for converting layouts from one type to another (for example converting a ConstraintLayout to a LinearLayout).

16.9 Displaying Sample Data

When designing layouts in Android Studio situations will arise where the content to be displayed within the user interface will not be available until the app is completed and running. This can sometimes make it difficult to assess from within the layout editor how the layout will appear at app runtime. To address this issue, the layout editor allows sample data to be specified that will populate views within the layout editor with sample images and data. This sample data only appears within the layout editor and is not displayed when the app runs. Sample data may be configured either by directly editing the XML for the layout, or visually using the design-time helper by right-clicking on the widget in the design area and selecting the *Set Sample Data* menu option. The design-time helper panel will display a range of preconfigured options for sample data to be displayed on the selected view item including combinations of text and images in a variety of configurations. Figure 16-14, for example, shows the sample data options displayed when selecting sample data to appear in a RecyclerView list:

Figure 16-14

Alternatively, custom text and images may be provided for display during the layout design process. An example of using sample data within the layout editor is included in a later chapter entitled *"A Layout Editor Sample Data Tutorial"*.

16.10 Creating a Custom Device Definition

The device menu in the Layout Editor toolbar (Figure 16-15) provides a list of preconfigured device types which, when selected, will appear as the device screen canvas. In addition to the pre-configured device types, any AVD instances that have previously been configured within the Android Studio environment will also be listed within the menu. To add additional device configurations, display the device menu, select the *Add Device Definition...* option and follow the steps outlined in the chapter entitled *"Creating an Android Virtual Device (AVD) in Android Studio"*.

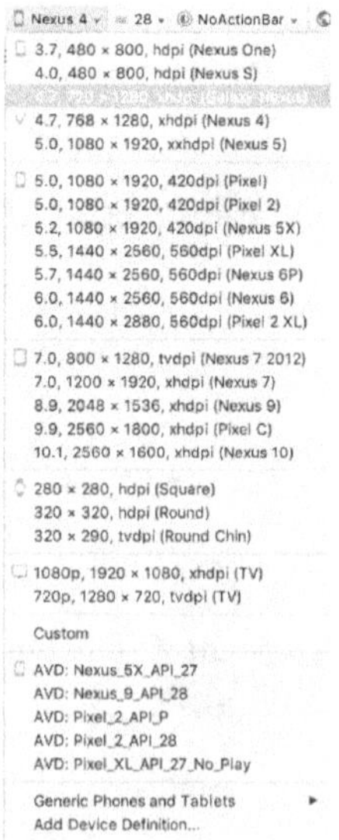

Figure 16-15

16.11 Changing the Current Device

As an alternative to the device selection menu, the current device format may be changed by selecting the *Custom* option from the device menu, clicking on the resize handle located next to the bottom right-hand corner of the device screen (Figure 16-16) and dragging to select an alternate device display format. As the screen resizes, markers will appear indicating the various size options and orientations available for selection:

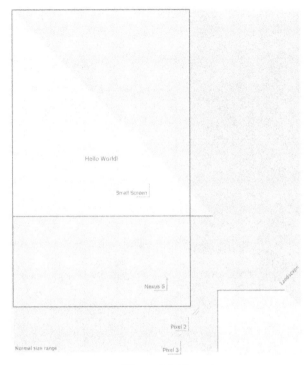

Figure 16-16

16.12 Summary

A key part of developing Android applications involves the creation of the user interface. Within the Android Studio environment, this is performed using the Layout Editor tool which operates in two modes. In design mode, view components are selected from a palette and positioned on a layout representing an Android device screen and configured using a list of attributes. In text mode, the underlying XML that represents the user interface layout can be directly edited, with changes reflected in a preview screen. These modes combine to provide an extensive and intuitive user interface design environment.

17. A Guide to the Android ConstraintLayout

As discussed in the chapter entitled *"Understanding Android Views, View Groups and Layouts"*, Android provides a number of layout managers for the purpose of designing user interfaces. With Android 7, Google introduced a new layout that is intended to address many of the shortcomings of the older layout managers. This new layout, called ConstraintLayout, combines a simple, expressive and flexible layout system with powerful features built into the Android Studio Layout Editor tool to ease the creation of responsive user interface layouts that adapt automatically to different screen sizes and changes in device orientation.

This chapter will outline the basic concepts of ConstraintLayout while the next chapter will provide a detailed overview of how constraint-based layouts can be created using ConstraintLayout within the Android Studio Layout Editor tool.

17.1 How ConstraintLayout Works

In common with all other layouts, ConstraintLayout is responsible for managing the positioning and sizing behavior of the visual components (also referred to as widgets) it contains. It does this based on the constraint connections that are set on each child widget.

In order to fully understand and use ConstraintLayout, it is important to gain an appreciation of the following key concepts:

- Constraints

- Margins

- Opposing Constraints

- Constraint Bias

- Chains

- Chain Styles

- Barriers

17.1.1 Constraints

Constraints are essentially sets of rules that dictate the way in which a widget is aligned and distanced in relation to other widgets, the sides of the containing ConstraintLayout and special elements called *guidelines*. Constraints also dictate how the user interface layout of an activity will respond to changes in device orientation, or when displayed on devices of differing screen sizes. In order to be adequately configured, a widget must have sufficient constraint connections such that it's position can be resolved by the ConstraintLayout layout engine in both the horizontal and vertical planes.

17.1.2 Margins

A margin is a form of constraint that specifies a fixed distance. Consider a Button object that needs to be positioned near the top right-hand corner of the device screen. This might be achieved by implementing margin constraints from the top and right-hand edges of the Button connected to the corresponding sides of the parent ConstraintLayout as illustrated in Figure 17-1:

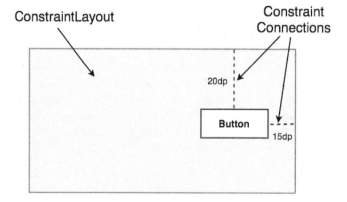

Figure 17-1

As indicated in the above diagram, each of these constraint connections has associated with it a margin value dictating the fixed distances of the widget from two sides of the parent layout. Under this configuration, regardless of screen size or the device orientation, the Button object will always be positioned 20 and 15 device-independent pixels (dp) from the top and right-hand edges of the parent ConstraintLayout respectively as specified by the two constraint connections.

While the above configuration will be acceptable for some situations, it does not provide any flexibility in terms of allowing the ConstraintLayout layout engine to adapt the position of the widget in order to respond to device rotation and to support screens of different sizes. To add this responsiveness to the layout it is necessary to implement opposing constraints.

17.1.3 Opposing Constraints

Two constraints operating along the same axis on a single widget are referred to as *opposing constraints*. In other words, a widget with constraints on both its left and right-hand sides is considered to have horizontally opposing constraints. Figure 17-2, for example, illustrates the addition of both horizontally and vertically opposing constraints to the previous layout:

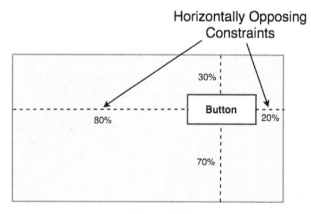

Figure 17-2

The key point to understand here is that once opposing constraints are implemented on a particular axis, the positioning of the widget becomes percentage rather than coordinate based. Instead of being fixed at 20dp from the top of the layout, for example, the widget is now positioned at a point 30% from the top of the layout. In different orientations and when running on larger or smaller screens, the Button will always be in the same location relative to the dimensions of the parent layout.

It is now important to understand that the layout outlined in Figure 17-2 has been implemented using not only opposing constraints, but also by applying *constraint bias*.

17.1.4 Constraint Bias

It has now been established that a widget in a ConstraintLayout can potentially be subject to opposing constraint connections. By default, opposing constraints are equal, resulting in the corresponding widget being centered along the axis of opposition. Figure 17-3, for example, shows a widget centered within the containing ConstraintLayout using opposing horizontal and vertical constraints:

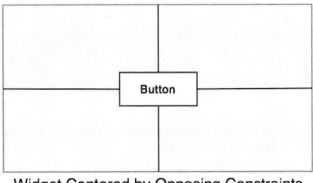

Widget Centered by Opposing Constraints

Figure 17-3

To allow for the adjustment of widget position in the case of opposing constraints, the ConstraintLayout implements a feature known as *constraint bias*. Constraint bias allows the positioning of a widget along the axis of opposition to be biased by a specified percentage in favor of one constraint. Figure 17-4, for example, shows the previous constraint layout with a 75% horizontal bias and 10% vertical bias:

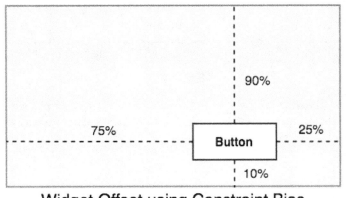

Widget Offset using Constraint Bias

Figure 17-4

The next chapter, entitled *"A Guide to using ConstraintLayout in Android Studio"*, will cover these concepts in greater detail and explain how these features have been integrated into the Android Studio Layout Editor tool. In the meantime, however, a few more areas of the ConstraintLayout class need to be covered.

17.1.5 Chains

ConstraintLayout chains provide a way for the layout behavior of two or more widgets to be defined as a group. Chains can be declared in either the vertical or horizontal axis and configured to define how the widgets in the chain are spaced and sized.

Widgets are chained when connected together by bi-directional constraints. Figure 17-5, for example, illustrates three widgets chained in this way:

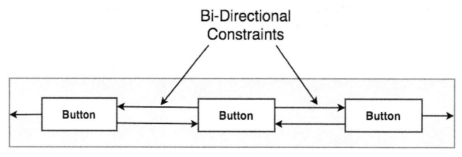

Figure 17-5

The first element in the chain is the *chain head* which translates to the top widget in a vertical chain or, in the case of a horizontal chain, the left-most widget. The layout behavior of the entire chain is primarily configured by setting attributes on the chain head widget.

17.1.6 Chain Styles

The layout behavior of a ConstraintLayout chain is dictated by the *chain style* setting applied to the chain head widget. The ConstraintLayout class currently supports the following chain layout styles:

- **Spread Chain** – The widgets contained within the chain are distributed evenly across the available space. This is the default behavior for chains.

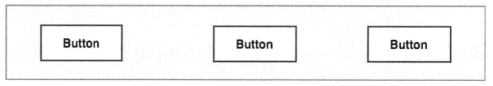

Figure 17-6

- **Spread Inside Chain** – The widgets contained within the chain are spread evenly between the chain head and the last widget in the chain. The head and last widgets are not included in the distribution of spacing.

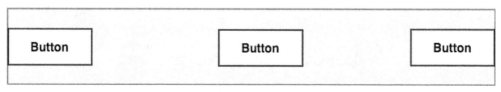

Figure 17-7

- **Weighted Chain** – Allows the space taken up by each widget in the chain to be defined via weighting properties.

Figure 17-8

- **Packed Chain** – The widgets that make up the chain are packed together without any spacing. A bias may be applied to control the horizontal or vertical positioning of the chain in relation to the parent container.

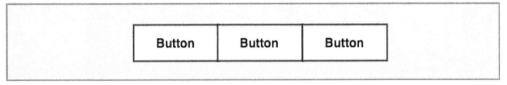

Figure 17-9

17.2 Baseline Alignment

So far, this chapter has only referred to constraints that dictate alignment relative to the sides of a widget (typically referred to as side constraints). A common requirement, however, is for a widget to be aligned relative to the content that it displays rather than the boundaries of the widget itself. To address this need, ConstraintLayout provides *baseline alignment* support.

As an example, assume that the previous theoretical layout from Figure 17-1 requires a TextView widget to be positioned 40dp to the left of the Button. In this case, the TextView needs to be *baseline aligned* with the Button view. This means that the text within the Button needs to be vertically aligned with the text within the TextView. The additional constraints for this layout would need to be connected as illustrated in Figure 17-10:

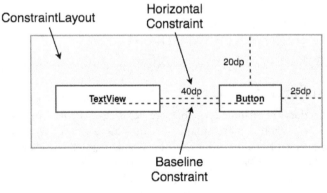

Figure 17-10

The TextView is now aligned vertically along the baseline of the Button and positioned 40dp horizontally from the Button object's left-hand edge.

17.3 Working with Guidelines

Guidelines are special elements available within the ConstraintLayout that provide an additional target to which constraints may be connected. Multiple guidelines may be added to a ConstraintLayout instance which may, in turn, be configured in horizontal or vertical orientations. Once added, constraint connections may be established from widgets in the layout to the guidelines. This is particularly useful when multiple widgets need to be aligned along an axis. In Figure 17-11, for example, three Button objects contained within a ConstraintLayout are constrained along a vertical guideline:

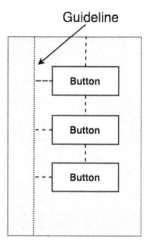

Figure 17-11

17.4 Configuring Widget Dimensions

Controlling the dimensions of a widget is a key element of the user interface design process. The ConstraintLayout provides three options which can be set on individual widgets to manage sizing behavior. These settings are configured individually for height and width dimensions:

- **Fixed** – The widget is fixed to specified dimensions.

- **Match Constraint** – Allows the widget to be resized by the layout engine to satisfy the prevailing constraints. Also referred to as the *AnySize* or MATCH_CONSTRAINT option.

- **Wrap Content** – The size of the widget is dictated by the content it contains (i.e. text or graphics).

17.5 Working with Barriers

Rather like guidelines, barriers are virtual views that can be used to constrain views within a layout. As with guidelines, a barrier can be vertical or horizontal and one or more views may be constrained to it (to avoid confusion, these will be referred to as *constrained views*). Unlike guidelines where the guideline remains at a fixed position within the layout, however, the position of a barrier is defined by a set of so called *reference views*. Barriers were introduced to address an issue that occurs with some frequency involving overlapping views. Consider, for example, the layout illustrated in Figure 17-12 below:

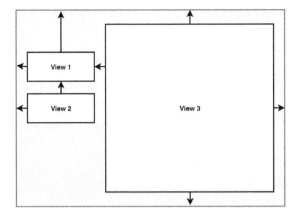

Figure 17-12

The key points to note about the above layout is that the width of View 3 is set to match constraint mode, and the left-hand edge of the view is connected to the right hand edge of View 1. As currently implemented, an increase in width of View 1 will have the desired effect of reducing the width of View 3:

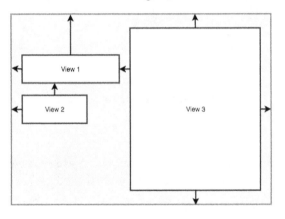

Figure 17-13

A problem arises, however, if View 2 increases in width instead of View 1:

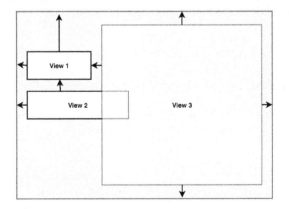

Figure 17-14

Clearly because View 3 is only constrained by View 1, it does not resize to accommodate the increase in width of View 2 causing the views to overlap.

A solution to this problem is to add a vertical barrier and assign Views 1 and 2 as the barrier's *reference views* so that they control the barrier position. The left-hand edge of View 3 will then be constrained in relation to the barrier, making it a *constrained view*.

Now when either View 1 or View 2 increase in width, the barrier will move to accommodate the widest of the two views, causing the width of View 3 change in relation to the new barrier position:

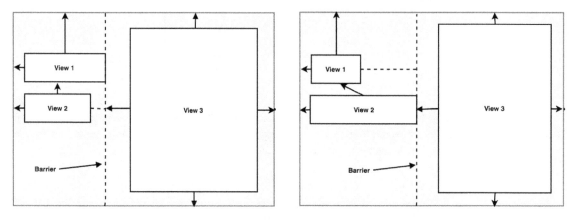

Figure 17-15

When working with barriers there is no limit to the number of reference views and constrained views that can be associated with a single barrier.

17.6 Ratios

The dimensions of a widget may be defined using ratio settings. A widget could, for example, be constrained using a ratio setting such that, regardless of any resizing behavior, the width is always twice the height dimension.

17.7 ConstraintLayout Advantages

ConstraintLayout provides a level of flexibility that allows many of the features of older layouts to be achieved with a single layout instance where it would previously have been necessary to nest multiple layouts. This has the benefit of avoiding the problems inherent in layout nesting by allowing so called "flat" or "shallow" layout hierarchies to be designed leading both to less complex layouts and improved user interface rendering performance at runtime.

ConstraintLayout was also implemented with a view to addressing the wide range of Android device screen sizes available on the market today. The flexibility of ConstraintLayout makes it easier for user interfaces to be designed that respond and adapt to the device on which the app is running.

Finally, as will be demonstrated in the chapter entitled *"A Guide to using ConstraintLayout in Android Studio"*, the Android Studio Layout Editor tool has been enhanced specifically for ConstraintLayout-based user interface design.

17.8 ConstraintLayout Availability

Although introduced with Android 7, ConstraintLayout is provided as a separate support library from the main Android SDK and is compatible with older Android versions as far back as API Level 9 (Gingerbread). This allows apps that make use of this new layout to run on devices running much older versions of Android.

17.9 Summary

ConstraintLayout is a layout manager introduced with Android 7. It is designed to ease the creation of flexible layouts that adapt to the size and orientation of the many Android devices now on the market. ConstraintLayout uses constraints to control the alignment and positioning of widgets in relation to the parent ConstraintLayout instance, guidelines, barriers and the other widgets in the layout. ConstraintLayout is the default layout for newly created Android Studio projects and is the recommended choice when designing user interface layouts. With this simple yet flexible approach to layout management, complex and responsive user interfaces can be implemented with surprising ease.

18. A Guide to using ConstraintLayout in Android Studio

As mentioned more than once in previous chapters, Google has made significant changes to the Android Studio Layout Editor tool, many of which were made solely to support user interface layout design using ConstraintLayout. Now that the basic concepts of ConstraintLayout have been outlined in the previous chapter, this chapter will explore these concepts in more detail while also outlining the ways in which the Layout Editor tool allows ConstraintLayout-based user interfaces to be designed and implemented.

18.1 Design and Layout Views

The chapter entitled *"A Guide to the Android Studio Layout Editor Tool"* explained that the Android Studio Layout Editor tool provides two ways to view the user interface layout of an activity in the form of Design and Layout (also known as blueprint) views. These views of the layout may be displayed individually or, as in Figure 18-1, side by side:

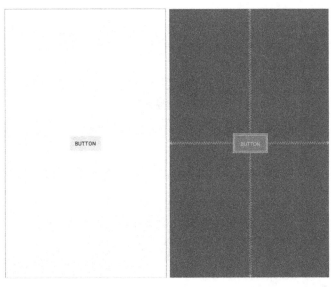

Figure 18-1

The Design view (positioned on the left in the above figure) presents a "what you see is what you get" representation of the layout, wherein the layout appears as it will within the running app. The Layout view, on the other hand, displays a blueprint style of view where the widgets are represented by shaded outlines. As can be seen in Figure 18-1 above, Layout view also displays the constraint connections (in this case opposing constraints used to center a button within the layout). These constraints are also overlaid onto the Design view when a specific widget in the layout is selected or when the mouse pointer hovers over the design area as illustrated in Figure 18-2:

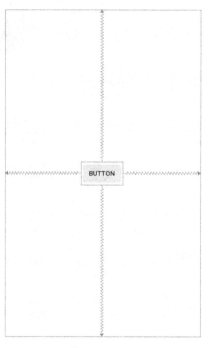

Figure 18-2

The appearance of constraint connections in both views can be changed using the View Options menu shown in Figure 18-3:

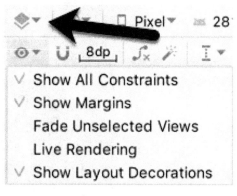

Figure 18-3

In addition to the two modes of displaying the user interface layout, the Layout Editor tool also provides three different ways of establishing the constraints required for a specific layout design.

18.2 Autoconnect Mode

Autoconnect, as the name suggests, automatically establishes constraint connections as items are added to the layout. Autoconnect mode may be enabled and disabled using the toolbar button indicated in Figure 18-4:

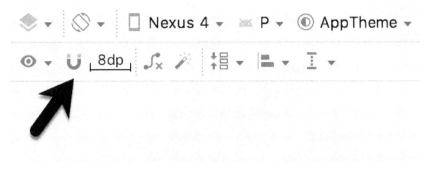

Figure 18-4

Autoconnect mode uses algorithms to decide the best constraints to establish based on the position of the widget and the widget's proximity to both the sides of the parent layout and other elements in the layout. In the event that any of the automatic constraint connections fail to provide the desired behavior, these may be changed manually as outlined later in this chapter.

18.3 Inference Mode

Inference mode uses a heuristic approach involving algorithms and probabilities to automatically implement constraint connections after widgets have already been added to the layout. This mode is usually used when the Autoconnect feature has been turned off and objects have been added to the layout without any constraint connections. This allows the layout to be designed simply by dragging and dropping objects from the palette onto the layout canvas and making size and positioning changes until the layout appears as required. In essence this involves "painting" the layout without worrying about constraints. Inference mode may also be used at any time during the design process to fill in missing constraints within a layout.

Constraints are automatically added to a layout when the *Infer constraints* button (Figure 18-5) is clicked:

Figure 18-5

As with Autoconnect mode, there is always the possibility that the Layout Editor tool will infer incorrect constraints, though these may be modified and corrected manually.

18.4 Manipulating Constraints Manually

The third option for implementing constraint connections is to do so manually. When doing so, it will be helpful to understand the various handles that appear around a widget within the Layout Editor tool. Consider, for example, the widget shown in Figure 18-6:

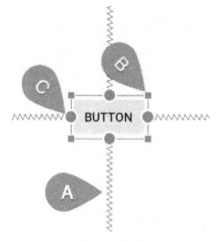

Figure 18-6

Clearly the spring-like lines (A) represent established constraint connections leading from the sides of the widget to the targets. The small square markers (B) in each corner of the object are resize handles which, when clicked and dragged, serve to resize the widget. The small circle handles (C) located on each side of the widget are the side constraint anchors. To create a constraint connection, click on the handle and drag the resulting line to the element to which the constraint is to be connected (such as a guideline or the side of either the parent layout or another widget) as outlined in Figure 18-7. When connecting to the side of another widget, simply drag the line to the side constraint handle of that widget and release the line when the widget and handle highlight.

Figure 18-7

If the constraint line is dragged to a widget and released, but not attached to a constraint handle, the layout editor will display a menu containing a list of the sides to which the constraint may be attached. In Figure 18-8, for example, the constraint can be attached to the top or bottom edge of the destination button widget:

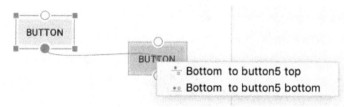

Figure 18-8

An additional marker indicates the anchor point for baseline constraints whereby the content within the widget (as opposed to outside edges) is used as the alignment point. To display this marker, simply right-click on the widget and select the *Show Baseline* menu option. To establish a constraint connection from a baseline constraint handle, simply hover the mouse pointer over the handle until it begins to flash before clicking and dragging to the target (such as the baseline anchor of another widget as shown in Figure 18-9). When the destination anchor begins to flash green, release the mouse button to make the constraint connection:

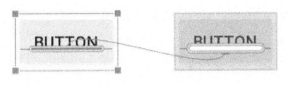

Figure 18-9

To hide the baseline anchors, right click on the widget a second time and select the *Hide Baseline* menu option.

18.5 Adding Constraints in the Inspector

Constraints may also be added to a view within the Android Studio Layout Editor tool using the *Inspector* panel located in the Attributes tool window as shown in Figure 18-10. The square in the center represents the currently selected view and the areas around the square the constraints, if any, applied to the corresponding sides of the view:

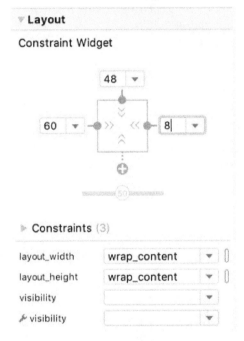

Figure 18-10

The absence of a constraint on a side of the view is represented by a dotted line leading to a blue circle containing a plus sign (as is the case with the bottom edge of the view in the above figure). To add a constraint, simply click on this blue circle and the layout editor will add a constraint connected to what it considers to be the most appropriate target within the layout.

18.6 Viewing Constraints in the Attributes Window

A list of constraints configured on the currently select widget can be viewing by displaying the Constraints section of the Attributes tool window as shown in Figure 18-11 below:

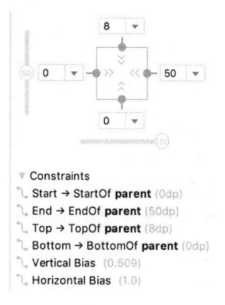

Figure 18-11

Clicking on a constraint in the list will select that constraint within the design layout.

18.7 Deleting Constraints

To delete an individual constraint, simply select the constraint either within the design layout or the Attributes tool window so that it highlights (in Figure 18-12, for example, the right-most constraint has been selected) and tap the keyboard delete key. The constraint will then be removed from the layout.

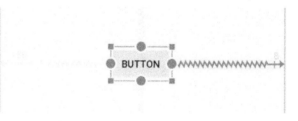

Figure 18-12

Another option is to hover the mouse pointer over the constraint anchor while holding down the Ctrl (Cmd on macOS) key and clicking on the anchor after it turns red:

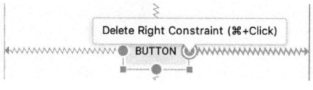

Figure 18-13

Alternatively, remove all of the constraints on a widget by right-clicking on it selecting the *Clear Constraints of Selection* menu option.

To remove all of the constraints from every widget in a layout, use the toolbar button highlighted in Figure 18-

14:

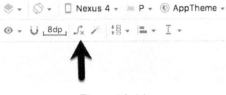

Figure 18-14

18.8 Adjusting Constraint Bias

In the previous chapter, the concept of using bias settings to favor one opposing constraint over another was outlined. Bias within the Android Studio Layout Editor tool is adjusted using the *Inspector* located in the Attributes tool window and shown in Figure 18-15. The two sliders indicated by the arrows in the figure are used to control the bias of the vertical and horizontal opposing constraints of the currently selected widget.

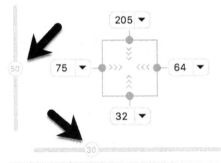

Figure 18-15

18.9 Understanding ConstraintLayout Margins

Constraints can be used in conjunction with margins to implement fixed gaps between a widget and another element (such as another widget, a guideline or the side of the parent layout). Consider, for example, the horizontal constraints applied to the Button object in Figure 18-16:

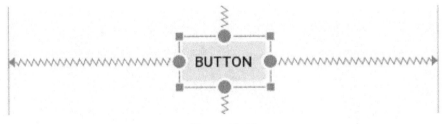

Figure 18-16

As currently configured, horizontal constraints run to the left and right edges of the parent ConstraintLayout. As such, the widget has opposing horizontal constraints indicating that the ConstraintLayout layout engine has some discretion in terms of the actual positioning of the widget at runtime. This allows the layout some flexibility to accommodate different screen sizes and device orientation. The horizontal bias setting is also able to control the position of the widget right up to the right-hand side of the layout. Figure 18-17, for example, shows the same button with 100% horizontal bias applied:

Figure 18-17

ConstraintLayout margins can appear at the end of constraint connections and represent a fixed gap into which the widget cannot be moved even when adjusting bias or in response to layout changes elsewhere in the activity. In Figure 18-18, the right-hand constraint now includes a 50dp margin into which the widget cannot be moved even though the bias is still set at 100%.

Figure 18-18

Existing margin values on a widget can be modified from within the Inspector. As can be seen in Figure 18-19, a dropdown menu is being used to change the right-hand margin on the currently selected widget to 16dp. Alternatively, clicking on the current value also allows a number to be typed into the field.

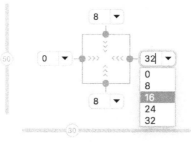

Figure 18-19

The default margin for new constraints can be changed at any time using the option in the toolbar highlighted in Figure 18-20:

Figure 18-20

18.10 The Importance of Opposing Constraints and Bias

As discussed in the previous chapter, opposing constraints, margins and bias form the cornerstone of responsive layout design in Android when using the ConstraintLayout. When a widget is constrained without opposing constraint connections, those constraints are essentially margin constraints. This is indicated visually within the Layout Editor tool by solid straight lines accompanied by margin measurements as shown in Figure 18-21.

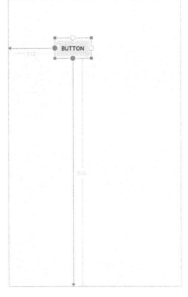

Figure 18-21

The above constraints essentially fix the widget at that position. The result of this is that if the device is rotated to landscape orientation, the widget will no longer be visible since the vertical constraint pushes it beyond the top edge of the device screen (as is the case in Figure 18-22). A similar problem will arise if the app is run on a device with a smaller screen than that used during the design process.

Figure 18-22

When opposing constraints are implemented, the constraint connection is represented by the spring-like jagged line (the spring metaphor is intended to indicate that the position of the widget is not fixed to absolute X and Y coordinates):

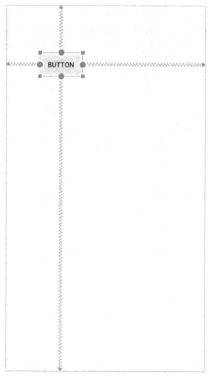

Figure 18-23

In the above layout, vertical and horizontal bias settings have been configured such that the widget will always be positioned 90% of the distance from the bottom and 35% from the left-hand edge of the parent layout. When rotated, therefore, the widget is still visible and positioned in the same location relative to the dimensions of the screen:

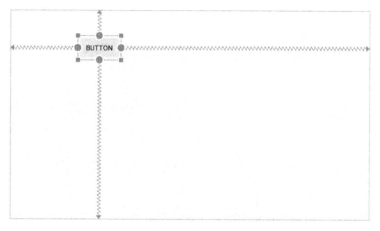

Figure 18-24

When designing a responsive and adaptable user interface layout, it is important to take into consideration both bias and opposing constraints when manually designing a user interface layout and making corrections to automatically created constraints.

18.11 Configuring Widget Dimensions

The inner dimensions of a widget within a ConstraintLayout can also be configured using the Inspector. As outlined in the previous chapter, widget dimensions can be set to wrap content, fixed or match constraint modes. The prevailing settings for each dimension on the currently selected widget are shown within the square representing the widget in the Inspector as illustrated in Figure 18-25:

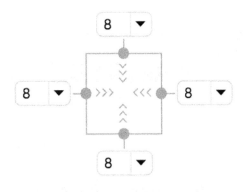

Figure 18-25

In the above figure, both the horizontal and vertical dimensions are set to wrap content mode (indicated by the inward pointing chevrons). The inspector uses the following visual indicators to represent the three dimension modes:

Fixed Size	
Match Constraint	⟞⋀⋀⟝
Wrap Content	

Table 18-1

To change the current setting, simply click on the indicator to cycle through the three different settings. When the dimension of a view within the layout editor is set to match constraint mode, the corresponding sides of the view are drawn with the spring-like line instead of the usual straight lines. In Figure 18-26, for example, only the width of the view has been set to match constraint:

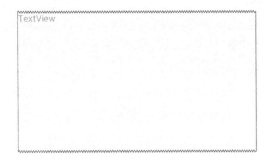

Figure 18-26

In addition, the size of a widget can be expanded either horizontally or vertically to the maximum amount allowed by the constraints and other widgets in the layout using the *Expand horizontally* and *Expand vertically* options. These are accessible by right clicking on a widget within the layout and selecting the *Organize* option from the resulting menu (Figure 18-27). When used, the currently selected widget will increase in size horizontally or vertically to fill the available space around it.

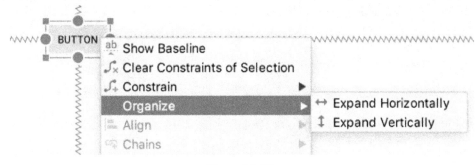

Figure 18-27

18.12 Adding Guidelines

Guidelines provide additional elements to which constraints may be anchored. Guidelines are added by right-clicking on the layout and selecting either the *Add Vertical Guideline* or *Add Horizontal Guideline* menu option or using the toolbar menu options as shown in Figure 18-28:

Figure 18-28

Once added, a guideline will appear as a dashed line in the layout and may be moved simply by clicking and dragging the line. To establish a constraint connection to a guideline, click in the constraint handler of a widget and drag to the guideline before releasing. In Figure 18-29, the left sides of two Buttons are connected by constraints to a vertical guideline.

The position of a vertical guideline can be specified as an absolute distance from either the left or the right of the parent layout (or the top or bottom for a horizontal guideline). The vertical guideline in the above figure, for example, is positioned 96dp from the left-hand edge of the parent.

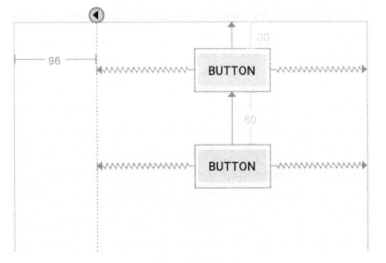

Figure 18-29

Alternatively, the guideline may be positioned as a percentage of the overall width or height of the parent layout. To switch between these three modes, select the guideline and click on the circle at the top or start of the guideline (depending on whether the guideline is vertical or horizontal). Figure 18-30, for example, shows a guideline positioned based on percentage:

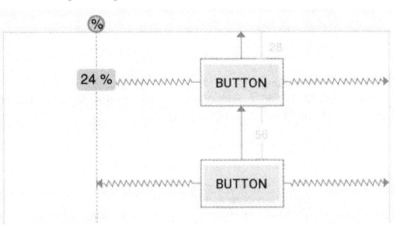

Figure 18-30

18.13 Adding Barriers

Barriers are added by right-clicking on the layout and selecting either the *Add Vertical Barrier* or *Add Horizontal Barrier* option from the *Helpers* menu, or using the toolbar menu options as shown previously in Figure 18-28.

Once a barrier has been added to the layout, it will appear as an entry in the Component Tree panel:

Figure 18-31

To add views as reference views (in other words, the views that control the position of the barrier), simply drag the widgets from within the Component Tree onto the barrier entry. In Figure 18-32, for example, widgets named textView1 and textView2 have been assigned as the reference widgets for barrier1:

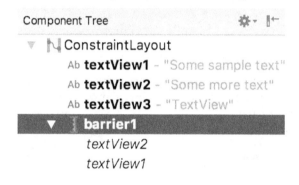

Figure 18-32

After the reference views have been added, the barrier needs to be configured to specify the direction of the barrier in relation those views. This is the *barrier direction* setting and is defined within the Attributes tool window when the barrier is selected in the Component Tree panel:

Figure 18-33

The following figure shows a layout containing a barrier declared with textView1 and textView2 acting as the reference views and textview3 as the constrained view. Since the barrier is pushing from the end of the reference views towards the constrained view, the barrier direction has been set to *end*:

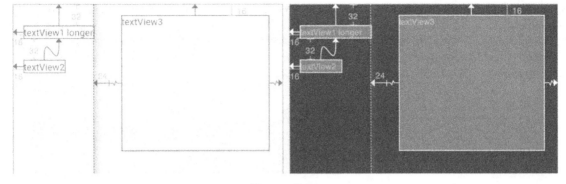

Figure 18-34

18.14 Widget Group Alignment and Distribution

The Android Studio Layout Editor tool provides a range of alignment and distribution actions that can be performed when two or more widgets are selected in the layout. Simply shift-click on each of the widgets to be included in the action, right-click on the layout and make a selection from the many options displayed in the Align menu:

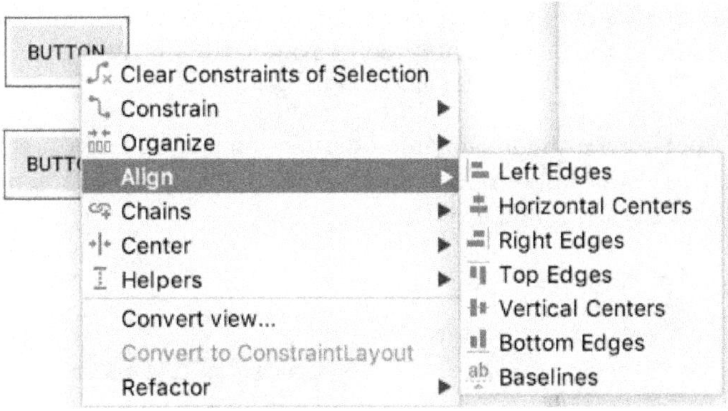

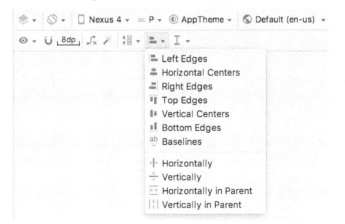

Figure 18-35

As shown in Figure 18-36 below, these options are also available as buttons in the Layout Editor toolbar:

Figure 18-36

Similarly, the Pack menu (Figure 18-37) can be used to collectively reposition the selected widgets so that they are packed tightly together either vertically or horizontally. It achieves this by changing the absolute x and y coordinates of the widgets but does not apply any constraints. The two distribution options in the Pack menu, on the other hand, move the selected widgets so that they are spaced evenly apart in either vertical or horizontal axis and applies constraints between the views to maintain this spacing.

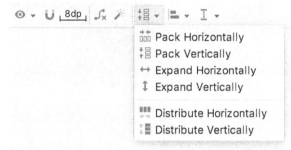

Figure 18-37

18.15 Converting other Layouts to ConstraintLayout

For existing user interface layouts that make use of one or more of the other Android layout classes (such as RelativeLayout or LinearLayout), the Layout Editor tool provides an option to convert the user interface to use the ConstraintLayout.

When the Layout Editor tool is open and in Design mode, the Component Tree panel is displayed beneath the Palette. To convert a layout to ConstraintLayout, locate it within the Component Tree, right-click on it and select the *Convert <current layout> to Constraint Layout* menu option:

Figure 18-38

When this menu option is selected, Android Studio will convert the selected layout to a ConstraintLayout and use inference to establish constraints designed to match the layout behavior of the original layout type.

18.16 Summary

A redesigned Layout Editor tool combined with ConstraintLayout makes designing complex user interface layouts with Android Studio a relatively fast and intuitive process. This chapter has covered the concepts of constraints, margins and bias in more detail while also exploring the ways in which ConstraintLayout-based design has been integrated into the Layout Editor tool.

19. Working with ConstraintLayout Chains and Ratios in Android Studio

The previous chapters have introduced the key features of the ConstraintLayout class and outlined the best practices for ConstraintLayout-based user interface design within the Android Studio Layout Editor. Although the concepts of ConstraintLayout chains and ratios were outlined in the chapter entitled *"A Guide to the Android ConstraintLayout"*, we have not yet addressed how to make use of these features within the Layout Editor. The focus of this chapter, therefore, is to provide practical steps on how to create and manage chains and ratios when using the ConstraintLayout class.

19.1 Creating a Chain

Chains may be implemented either by adding a few lines to the XML layout resource file of an activity or by using some chain specific features of the Layout Editor.

Consider a layout consisting of three Button widgets constrained so as to be positioned in the top-left, top-center and top-right of the ConstraintLayout parent as illustrated in Figure 19-1:

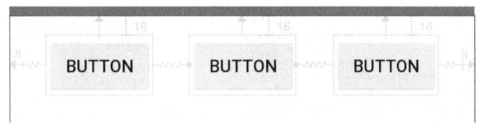

Figure 19-1

To represent such a layout, the XML resource layout file might contain the following entries for the button widgets:

```
<Button
    android:id="@+id/button1"
    android:layout_width="wrap_content"
    android:layout_height="wrap_content"
    android:layout_marginStart="8dp"
    android:layout_marginTop="16dp"
    android:text="Button"
    app:layout_constraintHorizontal_bias="0.5"
    app:layout_constraintStart_toStartOf="parent"
    app:layout_constraintTop_toTopOf="parent" />

<Button
    android:id="@+id/button2"
    android:layout_width="wrap_content"
```

```
    android:layout_height="wrap_content"
    android:layout_marginEnd="8dp"
    android:layout_marginStart="8dp"
    android:layout_marginTop="16dp"
    android:text="Button"
    app:layout_constraintHorizontal_bias="0.5"
    app:layout_constraintEnd_toStartOf="@+id/button3"
    app:layout_constraintStart_toEndOf="@+id/button1"
    app:layout_constraintTop_toTopOf="parent" />

<Button
    android:id="@+id/button3"
    android:layout_width="wrap_content"
    android:layout_height="wrap_content"
    android:layout_marginEnd="8dp"
    android:layout_marginTop="16dp"
    android:text="Button"
    app:layout_constraintHorizontal_bias="0.5"
    app:layout_constraintEnd_toEndOf="parent"
    app:layout_constraintTop_toTopOf="parent" />
```

As currently configured, there are no bi-directional constraints to group these widgets into a chain. To address this, additional constraints need to be added from the right-hand side of button1 to the left side of button2, and from the left side of button3 to the right side of button2 as follows:

```
<Button
    android:id="@+id/button1"
    android:layout_width="wrap_content"
    android:layout_height="wrap_content"
    android:layout_marginStart="8dp"
    android:layout_marginTop="16dp"
    android:text="Button"
    app:layout_constraintHorizontal_bias="0.5"
    app:layout_constraintStart_toStartOf="parent"
    app:layout_constraintTop_toTopOf="parent"
    app:layout_constraintEnd_toStartOf="@+id/button2" />

<Button
    android:id="@+id/button2"
    android:layout_width="wrap_content"
    android:layout_height="wrap_content"
    android:layout_marginEnd="8dp"
    android:layout_marginStart="8dp"
    android:layout_marginTop="16dp"
    android:text="Button"
    app:layout_constraintHorizontal_bias="0.5"
    app:layout_constraintEnd_toStartOf="@+id/button3"
```

```
app:layout_constraintStart_toEndOf="@+id/button1"
app:layout_constraintTop_toTopOf="parent" />

<Button
    android:id="@+id/button3"
    android:layout_width="wrap_content"
    android:layout_height="wrap_content"
    android:layout_marginEnd="8dp"
    android:layout_marginTop="16dp"
    android:text="Button"
    app:layout_constraintHorizontal_bias="0.5"
    app:layout_constraintEnd_toEndOf="parent"
    app:layout_constraintTop_toTopOf="parent"
    app:layout_constraintStart_toEndOf="@+id/button2" />
```

With these changes, the widgets now have bi-directional horizontal constraints configured. This essentially constitutes a ConstraintLayout chain which is represented visually within the Layout Editor by chain connections as shown in Figure 19-2 below. Note that in this configuration the chain has defaulted to the *spread* chain style.

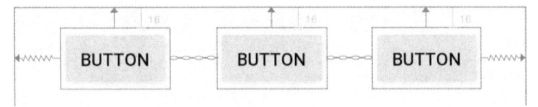

Figure 19-2

A chain may also be created by right-clicking on one of the views and selecting the *Chains -> Create Horizontal Chain* or *Chains -> Create Vertical Chain* menu options.

19.2 Changing the Chain Style

If no chain style is configured, the ConstraintLayout will default to the spread chain style. The chain style can be altered by right-clicking any of the widgets in the chain and selecting the *Cycle Chain Mode* menu option. Each time the menu option is clicked the style will switch to another setting in the order of spread, spread inside and packed.

Alternatively, the style may be specified in the Attributes tool window unfolding the *layout_constraints* property and changing either the *horizontal_chainStyle* or *vertical_chainStyle* property depending on the orientation of the chain:

Figure 19-3

19.3 Spread Inside Chain Style

Figure 19-4 illustrates the effect of changing the chain style to the *spread inside* chain style using the above techniques:

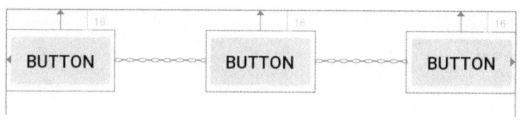

Figure 19-4

19.4 Packed Chain Style

Using the same technique, changing the chain style property to *packed* causes the layout to change as shown in Figure 19-5:

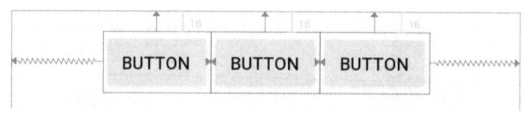

Figure 19-5

19.5 Packed Chain Style with Bias

The positioning of the packed chain may be influenced by applying a bias value. The bias can be any value between 0.0 and 1.0, with 0.5 representing the center of the parent. Bias is controlled by selecting the chain head widget and assigning a value to the *horizontal_bias* or *vertical_bias* attribute in the Attributes panel. Figure 19-6 shows a packed chain with a horizontal bias setting of 0.2:

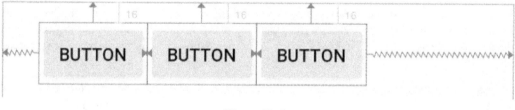

Figure 19-6

19.6 Weighted Chain

The final area of chains to explore involves weighting of the individual widgets to control how much space each widget in the chain occupies within the available space. A weighted chain may only be implemented using the *spread* chain style and any widget within the chain that is to respond to the weight property must have the corresponding dimension property (height for a vertical chain and width for a horizontal chain) configured for *match constraint* mode. Match constraint mode for a widget dimension may be configured by selecting the widget, displaying the Attributes panel and changing the dimension to *match_constraint* (equivalent to 0dp). In Figure 19-7, for example, the *layout_width* constraint for a button has been set to *match_constraint (0dp)* to indicate that the width of the widget is to be determined based on the prevailing constraint settings:

Figure 19-7

Assuming that the spread chain style has been selected, and all three buttons have been configured such that the width dimension is set to match the constraints, the widgets in the chain will expand equally to fill the available space:

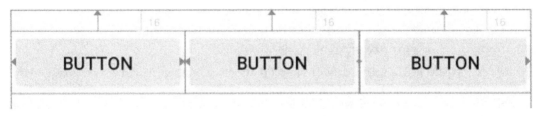

Figure 19-8

The amount of space occupied by each widget relative to the other widgets in the chain can be controlled by adding weight properties to the widgets. Figure 19-9 shows the effect of setting the *horizontal_weight* property to 4 on button1, and to 2 on both button2 and button3:

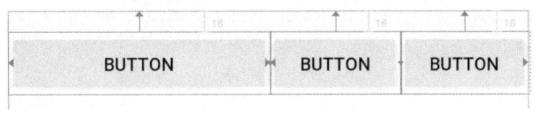

Figure 19-9

As a result of these weighting values, button1 occupies half of the space (4/8), while button2 and button3 each occupy one quarter (2/8) of the space.

19.7 Working with Ratios

ConstraintLayout ratios allow one dimension of a widget to be sized relative to the widget's other dimension (otherwise known as aspect ratio). An aspect ratio setting could, for example, be applied to an ImageView to ensure that its width is always twice its height.

A dimension ratio constraint is configured by setting the constrained dimension to match constraint mode and configuring the *layout_constraintDimensionRatio* attribute on that widget to the required ratio. This ratio value may be specified either as a float value or a *width:height* ratio setting. The following XML excerpt, for example, configures a ratio of 2:1 on an ImageView widget:

```
<ImageView
        android:layout_width="0dp"
        android:layout_height="100dp"
        android:id="@+id/imageView"
        app:layout_constraintDimensionRatio="2:1" />
```

The above example demonstrates how to configure a ratio when only one dimension is set to match constraint. A ratio may also be applied when both dimensions are set to match constraint mode. This involves specifying the ratio preceded with either an H or a W to indicate which of the dimensions is constrained relative to the other.

Consider, for example, the following XML excerpt for an ImageView object:

```
<ImageView
    android:layout_width="0dp"
    android:layout_height="0dp"
    android:id="@+id/imageView"
    app:layout_constraintBottom_toBottomOf="parent"
    app:layout_constraintRight_toRightOf="parent"
    app:layout_constraintLeft_toLeftOf="parent"
    app:layout_constraintTop_toTopOf="parent"
    app:layout_constraintDimensionRatio="W,1:3" />
```

In the above example the height will be defined subject to the constraints applied to it. In this case constraints have been configured such that it is attached to the top and bottom of the parent view, essentially stretching the widget to fill the entire height of the parent. The width dimension, on the other hand, has been constrained to be one third of the ImageView's height dimension. Consequently, whatever size screen or orientation the layout appears on, the ImageView will always be the same height as the parent and the width one third of that height.

The same results may also be achieved without the need to manually edit the XML resource file. Whenever a widget dimension is set to match constraint mode, a ratio control toggle appears in the Inspector area of the property panel. Figure 19-10, for example, shows the layout width and height attributes of a button widget set to match constraint mode and 100dp respectively, and highlights the ratio control toggle in the widget sizing preview:

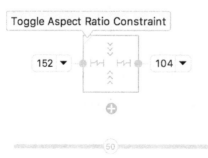

Figure 19-10

By default the ratio sizing control is toggled off. Clicking on the control enables the ratio constraint and displays an additional field where the ratio may be changed:

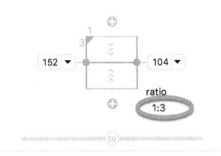

Figure 19-11

19.8 Summary

Both chains and ratios are powerful features of the ConstraintLayout class intended to provide additional options for designing flexible and responsive user interface layouts within Android applications. As outlined in this chapter, the Android Studio Layout Editor has been enhanced to make it easier to use these features during the user interface design process.

20. An Android Studio Layout Editor ConstraintLayout Tutorial

By far the easiest and most productive way to design a user interface for an Android application is to make use of the Android Studio Layout Editor tool. The goal of this chapter is to provide an overview of how to create a ConstraintLayout-based user interface using this approach. The exercise included in this chapter will also be used as an opportunity to outline the creation of an activity starting with a "bare-bones" Android Studio project.

Having covered the use of the Android Studio Layout Editor, the chapter will also introduce the Layout Inspector tool.

20.1 An Android Studio Layout Editor Tool Example

The first step in this phase of the example is to create a new Android Studio project. Begin, therefore, by launching Android Studio and closing any previously opened projects by selecting the *File -> Close Project* menu option.

Select the *Start a new Android Studio project* quick start option from the welcome screen. In previous examples, we have requested that Android Studio create a template activity for the project. We will, however, be using this tutorial to learn how to create an entirely new activity and corresponding layout resource file manually, so make sure that the *Add No Activity* option is selected before clicking on the Next button

Enter *LayoutSample* into the Name field and specify *com.ebookfrenzy.layoutsample* as the package name. Before clicking on the Finish button, change the Minimum API level setting to API 26: Android 8.0 (Oreo) and the Language menu to Java.

20.2 Creating a New Activity

Once the project creation process is complete, the Android Studio main window should appear with no tool windows open.

The next step in the project is to create a new activity. This will be a valuable learning exercise since there are many instances in the course of developing Android applications where new activities need to be created from the ground up.

Begin by displaying the Project tool window using the Alt-1/Cmd-1 keyboard shortcut. Once displayed, unfold the hierarchy by clicking on the right facing arrows next to the entries in the Project window. The objective here is to gain access to the *app -> java -> com.ebookfrenzy.layoutsample* folder in the project hierarchy. Once the package name is visible, right-click on it and select the *New -> Activity -> Empty Activity* menu option as illustrated in Figure 20-1:

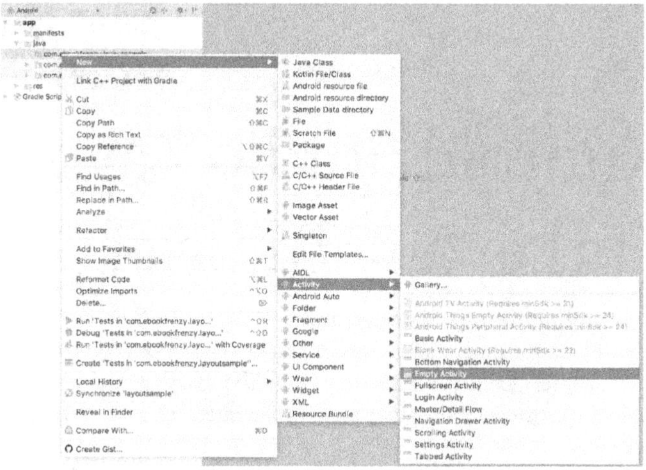

Figure 20-1

In the resulting *New Android Activity* dialog, name the new activity *MainActivity* and the layout *activity_main*. The activity will, of course, need a layout resource file so make sure that the *Generate Layout File* option is enabled.

In order for an application to be able to run on a device it needs to have an activity designated as the *launcher activity*. Without a launcher activity, the operating system will not know which activity to start up when the application first launches and the application will fail to start. Since this example only has one activity, it needs to be designated as the launcher activity for the application so make sure that the *Launcher Activity* option is enabled before clicking on the *Finish* button.

At this point Android Studio should have added two files to the project. The Java source code file for the activity should be located in the *app -> java -> com.ebookfrenzy.layoutsample* folder.

In addition, the XML layout file for the user interface should have been created in the *app -> res -> layout* folder. Note that the Empty Activity template was chosen for this activity so the layout is contained entirely within the *activity_main.xml* file and there is no separate content layout file.

Finally, the new activity should have been added to the *AndroidManifest.xml* file and designated as the launcher activity. The manifest file can be found in the project window under the *app -> manifests* folder and should contain the following XML:

```
<?xml version="1.0" encoding="utf-8"?>
<manifest xmlns:android="http://schemas.android.com/apk/res/android"
    package="com.ebookfrenzy.layoutsample">

    <application
        android:allowBackup="true"
        android:icon="@mipmap/ic_launcher"
        android:label="@string/app_name"
        android:roundIcon="@mipmap/ic_launcher_round"
        android:supportsRtl="true"
        android:theme="@style/AppTheme">
        <activity android:name=".MainActivity">
            <intent-filter>
```

```
        <action android:name="android.intent.action.MAIN" />

        <category
    android:name="android.intent.category.LAUNCHER" />
        </intent-filter>
      </activity>
    </application>

</manifest>
```

20.3 Preparing the Layout Editor Environment

Locate and double-click on the *activity_main.xml* layout file located in the *app -> res -> layout* folder to load it into the Layout Editor tool. Since the purpose of this tutorial is to gain experience with the use of constraints, turn off the Autoconnect feature using the button located in the Layout Editor toolbar. Once disabled, the button will appear with a line through it as is the case in Figure 20-2:

Figure 20-2

If the default margin value to the right of the Autoconnect button is not set to 8dp, click on it and select 8dp from the resulting panel.

The user interface design will also make use of the ImageView object to display an image. Before proceeding, this image should be added to the project ready for use later in the chapter. This file is named *galaxys6.png* and can be found in the *project_icons* folder of the sample code download available from the following URL:

https://www.ebookfrenzy.com/retail/androidstudio35/index.php

Within Android Studio, display the Resource Manager tool window (*View -> Tool Windows -> Resource Manager*). Locate the *galaxy6s.png* image in the file system navigator for your operating system and drag and drop the image onto the Resource Manager tool window. In the resulting dialog, select the *Import* button to add the image to project. The image should now appear in the Resource Manager as shown in Figure 20-3 below:

Figure 20-3

The image will also appear in the *res -> drawables* section of the Project tool window:

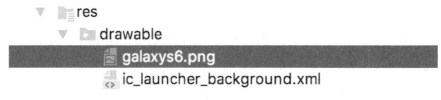

▼ ▓ res
  ▼ ▓ drawable
        ▓ galaxys6.png
        ▓ ic_launcher_background.xml

Figure 20-4

20.4 Adding the Widgets to the User Interface

From within the *Common* palette category, drag an ImageView object into the center of the display view. Note that horizontal and vertical dashed lines appear indicating the center axes of the display. When centered, release the mouse button to drop the view into position. Once placed within the layout, the Resources dialog will appear seeking the image to be displayed within the view. In the search bar located at the top of the dialog, enter "galaxy" to locate the *galaxys6.png* resource as illustrated in Figure 20-5.

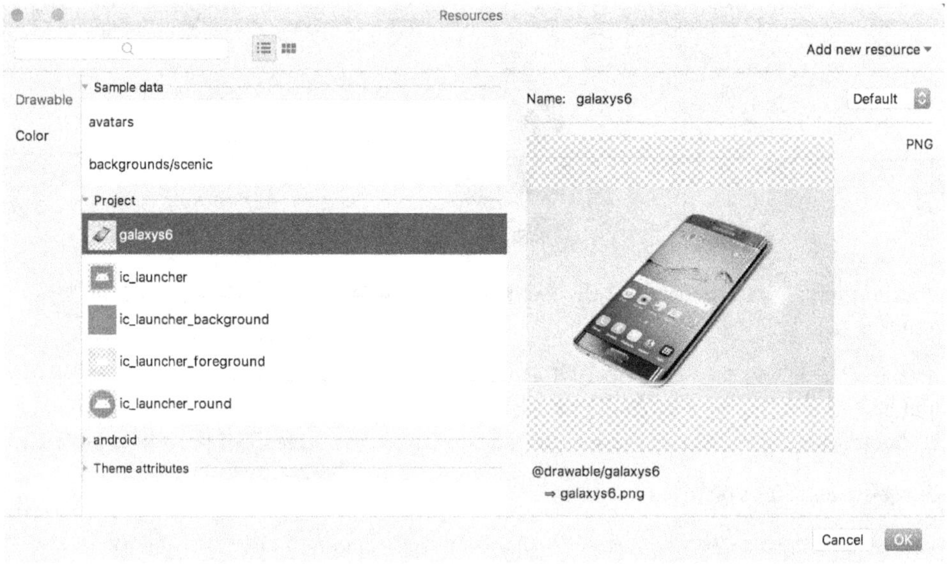

Figure 20-5

Select the image and click on OK to assign it to the ImageView object. If necessary, adjust the size of the ImageView using the resize handles and reposition it in the center of the layout. At this point the layout should match Figure 20-6:

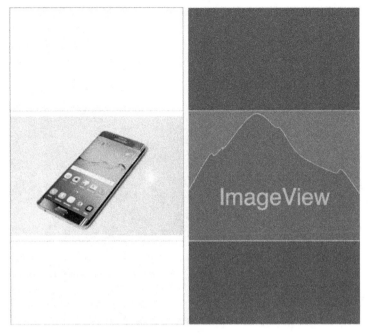

Figure 20-6

Click and drag a TextView object from the *Common* section of the palette and position it so that it appears above the ImageView as illustrated in Figure 20-7.

Using the Attributes panel, change the *textSize* property to 24sp, the *textAlignment* setting to center and the text to "Samsung Galaxy S6".

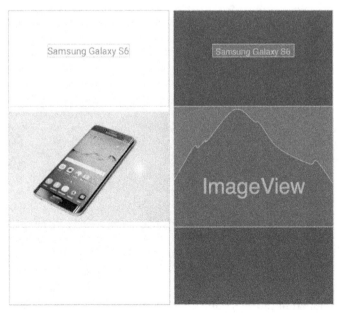

Figure 20-7

Next, add three Button widgets along the bottom of the layout and set the text attributes of these views to "Buy

Now", "Pricing" and "Details". The completed layout should now match Figure 20-8:

Figure 20-8

At this point, the widgets are not sufficiently constrained for the layout engine to be able to position and size the widgets at runtime. Were the app to run now, all of the widgets would be positioned in the top left-hand corner of the display.

With the widgets added to the layout, use the device rotation button located in the Layout Editor toolbar (indicated by the arrow in Figure 20-9) to view the user interface in landscape orientation:

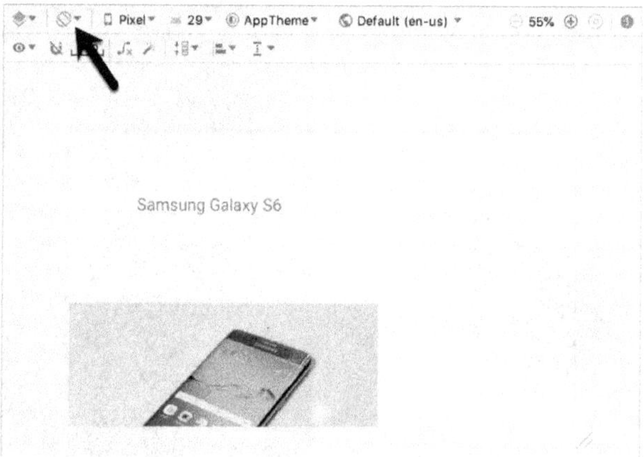

Figure 20-9

The absence of constraints results in a layout that fails to adapt to the change in device orientation, leaving the content off center and with part of the image and all three buttons positioned beyond the viewable area of the screen. Clearly some work still needs to be done to make this into a responsive user interface.

20.5 Adding the Constraints

Constraints are the key to creating layouts that can adapt to device orientation changes and different screen sizes. Begin by rotating the layout back to portrait orientation and selecting the TextView widget located above the ImageView. With the widget selected, establish constraints from the left, right and top sides of the TextView to the corresponding sides of the parent ConstraintLayout as shown in Figure 20-10:

Figure 20-10

With the TextView widget constrained, select the ImageView instance and establish opposing constraints on the left and right-hand sides with each connected to the corresponding sides of the parent layout. Next, establish a constraint connection from the top of the ImageView to the bottom of the TextView and from the bottom of the ImageView to the top of the center Button widget. If necessary, click and drag the ImageView so that it is still positioned in the vertical center of the layout. Next, establish constraints on the left and right hand sides of the ImageView to the corresponding sides of the ConstraintLayout container.

With the ImageView still selected, use the Inspector in the attributes panel to change the top and bottom margins on the ImageView to 24 and 8 respectively and to change both the widget height and width dimension properties to *match_constraint* so that the widget will resize to match the constraints. These settings will allow the layout engine to enlarge and reduce the size of the ImageView when necessary to accommodate layout changes:

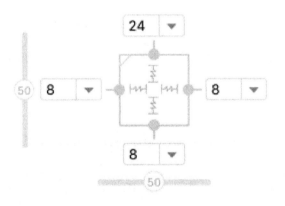

Figure 20-11

Figure 20-12, shows the currently implemented constraints for the ImageView in relation to the other elements in the layout:

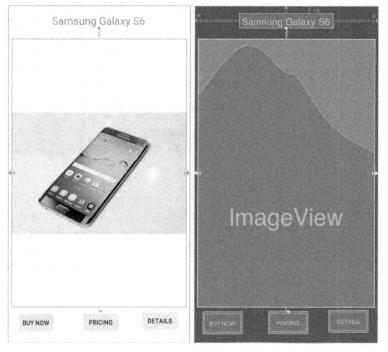

Figure 20-12

The final task is to add constraints to the three Button widgets. For this example, the buttons will be placed in a chain. Begin by turning on Autoconnect within the Layout Editor by clicking the toolbar button highlighted in Figure 20-2.

Next, click on the Buy Now button and then shift-click on the other two buttons so that all three are selected. Right-click on the Buy Now button and select the *Chains -> Create Horizontal Chain* menu option from the resulting menu. By default, the chain will be displayed using the spread style which is the correct behavior for this example.

Finally, establish a constraint between the bottom of the Buy Now button and the bottom of the layout. Repeat this step for the remaining buttons.

On completion of these steps the buttons should be constrained as outlined in Figure 20-13:

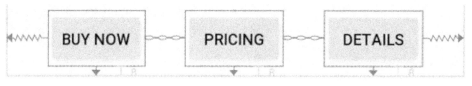

Figure 20-13

20.6 Testing the Layout

With the constraints added to the layout, rotate the screen into landscape orientation and verify that the layout adapts to accommodate the new screen dimensions.

While the Layout Editor tool provides a useful visual environment in which to design user interface layouts, when it comes to testing there is no substitute for testing the running app. Launch the app on a physical Android device or emulator session and verify that the user interface reflects the layout created in the Layout Editor.

Figure 20-14, for example, shows the running app in landscape orientation:

Figure 20-14

The very simple user interface design is now complete. Designing a more complex user interface layout is a continuation of the steps outlined above. Simply drag and drop views onto the display, position, constrain and set properties as needed.

20.7 Using the Layout Inspector

The hierarchy of components that make up a user interface layout may be viewed at any time using the Layout Inspector tool. In order to access this information the app must be running on a device or emulator. Once the app is running, select the *Tools -> Layout Inspector* menu option followed by the process to be inspected.

Once the inspector loads, the left most panel (A) shows the hierarchy of components that make up the user interface layout. The center panel (B) shows a visual representation of the layout design. Clicking on a widget in the visual layout will cause that item to highlight in the hierarchy list making it easy to find where a visual component is situated relative to the overall layout hierarchy.

Finally, the rightmost panel (marked C in Figure 20-15) contains all of the property settings for the currently selected component, allowing for in-depth analysis of the component's internal configuration.

Figure 20-15

20.8 Summary

The Layout Editor tool in Android Studio has been tightly integrated with the ConstraintLayout class. This chapter has worked through the creation of an example user interface intended to outline the ways in which a ConstraintLayout-based user interface can be implemented using the Layout Editor tool in terms of adding widgets and setting constraints. This chapter also introduced the Layout Inspector tool which is useful for analyzing the structural composition of a user interface layout.

21. Manual XML Layout Design in Android Studio

While the design of layouts using the Android Studio Layout Editor tool greatly improves productivity, it is still possible to create XML layouts by manually editing the underlying XML. This chapter will introduce the basics of the Android XML layout file format.

21.1 Manually Creating an XML Layout

The structure of an XML layout file is actually quite straightforward and follows the hierarchical approach of the view tree. The first line of an XML resource file should ideally include the following standard declaration:

```
<?xml version="1.0" encoding="utf-8"?>
```

This declaration should be followed by the root element of the layout, typically a container view such as a layout manager. This is represented by both opening and closing tags and any properties that need to be set on the view. The following XML, for example, declares a ConstraintLayout view as the root element, assigns the ID *activity_main* and sets *match_parent* attributes such that it fills all the available space of the device display:

```
<?xml version="1.0" encoding="utf-8"?>
<androidx.constraintlayout.widget.ConstraintLayout
    xmlns:android="http://schemas.android.com/apk/res/android"
    xmlns:app="http://schemas.android.com/apk/res-auto"
    xmlns:tools="http://schemas.android.com/tools"
    android:layout_width="match_parent"
    android:layout_height="match_parent"
    android:paddingLeft="16dp"
    android:paddingRight="16dp"
    android:paddingTop="16dp"
    android:paddingBottom="16dp"
    tools:context=".MainActivity">

</androidx.constraintlayout.widget.ConstraintLayout>
```

Note that in the above example the layout element is also configured with padding on each side of 16dp (density independent pixels). Any specification of spacing in an Android layout must be specified using one of the following units of measurement:

• **in** – Inches.

• **mm** – Millimeters.

• **pt** – Points (1/72 of an inch).

• **dp** – Density-independent pixels. An abstract unit of measurement based on the physical density of the device display relative to a 160dpi display baseline.

- **sp** – Scale-independent pixels. Similar to dp but scaled based on the user's font preference.

- **px** – Actual screen pixels. Use is not recommended since different displays will have different pixels per inch. Use *dp* in preference to this unit.

Any children that need to be added to the ConstraintLayout parent must be *nested* within the opening and closing tags. In the following example a Button widget has been added as a child of the ConstraintLayout:

```xml
<?xml version="1.0" encoding="utf-8"?>
<androidx.constraintlayout.widget.ConstraintLayout
    xmlns:android="http://schemas.android.com/apk/res/android"
    xmlns:app="http://schemas.android.com/apk/res-auto"
    xmlns:tools="http://schemas.android.com/tools"
    android:id="@+id/activity_main"
    android:layout_width="match_parent"
    android:layout_height="match_parent"
    android:paddingLeft="16dp"
    android:paddingRight="16dp"
    android:paddingTop="16dp"
    android:paddingBottom="16dp"
    tools:context=".MainActivity">

    <Button
        android:text="@string/button_string"
        android:layout_width="wrap_content"
        android:layout_height="wrap_content"
        android:id="@+id/button" />

</androidx.constraintlayout.widget.ConstraintLayout>
```

As currently implemented, the button has no constraint connections. At runtime, therefore, the button will appear in the top left-hand corner of the screen (though indented 16dp by the padding assigned to the parent layout). If opposing constraints are added to the sides of the button, however, it will appear centered within the layout:

```xml
<Button
    android:text="@string/button_string"
    android:layout_width="wrap_content"
    android:layout_height="wrap_content"
    android:id="@+id/button"
    app:layout_constraintBottom_toBottomOf="parent"
    app:layout_constraintEnd_toEndOf="parent"
    app:layout_constraintStart_toStartOf="parent"
    app:layout_constraintTop_toTopOf="parent" />
```

Note that each of the constraints is attached to the element named *activity_main* which is, in this case, the parent ConstraintLayout instance.

To add a second widget to the layout, simply embed it within the body of the ConstraintLayout element. The following modification, for example, adds a TextView widget to the layout:

```xml
<?xml version="1.0" encoding="utf-8"?>
<androidx.constraintlayout.widget.ConstraintLayout
    xmlns:android="http://schemas.android.com/apk/res/android"
    xmlns:app="http://schemas.android.com/apk/res-auto"
    xmlns:tools="http://schemas.android.com/tools"
    android:id="@+id/activity_main"
    android:layout_width="match_parent"
    android:layout_height="match_parent"
    android:paddingLeft="16dp"
    android:paddingTop="16dp"
    android:paddingRight="16dp"
    android:paddingBottom="16dp"
    tools:context=".MainActivity">

    <Button
        android:text="@string/button_string"
        android:layout_width="wrap_content"
        android:layout_height="wrap_content"
        android:id="@+id/button"
        app:layout_constraintBottom_toBottomOf="parent"
        app:layout_constraintEnd_toEndOf="parent"
        app:layout_constraintStart_toStartOf="parent"
        app:layout_constraintTop_toTopOf="parent" />

    <TextView
        android:text="@string/text_string"
        android:layout_width="wrap_content"
        android:layout_height="wrap_content"
        android:id="@+id/textView" />

</androidx.constraintlayout.widget.ConstraintLayout>
```

Once again, the absence of constraints on the newly added TextView will cause it to appear in the top left-hand corner of the layout at runtime. The following modifications add opposing constraints connected to the parent layout to center the widget horizontally, together with a constraint connecting the bottom of the TextView to the top of the button with a margin of 72dp:

```xml
<TextView
    android:text="@string/text_string"
    android:layout_width="wrap_content"
    android:layout_height="wrap_content"
    android:id="@+id/textView" />
```

Also, note that the Button and TextView views have a number of attributes declared. Both views have been assigned IDs and configured to display text strings represented by string resources named *button_string* and *text_string* respectively. Additionally, the *wrap_content* height and width properties have been declared on both objects so that they are sized to accommodate the content (in this case the text referenced by the string resource value).

Viewed from within the Preview panel of the Layout Editor in Text mode, the above layout will be rendered as shown in Figure 21-1:

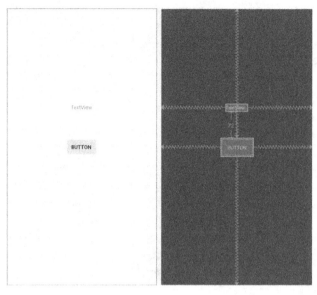

Figure 21-1

21.2 Manual XML vs. Visual Layout Design

When to write XML manually as opposed to using the Layout Editor tool in design mode is a matter of personal preference. There are, however, advantages to using design mode.

First, design mode will generally be quicker given that it avoids the necessity to type lines of XML. Additionally, design mode avoids the need to learn the intricacies of the various property values of the Android SDK view classes. Rather than continually refer to the Android documentation to find the correct keywords and values, most properties can be located by referring to the Attributes panel.

All the advantages of design mode aside, it is important to keep in mind that the two approaches to user interface design are in no way mutually exclusive. As an application developer, it is quite likely that you will end up creating user interfaces within design mode while performing fine-tuning and layout tweaks of the design by directly editing the generated XML resources. Both views of the interface design are, after all, displayed side by side within the Android Studio environment making it easy to work seamlessly on both the XML and the visual layout.

21.3 Summary

The Android Studio Layout Editor tool provides a visually intuitive method for designing user interfaces. Using a drag and drop paradigm combined with a set of property editors, the tool provides considerable productivity benefits to the application developer.

User interface designs may also be implemented by manually writing the XML layout resource files, the format of which is well structured and easily understood.

The fact that the Layout Editor tool generates XML resource files means that these two approaches to interface design can be combined to provide a "best of both worlds" approach to user interface development.

22. Managing Constraints using Constraint Sets

Up until this point in the book, all user interface design tasks have been performed using the Android Studio Layout Editor tool, either in text or design mode. An alternative to writing XML resource files or using the Android Studio Layout Editor is to write Java code to directly create, configure and manipulate the view objects that comprise the user interface of an Android activity. Within the context of this chapter, we will explore some of the advantages and disadvantages of writing Java code to create a user interface before describing some of the key concepts such as view properties and the creation and management of layout constraints.

In the next chapter, an example project will be created and used to demonstrate some of the typical steps involved in this approach to Android user interface creation.

22.1 Java Code vs. XML Layout Files

There are a number of key advantages to using XML resource files to design a user interface as opposed to writing Java code. In fact, Google goes to considerable lengths in the Android documentation to extol the virtues of XML resources over Java code. As discussed in the previous chapter, one key advantage to the XML approach includes the ability to use the Android Studio Layout Editor tool, which, itself, generates XML resources. A second advantage is that once an application has been created, changes to user interface screens can be made by simply modifying the XML file, thereby avoiding the necessity to recompile the application. Also, even when hand writing XML layouts, it is possible to get instant feedback on the appearance of the user interface using the preview feature of the Android Studio Layout Editor tool. In order to test the appearance of a Java created user interface the developer will, inevitably, repeatedly cycle through a loop of writing code, compiling and testing in order to complete the design work.

In terms of the strengths of the Java coding approach to layout creation, perhaps the most significant advantage that Java has over XML resource files comes into play when dealing with dynamic user interfaces. XML resource files are inherently most useful when defining static layouts, in other words layouts that are unlikely to change significantly from one invocation of an activity to the next. Java code, on the other hand, is ideal for creating user interfaces dynamically at run-time. This is particularly useful in situations where the user interface may appear differently each time the activity executes subject to external factors.

A knowledge of working with user interface components in Java code can also be useful when dynamic changes to a static XML resource based layout need to be performed in real-time as the activity is running.

Finally, some developers simply prefer to write Java code than to use layout tools and XML, regardless of the advantages offered by the latter approaches.

22.2 Creating Views

As previously established, the Android SDK includes a toolbox of view classes designed to meet most of the basic user interface design needs. The creation of a view in Java is simply a matter of creating instances of these classes, passing through as an argument a reference to the activity with which that view is to be associated.

The first view (typically a container view to which additional child views can be added) is displayed to the user via a call to the *setContentView()* method of the activity. Additional views may be added to the root view via calls to the object's *addView()* method.

When working with Java code to manipulate views contained in XML layout resource files, it is necessary to obtain the ID of the view. The same rule holds true for views created in Java. As such, it is necessary to assign an ID to any view for which certain types of access will be required in subsequent Java code. This is achieved via a call to the *setId()* method of the view object in question. In later code, the ID for a view may be obtained via the object's *getId()* method.

22.3 View Attributes

Each view class has associated with it a range of *attributes*. These property settings are set directly on the view instances and generally define how the view object will appear or behave. Examples of attributes are the text that appears on a Button object, or the background color of a ConstraintLayout view. Each view class within the Android SDK has a pre-defined set of methods that allow the user to *set* and *get* these property values. The Button class, for example, has a *setText()* method which can be called from within Java code to set the text displayed on the button to a specific string value. The background color of a *ConstraintLayout* object, on the other hand, can be set with a call to the object's *setBackgroundColor()* method.

22.4 Constraint Sets

While property settings are internal to view objects and dictate how a view appears and behaves, *constraint sets* are used to control how a view appears relative to its parent view and other sibling views. Every ConstraintLayout instance has associated with it a set of constraints that define how its child views are positioned and constrained.

The key to working with constraint sets in Java code is the *ConstraintSet* class. This class contains a range of methods that allow tasks such as creating, configuring and applying constraints to a ConstraintLayout instance. In addition, the current constraints for a ConstraintLayout instance may be copied into a ConstraintSet object and used to apply the same constraints to other layouts (with or without modifications).

A ConstraintSet instance is created just like any other Java object:

```
ConstraintSet set = new ConstraintSet();
```

Once a constraint set has been created, methods can be called on the instance to perform a wide range of tasks.

22.4.1 Establishing Connections

The *connect()* method of the ConstraintSet class is used to establish constraint connections between views. The following code configures a constraint set in which the left-hand side of a Button view is connected to the right-hand side of an EditText view with a margin of 70dp:

```
set.connect(button1.getId(), ConstraintSet.LEFT,
            editText1.getId(), ConstraintSet.RIGHT, 70);
```

22.4.2 Applying Constraints to a Layout

Once the constraint set is configured, it must be applied to a ConstraintLayout instance before it will take effect. A constraint set is applied via a call to the *applyTo()* method, passing through a reference to the layout object to which the settings are to be applied:

```
set.applyTo(myLayout);
```

22.4.3 Parent Constraint Connections

Connections may also be established between a child view and its parent ConstraintLayout by referencing the ConstraintSet.PARENT_ID constant. In the following example, the constraint set is configured to connect the top edge of a Button view to the top of the parent layout with a margin of 100dp:

```
set.connect(button1.getId(), ConstraintSet.TOP,
```

```
ConstraintSet.PARENT_ID, ConstraintSet.TOP, 100);
```

22.4.4 Sizing Constraints

A number of methods are available for controlling the sizing behavior of views. The following code, for example, sets the horizontal size of a Button view to *wrap_content* and the vertical size of an ImageView instance to a maximum of 250dp:

```
set.constrainWidth(button1.getId(), ConstraintSet.WRAP_CONTENT);
set.constrainMaxHeight(imageView1.getId(), 250);
```

22.4.5 Constraint Bias

As outlined in the chapter entitled *"A Guide to using ConstraintLayout in Android Studio"*, when a view has opposing constraints it is centered along the axis of the constraints (i.e. horizontally or vertically). This centering can be adjusted by applying a bias along the particular axis of constraint. When using the Android Studio Layout Editor, this is achieved using the controls in the Attributes tool window. When working with a constraint set, however, bias can be added using the *setHorizontalBias()* and *setVerticalBias()* methods, referencing the view ID and the bias as a floating point value between 0 and 1.

The following code, for example, constrains the left and right-hand sides of a Button to the corresponding sides of the parent layout before applying a 25% horizontal bias:

```
set.connect(button1.getId(), ConstraintSet.LEFT,
            ConstraintSet.PARENT_ID, ConstraintSet.LEFT, 0);
set.connect(button1.getId(), ConstraintSet.RIGHT,
            ConstraintSet.PARENT_ID, ConstraintSet.RIGHT, 0);
set.setHorizontalBias(button1.getId(), 0.25f);
```

22.4.6 Alignment Constraints

Alignments may also be applied using a constraint set. The full set of alignment options available with the Android Studio Layout Editor may also be configured using a constraint set via the *centerVertically()* and *centerHorizontally()* methods, both of which take a variety of arguments depending on the alignment being configured. In addition, the *center()* method may be used to center a view between two other views.

In the code below, button2 is positioned so that it is aligned horizontally with button1:

```
set.centerHorizontally(button2.getId(), button1.getId());
```

22.4.7 Copying and Applying Constraint Sets

The current constraint set for a ConstraintLayout instance may be copied into a constraint set object using the *clone()* method. The following line of code, for example, copies the constraint settings from a ConstraintLayout instance named *myLayout* into a constraint set object:

```
set.clone(myLayout);
```

Once copied, the constraint set may be applied directly to another layout or, as in the following example, modified before being applied to the second layout:

```
ConstraintSet set = new ConstraintSet();
set.clone(myLayout);
set.constrainWidth(button1.getId(), ConstraintSet.WRAP_CONTENT);
set.applyTo(mySecondLayout);
```

22.4.8 ConstraintLayout Chains

Vertical and horizontal chains may also be created within a constraint set using the *createHorizontalChain()* and *createVerticalChain()* methods. The syntax for using these methods is as follows:

```
createHorizontalChain(int leftId, int leftSide, int rightId,
    int rightSide, int[] chainIds, float[] weights, int style);
```

Based on the above syntax, the following example creates a horizontal spread chain that starts with button1 and ends with button4. In between these views are button2 and button3 with weighting set to zero for both:

```
int[] chainViews = {button2.getId(), button3.getId()};
float[] chainWeights = {0, 0};

set.createHorizontalChain(button1.getId(), ConstraintSet.LEFT,
                          button4.getId(), ConstraintSet.RIGHT,
                          chainViews, chainWeights,
                          ConstraintSet.CHAIN_SPREAD);
```

A view can be removed from a chain by passing the ID of the view to be removed through to either the *removeFromHorizontalChain()* or *removeFromVerticalChain()* methods. A view may be added to an existing chain using either the *addToHorizontalChain()* or *addToVerticalChain()* methods. In both cases the methods take as arguments the IDs of the views between which the new view is to be inserted as follows:

```
set.addToHorizontalChain(newViewId, leftViewId, rightViewId);
```

22.4.9 Guidelines

Guidelines are added to a constraint set using the *create()* method and then positioned using the *setGuidelineBegin()*, *setGuidelineEnd()* or *setGuidelinePercent()* methods. In the following code, a vertical guideline is created and positioned 50% across the width of the parent layout. The left side of a button view is then connected to the guideline with no margin:

```
set.create(R.id.myGuideline, ConstraintSet.VERTICAL_GUIDELINE);
set.setGuidelinePercent(R.id.myGuideline, 0.5f);

set.connect(button.getId(), ConstraintSet.LEFT,
        R.id.myGuideline, ConstraintSet.RIGHT, 0);

set.applyTo(layout);
```

22.4.10 Removing Constraints

A constraint may be removed from a view in a constraint set using the *clear()* method, passing through as arguments the view ID and the anchor point for which the constraint is to be removed:

```
set.clear(button.getId(), ConstraintSet.LEFT);
```

Similarly, all of the constraints on a view may be removed in a single step by referencing only the view in the *clear()* method call:

```
set.clear(button.getId());
```

22.4.11 Scaling

The scale of a view within a layout may be adjusted using the ConstraintSet *setScaleX()* and *setScaleY()* methods which take as arguments the view on which the operation is to be performed together with a float value indicating the scale. In the following code, a button object is scaled to twice its original width and half the height:

```
set.setScaleX(myButton.getId(), 2f);
set.setScaleY(myButton.getId(), 0.5f);
```

22.4.12 Rotation

A view may be rotated on either the X or Y axis using the *setRotationX()* and *setRotationY()* methods respectively both of which must be passed the ID of the view to be rotated and a float value representing the degree of rotation to be performed. The pivot point on which the rotation is to take place may be defined via a call to the *setTransformPivot()*, *setTransformPivotX()* and *setTransformPivotY()* methods. The following code rotates a button view 30 degrees on the Y axis using a pivot point located at point 500, 500:

```
set.setTransformPivot(button.getId(), 500, 500);
set.setRotationY(button.getId(), 30);
set.applyTo(layout);
```

Having covered the theory of constraint sets and user interface creation from within Java code, the next chapter will work through the creation of an example application with the objective of putting this theory into practice. For more details on the ConstraintSet class, refer to the reference guide at the following URL:

https://developer.android.com/reference/android/support/constraint/ConstraintSet.html

22.5 Summary

As an alternative to writing XML layout resource files or using the Android Studio Layout Editor tool, Android user interfaces may also be dynamically created in Java code.

Creating layouts in Java code consists of creating instances of view classes and setting attributes on those objects to define required appearance and behavior.

How a view is positioned and sized relative to its ConstraintLayout parent view and any sibling views is defined through the use of constraint sets. A constraint set is represented by an instance of the ConstraintSet class which, once created, can be configured using a wide range of method calls to perform tasks such as establishing constraint connections, controlling view sizing behavior and creating chains.

With the basics of the ConstraintSet class covered in this chapter, the next chapter will work through a tutorial that puts these features to practical use.

23. An Android ConstraintSet Tutorial

The previous chapter introduced the basic concepts of creating and modifying user interface layouts in Java code using the ConstraintLayout and ConstraintSet classes. This chapter will take these concepts and put them into practice through the creation of an example layout created entirely in Java code and without using the Android Studio Layout Editor tool.

23.1 Creating the Example Project in Android Studio

Launch Android Studio and select the *Start a new Android Studio project* option from the quick start menu in the welcome screen and, within the resulting new project dialog, choose the Empty Activity template before clicking on the Next button.

Enter *JavaLayout* into the Name field and specify *com.ebookfrenzy.javalayout* as the package name. Before clicking on the Finish button, change the Minimum API level setting to API 26: Android 8.0 (Oreo) and the Language menu to Java.

Once the project has been created, the *MainActivity.java* file should automatically load into the editing panel. As we have come to expect, Android Studio has created a template activity and overridden the *onCreate()* method, providing an ideal location for Java code to be added to create a user interface.

23.2 Adding Views to an Activity

The *onCreate()* method is currently designed to use a resource layout file for the user interface. Begin, therefore, by deleting this line from the method:

```
@Override
protected void onCreate(Bundle savedInstanceState) {
        super.onCreate(savedInstanceState);
        setContentView(R.layout.activity_main);
}
```

The next modification is to add a ConstraintLayout object with a single Button view child to the activity. This involves the creation of new instances of the ConstraintLayout and Button classes. The Button view then needs to be added as a child to the ConstraintLayout view which, in turn, is displayed via a call to the *setContentView()* method of the activity instance:

```
package com.ebookfrenzy.javalayout;

import androidx.appcompat.app.AppCompatActivity;

import android.os.Bundle;
import androidx.constraintlayout.widget.ConstraintLayout;
import android.widget.Button;
import android.widget.EditText;
```

```
public class MainActivity extends AppCompatActivity {

    @Override
    protected void onCreate(Bundle savedInstanceState) {
        super.onCreate(savedInstanceState);
        configureLayout();
    }

    private void configureLayout() {
        Button myButton = new Button(this);
        ConstraintLayout myLayout = new ConstraintLayout(this);
        myLayout.addView(myButton);
        setContentView(myLayout);
    }
}
```

When new instances of user interface objects are created in this way, the constructor methods must be passed the context within which the object is being created which, in this case, is the current activity. Since the above code resides within the activity class, the context is simply referenced by the standard *this* keyword:

```
Button myButton = new Button(this);
```

Once the above additions have been made, compile and run the application (either on a physical device or an emulator). Once launched, the visible result will be a button containing no text appearing in the top left-hand corner of the ConstraintLayout view as shown in Figure 23-1:

Figure 23-1

23.3 Setting View Attributes

For the purposes of this exercise, we need the background of the ConstraintLayout view to be blue and the Button view to display text that reads "Press Me" on a yellow background. Both of these tasks can be achieved by setting attributes on the views in the Java code as outlined in the following code fragment. In order to allow the text on the button to be easily translated to other languages it will be added as a String resource. Within the Project tool window, locate the *app -> res -> values -> strings.xml* file and modify it to add a resource value for the "Press Me" string:

```
<resources>
    <string name="app_name">JavaLayout</string>
    <string name="press_me">Press Me</string>
</resources>
```

Although this is the recommended way to handle strings that are directly referenced in code, to avoid repetition of this step throughout the remainder of the book, many subsequent code samples will directly enter strings into the code.

Once the string is stored as a resource it can be accessed from within code as follows:

```
getString(R.string.press_me);
```

With the string resource created, add code to the *configureLayout()* method to set the button text and color attributes:

```
.

.

import android.graphics.Color;

public class MainActivity extends AppCompatActivity {

    private void configureLayout() {
        Button myButton = new Button(this);
        myButton.setText(getString(R.string.press_me));
        myButton.setBackgroundColor(Color.YELLOW);

        ConstraintLayout myLayout = new ConstraintLayout(this);
        myLayout.setBackgroundColor(Color.BLUE);

        myLayout.addView(myButton);
        setContentView(myLayout);
}
```

When the application is now compiled and run, the layout will reflect the property settings such that the layout will appear with a blue background and the button will display the assigned text on a yellow background.

23.4 Creating View IDs

When the layout is complete it will consist of a Button and an EditText view. Before these views can be referenced within the methods of the ConstraintSet class, they must be assigned unique view IDs. The first step in this process is to create a new resource file containing these ID values.

Right click on the *app -> res -> values* folder, select the *New -> Values resource file* menu option and name the new resource file *id.xml*. With the resource file created, edit it so that it reads as follows:

```
<?xml version="1.0" encoding="utf-8"?>
<resources>
    <item name="myButton" type="id" />
    <item name="myEditText" type="id" />
</resources>
```

At this point in the tutorial, only the Button has been created, so edit the *createLayout()* method to assign the corresponding ID to the object:

```
private void configureLayout() {
    Button myButton = new Button(this);
    myButton.setText(getString(R.string.press_me));
    myButton.setBackgroundColor(Color.YELLOW);
    myButton.setId(R.id.myButton);
```

·

·

23.5 Configuring the Constraint Set

In the absence of any constraints, the ConstraintLayout view has placed the Button view in the top left corner of the display. In order to instruct the layout view to place the button in a different location, in this case centered both horizontally and vertically, it will be necessary to create a ConstraintSet instance, initialize it with the appropriate settings and apply it to the parent layout.

For this example, the button needs to be configured so that the width and height are constrained to the size of the text it is displaying and the view centered within the parent layout. Edit the *onCreate()* method once more to make these changes:

·

·

```
import androidx.constraintlayout.widget.ConstraintSet;
```

·

·

```
private void configureLayout() {
    Button myButton = new Button(this);
    myButton.setText(getString(R.string.press_me));
    myButton.setBackgroundColor(Color.YELLOW);
    myButton.setId(R.id.myButton);

    ConstraintLayout myLayout = new ConstraintLayout(this);
    myLayout.setBackgroundColor(Color.BLUE);

    myLayout.addView(myButton);
    setContentView(myLayout);

    ConstraintSet set = new ConstraintSet();

    set.constrainHeight(myButton.getId(),
            ConstraintSet.WRAP_CONTENT);
    set.constrainWidth(myButton.getId(),
            ConstraintSet.WRAP_CONTENT);

    set.connect(myButton.getId(), ConstraintSet.START,
            ConstraintSet.PARENT_ID, ConstraintSet.START, 0);
    set.connect(myButton.getId(), ConstraintSet.END,
            ConstraintSet.PARENT_ID, ConstraintSet.END, 0);
    set.connect(myButton.getId(), ConstraintSet.TOP,
            ConstraintSet.PARENT_ID, ConstraintSet.TOP, 0);
    set.connect(myButton.getId(), ConstraintSet.BOTTOM,
            ConstraintSet.PARENT_ID, ConstraintSet.BOTTOM, 0);

    set.applyTo(myLayout);
```

}

With the initial constraints configured, compile and run the application and verify that the Button view now appears in the center of the layout:

Figure 23-2

23.6 Adding the EditText View

The next item to be added to the layout is the EditText view. The first step is to create the EditText object, assign it the ID as declared in the *id.xml* resource file and add it to the layout. The code changes to achieve these steps now need to be made to the *onCreate()* method as follows:

```
private void configureLayout() {
    Button myButton = new Button(this);
    myButton.setText(getString(R.string.press_me));
    myButton.setBackgroundColor(Color.YELLOW);
    myButton.setId(R.id.myButton);

    EditText myEditText = new EditText(this);
    myEditText.setId(R.id.myEditText);

    ConstraintLayout myLayout = new ConstraintLayout(this);
    myLayout.setBackgroundColor(Color.BLUE);

    myLayout.addView(myButton);
    myLayout.addView(myEditText);

    setContentView(myLayout);
    .
    .
    .
}
```

The EditText widget is intended to be sized subject to the content it is displaying, centered horizontally within the layout and positioned 70dp above the existing Button view. Add code to the *configureLayout()* method so that it reads as follows:

.

.

```
set.connect(myButton.getId(), ConstraintSet.START,
            ConstraintSet.PARENT_ID, ConstraintSet.START, 0);
set.connect(myButton.getId(), ConstraintSet.END,
            ConstraintSet.PARENT_ID, ConstraintSet.END, 0);
set.connect(myButton.getId(), ConstraintSet.TOP,
            ConstraintSet.PARENT_ID, ConstraintSet.TOP, 0);
set.connect(myButton.getId(), ConstraintSet.BOTTOM,
            ConstraintSet.PARENT_ID, ConstraintSet.BOTTOM, 0);

set.constrainHeight(myEditText.getId(),
                    ConstraintSet.WRAP_CONTENT);
set.constrainWidth(myEditText.getId(),
                    ConstraintSet.WRAP_CONTENT);

set.connect(myEditText.getId(), ConstraintSet.START,
            ConstraintSet.PARENT_ID, ConstraintSet.START, 0);
set.connect(myEditText.getId(), ConstraintSet.END,
            ConstraintSet.PARENT_ID, ConstraintSet.END, 0);
set.connect(myEditText.getId(), ConstraintSet.BOTTOM,
            myButton.getId(), ConstraintSet.TOP, 70);

set.applyTo(myLayout);
```

A test run of the application should show the EditText field centered above the button with a margin of 70dp.

23.7 Converting Density Independent Pixels (dp) to Pixels (px)

The next task in this exercise is to set the width of the EditText view to 200dp. As outlined in the chapter entitled *"An Android Studio Layout Editor ConstraintLayout Tutorial"* when setting sizes and positions in user interface layouts it is better to use density independent pixels (dp) rather than pixels (px). In order to set a position using dp it is necessary to convert a dp value to a px value at runtime, taking into consideration the density of the device display. In order, therefore, to set the width of the EditText view to 200dp, the following code needs to be added to the class:

```
package com.ebookfrenzy.javalayout;

.

.

import android.content.res.Resources;
import android.util.TypedValue;

public class MainActivity extends AppCompatActivity {

    private int convertToPx(int value) {
        Resources r = getResources();
        int px = (int) TypedValue.applyDimension(
                TypedValue.COMPLEX_UNIT_DIP, value,
```

```
            r.getDisplayMetrics());
        return px;

    }


    private void configureLayout() {
        Button myButton = new Button(this);
        myButton.setText(getString(R.string.press_me));
        myButton.setBackgroundColor(Color.YELLOW);
        myButton.setId(R.id.myButton);

        EditText myEditText = new EditText(this);
        myEditText.setId(R.id.myEditText);

        int px = convertToPx(200);
        myEditText.setWidth(px);
.
.
.
}
```

Compile and run the application one more time and note that the width of the EditText view has changed as illustrated in Figure 23-3:

Figure 23-3

23.8 Summary

The example activity created in this chapter has, of course, created a similar user interface (the change in background color and view type notwithstanding) as that created in the earlier *"Manual XML Layout Design in Android Studio"* chapter. If nothing else, this chapter should have provided an appreciation of the level to which the Android Studio Layout Editor tool and XML resources shield the developer from many of the complexities of creating Android user interface layouts.

There are, however, instances where it makes sense to create a user interface in Java. This approach is most useful, for example, when creating dynamic user interface layouts.

24. A Guide to using Apply Changes in Android Studio

Now that some of the basic concepts of Android development using Android Studio have been covered, now is a good time to introduce the Android Studio Apply Changes feature. As all experienced developers know, every second spent waiting for an app to compile and run is time better spent writing and refining code.

24.1 Introducing Apply Changes

In early versions of Android Studio, each time a change to a project needed to be tested Android Studio would recompile the code, convert it to Dex format, generate the APK package file and install it on the device or emulator. Having performed these steps the app would finally be launched ready for testing. Even on a fast development system this is a process that takes a considerable amount of time to complete. It is not uncommon for it to take a minute or more for this process to complete for a large application.

Apply Changes, in contrast, allows many code and resource changes within a project to be reflected nearly instantaneously within the app while it is already running on a device or emulator session.

Consider, for the purposes of an example, an app being developed in Android Studio which has already been launched on a device or emulator. If changes are made to resource settings or the code within a method, Apply Changes will push the updated code and resources to the running app and dynamically "swap" the changes. The changes are then reflected in the running app without the need to build, deploy and relaunch the entire app. In many cases, this allows changes to be tested in a fraction of the time it would take without Apply Changes.

24.2 Understanding Apply Changes Options

Android Studio provides three options in terms of applying changes to a running app in the form of *Run App*, *Apply Changes and Restart Activity* and *Apply Code Changes*. These options can be summarized as follows:

- **Run App** - Stops the currently running app and restarts it. If no changes have been made to the project since it was last launched, this option will simply restart the app. If, on the other hand, changes have been made to the project, Android Studio will rebuild and reinstall the app onto the device or emulator before launching it.

- **Apply Code Changes** - This option can be used when the only changes made to a project involve modifications to the body of existing methods. When selected, the changes will be applied to the running app without the need to restart either the app or the currently running activity. This mode cannot, however, be used when changes have been made to any project resources such as a layout file. Other restrictions include the addition or removal of methods, changes to a method signature, renaming of classes and other structural code changes. It is also not possible to use this option when changes have been made to the project manifest.

- **Apply Changes and Restart Activity** - When selected, this mode will dynamically apply any code or resource changes made within the project and restart the activity without reinstalling or restarting the app. Unlike the Apply Code changes option, this can be used when changes have been made to the code and resources of the project, though the same restrictions involving structural code changes and manifest modifications apply.

24.3 Using Apply Changes

When a project has been loaded into Android Studio, but is not yet running on a device or emulator, it can be launched as usual using either the run (marked A in Figure 24-1) or debug (B) button located in the toolbar:

Figure 24-1

After the app has launched and is running, the icon on the run button will change to indicate that the app is running and the *Apply Changes and Restart Activity* and *Apply Code Changes* buttons will be enabled as indicated in Figure 24-2 below:

Figure 24-2

If the changes are unable to be applied when one of the Apply Changes buttons is selected, Android Studio will display a message indicating the failure together with an explanation. Figure 24-3, for example, shows the message displayed by Android Studio when the *Apply Code Changes* option is selected after a change has been made to a resource file:

Figure 24-3

In this situation, the solution is to use the *Apply Changes and Restart Activity* option (for which a link is provided). Similarly, the following message will appear when an attempt to apply changes that involve the addition or removal of a method is made:

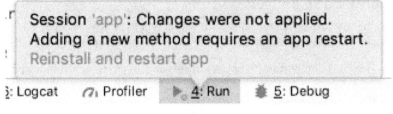

Figure 24-4

In this case, the only option is to click on the *Run App* button to reinstall and restart the app. As an alternative to manually selecting the correct option in these situations, Android Studio may be configured to automatically fall back to performing a Run App operation.

24.4 Configuring Apply Changes Fallback Settings

The Apply Changes fallback settings are located in the Android Studio Preferences window which is displayed by selecting the *File -> Settings* menu option (*Android Studio -> Preferences* on macOS). Within the Preferences dialog, select the *Build, Execution, Deployment* entry in the left-hand panel followed by *Deployment* as shown in Figure 24-5:

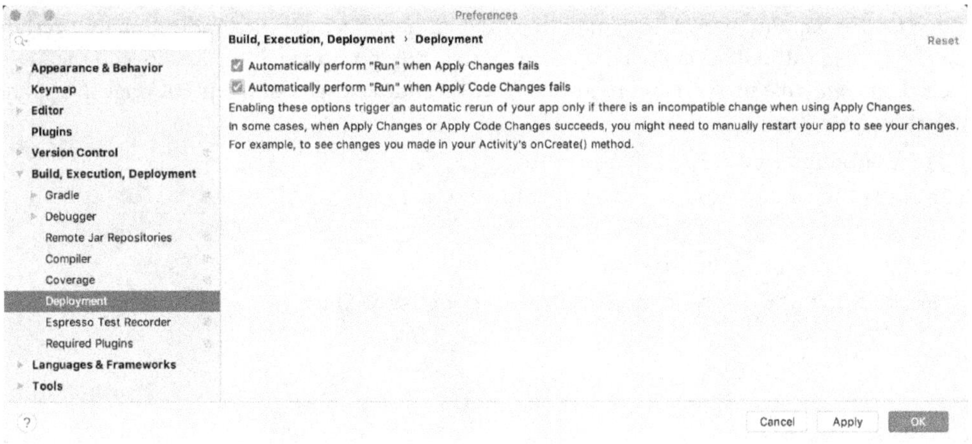

Figure 24-5

Once the required options have been enabled, click on Apply followed by the OK button to commit the changes and dismiss the dialog. After these defaults have been enabled, Android Studio will automatically reinstall and restart the app when necessary.

24.5 An Apply Changes Tutorial

Launch Android Studio, select the *Start a new Android Studio project* quick start option from the welcome screen and, within the resulting new project dialog, choose the Basic Activity template before clicking on the Next button.

Enter *ApplyChanges* into the Name field and specify *com.ebookfrenzy.applychanges* as the package name. Before clicking on the Finish button, change the Minimum API level setting to API 26: Android 8.0 (Oreo) and the Language menu to Java.

24.6 Using Apply Code Changes

Begin by clicking on the run button and selecting a suitable emulator or physical device as the run target. After clicking the run button, track the amount of time before the example app appears on the device or emulator.

Once running, click on the action button (the button displaying an envelope icon located in the lower right-hand corner of the screen). Note that a Snackbar instance appears displaying text which reads "Replace with your own action" as shown in Figure 24-6:

Figure 24-6

Once the app is running, the Apply Changes buttons should have been enabled indicating that certain project changes can be applied without having to reinstall and restart the app. To see this in action, edit the *MainActivity. java* file, locate the *onCreate* method and modify the action code so that a different message is displayed when the action button is selected:

```
FloatingActionButton fab = findViewById(R.id.fab);
fab.setOnClickListener(new View.OnClickListener() {
    @Override
    public void onClick(View view) {
        Snackbar.make(view, "Apply Changes is Amazing!",
                        Snackbar.LENGTH_LONG)
                .setAction("Action", null).show();
    }
});
```

With the code change implemented, click on the *Apply Code Changes* button and note that a message appears within a few seconds indicating the app has been updated. Tap the action button and note that the new message is now displayed in the Snackbar.

24.7 Using Apply Changes and Restart Activity

Any resource change will require use of the *Apply Changes and Restart Activity* option. Within Android Studio select the *app -> res -> layout -> content_main.xml* layout file. With the Layout Editor tool in Design mode, select the default TextView component and change the text property in the attributes tool window to "Hello Android".

Make sure that the fallback options outlined in *"Configuring Apply Changes Fallback Settings"* above are turned off before clicking on the *Apply Code Changes* button. Note that the request fails because this change involves project resources. Click on the *Apply Changes and Restart Activity* button and verify that the activity restarts and displays the new text on the TextView widget.

24.8 Using Run App

As previously described, the addition or removal of a method requires the complete re-installation and restart of the running app. To experience this, edit the *MainActivity.java* file and add a new method after the *onCreate* method as follows:

```
public void demoMethod() {

}
```

Clicking on either of the two Apply Changes buttons will result in the request failing. The only way to run the app after such a change is to click on the Run App button.

24.9 Summary

Apply Changes is a feature of Android Studio designed to significantly accelerate the code, build and run cycle performed when developing an app. The Apply Changes feature is able to push updates to the running application, in many cases without the need to re-install or even restart the app. Apply Changes provides a number of different levels of support depending on the nature of the modification being applied to the project.

25. An Overview and Example of Android Event Handling

Much has been covered in the previous chapters relating to the design of user interfaces for Android applications. An area that has yet to be covered, however, involves the way in which a user's interaction with the user interface triggers the underlying activity to perform a task. In other words, we know from the previous chapters how to create a user interface containing a button view, but not how to make something happen within the application when it is touched by the user.

The primary objective of this chapter, therefore, is to provide an overview of event handling in Android applications together with an Android Studio based example project.

25.1 Understanding Android Events

Events in Android can take a variety of different forms, but are usually generated in response to an external action. The most common form of events, particularly for devices such as tablets and smartphones, involve some form of interaction with the touch screen. Such events fall into the category of *input events*.

The Android framework maintains an *event queue* into which events are placed as they occur. Events are then removed from the queue on a first-in, first-out (FIFO) basis. In the case of an input event such as a touch on the screen, the event is passed to the view positioned at the location on the screen where the touch took place. In addition to the event notification, the view is also passed a range of information (depending on the event type) about the nature of the event such as the coordinates of the point of contact between the user's fingertip and the screen.

In order to be able to handle the event that it has been passed, the view must have in place an *event listener*. The Android View class, from which all user interface components are derived, contains a range of event listener interfaces, each of which contains an abstract declaration for a callback method. In order to be able to respond to an event of a particular type, a view must register the appropriate event listener and implement the corresponding callback. For example, if a button is to respond to a *click* event (the equivalent to the user touching and releasing the button view as though clicking on a physical button) it must both register the *View.onClickListener* event listener (via a call to the target view's *setOnClickListener()* method) and implement the corresponding *onClick()* callback method. In the event that a "click" event is detected on the screen at the location of the button view, the Android framework will call the *onClick()* method of that view when that event is removed from the event queue. It is, of course, within the implementation of the *onClick()* callback method that any tasks should be performed or other methods called in response to the button click.

25.2 Using the android:onClick Resource

Before exploring event listeners in more detail it is worth noting that a shortcut is available when all that is required is for a callback method to be called when a user "clicks" on a button view in the user interface. Consider a user interface layout containing a button view named *button1* with the requirement that when the user touches the button, a method called *buttonClick()* declared in the activity class is called. All that is required to implement this behavior is to write the *buttonClick()* method (which takes as an argument a reference to the view that triggered the click event) and add a single line to the declaration of the button view in the XML file. For example:

```
<Button
```

```
android:id="@+id/button1"
android:layout_width="wrap_content"
android:layout_height="wrap_content"
android:onClick="buttonClick"
android:text="Click me" />
```

This provides a simple way to capture click events. It does not, however, provide the range of options offered by event handlers, which are the topic of the rest of this chapter. As will be outlined in later chapters, the onClick property also has limitations in layouts involving fragments. When working within Android Studio Layout Editor, the onClick property can be found and configured in the Attributes panel when a suitable view type is selected in the device screen layout.

25.3 Event Listeners and Callback Methods

In the example activity outlined later in this chapter the steps involved in registering an event listener and implementing the callback method will be covered in detail. Before doing so, however, it is worth taking some time to outline the event listeners that are available in the Android framework and the callback methods associated with each one.

- **onClickListener** – Used to detect click style events whereby the user touches and then releases an area of the device display occupied by a view. Corresponds to the *onClick()* callback method which is passed a reference to the view that received the event as an argument.

- **onLongClickListener** – Used to detect when the user maintains the touch over a view for an extended period. Corresponds to the *onLongClick()* callback method which is passed as an argument the view that received the event.

- **onTouchListener** – Used to detect any form of contact with the touch screen including individual or multiple touches and gesture motions. Corresponding with the *onTouch()* callback, this topic will be covered in greater detail in the chapter entitled *"Android Touch and Multi-touch Event Handling"*. The callback method is passed as arguments the view that received the event and a MotionEvent object.

- **onCreateContextMenuListener** – Listens for the creation of a context menu as the result of a long click. Corresponds to the *onCreateContextMenu()* callback method. The callback is passed the menu, the view that received the event and a menu context object.

- **onFocusChangeListener** – Detects when focus moves away from the current view as the result of interaction with a track-ball or navigation key. Corresponds to the *onFocusChange()* callback method which is passed the view that received the event and a Boolean value to indicate whether focus was gained or lost.

- **onKeyListener** – Used to detect when a key on a device is pressed while a view has focus. Corresponds to the *onKey()* callback method. Passed as arguments are the view that received the event, the KeyCode of the physical key that was pressed and a KeyEvent object.

25.4 An Event Handling Example

In the remainder of this chapter, we will work through the creation of a simple Android Studio project designed to demonstrate the implementation of an event listener and corresponding callback method to detect when the user has clicked on a button. The code within the callback method will update a text view to indicate that the event has been processed.

Select the *Start a new Android Studio project* quick start option from the welcome screen and, within the resulting new project dialog, choose the Empty Activity template before clicking on the Next button.

Enter *EventExample* into the Name field and specify *com.ebookfrenzy.eventexample* as the package name. Before clicking on the Finish button, change the Minimum API level setting to API 26: Android 8.0 (Oreo) and the Language menu to Java.

25.5 Designing the User Interface

The user interface layout for the *MainActivity* class in this example is to consist of a ConstraintLayout, a Button and a TextView as illustrated in Figure 25-1.

Hello World!

PRESS ME

Figure 25-1

Locate and select the *activity_main.xml* file created by Android Studio (located in the Project tool window under *app -> res -> layouts*) and double-click on it to load it into the Layout Editor tool.

Make sure that Autoconnect is enabled, then drag a Button widget from the palette and move it so that it is positioned in the horizontal center of the layout and beneath the existing TextView widget. When correctly positioned, drop the widget into place so that appropriate constraints are added by the autoconnect system. Add any missing constraints by clicking on the *Infer Constraints* button in the layout editor toolbar.

With the Button widget selected, use the Attributes panel to set the text property to Press Me. Using the yellow warning button located in the top right-hand corner of the Layout Editor (Figure 25-2), display the warnings list and click on the *Fix* button to extract the text string on the button to a resource named *press_me*:

Figure 25-2

Select the "Hello World!" TextView widget and use the Attributes panel to set the ID to *statusText*. Repeat this step to change the ID of the Button widget to *myButton*.

With the user interface layout now completed, the next step is to register the event listener and callback method.

25.6 The Event Listener and Callback Method

For the purposes of this example, an *onClickListener* needs to be registered for the *myButton* view. This is achieved by making a call to the *setOnClickListener()* method of the button view, passing through a new *onClickListener* object as an argument and implementing the *onClick()* callback method. Since this is a task that only needs to be performed when the activity is created, a good location is the *onCreate()* method of the MainActivity class.

If the *MainActivity.java* file is already open within an editor session, select it by clicking on the tab in the editor panel. Alternatively locate it within the Project tool window by navigating to (*app -> java -> com.ebookfrenzy. eventexample -> MainActivity*) and double-click on it to load it into the code editor. Once loaded, locate the template *onCreate()* method and modify it to obtain a reference to the button view, register the event listener and implement the *onClick()* callback method:

```
package com.ebookfrenzy.eventexample;

import androidx.appcompat.app.AppCompatActivity;

import android.os.Bundle;
import android.view.View;
import android.widget.Button;
import android.widget.TextView;

public class MainActivity extends AppCompatActivity {

    @Override
    protected void onCreate(Bundle savedInstanceState) {
        super.onCreate(savedInstanceState);
        setContentView(R.layout.activity_event_example);
        Button button = findViewById(R.id.myButton);

        button.setOnClickListener(
                new Button.OnClickListener() {
                    public void onClick(View v) {


                    }
                }
        );
    }
    .
    .
    .
}
```

The above code has now registered the event listener on the button and implemented the *onClick()* method. If the application were to be run at this point, however, there would be no indication that the event listener installed on the button was working since there is, as yet, no code implemented within the body of the *onClick()*

callback method. The goal for the example is to have a message appear on the TextView when the button is clicked, so some further code changes need to be made:

```
@Override
protected void onCreate(Bundle savedInstanceState) {
        super.onCreate(savedInstanceState);
        setContentView(R.layout.activity_event_example);

        Button button = findViewById(R.id.myButton);

    button.setOnClickListener(
            new Button.OnClickListener() {
                public void onClick(View v) {
                    TextView statusText =
                            findViewById(R.id.statusText);
                    statusText.setText("Button clicked");
                }
            }
        );
}
```

Complete this phase of the tutorial by compiling and running the application on either an AVD emulator or physical Android device. On touching and releasing the button view (otherwise known as "clicking") the text view should change to display the "Button clicked" text.

25.7 Consuming Events

The detection of standard clicks (as opposed to long clicks) on views is a very simple case of event handling. The example will now be extended to include the detection of long click events which occur when the user clicks and holds a view on the screen and, in doing so, cover the topic of event consumption.

Consider the code for the *onClick()* method in the above section of this chapter. The callback is declared as *void* and, as such, does not return a value to the Android framework after it has finished executing.

The code assigned to the *onLongClickListener*, on the other hand, is required to return a Boolean value to the Android framework. The purpose of this return value is to indicate to the Android runtime whether or not the callback has *consumed* the event. If the callback returns a *true* value, the event is discarded by the framework. If, on the other hand, the callback returns a *false* value the Android framework will consider the event still to be active and will consequently pass it along to the next matching event listener that is registered on the same view.

As with many programming concepts this is, perhaps, best demonstrated with an example. The first step is to add an event listener and callback method for long clicks to the button view in the example activity:

```
@Override
protected void onCreate(Bundle savedInstanceState) {
        super.onCreate(savedInstanceState);
        setContentView(R.layout.activity_event_example);

        Button button = findViewById(R.id.myButton);

    button.setOnClickListener(
```

```
                    new Button.OnClickListener() {
                        public void onClick(View v) {
                            TextView statusText =
                                findViewById(R.id.statusText);
                            statusText.setText("Button clicked");
                        }
                    }
                );


        button.setOnLongClickListener(
                new Button.OnLongClickListener() {
                    public boolean onLongClick(View v) {
                        TextView statusText =
                                findViewById(R.id.statusText);
                        statusText.setText("Long button click");
                        return true;

                    }
                }
            );
        }
    }
```

Clearly, when a long click is detected, the *onLongClick()* callback method will display "Long button click" on the text view. Note, however, that the callback method also returns a value of *true* to indicate that it has consumed the event. Run the application and press and hold the Button view until the "Long button click" text appears in the text view. On releasing the button, the text view continues to display the "Long button click" text indicating that the onClick listener code was not called.

Next, modify the code so that the onLongClick listener now returns a *false* value:

```
button.setOnLongClickListener(
    new Button.OnLongClickListener() {
        public boolean onLongClick(View v) {
                TextView myTextView = findViewById(R.id.myTextView);
                myTextView.setText("Long button click");
                return false;
        }
    }
);
```

Once again, compile and run the application and perform a long click on the button until the long click message appears. Upon releasing the button this time, however, note that the *onClick* listener is also triggered and the text changes to "Button click". This is because the *false* value returned by the *onLongClick* listener code indicated to the Android framework that the event was not consumed by the method and was eligible to be passed on to the next registered listener on the view. In this case, the runtime ascertained that the onClickListener on the button was also interested in events of this type and subsequently called the *onClick* listener code.

25.8 Summary

A user interface is of little practical use if the views it contains do not do anything in response to user interaction. Android bridges the gap between the user interface and the back end code of the application through the concepts of event listeners and callback methods. The Android View class defines a set of event listeners, which can be registered on view objects. Each event listener also has associated with it a callback method.

When an event takes place on a view in a user interface, that event is placed into an event queue and handled on a first in, first out basis by the Android runtime. If the view on which the event took place has registered a listener that matches the type of event, the corresponding callback method is called. This code then performs any tasks required by the activity before returning. Some callback methods are required to return a Boolean value to indicate whether the event needs to be passed on to any other event listeners registered on the view or discarded by the system.

Having covered the basics of event handling, the next chapter will explore in some depth the topic of touch events with a particular emphasis on handling multiple touches.

26. Android Touch and Multi-touch Event Handling

Most Android based devices use a touch screen as the primary interface between user and device. The previous chapter introduced the mechanism by which a touch on the screen translates into an action within a running Android application. There is, however, much more to touch event handling than responding to a single finger tap on a view object. Most Android devices can, for example, detect more than one touch at a time. Nor are touches limited to a single point on the device display. Touches can, of course, be dynamic as the user slides one or more points of contact across the surface of the screen.

Touches can also be interpreted by an application as a *gesture*. Consider, for example, that a horizontal swipe is typically used to turn the page of an eBook, or how a pinching motion can be used to zoom in and out of an image displayed on the screen.

This chapter will explain the handling of touches that involve motion and explore the concept of intercepting multiple concurrent touches. The topic of identifying distinct gestures will be covered in the next chapter.

26.1 Intercepting Touch Events

Touch events can be intercepted by a view object through the registration of an *onTouchListener* event listener and the implementation of the corresponding *onTouch()* callback method. The following code, for example, ensures that any touches on a ConstraintLayout view instance named *myLayout* result in a call to the *onTouch()* method:

```
myLayout.setOnTouchListener(
        new ConstraintLayout.OnTouchListener() {
                public boolean onTouch(View v, MotionEvent m) {
                        // Perform tasks here
                        return true;
                }
        }
);
```

As indicated in the code example, the *onTouch()* callback is required to return a Boolean value indicating to the Android runtime system whether or not the event should be passed on to other event listeners registered on the same view or discarded. The method is passed both a reference to the view on which the event was triggered and an object of type *MotionEvent*.

26.2 The MotionEvent Object

The MotionEvent object passed through to the *onTouch()* callback method is the key to obtaining information about the event. Information contained within the object includes the location of the touch within the view and the type of action performed. The MotionEvent object is also the key to handling multiple touches.

26.3 Understanding Touch Actions

An important aspect of touch event handling involves being able to identify the type of action performed by the user. The type of action associated with an event can be obtained by making a call to the *getActionMasked()* method of the MotionEvent object which was passed through to the *onTouch()* callback method. When the first touch on a view occurs, the MotionEvent object will contain an action type of ACTION_DOWN together with the coordinates of the touch. When that touch is lifted from the screen, an ACTION_UP event is generated. Any motion of the touch between the ACTION_DOWN and ACTION_UP events will be represented by ACTION_MOVE events.

When more than one touch is performed simultaneously on a view, the touches are referred to as *pointers*. In a multi-touch scenario, pointers begin and end with event actions of type ACTION_POINTER_DOWN and ACTION_POINTER_UP respectively. In order to identify the index of the pointer that triggered the event, the *getActionIndex()* callback method of the MotionEvent object must be called.

26.4 Handling Multiple Touches

The chapter entitled *"An Overview and Example of Android Event Handling"* began exploring event handling within the narrow context of a single touch event. In practice, most Android devices possess the ability to respond to multiple consecutive touches (though it is important to note that the number of simultaneous touches that can be detected varies depending on the device).

As previously discussed, each touch in a multi-touch situation is considered by the Android framework to be a *pointer*. Each pointer, in turn, is referenced by an *index* value and assigned an *ID*. The current number of pointers can be obtained via a call to the *getPointerCount()* method of the current MotionEvent object. The ID for a pointer at a particular index in the list of current pointers may be obtained via a call to the MotionEvent *getPointerId()* method. For example, the following code excerpt obtains a count of pointers and the ID of the pointer at index 0:

```
public boolean onTouch(View v, MotionEvent m) {
        int pointerCount = m.getPointerCount();
        int pointerId = m.getPointerId(0);
        return true;
}
```

Note that the pointer count will always be greater than or equal to 1 when the *onTouch* listener is triggered (since at least one touch must have occurred for the callback to be triggered).

A touch on a view, particularly one involving motion across the screen, will generate a stream of events before the point of contact with the screen is lifted. As such, it is likely that an application will need to track individual touches over multiple touch events. While the ID of a specific touch gesture will not change from one event to the next, it is important to keep in mind that the index value will change as other touch events come and go. When working with a touch gesture over multiple events, therefore, it is essential that the ID value be used as the touch reference in order to make sure the same touch is being tracked. When calling methods that require an index value, this should be obtained by converting the ID for a touch to the corresponding index value via a call to the *findPointerIndex()* method of the *MotionEvent* object.

26.5 An Example Multi-Touch Application

The example application created in the remainder of this chapter will track up to two touch gestures as they move across a layout view. As the events for each touch are triggered, the coordinates, index and ID for each touch will be displayed on the screen.

Select the *Start a new Android Studio project* quick start option from the welcome screen and, within the resulting new project dialog, choose the Empty Activity template before clicking on the Next button.

Enter *MotionEvent* into the Name field and specify *com.ebookfrenzy.motionevent* as the package name. Before clicking on the Finish button, change the Minimum API level setting to API 26: Android 8.0 (Oreo) and the Language menu to Java.

26.6 Designing the Activity User Interface

The user interface for the application's sole activity is to consist of a ConstraintLayout view containing two TextView objects. Within the Project tool window, navigate to *app -> res -> layout* and double-click on the *activity_main.xml* layout resource file to load it into the Android Studio Layout Editor tool.

Select and delete the default "Hello World!" TextView widget and then, with autoconnect enabled, drag and drop a new TextView widget so that it is centered horizontally and positioned at the 16dp margin line on the top edge of the layout:

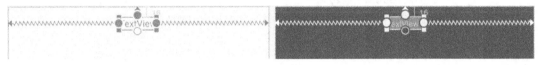

Figure 26-1

Drag a second TextView widget and position and constrain it so that it is distanced by a 32dp margin from the bottom of the first widget:

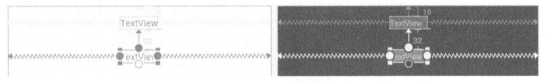

Figure 26-2

Using the Attributes tool window, change the IDs for the TextView widgets to *textView1* and *textView2* respectively. Change the text displayed on the widgets to read "Touch One Status" and "Touch Two Status" and extract the strings to resources using the warning button in the top right-hand corner of the Layout Editor.

Select the ConstraintLayout entry in the Component Tree and use the Attributes panel to change the ID to *activity_main*.

26.7 Implementing the Touch Event Listener

In order to receive touch event notifications it will be necessary to register a touch listener on the layout view within the *onCreate()* method of the *MainActivity* activity class. Select the *MainActivity.java* tab from the Android Studio editor panel to display the source code. Within the *onCreate()* method, add code to identify the ConstraintLayout view object, register the touch listener and implement code which, in this case, is going to call a second method named *handleTouch()* to which is passed the MotionEvent object:

```
package com.ebookfrenzy.motionevent;

import androidx.appcompat.app.AppCompatActivity;
import android.os.Bundle;
import android.view.MotionEvent;
import android.view.View;
import androidx.constraintlayout.widget.ConstraintLayout;
```

```
import android.widget.TextView;

public class MainActivity extends AppCompatActivity {

    @Override
    protected void onCreate(Bundle savedInstanceState) {
        super.onCreate(savedInstanceState);
        setContentView(R.layout.activity_main);

        ConstraintLayout myLayout =
                    findViewById(R.id.activity_main);

        myLayout.setOnTouchListener(
                new ConstraintLayout.OnTouchListener() {
                    public boolean onTouch(View v,
                                            MotionEvent m) {
                        handleTouch(m);
                        return true;
                    }
                }
        );
    }
    .
    .
    .
}
```

The final task before testing the application is to implement the *handleTouch()* method called by the listener. The code for this method reads as follows:

```
void handleTouch(MotionEvent m)
{
            TextView textView1 = findViewById(R.id.textView1);
            TextView textView2 = findViewById(R.id.textView2);

            int pointerCount = m.getPointerCount();

            for (int i = 0; i < pointerCount; i++)
            {
                    int x = (int) m.getX(i);
                    int y = (int) m.getY(i);
                    int id = m.getPointerId(i);
                    int action = m.getActionMasked();
                    int actionIndex = m.getActionIndex();
                    String actionString;


                    switch (action)
```

```
{
        case MotionEvent.ACTION_DOWN:
                actionString = "DOWN";
                break;
        case MotionEvent.ACTION_UP:
                actionString = "UP";
                break;
        case MotionEvent.ACTION_POINTER_DOWN:
                actionString = "PNTR DOWN";
                break;
        case MotionEvent.ACTION_POINTER_UP:
            actionString = "PNTR UP";
            break;
        case MotionEvent.ACTION_MOVE:
                actionString = "MOVE";
                break;
        default:
                actionString = "";
    }

    String touchStatus = "Action: " + actionString + " Index: " +
actionIndex + " ID: " + id + " X: " + x + " Y: " + y;

    if (id == 0)
            textView1.setText(touchStatus);
    else
            textView2.setText(touchStatus);

    }
}
```

Before compiling and running the application, it is worth taking the time to walk through this code systematically to highlight the tasks that are being performed.

The code begins by obtaining references to the two TextView objects in the user interface and identifying how many pointers are currently active on the view:

```
TextView textView1 = findViewById(R.id.textView1);
TextView textView2 = findViewById(R.id.textView2);

int pointerCount = m.getPointerCount();
```

Next, the *pointerCount* variable is used to initiate a *for* loop which performs a set of tasks for each active pointer. The first few lines of the loop obtain the X and Y coordinates of the touch together with the corresponding event ID, action type and action index. Lastly, a string variable is declared:

```
for (int i = 0; i < pointerCount; i++)
{
                int x = (int) m.getX(i);
                int y = (int) m.getY(i);
```

```
        int id = m.getPointerId(i);
        int action = m.getActionMasked();
        int actionIndex = m.getActionIndex();
        String actionString;
```

Since action types equate to integer values, a *switch* statement is used to convert the action type to a more meaningful string value, which is stored in the previously declared *actionString* variable:

```
switch (action)
    {
        case MotionEvent.ACTION_DOWN:
            actionString = "DOWN";
            break;
        case MotionEvent.ACTION_UP:
            actionString = "UP";
            break;
        case MotionEvent.ACTION_POINTER_DOWN:
            actionString = "PNTR DOWN";
            break;
        case MotionEvent.ACTION_POINTER_UP:
            actionString = "PNTR UP";
            break;
        case MotionEvent.ACTION_MOVE:
            actionString = "MOVE";
            break;
        default:
            actionString = "";
    }
```

Finally, the string message is constructed using the *actionString* value, the action index, touch ID and X and Y coordinates. The ID value is then used to decide whether the string should be displayed on the first or second TextView object:

```
String touchStatus = "Action: " + actionString + " Index: "
        + actionIndex + " ID: " + id + " X: " + x + " Y: " + y;

        if (id == 0)
                textView1.setText(touchStatus);
        else
                textView2.setText(touchStatus);
```

26.8 Running the Example Application

Compile and run the application and, once launched, experiment with single and multiple touches on the screen and note that the text views update to reflect the events as illustrated in Figure 26-3. When running on an emulator, multiple touches may be simulated by holding down the Ctrl (Cmd on macOS) key while clicking the mouse button:

Action: PNTR UP Index: 0 ID: 0 X: 633 Y: 806

Action: UP Index: 0 ID: 1 X: 438 Y: 686

Figure 26-3

26.9 Summary

Activities receive notifications of touch events by registering an onTouchListener event listener and implementing the *onTouch()* callback method which, in turn, is passed a MotionEvent object when called by the Android runtime. This object contains information about the touch such as the type of touch event, the coordinates of the touch and a count of the number of touches currently in contact with the view.

When multiple touches are involved, each point of contact is referred to as a pointer with each assigned an index and an ID. While the index of a touch can change from one event to another, the ID will remain unchanged until the touch ends.

This chapter has worked through the creation of an example Android application designed to display the coordinates and action type of up to two simultaneous touches on a device display.

Having covered touches in general, the next chapter (entitled *"Detecting Common Gestures using the Android Gesture Detector Class"*) will look further at touch screen event handling through the implementation of gesture recognition.

27. Detecting Common Gestures using the Android Gesture Detector Class

The term "gesture" is used to define a contiguous sequence of interactions between the touch screen and the user. A typical gesture begins at the point that the screen is first touched and ends when the last finger or pointing device leaves the display surface. When correctly harnessed, gestures can be implemented as a form of communication between user and application. Swiping motions to turn the pages of an eBook, or a pinching movement involving two touches to zoom in or out of an image are prime examples of the ways in which gestures can be used to interact with an application.

The Android SDK provides mechanisms for the detection of both common and custom gestures within an application. Common gestures involve interactions such as a tap, double tap, long press or a swiping motion in either a horizontal or a vertical direction (referred to in Android nomenclature as a *fling*).

The goal of this chapter is to explore the use of the Android GestureDetector class to detect common gestures performed on the display of an Android device. The next chapter, entitled *"Implementing Custom Gesture and Pinch Recognition on Android"*, will cover the detection of more complex, custom gestures such as circular motions and pinches.

27.1 Implementing Common Gesture Detection

When a user interacts with the display of an Android device, the *onTouchEvent()* method of the currently active application is called by the system and passed MotionEvent objects containing data about the user's contact with the screen. This data can be interpreted to identify if the motion on the screen matches a common gesture such as a tap or a swipe. This can be achieved with very little programming effort by making use of the Android GestureDetectorCompat class. This class is designed specifically to receive motion event information from the application and to trigger method calls based on the type of common gesture, if any, detected.

The basic steps in detecting common gestures are as follows:

1. Declaration of a class which implements the GestureDetector.OnGestureListener interface including the required *onFling()*, *onDown()*, *onScroll()*, *onShowPress()*, *onSingleTapUp()* and *onLongPress()* callback methods. Note that this can be either an entirely new class, or the enclosing activity class. In the event that double tap gesture detection is required, the class must also implement the GestureDetector. OnDoubleTapListener interface and include the corresponding *onDoubleTap()* method.

2. Creation of an instance of the Android GestureDetectorCompat class, passing through an instance of the class created in step 1 as an argument.

3. An optional call to the *setOnDoubleTapListener()* method of the GestureDetectorCompat instance to enable double tap detection if required.

4. Implementation of the *onTouchEvent()* callback method on the enclosing activity which, in turn, must call the *onTouchEvent()* method of the GestureDetectorCompat instance, passing through the current motion

event object as an argument to the method.

Once implemented, the result is a set of methods within the application code that will be called when a gesture of a particular type is detected. The code within these methods can then be implemented to perform any tasks that need to be performed in response to the corresponding gesture.

In the remainder of this chapter, we will work through the creation of an example project intended to put the above steps into practice.

27.2 Creating an Example Gesture Detection Project

The goal of this project is to detect the full range of common gestures currently supported by the GestureDetectorCompat class and to display status information to the user indicating the type of gesture that has been detected.

Select the *Start a new Android Studio project* quick start option from the welcome screen and, within the resulting new project dialog, choose the Empty Activity template before clicking on the Next button.

Enter *CommonGestures* into the Name field and specify *com.ebookfrenzy.commongestures* as the package name. Before clicking on the Finish button, change the Minimum API level setting to API 26: Android 8.0 (Oreo) and the Language menu to Java.

Once the new project has been created, navigate to the *app -> res -> layout -> activity_main.xml* file in the Project tool window and double-click on it to load it into the Layout Editor tool.

Within the Layout Editor tool, select the "Hello, World!" TextView component and, in the Attributes tool window, enter *gestureStatusText* as the ID.

27.3 Implementing the Listener Class

As previously outlined, it is necessary to create a class that implements the GestureDetector.OnGestureListener interface and, if double tap detection is required, the GestureDetector.OnDoubleTapListener interface. While this can be an entirely new class, it is also perfectly valid to implement this within the current activity class. For the purposes of this example, therefore, we will modify the MainActivity class to implement these listener interfaces. Edit the *MainActivity.java* file so that it reads as follows to declare the interfaces and to extract and store a reference to the TextView component in the user interface:

```
package com.ebookfrenzy.commongestures;

import androidx.appcompat.app.AppCompatActivity;
import android.os.Bundle;
import android.view.GestureDetector;
import android.widget.TextView;

public class MainActivity extends AppCompatActivity
        implements GestureDetector.OnGestureListener,
        GestureDetector.OnDoubleTapListener
{
    private TextView gestureText;

    @Override
    protected void onCreate(Bundle savedInstanceState) {
        super.onCreate(savedInstanceState);
```

```
        setContentView(R.layout.activity_common_gestures);

        gestureText = findViewById(R.id.gestureStatusText);

    }
.
.
.
}
```

Declaring that the class implements the listener interfaces mandates that the corresponding methods also be implemented in the class:

```
package com.ebookfrenzy.commongestures;

import androidx.appcompat.app.AppCompatActivity;
import android.os.Bundle;
import android.view.GestureDetector;
import android.widget.TextView;
import android.view.MotionEvent;


public class MainActivity extends AppCompatActivity
        implements GestureDetector.OnGestureListener,
        GestureDetector.OnDoubleTapListener {

    private TextView gestureText;

    @Override
    protected void onCreate(Bundle savedInstanceState) {
        super.onCreate(savedInstanceState);
        setContentView(R.layout.activity_common_gestures);
        gestureText = findViewById(R.id.gestureStatusText);
    }

    @Override
    public boolean onDown(MotionEvent event) {
        gestureText.setText ("onDown");
        return true;
    }

    @Override
    public boolean onFling(MotionEvent event1, MotionEvent event2,
                           float velocityX, float velocityY) {
        gestureText.setText("onFling");
        return true;
    }
```

```
@Override
public void onLongPress(MotionEvent event) {
    gestureText.setText("onLongPress");
}

@Override
public boolean onScroll(MotionEvent e1, MotionEvent e2,
                        float distanceX, float distanceY) {
    gestureText.setText("onScroll");
    return true;
}

@Override
public void onShowPress(MotionEvent event) {
    gestureText.setText("onShowPress");
}

@Override
public boolean onSingleTapUp(MotionEvent event) {
    gestureText.setText("onSingleTapUp");
    return true;
}

@Override
public boolean onDoubleTap(MotionEvent event) {
    gestureText.setText("onDoubleTap");
    return true;
}

@Override
public boolean onDoubleTapEvent(MotionEvent event) {
    gestureText.setText("onDoubleTapEvent");
    return true;
}

@Override
public boolean onSingleTapConfirmed(MotionEvent event) {
    gestureText.setText("onSingleTapConfirmed");
    return true;
}
    .
    .
    .
}
```

Note that many of these methods return *true*. This indicates to the Android Framework that the event has been consumed by the method and does not need to be passed to the next event handler in the stack.

27.4 Creating the GestureDetectorCompat Instance

With the activity class now updated to implement the listener interfaces, the next step is to create an instance of the GestureDetectorCompat class. Since this only needs to be performed once at the point that the activity is created, the best place for this code is in the *onCreate()* method. Since we also want to detect double taps, the code also needs to call the *setOnDoubleTapListener()* method of the GestureDetectorCompat instance:

```
package com.ebookfrenzy.commongestures;

import androidx.appcompat.app.AppCompatActivity;
import android.os.Bundle;
import android.view.GestureDetector;
import android.widget.TextView;
import android.view.MotionEvent;
import androidx.core.view.GestureDetectorCompat;

public class MainActivity extends AppCompatActivity
        implements GestureDetector.OnGestureListener,
        GestureDetector.OnDoubleTapListener {

    private TextView gestureText;
    private GestureDetectorCompat gDetector;

    @Override
    protected void onCreate(Bundle savedInstanceState) {
        super.onCreate(savedInstanceState);
        setContentView(R.layout.activity_common_gestures);
        gestureText = findViewById(R.id.gestureStatusText);

        this.gDetector = new GestureDetectorCompat(this,this);
        gDetector.setOnDoubleTapListener(this);
    }
.
.
.
}
```

27.5 Implementing the onTouchEvent() Method

If the application were to be compiled and run at this point, nothing would happen if gestures were performed on the device display. This is because no code has been added to intercept touch events and to pass them through to the GestureDetectorCompat instance. In order to achieve this, it is necessary to override the *onTouchEvent()* method within the activity class and implement it such that it calls the *onTouchEvent()* method of the GestureDetectorCompat instance. Remaining in the *MainActivity.java* file, therefore, implement this method so that it reads as follows:

```
@Override
public boolean onTouchEvent(MotionEvent event) {
        this.gDetector.onTouchEvent(event);
```

```
        // Be sure to call the superclass implementation
        return super.onTouchEvent(event);
}
```

27.6 Testing the Application

Compile and run the application on either a physical Android device or an AVD emulator. Once launched, experiment with swipes, presses, scrolling motions and double and single taps. Note that the text view updates to reflect the events as illustrated in Figure 27-1:

Figure 27-1

27.7 Summary

Any physical contact between the user and the touch screen display of a device can be considered a "gesture". Lacking the physical keyboard and mouse pointer of a traditional computer system, gestures are widely used as a method of interaction between user and application. While a gesture can be comprised of just about any sequence of motions, there is a widely used set of gestures with which users of touch screen devices have become familiar. A number of these so-called "common gestures" can be easily detected within an application by making use of the Android Gesture Detector classes. In this chapter, the use of this technique has been outlined both in theory and through the implementation of an example project.

Having covered common gestures in this chapter, the next chapter will look at detecting a wider range of gesture types including the ability to both design and detect your own gestures.

28. Implementing Custom Gesture and Pinch Recognition on Android

The previous chapter covered the detection of what are referred to as "common gestures" from within an Android application. In practice, however, a gesture can conceivably involve just about any sequence of touch motions on the display of an Android device. In recognition of this fact, the Android SDK allows custom gestures of just about any nature to be defined by the application developer and used to trigger events when performed by the user. This is a multistage process, the details of which are the topic of this chapter.

28.1 The Android Gesture Builder Application

The Android SDK allows developers to design custom gestures which are then stored in a gesture file bundled with an Android application package. These custom gesture files are most easily created using the *Gesture Builder* application which is bundled with the samples package supplied as part of the Android SDK. The creation of a gestures file involves launching the Gesture Builder application, either on a physical device or emulator, and "drawing" the gestures that will need to be detected by the application. Once the gestures have been designed, the file containing the gesture data can be pulled off the SD card of the device or emulator and added to the application project. Within the application code, the file is then loaded into an instance of the *GestureLibrary* class where it can be used to search for matches to any gestures performed by the user on the device display.

28.2 The GestureOverlayView Class

In order to facilitate the detection of gestures within an application, the Android SDK provides the GestureOverlayView class. This is a transparent view that can be placed over other views in the user interface for the sole purpose of detecting gestures.

28.3 Detecting Gestures

Gestures are detected by loading the gestures file created using the Gesture Builder app and then registering a *GesturePerformedListener* event listener on an instance of the GestureOverlayView class. The enclosing class is then declared to implement both the *OnGesturePerformedListener* interface and the corresponding *onGesturePerformed* callback method required by that interface. In the event that a gesture is detected by the listener, a call to the *onGesturePerformed* callback method is triggered by the Android runtime system.

28.4 Identifying Specific Gestures

When a gesture is detected, the *onGesturePerformed* callback method is called and passed as arguments a reference to the GestureOverlayView object on which the gesture was detected, together with a Gesture object containing information about the gesture.

With access to the Gesture object, the GestureLibrary can then be used to compare the detected gesture to those contained in the gestures file previously loaded into the application. The GestureLibrary reports the probability that the gesture performed by the user matches an entry in the gestures file by calculating a *prediction score* for each gesture. A prediction score of 1.0 or greater is generally accepted to be a good match between a gesture stored in the file and that performed by the user on the device display.

28.5 Installing and Running the Gesture Builder Application

The easiest way to create a gestures file is to use an app that will allow gesture motions to be captured and saved. Although Google originally provided an app for this purpose, it has not been maintained adequately for use on more recent versions of Android. Fortunately, an alternative is available in the form of the Gesture Builder app developed by Manan Gandhi which is available from the Google Play Store at the following URL:

https://play.google.com/store/apps/details?id=pack.GestureApp

Note that the app works best on devices or emulators running Android 9.0 (API 28) or older.

28.6 Creating a Gestures File

Once the Gesture Builder application has loaded, click on the *Add* button located at the bottom of the device screen and, on the subsequent screen, "draw" a gesture using a circular motion on the screen as illustrated in Figure 28-1. Assuming that the gesture appears as required (represented by the yellow line on the device screen), click on the save button to add the gesture to the gestures file, entering "Circle Gesture" when prompted for a name:

Figure 28-1

After the gesture has been saved, return to the main screen where the Gesture Builder app will display a list of currently defined gestures which, at this point, will consist solely of the new *Circle Gesture*. Before proceeding, use the *Test* button to verify that the gesture works as intended.

28.7 Creating the Example Project

Select the *Start a new Android Studio project* quick start option from the welcome screen and, within the resulting new project dialog, choose the Empty Activity template before clicking on the Next button.

Enter *CustomGestures* into the Name field and specify *com.ebookfrenzy.customgestures* as the package name. Before clicking on the Finish button, change the Minimum API level setting to API 26: Android 8.0 (Oreo) and the Language menu to Java.

28.8 Extracting the Gestures File from the SD Card

As each gesture was created within the Gesture Builder application, it was added to a file named *gesture.txt* located in the storage of the emulator or device on which the app was running. Before this file can be added to an Android Studio project, however, it must first be copied off the device storage and saved to the local file system. This is most easily achieved by using the Android Studio Device File Explorer tool window. Display this tool using the *View -> Tool Windows -> Device File Explorer* menu option. Once displayed, select the device or emulator on which the gesture file was created from the dropdown menu, then navigate through the filesystem to the following folder:

```
sdcard/Android/data/pack.GestureApp/files
```

Locate the *gesture.txt* file in this folder, right-click on it, select the *Save as...* menu option and save the file to a temporary location as a file named *gestures*.

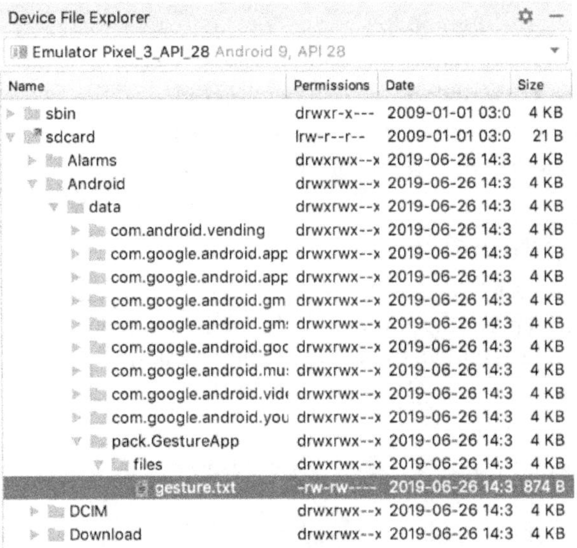

Figure 28-2

Once the gestures file has been created and pulled from the device storage, it is ready to be added to an Android Studio project as a resource file.

28.9 Adding the Gestures File to the Project

Within the Android Studio Project tool window, locate and right-click on the *res* folder (located under *app*) and select *New -> Directory* from the resulting menu. In the New Directory dialog, enter *raw* as the folder name and click on the *OK* button. Using the appropriate file explorer utility for your operating system type, locate the *gesture* file previously pulled from the device storage and copy and paste it into the new *raw* folder in the Project tool window.

28.10 Designing the User Interface

This example application calls for a very simple user interface consisting of a LinearLayout view with a GestureOverlayView layered on top of it to intercept any gestures performed by the user. Locate the *app -> res -> layout -> activity_main.xml* file, double-click on it to load it into the Layout Editor tool and select and delete the default TextView widget.

Switch the layout editor Text mode and modify the XML so that it reads as follows:

```xml
<?xml version="1.0" encoding="utf-8"?>
<androidx.constraintlayout.widget.ConstraintLayout
    xmlns:android="http://schemas.android.com/apk/res/android"
    xmlns:app="http://schemas.android.com/apk/res-auto"
    xmlns:tools="http://schemas.android.com/tools"
    android:layout_width="match_parent"
    android:layout_height="match_parent"
    tools:context=".MainActivity">

    <android.gesture.GestureOverlayView
        android:id="@+id/gOverlay"
        android:layout_width="0dp"
        android:layout_height="0dp"
        app:layout_constraintBottom_toBottomOf="parent"
        app:layout_constraintEnd_toEndOf="parent"
        app:layout_constraintStart_toStartOf="parent"
        app:layout_constraintTop_toTopOf="parent" />
</androidx.constraintlayout.widget.ConstraintLayout>
```

28.11 Loading the Gestures File

Now that the gestures file has been added to the project, the next step is to write some code so that the file is loaded when the activity starts up. For the purposes of this project, the code to achieve this will be added to the *MainActivity* class located in the *MainActivity.java* source file as follows:

```java
package com.ebookfrenzy.customgestures;

import androidx.appcompat.app.AppCompatActivity;
import android.os.Bundle;
import android.gesture.GestureLibraries;
import android.gesture.GestureLibrary;
import android.gesture.GestureOverlayView;
import android.gesture.GestureOverlayView.OnGesturePerformedListener;

public class MainActivity extends AppCompatActivity
        implements OnGesturePerformedListener {

    private GestureLibrary gLibrary;

    @Override
    protected void onCreate(Bundle savedInstanceState) {
        super.onCreate(savedInstanceState);
        setContentView(R.layout.activity_custom_gestures);

        gestureSetup();
    }

    private void gestureSetup() {
```

```
        gLibrary =
                GestureLibraries.fromRawResource(this,
                        R.raw.gestures);
        if (!gLibrary.load()) {
            finish();
        }
    }

    .

    .

}
```

In addition to some necessary import directives, the above code also creates a *GestureLibrary* instance named *gLibrary* and then loads into it the contents of the *gesture* file located in the *raw* resources folder. The activity class has also been modified to implement the *OnGesturePerformedListener* interface, which requires the implementation of the *onGesturePerformed* callback method (which will be created in a later section of this chapter).

28.12 Registering the Event Listener

In order for the activity to receive notification that the user has performed a gesture on the screen, it is necessary to register the *OnGesturePerformedListener* event listener on the *gLayout* view, a reference to which can be obtained using the *findViewById* method as outlined in the following code fragment:

```
private void gestureSetup() {
    gLibrary =
            GestureLibraries.fromRawResource(this,
                    R.raw.gestures);
    if (!gLibrary.load()) {
        finish();
    }


    GestureOverlayView gOverlay = findViewById(R.id.gOverlay);
    gOverlay.addOnGesturePerformedListener(this);
}
```

28.13 Implementing the onGesturePerformed Method

All that remains before an initial test run of the application can be performed is to implement the *OnGesturePerformed* callback method. This is the method which will be called when a gesture is performed on the GestureOverlayView instance:

```
package com.ebookfrenzy.customgestures;

import androidx.appcompat.app.AppCompatActivity;
import android.os.Bundle;
import android.gesture.GestureLibraries;
import android.gesture.GestureLibrary;
import android.gesture.GestureOverlayView;
import android.gesture.GestureOverlayView.OnGesturePerformedListener;
import android.gesture.Prediction;
import android.widget.Toast;
```

```java
import android.gesture.Gesture;
import java.util.ArrayList;

public class MainActivity extends AppCompatActivity implements
OnGesturePerformedListener {

    private GestureLibrary gLibrary;

.
.

    public void onGesturePerformed(GestureOverlayView overlay, Gesture
            gesture) {
        ArrayList<Prediction> predictions =
                gLibrary.recognize(gesture);

        if (predictions.size() > 0 && predictions.get(0).score > 1.0)
        {

            String action = predictions.get(0).name;

            Toast.makeText(this, action, Toast.LENGTH_SHORT).show();
        }
    }

.
.
.
.

}
```

When a gesture on the gesture overlay view object is detected by the Android runtime, the *onGesturePerformed* method is called. Passed through as arguments are a reference to the GestureOverlayView object on which the gesture was detected together with an object of type *Gesture*. The Gesture class is designed to hold the information that defines a specific gesture (essentially a sequence of timed points on the screen depicting the path of the strokes that comprise a gesture).

The Gesture object is passed through to the *recognize()* method of our *gLibrary* instance, the purpose of which is to compare the current gesture with each gesture loaded from the *gesture* file. Once this task is complete, the *recognize()* method returns an ArrayList object containing a Prediction object for each comparison performed. The list is ranked in order from the best match (at position 0 in the array) to the worst. Contained within each prediction object is the name of the corresponding gesture from the *gesture* file and a prediction score indicating how closely it matches the current gesture.

The code in the above method, therefore, takes the prediction at position 0 (the closest match) makes sure it has a score of greater than 1.0 and then displays a Toast message (an Android class designed to display notification pop ups to the user) displaying the name of the matching gesture.

28.14 Testing the Application

Build and run the application on either an emulator or a physical Android device and perform the circle gesture on the display. When performed, the toast notification should appear containing the name of the detected gesture. Note that when a gesture is recognized, it is outlined on the display with a bright yellow line while gestures about which the overlay is uncertain appear as a faded yellow line. While useful during development, this is probably not ideal for a real world application. Clearly, therefore, there is still some more configuration work to do.

28.15 Configuring the GestureOverlayView

By default, the GestureOverlayView is configured to display yellow lines during gestures. The color used to draw recognized and unrecognized gestures can be defined via the *android:gestureColor* and *android:uncertainGestureColor* attributes. For example, to hide the gesture lines, modify the *activity_main.xml* file in the example project as follows:

```
<android.gesture.GestureOverlayView
    android:id="@+id/gOverlay"
    android:layout_width="0dp"
    android:layout_height="0dp"
    app:layout_constraintBottom_toBottomOf="parent"
    app:layout_constraintEnd_toEndOf="parent"
    app:layout_constraintStart_toStartOf="parent"
    app:layout_constraintTop_toTopOf="parent"
    android:gestureColor="#00000000"
    android:uncertainGestureColor="#00000000" />
```

On re-running the application, gestures should now be invisible (since they are drawn in white on the white background of the LinearLayout view).

28.16 Intercepting Gestures

The GestureOverlayView is, as previously described, a transparent overlay that may be positioned over the top of other views. This leads to the question as to whether events intercepted by the gesture overlay should then be passed on to the underlying views when a gesture has been recognized. This is controlled via the *android:eventsInterceptionEnabled* property of the GestureOverlayView instance. When set to true, the gesture events are not passed to the underlying views when a gesture is recognized. This can be a particularly useful setting when gestures are being performed over a view that might be configured to scroll in response to certain gestures. Setting this property to *true* will avoid gestures also being interpreted as instructions to the underlying view to scroll in a particular direction.

28.17 Detecting Pinch Gestures

Before moving on from touch handling in general and gesture recognition in particular, the last topic of this chapter is that of handling pinch gestures. While it is possible to create and detect a wide range of gestures using the steps outlined in the previous sections of this chapter it is, in fact, not possible to detect a pinching gesture (where two fingers are used in a stretching and pinching motion, typically to zoom in and out of a view or image) using the techniques discussed so far.

The simplest method for detecting pinch gestures is to use the Android *ScaleGestureDetector* class. In general terms, detecting pinch gestures involves the following three steps:

1. Declaration of a new class which implements the SimpleOnScaleGestureListener interface including the required *onScale()*, *onScaleBegin()* and *onScaleEnd()* callback methods.

2. Creation of an instance of the ScaleGestureDetector class, passing through an instance of the class created in step 1 as an argument.

3. Implementing the *onTouchEvent()* callback method on the enclosing activity which, in turn, calls the *onTouchEvent()* method of the ScaleGestureDetector class.

In the remainder of this chapter, we will create a very simple example designed to demonstrate the implementation of pinch gesture recognition.

28.18 A Pinch Gesture Example Project

Select the *Start a new Android Studio project* quick start option from the welcome screen and, within the resulting new project dialog, choose the Empty Activity template before clicking on the Next button.

Enter *PinchExample* into the Name field and specify *com.ebookfrenzy.pinchexample* as the package name. Before clicking on the Finish button, change the Minimum API level setting to API 26: Android 8.0 (Oreo) and the Language menu to Java.

Within the *activity_main.xml* file, select the default TextView object and use the Attributes tool window to set the ID to *myTextView*.

Locate and load the *MainActivity.java* file into the Android Studio editor and modify the file as follows:

```java
package com.ebookfrenzy.pinchexample;

import androidx.appcompat.app.AppCompatActivity;
import android.os.Bundle;
import android.view.MotionEvent;
import android.view.ScaleGestureDetector;
import android.view.ScaleGestureDetector.SimpleOnScaleGestureListener;
import android.widget.TextView;

public class MainActivity extends AppCompatActivity {

    TextView scaleText;
    ScaleGestureDetector scaleGestureDetector;

    @Override
    protected void onCreate(Bundle savedInstanceState) {
        super.onCreate(savedInstanceState);
        setContentView(R.layout.activity_pinch_example);

        scaleText = findViewById(R.id.myTextView);

        scaleGestureDetector =
                new ScaleGestureDetector(this,
                        new MyOnScaleGestureListener());
    }

    @Override
    public boolean onTouchEvent(MotionEvent event) {
        scaleGestureDetector.onTouchEvent(event);
        return true;
    }
```

```
public class MyOnScaleGestureListener extends
        SimpleOnScaleGestureListener {

    @Override
    public boolean onScale(ScaleGestureDetector detector) {

        float scaleFactor = detector.getScaleFactor();

        if (scaleFactor > 1) {
            scaleText.setText("Zooming Out");
        } else {
            scaleText.setText("Zooming In");
        }
        return true;
    }

    @Override
    public boolean onScaleBegin(ScaleGestureDetector detector) {
        return true;
    }

    @Override
    public void onScaleEnd(ScaleGestureDetector detector) {

    }
}
.
.
.
}
```

The code declares a new class named MyOnScaleGestureListener which extends the Android SimpleOnScaleGestureListener class. This interface requires that three methods (*onScale()*, *onScaleBegin()* and *onScaleEnd()*) be implemented. In this instance the *onScale()* method identifies the scale factor and displays a message on the text view indicating the type of pinch gesture detected.

Within the *onCreate()* method, a reference to the text view object is obtained and assigned to the scaleText variable. Next, a new *ScaleGestureDetector* instance is created, passing through a reference to the enclosing activity and an instance of our new *MyOnScaleGestureListener* class as arguments. Finally, an *onTouchEvent()* callback method is implemented for the activity, which simply calls the corresponding *onTouchEvent()* method of the *ScaleGestureDetector* object, passing through the MotionEvent object as an argument.

Compile and run the application on an emulator or physical Android device and perform pinching gestures on the screen, noting that the text view displays either the zoom in or zoom out message depending on the pinching motion. Pinching gestures may be simulated within the emulator by holding down the Ctrl (or Cmd) key and clicking and dragging the mouse pointer as shown in Figure 28-3:

Figure 28-3

28.19 Summary

A gesture is essentially the motion of points of contact on a touch screen involving one or more strokes and can be used as a method of communication between user and application. Android allows gestures to be designed using the Gesture Builder application. Once created, gestures can be saved to a gestures file and loaded into an activity at application runtime using the GestureLibrary.

Gestures can be detected on areas of the display by overlaying existing views with instances of the transparent *GestureOverlayView* class and implementing an *OnGesturePerformedListener* event listener. Using the GestureLibrary, a ranked list of matches between a gesture performed by the user and the gestures stored in a gestures file may be generated, using a prediction score to decide whether a gesture is a close enough match.

Pinch gestures may be detected through the implementation of the ScaleGestureDetector class, an example of which was also provided in this chapter.

29. An Introduction to Android Fragments

As you progress through the chapters of this book it will become increasingly evident that many of the design concepts behind the Android system were conceived with the goal of promoting reuse of, and interaction between, the different elements that make up an application. One such area that will be explored in this chapter involves the use of Fragments.

This chapter will provide an overview of the basics of fragments in terms of what they are and how they can be created and used within applications. The next chapter will work through a tutorial designed to show fragments in action when developing applications in Android Studio, including the implementation of communication between fragments.

29.1 What is a Fragment?

A fragment is a self-contained, modular section of an application's user interface and corresponding behavior that can be embedded within an activity. Fragments can be assembled to create an activity during the application design phase, and added to or removed from an activity during application runtime to create a dynamically changing user interface.

Fragments may only be used as part of an activity and cannot be instantiated as standalone application elements. That being said, however, a fragment can be thought of as a functional "sub-activity" with its own lifecycle similar to that of a full activity.

Fragments are stored in the form of XML layout files and may be added to an activity either by placing appropriate <fragment> elements in the activity's layout file, or directly through code within the activity's class implementation.

29.2 Creating a Fragment

The two components that make up a fragment are an XML layout file and a corresponding Java class. The XML layout file for a fragment takes the same format as a layout for any other activity layout and can contain any combination and complexity of layout managers and views. The following XML layout, for example, is for a fragment consisting simply of a RelativeLayout with a red background containing a single TextView:

```xml
<?xml version="1.0" encoding="utf-8"?>
<RelativeLayout xmlns:android="http://schemas.android.com/apk/res/android"
    android:layout_width="match_parent"
    android:layout_height="match_parent"
    android:background="@color/red" >

    <TextView
        android:id="@+id/textView1"
        android:layout_width="wrap_content"
        android:layout_height="wrap_content"
        android:layout_centerHorizontal="true"
```

```
        android:layout_centerVertical="true"
        android:text="@string/fragone_label_text"
        android:textAppearance="?android:attr/textAppearanceLarge" />
</RelativeLayout>
```

The corresponding class to go with the layout must be a subclass of the Android *Fragment* class. This class should, at a minimum, override the *onCreateView()* method which is responsible for loading the fragment layout. For example:

```
package com.example.myfragmentdemo;


import android.os.Bundle;
import android.view.LayoutInflater;
import android.view.View;
import android.view.ViewGroup;
import androidx.fragment.app.Fragment;


public class FragmentOne extends Fragment {

    @Override
    public View onCreateView(LayoutInflater inflater,
            ViewGroup container,
            Bundle savedInstanceState) {
        // Inflate the layout for this fragment
        return inflater.inflate(R.layout.fragment_one_layout,
                container, false);
    }

}
```

In addition to the *onCreateView()* method, the class may also override the standard lifecycle methods.

Once the fragment layout and class have been created, the fragment is ready to be used within application activities.

29.3 Adding a Fragment to an Activity using the Layout XML File

Fragments may be incorporated into an activity either by writing Java code or by embedding the fragment into the activity's XML layout file. Regardless of the approach used, a key point to be aware of is that when the support library is being used for compatibility with older Android releases, any activities using fragments must be implemented as a subclass of *FragmentActivity* instead of the *AppCompatActivity* class:

```
package com.example.myfragmentdemo;


import android.os.Bundle;
import androidx.fragment.app.FragmentActivity;
import android.view.Menu;


public class MainActivity extends FragmentActivity {

        @Override
        protected void onCreate(Bundle savedInstanceState) {
```

```
            super.onCreate(savedInstanceState);
            setContentView(R.layout.activity_fragment_demo);
        }
}
```

Fragments are embedded into activity layout files using the <fragment> element. The following example layout embeds the fragment created in the previous section of this chapter into an activity layout:

```
<RelativeLayout xmlns:android="http://schemas.android.com/apk/res/android"
    xmlns:tools="http://schemas.android.com/tools"
    android:layout_width="match_parent"
    android:layout_height="match_parent"
    tools:context=".MainActivity" >

    <fragment
        android:id="@+id/fragment_one"
        android:name="com.example.myfragmentdemo.myfragmentdemo.FragmentOne"
        android:layout_width="match_parent"
        android:layout_height="wrap_content"
        android:layout_alignParentLeft="true"
        android:layout_centerVertical="true"
        tools:layout="@layout/fragment_one_layout" />

</RelativeLayout>
```

The key properties within the <fragment> element are *android:name*, which must reference the class associated with the fragment, and *tools:layout*, which must reference the XML resource file containing the layout of the fragment.

Once added to the layout of an activity, fragments may be viewed and manipulated within the Android Studio Layout Editor tool. Figure 29-1, for example, shows the above layout with the embedded fragment within the Android Studio Layout Editor:

Figure 29-1

29.4 Adding and Managing Fragments in Code

The ease of adding a fragment to an activity via the activity's XML layout file comes at the cost of the activity not being able to remove the fragment at runtime. In order to achieve full dynamic control of fragments during runtime, those activities must be added via code. This has the advantage that the fragments can be added, removed and even made to replace one another dynamically while the application is running.

When using code to manage fragments, the fragment itself will still consist of an XML layout file and a corresponding class. The difference comes when working with the fragment within the hosting activity. There is a standard sequence of steps when adding a fragment to an activity using code:

1. Create an instance of the fragment's class.

2. Pass any additional intent arguments through to the class instance.

3. Obtain a reference to the fragment manager instance.

4. Call the *beginTransaction()* method on the fragment manager instance. This returns a fragment transaction instance.

5. Call the *add()* method of the fragment transaction instance, passing through as arguments the resource ID of the view that is to contain the fragment and the fragment class instance.

6. Call the *commit()* method of the fragment transaction.

The following code, for example, adds a fragment defined by the FragmentOne class so that it appears in the container view with an ID of LinearLayout1:

```
FragmentOne firstFragment = new FragmentOne();
firstFragment.setArguments(getIntent().getExtras());


FragmentManager fragManager = getSupportFragmentManager();
FragmentTransaction transaction = fragManager.beginTransaction();


transaction.add(R.id.LinearLayout1, firstFragment);
transaction.commit();
```

The above code breaks down each step into a separate statement for the purposes of clarity. The last four lines can, however, be abbreviated into a single line of code as follows:

```
getSupportFragmentManager().beginTransaction()
        .add(R.id.LinearLayout1, firstFragment).commit();
```

Once added to a container, a fragment may subsequently be removed via a call to the *remove()* method of the fragment transaction instance, passing through a reference to the fragment instance that is to be removed:

```
transaction.remove(firstFragment);
```

Similarly, one fragment may be replaced with another by a call to the *replace()* method of the fragment transaction instance. This takes as arguments the ID of the view containing the fragment and an instance of the new fragment. The replaced fragment may also be placed on what is referred to as the *back* stack so that it can be quickly restored in the event that the user navigates back to it. This is achieved by making a call to the *addToBackStack()* method of the fragment transaction object before making the *commit()* method call:

```
FragmentTwo secondFragment = new FragmentTwo();
transaction.replace(R.id.LinearLayout1, secondFragment);
```

```
transaction.addToBackStack(null);
transaction.commit();
```

29.5 Handling Fragment Events

As previously discussed, a fragment is very much like a sub-activity with its own layout, class and lifecycle. The view components (such as buttons and text views) within a fragment are able to generate events just like those in a regular activity. This raises the question as to which class receives an event from a view in a fragment; the fragment itself, or the activity in which the fragment is embedded. The answer to this question depends on how the event handler is declared.

In the chapter entitled *"An Overview and Example of Android Event Handling"*, two approaches to event handling were discussed. The first method involved configuring an event listener and callback method within the code of the activity. For example:

```
button.setOnClickListener(
        new Button.OnClickListener() {
                public void onClick(View v) {
                        // Code to be performed when
                        // the button is clicked
                }
        }
    );
```

In the case of intercepting click events, the second approach involved setting the *android:onClick* property within the XML layout file:

```
<Button
    android:id="@+id/button1"
    android:layout_width="wrap_content"
    android:layout_height="wrap_content"
    android:onClick="onClick"
    android:text="Click me" />
```

The general rule for events generated by a view in a fragment is that if the event listener was declared in the fragment class using the event listener and callback method approach, then the event will be handled first by the fragment. If the *android:onClick* resource is used, however, the event will be passed directly to the activity containing the fragment.

29.6 Implementing Fragment Communication

Once one or more fragments are embedded within an activity, the chances are good that some form of communication will need to take place both between the fragments and the activity, and between one fragment and another. In fact, good practice dictates that fragments do not communicate directly with one another. All communication should take place via the encapsulating activity.

In order for an activity to communicate with a fragment, the activity must identify the fragment object via the ID assigned to it. Once this reference has been obtained, the activity can simply call the public methods of the fragment object.

Communicating in the other direction (from fragment to activity) is a little more complicated. In the first instance, the fragment must define a listener interface, which is then implemented within the activity class. For example, the following code declares an interface named ToolbarListener on a fragment class named ToolbarFragment. The code also declares a variable in which a reference to the activity will later be stored:

```
public class ToolbarFragment extends Fragment {


        ToolbarListener activityCallback;


        public interface ToolbarListener {
                public void onButtonClick(int position, String text);
        }

  .

  .

}
```

The above code dictates that any class that implements the ToolbarListener interface must also implement a callback method named *onButtonClick* which, in turn, accepts an integer and a String as arguments.

Next, the *onAttach()* method of the fragment class needs to be overridden and implemented. This method is called automatically by the Android system when the fragment has been initialized and associated with an activity. The method is passed a reference to the activity in which the fragment is contained. The method must store a local reference to this activity and verify that it implements the ToolbarListener interface:

```
@Override
public void onAttach(Context context) {
    super.onAttach(context);

    try {
       activityCallback = (ToolbarListener) activity;
    } catch (ClassCastException e) {
        throw new ClassCastException(activity.toString()
                + " must implement ToolbarListener");
    }
}
```

Upon execution of this example, a reference to the activity will be stored in the local *activityCallback* variable, and an exception will be thrown if that activity does not implement the ToolbarListener interface.

The next step is to call the callback method of the activity from within the fragment. When and how this happens is entirely dependent on the circumstances under which the activity needs to be contacted by the fragment. The following code, for example, calls the callback method on the activity when a button is clicked:

```
public void buttonClicked (View view) {
   activityCallback.onButtonClick(arg1, arg2);
}
```

All that remains is to modify the activity class so that it implements the ToolbarListener interface. For example:

```
public class MainActivity extends FragmentActivity
                    implements ToolbarFragment.ToolbarListener {


        public void onButtonClick(String arg1, int arg2) {
                // Implement code for callback method

        }

  .
```

.

}

As we can see from the above code, the activity declares that it implements the ToolbarListener interface of the ToolbarFragment class and then proceeds to implement the *onButtonClick()* method as required by the interface.

29.7 Summary

Fragments provide a powerful mechanism for creating re-usable modules of user interface layout and application behavior, which, once created, can be embedded in activities. A fragment consists of a user interface layout file and a class. Fragments may be utilized in an activity either by adding the fragment to the activity's layout file, or by writing code to manage the fragments at runtime. Fragments added to an activity in code can be removed and replaced dynamically at runtime. All communication between fragments should be performed via the activity within which the fragments are embedded.

Having covered the basics of fragments in this chapter, the next chapter will work through a tutorial designed to reinforce the techniques outlined in this chapter.

30. Using Fragments in Android Studio - An Example

As outlined in the previous chapter, fragments provide a convenient mechanism for creating reusable modules of application functionality consisting of both sections of a user interface and the corresponding behavior. Once created, fragments can be embedded within activities.

Having explored the overall theory of fragments in the previous chapter, the objective of this chapter is to create an example Android application using Android Studio designed to demonstrate the actual steps involved in both creating and using fragments, and also implementing communication between one fragment and another within an activity.

30.1 About the Example Fragment Application

The application created in this chapter will consist of a single activity and two fragments. The user interface for the first fragment will contain a toolbar of sorts consisting of an EditText view, a SeekBar and a Button, all contained within a RelativeLayout view. The second fragment will consist solely of a TextView object, also contained within a RelativeLayout view.

The two fragments will be embedded within the main activity of the application and communication implemented such that when the button in the first fragment is pressed, the text entered into the EditText view will appear on the TextView of the second fragment using a font size dictated by the position of the SeekBar in the first fragment.

Since this application is intended to work on earlier versions of Android, it will also be necessary to make use of the appropriate Android support library.

30.2 Creating the Example Project

Select the *Start a new Android Studio project* quick start option from the welcome screen and, within the resulting new project dialog, choose the Empty Activity template before clicking on the Next button.

Enter *FragmentExample* into the Name field and specify *com.ebookfrenzy.fragmentexample* as the package name. Before clicking on the Finish button, change the Minimum API level setting to API 26: Android 8.0 (Oreo) and the Language menu to Java.

30.3 Creating the First Fragment Layout

The next step is to create the user interface for the first fragment that will be used within our activity.

This user interface will, of course, reside in an XML layout file so begin by navigating to the *layout* folder located under *app -> res* in the Project tool window. Once located, right-click on the *layout* entry and select the *New -> Layout resource file* menu option as illustrated in Figure 30-1:

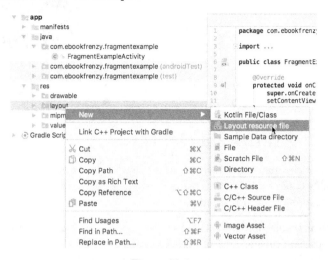

Figure 30-1

In the resulting dialog, name the layout *toolbar_fragment* and change the root element to RelativeLayout before clicking on OK to create the new resource file.

The new resource file will appear within the Layout Editor tool ready to be designed. Switch the Layout Editor to Text mode and modify the XML so that it reads as outlined in the following listing to add three new view elements to the layout:

```xml
<?xml version="1.0" encoding="utf-8"?>

<RelativeLayout
    xmlns:android="http://schemas.android.com/apk/res/android"
    android:layout_width="match_parent"
    android:layout_height="match_parent">

    <Button
        android:id="@+id/button1"
        android:layout_width="wrap_content"
        android:layout_height="wrap_content"
        android:layout_below="@+id/seekBar1"
        android:layout_centerHorizontal="true"
        android:layout_marginTop="17dp"
        android:text="Change Text" />

    <EditText
        android:id="@+id/editText1"
        android:layout_width="wrap_content"
        android:layout_height="wrap_content"
        android:layout_alignParentTop="true"
        android:layout_centerHorizontal="true"
        android:layout_marginTop="16dp"
        android:ems="10"
```

```
    android:inputType="text" >
    <requestFocus />
</EditText>

<SeekBar
    android:id="@+id/seekBar1"
    android:layout_width="match_parent"
    android:layout_height="wrap_content"
    android:layout_alignParentStart="true"
    android:layout_below="@+id/editText1"
    android:layout_marginTop="14dp" />
</RelativeLayout>
```

Once the changes have been made, switch the Layout Editor tool back to Design mode and click on the warning button in the top right-hand corner of the design area. Select the hardcoded text warning, click the *Fix* button and assign the string to a resource named *change_text*.

Upon completion of these steps, the user interface layout should resemble that of Figure 30-2:

Figure 30-2

With the layout for the first fragment implemented, the next step is to create a class to go with it.

30.4 Creating the First Fragment Class

In addition to a user interface layout, a fragment also needs to have a class associated with it to do the actual work behind the scenes. Add a class for this purpose to the project by unfolding the *app -> java* folder in the Project tool window and right-clicking on the package name given to the project when it was created (in this instance *com.ebookfrenzy.fragmentexample*). From the resulting menu, select the *New -> Java Class* option. In the resulting *Create New Class* dialog, name the class *ToolbarFragment* and click on *OK* to create the new class.

Once the class has been created it should, by default, appear in the editing panel where it will read as follows:

```
package com.ebookfrenzy.fragmentexample;
```

```
public class ToolbarFragment {
}
```

For the time being, the only changes to this class are the addition of some import directives and the overriding of the *onCreateView()* method to make sure the layout file is inflated and displayed when the fragment is used within an activity. The class declaration also needs to indicate that the class extends the Android Fragment class:

```
package com.ebookfrenzy.fragmentexample;

import android.os.Bundle;
import androidx.fragment.app.Fragment;
import android.view.LayoutInflater;
import android.view.View;
import android.view.ViewGroup;

public class ToolbarFragment extends Fragment {

    @Override
    public View onCreateView(LayoutInflater inflater,
                             ViewGroup container, Bundle
                             savedInstanceState) {

        // Inflate the layout for this fragment
        View view =  inflater.inflate(R.layout.toolbar_fragment,
                container, false);
        return view;

    }

}
```

Later in this chapter, more functionality will be added to this class. Before that, however, we need to create the second fragment.

30.5 Creating the Second Fragment Layout

Add a second new Android XML layout resource file to the project, once again selecting a RelativeLayout as the root element. Name the layout *text_fragment* and click *OK*. When the layout loads into the Layout Editor tool, change to Text mode and modify the XML to add a TextView to the fragment layout as follows:

```
<?xml version="1.0" encoding="utf-8"?>
<RelativeLayout
    xmlns:android="http://schemas.android.com/apk/res/android"
    android:layout_width="match_parent"
    android:layout_height="match_parent">
    <TextView
        android:id="@+id/textView1"
        android:layout_width="wrap_content"
        android:layout_height="wrap_content"
        android:layout_centerHorizontal="true"
        android:layout_centerVertical="true"
```

```
        android:text="Fragment Two"
        android:textAppearance="?android:attr/textAppearanceLarge" />
</RelativeLayout>
```

Once the XML changes have been made, switch back to Design mode and extract the string to a resource named *fragment_two*. Upon completion of these steps, the user interface layout for this second fragment should resemble that of Figure 30-3.

As with the first fragment, this one will also need to have a class associated with it. Right-click on *app -> java -> com.ebookfrenzy.fragmentexample* in the Project tool window. From the resulting menu, select the *New -> Java Class* option. Name the fragment *TextFragment* and click *OK* to create the class.

Fragment Two

Figure 30-3

Edit the new *TextFragment.java* class file and modify it to implement the *onCreateView()* method and designate the class as extending the Android *Fragment* class:

```
package com.ebookfrenzy.fragmentexample;

import android.os.Bundle;
import androidx.fragment.app.Fragment;
import android.view.LayoutInflater;
import android.view.View;
import android.view.ViewGroup;

public class TextFragment extends Fragment {

    @Override
    public View onCreateView(LayoutInflater inflater,
                             ViewGroup container,
                             Bundle savedInstanceState) {
        View view = inflater.inflate(R.layout.text_fragment,
```

```
                    container, false);

        return view;
    }
}
```

Now that the basic structure of the two fragments has been implemented, they are ready to be embedded in the application's main activity.

30.6 Adding the Fragments to the Activity

The main activity for the application has associated with it an XML layout file named *activity_main.xml*. For the purposes of this example, the fragments will be added to the activity using the <fragment> element within this file. Using the Project tool window, navigate to the *app -> res -> layout* section of the *FragmentExample* project and double-click on the *activity_main.xml* file to load it into the Android Studio Layout Editor tool.

With the Layout Editor tool in Design mode, select and delete the default TextView object from the layout and select the *Common* category in the palette. Drag the *<fragment>* component from the list of layouts and drop it onto the layout so that it is centered horizontally and positioned such that the dashed line appears indicating the top layout margin:

Figure 30-4

On dropping the fragment onto the layout, a dialog will appear displaying a list of Fragments available within the current project as illustrated in Figure 30-5:

Figure 30-5

Select the ToolbarFragment entry from the list and click on the OK button to dismiss the Fragments dialog. Once added, click on the red warning button in the top right-hand corner of the layout editor to display the warnings panel. An *unknown fragments* message (Figure 30-6) will be listed indicating that the Layout Editor tool needs to know which fragment to display during the preview session. Display the ToolbarFragment fragment by clicking on the *Use @layout/toolbar_fragment* link within the message:

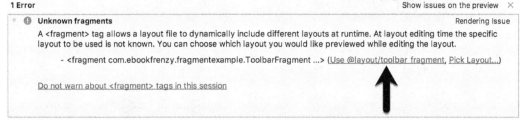

Figure 30-6

Click and drag another <fragment> entry from the panel and position it so that it is centered horizontally and located beneath the bottom edge of the first fragment. When prompted, select the *TextFragment* entry from the fragment dialog before clicking on the OK button. When the rendering message appears, click on the *Use @ layout/text_fragment* option. Use the Infer Constraints button to establish any missing layout constraints.

Note that the fragments are now visible in the layout as demonstrated in Figure 30-7:

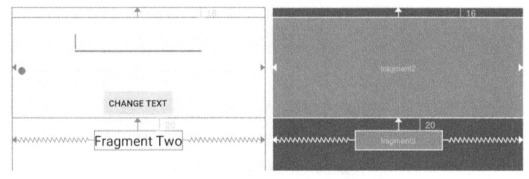

Figure 30-7

Before proceeding to the next step, select the TextFragment instance in the layout and, within the Attributes tool window, change the ID of the fragment to *text_fragment*.

30.7 Making the Toolbar Fragment Talk to the Activity

When the user touches the button in the toolbar fragment, the fragment class is going to need to get the text from the EditText view and the current value of the SeekBar and send them to the text fragment. As outlined in *"An Introduction to Android Fragments"*, fragments should not communicate with each other directly, instead using the activity in which they are embedded as an intermediary.

The first step in this process is to make sure that the toolbar fragment responds to the button being clicked. We also need to implement some code to keep track of the value of the SeekBar view. For the purposes of this example, we will implement these listeners within the ToolbarFragment class. Select the *ToolbarFragment.java* file and modify it so that it reads as shown in the following listing:

```
package com.ebookfrenzy.fragmentexample;

import android.os.Bundle;
import androidx.fragment.app.Fragment;
import android.view.LayoutInflater;
import android.view.View;
import android.view.ViewGroup;
```

```java
import android.content.Context;
import android.widget.Button;
import android.widget.EditText;
import android.widget.SeekBar;
import android.widget.SeekBar.OnSeekBarChangeListener;

public class ToolbarFragment extends Fragment implements OnSeekBarChangeListener
{

    private static int seekvalue = 10;
    private static EditText edittext;

    @Override
    public View onCreateView(LayoutInflater inflater,
                        ViewGroup container, Bundle
                        savedInstanceState) {

        // Inflate the layout for this fragment
        View view =  inflater.inflate(R.layout.toolbar_fragment,
                container, false);

        edittext = view.findViewById(R.id.editText1);
        final SeekBar seekbar = view.findViewById(R.id.seekBar1);

        seekbar.setOnSeekBarChangeListener(this);

        final Button button = view.findViewById(R.id.button1);

        button.setOnClickListener(new View.OnClickListener() {
            public void onClick(View v) {
                buttonClicked(v);
            }
        });

        return view;
    }

    public void buttonClicked (View view) {

    }

    @Override
    public void onProgressChanged(SeekBar seekBar, int progress,
                            boolean fromUser) {
        seekvalue = progress;
```

```
    }

    @Override
    public void onStartTrackingTouch(SeekBar arg0) {

    }

    @Override
    public void onStopTrackingTouch(SeekBar arg0) {

    }
}
```

Before moving on, we need to take some time to explain the above code changes. First, the class is declared as implementing the OnSeekBarChangeListener interface. This is because the user interface contains a SeekBar instance and the fragment needs to receive notifications when the user slides the bar to change the font size. Implementation of the OnSeekBarChangeListener interface requires that the *onProgressChanged()*, *onStartTrackingTouch()* and *onStopTrackingTouch()* methods be implemented. These methods have been implemented but only the *onProgressChanged()* method is actually required to perform a task, in this case storing the new value in a variable named seekvalue which has been declared at the start of the class. Also declared is a variable in which to store a reference to the EditText object.

The *onCreateView()* method has been modified to obtain references to the EditText, SeekBar and Button views in the layout. Once a reference to the button has been obtained it is used to set up an onClickListener on the button which is configured to call a method named *buttonClicked()* when a click event is detected. This method is also then implemented, though at this point it does not do anything.

The next phase of this process is to set up the listener that will allow the fragment to call the activity when the button is clicked. This follows the mechanism outlined in the previous chapter:

```
public class ToolbarFragment extends Fragment
    implements OnSeekBarChangeListener {

        private static int seekvalue = 10;
        private static EditText edittext;

        ToolbarListener activityCallback;

        public interface ToolbarListener {
            public void onButtonClick(int position, String text);
        }

        @Override
        public void onAttach(Context context) {
            super.onAttach(context);
            try {
                activityCallback = (ToolbarListener) context;
            } catch (ClassCastException e) {
                throw new ClassCastException(context.toString()
```

```
                                    + " must implement ToolbarListener");
                }
            }


            public void buttonClicked (View view) {
                    activityCallback.onButtonClick(seekvalue,
                            edittext.getText().toString());
            }




}
```

The above implementation will result in a method named *onButtonClick()* belonging to the activity class being called when the button is clicked by the user. All that remains, therefore, is to declare that the activity class implements the newly created ToolbarListener interface and to implement the *onButtonClick()* method.

Since the Android Support Library is being used for fragment support in earlier Android versions, the activity also needs to be changed to subclass from *FragmentActivity* instead of *AppCompatActivity*. Bringing these requirements together results in the following modified *MainActivity.java* file:

```
package com.ebookfrenzy.fragmentexample;


import androidx.appcompat.app.AppCompatActivity;
import androidx.fragment.app.FragmentActivity;
import android.os.Bundle;


public class MainActivity extends FragmentActivity implements ToolbarFragment.
ToolbarListener {

    @Override
    protected void onCreate(Bundle savedInstanceState) {
        super.onCreate(savedInstanceState);
        setContentView(R.layout.activity_fragment_example);
    }

    public void onButtonClick(int fontsize, String text) {

    }
}
```

With the code changes as they currently stand, the toolbar fragment will detect when the button is clicked by the user and call a method on the activity passing through the content of the EditText field and the current setting of the SeekBar view. It is now the job of the activity to communicate with the Text Fragment and to pass along these values so that the fragment can update the TextView object accordingly.

30.8 Making the Activity Talk to the Text Fragment

As outlined in *"An Introduction to Android Fragments"*, an activity can communicate with a fragment by obtaining a reference to the fragment class instance and then calling public methods on the object. As such, within the TextFragment class we will now implement a public method named *changeTextProperties()* which takes as arguments an integer for the font size and a string for the new text to be displayed. The method will then use these values to modify the TextView object. Within the Android Studio editing panel, locate and modify the *TextFragment.java* file to add this new method and to add code to the *onCreateView()* method to obtain the ID of the TextView object:

```
package com.ebookfrenzy.fragmentexample;


import android.os.Bundle;
import androidx.fragment.app.Fragment;
import android.view.LayoutInflater;
import android.view.View;
import android.view.ViewGroup;
import android.widget.TextView;


public class TextFragment extends Fragment {

    private static TextView textview;

    @Override
    public View onCreateView(LayoutInflater inflater,
                             ViewGroup container,
                             Bundle savedInstanceState) {
        View view = inflater.inflate(R.layout.text_fragment,
                container, false);

        textview = view.findViewById(R.id.textView1);

        return view;
    }

    public void changeTextProperties(int fontsize, String text)
    {
        textview.setTextSize(fontsize);
        textview.setText(text);
    }
}
```

When the TextFragment fragment was placed in the layout of the activity, it was given an ID of *text_fragment*. Using this ID, it is now possible for the activity to obtain a reference to the fragment instance and call the *changeTextProperties()* method on the object. Edit the *MainActivity.java* file and modify the *onButtonClick()* method as follows:

```
public void onButtonClick(int fontsize, String text) {
```

```
TextFragment textFragment =
  (TextFragment)
    getSupportFragmentManager().findFragmentById(R.id.text_fragment);

textFragment.changeTextProperties(fontsize, text);
}
```

30.9 Testing the Application

With the coding for this project now complete, the last remaining task is to run the application. When the application is launched, the main activity will start and will, in turn, create and display the two fragments. When the user touches the button in the toolbar fragment, the *onButtonClick()* method of the activity will be called by the toolbar fragment and passed the text from the EditText view and the current value of the SeekBar. The activity will then call the *changeTextProperties()* method of the second fragment, which will modify the TextView to reflect the new text and font size:

Figure 30-8

30.10 Summary

The goal of this chapter was to work through the creation of an example project intended specifically to demonstrate the steps involved in using fragments within an Android application. Topics covered included the use of the Android Support Library for compatibility with Android versions predating the introduction of fragments, the inclusion of fragments within an activity layout and the implementation of inter-fragment communication.

31. Modern Android App Architecture with Jetpack

Until recently, Google did not recommend a specific approach to building Android apps other than to provide tools and development kits while letting developers decide what worked best for a particular project or individual programming style. That changed in 2017 with the introduction of the Android Architecture Components which, in turn, became part of Android Jetpack when it was released in 2018.

The purpose of this chapter is to provide an overview of the concepts of Jetpack, Android app architecture recommendations and some of the key architecture components. Once the basics have been covered, these topics will be covered in more detail and demonstrated through practical examples in later chapters.

31.1 What is Android Jetpack?

Android Jetpack consists of Android Studio, the Android Architecture Components and Android Support Library together with a set of guidelines that recommend how an Android App should be structured. The Android Architecture Components are designed to make it quicker and easier both to perform common tasks when developing Android apps while also conforming to the key principle of the architectural guidelines.

While all of the Android Architecture Components will be covered in this book, the objective of this chapter is to introduce the key architectural guidelines together with the ViewModel, LiveData, Lifecycle components while also introducing Data Binding and the use of Repositories.

Before moving on, it is important to understand the Jetpack approach to app development is not mandatory. While highlighting some of the shortcoming of other techniques that have gained popularity of the years, Google stopped short of completely condemning those approaches to app development. Google appears to be taking the position that while there is no right or wrong way to develop an app, there is a recommended way.

31.2 The "Old" Architecture

In the chapter entitled *"Creating an Example Android App in Android Studio"*, an Android project was created consisting of a single activity which contained all of the code for presenting and managing the user interface together with the back-end logic of the app. Up until the introduction of Jetpack, the most common architecture followed this paradigm with apps consisting of multiple activities (one for each screen within the app) with each activity class to some degree mixing user interface and back-end code.

This approach led to a range of problems related to the lifecycle of an app (for example an activity is destroyed and recreated each time the user rotates the device leading to the loss of any app data that had not been saved to some form of persistent storage) as well as issues such inefficient navigation involving launching a new activity for each app screen accessed by the user.

31.3 Modern Android Architecture

At the most basic level, Google now advocates single activity apps where different screens are loaded as content within the same activity.

Modern architecture guidelines also recommend separating different areas of responsibility within an app into entirely separate modules (a concept Google refers to as "separation of concerns"). One of the keys to this approach is the ViewModel component.

31.4 The ViewModel Component

The purpose of ViewModel is to separate the user interface-related data model and logic of an app from the code responsible for actually displaying and managing the user interface and interacting with the operating system. When designed in this way, an app will consist of one or more *UI Controllers,* such as an activity, together with ViewModel instances responsible for handling the data needed by those controllers.

In effect, the ViewModel only knows about the data model and corresponding logic. It knows nothing about the user interface and makes no attempt to directly access or respond to events relating to views within the user interface. When a UI controller needs data to display, it simply asks the ViewModel to provide it. Similarly, when the user enters data into a view within the user interface, the UI controller passes it to the ViewModel for handling.

This separation of responsibility addresses the issues relating to the lifecycle of UI controllers. Regardless of how many times a UI controller is recreated during the lifecycle of an app, the ViewModel instances remain in memory thereby maintaining data consistency. A ViewModel used by an activity, for example, will remain in memory until the activity completely finishes which, in the single activity app, is not until the app exits.

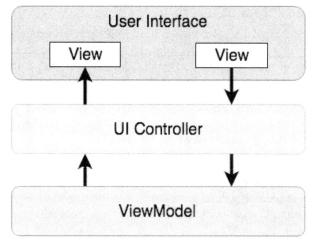

Figure 31-1

31.5 The LiveData Component

Consider an app that displays realtime data such as the current price of a financial stock. The app would probably use some form of stock price web service to continuously update the data model within the ViewModel with the latest information. Obviously, this realtime data is of little use unless it is displayed to the user in a timely manner. There are only two ways that the UI controller can ensure that the latest data is displayed in the user interface. One option is for the controller to continuously check with the ViewModel to find out if the data has changed since it was last displayed. The problem with this approach, however, is that it is inefficient. To maintain the realtime nature of the data feed, the UI controller would have to run on a loop, continuously checking for the data to change.

A better solution would be for the UI controller to receive a notification when a specific data item within a ViewModel changes. This is made possible by using the LiveData component. LiveData is a data holder that allows a value to become *observable* . In basic terms, an observable object has the ability to notify other objects when changes to its data occur thereby solving the problem of making sure that the user interface always matches the data within the ViewModel

This means, for example, that a UI controller that is interested a ViewModel value can set up an *observer* which will, in turn, be notified when that value changes. In our hypothetical application, for example, the stock price would be wrapped in a LiveData object within the ViewModel and the UI controller would assign an observer to the value, declaring a method to be called when the value changes. This method will, when triggered by data change, read the updated value from the ViewModel and use it to update the user interface.

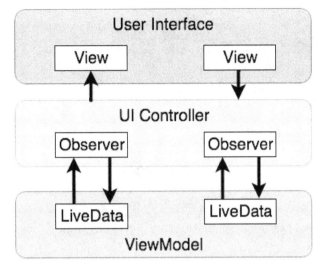

Figure 31-2

A LiveData instance may also be declared as being mutable, allowing the observing entity to update the underlying value held within the LiveData object. The user might, for example, enter a value in the user interface that needs to overwrite the value stored in the ViewModel.

Another of the key advantages of using LiveData is that it is aware of the *lifecycle state* of its observers. If, for example, an activity contains a LiveData observer, the corresponding LiveData object will know when the activity's lifecycle state changes and respond accordingly. If the activity is paused (perhaps the app is put into the background), the LiveData object will stop sending events to the observer. If the activity has just started or resumes after being paused, the LiveData object will send a LiveData event to the observer so that the activity has the most up to date value. Similarly, the LiveData instance will know when the activity is destroyed and remove the observer to free up resources.

So far, we've only talked about UI controllers using observers. In practice, however, an observer can be used within any object that conforms to the Jetpack approach to lifecycle management.

31.6 LiveData and Data Binding

Android Jetpack includes the Data Binding Library which allows data in a ViewModel to be mapped directly to specific views within the XML user interface layout file. In the AndroidSample project created earlier, code had to be written both to obtain references to the EditText and TextView views and to set and get the text properties to reflect data changes. Data binding allows the LiveData value stored in the ViewModel to be referenced directly within the XML layout file avoiding the need to write code to keep the layout views updated.

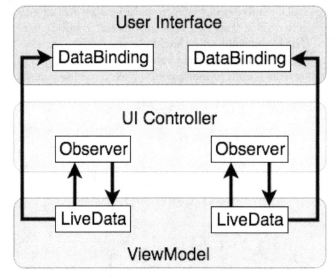

Figure 31-3

Data binding will be covered in greater detail starting with the chapter entitled *"An Overview of Android Jetpack Data Binding"*.

31.7 Android Lifecycles

The duration from when an Android component is created to the point that it is destroyed is referred to as the *lifecycle*. During this lifecycle, the component will change between different lifecycle states, usually under the control of the operating system and in response to user actions. An activity, for example, will begin in the *initialized* state before transitioning to the *created* state. Once the activity is running it will switch to the *started* state from which it will cycle through various states including *created*, *started*, *resumed* and *destroyed*.

Many Android Framework classes and components allow other objects to access their current state. *Lifecycle observers* may also be used so that an object receives notification when the lifecycle state of another object changes. This is the technique used behind the scenes by the ViewModel component to identify when an observer has restarted or been destroyed. This functionality is not limited to Android framework and architecture components and may also be built into any other classes using a set lifecycle components included with the architecture components.

Objects that are able to detect and react to lifecycle state changes in other objects are said to be *lifecycle-aware*, while objects that provide access to their lifecycle state are called *lifecycle-owners*. Lifecycles will be covered in greater detail in the chapter entitled *"Working with Android Lifecycle-Aware Components"*.

31.8 Repository Modules

If a ViewModel obtains data from one or more external sources (such as databases or web services) it is important to separate the code involved in handling those data sources from the ViewModel class. Failure to do this would, after all, violate the separation of concerns guidelines. To avoid mixing this functionality in with the ViewModel, Google's architecture guidelines recommend placing this code in a separate *Repository* module.

A repository is not an Android architecture component, but rather a Java class created by the app developer that is responsible for interfacing with the various data sources. The class then provides an interface to the ViewModel allowing that data to be stored in the model.

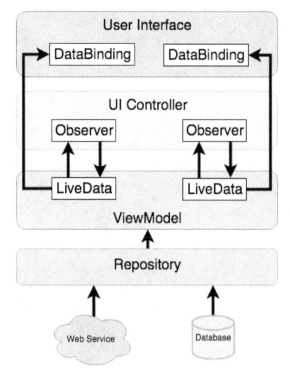

Figure 31-4

31.9 Summary

Until the last year, Google has tended not to recommend any particular approach to structuring an Android app. That has now changed with the introduction of Android Jetpack which consists of a set of tools, components, libraries and architecture guidelines. Google now recommends that an app project be divided into separate modules, each being responsible for a particular area of functionality otherwise known as "separation of concerns".

In particular, the guidelines recommend separating the view data model of an app from the code responsible for handling the user interface. In addition, the code responsible for gathering data from data sources such as web services or databases should be built into a separate repository module instead of being bundled with the view model.

Android Jetpack includes the Android Architecture Components which have been designed specifically to make it easier to develop apps that conform to the recommended guidelines. This chapter has introduced the ViewModel, LiveData and Lifecycle components. These will be covered in more detail starting with the next chapter. Other architecture components not mentioned in this chapter will be covered later in the book.

32. An Android Jetpack ViewModel Tutorial

The previous chapter introduced the key concepts of Android Jetpack and outlined the basics of modern Android app architecture. Jetpack essentially defines a set of recommendations describing how an Android app project should be structured while providing a set of libraries and components that make it easier to conform with these guidelines with the goal of developing reliable apps with less coding and fewer errors.

To help re-enforce and clarify the information provided in the previous chapter, this chapter will step through the creation of an example app project that makes use of the ViewModel component. This example will be further enhanced in the next chapter with the inclusion of LiveData and data binding support.

32.1 About the Project

In the chapter entitled *"Creating an Example Android App in Android Studio"*, a project named AndroidSample was created in which all of the code for the app was bundled into the main Activity class file. In the chapter that followed, an AVD emulator was created and used to run the app. While the app was running, we experienced first-hand the kind of problems that occur when developing apps in this way when the data displayed on a TextView widget was lost during a device rotation.

This chapter will implement the same currency converter app, this time using the ViewModel component and following the Google app architecture guidelines to avoid Activity lifecycle complications.

32.2 Creating the ViewModel Example Project

The first step in this exercise is to create the new project. Begin by launching Android Studio and, if necessary, closing any currently open projects using the *File -> Close Project* menu option so that the Welcome screen appears.

When the AndroidSample project was created, the Basic Activity template was chosen as the basis for the project. For this project, however, the *Fragment + ViewModel* template will be used. This will generate an Android Studio project structured to conform to the architectural guidelines.

Select the *Start a new Android Studio project* quick start option from the welcome screen and, within the resulting new project dialog, choose the Fragment + ViewModel template before clicking on the Next button.

Enter *ViewModelDemo* into the Name field and specify *com.ebookfrenzy.viewmodeldemo* as the package name. Before clicking on the Finish button, change the Minimum API level setting to API 26: Android 8.0 (Oreo) and the Language menu to Java.

32.3 Reviewing the Project

When a project is created using the *Fragment + ViewModel* template, the structure of the project differs in a number of ways from the Basic Activity used when the AndroidSample project was created. The key components of the project are as follows:

32.3.1 The Main Activity

The first point to note is that the user interface of the main activity has been structured so as to allow a single activity to act as a container for all of the screens that will eventually be needed for the completed app. The main user interface layout for the activity is contained within the *app -> res -> layout -> main_activity.xml* file and provides an empty container space in the form of a FrameLayout (highlighted in Figure 32-1) in which screen content will appear:

Figure 32-1

32.3.2 The Content Fragment

The FrameLayout container is just a placeholder which will be replaced at runtime by the content of the first screen that is to appear when the app launches. This content will typically take the form of a Fragment consisting of an XML layout resource file and corresponding class file. In fact, when the project was created, Android Studio created an initial fragment for this very purpose. The layout resource file for this fragment can be found at *app -> res -> layout -> main_fragment.xml* and will appear as shown in Figure 32-2 when loaded into the layout editor:

Figure 32-2

By default, the fragment simply contains a TextView displaying text which reads "MainFragment" but is otherwise ready to be modified to contain the layout of the first app screen. It is worth taking some time at this point to look at the code that has already been generated by Android Studio to display this fragment within the activity container area.

The process of replacing the FrameLayout placeholder with the fragment begins in the MainActivity class file (*app -> java -> <package name> -> MainActivity*). The key lines of code appear within the *onCreate()* method of this class and replace the object with the id of *container* (which has already been assigned to the FrameLayout placeholder view) with the MainFragment class:

```
@Override
protected void onCreate(Bundle savedInstanceState) {
    super.onCreate(savedInstanceState);
    setContentView(R.layout.main_activity);
    if (savedInstanceState == null) {
        getSupportFragmentManager().beginTransaction()
                .replace(R.id.container, MainFragment.newInstance())
                .commitNow();
    }
}
```

The code that accompanies the fragment can be found in the *MainFragment.java* file (*app -> <package name> -> ui.main -> MainFragment*). Within this class file is the *onCreateView()* method which is called when the fragment is created. This method inflates the *main_fragment.xml* layout file so that it is displayed within the container area of the main activity layout:

```
@Override
public View onCreateView(@NonNull LayoutInflater inflater, @Nullable ViewGroup
container, @Nullable Bundle savedInstanceState) {
    return inflater.inflate(R.layout.main_fragment, container, false);
}
```

32.3.3 The ViewModel

The ViewModel for the activity is contained within the *MainViewModel.java* class file located at *app -> java -> ui.main -> MainViewModel*. This is declared as a sub-class of the ViewModel Android architecture component class and is ready to be modified to store the data model for the app:

```
package com.ebookfrenzy.viewmodeldemo.ui.main;

import androidx.lifecycle.ViewModel;

public class  MainViewModel extends ViewModel {
    // TODO: Implement the ViewModel
}
```

32.4 Designing the Fragment Layout

The next step is to design the layout of the fragment. Locate the *main_fragment.xml* file in the Project tool window and double click on it to load it into the layout editor. Once the layout has loaded, select the existing TextView widget and use the Attributes tool window to change the id property to *resultText*.

Drag a Number (Decimal) view from the palette and position it above the existing TextView. With the view selected in the layout refer to the Attributes tool window and change the id to *dollarText*.

Drag a Button widget onto the layout so that it is positioned below the TextView, double-click on it to edit the text and change it to read "Convert". With the button still selected, change the id property to *convertButton*. At this point, the layout should resemble that illustrated in Figure 32-3:

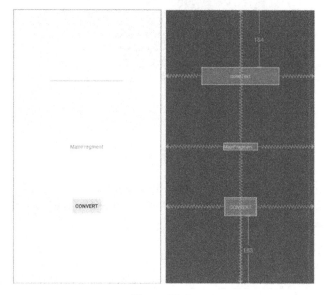

Figure 32-3

Click on the *Infer constraints* button (Figure 32-4) to add any missing layout constraints:

Figure 32-4

Finally, click on the warning icon in the top right-hand corner of the layout editor and convert the hardcoded strings to resources.

32.5 Implementing the View Model

With the user interface layout completed, the data model for the app needs to be created within the view model. Within the Project tool window, locate the *MainViewModel.java* file, double-click on it to load it into the code editor and modify the class so that it reads as follows:

```java
package com.ebookfrenzy.viewmodeldemo.ui.main;

import androidx.lifecycle.ViewModel;

public class  MainViewModel extends ViewModel {

    private static final Float usd_to_eu_rate = 0.74F;
    private String dollarText = "";
    private Float result = 0F;
```

```
public void setAmount(String value) {
    this.dollarText = value;
    result = Float.valueOf(dollarText)*usd_to_eu_rate;
}

public Float getResult()
{
    return result;
}
}
```

The class declares variables to store the current dollar string value and the converted amount together with getter and setter methods to provide access to those data values. When called, the *setAmount()* method takes as an argument the current dollar amount and stores it in the local *dollarText* variable. The dollar string value is converted to a floating point number, multiplied by a fictitious exchange rate and the resulting euro value stored in the *result* variable. The *getResult()* method, on the other hand, simply returns the current value assigned to the *result* variable.

32.6 Associating the Fragment with the View Model

Clearly, there needs to be some way for the fragment to obtain a reference to the ViewModel in order to be able to access the model and observe data changes. A Fragment or Activity maintains references to the ViewModels on which it relies for data using an instance of the ViewModelProvider class.

A ViewModelProvider instance is created via a call to the *ViewModelProviders.of()* method from within the Fragment. When called, the method is passed a reference to the current Fragment or Activity and returns a ViewModelProvider instance as follows:

```
ViewModelProvider viewModelProvider = ViewModelProviders.of(fragment);
```

Once the ViewModelProvider instance has been created, the *get()* method can be called on that instance passing through the class of specific ViewModel that is required. The provider will then either create a new instance of that ViewModel class, or return an existing instance:

```
ViewModel viewModel = viewModelProvider.get(MainViewModel.class);
```

Edit the *MainFragment.java* file and verify that Android Studio has already included this step within the *onActivityCreated()* method (albeit performing the operation in a single line of code for brevity):

```
viewModel = ViewModelProviders.of(this).get(MainViewModel.class);
```

With access to the model view, code can now be added to the Fragment to begin working with the data model.

32.7 Modifying the Fragment

The fragment class now needs to be updated to react to button clicks and to interact with the data values stored in the ViewModel. The class will also need references to the three views in the user interface layout to react to button clicks, extract the current dollar value and to display the converted currency amount. With the *MainFragment* class file loaded into the code editor, modify the *onActivityCreated()* method to obtain and store references to the three view objects as follows:

```
.
.
import android.widget.Button;
import android.widget.EditText;
```

```
import android.widget.TextView;

import com.ebookfrenzy.viewmodeldemo.R;

public class MainFragment extends Fragment {

    private MainViewModel mViewModel;
    private EditText dollarText;
    private TextView resultText;
    private Button convertButton;

    .
    .

    @Override
    public void onActivityCreated(@Nullable Bundle savedInstanceState) {
        super.onActivityCreated(savedInstanceState);
        mViewModel = ViewModelProviders.of(this).get(MainViewModel.class);

        dollarText = getView().findViewById(R.id.dollarText);
        resultText = getView().findViewById(R.id.resultText);
        convertButton = getView().findViewById(R.id.convertButton);
    }

    .
    .
```

In the chapter entitled *"Creating an Example Android App in Android Studio"*, the onClick property of the Button widget was used to designate the method to be called when the button is clicked by the user. Unfortunately, this property is only able to call methods on an Activity and cannot be used to call a method in a Fragment. To get around this limitation, we will need to add some code to the Fragment class to set up an onClick listener on the button. The code to do this can be added to the *onActivityCreated()* method of the *MainFragment.java* file as follows:

```
@Override
public void onActivityCreated(@Nullable Bundle savedInstanceState) {
    super.onActivityCreated(savedInstanceState);
    mViewModel = ViewModelProviders.of(this).get(MainViewModel.class);

    dollarText = getView().findViewById(R.id.dollarText);
    resultText = getView().findViewById(R.id.resultText);
    convertButton = getView().findViewById(R.id.convertButton);

    convertButton.setOnClickListener(new View.OnClickListener()
    {
        @Override
        public void onClick(View v) {

        }
    });
```

```
}
```

With the listener added, any code placed within the *onClick()* method will be called whenever the button is clicked by the user.

32.8 Accessing the ViewModel Data

When the button is clicked, the *onClick()* method needs to read the current value from the EditText view, confirm that the field is not empty and then call the *setAmount()* method of the ViewModel instance. The method will then need to call the ViewModel's *getResult()* method and display the converted value on the TextView widget.

Since LiveData is not yet being used in the project, it will also be necessary to get the latest result value from the ViewModel each time the Fragment is created.

Remaining in the *MainFragment.java* file, implement these requirements as follows in the *onActivityCreated()* method:

```
@Override
public void onActivityCreated(@Nullable Bundle savedInstanceState) {
    super.onActivityCreated(savedInstanceState);
    mViewModel = ViewModelProviders.of(this).get(MainViewModel.class);


    dollarText = getView().findViewById(R.id.dollarText);
    resultText = getView().findViewById(R.id.resultText);
    convertButton = getView().findViewById(R.id.convertButton);

    resultText.setText(mViewModel.getResult().toString());

    convertButton.setOnClickListener(new View.OnClickListener()
    {
        @Override
        public void onClick(View v) {

            if (!dollarText.getText().toString().equals("")) {
                mViewModel.setAmount(dollarText.getText().toString());
                resultText.setText(mViewModel.getResult().toString());
            } else {
                resultText.setText("No Value");
            }
        }
    });
}
```

32.9 Testing the Project

With this phase of the project development completed, build and run the app on the simulator or a physical device, enter a dollar value and click on the Convert button. The converted amount should appear on the TextView indicating that the UI controller and ViewModel re-structuring appears to be working as expected.

When the original AndroidSample app was run, rotating the device caused the value displayed on the *resultText* TextView widget to be lost. Repeat this test now with the ViewModelDemo app and note that the current euro value is retained after the rotation. This is because the ViewModel remained in memory as the Fragment was destroyed and recreated and code was added to the *onActivityCreated()* method to update the TextView with the result data value from the ViewModel each time the Fragment re-started.

While this is an improvement on the original AndroidSample app, there is much more that can be achieved to simplify the project by making use of LiveData and data binding, both of which are the topics of the next chapters.

32.10 Summary

In this chapter we revisited the AndroidSample project created earlier in the book and created a new version of the project structured to comply with the Android Jetpack architectural guidelines. The chapter outlined the structure of the Fragment + ViewModel project template and explained the concept of basing an app on a single Activity using Fragments to present different screens within a single Activity layout. The example project also demonstrated the use of ViewModels to separate data handling from user interface related code. Finally, the chapter showed how the ViewModel approach avoids some of the problems of handling Fragment and Activity lifecycles.

33. An Android Jetpack LiveData Tutorial

The previous chapter began the process of designing an app to conform to the recommended Jetpack architecture guidelines. These initial steps involved the selection of the Fragment+ViewModel project template and the implementation of the data model for the app user interface within a ViewModel instance.

This chapter will further enhance the app design by making use of the LiveData architecture component. Once LiveData support has been added to the project in this chapter, the next chapters (starting with *"An Overview of Android Jetpack Data Binding"*) will make use of the Jetpack Data Binding library to eliminate even more code from the project.

33.1 LiveData - A Recap

LiveData was introduced previously in the chapter entitled *"Modern Android App Architecture with Jetpack"*. As described earlier, the LiveData component can be used as a wrapper around data values within a view model. Once contained in a LiveData instance, those variables become observable to other objects within the app, typically UI controllers such as Activities and Fragments. This allows the UI controller to receive a notification whenever the underlying LiveData value changes. An observer is set up by creating an instance of the Observer class and defining an *onChange()* method to be called when the LiveData value changes. Once the Observer instance has been created, it is attached to the LiveData object via a call to the LiveData object's *observe()* method.

LiveData instances can be declared as being mutable using the MutableLiveData class, allowing both the ViewModel and UI controller to make changes to the underlying data value.

33.2 Adding LiveData to the ViewModel

Launch Android Studio, open the ViewModelDemo project created in the previous chapter and edit the *MainViewModel.java* file which should currently read as follows:

```
package com.ebookfrenzy.viewmodeldemo.ui.main;

import androidx.lifecycle.ViewModel;

public class  MainViewModel extends ViewModel {

    private static final Float usd_to_eu_rate = 0.74F;
    private String dollarText = "";
    private Float result = 0F;

    public void setAmount(String value) {
        this.dollarText = value;
        result = Float.valueOf(dollarText)*usd_to_eu_rate;
    }
```

```
    public Float getResult()
    {
        return result;
    }
}
```

The objective of this stage in the chapter is to wrap the *result* variable in a MutableLiveData instance (the object will need to be mutable so that the value can be changed each time the user requests a currency conversion). Begin by modifying the class so that it now reads as follows noting that an additional package needs to be imported when making use of LiveData:

```
package com.ebookfrenzy.viewmodeldemo.ui.main;

import androidx.lifecycle.MutableLiveData;
import androidx.lifecycle.ViewModel;

public class  MainViewModel extends ViewModel {

    private static final Float usd_to_eu_rate = 0.74F;
    private String dollarText = "";
    private Float result = 0F;
    private MutableLiveData<Float> result = new MutableLiveData<>();

    public void setAmount(String value) {
        this.dollarText = value;
        result = Float.valueOf(dollarText)*usd_to_eu_rate;
    }

    public Float getResult()
    {
        return result;
    }
}
```

Now that the result variable is contained in a mutable LiveData instance, both the *setAmount()* and *getResult()* methods need to modified. In the case of the *setAmount()* method, a value can no longer be assigned to the result variable using the assignment (=) operator. Instead, the LiveData *setValue()* method must be called, passing through the new value as an argument. As currently implemented, the *getResult()* method is declared as returning a Float value and now needs to be changed to return a MutableLiveData object. Making these remaining changes results in the following class file:

```
package com.ebookfrenzy.viewmodeldemo.ui.main;

import androidx.lifecycle.MutableLiveData;
import androidx.lifecycle.ViewModel;

public class  MainViewModel extends ViewModel {

    private static final Float usd_to_eu_rate = 0.74F;
```

```
private String dollarText = "";
private MutableLiveData<Float> result = new MutableLiveData<>();


public void setAmount(String value) {
    this.dollarText = value;
    result = Float.valueOf(dollarText)*usd_to_eu_rate;
    result.setValue(Float.valueOf(dollarText)*usd_to_eu_rate);
}


public Float getResult()
public MutableLiveData<Float> getResult()
{
    return result;
}
}
```

33.3 Implementing the Observer

Now that the conversion result is contained within a LiveData instance, the next step is to configure an observer within the UI controller which, in this example, is the MainFragment class. Locate the *MainFragment.java* class (*app -> java -> <package name> -> MainFragment*), double-click on it to load it into the editor and modify the *onActivityCreated()* method to create a new Observer instance named *resultObserver*:

```
package com.ebookfrenzy.viewmodeldemo.ui.main;

import androidx.lifecycle.Observer;
.

.

@Override
public void onActivityCreated(@Nullable Bundle savedInstanceState) {
.

.

    dollarText = getView().findViewById(R.id.dollarText);
    resultText = getView().findViewById(R.id.resultText);
    convertButton = getView().findViewById(R.id.convertButton);

    resultText.setText(mViewModel.getResult().toString());

    final Observer<Float> resultObserver = new Observer<Float>() {
        @Override
        public void onChanged(@Nullable final Float result) {
            resultText.setText(result.toString());
        }
    };
.

.

.

}
```

The *resultObserver* instance declares the *onChanged()* method which, when called, is passed the current result value which it then converts to a string and displays on the result TextView object. The next step is to add the observer to the result LiveData object, a reference to which can be obtained via a call to the *getResult()* method of the ViewModel object. Since updating the result TextView is now the responsibility of the *onChanged()* callback method, the existing lines of code to perform this task can now be deleted:

```
@Override
public void onActivityCreated(@Nullable Bundle savedInstanceState) {
    super.onActivityCreated(savedInstanceState);
    mViewModel = ViewModelProviders.of(this).get(MainViewModel.class);

    dollarText = getView().findViewById(R.id.dollarText);
    resultText = getView().findViewById(R.id.resultText);
    convertButton = getView().findViewById(R.id.convertButton);

    resultText.setText(mViewModel.getResult().toString());

    final Observer<Float> resultObserver = new Observer<Float>() {
        @Override
        public void onChanged(@Nullable final Float result) {
            resultText.setText(result.toString());
        }
    };

    mViewModel.getResult().observe(this, resultObserver);

    convertButton.setOnClickListener(new View.OnClickListener()
    {
        @Override
        public void onClick(View v) {

            if (!dollarText.getText().toString().equals("")) {
                mViewModel.setAmount(Float.valueOf(
                        dollarText.getText().toString()));
                resultText.setText(mViewModel.getResult().toString());
            } else {
                resultText.setText("No Value");
            }
        }
    });
}
```

Compile and run the app, enter a value into the dollar field, click on the Convert button and verify that the converted euro amount appears on the TextView. This confirms that the observer received notification that the result value had changed and called the *onChanged()* method to display the latest data.

Note in the above implementation of the *onActivityCreated()* method that the line of code responsible for displaying the current result value each time the method was called was removed. This was originally put in place to ensure that the displayed value was not lost in the event that the Fragment was recreated for any reason. Because LiveData monitors the lifecycle status of its observers, this step is no longer necessary. When LiveData detects that the UI controller was recreated, it automatically triggers any associated observers and provides the latest data. Verify this by rotating the device while a euro value is displayed on the TextView object and confirming that the value is not lost.

33.4 Summary

This chapter demonstrated the use of the Android LiveData component to make sure that the data displayed to the user always matches that stored in the ViewModel. This relatively simple process consisted of wrapping a ViewModel data value within a LiveData object and setting up an observer within the UI controller subscribed to the LiveData value. Each time the LiveData value changes, the observer is notified and the *onChanged()* method called and passed the updated value.

Adding LiveData support to the project has gone some way towards simplifying the design of the project. Additional and significant improvements are also possible by making use of the Data Binding Library, details of which will be covered in a later chapter. Before doing that, however, we will look saving ViewModel state.

34. An Overview of Android Jetpack Data Binding

In the chapter entitled *"Modern Android App Architecture with Jetpack"*, we introduced the concept of Android Data Binding and briefly explained how it is used to directly connect the views in a user interface layout to the methods and data located in other objects within an app without the need to write code. This chapter will provide more details on data binding with an emphasis on explaining how data binding is implemented within an Android Studio project. The tutorial in the next chapter (*"An Android Jetpack Data Binding Tutorial"*) will provide a practical example of data binding in action.

34.1 An Overview of Data Binding

Data binding support is provided by the Android Jetpack Data Binding Library, the primary purpose of which is to provide a simple way to connect the views in a user interface layout to the data that is stored within the code of the app (typically within ViewModel instances). Data binding also provides a convenient way to map user interface controls such as Button widgets to event and listener methods within other objects such as UI controllers and ViewModel instances.

Data binding becomes particularly powerful when used in conjunction with the LiveData component. Consider, for example, an EditText view bound to a LiveData variable within a ViewModel using data binding. When connected in this way, any changes to the data value in the ViewModel will automatically appear within the EditText view and, when using two-way binding, any data typed into the EditText will automatically be used to update the LiveData value. Perhaps most impressive is the fact that this can be achieved with no code beyond that necessary to initially set up the binding.

Connecting an interactive view such as a Button widget to a method within a UI controller traditionally required that the developer write code to implement a listener method to be called when the button is clicked. Data binding makes this as simple as referencing the method to be called within the Button element in the layout XML file.

34.2 The Key Components of Data Binding

By default, an Android Studio project is not configured for data binding support. In fact, a number of different elements need to be combined before an app can begin making use of data binding. These involve the project build configuration, the layout XML file, data binding classes and use of the data binding expression language. While this may appear to be a little overwhelming at first, when taken separately these are actually quite simple steps which, once completed, are more than worthwhile in terms of saved coding effort. In the remainder of this chapter, each of these elements will be covered in detail. Once these basics have been covered, the next chapter will work through a detailed tutorial demonstrating these steps in practical terms.

34.2.1 The Project Build Configuration

Before a project can make use of data binding it must first be configured to make use of the Android Data Binding Library and to enable support for data binding classes and the binding expression syntax. Fortunately this can be achieved with just a few lines added to the module level *build.gradle* file (the one listed as *build.gradle (Module: app)* under *Gradle Scripts* in the Project tool window). The following lists a partial build file with data binding enabled:

```
apply plugin: 'com.android.application'

android {
    compileSdkVersion 28

    dataBinding {
        enabled = true
    }
    defaultConfig {
        applicationId "com.ebookfrenzy.myapplication"
.
.
```

34.2.2 The Data Binding Layout File

As we have seen in previous chapters, the user interfaces for an app are typically contained within an XML layout file. Before the views contained within one of these layout files can take advantage of data binding, the layout file must first be converted to a *data binding layout file*.

As outlined earlier in the book, XML layout files define the hierarchy of components in the layout starting with a top-level or *root view*. Invariably, this root view takes the form of a layout container such as a ConstraintLayout, FrameLayout or LinearLayout instance, as is the case in the *main_fragment.xml* file for the ViewModelDemo project:

```
<?xml version="1.0" encoding="utf-8"?>
<androidx.constraintlayout.widget.ConstraintLayout
    xmlns:android="http://schemas.android.com/apk/res/android"
    xmlns:app="http://schemas.android.com/apk/res-auto"
    xmlns:tools="http://schemas.android.com/tools"
    android:id="@+id/main"
    android:layout_width="match_parent"
    android:layout_height="match_parent"
    tools:context=".ui.main.MainFragment">
.
.
</androidx.constraintlayout.widget.ConstraintLayout>
```

In order to be able to use data binding, the layout hierarchy must have a *layout* component as the root view which, in turn, becomes the parent of the current root view.

In the case of the above example, this would require that the following changes be made to the existing layout file:

```
<?xml version="1.0" encoding="utf-8"?>

<layout xmlns:app="http://schemas.android.com/apk/res-auto"
    xmlns:tools="http://schemas.android.com/tools"
    xmlns:android="http://schemas.android.com/apk/res/android">

        <androidx.constraintlayout.widget.ConstraintLayout
            xmlns:android="http://schemas.android.com/apk/res/android"
```

```
        xmlns:app="http://schemas.android.com/apk/res-auto"
        xmlns:tools="http://schemas.android.com/tools"
        android:id="@+id/main"
        android:layout_width="match_parent"
        android:layout_height="match_parent"
        tools:context=".ui.main.MainFragment">
    .
    .

        </androidx.constraintlayout.widget.ConstraintLayout>
</layout>
```

34.2.3 The Layout File Data Element

The data binding layout file needs some way to declare the classes within the project to which the views in the layout are to be bound (for example a ViewModel or UI controller). Having declared these classes, the layout file will also need a variable name by which to reference those instances within binding expressions.

This is achieved using the *data* element, an example of which is shown below:

```
<?xml version="1.0" encoding="utf-8"?>

<layout xmlns:app="http://schemas.android.com/apk/res-auto"
    xmlns:tools="http://schemas.android.com/tools"
    xmlns:android="http://schemas.android.com/apk/res/android">

    <data>
        <variable
            name="myViewModel"
            type="com.ebookfrenzy.myapp.ui.main.MainViewModel" />
    </data>

    <androidx.constraintlayout.widget.ConstraintLayout
        android:id="@+id/main"
        android:layout_width="match_parent"
        android:layout_height="match_parent"
        tools:context=".ui.main.MainFragment">
    .
    .

</layout>
```

The above data element declares a new variable named *myViewModel* of type MainViewModel (note that it is necessary to declare the full package name of the MyViewModel class when declaring the variable).

The data element can also import other classes that may then be referenced within binding expressions elsewhere in the layout file. For example, if you have a class containing a method that needs to be called on a value before it is displayed to the user, the class could be imported as follows:

```
<data>
        <import type="com.ebookfrenzy.MyFormattingTools" />
        <variable
            name="viewModel"
```

```
                type="com.ebookfrenzy.myapp.ui.main.MainViewModel" />
    </data>
```

34.2.4 The Binding Classes

For each class referenced in the *data* element within the binding layout file, Android Studio will automatically generate a corresponding *binding class*. This is a subclass of the Android ViewDataBinding class and will be named based on the layout filename using word capitalization and the *Binding* suffix. The binding class for a layout file named *main_fragment.xml* file, therefore, will be named *MainFragmentBinding*. The binding class contains the bindings specified within the layout file and maps them to the variables and methods within the bound objects.

Although the binding class is generated automatically, code still needs to be written to create an instance of the class based on the corresponding data binding layout file. Fortunately, this can be achieved by making use of the DataBindingUtil class.

The initialization code for an Activity or Fragment will typically set the content view or "inflate" the user interface layout file. This simply means that the code opens the layout file, parses the XML and creates and configures all of the view objects in memory. In the case of an existing Activity class, the code to achieve this can be found in the *onCreate()* method and will read as follows:

```
setContentView(R.layout.activity_main);
```

In the case of a Fragment, this takes place in the *onCreateView()* method:

```
return inflater.inflate(R.layout.main_fragment, container, false);
```

All that is needed to create the binding class instances within an Activity class is to modify this initialization code as follows:

```
MainFragmentBinding binding;

binding = DataBindingUtil.setContentView(this, R.layout.activity_main);
```

In the case of a Fragment, the code would read as follows:

```
MainFragmentBinding binding;

binding = DataBindingUtil.inflate(
        inflater, R.layout.main_fragment, container, false);

binding.setLifecycleOwner(this);
View view = binding.getRoot();
return view;
```

34.2.5 Data Binding Variable Configuration

As outlined above, the data binding layout file contains the *data* element which contains *variable* elements consisting of variable names and the class types to which the bindings are to be established. For example:

```
<data>
    <variable
        name="viewModel"
        type="com.ebookfrenzy.viewmodeldemo.ui.main.MainViewModel" />
    <variable
            name="uiController"
            type="com.ebookfrenzy.viewmodeldemo_databinding.ui.main.MainFragment"
```

```
/>
</data>
```

In the above example, the first variable knows that it will be binding to an instance of a ViewModel class of type MainViewModel but has not yet been connected to an actual MainViewModel object instance. This requires the additional step of assigning the MainViewModel instance used within the app to the variable declared in the layout file. This is performed via a call to the *setVariable()* method of the data binding instance, a reference to which was obtained in the previous chapter:

```
MainViewModel myViewModel = ViewModelProviders.of(this).get(MainViewModel.class);
binding.setVariable(viewModel, myViewModel);
```

The second variable in the above data element references a UI controller class in the form of a Fragment named MainFragment. In this situation the code within a UI controller (be it a Activity or Fragment) would simply need to assign itself to the variable as follows:

```
binding.setVariable(uiController, this);
```

34.2.6 Binding Expressions (One-Way)

Binding expressions define how a particular view interacts with bound objects. A binding expression on a Button, for example, might declare which method on an object is called in response to a click. Alternatively, a binding expression might define which data value stored in a ViewModel is to appear within a TextView and how it is to be presented and formatted.

Binding expressions use a declarative language that allows logic and access to other classes and methods to be used in deciding how bound data is used. Expressions can, for example, include mathematical expressions, method calls, string concatenations, access to array elements and comparison operations. In addition, all of the standard Java language libraries are imported by default so many things that can be achieved in Java can also be performed in a binding expression. As already discussed, the data element may also be used to import custom classes to add yet more capability to expressions.

A binding expression begins with an @ symbol followed by the expression enclosed in curly braces ({}).

Consider, for example, a ViewModel instance containing a variable named *result*. Assume that this class has been assigned to a variable named *viewModel* within the data binding layout file and needs to be bound to a TextView object so that the view always displays the latest result value. If this value was stored as a String object, this would be declared within the layout file as follows:

```
<TextView
    android:id="@+id/resultText"
    android:layout_width="wrap_content"
    android:layout_height="wrap_content"
    android:text="@{viewModel.result}"
    app:layout_constraintBottom_toBottomOf="parent"
    app:layout_constraintEnd_toEndOf="parent"
    app:layout_constraintStart_toStartOf="parent"
    app:layout_constraintTop_toTopOf="parent" />
```

In the above XML the *text* property is being set to the value stored in the *result* LiveData property of the viewModel object.

Consider, however, that the result is stored within the model as a Float value instead of a String. That being the case, the above expression would cause a compilation error. Clearly the Float value will need to be converted to a string before the TextView can display it. To resolve issues such as this, the binding expression can include the necessary steps to complete the conversion using the standard Java language classes:

```
android:text="@{String.valueOf(viewModel.result)}"
```

When running the app after making this change it is important to be aware that the following warning may appear in the Android Studio console:

```
warning: myViewModel.result.getValue() is a boxed field but needs to be un-boxed
to execute String.valueOf(viewModel.result.getValue()).
```

Values in Java can take the form of primitive values such as the *boolean* type (referred to as being *unboxed*) or wrapped in an Java object such as the *Boolean* type and accessed via reference to that object (i.e. *boxed*). The process of *unboxing* involves the unwrapping of the primitive value from the object.

To avoid this message, wrap the offending operation in a *safeUnbox()* call as follows:

```
android:text="@{String.valueOf(safeUnbox(myViewModel.result))}"
```

String concatenation may also be used. For example, to includes the word "dollars" after the result string value the following expression would be used:

```
android:text='@{String.valueOf(safeUnbox(myViewModel.result)) + " dollars"}'
```

Note that since the appended result string is wrapped in double quotes, the expression is now encapsulated with single quotes to avoid syntax errors.

The expression syntax also allows ternary statements to be declared. In the following expression the view will display different text depending on whether or not the result value is greater than 10.

```
@{myViewModel.result > 10 ? "Out of range" : "In range"}
```

Expressions may also be constructed to access specific elements in a data array:

```
@{myViewModel.resultsArray[3]}
```

34.2.7 Binding Expressions (Two-Way)

The type of expressions covered so far are referred to as a *one-way binding*. In other words, the layout is constantly updated as the corresponding value changes, but changes to the value from within the layout do not update the stored value.

A *two-way binding* on the other hand allows the data model to be updated in response to changes in the layout. An EditText view, for example, could be configured with a two-way binding so that when the user enters a different value, that value is used to update the corresponding data model value. When declaring a two-way expression, the syntax is similar to a one-way expression with the exception that it begins with @=. For example:

```
android:text="@={myViewModel.result}"
```

34.2.8 Event and Listener Bindings

Binding expressions may also be used to trigger method calls in response to events on a view. A Button view, for example, can be configured to call a method when clicked. Back in the chapter entitled *"Creating an Example Android App in Android Studio"*, for example, the onClick property of a button was configured to call a method within the app's main activity named *convertCurrency()*. Within the XML file this was represented as follows:

```
android:onClick="convertCurrency"
```

The *convertCurrency()* method was declared along the following lines:

```
public void convertCurrency(View view) {
    .
    .
    .
}
```

Note that this type of method call is always passed a reference to the view on which the event occurred. The same effect can be achieved in data binding using the following expression (assuming the layout has been bound to a class with a variable name of *uiController*):

```
android:onClick="@{uiController::convertCurrency}"
```

Another option, and one which provides the ability to pass parameters to the method, is referred to as a *listener binding*. The following expression uses this approach to call a method on the same viewModel instance with no parameters:

```
android:onClick='@{() -> myViewModel.methodOne()}'
```

The following expression calls a method that expects three parameters:

```
android:onClick='@{() -> myViewModel.methodTwo(viewModel.result, 10, "A
String")}'
```

Binding expressions provide a rich and flexible language in which to bind user interface views to data and methods in other objects and this chapter has only covered the most common use cases. To learn more about binding expressions, review the Android documentation online at:

```
https://developer.android.com/topic/libraries/data-binding/expressions
```

34.3 Summary

Android data bindings provide a system for creating connections between the views in a user interface layout and the data and methods of other objects within the app architecture without having to write code. Once some initial configuration steps have been performed, data binding simply involves the use of binding expressions within the view elements of the layout file. These binding expressions can be either one-way or two-way and may also be used to bind methods to be called in response to events such as button clicks within the user interface.

35. An Android Jetpack Data Binding Tutorial

So far in this book we have covered the basic concepts of modern Android app architecture and looked in more detail at the ViewModel and LiveData components. The concept of data binding was also covered in the previous chapter and will now be used in this chapter to further modify the ViewModelDemo app.

35.1 Removing the Redundant Code

Before implementing data binding within the ViewModelDemo app, the power of data binding will be demonstrated by deleting all of the code within the project that will no longer be needed by the end of this chapter.

Launch Android Studio, open the ViewModelDemo project, edit the *MainFragment.java* file and modify the code as follows:

```
package com.ebookfrenzy.viewmodeldemo.ui.main;

import android.arch.lifecycle.Observer;
import android.arch.lifecycle.ViewModelProviders;

import android.os.Bundle;

import android.support.annotation.NonNull;
import android.support.annotation.Nullable;
import android.support.v4.app.Fragment;

import android.view.LayoutInflater;
import android.view.View;
import android.view.ViewGroup;
import android.widget.Button;
import android.widget.EditText;
import android.widget.TextView;

import com.ebookfrenzy.viewmodeldemo.R;

public class MainFragment extends Fragment {

    private MainViewModel mViewModel;
    private EditText dollarText;
    private TextView resultText;
    private Button convertButton;
```

```
    @Override
    public void onActivityCreated(@Nullable Bundle savedInstanceState) {
        super.onActivityCreated(savedInstanceState);
        mViewModel = ViewModelProviders.of(this).get(MainViewModel.class);


        dollarText = getView().findViewById(R.id.dollarText);
        resultText = getView().findViewById(R.id.resultText);
        convertButton = getView().findViewById(R.id.convertButton);

        final Observer<Float> resultObserver = new Observer<Float>() {
            @Override
            public void onChanged(@Nullable final Float result) {
                resultText.setText(result.toString());
            }
        };

        mViewModel.getResult().observe(this, resultObserver);

        convertButton.setOnClickListener(new View.OnClickListener()
        {
            @Override
            public void onClick(View v) {

                if (!dollarText.getText().toString().equals("")) {
                    mViewModel.setAmount(dollarText.getText().toString());
                } else {
                    resultText.setText("No Value");
                }
            }
        });
    }
}
```

Next, edit the *MainViewModel.java* file and continue deleting code as follows (note also the conversion of the *dollarText* variable to LiveData):

```
package com.ebookfrenzy.viewmodeldemo.ui.main;

import android.arch.lifecycle.MutableLiveData;
import android.arch.lifecycle.ViewModel;

public class  MainViewModel extends ViewModel {

    private static final Float usd_to_eu_rate = 0.74F;
    public MutableLiveData<String> dollarValue = new MutableLiveData<>();
```

```
private String dollarText = "";
private public MutableLiveData<Float> result = new MutableLiveData<>();


public void setAmount(String value) {
    this.dollarText = value;
    result.setValue(Float.valueOf(dollarText)*usd_to_eu_rate);
}

public MutableLiveData<Float> getResult()
{
    return result;
}
}
```

Though we'll be adding a few additional lines of code in the course of implementing data binding, clearly data binding has significantly reduced the amount of code that needed to be written.

35.2 Enabling Data Binding

The first step in using data binding is to enable it within the Android Studio project. This involves adding a new property to the Module level *build.gradle* file, so open this file (*app -> Gradle Scripts -> build.gradle (Module: app)*) as highlighted in Figure 35-1:

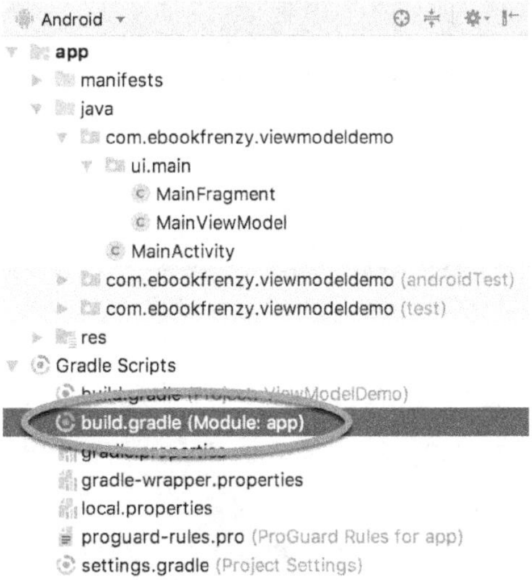

Figure 35-1

Within the *build.gradle* file, add the element shown below to enable data binding within the project:

```
apply plugin: 'com.android.application'

android {

    dataBinding {
        enabled = true
    }
```

```
compileSdkVersion 29
.
.
}
```

Once the entry has been added, a yellow bar will appear across the top of the editor screen containing a *Sync Now* link. Click this to resynchronize the project with the new build configuration settings:

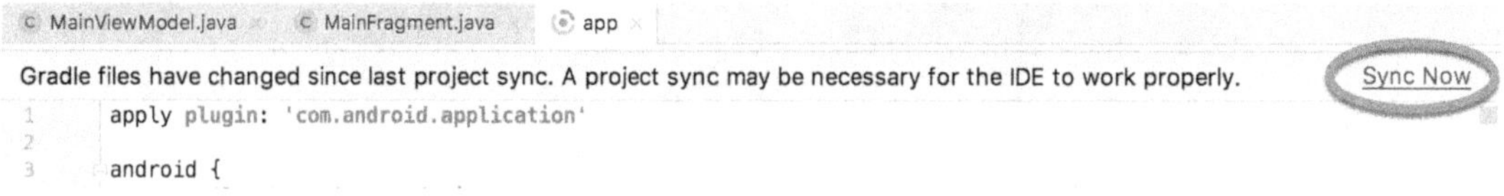

```
c MainViewModel.java     c MainFragment.java     app

Gradle files have changed since last project sync. A project sync may be necessary for the IDE to work properly.     Sync Now
1     apply plugin: 'com.android.application'
2
3     android {
```

Figure 35-2

35.3 Adding the Layout Element

As described in *"An Overview of Android Jetpack Data Binding"*, in order to be able to use data binding, the layout hierarchy must have a *layout* component as the root view. This requires that the following changes be made to the *main_fragment.xml* layout file (*app -> res -> layout -> main_fragment.xml*). Open this file in the layout editor tool, switch to Text mode and make these changes:

```
<?xml version="1.0" encoding="utf-8"?>

<layout xmlns:app="http://schemas.android.com/apk/res-auto"
    xmlns:tools="http://schemas.android.com/tools"
    xmlns:android="http://schemas.android.com/apk/res/android">

        <androidx.constraintlayout.widget.ConstraintLayout
            xmlns:android="http://schemas.android.com/apk/res/android"
            xmlns:app="http://schemas.android.com/apk/res-auto"
            xmlns:tools="http://schemas.android.com/tools"
            android:id="@+id/main"
            android:layout_width="match_parent"
            android:layout_height="match_parent"
            tools:context=".ui.main.MainFragment">

        .
        .

        </androidx.constraintlayout.widget.ConstraintLayout>
</layout>
```

Once these changes have been made, switch back to Design mode and note that the new root view, though invisible in the layout canvas, is now listed in the component tree as shown in Figure 35-3:

Figure 35-3

Build and run the app to verify that the addition of the layout element has not changed the user interface appearance in any way.

35.4 Adding the Data Element to Layout File

The next step in converting the layout file to a data binding layout file is to add the *data* element. For this example, the layout will be bound to MainViewModel so edit the *main_fragment.xml* file to add the data element as follows:

```xml
<?xml version="1.0" encoding="utf-8"?>

<layout xmlns:app="http://schemas.android.com/apk/res-auto"
    xmlns:tools="http://schemas.android.com/tools"
    xmlns:android="http://schemas.android.com/apk/res/android">

    <data>
        <variable
            name="myViewModel"
            type="com.ebookfrenzy.viewmodeldemo.ui.main.MainViewModel" />
    </data>

    <androidx.constraintlayout.widget.ConstraintLayout
        android:id="@+id/main"
        android:layout_width="match_parent"
        android:layout_height="match_parent"
        tools:context=".ui.main.MainFragment">
.
.
.
</layout>
```

Build and run the app once again to make sure that these changes take effect.

35.5 Working with the Binding Class

The next step is to modify the code within the *MainFragment.java* file to obtain a reference to the binding class instance. This is best achieved by rewriting the *onCreateView()* method:

```java
.
.
import androidx.databinding.DataBindingUtil;
import com.ebookfrenzy.viewmodeldemo.databinding.MainFragmentBinding;
```

```
.
public class MainFragment extends Fragment {

    private MainViewModel mViewModel;

    public MainFragmentBinding binding;

.

.

    @Nullable
    @Override
    public View onCreateView(@NonNull LayoutInflater inflater,
                        @Nullable ViewGroup container,
                        @Nullable Bundle savedInstanceState) {

        binding = DataBindingUtil.inflate(
                inflater, R.layout.main_fragment, container, false);

        binding.setLifecycleOwner(this);

        return binding.getRoot();
        return inflater.inflate(R.layout.main_fragment, container, false);
    }

.

.

}
```

The old code simply inflated the *main_fragment.xml* layout file (in other words created the layout containing all of the view objects) and returned a reference to the root view (the top level layout container). The Data Binding Library contains a utility class which provides a special inflation method which, in addition to constructing the UI, also initializes and returns an instance of the layout's data binding class. The new code calls this method and stores a reference to the binding class instance in a variable:

```
binding = DataBindingUtil.inflate(
                inflater, R.layout.main_fragment, container, false);
```

The binding object will only need to remain in memory for as long as the fragment is present. To ensure that the instance is destroyed when the fragment goes away, the current fragment is declared as the lifecycle owner for the binding object.

```
binding.setLifecycleOwner(this);
```

Although the code for the *onCreateView()* method has been rewritten, the basic requirement that it return the root view of the layout has not changed. Fortunately, this can be obtained via a call to the *getRoot()* method of the binding object:

```
return binding.getRoot();
```

35.6 Assigning the ViewModel Instance to the Data Binding Variable

At this point, the data binding knows that it will be binding to an instance of a class of type MainViewModel but has not yet been connected to an actual MainViewModel object. This requires the additional step of assigning the MainViewModel instance used within the app to the viewModel variable declared in the layout file. Since the reference to the ViewModel is obtained in the *onActivityCreated()* method, it makes sense to make the assignment there:

```
.
.
import static com.ebookfrenzy.viewmodeldemo.BR.myViewModel;
.
.
@Override
public void onActivityCreated(@Nullable Bundle savedInstanceState) {
    super.onActivityCreated(savedInstanceState);

    mViewModel = ViewModelProviders.of(this).get(MainViewModel.class);
    binding.setVariable(myViewModel, mViewModel);
}
```

With these changes made, the next step is to begin inserting some binding expressions into the view elements of the data binding layout file.

35.7 Adding Binding Expressions

The first binding expression will bind the resultText TextView to the result value within the model view. Edit the *main_fragment.xml* file, locate the resultText element and modify the text property so that the element reads as follows:

```
<TextView
    android:id="@+id/resultText"
    android:layout_width="wrap_content"
    android:layout_height="wrap_content"
    android:text="MainFragment"
    android:text='@{safeUnbox(myViewModel.result) == 0.0 ? "Enter value" :
String.valueOf(safeUnbox(myViewModel.result)) + " euros"}'
    app:layout_constraintBottom_toBottomOf="parent"
    app:layout_constraintEnd_toEndOf="parent"
    app:layout_constraintStart_toStartOf="parent"
    app:layout_constraintTop_toTopOf="parent" />
```

The expression begins by checking if the result value is currently zero and, if it is, displays a message instructing the user to enter a value. If the result is not zero, however, the value is converted to a string and concatenated with the word "euros" before being displayed to the user.

The result value only requires a one-way binding in that the layout does not ever need to update the value stored in the ViewModel. The *dollarValue* EditText view, on the other hand, needs to use two-way binding so that the data model can be updated with the latest value entered by the user, and to allow the current value to be redisplayed in the view in the event of a lifecycle event such as that triggered by a device rotation. The *dollarText* element should now be declared as follows:

```
<EditText
    android:id="@+id/dollarText"
    android:layout_width="wrap_content"
    android:layout_height="wrap_content"
    android:layout_marginTop="96dp"
```

```
android:ems="10"
android:importantForAutofill="no"
android:inputType="numberDecimal"
android:text="@={myViewModel.dollarValue}"
app:layout_constraintEnd_toEndOf="parent"
app:layout_constraintHorizontal_bias="0.502"
app:layout_constraintStart_toStartOf="parent"
app:layout_constraintTop_toTopOf="parent" />
```

Now that these initial binding expressions have been added a method now needs to be written to perform the conversion when the user clicks on the Button widget.

35.8 Adding the Conversion Method

When the Convert button is clicked, it is going to call a method on the ViewModel to perform the conversion calculation and place the euro value in the *result* LiveData variable. Add this method now within the *MainViewModel.java* file:

```
.
.
public class  MainViewModel extends ViewModel {

    private static final Float usd_to_eu_rate = 0.74F;
    public MutableLiveData<String> dollarValue = new MutableLiveData<>();
    public MutableLiveData<Float> result = new MutableLiveData<>();

    public void convertValue() {
        if ((dollarValue.getValue() != null) &&
                         (!dollarValue.getValue().equals(""))) {
            result.setValue(Float.valueOf(dollarValue.getValue())
                                        * usd_to_eu_rate);
        } else {
            result.setValue(0F);
        }
    }
}
```

Note that in the absence of a valid dollar value, a zero value is assigned to the *result* LiveData variable. This ensures that the binding expression assigned to the *resultText* TextView displays the "Enter value" message if no value has been entered by the user.

35.9 Adding a Listener Binding

The final step before testing the project is to add a listener binding expression to the Button element within the layout file to call the *convertValue()* method when the button is clicked. Edit the *main_fragment.xml* file in text mode once again, locate the *convertButton* element and add an onClick entry as follows:

```
<Button
    android:id="@+id/convertButton"
    android:layout_width="wrap_content"
    android:layout_height="wrap_content"
```

```
android:layout_marginTop="77dp"
android:onClick="@{() -> myViewModel.convertValue()}"
android:text="Convert"
app:layout_constraintEnd_toEndOf="parent"
app:layout_constraintStart_toStartOf="parent"
app:layout_constraintTop_toBottomOf="@+id/resultText" />
```

35.10 Testing the App

Compile and run the app and test that entering a value into the dollar field and clicking on the Convert button displays the correct result on the TextView (together with the "euros" suffix) and that the "Enter value" prompt appears if a conversion is attempted while the dollar field is empty. Also, verify that information displayed in the user interface is retained through a device rotation.

35.11 Summary

The primary goal of this chapter has been to work through the steps involved in setting up a project to use data binding and to demonstrate the use of one-way, two-way and listener binding expressions. The chapter also provided a practical example of how much code writing is saved by using data binding in conjunction with LiveData to connect the user interface views with the back-end data and logic of the app. In fact, 36 lines of code from the original app were replaced by just 12 lines when using data binding.

36. Working with Android Lifecycle-Aware Components

The earlier chapter entitled *"Understanding Android Application and Activity Lifecycles"* described the use of lifecycle methods to track lifecycle state changes within a UI controller such as an activity or fragment. One of the main problems with these methods is that they place the burden of handling lifecycle changes onto the UI controller. On the surface this might seem like the logical approach since the UI controller is, after all, the object going through the state change. The fact is, however, that the code that is typically impacted by the state change invariably resides in other classes within the app. This led to complex code appearing in the UI controller that needed to manage and manipulate other objects in response to changes in lifecycle state. Clearly this is a scenario best avoided when following the Android architectural guidelines.

A much cleaner and logical approach would be for the objects within an app to be able to observe the lifecycle state of other objects and to be responsible for taking any necessary actions in response to the changes. The class responsible for tracking a user's location, for example, could observe the lifecycle state of a UI controller and suspend location updates when the controller enters a paused state. Tracking would then be restarted when the controller enters the resumed state. This is made possible by the classes and interfaces provided by the Lifecycle package bundled with the Android architecture components.

This chapter will introduce the terminology and key components that enable lifecycle awareness to be built into Android apps.

36.1 Lifecycle Awareness

An object is said to be *lifecycle-aware* if it is able to detect and respond to changes in the lifecycle state of other objects within an app. Some Android components, LiveData being a prime example, are already lifecycle-aware. It is also possible to configure any class to be lifecycle-aware by implementing the LifecycleObserver interface within the class.

36.2 Lifecycle Owners

Lifecycle-aware components can only observe the status of objects that are *lifecycle owners*. Lifecycle owners implement the LifecycleOwner interface and are assigned a companion *Lifecycle object* which is responsible for storing the current state of the component and providing state information to *lifecycle observers*. Most standard Android Framework components (such as activity and fragment classes) are lifecycle owners. Custom classes may also be configured as lifecycle owners by using the LifecycleRegistry class and implementing the LifecycleObserver interface. For example:

```
public class SampleOwner implements LifecycleOwner {

    private LifecycleRegistry lifecycleRegistry;

    @Override
    protected void onCreate(Bundle savedInstanceState) {
        super.onCreate(savedInstanceState);
```

```
        lifecycleRegistry = new LifecycleRegistry(this);
    }


    @NonNull
    @Override
    public Lifecycle getLifecycle() {
        return lifecycleRegistry;
    }
}
```

Unless the lifecycle owner is a subclass of another lifecycle-aware component, the class will need to trigger lifecycle state changes itself via calls to methods of the LifecycleRegistry class. The *markState()* method can be used to trigger a lifecycle state change passing through the new state value:

```
public void resuming() {
    lifecycleRegistry.markState(Lifecycle.State.RESUMED);
}
```

The above call will also result in a call to the corresponding event handler. Alternatively, the LifecycleRegistry *handleLifecycleEvent()* method may be called and passed the lifecycle event to be triggered (which will also result in the lifecycle state changing). For example:

```
lifecycleRegistry.handleLifecycleEvent(Lifecycle.Event.ON_START);
```

36.3 Lifecycle Observers

In order for a lifecycle-aware component to observe the state of a lifecycle owner it must implement the LifecycleObserver interface and contain event listener handlers for any lifecycle change events it needs to observe.

```
public class SampleObserver implements LifecycleObserver {
    // Lifecycle event methods go here
}
```

An instance of this observer class is then created and added to the list of observers maintained by the Lifecycle object.

```
getLifecycle().addObserver(new SampleObserver());
```

An observer may also be removed from the Lifecycle object at any time if it no longer needs to track the lifecycle state.

Figure 36-1 illustrates the relationship between the key elements that provide lifecycle awareness:

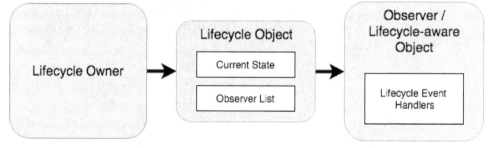

Figure 36-1

36.4 Lifecycle States and Events

When the status of a lifecycle owner changes, the assigned Lifecycle object will be updated with the new state. At any given time, a lifecycle owner will be in one of the following five states:

- Lifecycle.State.INITIALIZED

- Lifecycle.State.CREATED

- Lifecycle.State.STARTED

- Lifecycle.State.RESUMED

- Lifecycle.State.DESTROYED

As the component transitions through the different states, the Lifecycle object will trigger events on any observers that have been added to the list. The following events are available for implementation within the lifecycle observer:

- Lifecycle.Event.ON_CREATE

- Lifecycle.Event.ON_START

- Lifecycle.Event.ON_RESUME

- Lifecycle.Event.ON_PAUSE

- Lifecycle.Event.ON_STOP

- Lifecycle.Event.ON_DESTROY

- Lifecycle.Event.ON_ANY

Annotations are used within the observer class to associate methods with lifecycle events. The following code, for example, configures a method within a observer to be called in response to an ON_RESUME lifecycle event:

```
@OnLifecycleEvent(Lifecycle.Event.ON_RESUME)
public void onResume() {
    // Perform tasks in response to change to RESUMED status
}
```

The method assigned to the ON_ANY event will be called for all lifecycle events. The method for this event type is passed a reference to the lifecycle owner and an event object which can be used to find the current state and event type. The following method, for example, extracts the names of both the current state and event:

```
@OnLifecycleEvent(Lifecycle.Event.ON_ANY)
public void onAny(LifecycleOwner owner, Lifecycle.Event event) {
    String currentState = getLifecycle().getCurrentState().name();
    String eventName = event.name();
}
```

The *isAtLeast()* method of the current state object may also be used when the owner state needs to be at a certain lifecycle level:

```
if (getLifecycle().getCurrentState().isAtLeast(Lifecycle.State.STARTED)) {

}
```

The flowchart in Figure 36-2 illustrates the sequence of state changes for a lifecycle owner and the lifecycle events that will be triggered on observers between each state transition:

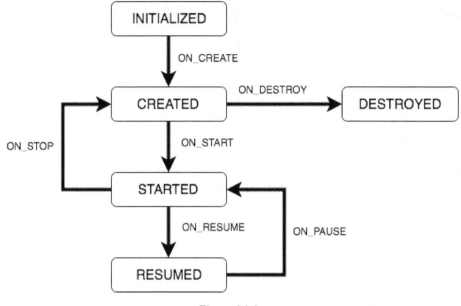

Figure 36-2

36.5 Summary

This chapter has introduced the basics of lifecycle awareness and the classes and interfaces of the Android Lifecycle package included with Android Jetpack. The package contains a number of classes and interfaces that are used to create lifecycle owners, lifecycle observers and lifecycle-aware components. A lifecycle owner has assigned to it a Lifecycle object that maintains a record of the owners state and a list of subscribed observers. When the owner's state changes, the observer is notified via lifecycle event methods so that it can respond to the change.

The next chapter will create an Android Studio project that demonstrates how to work with and create lifecycle-aware components including the creation of both lifecycle observers and owners, and the handling of lifecycle state changes and events.

37. An Android Jetpack Lifecycle Awareness Tutorial

The previous chapter provided an overview of lifecycle awareness and outlined the key classes and interfaces that make this possible within an Android app project. This chapter will build on this knowledge base by building an Android Studio project designed to highlight lifecycle awareness in action.

37.1 Creating the Example Lifecycle Project

Select the *Start a new Android Studio project* quick start option from the welcome screen and, within the resulting new project dialog, choose the Fragment + ViewModel template before clicking on the Next button.

Enter *LifecycleDemo* into the Name field and specify *com.ebookfrenzy.lifecycledemo* as the package name. Before clicking on the Finish button, change the Minimum API level setting to API 26: Android 8.0 (Oreo) and the Language menu to Java.

37.2 Creating a Lifecycle Observer

As previously discussed, activities and fragments already implement the LifecycleOwner interface and are ready to be observed by other objects. To see this in practice, the next step in this tutorial is to add a new class to the project that will be able to observe the MainFragment instance.

To add the new class, right-click on a*pp -> java -> com.ebookfrenzy.lifecycledemo* in the Project tool window and select *New -> Java Class...* from the resulting menu. In the Create New Class dialog, name the class DemoObserver and click on the OK button to create the *DemoObserver.java* file. The new file should automatically open in the editor where it will read as follows:

```
package com.ebookfrenzy.lifecycledemo;


public class DemoObserver {
}
```

Remaining in the editor, modify the class file to declare that it will be implementing the LifecycleObserver interface:

```
package com.ebookfrenzy.lifecycledemo;


import androidx.lifecycle.LifecycleObserver;


public class DemoObserver implements LifecycleObserver {


}
```

The next step is to add the lifecycle methods and assign them as the lifecycle event handlers. For the purposes of this example, all of the events will be handled, each outputting a message to the Logcat panel displaying the event type. Update the observer class as outlined in the following listing:

```
package com.ebookfrenzy.lifecycledemo;
```

```java
import android.util.Log;

import androidx.lifecycle.Lifecycle;
import androidx.lifecycle.LifecycleObserver;
import androidx.lifecycle.LifecycleOwner;
import androidx.lifecycle.OnLifecycleEvent;

public class DemoObserver implements LifecycleObserver {

    private String LOG_TAG = "DemoObserver";

    @OnLifecycleEvent(Lifecycle.Event.ON_RESUME)
    public void onResume() {
        Log.i(LOG_TAG, "onResume");
    }

    @OnLifecycleEvent(Lifecycle.Event.ON_PAUSE)
    public void onPause() {
        Log.i(LOG_TAG, "onPause");
    }

    @OnLifecycleEvent(Lifecycle.Event.ON_CREATE)
    public void onCreate() {
        Log.i(LOG_TAG, "onCreate");
    }

    @OnLifecycleEvent(Lifecycle.Event.ON_START)
    public void onStart() {
        Log.i(LOG_TAG, "onStart");
    }

    @OnLifecycleEvent(Lifecycle.Event.ON_STOP)
    public void onStop() {
        Log.i(LOG_TAG, "onStop");
    }

    @OnLifecycleEvent(Lifecycle.Event.ON_DESTROY)
    public void onDestroy() {
        Log.i(LOG_TAG, "onDestroy");
    }
}
```

So that we can track the events in relation to the current state of the fragment, an ON_ANY event handler will also be added. Since this method is passed a reference to the lifecycle owner, code can be added to obtain the current state. Remaining in the *DemoObserver.java* file, add the following method:

```
@OnLifecycleEvent(Lifecycle.Event.ON_ANY)
public void onAny(LifecycleOwner owner, Lifecycle.Event event) {
    Log.i(LOG_TAG, owner.getLifecycle().getCurrentState().name());
}
```

With the DemoObserver class completed the next step is to add it as an observer on the MainFragment class.

37.3 Adding the Observer

Observers are added to lifecycle owners via calls to the *addObserver()* method of the owner's Lifecycle object, a reference to which is obtained via a call to the *getLifecycle()* method. Edit the *MainFragment.java* class file and add code to the *onActivityCreated()* method to add the observer:

```
.
.
import com.ebookfrenzy.lifecycledemo.DemoObserver;
.
.
@Override
public void onActivityCreated(@Nullable Bundle savedInstanceState) {
    super.onActivityCreated(savedInstanceState);
    mViewModel = ViewModelProviders.of(this).get(MainViewModel.class);

    getLifecycle().addObserver(new DemoObserver());
}
```

With the observer class created and added to the lifecycle owner's Lifecycle object, the app is ready to be tested.

37.4 Testing the Observer

Since the DemoObserver class outputs diagnostic information to the Logcat console, it will be easier to see the output if a filter is configured to display only the DemoObserver messages. Using the steps outlined previously in *"Android Activity State Changes by Example"*, configure a filter for messages associated with the DemoObserver tag before running the app on a device or emulator.

On successful launch of the app, the Logcat output should indicate the following lifecycle state changes and events:

```
onCreate
CREATED
onStart
STARTED
onResume
RESUMED
```

With the app still running, perform a device rotation to trigger the destruction and recreation of the fragment, generating the following additional output:

```
onPause
STARTED
onStop
CREATED
onDestroy
```

```
DESTROYED
onCreate
CREATED
onStart
STARTED
onResume
RESUMED
```

Before moving to the next section in this chapter, take some time to compare the output from the app with the flow chart in Figure 36-2 of the previous chapter.

37.5 Creating a Lifecycle Owner

The final task in this chapter is to create a custom lifecycle owner class and demonstrate how to trigger events and modify the lifecycle state from within that class.

Add a new class by right-clicking on the *app -> java -> com.ebookfrenzy.lifecycledemo* entry in the Project tool window and selecting the *New -> Java Class...* menu option. Name the class DemoOwner in the Create Class dialog before clicking on the OK button. With the new *DemoOwner.java* file loaded into the code editor, modify it as follows:

```
package com.ebookfrenzy.lifecycledemo;

import androidx.lifecycle.Lifecycle;
import androidx.lifecycle.LifecycleOwner;
import androidx.lifecycle.LifecycleRegistry;

public class DemoOwner implements LifecycleOwner {
}
```

The class is going to need a LifecycleRegistry instance initialized with a reference to itself, and a *getLifecycle()* method configured to return the LifecycleRegistry instance. Declare a variable to store the LifecycleRegistry reference, a constructor to initialize the LifecycleRegistry instance and add the *getLifecycle()* method:

```
public class DemoOwner implements LifecycleOwner {

    private LifecycleRegistry lifecycleRegistry;

    public DemoOwner() {
        lifecycleRegistry = new LifecycleRegistry(this);
    }

    @Override
    public Lifecycle getLifecycle() {
        return lifecycleRegistry;
    }
}
```

Next, the class will need to notify the registry of lifecycle state changes. This can be achieved either by marking the state with the *markState()* method of the LifecycleRegistry object, or by triggering lifecycle events using the *handleLifecycleEvent()* method. What constitutes a state change within a custom class will depend on the purpose of the class. For this example, we will add some methods that simply trigger lifecycle events when called:

286

```
.
.
private LifecycleRegistry lifecycleRegistry;
.
.
    public void startOwner() {
        lifecycleRegistry.handleLifecycleEvent(Lifecycle.Event.ON_START);
    }

    public void stopOwner() {
        lifecycleRegistry.handleLifecycleEvent(Lifecycle.Event.ON_STOP);
    }

    @Override
    public Lifecycle getLifecycle() {
        return lifecycleRegistry;
    }
.
.
```

The final change within the DemoOwner class is to add the DemoObserver class as the observer. This call will be made within the constructor as follows:

```
public DemoOwner() {
    lifecycleRegistry = new LifecycleRegistry(this);
    getLifecycle().addObserver(new DemoObserver());
}
```

Load the *MainFragment.java* file into the code editor, locate the *onActivityCreated()* method and add code to create an instance of the DemoOwner class and to call the *startOwner()* and *stopOwner()* methods. Note also that the call to add the DemoObserver as an observer has been removed. Although a single observer can be used with multiple owners, it is removed in this case to avoid duplicated and confusing output within the Logcat tool window:

```
.
.
import com.ebookfrenzy.lifecycledemo.DemoOwner;
.
.
private DemoOwner demoOwner;
.
.
@Override
public void onActivityCreated(@Nullable Bundle savedInstanceState) {
    super.onActivityCreated(savedInstanceState);
    mViewModel = ViewModelProviders.of(this).get(MainViewModel.class);

    demoOwner = new DemoOwner();
    demoOwner.startOwner();
```

```
demoOwner.stopOwner();
getLifecycle().addObserver(new DemoObserver());
```

}

37.6 Testing the Custom Lifecycle Owner

Build and run the app one final time, refer to the Logcat tool window and confirm that the observer detected the create, start and stop lifecycle events in the following order:

```
onCreate
CREATED
onStart
STARTED
onStop
CREATED
```

Note that the "created" state changes were triggered even though code was not added to the DemoOwner class to do this manually. In fact, these were triggered automatically both when the owner instance was first created and subsequently when the ON_STOP event was handled.

37.7 Summary

This chapter has provided a practical demonstration of the steps involved in implementing lifecycle awareness within an Android app. This included the creation of a lifecycle observer and the design and implementation of a basic lifecycle owner class.

38. An Overview of the Navigation Architecture Component

Very few Android apps today consist of just a single screen. In reality, most apps comprise multiple screens through which the user navigates using screen gestures, button clicks and menu selections. Prior to the introduction of Android Jetpack, the implementation of navigation within an app was largely a manual coding process with no easy way to view and organize potentially complex navigation paths. This situation has improved considerably, however, with the introduction of the Android Navigation Architecture Component combined with support for navigation graphs in Android Studio.

38.1 Understanding Navigation

Every app has a home screen that appears after the app has launched and after any splash screen has appeared (a splash screen being the app branding screen that appears temporarily while the app loads). From this home screen, the user will typically perform tasks that will result in other screens appearing. These screens will usually take the form of other activities and fragments within the app. A messaging app, for example, might have a home screen listing current messages from which the user can navigate to either another screen to access a contact list or to a settings screen. The contacts list screen, in turn, might allow the user to navigate to other screens where new users can be added or existing contacts updated. Graphically, the app's *navigation graph* might be represented as shown in Figure 38-1:

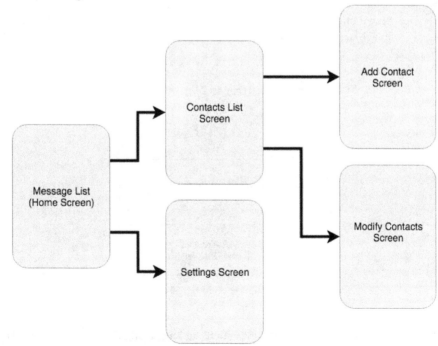

Figure 38-1

An Overview of the Navigation Architecture Component

Each screen that makes up an app, including the home screen, is referred to as a *destination* and is usually a fragment or activity. The Android navigation architecture uses a *navigation stack* to track the user's path through the destinations within the app. When the app first launches, the home screen is the first destination placed onto the stack and becomes the *current destination*. When the user navigates to another destination, that screen becomes the current destination and is *pushed* onto the stack above the home destination. As the user navigates to other screens, they are also pushed onto the stack. Figure 38-2, for example, shows the current state of the navigation stack for the hypothetical messaging app after the user has launched the app and is navigating to the "Add Contact" screen:

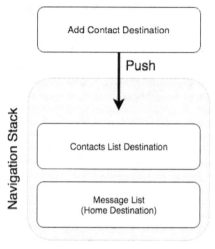

Figure 38-2

As the user navigates back through the screens using the system back button, each destination is *popped* off the stack until the home screen is once again the only destination on the stack. In Figure 38-3, the user has navigated back from the Add Contact screen, popping it off the stack and making the Contact List screen the current destination:

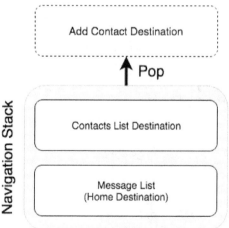

Figure 38-3

All of the work involved in navigating between destinations and managing the navigation stack is handled by a *navigation controller* which is represented by the NavController class.

Adding navigation to an Android project using the Navigation Architecture Component is a straightforward process involving a navigation host, navigation graph, navigation actions and a minimal amount of code writing to obtain a reference to, and interact with, the navigation controller instance.

38.2 Declaring a Navigation Host

A navigation host is simply a special fragment (NavHostFragment) that is embedded into the user interface layout of an activity and serves as a placeholder for the destinations through which the user will navigate. Figure 38-4, for example, shows a typical activity screen and highlights the area represented by the navigation host fragment:

Figure 38-4

A NavHostFragment can be placed into an activity layout within the Android Studio layout editor either by dragging and dropping an instance from the Containers section of the palette, or by manually editing the XML as follows:

```xml
<?xml version="1.0" encoding="utf-8"?>
<FrameLayout xmlns:android="http://schemas.android.com/apk/res/android"
    xmlns:app="http://schemas.android.com/apk/res-auto"
    xmlns:tools="http://schemas.android.com/tools"
    android:id="@+id/container"
    android:layout_width="match_parent"
    android:layout_height="match_parent"
    tools:context=".MainActivity" >

    <fragment
        android:id="@+id/demo_nav_host_fragment"
        android:name="androidx.navigation.fragment.NavHostFragment"
        android:layout_width="match_parent"
```

```
        android:layout_height="match_parent"
        app:defaultNavHost="true"
        app:navGraph="@navigation/navigation_graph" />
</FrameLayout>
```

The points of note in the above navigation host fragment element are the reference to the NavHostFragment in the *name* property, the setting of *defaultNavHost* to true and the assignment of the file containing the navigation graph to the *navGraph* property.

When the activity launches, this navigation host fragment is replaced by the home destination designated in the navigation graph. As the user navigates through the app screens, the host fragment will be replaced by the appropriate fragment for the destination.

38.3 The Navigation Graph

A navigation graph is an XML file which contains the destinations that will be included in the app navigation. In addition to these destinations, the file also contains navigation actions that define navigation between destinations, and optional arguments for passing data from one destination to another. Android Studio includes a navigation graph editor that can be used to design graphs and implement actions either visually or by manually editing the XML.

Figure 38-5, shows the Android Studio navigation graph editor in Design mode:

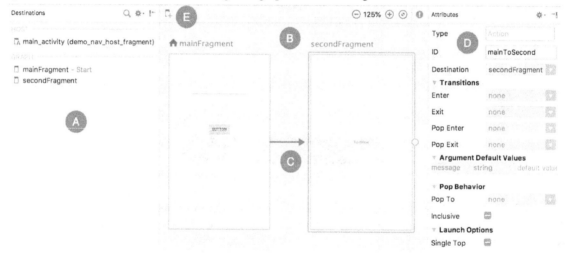

Figure 38-5

The destinations list (A) provides a list of all of the destinations currently contained within the graph. Selecting a destination from the list will locate and select the corresponding destination in the graph (particularly useful for locating specific destinations in a large graph). The navigation graph panel (B) contains a dialog for each destination showing a representation of the user interface layout. In this example, this graph contains two destinations named mainFragment and secondFragment. Arrows between destinations (C) represent navigation action connections. Actions are added by hovering the mouse pointer over the edge of the origin until a circle appears, then clicking and dragging from the circle to the destination. The Attributes panel (D) allows the properties of the currently selected destination or action connection to be viewed and modified. In the above figure, the attributes for the action are displayed. New destinations are added by clicking on the button marked E and selecting options from a menu. Options are available to add existing fragments or activities as destinations, or to create new blank fragment destinations.

The underlying XML for the navigation graph can be viewed and modified by switching the editor into Text mode. The following XML listing represents the navigation graph for the destinations and action connection shown in Figure 38-5 above:

```xml
<?xml version="1.0" encoding="utf-8"?>
<navigation xmlns:android="http://schemas.android.com/apk/res/android"
    xmlns:app="http://schemas.android.com/apk/res-auto"
    xmlns:tools="http://schemas.android.com/tools"
    android:id="@+id/navigation_graph"
    app:startDestination="@id/mainFragment">

    <fragment
        android:id="@+id/mainFragment"
        android:name="com.ebookfrenzy.navigationdemo.ui.main.MainFragment"
        android:label="main_fragment"
        tools:layout="@layout/main_fragment" >
        <action
            android:id="@+id/mainToSecond"
            app:destination="@id/secondFragment" />
    </fragment>
    <fragment
        android:id="@+id/secondFragment"
        android:name="com.ebookfrenzy.navigationdemo.SecondFragment"
        android:label="fragment_second"
        tools:layout="@layout/fragment_second" >
    </fragment>
</navigation>
```

If necessary, navigation graphs can also be split over multiple files to improve organization and promote reuse. When structured in this way, *nested graphs* are embedded into *root graphs*. To create a nested graph, simply shift-click on the destinations to be nested, right-click over the first destination and select the *Move to Nested Graph -> New Graph* menu option. The nested graph will then appear as a new node in the graph. To access the nested graph, simply double-click on the nested graph node to load the graph file into the editor.

38.4 Accessing the Navigation Controller

Navigating from one destination to another will usually take place in response to an event of some kind within an app such as a button click or menu selection. Before a navigation action can be triggered, the code must first obtain a reference to the navigation controller instance. This requires a call to the *findNavController()* method of the Navigation or NavHostFragment classes. The following code, for example, can be used to access the navigation controller of an activity. Note that for the code to work, the activity must contain a navigation host fragment:

```
NavController controller =
        Navigation.findNavController(activity, R.id.demo_nav_host_fragment);
```

In this case, the method call is passed a reference to the activity and the id of the NavHostFragment embedded in the activity's layout.

Alternatively, the navigation controller associated with any view may be identified simply by passing that view to the method:

```
Button button = getView().findViewById(R.id.button);
NavController controller = Navigation.findNavController(button);
```

The final option finds the navigation controller for a fragment by calling the *findNavController()* method of the NavHostFragment class, passing through a reference to the fragment:

```
NavController controller = NavHostFragment.findNavController(fragment);
```

38.5 Triggering a Navigation Action

Once the navigation controller has been found, a navigation action is triggered by calling the controller's *navigate()* method and passing through the resource id of the action to be performed. For example:

```
controller.navigate(R.id.goToContactsList);
```

The id of the action is defined within the Attributes panel of the navigation graph editor when an action connection is selected.

38.6 Passing Arguments

Data may be passed from one destination to another during a navigation action by making use of arguments which are declared within the navigation graph file. An argument consists of a name, type and an optional default value and may be added manually within the XML or using the Attributes panel when an action arrow or destination is selected within the graph. In Figure 38-6, for example, an integer argument named *contactsCount* has been declared with a default value of 0:

Figure 38-6

Once added, arguments are placed within the XML element of the receiving destination, for example:

```
<fragment
    android:id="@+id/secondFragment"
    android:name="com.ebookfrenzy.navigationdemo.SecondFragment"
    android:label="fragment_second"
    tools:layout="@layout/fragment_second" >
    <argument
        android:name="contactsCount"
        android:defaultValue=0
        app:type="integer" />
</fragment>
```

The Navigation Architecture Component provides two techniques for passing data between destinations. One approach involves placing the data into a Bundle object that is passed to the destination during an action where it is then unbundled and the arguments extracted.

The main drawback to this particular approach is that it is not "type safe". In other words, if the receiving destination treats an argument as being a different type than it was declared (for example treating a string as an integer) this error will not be caught by the compiler and will likely cause problems at runtime.

A better option, and the one used in this book is to make use of *safeargs*. Safeargs is a plugin for the Android Studio Gradle build system which automatically generates special classes that allow arguments to be passed in a type safe way. The safeargs approach to argument passing will be described and demonstrated in the next chapter (*"An Android Jetpack Navigation Component Tutorial"*).

38.7 Summary

The term Navigation within the context of an Android app user interface refers to the ability of a user to move back and forth between different screens. Once time consuming to implement and difficult to organize, Android Studio and the Navigation Architecture Component now make it easier to implement and manage navigation within Android app projects.

The different screens within an app are referred to as destinations and are usually represented by fragments or activities. All apps have a home destination which includes the screen displayed when the app first loads. The content area of this layout is replaced by a navigation host fragment which is swapped out for other destination fragments as the user navigates the app. The navigation path is defined by the navigation graph file consisting of destinations and the actions that connect them together with any arguments to be passed between destinations. Navigation is handled by navigation controllers which, in addition to managing the navigation stack, provide methods to initiate navigation actions from within app code.

39. An Android Jetpack Navigation Component Tutorial

The previous chapter described the Android Jetpack Navigation Component and how it integrates with the navigation graphing features of Android Studio to provide an easy way to implement navigation between the screens of an Android app. In this chapter a new Android Studio project will be created that makes use of these navigation features to implement a simple app containing multiple screens. In addition to demonstrating the use of the Android Studio navigation graph editor, the example project will also implement the passing of data between origin and destination screens using type-safe arguments.

39.1 Creating the NavigationDemo Project

Select the *Start a new Android Studio project* quick start option from the welcome screen and, within the resulting new project dialog, choose the Fragment + ViewModel template before clicking on the Next button.

Enter *NavigationDemo* into the Name field and specify *com.ebookfrenzy.navigationdemo* as the package name. Before clicking on the Finish button, change the Minimum API level setting to API 26: Android 8.0 (Oreo) and the Language menu to Java.

39.2 Adding Navigation to the Build Configuration

A new Android Studio project does not, by default, include the Navigation component libraries in the build configuration files. Before performing any other tasks, therefore, the first step is to modify the app level *build. gradle* file. Locate this file in the project tool window (*Gradle Scripts -> build.gradle (Module: app)*), double-click on it to load it into the code editor and modify the dependencies section to add the navigation libraries:

```
dependencies {
    implementation 'androidx.navigation:navigation-fragment:2.0.0'
    implementation 'androidx.navigation:navigation-ui:2.0.0'
    .
    .
    .
}
```

Note that newer versions of these libraries may have been released since this book was published. To identify and use newer versions of the libraries, add the above lines to the build file and then open the Project Structure dialog (*File -> Project Structure...*). In the Project Structure dialog, select the *Suggestions* option to display available updates. If new library versions are available, click the *Update* buttons to make sure these latest versions are used in the *build.gradle* file before clicking on the *Apply* button:

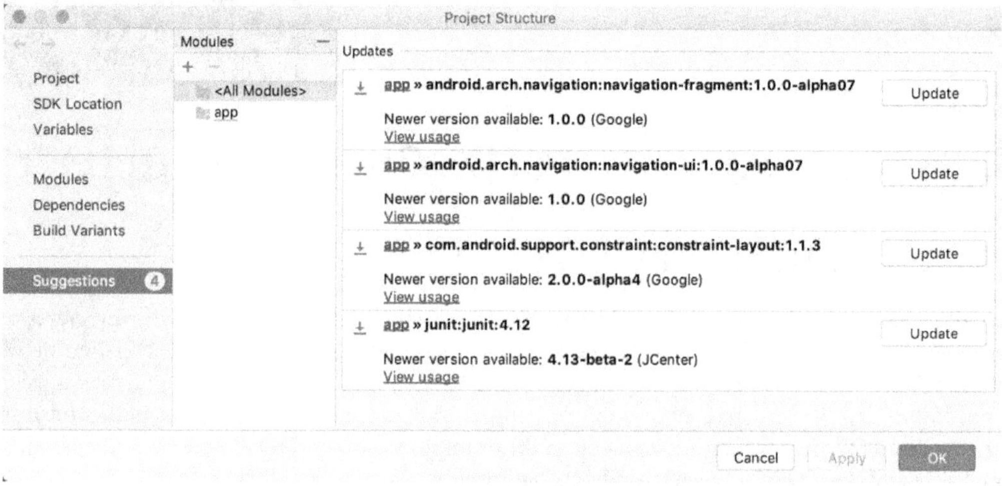

Figure 39-1

After adding the navigation dependencies to the file, click on the *Sync Now* link to resynchronize the build configuration for the project.

39.3 Creating the Navigation Graph Resource File

With the navigation libraries added to the build configuration the navigation graph resource file can now be added to the project. As outlined in *"An Overview of the Navigation Architecture Component"*, this is an XML file that contains the fragments and activities through which the user will be able to navigate, together with the actions to perform the transitions and any data to be passed between destinations.

Within the Project tool window, locate the *res* folder (*app -> res*), right-click on it and select the *New ->Android Resource File* menu option:

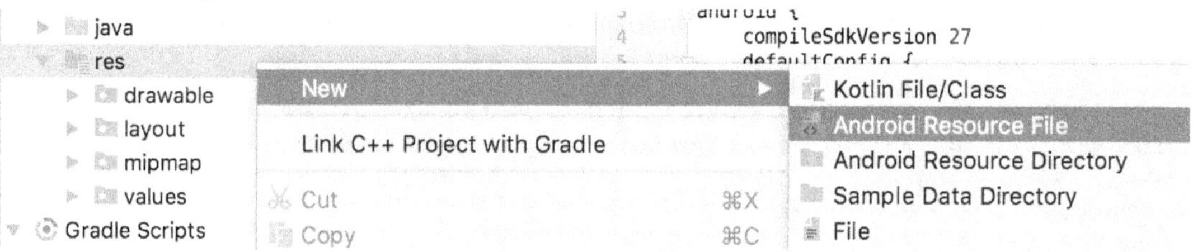

Figure 39-2

After the menu item has been selected, the New Resource File dialog will appear. In this dialog, name the file *navigation_graph* and change the Resource type menu to Navigation as outlined in Figure 39-3 before clicking on the OK button to create the file. If the Navigation type is not available, select the *File -> Settings* menu option (*Android Studio -> Preferences...* on macOS), display the *Experimental* screen and turn on the *Enable Navigation Editor* option.

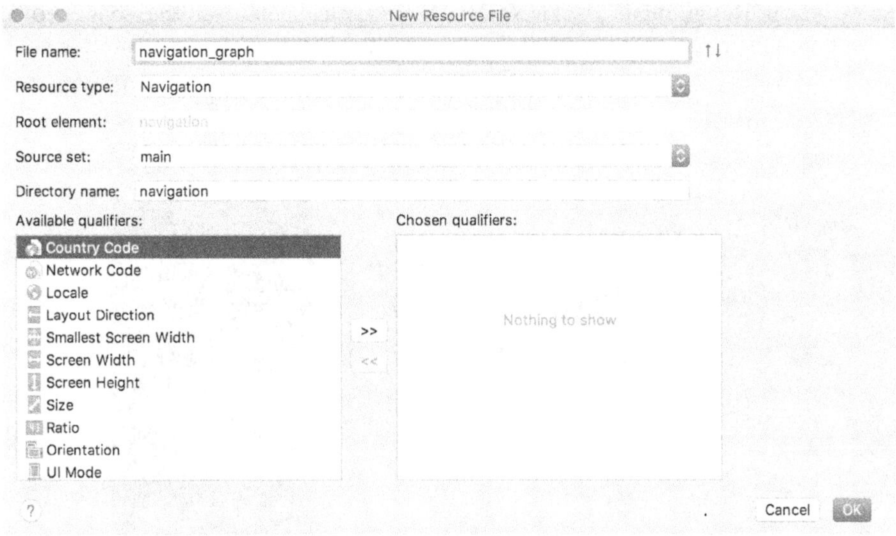

Figure 39-3

After the navigation graph resource file has been added to the project it will appear in the main panel ready for new destinations to be added. Switch the editor to Text mode and review the XML for the graph before any destinations are added:

```
<?xml version="1.0" encoding="utf-8"?>
<navigation xmlns:android="http://schemas.android.com/apk/res/android"
    xmlns:app="http://schemas.android.com/apk/res-auto"
    android:id="@+id/navigation_graph">


</navigation>
```

Switch back to Design mode within the editor and note that the Host section of the Destinations panel indicates that no navigation host fragments have been detected within the project:

Destinations   Q ✱⁃ ⊩

HOST ─────────────────────────────

No NavHostFragments found

GRAPH ────────────────────────────

Figure 39-4

Before adding any destinations to the navigation graph, the next step is to add a navigation host fragment to the project.

39.4 Declaring a Navigation Host

For this project, the navigation host fragment will be contained within the user interface layout of the main activity. This means that the destination fragments within the navigation graph will appear in the content area of the main activity currently occupied by the *main_fragment.xml* layout. Locate the main activity layout file in the Project tool window (*app -> res -> layout -> main_activity.xml*) and load it into the layout editor tool.

An Android Jetpack Navigation Component Tutorial

With the layout editor in Design mode, drag a NavHostFragment element from the Containers section of the Palette and drop it onto the container area of the activity layout as indicated by the arrow in Figure 39-5:

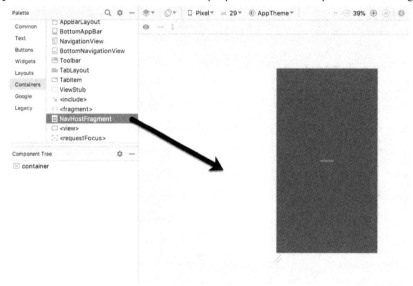

Figure 39-5

From the resulting Navigation Graphs dialog, select the *navigation_graph.xml* file created in the previous section and click on the OK button.

With the newly added NavHostFragment instance selected in the layout, use the Attributes tool window to change the ID of the element to *demo_nav_host_fragment*.

Switch the layout editor to Text mode and review the XML file. Note that the editor has correctly configured the navigation graph property to reference the *navigation_graph.xml* file and that the *defaultNavHost* property has been set to *true*:

```xml
<?xml version="1.0" encoding="utf-8"?>
<FrameLayout xmlns:android="http://schemas.android.com/apk/res/android"
    xmlns:app="http://schemas.android.com/apk/res-auto"
    xmlns:tools="http://schemas.android.com/tools"
    android:id="@+id/container"
    android:layout_width="match_parent"
    android:layout_height="match_parent"
    tools:context=".MainActivity" >

    <fragment
        android:id="@+id/demo_nav_host_fragment"
        android:name="androidx.navigation.fragment.NavHostFragment"
        android:layout_width="match_parent"
        android:layout_height="match_parent"
        app:defaultNavHost="true"
        app:navGraph="@navigation/navigation_graph" />
</FrameLayout>
```

With the NavHostFragment configured within the main activity layout file, some code needs to be removed from the *MainActivity.java* class file to prevent the activity from loading the *main_fragment.xml* file at runtime. Load this file into the code editor, locate the *onCreate()* method and remove the code responsible for displaying the main fragment:

```
@Override
protected void onCreate(Bundle savedInstanceState) {
    super.onCreate(savedInstanceState);
    setContentView(R.layout.main_activity);
    if (savedInstanceState == null) {
        getSupportFragmentManager().beginTransaction()
                .replace(R.id.container, MainFragment.newInstance())
                .commitNow();
    }
}
```

Return to the *navigation_graph.xml* file and confirm that the NavHostFragment instance has been detected (it may be necessary to close and reopen the file before the change appears):

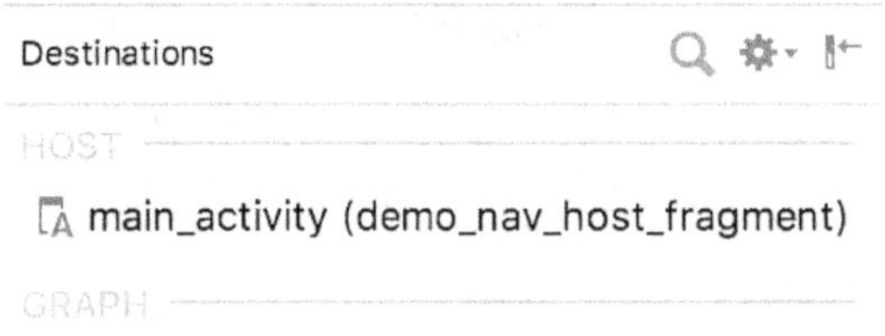

Destinations   Q   ✿▾   ⊩

HOST

⬜A main_activity (demo_nav_host_fragment)

GRAPH

Figure 39-6

39.5 Adding Navigation Destinations

Remaining in the navigation graph it is now time to add the first destination. Since the project already has a fragment for the first screen (*main_fragment.xml*) this will be the first destination to be added to the graph. Click on the new destination button highlighted in Figure 39-7 to select or create a destination:

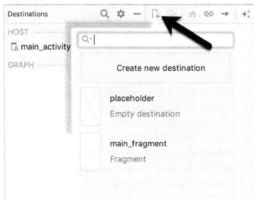

Figure 39-7

Select *main_fragment* as the destination so that it appears within the navigation graph:

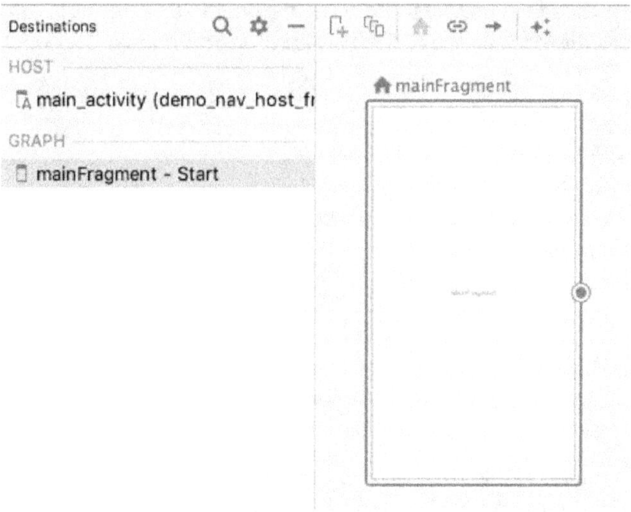

Figure 39-8

The home icon positioned above the destination node indicates that this is the *start destination*. This means that the destination will be the first displayed when the activity containing the NavHostFragment is created. To change the start destination to another destination, select that node in the graph and click on the *Set Start Destination* button located in the Attributes tool window.

Review the XML content of the navigation graph by switching the editor to Text mode:

```
<?xml version="1.0" encoding="utf-8"?>
<navigation xmlns:android="http://schemas.android.com/apk/res/android"
    xmlns:app="http://schemas.android.com/apk/res-auto"
    xmlns:tools="http://schemas.android.com/tools"
    android:id="@+id/navigation_graph"
    app:startDestination="@id/mainFragment">

    <fragment
        android:id="@+id/mainFragment"
        android:name="com.ebookfrenzy.navigationdemo.ui.main.MainFragment"
        android:label="main_fragment"
        tools:layout="@layout/main_fragment" />
</navigation>
```

Before any navigation can be performed, the graph needs at least one more destination. This time, the navigation graph editor will be used to create a new blank destination. Switch back to Design mode and click once again on the *New Destination* button, this time selecting the *Create new destination* option from the menu. In the resulting dialog, name the new fragment *SecondFragment* and the layout *fragment_second* before clicking on the Finish button. After a short delay while the project rebuilds, the new fragment will appear as another destination within the graph as shown in Figure 39-9:

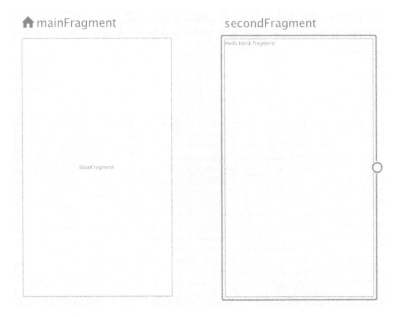

Figure 39-9

39.6 Designing the Destination Fragment Layouts

Before adding actions to navigate between destinations now is a good time to add some user interface components to the two destination fragments in the graph. Begin by double-clicking on the mainFragment destination so that the *main_fragment.xml* file loads into the layout editor. Select and delete the current TextView widget, then drag and drop Button and Plain Text EditText widgets onto the layout so that it resembles that shown in Figure 39-10 below:

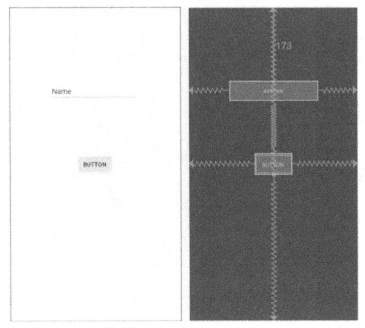

Figure 39-10

Once the views are correctly positioned, click on the *Infer constraints* button in the toolbar to add any missing constraints to the layout. Select the EditText view and use the Attributes tool window to delete the default "Name" text and to change the ID of the widget to *userText*.

Return to the *navigation_graph.xml* file and double-click on the secondFragment destination to load the *fragment_second.xml* file into the layout editor, then select and delete the default TextView instance. Within the Component Tree panel, right-click on the FrameLayout entry and select the *Convert from FrameLayout to ConstraintLayout...* menu option, accepting the default settings in the resulting conversion dialog:

Component Tree	🔧▾ |⊢
▣ FrameLayout	
Ab TextView	Convert view...
	Convert FrameLayout to ConstraintLayout
	Refactor ▶
	✂ Cut ⌘X
	🗐 Copy ⌘C
	🗐 Paste ⌘V
	Delete ⊠
	Go to XML ⌘B

Figure 39-11

Using the Attributes tool window, change the ID of the ConstraintLayout to *constraintLayout*. With the fragment's parent layout manager now converted to the more flexible ConstraintLayout, drag and drop a new TextView widget so that it is positioned in the center of the layout and click on the *Infer constraints* button to add any missing constraints. With the new TextView selected, use the Attributes panel to change the ID to *argText*.

39.7 Adding an Action to the Navigation Graph

Now that the two destinations have been added to the graph and the corresponding user interface layouts designed, the project now needs a way for the user to navigate from the main fragment to the second fragment. This will be achieved by adding an action to the graph which can then be referenced from within the app code.

To establish an action connection with the main fragment as the origin and second fragment as the destination, open the navigation graph and hover the mouse pointer over the vertical center of the right-hand edge of the mainFragment destination so that a circle appears as highlighted in Figure 39-12:

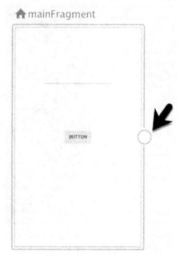

Figure 39-12

Click within the circle and drag the resulting line to the secondFragment destination:

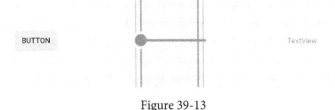

Figure 39-13

Release the line to establish the action connection between the origin and destination at which point the line will change into an arrow as shown in Figure 39-14:

Figure 39-14

An action connection may be deleted at any time by selecting it and pressing the keyboard Delete key. With the arrow selected, review the properties available within the Attributes tool window and change the ID to *mainToSecond*. This is the ID by which the action will be referenced within the code. Switch the editor to Text mode and note that the action is now included within the XML:

```xml
<?xml version="1.0" encoding="utf-8"?>
<navigation xmlns:android="http://schemas.android.com/apk/res/android"
    xmlns:app="http://schemas.android.com/apk/res-auto"
    xmlns:tools="http://schemas.android.com/tools"
    android:id="@+id/navigation_graph"
    app:startDestination="@id/mainFragment">

    <fragment
        android:id="@+id/mainFragment"
        android:name="com.ebookfrenzy.navigationdemo.ui.main.MainFragment"
        android:label="main_fragment"
        tools:layout="@layout/main_fragment" >
        <action
            android:id="@+id/mainToSecond"
            app:destination="@id/secondFragment" />
    </fragment>
    <fragment
        android:id="@+id/secondFragment"
        android:name="com.ebookfrenzy.navigationdemo.SecondFragment"
        android:label="fragment_second"
        tools:layout="@layout/fragment_second" />
```

39.8 Implement the OnFragmentInteractionListener

Before adding code to trigger the action, the MainActivity class will need to be modified to implement the OnFragmentInteractionListener interface. This is an interface that was generated within the SecondFragment class when the blank fragment was created within the navigation graph editor. In order to conform to the interface, the activity needs to implement a single method named *onFragmentInteraction()* and is used to implement communication between the fragment and the activity.

Edit the *MainActivity.java* file and modify it so that it reads as follows:

```
.
.
import android.net.Uri;
.
.
public class MainActivity extends AppCompatActivity implements SecondFragment.
OnFragmentInteractionListener {

    @Override
    protected void onCreate(Bundle savedInstanceState) {
        super.onCreate(savedInstanceState);
        setContentView(R.layout.main_activity);
    }

    @Override
    public void onFragmentInteraction(Uri uri) {
    }
}
```

39.9 Triggering the Action

Now that the action has been added to the navigation graph, the next step is to add some code within the main fragment to trigger the action when the Button widget is clicked. Locate the *MainFragment.java* file, load it into the code editor and modify the *onActivityCreated()* method to obtain a reference to the button instance and to configure an onClickListener instance to be called when the user clicks the button:

```
.
.
import android.widget.Button;
import androidx.navigation.Navigation;
.
.
public class MainFragment extends Fragment   {
.
.
    @Override
    public void onActivityCreated(@Nullable Bundle savedInstanceState) {
        super.onActivityCreated(savedInstanceState);
        mViewModel = ViewModelProviders.of(this).get(MainViewModel.class);

        Button button = getView().findViewById(R.id.button);

        button.setOnClickListener(new View.OnClickListener() {
```

```
        @Override
        public void onClick(View view) {
            Navigation.findNavController(view).navigate(
                                R.id.mainToSecond);
        }
    });
}
}
```

The above code obtains a reference to the navigation controller and calls the *navigate()* method on that instance, passing through the resource ID of the navigation action as an argument.

Compile and run the app and verify that clicking the button in the main fragment transitions to the second fragment.

As an alternative to this approach to setting up a listener, the Navigation class also includes a method named *createNavigateOnClickListener()* which provides a more efficient way of setting up a listener and navigating to a destination. The same result can be achieved, therefore, using the following single line of code to initiate the transition:

```
button.setOnClickListener(Navigation.createNavigateOnClickListener(
                                R.id.mainToSecond, null));
```

39.10 Passing Data Using Safeargs

The next objective in this tutorial is to pass the text entered into the EditText view in the main fragment to the second fragment where it will be displayed on the TextView widget. As outlined in the previous chapter, the Android Navigation component supports two approaches to passing data. This chapter will make use of type safe argument passing.

The first step in using safeargs is to add the safeargs plugin to the Gradle build configuration. Using the Project tool window, locate and edit the project level *build.gradle* file (*Gradle Scripts -> build.gradle (Project: NavigationDemo)*) to add the plugin to the dependencies as follows (once again keeping in mind that a more recent version may now be available):

```
buildscript {

    repositories {
        google()
        jcenter()
    }
    dependencies {
        classpath 'com.android.tools.build:gradle:3.2.1'
        classpath "androidx.navigation:navigation-safe-args-gradle-plugin:2.2.0-
alpha01"
    .
    .

```

Next, edit the app level *build.gradle* file (*Gradle Scripts -> build.gradle (Module: App)*) to apply the plugin as follows and resync the project when prompted to do so.

```
apply plugin: 'com.android.application'
apply plugin: 'androidx.navigation.safeargs'
```

```
.

.

android {

.

.
```

The next step is to define any arguments that will be received by the destination which, in this case, is the second fragment. Edit the navigation graph, select the secondFragment destination and locate the Arguments section within the Attributes tool window. Click on the + button (highlighted in Figure 39-15) to add a new argument to the destination:

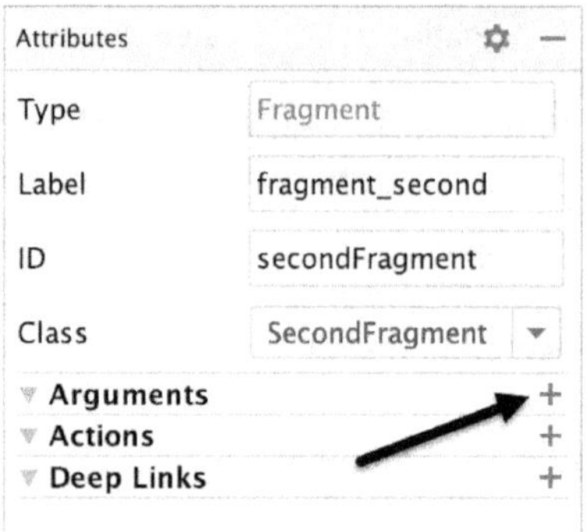

Attributes	⚙ —
Type	Fragment
Label	fragment_second
ID	secondFragment
Class	SecondFragment ▼
▼ **Arguments**	+
▼ **Actions**	+
▼ **Deep Links**	+

Figure 39-15

After the + button has been clicked, a dialog will appear into which the argument name, type and default value need to be entered. Name the argument *message*, set the type to *String* and enter *No Message* into the default value field:

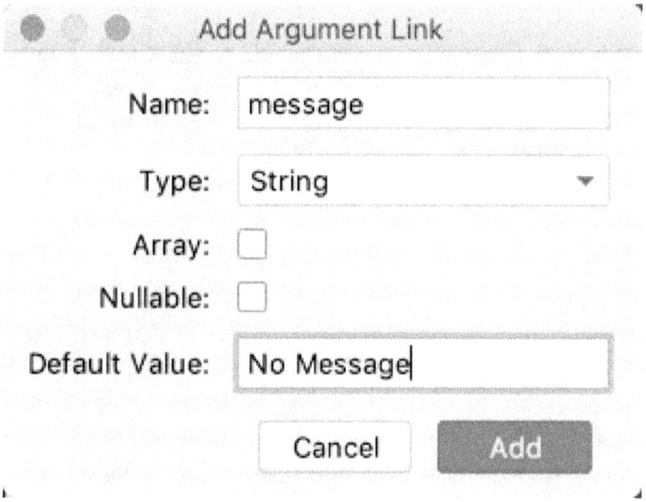

Add Argument Link

Name:	message
Type:	String ▼
Array:	☐
Nullable:	☐
Default Value:	No Message

Cancel   Add

Figure 39-16

The newly configured argument will appear in the secondFragment element of the *navigation_graph.xml* file as follows:

```
<fragment
    android:id="@+id/secondFragment"
    android:name="com.ebookfrenzy.navigationdemo.SecondFragment"
```

```
android:label="fragment_second"
tools:layout="@layout/fragment_second" >
<argument
    android:name="message"
    app:argType="string" />
    android:defaultValue="No Message"
</fragment>
```

The next step is to add code to the *Mainfragment.java* file to extract the text from the EditText view and pass it to the second fragment during the navigation action. This will involve using some special navigation classes that have been generated automatically by the safeargs plugin. Currently the navigation involves the MainFragment class, the SecondFragment class, a navigation action named *mainToSecond* and an argument named *message*.

When the project is built, the safeargs plugin will generate the following additional classes that can be used to pass and receive arguments during navigation.

- **MainFragmentDirections** - This class represents the origin for the navigation action (named using the class name of the navigation origin with "Directions" appended to the end) and provides access to the action object.

- **ActionMainToSecond** - The class that represents the action used to perform the transition (named based on the ID assigned to the action within the navigation graph file prefixed with "Action"). This class contains a setter method for each of the arguments configured on the destination. For example, since the second fragment destination contains an argument named *message*, the class includes a method named *setMessage()*. Once configured, an instance of this class is then passed to the *navigate()* method of the navigation controller to navigate to the destination.

- **SecondFragmentArgs** - The class used in the destination fragment to access the arguments passed from the origin (named using the class name of the navigation destination with "Args" appended to the end). This class includes a getter method for each of the arguments passed to the destination (i.e. *getMessage()*)

Using these classes, the *onClickListener* code within the *onActivityCreated()* method of the *MainFragment.java* file can be modified as follows to extract the current text from the EditText widget, apply it to the action and initiate the transition to the second fragment:

```
.
.
import android.widget.EditText;
.
.
button.setOnClickListener(new View.OnClickListener() {
    @Override
    public void onClick(View view) {
        EditText userText = getView().findViewById(R.id.userText);

        MainFragmentDirections.MainToSecond action =
                            MainFragmentDirections.mainToSecond();

        action.setMessage(userText.getText().toString());
        Navigation.findNavController(view).navigate(action);
    }
});
```

The above code obtains a reference to the action object, sets the message argument string using the *setMessage()* method and then calls the *navigate()* method of the navigation controller, passing through the action object.

All that remains is to modify the *SecondFragment.java* class file to receive the argument after the navigation has been performed and display it on the TextView widget. For this example, the code to achieve these tasks will be added using an *onStart()* lifecycle method. Edit the *SecondFragment.java* file and add this method so that it reads as follows:

```
.
.
import android.widget.TextView;
.
.
@Override
public void onStart() {
    super.onStart();

    TextView argText = getView().findViewById(R.id.argText);
    SecondFragmentArgs args = SecondFragmentArgs.fromBundle(getArguments());
    String message = args.getMessage();
    argText.setText(message);
}
```

The code in the above method begins by obtaining a reference to the TextView widget. Next, the *fromBundle()* method of the SecondFragmentArgs class is called to extract the SecondFragmentArgs object received from the origin. Since the argument in this example was named *message* in the *navigation_graph.xml* file, the corresponding *getMessage()* method is called on the args object to obtain the string value. This string is then displayed on the TextView widget.

Compile and run the app and enter some text before clicking on the Button widget. When the second fragment destination appears, the TextView should now display the text entered in the main fragment indicating that the data was successfully passed between navigation destinations.

39.11 Summary

This chapter has provided a practical example of how to implement Android app navigation using the Navigation Architecture Component together with the Android Studio navigation graph editor. Topics covered included the creation of a navigation graph containing both existing and new destination fragments, the embedding of a navigation host fragment within an activity layout, writing code to trigger navigation events and the passing of arguments between destinations using the Gradle safeargs plugin.

40. Creating and Managing Overflow Menus on Android

An area of user interface design that has not yet been covered in this book relates to the concept of menus within an Android application. Menus provide a mechanism for offering additional choices to the user beyond the view components that are present in the user interface layout. While there are a number of different menu systems available to the Android application developer, this chapter will focus on the more commonly used Overflow menu. The chapter will cover the creation of menus both manually via XML and visually using the Android Studio Layout Editor tool.

40.1 The Overflow Menu

The overflow menu (also referred to as the options menu) is a menu that is accessible to the user from the device display and allows the developer to include other application options beyond those included in the user interface of the application. The location of the overflow menu is dependent upon the version of Android that is running on the device. With the Android 4.0 release and later, the overflow menu button is located in the top right-hand corner (Figure 40-1) in the action toolbar represented by the stack of three squares:

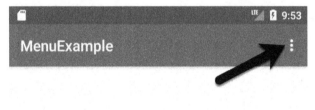

Figure 40-1

40.2 Creating an Overflow Menu

The items in a menu can be declared within an XML file, which is then inflated and displayed to the user on demand. This involves the use of the <menu> element, containing an <item> sub-element for each menu item. The following XML, for example, defines a menu consisting of two menu items relating to color choices:

```xml
<menu xmlns:android="http://schemas.android.com/apk/res/android"
    xmlns:app="http://schemas.android.com/apk/res-auto"
    xmlns:tools="http://schemas.android.com/tools"
    tools:context=".MainActivity" >
    <item
        android:id="@+id/menu_red"
        android:orderInCategory="1"
        app:showAsAction="never"
        android:title="@string/red_string"/>

        <item
            android:id="@+id/menu_green"
```

```
            android:orderInCategory="2"
            app:showAsAction="never"
            android:title="@string/green_string"/>
</menu>
```

In the above XML, the *android:orderInCategory* property dictates the order in which the menu items will appear within the menu when it is displayed. The *app:showAsAction* property, on the other hand, controls the conditions under which the corresponding item appears as an item within the action bar itself. If set to *if Room*, for example, the item will appear in the action bar if there is enough room. Figure 40-2 shows the effect of setting this property to *ifRoom* for both menu items:

Figure 40-2

This property should be used sparingly to avoid over cluttering the action bar.

By default, a menu XML file is created by Android Studio when a new Android application project is created. This file is located in the *app -> res -> menu* project folder and contains a single menu item entitled "Settings":

```
<menu xmlns:android="http://schemas.android.com/apk/res/android"
    xmlns:app="http://schemas.android.com/apk/res-auto"
    xmlns:tools="http://schemas.android.com/tools"
    tools:context=".MainActivity">
        <item android:id="@+id/action_settings"
            android:title="@string/action_settings"
            android:orderInCategory="100"
            app:showAsAction="never" />
</menu>
```

This menu is already configured to be displayed when the user selects the overflow menu on the user interface when the app is running, so simply modify this one to meet your needs.

40.3 Displaying an Overflow Menu

An overflow menu is created by overriding the *onCreateOptionsMenu()* method of the corresponding activity and then inflating the menu's XML file. For example, the following code creates the menu contained within a menu XML file named *menu_main*:

```
@Override
public boolean onCreateOptionsMenu(Menu menu) {
        getMenuInflater().inflate(R.menu.menu_main, menu);
        return true;
}
```

As with the menu XML file, Android Studio will already have overridden this method in the main activity of a newly created Android application project. In the event that an overflow menu is not required in your activity, either remove or comment out this method.

40.4 Responding to Menu Item Selections

Once a menu has been implemented, the question arises as to how the application receives notification when the user makes menu item selections. All that an activity needs to do to receive menu selection notifications is to override the *onOptionsItemSelected()* method. Passed as an argument to this method is a reference to the selected menu item. The *getItemId()* method may then be called on the item to obtain the ID which may, in turn, be used to identify which item was selected. For example:

```
@Override
public boolean onOptionsItemSelected(MenuItem item) {

        switch (item.getItemId()) {
         case R.id.menu_red:
             // Red item was selected
             return true;
         case R.id.menu_green:
             // Green item was selected
             return true;
         default:
             return super.onOptionsItemSelected(item);
        }

}
```

40.5 Creating Checkable Item Groups

In addition to configuring independent menu items, it is also possible to create groups of menu items. This is of particular use when creating checkable menu items whereby only one out of a number of choices can be selected at any one time. Menu items can be assigned to a group by wrapping them in the *<group>* tag. The group is declared as checkable using the *android:checkableBehavior* property, setting the value to either *single, all* or *none*. The following XML declares that two menu items make up a group wherein only one item may be selected at any given time:

```
<menu xmlns:android="http://schemas.android.com/apk/res/android"
    xmlns:app="http://schemas.android.com/apk/res-auto">
    <group android:checkableBehavior="single">
        <item
            android:id="@+id/menu_red"
            android:title="@string/red_string"/>
        <item
            android:id="@+id/menu_green"
            android:title="@string/green_string"/>
    </group>
</menu>
```

When a menu group is configured to be checkable, a small circle appears next to the item in the menu as illustrated in Figure 40-3. It is important to be aware that the setting and unsetting of this indicator does not take place automatically. It is, therefore, the responsibility of the application to check and uncheck the menu item.

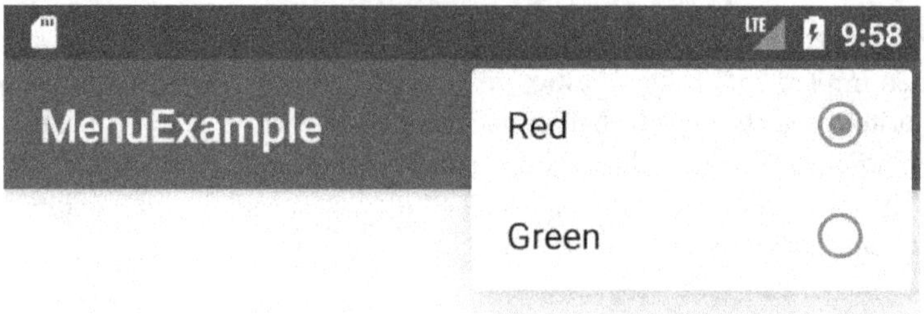

Figure 40-3

Continuing the color example used previously in this chapter, this would be implemented as follows:

```
@Override
public boolean onOptionsItemSelected(MenuItem item) {

    switch (item.getItemId()) {
        case R.id.menu_red:
            if (item.isChecked()) item.setChecked(false);
            else item.setChecked(true);
            return true;
        case R.id.menu_green:
            if (item.isChecked()) item.setChecked(false);
            else item.setChecked(true);
            return true;
        default:
            return super.onOptionsItemSelected(item);
    }
}
```

40.6 Menus and the Android Studio Menu Editor

Android Studio allows menus to be designed visually simply by loading the menu resource file into the Menu Editor tool, dragging and dropping menu elements from a palette and setting properties. This considerably eases the menu design process, though it is important to be aware that it is still necessary to write the code in the *onOptionsItemSelected()* method to implement the menu behavior.

To visually design a menu, locate the menu resource file and double-click on it to load it into the Menu Editor tool. Figure 40-4, for example, shows the default menu resource file for a basic activity loaded into the Menu Editor:

Figure 40-4

The palette (A) contains items that can be added to the menu contained in the design area (C). The Component Tree (B) is a useful tool for identifying the hierarchical structure of the menu. The Attributes panel (D) contains a subset of common attributes for the currently selected item. The view all attributes link (E) may be used to access the full list of attributes.

New elements may be added to the menu by dragging and dropping objects either onto the layout canvas or the Component Tree. When working with menus in the Layout Editor tool, it will sometimes be easier to drop the items onto the Component Tree since this provides greater control over where the item is placed within the tree. This is of particular use, for example, when adding items to a group.

Although the Menu Editor provides a visual approach to constructing menus, the underlying menu is still stored in XML format which may be viewed and edited manually by switching from Design to Text mode using the tab marked F in the above figure.

40.7 Creating the Example Project

To see the overflow menu in action, select the *Start a new Android Studio project* quick start option from the welcome screen and, within the resulting new project dialog, choose the Basic Activity template before clicking on the Next button.

Enter *MenuExample* into the Name field and specify *com.ebookfrenzy.menuexample* as the package name. Before clicking on the Finish button, change the Minimum API level setting to API 26: Android 8.0 (Oreo) and the Language menu to Java.

When the project has been created, navigate to the *app -> res -> layout* folder in the Project tool window and double-click on the *content_main.xml* file to load it into the Android Studio Menu Editor tool. Switch the tool to Design mode, select the ConstraintLayout from the Component Tree panel and enter *layoutView* into the ID field of the Attributes panel.

40.8 Designing the Menu

Within the Project tool window, locate the project's *app -> res -> menu -> menu_main.xml* file and double-click on it to load it into the Layout Editor tool. Switch to Design mode if necessary and select and delete the default Settings menu item added by Android Studio so that the menu currently has no items.

Creating and Managing Overflow Menus on Android

From the palette, click and drag a menu *group* object onto the title bar of the layout canvas as highlighted in Figure 40-5:

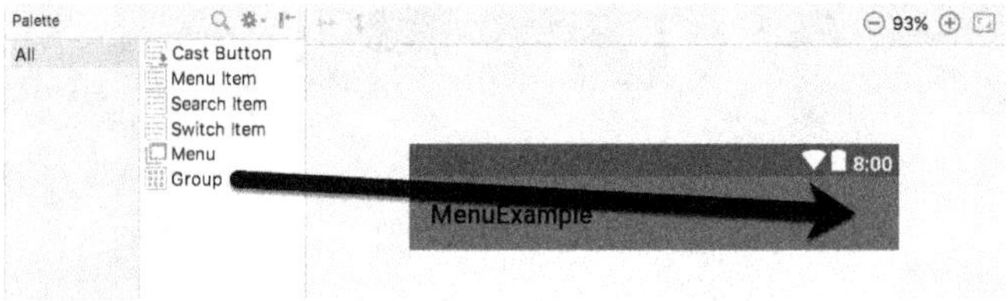

Figure 40-5

Although the group item has been added, it will be invisible within the layout. To verify the presence of the element, refer to the Component Tree panel where the group will be listed as a child of the menu:

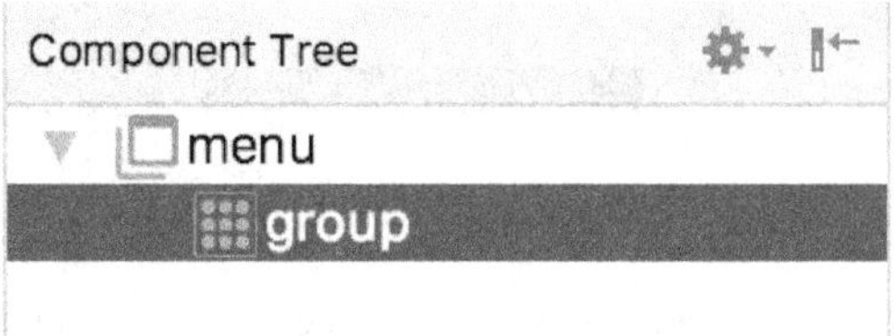

Component Tree

▼ menu
  ⠿ group

Figure 40-6

Select the *group* entry in the Component Tree and, referring to the Attributes panel, set the *checkableBehavior* property to *single* so that only one group menu item can be selected at any one time:

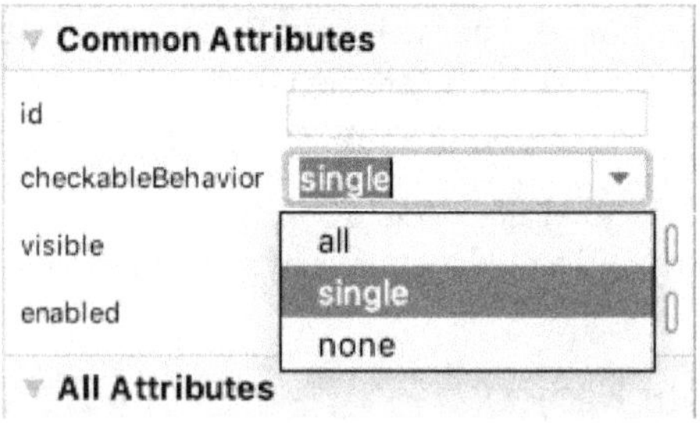

▼ **Common Attributes**

id	
checkableBehavior	single ▼
visible	all
enabled	single
	none

▼ **All Attributes**

Figure 40-7

Next, drag four *Menu Item* elements from the palette and drop them onto the *group* element in the Component Tree. Select the first item and use the Attributes panel to change the title to "Red" and the ID to *menu_red*:

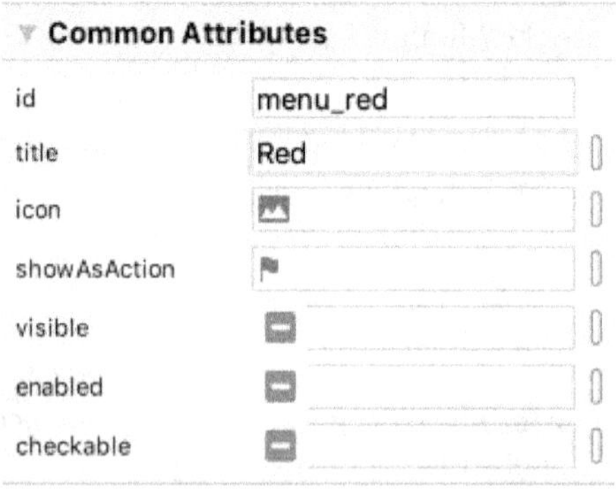

▼ **Common Attributes**

id	menu_red
title	Red
icon	
showAsAction	
visible	
enabled	
checkable	

Figure 40-8

Repeat these steps for the remaining three menu items setting the titles to "Green", "Yellow" and "Blue" with matching IDs of *menu_green, menu_yellow* and *menu_blue*. Use the warning buttons to the right of the menu items in the Component Tree panel to extract the strings to resources:

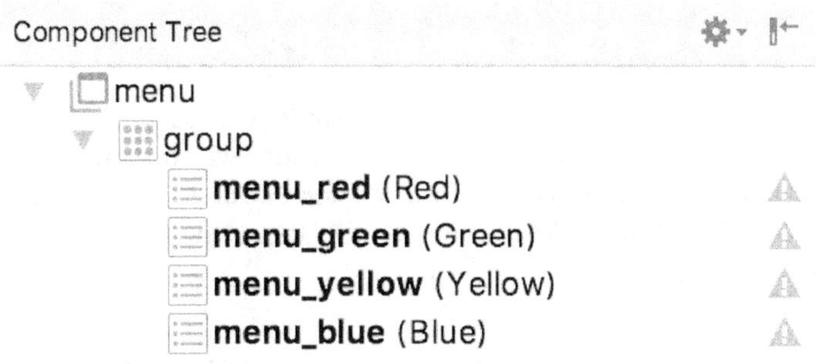

Figure 40-9

On completion of these steps, the menu layout should match that shown in Figure 40-10 below:

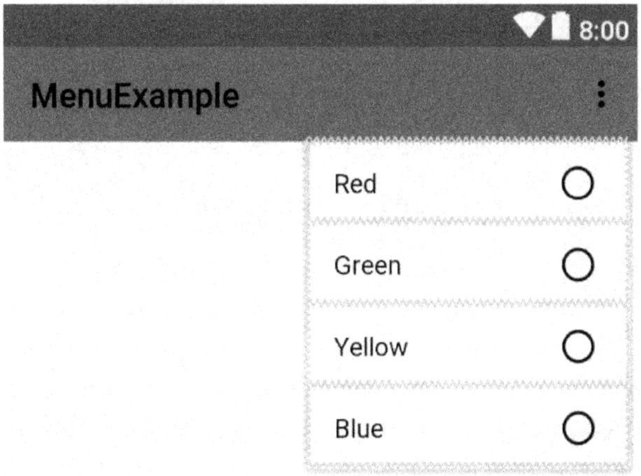

Figure 40-10

Switch the Layout Editor tool to Text mode and review the XML representation of the menu which should match the following listing:

```xml
<menu xmlns:android="http://schemas.android.com/apk/res/android"
    xmlns:app="http://schemas.android.com/apk/res-auto"
    xmlns:tools="http://schemas.android.com/tools"
    tools:context="com.ebookfrenzy.menuexample.MainActivity">

    <group android:checkableBehavior="single">
        <item android:title="@string/red_string"
            android:id="@+id/menu_red" />
        <item android:title="@string/green_string"
            android:id="@+id/menu_green" />
        <item android:title="@string/yellow_string"
            android:id="@+id/menu_yellow" />
```

```
        <item android:title="@string/blue_string"
            android:id="@+id/menu_blue" />
    </group>
</menu>
```

40.9 Modifying the onOptionsItemSelected() Method

When items are selected from the menu, the overridden *onOptionsItemsSelected()* method of the application's activity will be called. The role of this method will be to identify which item was selected and change the background color of the layout view to the corresponding color. Locate and double-click on the *app -> java -> com.ebookfrenzy.menuexample -> MainActivity* file and modify the method as follows:

```java
package com.ebookfrenzy.menuexample;

import com.google.android.material.floatingactionbutton.FloatingActionButton;
import com.google.android.material.snackbar.Snackbar;

import androidx.appcompat.app.AppCompatActivity;
import androidx.appcompat.widget.Toolbar;

import android.view.View;
import android.view.Menu;
import android.view.MenuItem;
import androidx.constraintlayout.widget.ConstraintLayout;

public class MainActivity extends AppCompatActivity {
    .
    .
    @Override
    public boolean onOptionsItemSelected(MenuItem item) {

        ConstraintLayout mainLayout =
                findViewById(R.id.layoutView);

        switch (item.getItemId()) {
            case R.id.menu_red:
                if (item.isChecked()) item.setChecked(false);
                else item.setChecked(true);
                mainLayout.setBackgroundColor(android.graphics.Color.RED);
                return true;
            case R.id.menu_green:
                if (item.isChecked()) item.setChecked(false);
                else item.setChecked(true);
                mainLayout.setBackgroundColor(android.graphics.Color.GREEN);
                return true;
            case R.id.menu_yellow:
                if (item.isChecked()) item.setChecked(false);
                else item.setChecked(true);
```

```
            mainLayout.setBackgroundColor(android.graphics.Color.YELLOW);
            return true;
        case R.id.menu_blue:
            if (item.isChecked()) item.setChecked(false);
            else item.setChecked(true);
            mainLayout.setBackgroundColor(android.graphics.Color.BLUE);
            return true;
        default:
            return super.onOptionsItemSelected(item);
    }
}
.
.
.
}
```

40.10 Testing the Application

Build and run the application on either an emulator or physical Android device. Using the overflow menu, select menu items and verify that the layout background color changes appropriately. Note that the currently selected color is displayed as the checked item in the menu.

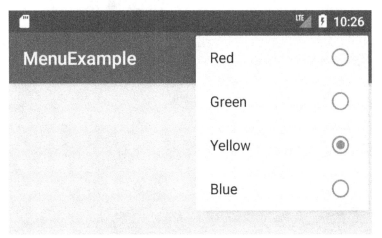

Figure 40-11

40.11 Summary

The Android overflow menu is accessed from the far right of the actions toolbar at the top of the display of the running app. This menu provides a location for applications to provide additional options to the user.

The structure of the menu is most easily defined within an XML file and the application activity receives notifications of menu item selections by overriding and implementing the *onOptionsItemSelected()* method.

41. Animating User Interfaces with the Android Transitions Framework

The Android Transitions framework was introduced as part of the Android 4.4 KitKat release and is designed to make it easy for you, as an Android developer, to add animation effects to the views that make up the screens of your applications. As will be outlined in both this and subsequent chapters, animated effects such as making the views in a user interface gently fade in and out of sight and glide smoothly to new positions on the screen can be implemented with just a few simple lines of code when using the Transitions framework in Android Studio.

41.1 Introducing Android Transitions and Scenes

Transitions allow the changes made to the layout and appearance of the views in a user interface to be animated during application runtime. While there are a number of different ways to implement Transitions from within application code, perhaps the most powerful mechanism involves the use of *Scenes*. A scene represents either the entire layout of a user interface screen, or a subset of the layout (represented by a ViewGroup).

To implement transitions using this approach, scenes are defined that reflect the two different user interface states (these can be thought of as the "before" and "after" scenes). One scene, for example, might consist of EditText, Button and TextView views positioned near the top of the screen. The second scene might remove the Button view and move the remaining EditText and TextView objects to the bottom of the screen to make room for the introduction of a MapView instance. Using the transition framework, the changes between these two scenes can be animated so that the Button fades from view, the EditText and TextView slide to the new locations and the map gently fades into view.

Scenes can be created in code from ViewGroups, or implemented in layout resource files that are loaded into Scene instances at application runtime.

Transitions can also be implemented dynamically from within application code. Using this approach, scenes are created by referencing collections of user interface views in the form of ViewGroups with transitions then being performed on those elements using the TransitionManager class, which provides a range of methods for triggering and managing the transitions between scenes.

Perhaps the simplest form of transition involves the use of the *beginDelayedTransition()* method of the TransitionManager class. When called and passed the ViewGroup representing a scene, any subsequent changes to any views within that scene (such as moving, resizing, adding or deleting views) will be animated by the Transition framework.

The actual animation is handled by the Transition framework via instances of the *Transition* class. Transition instances are responsible for detecting changes to the size, position and visibility of the views within a scene and animating those changes accordingly.

By default, transitions will be animated using a set of criteria defined by the AutoTransition class. Custom transitions can be created either via settings in XML transition files or directly within code. Multiple transitions can be combined together in a TransitionSet and configured to be performed either in parallel or sequentially.

41.2 Using Interpolators with Transitions

The Transitions framework makes extensive use of the Android Animation framework to implement animation effects. This fact is largely incidental when using transitions since most of this work happens behind the scenes, thereby shielding the developer from some of the complexities of the Animation framework. One area where some knowledge of the Animation framework is beneficial when using Transitions, however, involves the concept of interpolators.

Interpolators are a feature of the Android Animation framework that allow animations to be modified in a number of pre-defined ways. At present the Animation framework provides the following interpolators, all of which are available for use in customizing transitions:

- **AccelerateDecelerateInterpolator** – By default, animation is performed at a constant rate. The AccelerateDecelerateInterpolator can be used to cause the animation to begin slowly and then speed up in the middle before slowing down towards the end of the sequence.

- **AccelerateInterpolator** – As the name suggests, the AccelerateInterpolator begins the animation slowly and accelerates at a specified rate with no deceleration at the end.

- **AnticipateInterpolator** – The AnticipateInterpolator provides an effect similar to that of a sling shot. The animated view moves in the opposite direction to the configured animation for a short distance before being flung forward in the correct direction. The amount of backward force can be controlled through the specification of a tension value.

- **AnticipateOvershootInterpolator** – Combines the effect provided by the AnticipateInterpolator with the animated object overshooting and then returning to the destination position on the screen.

- **BounceInterpolator** – Causes the animated view to bounce on arrival at its destination position.

- **CycleInterpolator** – Configures the animation to be repeated a specified number of times.

- **DecelerateInterpolator** – The DecelerateInterpolator causes the animation to begin quickly and then decelerate by a specified factor as it nears the end.

- **LinearInterpolator** – Used to specify that the animation is to be performed at a constant rate.

- **OvershootInterpolator** – Causes the animated view to overshoot the specified destination position before returning. The overshoot can be configured by specifying a tension value.

As will be demonstrated in this and later chapters, interpolators can be specified both in code and XML files.

41.3 Working with Scene Transitions

Scenes can be represented by the content of an Android Studio XML layout file. The following XML, for example, could be used to represent a scene consisting of three button views within a RelativeLayout parent:

```xml
<?xml version="1.0" encoding="utf-8"?>
<RelativeLayout xmlns:android="http://schemas.android.com/apk/res/android"
    android:id="@+id/RelativeLayout1"
    android:layout_width="match_parent"
    android:layout_height="match_parent"
    android:orientation="vertical" >

    <Button
        android:id="@+id/button1"
```

```
        android:layout_width="wrap_content"
        android:layout_height="wrap_content"
        android:layout_alignParentLeft="true"
        android:layout_alignParentTop="true"
        android:onClick="goToScene2"
        android:text="@string/one_string" />

    <Button
        android:id="@+id/button2"
        android:layout_width="wrap_content"
        android:layout_height="wrap_content"
        android:layout_alignParentRight="true"
        android:layout_alignParentTop="true"
        android:onClick="goToScene1"
        android:text="@string/two_string" />

    <Button
        android:id="@+id/button3"
        android:layout_width="wrap_content"
        android:layout_height="wrap_content"
        android:layout_centerHorizontal="true"
        android:layout_centerVertical="true"
        android:text="@string/three_string" />

</RelativeLayout>
```

Assuming that the above layout resides in a file named *scene1_layout.xml* located in the *res/layout* folder of the project, the layout can be loaded into a scene using the *getSceneForLayout()* method of the Scene class. For example:

```
Scene scene1 = Scene.getSceneForLayout(rootContainer,
                R.layout.scene1_layout, this);
```

Note that the method call requires a reference to the root container. This is the view at the top of the view hierarchy in which the scene is to be displayed.

To display a scene to the user without any transition animation, the *enter()* method is called on the scene instance:

```
scene1.enter();
```

Transitions between two scenes using the default AutoTransition class can be triggered using the *go()* method of the TransitionManager class:

```
TransitionManager.go(scene2);
```

Scene instances can be created easily in code by bundling the view elements into one or more ViewGroups and then creating a scene from those groups. For example:

```
Scene scene1 = Scene(viewGroup1);
Scene scene2 = Scene(viewGroup2, viewGroup3);
```

41.4 Custom Transitions and TransitionSets in Code

The examples outlined so far in this chapter have used the default transition settings in which resizing, fading and motion are animated using pre-configured behavior. These can be modified by creating custom transitions which are then referenced during the transition process. Animations are categorized as either *change bounds* (relating to changes in the position and size of a view) and *fade* (relating to the visibility or otherwise of a view).

A single Transition can be created as follows:

```
Transition myChangeBounds = new ChangeBounds();
```

This new transition can then be used when performing a transition:

```
TransitionManager.go(scene2, myChangeBounds);
```

Multiple transitions may be bundled together into a TransitionSet instance. The following code, for example, creates a new TransitionSet object consisting of both change bounds and fade transition effects:

```
TransitionSet myTransition = new TransitionSet();
myTransition.addTransition(new ChangeBounds());
myTransition.addTransition(new Fade());
```

Transitions can be configured to target specific views (referenced by view ID). For example, the following code will configure the previous fade transition to target only the view with an ID that matches *myButton1*:

```
TransitionSet myTransition = new TransitionSet();
myTransition.addTransition(new ChangeBounds());
Transition fade = new Fade();
fade.addTarget(R.id.myButton1);
myTransition.addTransition(fade);
```

Additional aspects of the transition may also be customized, such as the duration of the animation. The following code specifies the duration over which the animation is to be performed:

```
Transition changeBounds = new ChangeBounds();
changeBounds.setDuration(2000);
```

As with Transition instances, once a TransitionSet instance has been created, it can be used in a transition via the TransitionManager class. For example:

```
TransitionManager.go(scene1, myTransition);
```

41.5 Custom Transitions and TransitionSets in XML

While custom transitions can be implemented in code, it is often easier to do so via XML transition files using the <fade> and <changeBounds> tags together with some additional options. The following XML includes a single changeBounds transition:

```
<?xml version="1.0" encoding="utf-8"?>
<changeBounds/>
```

As with the code based approach to working with transitions, each transition entry in a resource file may be customized. The XML below, for example, configures a duration for a change bounds transition:

```
<changeBounds android:duration="5000" >
```

Multiple transitions may be bundled together using the <transitionSet> element:

```
<?xml version="1.0" encoding="utf-8"?>
<transitionSet
  xmlns:android="http://schemas.android.com/apk/res/android" >
```

```
<fade
  android:duration="2000"
  android:fadingMode="fade_out" />

<changeBounds
  android:duration="5000" >

  <targets>
    <target android:targetId="@id/button2" />
  </targets>

</changeBounds>

<fade
  android:duration="2000"
  android:fadingMode="fade_in" />
</transitionSet>
```

Transitions contained within an XML resource file should be stored in the *res/transition* folder of the project in which they are being used and must be inflated before being referenced in the code of an application. The following code, for example, inflates the transition resources contained within a file named *transition.xml* and assigns the results to a reference named *myTransition*:

```
Transition myTransition = TransitionInflater.from(this)
    .inflateTransition(R.transition.transition);
```

Once inflated, the new transition can be referenced in the usual way:

```
TransitionManager.go(scene1, myTransition);
```

By default, transition effects within a TransitionSet are performed in parallel. To instruct the Transition framework to perform the animations sequentially, add the appropriate *android:transitionOrdering* property to the transitionSet element of the resource file:

```
<?xml version="1.0" encoding="utf-8"?>

<transitionSet
  xmlns:android="http://schemas.android.com/apk/res/android"
  android:transitionOrdering="sequential">

  <fade
    android:duration="2000"
    android:fadingMode="fade_out" />

  <changeBounds
    android:duration="5000" >
  </changeBounds>
</transitionSet>
```

Change the value from "sequential" to "together" to indicate that the animation sequences are to be performed in parallel.

41.6 Working with Interpolators

As previously discussed, interpolators can be used to modify the behavior of a transition in a variety of ways and may be specified either in code or via the settings within a transition XML resource file.

When working in code, new interpolator instances can be created by calling the constructor method of the required interpolator class and, where appropriate, passing through values to further modify the interpolator behavior:

· AccelerateDecelerateInterpolator()

· AccelerateInterpolator(float factor)

· AnticipateInterpolator(float tension)

· AnticipateOvershootInterpolator(float tension)

· BounceInterpolator()

· CycleInterpolator(float cycles)

· DecelerateInterpolator(float factor)

· LinearInterpolator()

· OvershootInterpolator(float tension)

Once created, an interpolator instance can be attached to a transition using the *setInterpolator()* method of the Transition class. The following code, for example, adds a bounce interpolator to a change bounds transition:

```
Transition changeBounds = new ChangeBounds();
changeBounds.setInterpolator(new BounceInterpolator());
```

Similarly, the following code adds an accelerate interpolator to the same transition, specifying an acceleration factor of 1.2:

```
changeBounds.setInterpolator(new AccelerateInterpolator(1.2f));
```

In the case of XML based transition resources, a default interpolator is declared using the following syntax:

```
android:interpolator="@android:anim/<interpolator_element>"
```

In the above syntax, *<interpolator_element>* must be replaced by the resource ID of the corresponding interpolator selected from the following list:

· accelerate_decelerate_interpolator

· accelerate_interpolator

· anticipate_interpolator

· anticipate_overshoot_interpolator

· bounce_interpolator

· cycle_interpolator

· decelerate_interpolator

· linear_interpolator

· overshoot_interpolator

The following XML fragment, for example, adds a bounce interpolator to a change bounds transition contained within a transition set:

```xml
<?xml version="1.0" encoding="utf-8"?>
<transitionSet
  xmlns:android="http://schemas.android.com/apk/res/android"
  android:transitionOrdering="sequential">

  <changeBounds
    android:interpolator="@android:anim/bounce_interpolator"
    android:duration="2000" />

  <fade
    android:duration="1000"
    android:fadingMode="fade_in" />
</transitionSet>
```

This approach to adding interpolators to transitions within XML resources works well when the default behavior of the interpolator is required. The task becomes a little more complex when the default behavior of an interpolator needs to be changed. Take, for example, the cycle interpolator. The purpose of this interpolator is to make an animation or transition repeat a specified number of times. In the absence of a *cycles* attribute setting, the cycle interpolator will perform only one cycle. Unfortunately, there is no way to directly specify the number of cycles (or any other interpolator attribute for that matter) when adding an interpolator using the above technique. Instead, a custom interpolator must be created and then referenced within the transition file.

41.7 Creating a Custom Interpolator

A custom interpolator must be declared in a separate XML file and stored within the *res/anim* folder of the project. The name of the XML file will be used by the Android system as the resource ID for the custom interpolator.

Within the custom interpolator XML resource file, the syntax should read as follows:

```xml
<?xml version="1.0" encoding="utf-8"?>
<interpolatorElement xmlns:android="http://schemas.android.com/apk/res/android"
android:attribute="value" />
```

In the above syntax, *interpolatorElement* must be replaced with the element name of the required interpolator selected from the following list:

- accelerateDecelerateInterpolator

- accelerateInterpolator

- anticipateInterpolator

- anticipateOvershootInterpolator

- bounceInterpolator

- cycleInterpolator

- decelerateInterpolator

- linearInterpolator

- overshootInterpolator

The *attribute* keyword is replaced by the name attribute of the interpolator for which the value is to be changed (for example *tension* to change the tension attribute of an overshoot interpolator). Finally, *value* represents the value to be assigned to the specified attribute. The following XML, for example, contains a custom cycle interpolator configured to cycle 7 times:

```
<?xml version="1.0" encoding="utf-8"?>
<cycleInterpolator xmlns:android="http://schemas.android.com/apk/res/android"
android:cycles="7" />
```

Assuming that the above XML was stored in a resource file named *my_cycle.xml* located in the *res/anim* project folder, the custom interpolator could be added to a transition resource file using the following XML syntax:

```
<changeBounds
  xmlns:android="http://schemas.android.com/apk/res/android"
  android:duration="5000"
  android:interpolator="@anim/my_cycle" >
```

41.8 Using the beginDelayedTransition Method

Perhaps the simplest form of Transition based user interface animation involves the use of the *beginDelayedTransition()* method of the TransitionManager class. This method is passed a reference to the root view of the viewgroup representing the scene for which animation is required. Subsequent changes to the views within that sub view will then be animated using the default transition settings:

```
myLayout = findViewById(R.id.myLayout);
TransitionManager.beginDelayedTransition(myLayout);
// Make changes to the scene here
```

If behavior other than the default animation behavior is required, simply pass a suitably configured Transition or TransitionSet instance through to the method call:

```
TransitionManager.beginDelayedTransition(myLayout, myTransition);
```

41.9 Summary

The Android 4.4 KitKat SDK release introduced the Transition Framework, the purpose of which is to simplify the task of adding animation to the views that make up the user interface of an Android application. With some simple configuration and a few lines of code, animation effects such as movement, visibility and resizing of views can be animated by making use of the Transition framework. A number of different approaches to implementing transitions are available involving a combination of Java code and XML resource files. The animation effects of transitions may also be enhanced through the use of a range of interpolators.

Having covered some of the theory of Transitions in Android, the next two chapters will put this theory into practice by working through some example Android Studio based transition implementations.

42. An Android Transition Tutorial using beginDelayedTransition

The previous chapter, entitled *"Animating User Interfaces with the Android Transitions Framework"*, provided an introduction to the animation of user interfaces using the Android Transitions framework. This chapter uses a tutorial based approach to demonstrate Android transitions in action using the *beginDelayedTransition()* method of the TransitionManager class.

The next chapter will create a more complex example that uses layout files and transition resource files to animate the transition from one scene to another within an application.

42.1 Creating the Android Studio TransitionDemo Project

Select the *Start a new Android Studio project* quick start option from the welcome screen and, within the resulting new project dialog, choose the Empty Activity template before clicking on the Next button.

Enter *TransitionDemo* into the Name field and specify *com.ebookfrenzy.transitiondemo* as the package name. Before clicking on the Finish button, change the Minimum API level setting to API 26: Android 8.0 (Oreo) and the Language menu to Java.

42.2 Preparing the Project Files

The first example transition animation will be implemented through the use of the *beginDelayedTransition()* method of the TransitionManager class. If Android Studio does not automatically load the file, locate and double-click on the *app -> res -> layout -> activity_main.xml* file in the Project tool window panel to load it into the Layout Editor tool.

Switch the Layout Editor to Design mode, delete the "Hello World!" TextView, drag a Button from the Widget section of the Layout Editor palette and position it in the top left-hand corner of the device screen layout. Once positioned, select the button and use the Attributes tool window to specify an ID value of *myButton*.

Select the ConstraintLayout entry in the Component Tree tool window and use the Attributes window to set the ID to *myLayout*.

42.3 Implementing beginDelayedTransition Animation

The objective for the initial phase of this tutorial is to implement a touch handler so that when the user taps on the layout view the button view moves to the lower right-hand corner of the screen.

Open the *MainActivity.java* file (located in the Project tool window under *app -> java -> com.ebookfrenzy. transitiondemo*) and modify the *onCreate()* method to implement the onTouch handler:

```
package com.ebookfrenzy.transitiondemo;

import androidx.appcompat.app.AppCompatActivity;
import android.os.Bundle;
import androidx.constraintlayout.widget.ConstraintLayout;
import androidx.constraintlayout.widget.ConstraintSet;
```

```
import android.view.MotionEvent;
import android.widget.Button;
import android.view.View;

public class MainActivity extends AppCompatActivity {

    ConstraintLayout myLayout;

    @Override
    protected void onCreate(Bundle savedInstanceState) {
        super.onCreate(savedInstanceState);
        setContentView(R.layout.activity_transition_demo);

        myLayout = findViewById(R.id.myLayout);

        myLayout.setOnTouchListener(
                new ConstraintLayout.OnTouchListener() {
                    public boolean onTouch(View v,
                                                MotionEvent m) {
                        handleTouch();
                        return true;
                    }
                }
        );
    }
}
```

The above code simply sets up a touch listener on the ConstraintLayout container and configures it to call a method named *handleTouch()* when a touch is detected. The next task, therefore, is to implement the *handleTouch()* method as follows:

```
public void handleTouch() {
    Button button = findViewById(R.id.myButton);

    button.setMinimumWidth(500);
    button.setMinimumHeight(350);

    ConstraintSet set = new ConstraintSet();

    set.connect(R.id.myButton, ConstraintSet.BOTTOM,
            ConstraintSet.PARENT_ID, ConstraintSet.BOTTOM, 0);

    set.connect(R.id.myButton, ConstraintSet.RIGHT,
            ConstraintSet.PARENT_ID, ConstraintSet.RIGHT, 0);

    set.constrainWidth(R.id.myButton, ConstraintSet.WRAP_CONTENT);
```

```
        set.applyTo(myLayout);
}
```

This method obtains a reference to the button view in the user interface layout and sets new minimum height and width attributes so that the button increases in size.

A ConstraintSet object is then created and configured with constraints that will position the button in the lower right-hand corner of the parent layout. This constraint set is then applied to the layout.

Test the code so far by compiling and running the application. Once launched, touch the background (not the button) and note that the button moves and resizes as illustrated in Figure 42-1:

Figure 42-1

Although the layout changes took effect, they did so instantly and without any form of animation. This is where the call to the *beginDelayedTransition()* method of the TransitionManager class comes in. All that is needed to add animation to this layout change is the addition of a single line of code before the layout changes are implemented. Remaining within the *MainActivity.java* file, modify the code as follows:

```
.

.
import android.transition.TransitionManager;

.

.
    public void handleTouch() {
        Button button = findViewById(R.id.myButton);

        TransitionManager.beginDelayedTransition(myLayout);
```

```
        ConstraintSet set = new ConstraintSet();

        button.setMinimumWidth(500);
        button.setMinimumHeight(350);

        set.connect(R.id.myButton, ConstraintSet.BOTTOM,
                ConstraintSet.PARENT_ID, ConstraintSet.BOTTOM, 0);

        set.connect(R.id.myButton, ConstraintSet.RIGHT,
                ConstraintSet.PARENT_ID, ConstraintSet.RIGHT, 0);

        set.constrainWidth(R.id.myButton, ConstraintSet.WRAP_CONTENT);

        set.applyTo(myLayout);
    }
}
```

Compile and run the application once again and note that the transition is now animated.

42.4 Customizing the Transition

The final task in this example is to modify the changeBounds transition so that it is performed over a longer duration and incorporates a bounce effect when the view reaches its new screen location. This involves the creation of a Transition instance with appropriate duration interpolator settings which is, in turn, passed through as an argument to the *beginDelayedTransition()* method:

```
.
.
import android.transition.ChangeBounds;
import android.transition.Transition;
import android.view.animation.BounceInterpolator;
.
.
public void handleTouch() {
    Button button = findViewById(R.id.myButton);

    Transition changeBounds = new ChangeBounds();
    changeBounds.setDuration(3000);
    changeBounds.setInterpolator(new BounceInterpolator());

    TransitionManager.beginDelayedTransition(myLayout,
            changeBounds);

    TransitionManager.beginDelayedTransition(myLayout);

    ConstraintSet set = new ConstraintSet();
```

```
button.setMinimumWidth(500);
button.setMinimumHeight(350);

set.connect(R.id.myButton, ConstraintSet.BOTTOM,
        ConstraintSet.PARENT_ID, ConstraintSet.BOTTOM, 0);

set.connect(R.id.myButton, ConstraintSet.RIGHT,
        ConstraintSet.PARENT_ID, ConstraintSet.RIGHT, 0);

set.constrainWidth(R.id.myButton, ConstraintSet.WRAP_CONTENT);

set.applyTo(myLayout);
}
```

When the application is now executed, the animation will slow to match the new duration setting and the button will bounce on arrival at the bottom right-hand corner of the display.

42.5 Summary

The most basic form of transition animation involves the use of the *beginDelayedTransition()* method of the TransitionManager class. Once called, any changes in size and position of the views in the next user interface rendering frame, and within a defined view group, will be animated using the specified transitions. This chapter has worked through a simple Android Studio example that demonstrates the use of this approach to implementing transitions.

43. Implementing Android Scene Transitions – A Tutorial

This chapter will build on the theory outlined in the chapter entitled *"Animating User Interfaces with the Android Transitions Framework"* by working through the creation of a project designed to demonstrate transitioning from one scene to another using the Android Transition framework.

43.1 An Overview of the Scene Transition Project

The application created in this chapter will consist of two scenes, each represented by an XML layout resource file. A transition will then be used to animate the changes from one scene to another. The first scene will consist of three button views. The second scene will contain two of the buttons from the first scene positioned at different locations on the screen. The third button will be absent from the second scene. Once the transition has been implemented, movement of the first two buttons will be animated with a bounce effect. The third button will gently fade into view as the application transitions back to the first scene from the second.

43.2 Creating the Android Studio SceneTransitions Project

Select the *Start a new Android Studio project* quick start option from the welcome screen and, within the resulting new project dialog, choose the Empty Activity template before clicking on the Next button.

Enter *SceneTransitions* into the Name field and specify *com.ebookfrenzy.scenetransitions* as the package name. Before clicking on the Finish button, change the Minimum API level setting to API 26: Android 8.0 (Oreo) and the Language menu to Java.

43.3 Identifying and Preparing the Root Container

When working with transitions it is important to identify the root container for the scenes. This is essentially the parent layout container into which the scenes are going to be displayed. When the project was created, Android Studio created a layout resource file in the *app -> res -> layout* folder named *activity_main.xml* and containing a single layout container and TextView. When the application is launched, this is the first layout that will be displayed to the user on the device screen.

Begin by locating the *activity_main.xml* layout resource file, loading it into the Android Studio Layout Editor tool and deleting the default TextView widget. Select the ConstraintLayout entry within the Component Tree window and change the ID property in the Attributes tool window to *rootContainer*.

43.4 Designing the First Scene

The first scene is going to consist of a layout containing three button views. Create this layout resource file by right-clicking on the *app -> res -> layout* entry in the Project tool window and selecting the *New -> Layout resource file...* menu option. In the resulting dialog, name the file *scene1_layout* and enter *androidx.constraintlayout.widget.ConstraintLayout* as the root element before clicking on *OK*.

When the newly created layout file has loaded into the Layout Editor tool, check that Autoconnect mode is enabled, drag a Button view from the Common section of the palette onto the layout canvas and position it in the top left-hand corner of the layout view so that the dashed margin guidelines appear as illustrated in Figure 43-1. Drop the Button view at this position, select it and change the text value in the Attributes tool window to

"One".

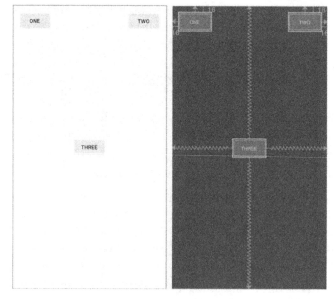

Figure 43-1

Drag a second Button view from the palette and position it in the top right-hand corner of the layout view so that the margin guidelines appear. Repeating the steps for the first button, assign text that reads "Two" on the button.

Drag a third Button view and position it so that it is centered both horizontally and vertically within the layout, this time configuring the button text to read "Three".

Click on the warning button in the top right-hand corner of the Layout Editor and work through the list of hardcoded text warnings, extracting the three button strings to resource values.

On completion of the above steps, the layout for the first scene should resemble that shown in Figure 43-2:

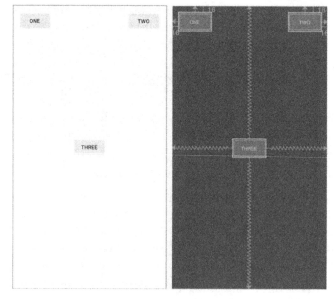

Figure 43-2

Select the "One" button and, using the Attributes tool window, configure the onClick attribute to call a method named *goToScene2*. Repeat this step for the "Two" button, this time entering a method named *goToScene1* into the *onClick* field.

43.5 Designing the Second Scene

The second scene is simply a modified version of the first scene. The first and second buttons will still be present but will be located in the bottom right and left-hand corners of the layout respectively. The third button, on the other hand, will no longer be present in the second scene.

For the purposes of avoiding duplicated effort, the layout file for the second scene will be created by copying and modifying the *scene1_layout.xml* file. Within the Project tool window, locate the *app -> res -> layout -> scene1_* *layout.xml* file, right-click on it and select the *Copy* menu option. Right-click on the *layout* folder, this time selecting the *Paste* menu option and change the name of the file to *scene2_layout.xml* when prompted to do so.

Double-click on the new *scene2_layout.xml* file to load it into the Layout Editor tool and switch to Design mode if necessary. Use the *Clear all Constraints* button located in the toolbar to remove the current constraints from the layout.

Select and delete the "Three" button and move the first and second buttons to the bottom right and bottom left locations as illustrated in Figure 43-3:

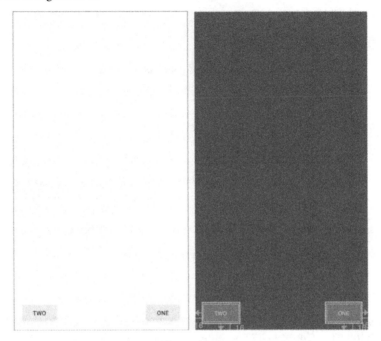

Figure 43-3

43.6 Entering the First Scene

If the application were to be run now, only the blank layout represented by the *activity_main.xml* file would be displayed. Some code must, therefore, be added to the *onCreate()* method located in the *MainActivity.java* file so that the first scene is presented when the activity is created. This can be achieved as follows:

```
package com.ebookfrenzy.scenetransitions;

import androidx.appcompat.app.AppCompatActivity;

import android.os.Bundle;
import android.transition.Scene;
import android.transition.Transition;
import android.transition.TransitionManager;
import android.view.ViewGroup;
import android.view.View;

public class MainActivity extends AppCompatActivity {
```

```
    ViewGroup rootContainer;
    Scene scene1;

    @Override
    protected void onCreate(Bundle savedInstanceState) {
        super.onCreate(savedInstanceState);
        setContentView(R.layout.activity_main);

        rootContainer =
                findViewById(R.id.rootContainer);

        scene1 = Scene.getSceneForLayout(rootContainer,
                R.layout.scene1_layout, this);

        scene1.enter();
    }
}
```

The code added to the activity class declares some variables in which to store references to the root container and first scene and obtains a reference to the root container view. The *getSceneForLayout()* method of the Scene class is then used to create a scene from the layout contained in the *scene1_layout.xml* file to convert that layout into a scene. The scene is then entered via the *enter()* method call so that it is displayed to the user.

Compile and run the application at this point and verify that scene 1 is displayed after the application has launched.

43.7 Loading Scene 2

Before implementing the transition between the first and second scene it is first necessary to add some code to load the layout from the *scene2_layout.xml* file into a Scene instance. Remaining in the *MainActivity.java* file, therefore, add this code as follows:

```
public class MainActivity extends AppCompatActivity {

    ViewGroup rootContainer;
    Scene scene1;
    Scene scene2;

    @Override
    protected void onCreate(Bundle savedInstanceState) {
        super.onCreate(savedInstanceState);
        setContentView(R.layout.activity_main);

        rootContainer =
                findViewById(R.id.rootContainer);

        scene1 = Scene.getSceneForLayout(rootContainer,
                R.layout.scene1_layout, this);
```

```
    scene2 = Scene.getSceneForLayout(rootContainer,
            R.layout.scene2_layout, this);


    scene1.enter();
    }
.
.
.
}
```

43.8 Implementing the Transitions

The first and second buttons have been configured to call methods named *goToScene2* and *goToScene1* respectively when selected. As the method names suggest, it is the responsibility of these methods to trigger the transitions between the two scenes. Add these two methods within the *MainActivity.java* file so that they read as follows:

```
public void goToScene2 (View view)
{
    TransitionManager.go(scene2);
}

public void goToScene1 (View view)
{
    TransitionManager.go(scene1);
}
```

Run the application and note that selecting the first two buttons causes the layout to switch between the two scenes. Since we have yet to configure any transitions, these layout changes are not yet animated.

43.9 Adding the Transition File

All of the transition effects for this project will be implemented within a single transition XML resource file. As outlined in the chapter entitled *"Animating User Interfaces with the Android Transitions Framework"*, transition resource files must be placed in the *app -> res -> transition* folder of the project. Begin, therefore, by right-clicking on the *res* folder in the Project tool window and selecting the *New -> Directory* menu option. In the resulting dialog, name the new folder *transition* and click on the *OK* button. Right-click on the new transition folder, this time selecting the *New -> Transition Resource File* option and name the new file *transition.xml*.

With the newly created *transition.xml* file selected and loaded into the editing panel, add the following XML content to add a transition set that enables the change bounds transition animation with a duration attribute setting:

```
<?xml version="1.0" encoding="utf-8"?>

<transitionSet
  xmlns:android="http://schemas.android.com/apk/res/android">

    <changeBounds
        android:duration="2000">
    </changeBounds>

</transitionSet>
```

43.10 Loading and Using the Transition Set

Although a transition resource file has been created and populated with a change bounds transition, this will have no effect until some code is added to load the transitions into a TransitionManager instance and reference it in the scene changes. The changes to achieve this are as follows:

```
package com.ebookfrenzy.scenetransitions;

import android.support.v7.app.AppCompatActivity;
import android.os.Bundle;
import android.transition.Scene;
import android.transition.Transition;
import android.transition.TransitionInflater;
import android.transition.TransitionManager;
import android.view.ViewGroup;
import android.view.View;

public class MainActivity extends AppCompatActivity {

        ViewGroup rootContainer;
        Scene scene1;
        Scene scene2;
        Transition transitionMgr;

        @Override
        protected void onCreate(Bundle savedInstanceState) {
                super.onCreate(savedInstanceState);
                setContentView(R.layout.activity_main);

                rootContainer =
                        findViewById(R.id.rootContainer);

                transitionMgr = TransitionInflater.from(this)
                        .inflateTransition(R.transition.transition);

                scene1 = Scene.getSceneForLayout(rootContainer,
                   R.layout.scene1_layout, this);

                scene2 = Scene.getSceneForLayout(rootContainer,
                   R.layout.scene2_layout, this);

                scene1.enter();
        }

        public void goToScene2 (View view)
        {
                TransitionManager.go(scene2, transitionMgr);
```

```
        }

    public void goToScene1 (View view)
    {
            TransitionManager.go(scene1, transitionMgr);
    }
.

.

}
```

When the application is now run the two buttons will gently glide to their new positions during the transition.

43.11 Configuring Additional Transitions

With the transition file integrated into the project, any number of additional transitions may be added to the file without the need to make any further changes to the Java source code of the activity. Take, for example, the following changes to the *transition.xml* file to add a bounce interpolator to the change bounds transition, introduce a fade-in transition targeted at the third button and to change the transitions such that they are performed sequentially:

```
<?xml version="1.0" encoding="utf-8"?>

<transitionSet
  xmlns:android="http://schemas.android.com/apk/res/android"
  android:transitionOrdering="sequential" >


        <fade
          android:duration="2000"
          android:fadingMode="fade_in">

          <targets>
              <target android:targetId="@id/button3" />
          </targets>
        </fade>

    <changeBounds
        android:duration="2000"
        android:interpolator="@android:anim/bounce_interpolator">
    </changeBounds>
</transitionSet>
```

Buttons one and two will now bounce on arriving at the end destinations and button three will gently fade back into view when transitioning to scene 1 from scene 2.

Take some time to experiment with different transitions and interpolators by making changes to the *transition. xml* file and re-running the application.

43.12 Summary

Scene based transitions provide a flexible approach to animating user interface layout changes within an Android application. This chapter has demonstrated the steps involved in animating the transition between the scenes represented by two layout resource files. In addition, the example also used a transition XML resource file to configure the transition animation effects between the two scenes.

44. Working with the Floating Action Button and Snackbar

One of the objectives of this chapter is to provide an overview of the concepts of material design. Originally introduced as part of Android 5.0, material design is a set of design guidelines that dictate how the Android user interface, and that of the apps running on Android, appear and behave.

As part of the implementation of the material design concepts, Google also introduced the Android Design Support Library. This library contains a number of different components that allow many of the key features of material design to be built into Android applications. Two of these components, the floating action button and Snackbar, will also be covered in this chapter prior to introducing many of the other components in subsequent chapters.

44.1 The Material Design

The overall appearance of the Android environment is defined by the principles of material design. Material design was created by the Android team at Google and dictates that the elements that make up the user interface of Android and the apps that run on it appear and behave in a certain way in terms of behavior, shadowing, animation and style. One of the tenets of the material design is that the elements of a user interface appear to have physical depth and a sense that items are constructed in layers of physical material. A button, for example, appears to be raised above the surface of the layout in which it resides through the use of shadowing effects. Pressing the button causes the button to flex and lift as though made of a thin material that ripples when released.

Material design also dictates the layout and behavior of many standard user interface elements. A key example is the way in which the app bar located at the top of the screen should appear and the way in which it should behave in relation to scrolling activities taking place within the main content of the activity.

In fact, material design covers a wide range of areas from recommended color styles to the way in which objects are animated. A full description of the material design concepts and guidelines can be found online at the following link and is recommended reading for all Android developers:

https://www.google.com/design/spec/material-design/introduction.html

44.2 The Design Library

Many of the building blocks needed to implement Android applications that adopt the principles of material design are contained within the Android Design Support Library. This library contains a collection of user interface components that can be included in Android applications to implement much of the look, feel and behavior of material design. Two of the components from this library, the floating action button and Snackbar, will be covered in this chapter, while others will be introduced in later chapters.

44.3 The Floating Action Button (FAB)

The floating action button is a button which appears to float above the surface of the user interface of an app and is generally used to promote the most common action within a user interface screen. A floating action button might, for example, be placed on a screen to allow the user to add an entry to a list of contacts or to send an email from within the app. Figure 44-1, for example, highlights the floating action button that allows the user to add a new contact within the standard Android Contacts app:

Figure 44-1

To conform with the material design guidelines, there are a number of rules that should be followed when using floating action buttons. Floating action buttons must be circular and can be either 56 x 56dp (Default) or 40 x 40dp (Mini) in size. The button should be positioned a minimum of 16dp from the edge of the screen on phones and 24dp on desktops and tablet devices. Regardless of the size, the button must contain an interior icon that is 24x24dp in size and it is recommended that each user interface screen have only one floating action button.

Floating action buttons can be animated or designed to morph into other items when touched. A floating action button could, for example, rotate when tapped or morph into another element such as a toolbar or panel listing related actions.

44.4 The Snackbar

The Snackbar component provides a way to present the user with information in the form of a panel that appears at the bottom of the screen as shown in Figure 44-2. Snackbar instances contain a brief text message and an optional action button which will perform a task when tapped by the user. Once displayed, a Snackbar will either timeout automatically or can be removed manually by the user via a swiping action. During the appearance of the Snackbar the app will continue to function and respond to user interactions in the normal manner.

Figure 44-2

In the remainder of this chapter an example application will be created that makes use of the basic features of the floating action button and Snackbar to add entries to a list of items.

344

44.5 Creating the Example Project

Select the *Start a new Android Studio project* quick start option from the welcome screen and, within the resulting new project dialog, choose the Basic Activity template before clicking on the Next button.

Enter *FabExample* into the Name field and specify *com.ebookfrenzy.fabexample* as the package name. Before clicking on the Finish button, change the Minimum API level setting to API 26: Android 8.0 (Oreo) and the Language menu to Java.

44.6 Reviewing the Project

Since the Basic Activity template was selected, the activity contains two layout files. The *activity_main.xml* file consists of a CoordinatorLayout manager containing entries for an app bar, a toolbar and a floating action button.

The *content_main.xml* file represents the layout of the content area of the activity and contains a ConstraintLayout instance and a TextView. This file is embedded into the *activity_main.xml* file via the following include directive:

```
<include layout="@layout/content_fab_example" />
```

The floating action button element within the *activity_main.xml* file reads as follows:

```
<com.google.android.material.floatingactionbutton.FloatingActionButton
    android:id="@+id/fab"
    android:layout_width="wrap_content"
    android:layout_height="wrap_content"
    android:layout_gravity="bottom|end"
    android:layout_margin="@dimen/fab_margin"
    app:srcCompat="@android:drawable/ic_dialog_email" />
```

This declares that the button is to appear in the bottom right-hand corner of the screen with margins represented by the *fab_margin* identifier in the *values/dimens.xml* file (which in this case is set to 16dp). The XML further declares that the interior icon for the button is to take the form of the standard drawable built-in email icon.

The blank template has also configured the floating action button to display a Snackbar instance when tapped by the user. The code to implement this can be found in the *onCreate()* method of the *MainActivity.java* file and reads as follows:

```
FloatingActionButton fab =
                findViewById(R.id.fab);


fab.setOnClickListener(new View.OnClickListener() {
    @Override
    public void onClick(View view) {
        Snackbar.make(view, "Replace with your own action",
            Snackbar.LENGTH_LONG)
                .setAction("Action", null).show();
    }
});
```

The code obtains a reference to the floating action button via the button's ID and adds to it an onClickListener handler to be called when the button is tapped. This method simply displays a Snackbar instance configured with a message but no actions.

When the project is compiled and run the floating action button will appear at the bottom of the screen as shown in Figure 44-3:

Figure 44-3

Tapping the floating action button will trigger the onClickListener handler method causing the Snackbar to appear at the bottom of the screen:

Figure 44-4

When the Snackbar appears on a narrower device (as is the case in Figure 44-4 above) note that the floating action button is moved up to make room for the Snackbar to appear. This is handled for us automatically by the CoordinatorLayout container in the *activity_main.xml* layout resource file.

44.7 Changing the Floating Action Button

Since the objective of this example is to configure the floating action button to add entries to a list, the email icon currently displayed on the button needs to be changed to something more indicative of the action being performed. The icon that will be used for the button is named *ic_add_entry.png* and can be found in the *project_icons* folder of the sample code download available from the following URL:

https://www.ebookfrenzy.com/retail/androidstudio35/index.php

Locate this image in the file system navigator for your operating system and copy the image file. Right-click on the *app -> res -> drawable* entry in the Project tool window and select Paste from the menu to add the file to the folder:

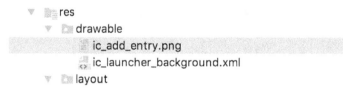

Figure 44-5

Next, edit the *activity_main.xml* file and change the image source for the icon from *@android:drawable/ic_dialog_email* to *@drawable/ic_add_entry* as follows:

```
<com.google.android.material.floatingactionbutton.FloatingActionButton
    android:id="@+id/fab"
    android:layout_width="wrap_content"
```

```
android:layout_height="wrap_content"
android:layout_gravity="bottom|end"
android:layout_margin="@dimen/fab_margin"
app:srcCompat="@drawable/ic_add_entry" />
```

Within the layout preview, the interior icon for the button will have changed to a plus sign.

The background color of the floating action button is defined by the *colorAccent* property of the prevailing theme used by the application. The color assigned to this value is declared in the *colors.xml* file located under *app -> res -> values* in the Project tool window. Edit this file and change the *colorAccent* property to a different color value:

```
<?xml version="1.0" encoding="utf-8"?>
<resources>
    <color name="colorPrimary">#008577</color>
    <color name="colorPrimaryDark">#00574B</color>
    <color name="colorAccent">#FFDE03</color>
</resources>
```

Return to the *activity_main.xml* file and verify that the floating action button now appears with a yellow background.

44.8 Adding the ListView to the Content Layout

The next step in this tutorial is to add the ListView instance to the *content_main.xml* file. The ListView class provides a way to display items in a list format and can be found in the *Legacy* section of the Layout Editor tool palette.

Load the *content_main.xml* file into the Layout Editor tool, select Design mode if necessary, and select and delete the default TextView object. Locate the ListView object in the Legacy category of the palette and, with autoconnect mode enabled, drag and drop it onto the center of the layout canvas. Select the ListView object and change the ID to *listView* within the Attributes tool window. The Layout Editor should have sized the ListView to fill the entire container and established constraints on all four edges as illustrated in Figure 44-6:

Figure 44-6

44.9 Adding Items to the ListView

Each time the floating action button is tapped by the user, a new item will be added to the ListView in the form of the prevailing time and date. To achieve this, some changes need to be made to the *MainActivity.java* file.

Begin by modifying the *onCreate()* method to obtain a reference to the ListView instance and to initialize an adapter instance to allow us to add items to the list in the form of an array:

```java
import android.os.Bundle;

import com.google.android.material.floatingactionbutton.FloatingActionButton;
import com.google.android.material.snackbar.Snackbar;

import androidx.appcompat.app.AppCompatActivity;
import androidx.appcompat.widget.Toolbar;

import android.view.View;
import android.view.Menu;
import android.view.MenuItem;
import android.widget.ArrayAdapter;
import android.widget.ListView;

import java.util.ArrayList;

public class MainActivity extends AppCompatActivity {

    ArrayList<String> listItems = new ArrayList<String>();
    ArrayAdapter<String> adapter;
    private ListView myListView;

    @Override
    protected void onCreate(Bundle savedInstanceState) {
        super.onCreate(savedInstanceState);
        setContentView(R.layout.activity_fab_example);
        Toolbar toolbar = findViewById(R.id.toolbar);
        setSupportActionBar(toolbar);

        myListView = findViewById(R.id.listView);

        adapter = new ArrayAdapter<String>(this,
                android.R.layout.simple_list_item_1,
                listItems);
        myListView.setAdapter(adapter);

        FloatingActionButton fab = findViewById(R.id.fab);

        fab.setOnClickListener(new View.OnClickListener() {
```

```
        @Override
        public void onClick(View view) {
            Snackbar.make(view, "Replace with your own action",
                Snackbar.LENGTH_LONG)
                    .setAction("Action", null).show();
        }
    });
}
.
.
}
```

The ListView needs an array of items to display, an adapter to manage the items in that array and a layout definition to dictate how items are to be presented to the user.

In the above code changes, the items are stored in an ArrayList instance assigned to an adapter that takes the form of an ArrayAdapter. The items added to the list will be displayed in the ListView using the *simple_list_item_1* layout, a built-in layout that is provided with Android to display simple string based items in a ListView instance.

Next, edit the onClickListener code for the floating action button to display a different message in the Snackbar and to call a method to add an item to the list:

```
FloatingActionButton fab = findViewById(R.id.fab);

fab.setOnClickListener(new View.OnClickListener() {
    @Override
    public void onClick(View view) {
        addListItem();
        Snackbar.make(view, "Item added to list",
                Snackbar.LENGTH_LONG)
                    .setAction("Action", null).show();

    }
});
```

Remaining within the *MainActivity.java* file, add the *addListItem()* method as follows:

```
package com.ebookfrenzy.fabexample;
.
.
import java.text.SimpleDateFormat;
import java.util.Date;
import java.util.Locale;

public class MainActivity extends AppCompatActivity {
.
.
    private void addListItem() {
```

```
SimpleDateFormat dateformat =
        new SimpleDateFormat("HH:mm:ss MM/dd/yyyy",
                Locale.US);
listItems.add(dateformat.format(new Date()));
adapter.notifyDataSetChanged();
    }
    .
    .
    .
}
```

The code in the *addListItem()* method identifies and formats the current date and time and adds it to the list items array. The array adapter assigned to the ListView is then notified that the list data has changed, causing the ListView to update to display the latest list items.

Compile and run the app and test that tapping the floating action button adds new time and date entries to the ListView, displaying the Snackbar each time as shown in Figure 44-7:

Figure 44-7

44.10 Adding an Action to the Snackbar

The final task in this project is to add an action to the Snackbar that allows the user to undo the most recent addition to the list. Edit the *MainActivity.java* file and modify the Snackbar creation code to add an action titled "Undo" configured with an onClickListener named *undoOnClickListener*:

```
fab.setOnClickListener(new View.OnClickListener() {
    @Override
    public void onClick(View view) {
```

```
        addListItem();
        Snackbar.make(view, "Item added to list",
            Snackbar.LENGTH_LONG)
                .setAction("Undo", undoOnClickListener).show();


    }
});
```

Within the *MainActivity.java* file add the listener handler:

```
View.OnClickListener undoOnClickListener = new View.OnClickListener() {
    @Override
    public void onClick(View view) {
        listItems.remove(listItems.size() -1);
        adapter.notifyDataSetChanged();
        Snackbar.make(view, "Item removed", Snackbar.LENGTH_LONG)
                .setAction("Action", null).show();
    }
};
```

The code in the onClick method identifies the location of the last item in the list array and removes it from the list before triggering the list view to perform an update. A new Snackbar is then displayed indicating that the last item has been removed from the list.

Run the app once again and add some items to the list. On the final addition, tap the Undo button in the Snackbar (Figure 44-8) to remove the last item from the list:

Figure 44-8

It is also worth noting that the Undo button appears using the same color assigned to the accentColor property via the Theme Editor earlier in the chapter.

44.11 Summary

This chapter has provided a general overview of material design, the floating action button and Snackbar before working through an example project that makes use of these features.

Both the floating action button and the Snackbar are part of the material design approach to user interface implementation in Android. The floating action button provides a way to promote the most common action within a particular screen of an Android application. The Snackbar provides a way for an application to both present information to the user and also allow the user to take action upon it.

45. Creating a Tabbed Interface using the TabLayout Component

The previous chapter outlined the concept of material design in Android and introduced two of the components provided by the design support library in the form of the floating action button and the Snackbar. This chapter will demonstrate how to use another of the design library components, the TabLayout, which can be combined with the ViewPager class to create a tab based interface within an Android activity.

45.1 An Introduction to the ViewPager

Although not part of the design support library, the ViewPager is a useful companion class when used in conjunction with the TabLayout component to implement a tabbed user interface. The primary role of the ViewPager is to allow the user to flip through different pages of information where each page is most typically represented by a layout fragment. The fragments that are associated with the ViewPager are managed by an instance of the FragmentPagerAdapter class.

At a minimum the pager adapter assigned to a ViewPager must implement two methods. The first, named *getCount()*, must return the total number of page fragments available to be displayed to the user. The second method, *getItem()*, is passed a page number and must return the corresponding fragment object ready to be presented to the user.

45.2 An Overview of the TabLayout Component

As previously discussed, TabLayout is one of the components introduced as part of material design and is included in the design support library. The purpose of the TabLayout is to present the user with a row of tabs which can be selected to display different pages to the user. The tabs can be fixed or scrollable, whereby the user can swipe left or right to view more tabs than will currently fit on the display. The information displayed on a tab can be text-based, an image or a combination of text and images. Figure 45-1, for example, shows the tab bar for the Android phone app consisting of three tabs displaying images:

Figure 45-1

Figure 45-2, on the other hand, shows a TabLayout configuration consisting of four tabs displaying text in a scrollable configuration:

Figure 45-2

The remainder of this chapter will work through the creation of an example project that demonstrates the use of the TabLayout component together with a ViewPager and four fragments.

45.3 Creating the TabLayoutDemo Project

Select the *Start a new Android Studio project* quick start option from the welcome screen and, within the resulting new project dialog, choose the Basic Activity template before clicking on the Next button.

Enter *TabLayoutDemo* into the Name field and specify *com.ebookfrenzy.tablayoutdemo* as the package name. Before clicking on the Finish button, change the Minimum API level setting to API 26: Android 8.0 (Oreo) and the Language menu to Java.

Once the project has been created, load the *content_main.xml* file into the Layout Editor tool, select the "Hello World" TextView object, and then delete it.

45.4 Creating the First Fragment

Each of the tabs on the TabLayout will display a different fragment when selected. Create the first of these fragments by right-clicking on the *app -> java -> com.ebookfrenzy.tablayoutdemo* entry in the Project tool window and selecting the *New -> Fragment -> Fragment (Blank)* option. In the resulting dialog, enter *Tab1Fragment* into the *Fragment Name:* field and *fragment_tab1* into the *Fragment Layout Name:* field. Enable the *Create layout XML?* option, while disabling the *Include fragment factory methods?* and *Include interface callbacks?* options. Click on the *Finish* button to create the new fragment:

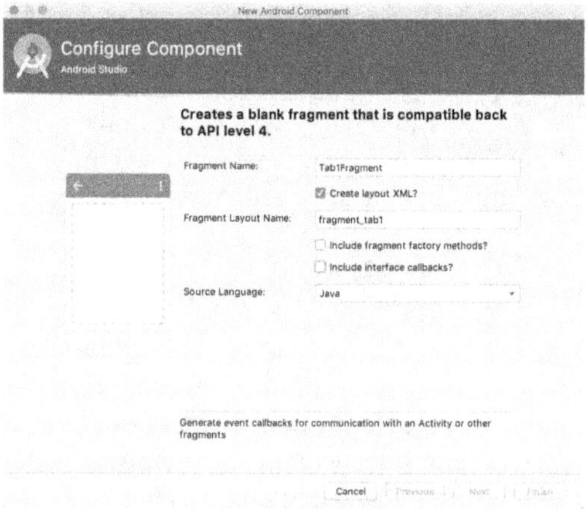

Figure 45-3

Load the newly created *fragment_tab1.xml* file (located under *app -> res -> layout*) into the Layout Editor tool, right-click on the FrameLayout entry in the Component Tree panel and select the *Convert FrameLayout to ConstraintLayout* menu option. In the resulting dialog, verify that all conversion options are selected before clicking on OK. Change the ID of the layout to *constraintLayout*.

Once the layout has been converted to a ConstraintLayout, delete the TextView from the layout. From the Palette, locate the TextView widget and drag and drop it so that it is positioned in the center of the layout. Edit the text property on the object so that it reads "Tab 1 Fragment" and extract the string to a resource named *tab_1_fragment*, at which point the layout should match that of Figure 45-4:

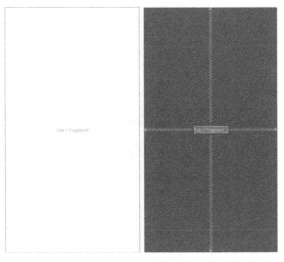

Figure 45-4

45.5 Duplicating the Fragments

So far, the project contains one of the four required fragments. Instead of creating the remaining three fragments using the previous steps it would be quicker to duplicate the first fragment. Each fragment consists of a layout XML file and a Java class file, each of which needs to be duplicated.

Right-click on the *fragment_tab1.xml* file in the Project tool window and select the Copy option from the resulting menu. Right-click on the *layout* entry, this time selecting the Paste option. In the resulting dialog, name the new layout file *fragment_tab2.xml* before clicking the *OK* button. Edit the new *fragment_tab2.xml* file and change the text on the Text View to "Tab 2 Fragment", following the usual steps to extract the string to a resource named *tab_2_fragment*.

To duplicate the Tab1Fragment class file, right-click on the class listed under *app -> java -> com.ebookfrenzy. tablayoutdemo* and select Copy. Right-click on the *com.ebookfrenzy.tablayoutdemo* entry and select Paste. In the Copy Class dialog, enter Tab2Fragment into the *New name:* field and click on OK. Edit the new *Tab2Fragment. java* file and change the class name and *onCreateView()* method to inflate the *fragment_tab2* layout file:

```
@Override
public View onCreateView(LayoutInflater inflater, ViewGroup container,
                        Bundle savedInstanceState) {
    // Inflate the layout for this fragment
    return inflater.inflate(R.layout.fragment_tab2, container, false);
}
```

Perform the above duplication steps twice more to create the fragment layout and class files for the remaining two fragments. On completion of these steps the project structure should match that of Figure 45-5:

Figure 45-5

45.6 Adding the TabLayout and ViewPager

With the fragment creation process now complete, the next step is to add the TabLayout and ViewPager to the main activity layout file. Edit the *activity_main.xml* file and add these elements as outlined in the following XML listing. Note that the TabLayout component is embedded into the AppBarLayout element while the ViewPager is placed after the AppBarLayout:

```
<?xml version="1.0" encoding="utf-8"?>
<androidx.coordinatorlayout.widget.CoordinatorLayout xmlns:android="http://
schemas.android.com/apk/res/android"
    xmlns:app="http://schemas.android.com/apk/res-auto"
    xmlns:tools="http://schemas.android.com/tools"
    android:layout_width="match_parent"
    android:layout_height="match_parent"
    tools:context=".MainActivity">

    <com.google.android.material.appbar.AppBarLayout
        android:layout_width="match_parent"
        android:layout_height="wrap_content"
        android:theme="@style/AppTheme.AppBarOverlay">

        <androidx.appcompat.widget.Toolbar
            android:id="@+id/toolbar"
            android:layout_width="match_parent"
            android:layout_height="?attr/actionBarSize"
            android:background="?attr/colorPrimary"
            app:popupTheme="@style/AppTheme.PopupOverlay" />

        <com.google.android.material.tabs.TabLayout
            android:id="@+id/tab_layout"
            android:layout_width="match_parent"
```

```
            android:layout_height="wrap_content"
            app:tabMode="fixed"
            app:tabGravity="fill"/>

    </com.google.android.material.appbar.AppBarLayout>

    <androidx.viewpager.widget.ViewPager
        android:id="@+id/pager"
        android:layout_width="match_parent"
        android:layout_height="match_parent"
        app:layout_behavior="@string/appbar_scrolling_view_behavior" />

    <include layout="@layout/content_main" />

    <com.google.android.material.floatingactionbutton.FloatingActionButton
        android:id="@+id/fab"
        android:layout_width="wrap_content"
        android:layout_height="wrap_content"
        android:layout_gravity="bottom|end"
        android:layout_margin="@dimen/fab_margin"
        app:srcCompat="@android:drawable/ic_dialog_email" />

</androidx.coordinatorlayout.widget.CoordinatorLayout>
```

45.7 Creating the Pager Adapter

This example will use the ViewPager approach to handling the fragments assigned to the TabLayout tabs. With the ViewPager added to the layout resource file, a new class which subclasses FragmentPagerAdapter needs to be added to the project to manage the fragments that will be displayed when the tab items are selected by the user.

Add a new class to the project by right-clicking on the *com.ebookfrenzy.tablayoutdemo* entry in the Project tool window and selecting the *New -> Java Class* menu option. In the new class dialog, enter *TabPagerAdapter* into the *Name:* field and click *OK*.

Edit the *TabPagerAdapter.java* file so that it reads as follows:

```
package com.ebookfrenzy.tablayoutdemo;

import androidx.fragment.app.Fragment;
import androidx.fragment.app.FragmentManager;
import androidx.fragment.app.FragmentPagerAdapter;

public class TabPagerAdapter extends FragmentPagerAdapter {

    int tabCount;

    public TabPagerAdapter(FragmentManager fm, int numberOfTabs) {
        super(fm);
        this.tabCount = numberOfTabs;
```

```
    }

    @Override
    public Fragment getItem(int position) {

        switch (position) {
            case 0:
                return new Tab1Fragment();
            case 1:
                return new Tab2Fragment();
            case 2:
                return new Tab3Fragment();
            case 3:
                return new Tab4Fragment();
            default:
                return null;
        }
    }


    @Override
    public int getCount() {
        return tabCount;
    }
}
```

The class is declared as extending the FragmentPagerAdapter class and a constructor is implemented allowing the number of pages required to be passed to the class when an instance is created. The *getItem()* method will be called when a specific page is required. A switch statement is used to identify the page number being requested and to return a corresponding fragment instance. Finally, the *getCount()* method simply returns the count value passed through when the object instance was created.

45.8 Performing the Initialization Tasks

The remaining tasks involve initializing the TabLayout, ViewPager and TabPagerAdapter instances and declaring the main activity class as implementing fragment interaction listeners for each of the four tab fragments. Edit the *MainActivity.java* file so that it reads as follows:

```
package com.ebookfrenzy.tablayoutdemo;

import android.os.Bundle;

import com.google.android.material.floatingactionbutton.FloatingActionButton;
import com.google.android.material.snackbar.Snackbar;

import androidx.appcompat.app.AppCompatActivity;
import androidx.appcompat.widget.Toolbar;

import android.view.View;
import android.view.Menu;
```

```java
import android.view.MenuItem;

import com.google.android.material.tabs.TabLayout;
import androidx.viewpager.widget.ViewPager;
import androidx.viewpager.widget.PagerAdapter;
.
.
public class MainActivity extends AppCompatActivity implements
        Tab1Fragment.OnFragmentInteractionListener,
        Tab2Fragment.OnFragmentInteractionListener,
        Tab3Fragment.OnFragmentInteractionListener,
        Tab4Fragment.OnFragmentInteractionListener {

    @Override
    protected void onCreate(Bundle savedInstanceState) {
        super.onCreate(savedInstanceState);
        setContentView(R.layout.activity_tab_layout_demo);
        Toolbar toolbar = findViewById(R.id.toolbar);
        setSupportActionBar(toolbar);

        FloatingActionButton fab = findViewById(R.id.fab);

        fab.setOnClickListener(new View.OnClickListener() {
            @Override
            public void onClick(View view) {
                Snackbar.make(view, "Replace with your own action",
                                Snackbar.LENGTH_LONG)
                        .setAction("Action", null).show();
            }
        });
        configureTabLayout();
    }

    private void configureTabLayout() {
                TabLayout tabLayout = findViewById(R.id.tab_layout);

        tabLayout.addTab(tabLayout.newTab().setText("Tab 1 Item"));
        tabLayout.addTab(tabLayout.newTab().setText("Tab 2 Item"));
        tabLayout.addTab(tabLayout.newTab().setText("Tab 3 Item"));
        tabLayout.addTab(tabLayout.newTab().setText("Tab 4 Item"));

        final ViewPager viewPager = findViewById(R.id.pager);
        final PagerAdapter adapter = new TabPagerAdapter
                (getSupportFragmentManager(),
                        tabLayout.getTabCount());
```

```
        viewPager.setAdapter(adapter);

        viewPager.addOnPageChangeListener(new
            TabLayout.TabLayoutOnPageChangeListener(tabLayout));
        tabLayout.addOnTabSelectedListener(new
            TabLayout.OnTabSelectedListener() {
          @Override
          public void onTabSelected(TabLayout.Tab tab) {
              viewPager.setCurrentItem(tab.getPosition());
          }

          @Override
          public void onTabUnselected(TabLayout.Tab tab) {

          }

          @Override
          public void onTabReselected(TabLayout.Tab tab) {

          }

        });
    }

    @Override
    public void onFragmentInteraction(Uri uri) {
    }
    .
    .
    .
}
```

The code begins by obtaining a reference to the TabLayout object that was added to the *activity_main.xml* file and creating four tabs, assigning the text to appear on each:

```
tabLayout.addTab(tabLayout.newTab().setText("Tab 1 Item"));
tabLayout.addTab(tabLayout.newTab().setText("Tab 2 Item"));
tabLayout.addTab(tabLayout.newTab().setText("Tab 3 Item"));
tabLayout.addTab(tabLayout.newTab().setText("Tab 4 Item"));
```

A reference to the ViewPager instance in the layout file is then obtained and an instance of the TabPagerAdapter class created. Note that the code to create the TabPagerAdapter instance passes through the number of tabs that have been assigned to the TabLayout component. The TabPagerAdapter instance is then assigned as the adapter for the ViewPager and the TabLayout component added to the page change listener:

```
final ViewPager viewPager = findViewById(R.id.pager);
final PagerAdapter adapter = new TabPagerAdapter
                (getSupportFragmentManager(),
                     tabLayout.getTabCount());
viewPager.setAdapter(adapter);
```

```
viewPager.addOnPageChangeListener(new
        TabLayout.TabLayoutOnPageChangeListener(tabLayout));
```

Finally, the onTabSelectedListener is configured on the TabLayout instance and the *onTabSelected()* method implemented to set the current page on the ViewPager based on the currently selected tab number. For the sake of completeness the other listener methods are added as stubs:

```
tabLayout.setOnTabSelectedListener(new
                    TabLayout.OnTabSelectedListener()
{
        @Override
        public void onTabSelected(TabLayout.Tab tab) {
                    viewPager.setCurrentItem(tab.getPosition());
        }

        @Override
        public void onTabUnselected(TabLayout.Tab tab) {

        }

        @Override
        public void onTabReselected(TabLayout.Tab tab) {

        }
});
```

45.9 Testing the Application

Compile and run the app on a device or emulator and make sure that selecting a tab causes the corresponding fragment to appear in the content area of the screen:

Figure 45-6

45.10 Customizing the TabLayout

The TabLayout in this example project is configured using *fixed* mode. This mode works well for a limited number of tabs with short titles. A greater number of tabs or longer titles can quickly become a problem when using fixed mode as illustrated by Figure 45-7:

Figure 45-7

In an effort to fit the tabs into the available display width the TabLayout has used multiple lines of text. Even so, the second line is clearly truncated making it impossible to see the full title. The best solution to this problem is to switch the TabLayout to *scrollable* mode. In this mode the titles appear in full length, single line format allowing the user to swipe to scroll horizontally through the available items as demonstrated in Figure 45-8:

Figure 45-8

To switch a TabLayout to scrollable mode, simply change the *app:tabMode* property in the *activity_main.xml* layout resource file from "fixed" to "scrollable":

```
<android.support.design.widget.TabLayout
    android:id="@+id/tab_layout"
    android:layout_width="match_parent"
    android:layout_height="wrap_content"
    app:tabMode="scrollable"
    app:tabGravity="fill"/>
</android.support.design.widget.AppBarLayout>
```

When in fixed mode, the TabLayout may be configured to control how the tab items are displayed to take up the available space on the screen. This is controlled via the *app:tabGravity* property, the results of which are more noticeable on wider displays such as tablets in landscape orientation. When set to "fill", for example, the items will be distributed evenly across the width of the TabLayout as shown in Figure 45-9:

Figure 45-9

Changing the property value to "center" will cause the items to be positioned relative to the center of the tab bar:

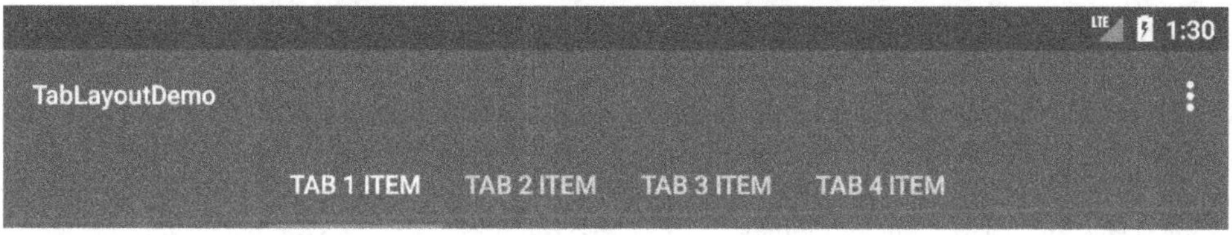

Figure 45-10

Before proceeding to the final step in this chapter, revert the tabMode and tabGravity attributes in the *activity_main.xml* file to "fixed" and "fill" respectively.

45.11 Displaying Icon Tab Items

The last step in this tutorial is to replace the text based tabs with icons. Achieve this by modifying the *onCreate()* method in the *MainActivity.java* file to assign some built-in drawable icons to the tab items:

```
private void configureTabLayout() {

    TabLayout tabLayout = findViewById(R.id.tab_layout);

    tabLayout.addTab(tabLayout.newTab().setIcon(
                    android.R.drawable.ic_dialog_email));
    tabLayout.addTab(tabLayout.newTab().setIcon(
                    android.R.drawable.ic_dialog_dialer));
    tabLayout.addTab(tabLayout.newTab().setIcon(
                    android.R.drawable.ic_dialog_map));
    tabLayout.addTab(tabLayout.newTab().setIcon(
                    android.R.drawable.ic_dialog_info));

    final ViewPager viewPager = findViewById(R.id.pager);
    .
    .
```

Instead of using the *setText()* method of the tab item, the code is now calling the *setIcon()* method and passing through a drawable icon reference. When compiled and run, the tab bar should now appear as shown in Figure 45-11. Note if using Instant Run that it will be necessary to trigger a warm swap using Ctrl-Shift-R for the changes to take effect:

Figure 45-11

45.12 Summary

TabLayout is one of the components introduced as part of the Android material design implementation. The purpose of the TabLayout component is to present a series of tab items which, when selected, display different content to the user. The tab items can display text, images or a combination of both. When combined with the ViewPager class and fragments, tab layouts can be created with relative ease, with each tab item selection displaying a different fragment.

46. Working with the RecyclerView and CardView Widgets

The RecyclerView and CardView widgets work together to provide scrollable lists of information to the user in which the information is presented in the form of individual cards. Details of both classes will be covered in this chapter before working through the design and implementation of an example project.

46.1 An Overview of the RecyclerView

Much like the ListView class outlined in the chapter entitled *"Working with the Floating Action Button and Snackbar"*, the purpose of the RecyclerView is to allow information to be presented to the user in the form of a scrollable list. The RecyclerView, however, provides a number of advantages over the ListView. In particular, the RecyclerView is significantly more efficient in the way it manages the views that make up a list, essentially reusing existing views that make up list items as they scroll off the screen instead if creating new ones (hence the name "recycler"). This both increases the performance and reduces the resources used by a list, a feature that is of particular benefit when presenting large amounts of data to the user.

Unlike the ListView, the RecyclerView also provides a choice of three built-in layout managers to control the way in which the list items are presented to the user:

- **LinearLayoutManager** – The list items are presented as either a horizontal or vertical scrolling list.

Figure 46-1

- **GridLayoutManager** – The list items are presented in grid format. This manager is best used when the list items are of uniform size.

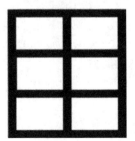

Figure 46-2

- **StaggeredGridLayoutManager** - The list items are presented in a staggered grid format. This manager is best used when the list items are not of uniform size.

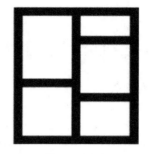

Figure 46-3

For situations where none of the three built-in managers provide the necessary layout, custom layout managers may be implemented by subclassing the RecyclerView.LayoutManager class.

Each list item displayed in a RecyclerView is created as an instance of the ViewHolder class. The ViewHolder instance contains everything necessary for the RecyclerView to display the list item, including the information to be displayed and the view layout used to display the item.

As with the ListView, the RecyclerView depends on an adapter to act as the intermediary between the RecyclerView instance and the data that is to be displayed to the user. The adapter is created as a subclass of the RecyclerView.Adapter class and must, at a minimum, implement the following methods, which will be called at various points by the RecyclerView object to which the adapter is assigned:

- **getItemCount()** – This method must return a count of the number of items that are to be displayed in the list.

- **onCreateViewHolder()** – This method creates and returns a ViewHolder object initialized with the view that is to be used to display the data. This view is typically created by inflating the XML layout file.

- **onBindViewHolder()** – This method is passed the ViewHolder object created by the *onCreateViewHolder()* method together with an integer value indicating the list item that is about to be displayed. Contained within the ViewHolder object is the layout assigned by the *onCreateViewHolder()* method. It is the responsibility of the *onBindViewHolder()* method to populate the views in the layout with the text and graphics corresponding to the specified item and to return the object to the RecyclerView where it will be presented to the user.

Adding a RecyclerView to a layout is simply a matter of adding the appropriate element to the XML content layout file of the activity in which it is to appear. For example:

```
<?xml version="1.0" encoding="utf-8"?>
<androidx.constraintlayout.widget.ConstraintLayout
    xmlns:android="http://schemas.android.com/apk/res/android"
    xmlns:app="http://schemas.android.com/apk/res-auto"
    xmlns:tools="http://schemas.android.com/tools"
    android:layout_width="match_parent"
    android:layout_height="match_parent"
    app:layout_behavior="@string/appbar_scrolling_view_behavior"
    tools:context=".MainActivity"
    tools:showIn="@layout/activity_card_demo">

    <android.support.v7.widget.RecyclerView
```

```
        android:id="@+id/recycler_view"
        android:layout_width="0dp"
        android:layout_height="0dp"
        app:layout_constraintBottom_toBottomOf="parent"
        app:layout_constraintEnd_toEndOf="parent"
        app:layout_constraintStart_toStartOf="parent"
        app:layout_constraintTop_toTopOf="parent"
        tools:listItem="@layout/card_layout" />

</androidx.constraintlayout.widget.ConstraintLayout>
.
.
```

In the above example the RecyclerView has been embedded into the CoordinatorLayout of a main activity layout file along with the AppBar and Toolbar. This provides some additional features, such as configuring the Toolbar and AppBar to scroll off the screen when the user scrolls up within the RecyclerView (a topic covered in more detail in the chapter entitled *"Working with the AppBar and Collapsing Toolbar Layouts"*).

46.2 An Overview of the CardView

The CardView class is a user interface view that allows information to be presented in groups using a card metaphor. Cards are usually presented in lists using a RecyclerView instance and may be configured to appear with shadow effects and rounded corners. Figure 46-4, for example, shows three CardView instances configured to display a layout consisting of an ImageView and two TextViews:

Figure 46-4

The user interface layout to be presented with a CardView instance is defined within an XML layout resource file and loaded into the CardView at runtime. The CardView layout can contain a layout of any complexity using the standard layout managers such as RelativeLayout and LinearLayout. The following XML layout file represents a card view layout consisting of a RelativeLayout and a single ImageView. The card is configured to be elevated to create shadowing effect and to appear with rounded corners:

```
<?xml version="1.0" encoding="utf-8"?>
    <android.support.v7.widget.CardView
        xmlns:card_view="http://schemas.android.com/apk/res-auto"
        xmlns:android="http://schemas.android.com/apk/res/android"
        android:id="@+id/card_view"
        android:layout_width="match_parent"
```

```
            android:layout_height="wrap_content"
            android:layout_margin="5dp"
            card_view:cardCornerRadius="12dp"
            card_view:cardElevation="3dp"
            card_view:contentPadding="4dp">

        <RelativeLayout
            android:layout_width="match_parent"
            android:layout_height="wrap_content"
            android:padding="16dp" >

        <ImageView
            android:layout_width="100dp"
            android:layout_height="100dp"
            android:id="@+id/item_image"
            android:layout_alignParentLeft="true"
            android:layout_alignParentTop="true"
            android:layout_marginRight="16dp" />
        </RelativeLayout>
</android.support.v7.widget.CardView>
```

When combined with the RecyclerView to create a scrollable list of cards, the *onCreateViewHolder()* method of the recycler view inflates the layout resource file for the card, assigns it to the ViewHolder instance and returns it to the RecyclerView instance.

46.3 Summary

This chapter has introduced the Android RecyclerView and CardView components. The RecyclerView provides a resource efficient way to display scrollable lists of views within an Android app. The CardView is useful when presenting groups of data (such as a list of names and addresses) in the form of cards. As previously outlined, and demonstrated in the tutorial contained in the next chapter, the RecyclerView and CardView are particularly useful when combined.

47. An Android RecyclerView and CardView Tutorial

In this chapter an example project will be created that makes use of both the CardView and RecyclerView components to create a scrollable list of cards. The completed app will display a list of cards containing images and text. In addition to displaying the list of cards, the project will be implemented such that selecting a card causes messages to be displayed to the user indicating which card was tapped.

47.1 Creating the CardDemo Project

Select the *Start a new Android Studio project* quick start option from the welcome screen and, within the resulting new project dialog, choose the Basic Activity template before clicking on the Next button.

Enter *CardDemo* into the Name field and specify *com.ebookfrenzy.carddemo* as the package name. Before clicking on the Finish button, change the Minimum API level setting to API 26: Android 8.0 (Oreo) and the Language menu to Java.

Once the project has been created, load the *content_main.xml* file into the Layout Editor tool and select and delete the "Hello World" TextView object.

47.2 Removing the Floating Action Button

Since the Basic Activity was selected, the layout includes a floating action button which is not required for this project. Load the *activity_main.xml* layout file into the Layout Editor tool, select the floating action button and tap the keyboard delete key to remove the object from the layout. Edit the *MainActivity.java* file and remove the floating action button code from the onCreate method as follows:

```
@Override
protected void onCreate(Bundle savedInstanceState) {
    super.onCreate(savedInstanceState);
    setContentView(R.layout.activity_card_demo);
    Toolbar toolbar = findViewById(R.id.toolbar);
    setSupportActionBar(toolbar);

    FloatingActionButton fab = findViewById(R.id.fab);

    fab.setOnClickListener(new View.OnClickListener() {
        @Override
        public void onClick(View view) {
            Snackbar.make(view, "Replace with your own action",
                Snackbar.LENGTH_LONG)
                    .setAction("Action", null).show();
        }
    });
}
```

47.3 Designing the CardView Layout

The layout of the views contained within the cards will be defined within a separate XML layout file. Within the Project tool window right-click on the *app -> res -> layout* entry and select the *New -> Layout resource file* menu option. In the New Resource Dialog enter *card_layout* into the *File name:* field and *androidx.cardview.widget. CardView* into the root element field before clicking on the *OK* button.

Load the *card_layout.xml* file into the Layout Editor tool, switch to Text mode and modify the layout so that it reads as follows:

```xml
<?xml version="1.0" encoding="utf-8"?>
<androidx.cardview.widget.CardView
    xmlns:android="http://schemas.android.com/apk/res/android"
    xmlns:app="http://schemas.android.com/apk/res-auto"
    android:layout_width="match_parent"
    android:layout_height="wrap_content"
    android:id="@+id/card_view"
    android:layout_margin="5dp"
    app:cardBackgroundColor="#81C784"
    app:cardCornerRadius="12dp"
    app:cardElevation="3dp"
    app:contentPadding="4dp" >


    <androidx.constraintlayout.widget.ConstraintLayout
        android:id="@+id/relativeLayout"
        android:layout_width="match_parent"
        android:layout_height="wrap_content"
        android:padding="16dp">


        <ImageView
            android:id="@+id/item_image"
            android:layout_width="100dp"
            android:layout_height="100dp"
            app:layout_constraintLeft_toLeftOf="parent"
            app:layout_constraintStart_toStartOf="parent"
            app:layout_constraintTop_toTopOf="parent" />


        <TextView
            android:id="@+id/item_title"
            android:layout_width="236dp"
            android:layout_height="39dp"
            android:layout_marginStart="16dp"
            android:textSize="30sp"
            app:layout_constraintLeft_toRightOf="@+id/item_image"
            app:layout_constraintStart_toEndOf="@+id/item_image"
            app:layout_constraintTop_toTopOf="parent" />
```

```
    <TextView
        android:id="@+id/item_detail"
        android:layout_width="236dp"
        android:layout_height="16dp"
        android:layout_marginStart="16dp"
        android:layout_marginTop="8dp"
        app:layout_constraintLeft_toRightOf="@+id/item_image"
        app:layout_constraintStart_toEndOf="@+id/item_image"
        app:layout_constraintTop_toBottomOf="@+id/item_title" />
    </androidx.constraintlayout.widget.ConstraintLayout>
</androidx.cardview.widget.CardView>
```

47.4 Adding the RecyclerView

Select the *content_main.xml* layout file and drag and drop a RecyclerView object from the *Containers* section of the palette onto the layout so that it is positioned in the center of the screen where it should automatically resize to fill the entire screen. Use the *Infer constraints* toolbar button to add any missing layout constraints to the view. Using the Attributes tool window, change the ID of the RecyclerView instance to *recycler_view* and the layout_width and layout_height properties to *match_constraint*.

47.5 Creating the RecyclerView Adapter

As outlined in the previous chapter, the RecyclerView needs to have an adapter to handle the creation of the list items. Add this new class to the project by right-clicking on the *app -> java -> com.ebookfrenzy.carddemo* entry in the Project tool window and selecting the *New -> Java Class* menu option. In the Create New Class dialog, enter *RecyclerAdapter* into the *Name:* field and change the Kind menu to *Class* before clicking on the *OK* button to create the new Java class file.

Edit the new *RecyclerAdapter.java* file to add some import directives and to declare that the class now extends *RecyclerView.Adapter*. Rather than create a separate class to provide the data to be displayed, some basic arrays will also be added to the adapter to act as the data for the app:

```
package com.ebookfrenzy.carddemo;

import android.view.LayoutInflater;
import android.view.View;
import android.view.ViewGroup;
import android.widget.ImageView;
import android.widget.TextView;
import androidx.recyclerview.widget.RecyclerView;

public class RecyclerAdapter extends RecyclerView.Adapter<RecyclerAdapter.
ViewHolder> {

    private String[] titles = {"Chapter One",
            "Chapter Two",
            "Chapter Three",
            "Chapter Four",
            "Chapter Five",
            "Chapter Six",
```

```
                "Chapter Seven",
                "Chapter Eight"};

   private String[] details = {"Item one details",
            "Item two details", "Item three details",
            "Item four details", "Item five details",
            "Item six details", "Item seven details",
            "Item eight details"};

   private int[] images = { R.drawable.android_image_1,
                            R.drawable.android_image_2,
                            R.drawable.android_image_3,
                            R.drawable.android_image_4,
                            R.drawable.android_image_5,
                            R.drawable.android_image_6,
                            R.drawable.android_image_7,
                            R.drawable.android_image_8 };
}
```

Within the RecyclerAdapter class we now need our own implementation of the ViewHolder class configured to reference the view elements in the *card_layout.xml* file. Remaining within the *RecyclerAdapter.java* file implement this class as follows:

```
public class RecyclerAdapter extends RecyclerView.Adapter<RecyclerAdapter.
ViewHolder> {
    .

    .

    class ViewHolder extends RecyclerView.ViewHolder {

        ImageView itemImage;
        TextView itemTitle;
        TextView itemDetail;

        ViewHolder(View itemView) {
            super(itemView);
            itemImage = itemView.findViewById(R.id.item_image);
            itemTitle = itemView.findViewById(R.id.item_title);
            itemDetail = itemView.findViewById(R.id.item_detail);
        }
    }
    .

    .

}
```

The ViewHolder class contains an ImageView and two TextView variables together with a constructor method that initializes those variables with references to the three view items in the *card_layout.xml* file.

The next item to be added to the *RecyclerAdapter.java* file is the implementation of the *onCreateViewHolder()*

method:

```
@Override
public ViewHolder onCreateViewHolder(ViewGroup viewGroup, int i) {
    View v = LayoutInflater.from(viewGroup.getContext())
                .inflate(R.layout.card_layout, viewGroup, false);
    ViewHolder viewHolder = new ViewHolder(v);
    return viewHolder;
}
```

This method will be called by the RecyclerView to obtain a ViewHolder object. It inflates the view hierarchy *card_layout.xml* file and creates an instance of our ViewHolder class initialized with the view hierarchy before returning it to the RecyclerView.

The purpose of the *onBindViewHolder()* method is to populate the view hierarchy within the ViewHolder object with the data to be displayed. It is passed the ViewHolder object and an integer value indicating the list item that is to be displayed. This method should now be added, using the item number as an index into the data arrays. This data is then displayed on the layout views using the references created in the constructor method of the ViewHolder class:

```
@Override
public void onBindViewHolder(ViewHolder viewHolder, int i) {
    viewHolder.itemTitle.setText(titles[i]);
    viewHolder.itemDetail.setText(details[i]);
    viewHolder.itemImage.setImageResource(images[i]);
}
```

The final requirement for the adapter class is an implementation of the *getItem()* method which, in this case, simply returns the number of items in the *titles* array:

```
@Override
public int getItemCount() {
    return titles.length;
}
```

47.6 Adding the Image Files

In addition to the two TextViews, the card layout also contains an ImageView on which the Recycler adapter has been configured to display images. Before the project can be tested these images must be added. The images that will be used for the project are named *android_image_<n>.jpg* and can be found in the *project_icons* folder of the sample code download available from the following URL:

https://www.ebookfrenzy.com/retail/androidstudio35/index.php

Locate these images in the file system navigator for your operating system and select and copy the eight images. Right click on the *app -> res -> drawable* entry in the Project tool window and select Paste to add the files to the folder:

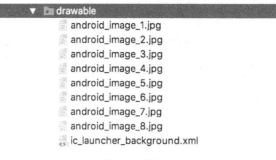

Figure 47-1

47.7 Initializing the RecyclerView Component

At this point the project consists of a RecyclerView instance, an XML layout file for the CardView instances and an adapter for the RecyclerView. The last step before testing the progress so far is to initialize the RecyclerView with a layout manager, create an instance of the adapter and assign that instance to the RecyclerView object. For the purposes of this example, the RecyclerView will be configured to use the LinearLayoutManager layout option. Edit the *MainActivity.java* file and modify the *onCreate()* method to implement this initialization code:

```
package com.ebookfrenzy.carddemo;
.
.
import androidx.appcompat.app.AppCompatActivity;
import androidx.appcompat.widget.Toolbar;
import androidx.recyclerview.widget.LinearLayoutManager;
import androidx.recyclerview.widget.RecyclerView;

import android.view.View;
import android.view.Menu;
import android.view.MenuItem;

public class MainActivity extends AppCompatActivity {

    RecyclerView recyclerView;
    RecyclerView.LayoutManager layoutManager;
    RecyclerView.Adapter adapter;

    @Override
    protected void onCreate(Bundle savedInstanceState) {
        super.onCreate(savedInstanceState);
        setContentView(R.layout.activity_card_demo);
        Toolbar toolbar = findViewById(R.id.toolbar);
        setSupportActionBar(toolbar);

        recyclerView = findViewById(R.id.recycler_view);

        layoutManager = new LinearLayoutManager(this);
        recyclerView.setLayoutManager(layoutManager);
```

```
        adapter = new RecyclerAdapter();
        recyclerView.setAdapter(adapter);
    }
.
.

}
```

47.8 Testing the Application

Compile and run the app on a physical device or emulator session and scroll through the different card items in the list:

Figure 47-2

47.9 Responding to Card Selections

The last phase of this project is to make the cards in the list selectable so that clicking on a card triggers an event within the app. For this example, the cards will be configured to present a message on the display when tapped by the user. To respond to clicks, the ViewHolder class needs to be modified to assign an onClickListener on each item view. Edit the *RecyclerAdapter.java* file and modify the ViewHolder class declaration so that it reads as follows:

```
.
.
import com.google.android.material.snackbar.Snackbar;
.
.
class ViewHolder extends RecyclerView.ViewHolder{

    ImageView itemImage;
    TextView itemTitle;
    TextView itemDetail;

    ViewHolder(View itemView) {
```

```
        super(itemView);
        itemImage = itemView.findViewById(R.id.item_image);
        itemTitle = itemView.findViewById(R.id.item_title);
        itemDetail = itemView.findViewById(R.id.item_detail);

        itemView.setOnClickListener(new View.OnClickListener() {
            @Override public void onClick(View v) {


            }
        });
    }
}
```

Within the body of the onClick handler, code can now be added to display a message indicating that the card has been clicked. Given that the actions performed as a result of a click will likely depend on which card was tapped it is also important to identify the selected card. This information can be obtained via a call to the *getAdapterPosition()* method of the *RecyclerView.ViewHolder* class. Remaining within the *RecyclerAdapter.java* file, add code to the *onClick* handler so it reads as follows:

```
@override
public void onClick(View v) {

    int position = getAdapterPosition();

    Snackbar.make(v, "Click detected on item " + position,
            Snackbar.LENGTH_LONG)
            .setAction("Action", null).show();
    }
});
```

The last task is to enable the material design ripple effect that appears when items are tapped within Android applications. This simply involves the addition of some properties to the declaration of the CardView instance in the *card_layout.xml* file as follows:

```
<?xml version="1.0" encoding="utf-8"?>
<androidx.cardview.widget.CardView
    xmlns:android="http://schemas.android.com/apk/res/android"
    xmlns:card_view="http://schemas.android.com/apk/res-auto"
    android:layout_width="match_parent"
    android:layout_height="match_parent"
    android:id="@+id/card_view"
    android:layout_margin="5dp"
    app:cardBackgroundColor="#81C784"
    app:cardCornerRadius="12dp"
    app:cardElevation="3dp"
    app:contentPadding="4dp"
    android:foreground="?selectableItemBackground"
    android:clickable="true" >
```

Run the app once again and verify that tapping a card in the list triggers both the standard ripple effect at the point of contact and the appearance of a Snackbar reporting the number of the selected item.

47.10 Summary

This chapter has worked through the steps involved in combining the CardView and RecyclerView components to display a scrollable list of card based items. The example also covered the detection of clicks on list items, including the identification of the selected item and the enabling of the ripple effect visual feedback on the tapped CardView instance.

48. A Layout Editor Sample Data Tutorial

The CardDemo project created in the previous chapter has provided a good example of how it can be difficult to assess from within the layout editor exactly how a user interface is going to appear until the completed app is tested. This is a problem that frequently occurs when the content to be displayed in a user interface is only generated or acquired once the user has the app installed and running.

For some time now, the Android Studio layout editor has provided the ability to specify simple attributes that are active only when the layout is being designed. A design-time only string resource could, for example, be assigned to a TextView within the layout editor that would not appear when the app runs. This capability has been extended significantly with the introduction of sample data support within the Android Studio layout editor and will be used in this chapter to improve the layout editor experience in the CardDemo project.

48.1 Adding Sample Data to a Project

During the design phase of the user interface layout, the RecyclerView instance (Figure 48-1) bears little resemblance to the running app tested at the end of the previous chapter:

Figure 48-1

In the *"Modern Android App Architecture with Jetpack"* chapter earlier in the book the concept of sample data was introduced. To demonstrate sample data in use, the project will now be modified so that the fully populated cards appear within the RecyclerView from within the layout editor. Before doing that, however, it is worth noting that the layout editor has a collection of preconfigured sample data templates that can be used when designing user interfaces. To see some of these in action, load the *content_main.xml* layout file into the layout editor and select the RecyclerView instance. Right-click on the RecyclerView and select the *Set Sample Data* menu option to display the Design-time View Attributes panel:

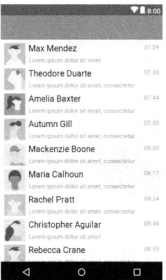

Figure 48-2

Change the template to the Email Client option and the item count to 12 and note that the RecyclerView changes to display data from the template:

Figure 48-3

These templates can be useful for displaying sample data without any additional work and will often provide enough to complete the layout design. For this example, however, sample data is going to be used to display the cards within the RecyclerView as they are intended to appear in the running app. With the *content_main.xml* file still loaded in the layout editor, switch to Text mode and locate the RecyclerView element which should read as follows:

```
<androidx.recyclerview.widget.RecyclerView
    android:id="@+id/recycler_view"
    android:layout_width="0dp"
    android:layout_height="0dp"
    app:layout_constraintBottom_toBottomOf="parent"
    app:layout_constraintEnd_toEndOf="parent"
    app:layout_constraintStart_toStartOf="parent"
    app:layout_constraintTop_toTopOf="parent"
    tools:itemCount="12"
```

```
tools:listitem="@layout/recycler_view_item" />
```

Note the two special *tools* properties currently configured to display 12 items in the list, each using a layout contained within a file named *recycler_view_item.xml*. The layout editor provides a range of tools options that may be configured within a layout file. Though coverage of all of these settings is beyond the scope of this book, a full description of each can be found at the following URL:

https://developer.android.com/studio/write/tool-attributes#toolssample_resources

The *recycler_view_item.xml* file referenced above was generated automatically by the layout editor when the sample data template was selected and can be found in the project tool window.

Switch back to Design mode and, with the RecyclerView selected, use the Design-time View Attributes panel to switch the template back to the default settings. The *recycler_view_item.xml* file will be removed from the project along with the two *tools* property lines within the *content_main.xml* XML file.

To switch to using the card layout for the sample data display, add a *listitem* property to reference the *card_layout.xml* file. With the RecyclerView selected in the layout, search for the *listItem* property in the Attributes tool window and enter *@layout/card_layout* into the property field as illustrated in Figure 48-4:

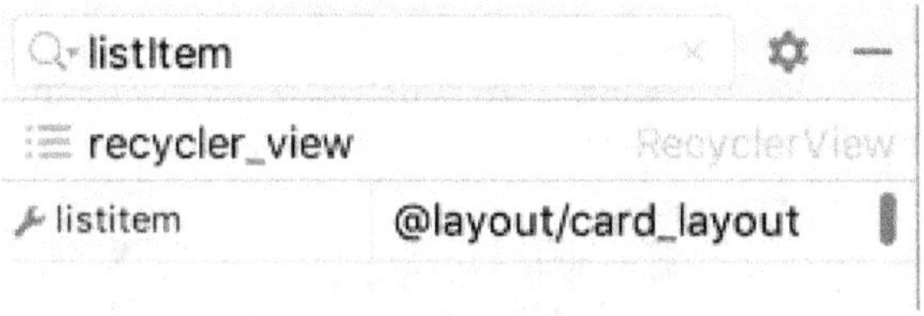

Figure 48-4

Switch back to Design mode and note the card layout is now appearing for each list item, though without any images and using sample text data:

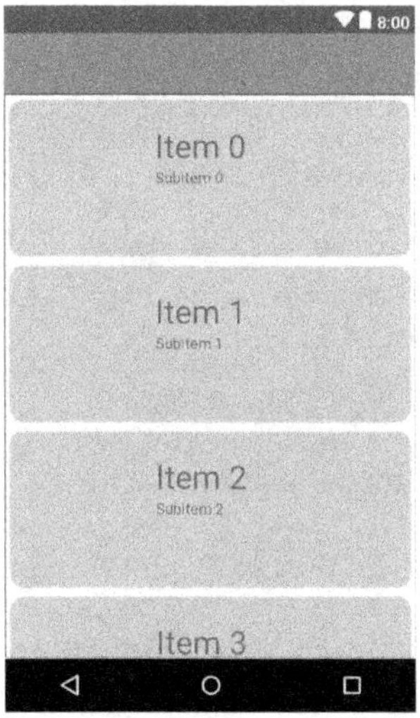

Figure 48-5

The next step is to display some images and different text on the views within the card layout. This can either take the form of template sample data provided by the layout editor, or custom sample data added specifically for this project. Load the *card_layout.xml* file into the layout editor, select the ImageView and display the Design-time View Attributes panel as outlined earlier in the chapter. From the srcCompat menu, select the built-in

A Layout Editor Sample Data Tutorial

backgrounds/scenic image set as illustrated in Figure 48-6 below:

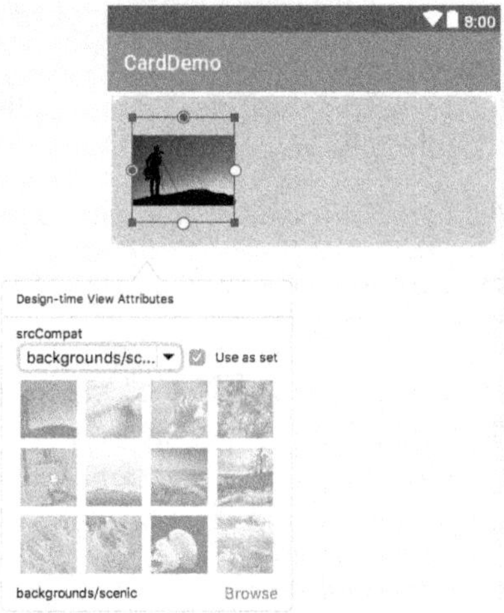

Figure 48-6

Next, right-click on the *item_title* TextView object, select the *Set Sample Data* menu option and, in the Design-time attributes panel, select the *cities* text option. Repeat this step for the *item_detail* view, this time selecting the *full_names* option as shown in Figure 48-7:

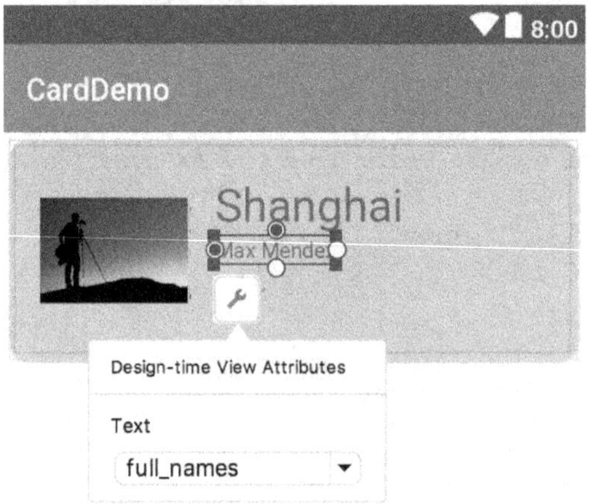

Figure 48-7

Open the *content_main.xml* file in Design mode and note that the RecyclerView is now using the built-in images and sample text data:

Figure 48-8

48.2 Using Custom Sample Data

The final step in this chapter is to demonstrate the use of custom sample data and images within the layout editor. This requires the creation of a sample data directory and the addition of some text and image files. Within the Project tool window, right-click on the *app* entry and select the *New -> Sample Data Directory* menu option, at which point a new directory named *sampledata* will appear within the Project tool window.

Right-click on the *sampledata* directory, create a subdirectory named *images* and copy and paste the Android images into the new folder using the same steps outlined in the previous chapter. Display the Design-time View Attributes panel for the ImageView once again, this time clicking the Browse link and selecting the newly added Android images in the *Resources* dialog (if the images folder does not appear try rebuilding the project):

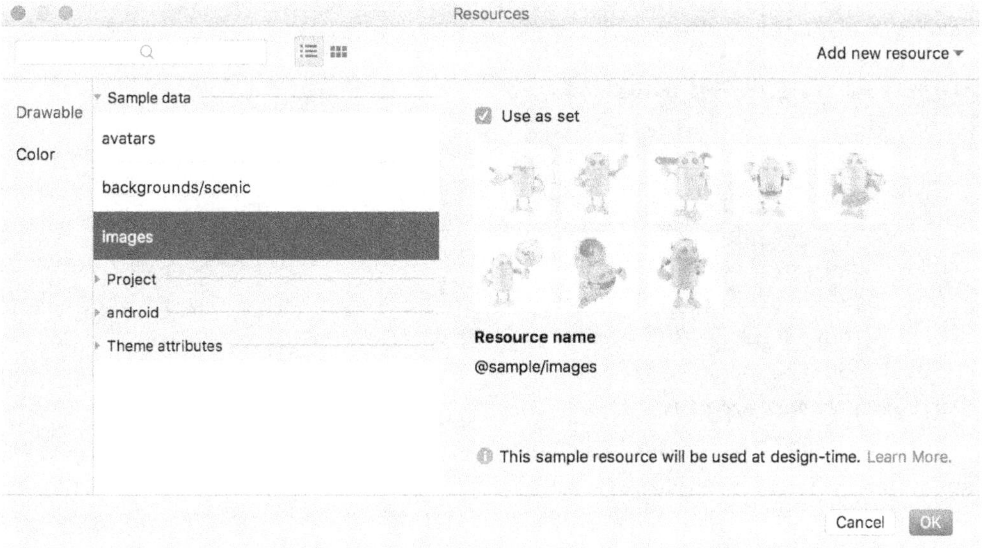

![Resources dialog showing Sample data with images selected and Resource name @sample/images]

Figure 48-9

A Layout Editor Sample Data Tutorial

Right-click once again on the *sampledata* directory, select the New File option, name the file *chapters* and set the type to *Text*. After the file has been created, enter the following content:

```
Chapter One
Chapter Two
Chapter Three
Chapter Four
Chapter Five
Chapter Six
Chapter Seven
Chapter Eight
```

Next, create a second text file named *items* with the following content:

```
Item one details
Item two details
Item three details
Item four details
Item five details
Item six details
Item seven details
Item eight details
```

With the sample data text files created, all that remains is to reference them in the view elements of the *card_layout.xml* file as follows:

```
<TextView
    android:layout_width="wrap_content"
    android:layout_height="wrap_content"
    android:id="@+id/item_title"
    android:layout_toEndOf="@+id/item_image"
    android:layout_toRightOf="@+id/item_image"
    android:layout_alignParentTop="true"
    android:textSize="30sp"
    tools:text="@sample/chapters" />


<TextView
    android:layout_width="wrap_content"
    android:layout_height="wrap_content"
    android:id="@+id/item_detail"
    android:layout_toEndOf="@+id/item_image"
    android:layout_toRightOf="@+id/item_image"
    android:layout_below="@+id/item_title"
    tools:text="@sample/items" />
```

Return to the layout design in the *content_main.xml* file where the custom sample data and images should now be displayed within the RecyclerView list:

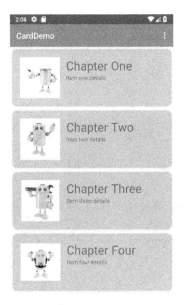

Figure 48-10

Instead of having two separate text files and a reference to the image set, another option is to declare the sample data within a JSON file. For example:

```
{
  "mydata": [
    {
      "chapter" : "Chapter One",
      "details": "Item one details",
      "image": "@sample/images"
    },
    {
      "chapter" : "Chapter Two",
      "details": "Item two details",
      "image": "@sample/images"
    },
    .
    .
}
```

Assuming the above was contained within a file named *chapterdata.json*, the sample data would then be referenced within the view XML elements as follows:

```
.
.
<ImageView
  .
  .
    tools:src="@sample/chapterdata.json/mydata/image" />
<TextView
  .
```

.

```
        tools:text="@sample/chapterdata.json/mydata/chapter" />

<TextView

.

.

        tools:text="@sample/chapterdata.json/mydata/details" />

.

.
```

48.3 Summary

This chapter has demonstrated the use of sample data within the layout editor to provide a more realistic representation of how the user interface will appear at runtime. The steps covered in this tutorial included the use of both pre-existing sample data templates and the integration of custom sample data.

49. Working with the AppBar and Collapsing Toolbar Layouts

In this chapter we will be exploring the ways in which the app bar within an activity layout can be customized and made to react to the scrolling events taking place within other views on the screen. By making use of the CoordinatorLayout in conjunction with the AppBarLayout and CollapsingToolbarLayout containers, the app bar can be configured to display an image and to animate in and out of view. An upward scrolling motion on a list, for example, can be configured so that the app bar recedes from view and then reappears when a downward scrolling motion is performed.

Beginning with an overview of the elements that can comprise an app bar, this chapter will then work through a variety of examples of app bar configuration.

49.1 The Anatomy of an AppBar

The app bar is the area that appears at the top of the display when an app is running and can be configured to contain a variety of different items including the status bar, toolbar, tab bar and a flexible space area. Figure 49-1, for example, shows an app bar containing a status bar, toolbar and tab bar:

Figure 49-1

The flexible space area can be filled by a blank background color, or as shown in Figure 49-2, an image displayed on an ImageView object:

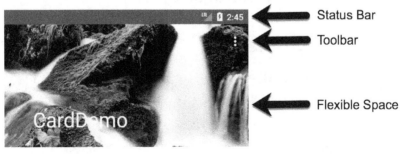

Figure 49-2

As will be demonstrated in the remainder of this chapter, if the main content area of the activity user interface layout contains scrollable content, the elements of the app bar can be configured to expand and contract as the content on the screen is scrolled.

49.2 The Example Project

For the purposes of this example, changes will be made to the CardDemo project created in the earlier chapter entitled *"An Android RecyclerView and CardView Tutorial"*. Begin by launching Android Studio and loading this project.

Once the project has loaded, run the app and note when scrolling the list upwards that the toolbar remains visible as shown in Figure 49-3:

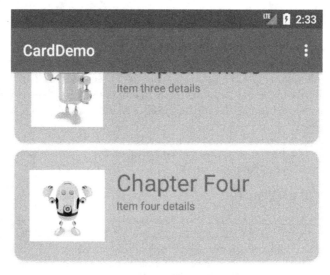

Figure 49-3

The first step is to make some configuration changes so that the toolbar contracts during an upward scrolling motion, and then expands on a downward scroll.

49.3 Coordinating the RecyclerView and Toolbar

Load the *activity_main.xml* file into the Layout Editor tool, switch to text mode and review the XML layout design, the hierarchy of which is represented by the diagram in Figure 49-4:

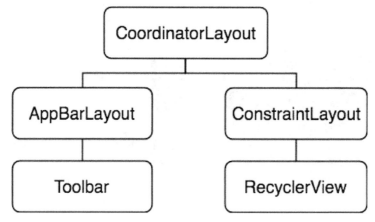

Figure 49-4

At the top level of the hierarchy is the CoordinatorLayout which, as the name suggests, coordinates the interactions between the various child view elements it contains. As highlighted in *"Working with the Floating*

Action Button and Snackbar" for example, the CoordinatorLayout automatically slides the floating action button upwards to accommodate the appearance of a Snackbar when it appears, then moves the button back down after the bar is dismissed.

The CoordinatorLayout can similarly be used to cause elements of the app bar to slide in and out of view based on the scrolling action of certain views within the view hierarchy. One such element within the layout hierarchy shown in Figure 49-4 is the ConstraintLayout. To achieve this coordinated behavior, it is necessary to set properties on both the element on which scrolling takes place and the elements with which the scrolling is to be coordinated.

On the scrolling element (in this case the RecyclerView) the *android:layout_behavior* property must be set to *appbar_scrolling_view_behavior*. Within the *content_main.xml* file, locate the top level ConstraintLayout element and note that this property has been set by default:

```
<androidx.constraintlayout.widget.ConstraintLayout
    xmlns:android="http://schemas.android.com/apk/res/android"
    xmlns:app="http://schemas.android.com/apk/res-auto"
    xmlns:tools="http://schemas.android.com/tools"
    android:layout_width="match_parent"
    android:layout_height="match_parent"
    app:layout_behavior="@string/appbar_scrolling_view_behavior"
    tools:context=".MainActivity"
    tools:showIn="@layout/activity_card_demo">
```

Next, open the *activity_main.xml* file in the layout editor, switch to Text mode and locate the AppBarLayout element. Note that the only child of AppBarLayout in the view hierarchy is the Toolbar. To make the toolbar react to the scroll events taking place in the RecyclerView the *app:layout_scrollFlags* property must be set on this element. The value assigned to this property will depend on the nature of the interaction required and must consist of one or more of the following:

- **scroll** – Indicates that the view is to be scrolled off the screen. If this is not set the view will remain pinned at the top of the screen during scrolling events.

- **enterAlways** – When used in conjunction with the *scroll* option, an upward scrolling motion will cause the view to retract. Any downward scrolling motion in this mode will cause the view to re-appear.

- **enterAlwaysCollapsed** – When set on a view, that view will not expand from the collapsed state until the downward scrolling motion reaches the limit of the list. If the *minHeight* property is set, the view will appear during the initial scrolling motion but only until the minimum height is reached. It will then remain at that height and will not expand fully until the top of the list is reached. Note this option only works when used in conjunction with both the *enterAlways* and *scroll* options. For example:

```
app:layout_scrollFlags="scroll|enterAlways|enterAlwaysCollapsed"
android:minHeight="20dp"
```

- **exitUntilCollapsed** – When set, the view will collapse during an upward scrolling motion until the minHeight threshold is met, at which point it will remain at that height until the scroll direction changes.

For the purposes of this example, the *scroll* and *enterAlways* options will be set on the Toolbar as follows:

```
<androidx.appcompat.widget.Toolbar
    android:id="@+id/toolbar"
    android:layout_width="match_parent"
    android:layout_height="?attr/actionBarSize"
```

```
android:background="?attr/colorPrimary"
app:popupTheme="@style/AppTheme.PopupOverlay"
app:layout_scrollFlags="scroll|enterAlways" />
```

With the appropriate properties set, run the app once again and make an upward scrolling motion in the RecyclerView list. This should cause the toolbar to collapse out of view (Figure 49-5). A downward scrolling motion should cause the toolbar to re-appear.

Figure 49-5

49.4 Introducing the Collapsing Toolbar Layout

The CollapsingToolbarLayout container enhances the standard toolbar by providing a greater range of options and level of control over the collapsing of the app bar and its children in response to coordinated scrolling actions. The CollapsingToolbarLayout class is intended to be added as a child of the AppBarLayout and provides features such as automatically adjusting the font size of the toolbar title as the toolbar collapses and expands. A *parallax* mode allows designated content in the app bar to fade from view as it collapses while a *pin* mode allows elements of the app bar to remain in fixed position during the contraction.

A *scrim* option is also available to designate the color to which the toolbar should transition during the collapse sequence.

To see these features in action, the app bar contained in the *activity_main.xml* file will be modified to use the CollapsingToolbarLayout class together with the addition of an ImageView to better demonstrate the effect of parallax mode. The new view hierarchy that makes use of the CollapsingToolbarLayout is represented by the diagram in Figure 49-6:

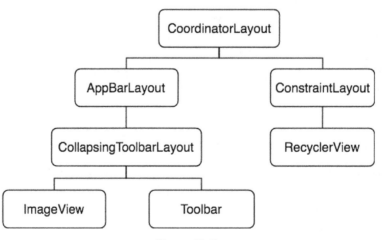

Figure 49-6

Load the *activity_main.xml* file into the Layout Editor tool in Text mode and modify the layout so that it reads as follows:

```xml
<?xml version="1.0" encoding="utf-8"?>
<androidx.coordinatorlayout.widget.CoordinatorLayout
    xmlns:android="http://schemas.android.com/apk/res/android"
    xmlns:app="http://schemas.android.com/apk/res-auto"
    xmlns:tools="http://schemas.android.com/tools"
    android:layout_width="match_parent"
    android:layout_height="match_parent"
    tools:context=".MainActivity">

    <com.google.android.material.appbar.AppBarLayout
        android:layout_width="match_parent"
        android:layout_height="wrap_content"
        android:theme="@style/AppTheme.AppBarOverlay">

        <com.google.android.material.appbar.CollapsingToolbarLayout
            android:id="@+id/collapsing_toolbar"
            android:layout_width="match_parent"
            android:layout_height="match_parent"
            app:layout_scrollFlags="scroll|enterAlways"
            android:fitsSystemWindows="true"
            app:contentScrim="?attr/colorPrimary"
            app:expandedTitleMarginStart="48dp"
            app:expandedTitleMarginEnd="64dp">

            <ImageView
                android:id="@+id/backdrop"
                android:layout_width="match_parent"
                android:layout_height="200dp"
                android:scaleType="centerCrop"
                android:fitsSystemWindows="true"
                app:layout_collapseMode="parallax"
                android:src="@drawable/appbar_image" />

            <androidx.appcompat.widget.Toolbar
                android:id="@+id/toolbar"
                android:layout_width="match_parent"
                android:layout_height="?attr/actionBarSize"
                android:background="?attr/colorPrimary"
                app:popupTheme="@style/AppTheme.PopupOverlay"
                app:layout_scrollFlags="scroll|enterAlways"
                app:layout_collapseMode="pin" />
        </com.google.android.material.appbar.CollapsingToolbarLayout>
```

```
    </com.google.android.material.appbar.AppBarLayout>

    <include layout="@layout/content_main" />

</androidx.coordinatorlayout.widget.CoordinatorLayout>
```

In addition to adding the new elements to the layout above, the background color property setting has been removed. This change has the advantage of providing a transparent toolbar allowing more of the image to be visible in the app bar.

Using the file system navigator for your operating system, locate the *appbar_image.jpg* image file in the *project_icons* folder of the code sample download for the book and copy it. Right-click on the *app -> res -> drawable* entry in the Project tool window and select *Paste* from the resulting menu.

When run, the app bar should appear as illustrated in Figure 49-7:

Figure 49-7

Scrolling the list upwards will cause the app bar to gradually collapse. During the contraction, the image will fade to the color defined by the scrim property while the title text font size reduces at a corresponding rate until only the toolbar is visible:

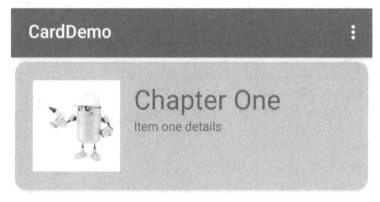

Figure 49-8

The toolbar has remained visible during the initial stages of the scrolling motion (the toolbar will also recede from view if the upward scrolling motion continues) as the flexible area collapses because the toolbar element in the *activity_main.xml* file was configured to use pin mode:

```
app:layout_collapseMode="pin"
```

Had the collapse mode been set to parallax the toolbar would have retracted along with the image view.

Continuing the upward scrolling motion will cause the toolbar to also collapse leaving only the status bar visible:

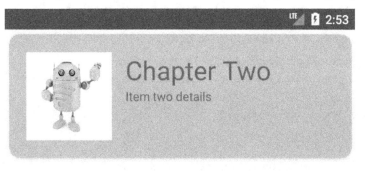

Figure 49-9

Since the scroll flags property for the CollapsingToolbarLayout element includes the enterAlways option, a downward scrolling motion will cause the app bar to expand once again.

To fix the toolbar in place so that it no longer recedes from view during the upward scrolling motion, replace *enterAlways* with *exitUntilCollapsed* in the *layout_scrollFlags* property of the CollapsingToolbarLayout element in the *activity_main.xml* file as follows:

```
<com.google.android.material.appbar.CollapsingToolbarLayout
    android:id="@+id/collapsing_toolbar"
    android:layout_width="match_parent"
    android:layout_height="match_parent"
    app:layout_scrollFlags="scroll|exitUntilCollapsed"
    android:fitsSystemWindows="true"
    app:contentScrim="?attr/colorPrimary"
    app:expandedTitleMarginStart="48dp"
    app:expandedTitleMarginEnd="64dp">
```

49.5 Changing the Title and Scrim Color

As a final task, edit the *MainActivity.java* file and add some code to the *onCreate()* method to change the title text on the collapsing layout manager instance and to set a different scrim color (note that the scrim color may also be set within the layout resource file):

```
package com.ebookfrenzy.carddemo;
.
.
import com.google.android.material.appbar.CollapsingToolbarLayout;
import android.graphics.Color;
.
.
.
    @Override
    protected void onCreate(Bundle savedInstanceState) {
        super.onCreate(savedInstanceState);
        setContentView(R.layout.activity_card_demo);
        Toolbar toolbar = findViewById(R.id.toolbar);
        setSupportActionBar(toolbar);
```

```
    CollapsingToolbarLayout collapsingToolbarLayout =
            findViewById(R.id.collapsing_toolbar);

    collapsingToolbarLayout.setTitle("My Toolbar Title");
    collapsingToolbarLayout.setContentScrimColor(Color.GREEN);

    recyclerView = findViewById(R.id.recycler_view);

    layoutManager = new LinearLayoutManager(this);
    recyclerView.setLayoutManager(layoutManager);

    adapter = new RecyclerAdapter();
    recyclerView.setAdapter(adapter);
}
    .
    .
    .
}
```

Run the app one last time and note that the new title appears in the app bar and that scrolling now causes the toolbar to transition to green as it retracts from view.

49.6 Summary

The app bar that appears at the top of most Android apps can consist of a number of different elements including a toolbar, tab layout and even an image view. When embedded in a CoordinatorLayout parent, a number of different options are available to control the way in which the app bar behaves in response to scrolling events in the main content of the activity. For greater control over this behavior, the CollapsingToolbarLayout manager provides a range of additional levels of control over the way the app bar content expands and contracts in relation to scrolling activity.

50. An Android Studio Master/Detail Flow Tutorial

This chapter will explain the concept of the Master/Detail user interface design before exploring, in detail, the elements that make up the Master/Detail Flow template included with Android Studio. An example application will then be created that demonstrates the steps involved in modifying the template to meet the specific needs of the application developer.

50.1 The Master/Detail Flow

A master/detail flow is an interface design concept whereby a list of items (referred to as the *master list*) is displayed to the user. On selecting an item from the list, additional information relating to that item is then presented to the user within a *detail* pane. An email application might, for example, consist of a master list of received messages consisting of the address of the sender and the subject of the message. Upon selection of a message from the master list, the body of the email message would appear within the detail pane.

On tablet sized Android device displays in landscape orientation, the master list appears in a narrow vertical panel along the left-hand edge of the screen. The remainder of the display is devoted to the detail pane in an arrangement referred to as *two-pane mode*. Figure 50-1, for example, shows the master/detail, two-pane arrangement with master items listed and the content of item one displayed in the detail pane:

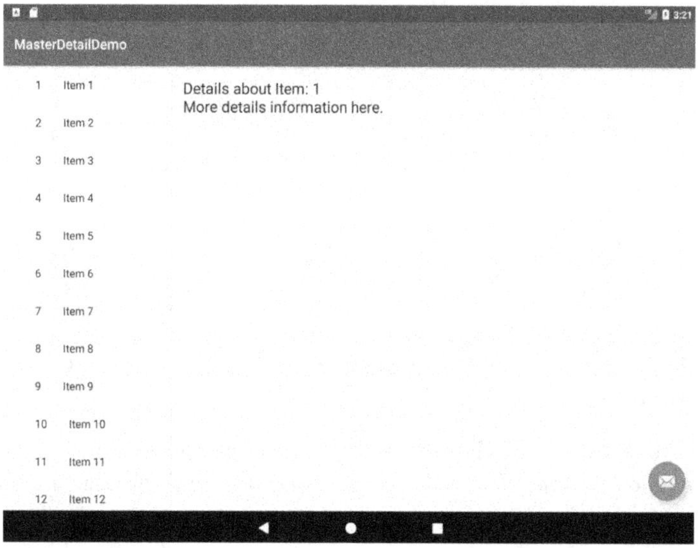

Figure 50-1

On smaller, phone sized Android devices, the master list takes up the entire screen and the detail pane appears on a separate screen which appears when a selection is made from the master list. In this mode, the detail screen includes an action bar entry to return to the master list. Figure 50-2 for example, illustrates both the master and detail screens for the same item list on a 4" phone screen:

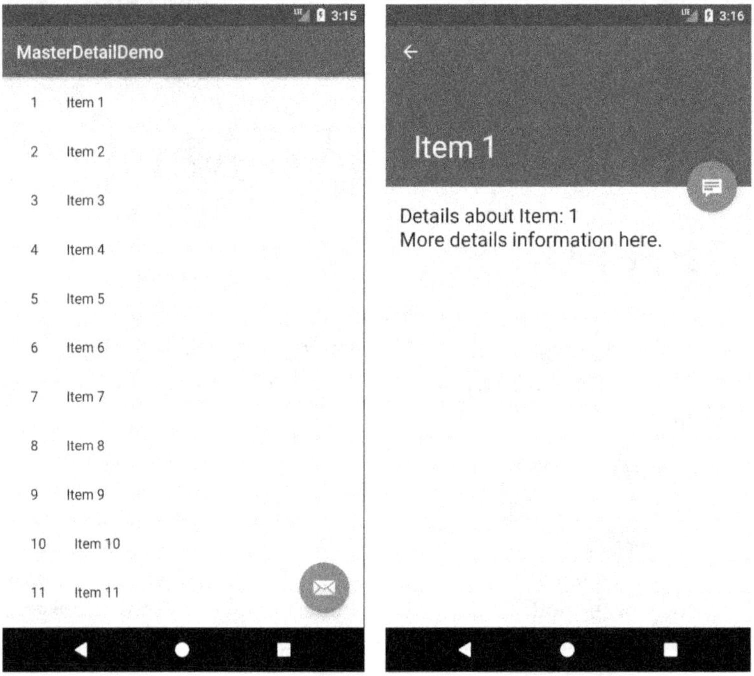

Figure 50-2

50.2 Creating a Master/Detail Flow Activity

In the next section of this chapter, the different elements that comprise the Master/Detail Flow template will be covered in some detail. This is best achieved by creating a project using the Master/Detail Flow template to use while working through the information. This project will subsequently be used as the basis for the tutorial at the end of the chapter.

Although the project creation wizard includes the option to select the Master/Detail Flow template, greater flexibility in terms of configuring the template is available by adding the activity after the project has been created.

Select the *Start a new Android Studio project* quick start option from the welcome screen and, within the resulting new project dialog, choose the Add No Activity template before clicking on the Next button.

Enter *MasterDetailFlow* into the Name field and specify *com.ebookfrenzy.masterdetailflow* as the package name. Before clicking on the Finish button, change the Minimum API level setting to API 26: Android 8.0 (Oreo) and the Language menu to Java.

Once the project has been created, right-click on the *app -> java -> com.ebookfrenzy.masterdetailflow* entry in the Project tool window and select the *New -> Activity -> Master/Detail Flow* menu option.

The New Android Activity screen (Figure 50-3) provides the opportunity to configure the objects that will be displayed within the Master/Detail activity. In the tutorial later in this chapter, the master list will contain a number of web site names which, when selected, will load the chosen web site into a web view within the detail pane. With these requirements in mind, set the *Object Kind* field to "Website", and the *Object Kind Plural* and *Title* settings to "Websites".

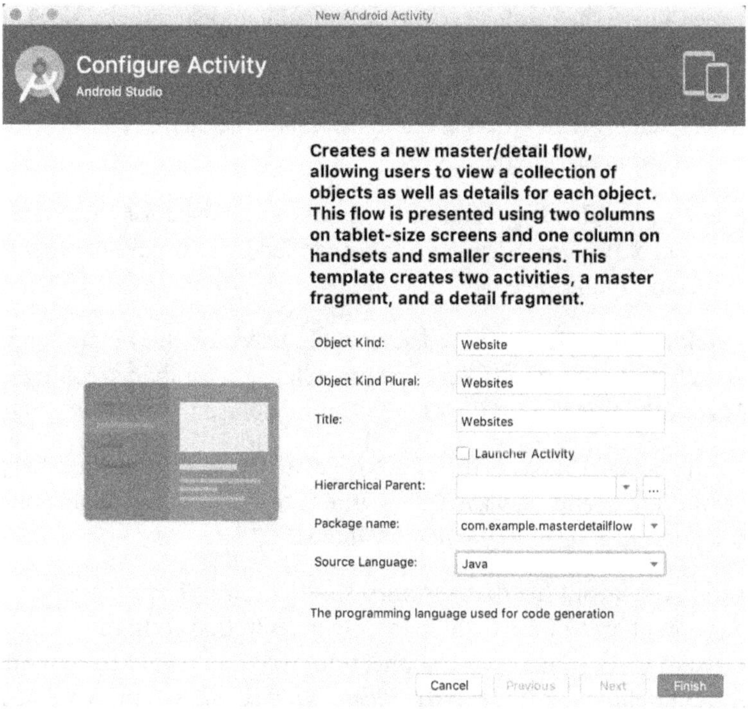

Figure 50-3

Be sure to enable the *Launcher Activity* option and set the Source Language menu to Java before clicking on the Finish button.

50.3 The Anatomy of the Master/Detail Flow Template

Once a new project has been created using the Master/Detail Flow template, a number of Java and XML layout resource files will have been created automatically. It is important to gain an understanding of these different files in order to be able to adapt the template to specific requirements. A review of the project within the Android Studio Project tool window will reveal the following files, where *<item>* is replaced by the Object Kind name that was specified when the project was created (this being "Website" in the case of the *MasterDetailFlow* example project):

- **activity_<item>_list.xml** – The top level layout file for the master list, this file is loaded by the *<item>ListActivity* class. This layout contains a toolbar, a floating action button and includes the *<item>_list.xml* file.

- **<item>ListActivity.java** – The activity class responsible for displaying and managing the master list (declared in the *activity_<item>_list.xml* file) and for both displaying and responding to the selection of items within that list.

- **<item>_list.xml** – The layout file used to display the master list of items in single-pane mode where the master list and detail pane appear on different screens. This file consists of a RecyclerView object configured to use the LinearLayoutManager. The RecyclerView element declares that each item in the master list is to be displayed using the layout declared within the *<item>_list_content.xml* file.

- **<item>_list.xml (w900dp)** – The layout file for the master list in the two-pane mode used on tablets in landscape (where the master list and detail pane appear side by side). This file contains a horizontal LinearLayout parent within which resides a RecyclerView to display the master list, and a FrameLayout to contain the content of the detail pane. As with the single-pane variant of this file, the RecyclerView element declares that each item in the list be displayed using the layout contained within the *<item>_list_content.xml* file.

- **<item>_list_content.xml** – This file contains the layout to be used for each item in the master list. By default, this consists of two TextView objects embedded in a horizontal LinearLayout but may be changed to meet specific application needs.

- **activity_<item>_detail.xml** – The top level layout file used for the detail pane when running in single-pane mode. This layout contains an app bar, collapsing toolbar, scrolling view and a floating action button. At runtime this layout file is loaded and displayed by the *<item>DetailActivity* class.

- **<item>DetailActivity.java** – This class displays the layout defined in the *activity_<item>_detail.xml* file. The class also initializes and displays the fragment containing the detail content defined in the *<item>_detail.xml* and *<item>DetailFragment.java* files.

- **<item>_detail.xml** – The layout file that accompanies the *<item>DetailFragment* class and contains the layout for the content area of the detail pane. By default, this contains a single TextView object, but may be changed to meet your specific application needs. In single-pane mode, this fragment is loaded into the layout defined by the *activity_<item>_detail.xml* file. In two-pane mode, this layout is loaded into the FrameLayout area of the *<item>_list.xml (w900dp)* file so that it appears adjacent to the master list.

- **<item>DetailFragment.java** – The fragment class file responsible for displaying the *<item>_detail.xml* layout and populating it with the content to be displayed in the detail pane. This fragment is initialized and displayed within the *<item>DetailActivity.java* file to provide the content displayed within the *activity_<item>_detail.xml* layout for single-pane mode and the *<item>_list.xml (w900dp)* layout for two-pane mode.

- **DummyContent.java** – A class file intended to provide sample data for the template. This class can either be modified to meet application needs, or replaced entirely. By default, the content provided by this class simply consists of a number of string items.

50.4 Modifying the Master/Detail Flow Template

While the structure of the Master/Detail Flow template can appear confusing at first, the concepts will become clearer as the default template is modified in the remainder of this chapter. As will become evident, much of the functionality provided by the template can remain unchanged for many master/detail implementation requirements.

In the rest of this chapter, the *MasterDetailFlow* project will be modified such that the master list displays a list of web site names and the detail pane altered to contain a WebView object instead of the current TextView. When a web site is selected by the user, the corresponding web page will subsequently load and display in the detail pane.

50.5 Changing the Content Model

The content for the example as it currently stands is defined by the *DummyContent* class file. Begin, therefore, by selecting the *DummyContent.java* file (located in the Project tool window in the *app -> java -> com.ebookfrenzy. masterdetailflow -> dummy* folder) and reviewing the code. At the bottom of the file is a declaration for a class named *DummyItem* which is currently able to store two String objects representing a content string and an ID. The updated project, on the other hand, will need each item object to contain an ID string, a string for the web site name, and a string for the corresponding URL of the web site. To add these features, modify the *DummyItem* class so that it reads as follows:

```
public static class DummyItem {
        public String id;
        public String website_name;
        public String website_url;

        public DummyItem(String id, String website_name,
                String website_url)
        {
                this.id = id;
                this.website_name = website_name;
                this.website_url = website_url;
        }

        @Override
        public String toString() {
                return website_name;
        }
}
```

Note that the encapsulating DummyContent class currently contains a *for* loop that adds 25 items by making multiple calls to methods named *createDummyItem()* and *makeDetails()*. Much of this code will no longer be required and should be deleted from the class as follows:

```
public static Map<String, DummyItem> ITEM_MAP = new HashMap<String, DummyItem>();

private static final int COUNT = 25;

static {
    // Add some sample items.
    for (int i = 1; i <= COUNT; i++) {
        addItem(createDummyItem(i));
    }
}

private static void addItem(DummyItem item) {
    ITEMS.add(item);
    ITEM_MAP.put(item.id, item);
}

private static DummyItem createDummyItem(int position) {
    return new DummyItem(String.valueOf(position), "Item " + position,
makeDetails(position));
}
```

—

```
private static String makeDetails(int position) {
    StringBuilder builder = new StringBuilder();
    builder.append("Details about Item: ").append(position);
    for (int i = 0; i < position; i++) {
        builder.append("\nMore details information here.");
    }
    return builder.toString();
}
```

This code needs to be modified to initialize the data model with the required web site data:

```
public static final Map<String, DummyItem> ITEM_MAP =
        new HashMap<String, DummyItem>();


static {
    // Add 3 sample items.
    addItem(new DummyItem("1", "eBookFrenzy",
            "https://www.ebookfrenzy.com"));
    addItem(new DummyItem("2", "Amazon",
            "https://www.amazon.com"));
    addItem(new DummyItem("3", "New York Times",
            "https://www.nytimes.com"));
}
```

The code now takes advantage of the modified DummyItem class to store an ID, web site name and URL for each item.

50.6 Changing the Detail Pane

The detail information shown to the user when an item is selected from the master list is currently displayed via the layout contained in the *website_detail.xml* file. By default, this contains a single view in the form of a TextView. Since the TextView class is not capable of displaying a web page, this needs to be changed to a WebView object for this tutorial. To achieve this, navigate to the *app -> res -> layout -> website_detail.xml* file in the Project tool window and double-click on it to load it into the Layout Editor tool. Switch to Text mode and delete the current XML content from the file. Replace this content with the following XML:

```
<WebView xmlns:android="http://schemas.android.com/apk/res/android"
    xmlns:tools="http://schemas.android.com/tools"
    android:layout_width="match_parent"
    android:layout_height="match_parent"
    android:id="@+id/website_detail"
    tools:context= ".WebsiteDetailFragment">
</WebView>
```

Switch to Design mode and verify that the layout now matches that shown in Figure 50-4:

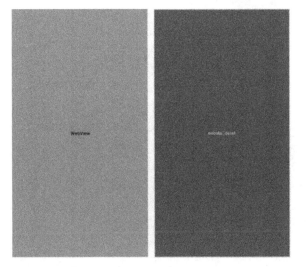

Figure 50-4

50.7 Modifying the WebsiteDetailFragment Class

At this point the user interface detail pane has been modified but the corresponding Java class is still designed for working with a TextView object instead of a WebView. Load the source code for this class by double-clicking on the *WebsiteDetailFragment.java* file in the Project tool window.

In order to load the web page URL corresponding to the currently selected item only a few lines of code need to be changed. Once this change has been made, the code should read as follows:

```
package com.ebookfrenzy.masterdetailflow;
.
.
import android.webkit.WebViewClient;
import android.webkit.WebView;
import android.webkit.WebResourceRequest;
.
.
public class WebSiteDetailFragment extends Fragment {
.
.
.
    public void onCreate(Bundle savedInstanceState) {
        super.onCreate(savedInstanceState);

        if (getArguments().containsKey(ARG_ITEM_ID)) {
            // Load the dummy content specified by the fragment
            // arguments. In a real-world scenario, use a Loader
            // to load content from a content provider.
            mItem = DummyContent.ITEM_MAP.get(getArguments().getString(ARG_ITEM_
ID));
```

```
                Activity activity = this.getActivity();
                CollapsingToolbarLayout appBarLayout =
                        activity.findViewById(R.id.toolbar_layout);
                if (appBarLayout != null) {
                    appBarLayout.setTitle(mItem.website_name);
                }
            }
        }


        @Override
        public View onCreateView(LayoutInflater inflater,
                ViewGroup container, Bundle savedInstanceState) {
            View rootView = inflater.inflate(
                R.layout.fragment_website_detail, container, false);

            // Show the dummy content as text in a TextView.
            if (mItem != null) {
                ((WebView) rootView.findViewById(R.id.website_detail))
                        .loadUrl(mItem.website_url);
                WebView webView = rootView.findViewById(R.id.website_detail);
                webView.setWebViewClient(new WebViewClient(){
                    @Override
                    public boolean shouldOverrideUrlLoading(
                        WebView view, WebResourceRequest request) {
                        return super.shouldOverrideUrlLoading(
                                    view, request);
                    }
                });
                webView.loadUrl(mItem.website_url);
            }

            return rootView;
        }
    }
}
```

The above changes modify the *onCreate()* method to display the web site name on the app bar:

```
appBarLayout.setTitle(mItem.website_name);
```

The *onCreateView()* method is then modified to find the view with the ID of *website_detail* (this was formally the TextView but is now a WebView) and extract the URL of the web site from the selected item. An instance of the WebViewClient class is created and assigned the *shouldOverrideUrlLoading()* callback method. This method is implemented so as to force the system to use the WebView instance to load the page instead of the Chrome browser. Finally, JavaScript support is enabled on the webView instance and the web page loaded.

50.8 Modifying the WebsiteListActivity Class

A minor change also needs to be made to the *WebsiteListActivity.java* file to make sure that the web site names appear in the master list. Edit this file, locate the *onBindViewHolder()* method and modify the *setText()* method call to reference the web site name as follows:

```
public void onBindViewHolder(final ViewHolder holder, int position) {
    holder.mItem = mValues.get(position);
    holder.mIdView.setText(mValues.get(position).id);
    holder.mContentView.setText(mValues.get(position).website_name);
    .
    .
}
```

50.9 Adding Manifest Permissions

The final step is to add internet permission to the application via the manifest file. This will enable the WebView object to access the internet and download web pages. Navigate to, and load the *AndroidManifest.xml* file in the Project tool window (*app -> manifests*), and double-click on it to load it into the editor. Once loaded, add the appropriate permission line to the file:

```
<?xml version="1.0" encoding="utf-8"?>
<manifest xmlns:android="http://schemas.android.com/apk/res/android"
    package="com.example.masterdetailflow" >

    <uses-permission android:name="android.permission.INTERNET" />

    <application
        android:allowBackup="true"
        android:icon="@mipmap/ic_launcher"
        android:label="@string/app_name"
        android:theme="@style/AppTheme" >
    .
    .
```

50.10 Running the Application

Compile and run the application on a suitably configured emulator or an attached Android device. Depending on the size of the display, the application will appear either in small screen or two-pane mode. Regardless, the master list should appear primed with the names of the three web sites defined in the content model. Selecting an item should cause the corresponding web site to appear in the detail pane as illustrated in two-pane mode in Figure 50-5:

Figure 50-5

50.11 Summary

A master/detail user interface consists of a master list of items which, when selected, displays additional information about that selection within a detail pane. The Master/Detail Flow is a template provided with Android Studio that allows a master/detail arrangement to be created quickly and with relative ease. As demonstrated in this chapter, with minor modifications to the default template files, a wide range of master/detail based functionality can be implemented with minimal coding and design effort.

51. An Overview of Android Intents

By this stage of the book, it should be clear that Android applications are comprised, among other things, of one or more activities. An area that has yet to be covered in extensive detail, however, is the mechanism by which one activity can trigger the launch of another activity. As outlined briefly in the chapter entitled *"The Anatomy of an Android Application"*, this is achieved primarily by using *Intents*.

Prior to working through some Android Studio based example implementations of intents in the following chapters, the goal of this chapter is to provide an overview of intents in the form of *explicit intents* and *implicit intents* together with an introduction to *intent filters*.

51.1 An Overview of Intents

Intents (*android.content.Intent*) are the messaging system by which one activity is able to launch another activity. An activity can, for example, issue an intent to request the launch of another activity contained within the same application. Intents also, however, go beyond this concept by allowing an activity to request the services of any other appropriately registered activity on the device for which permissions are configured. Consider, for example, an activity contained within an application that requires a web page to be loaded and displayed to the user. Rather than the application having to contain a second activity to perform this task, the code can simply send an intent to the Android runtime requesting the services of any activity that has registered the ability to display a web page. The runtime system will match the request to available activities on the device and either launch the activity that matches or, in the event of multiple matches, allow the user to decide which activity to use.

Intents also allow for the transfer of data from the sending activity to the receiving activity. In the previously outlined scenario, for example, the sending activity would need to send the URL of the web page to be displayed to the second activity. Similarly, the receiving activity may also be configured to return data to the sending activity when the required tasks are completed.

Though not covered until later chapters, it is also worth highlighting the fact that, in addition to launching activities, intents are also used to launch and communicate with services and broadcast receivers.

Intents are categorized as either *explicit* or *implicit*.

51.2 Explicit Intents

An *explicit intent* requests the launch of a specific activity by referencing the *component name* (which is actually the class name) of the target activity. This approach is most common when launching an activity residing in the same application as the sending activity (since the class name is known to the application developer).

An explicit intent is issued by creating an instance of the Intent class, passing through the activity context and the component name of the activity to be launched. A call is then made to the *startActivity()* method, passing the intent object as an argument. For example, the following code fragment issues an intent for the activity with the class name ActivityB to be launched:

```
Intent i = new Intent(this, ActivityB.class);
startActivity(i);
```

Data may be transmitted to the receiving activity by adding it to the intent object before it is started via calls to the *putExtra()* method of the intent object. Data must be added in the form of key-value pairs. The following code extends the previous example to add String and integer values with the keys "myString" and "myInt" respectively to the intent:

```
Intent i = new Intent(this, ActivityB.class);
i.putExtra("myString", "This is a message for ActivityB");
i.putExtra("myInt", 100);

startActivity(i);
```

The data is received by the target activity as part of a Bundle object which can be obtained via a call to *getIntent().getExtras()*. The *getIntent()* method of the Activity class returns the intent that started the activity, while the *getExtras()* method (of the Intent class) returns a Bundle object containing the data. For example, to extract the data values passed to ActivityB:

```
Bundle extras = getIntent().getExtras();
if (extras != null) {
    String myString = extras.getString("myString");
    int myInt = extras.getInt("myInt");
}
```

When using intents to launch other activities within the same application, it is essential that those activities be listed in the application manifest file. The following *AndroidManifest.xml* contents are correctly configured for an application containing activities named ActivityA and ActivityB:

```
<?xml version="1.0" encoding="utf-8"?>
<manifest xmlns:android="http://schemas.android.com/apk/res/android"
    package="com.ebookfrenzy.intent1.intent1" >

    <application
        android:icon="@mipmap/ic_launcher"
        android:label="@string/app_name" >
        <activity
            android:label="@string/app_name"
            android:name="com.ebookfrenzy.intent1.intent1.ActivityA" >
            <intent-filter>
              <action android:name="android.intent.action.MAIN" />
              <category android:name="android.intent.category.LAUNCHER" />
            </intent-filter>
        </activity>
        <activity
            android:name="ActivityB"
            android:label="ActivityB" >
        </activity>
    </application>
</manifest>
```

51.3 Returning Data from an Activity

As the example in the previous section stands, while data is transferred to ActivityB, there is no way for data to be returned to the first activity (which we will call ActivityA). This can, however, be achieved by launching ActivityB as a *sub-activity* of ActivityA. An activity is started as a sub-activity by starting the intent with a call to the *startActivityForResult()* method instead of using *startActivity()*. In addition to the intent object, this method is also passed a *request code* value which can be used to identify the return data when the sub-activity returns. For example:

```
startActivityForResult(i, REQUEST_CODE);
```

In order to return data to the parent activity, the sub-activity must implement the *finish()* method, the purpose of which is to create a new intent object containing the data to be returned, and then calling the *setResult()* method of the enclosing activity, passing through a *result code* and the intent containing the return data. The result code is typically *RESULT_OK,* or *RESULT_CANCELED*, but may also be a custom value subject to the requirements of the developer. In the event that a sub-activity crashes, the parent activity will receive a *RESULT_CANCELED* result code.

The following code, for example, illustrates the code for a typical sub-activity *finish()* method:

```
public void finish() {
        Intent data = new Intent();

        data.putExtra("returnString1", "Message to parent activity");
        setResult(RESULT_OK, data);
        super.finish();
}
```

In order to obtain and extract the returned data, the parent activity must implement the *onActivityResult()* method, for example:

```
protected void onActivityResult(int requestCode, int resultCode, Intent data)
{
   String returnString;
   if (requestCode == REQUEST_CODE && resultCode == RESULT_OK) {
      if (data.hasExtra("returnString1")) {
            returnString = data.getExtras().getString("returnString1");
      }
   }
}
```

Note that the above method checks the returned request code value to make sure that it matches that passed through to the *startActivityForResult()* method. When starting multiple sub-activities it is especially important to use the request code to track which activity is currently returning results, since all will call the same *onActivityResult()* method on exit.

51.4 Implicit Intents

Unlike explicit intents, which reference the class name of the activity to be launched, implicit intents identify the activity to be launched by specifying the action to be performed and the type of data to be handled by the receiving activity. For example, an action type of ACTION_VIEW accompanied by the URL of a web page in the form of a URI object will instruct the Android system to search for, and subsequently launch, a web browser capable activity. The following implicit intent will, when executed on an Android device, result in the designated web page appearing in a web browser activity:

```
Intent intent = new Intent(Intent.ACTION_VIEW,
        Uri.parse("https://www.ebookfrenzy.com"));

startActivity(intent);
```

When the above implicit intent is issued by an activity, the Android system will search for activities on the device that have registered the ability to handle ACTION_VIEW requests on *http* scheme data using a process referred to as *intent resolution*. In the event that a single match is found, that activity will be launched. If more than one match is found, the user will be prompted to choose from the available activity options.

51.5 Using Intent Filters

Intent filters are the mechanism by which activities "advertise" supported actions and data handling capabilities to the Android intent resolution process. Continuing the example in the previous section, an activity capable of displaying web pages would include an intent filter section in its manifest file indicating support for the ACTION_VIEW type of intent requests on http scheme data.

It is important to note that both the sending and receiving activities must have requested permission for the type of action to be performed. This is achieved by adding *<uses-permission>* tags to the manifest files of both activities. For example, the following manifest lines request permission to access the internet and contacts database:

```
<uses-permission android:name="android.permission.READ_CONTACTS" />
<uses-permission android:name="android.permission.INTERNET"/>
```

The following *AndroidManifest.xml* file illustrates a configuration for an activity named *WebViewActivity* with intent filters and permissions enabled for internet access:

```
<?xml version="1.0" encoding="utf-8"?>
<manifest xmlns:android="http://schemas.android.com/apk/res/android"
    package="com.ebookfreny.WebView"
    android:versionCode="1"
    android:versionName="1.0" >

    <uses-sdk android:minSdkVersion="10" />

    <uses-permission android:name="android.permission.INTERNET" />

    <application
        android:icon="@mipmap/ic_launcher"
        android:label="@string/app_name" >
        <activity
            android:label="@string/app_name"
            android:name=".MainActivity" >
            <intent-filter>
                <action android:name="android.intent.action.VIEW" />
                <category android:name="android.intent.category.DEFAULT" />
                <data android:scheme="http" />
            </intent-filter>
        </activity>
    </application>

</manifest>
```

51.6 Checking Intent Availability

It is generally unwise to assume that an activity will be available for a particular intent, especially since the absence of a matching action will typically result in the application crashing. Fortunately, it is possible to identify the availability of an activity for a specific intent before it is sent to the runtime system. The following method can be used to identify the availability of an activity for a specified intent action type:

```
public static boolean isIntentAvailable(Context context, String action) {
    final PackageManager packageManager = context.getPackageManager();
    final Intent intent = new Intent(action);
    List<ResolveInfo> list =
            packageManager.queryIntentActivities(intent,
                    PackageManager.MATCH_DEFAULT_ONLY);
    return list.size() > 0;
}
```

51.7 Summary

Intents are the messaging mechanism by which one Android activity can launch another. An explicit intent references a specific activity to be launched by referencing the receiving activity by class name. Explicit intents are typically, though not exclusively, used when launching activities contained within the same application. An implicit intent specifies the action to be performed and the type of data to be handled, and lets the Android runtime find a matching activity to launch. Implicit intents are generally used when launching activities that reside in different applications.

An activity can send data to the receiving activity by bundling data into the intent object in the form of key-value pairs. Data can only be returned from an activity if it is started as a *sub-activity* of the sending activity.

Activities advertise capabilities to the Android intent resolution process through the specification of intent-filters in the application manifest file. Both sending and receiving activities must also request appropriate permissions to perform tasks such as accessing the device contact database or the internet.

Having covered the theory of intents, the next few chapters will work through the creation of some examples in Android Studio that put both explicit and implicit intents into action.

52. Android Explicit Intents – A Worked Example

The chapter entitled *"An Overview of Android Intents"* covered the theory of using intents to launch activities. This chapter will put that theory into practice through the creation of an example application.

The example Android Studio application project created in this chapter will demonstrate the use of an explicit intent to launch an activity, including the transfer of data between sending and receiving activities. The next chapter (*"Android Implicit Intents – A Worked Example"*) will demonstrate the use of implicit intents.

52.1 Creating the Explicit Intent Example Application

Select the *Start a new Android Studio project* quick start option from the welcome screen and, within the resulting new project dialog, choose the Empty Activity template before clicking on the Next button.

Enter *ExplicitIntent* into the Name field and specify *com.ebookfrenzy.explicitintent* as the package name. Before clicking on the Finish button, change the Minimum API level setting to API 26: Android 8.0 (Oreo) and the Language menu to Java.

52.2 Designing the User Interface Layout for MainActivity

The user interface for MainActivity will consist of a ConstraintLayout view containing EditText (Plain Text), TextView and Button views named *editText1*, *textView1* and *button1* respectively. Using the Project tool window, locate the *activity_main.xml* resource file for MainActivity (located under *app -> res -> layout*) and double-click on it to load it into the Android Studio Layout Editor tool. Select and delete the default "Hello World!" TextView.

Drag a TextView widget from the palette and drop it so that it is centered within the layout and use the Attributes tool window to assign an ID of *textView1*.

Drag a Button object from the palette and position it so that it is centered horizontally and located beneath the bottom edge of the TextView. Change the text property so that it reads "Ask Question" and configure the *onClick* property to call a method named *askQuestion*.

Next, add a Plain Text object so that it is centered horizontally and positioned above the top edge of the TextView. Using the Attributes tool window, remove the "Name" string assigned to the text property and set the ID to *editText1*. With the layout completed, click on the toolbar *Infer constraints* button to add appropriate constraints:

Figure 52-1

Finally, click on the red warning button in the top right-hand corner of the Layout Editor window and use the resulting panel to extract the "Ask Question" string to a resource named *ask_question*.

Once the layout is complete, the user interface should resemble that illustrated in Figure 52-2:

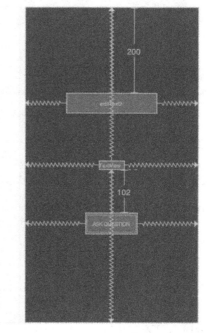

Figure 52-2

52.3 Creating the Second Activity Class

When the "Ask Question" button is touched by the user, an intent will be issued requesting that a second activity be launched into which an answer can be entered by the user. The next step, therefore, is to create the second activity. Within the Project tool window, right-click on the *com.ebookfrenzy.explicitintent* package name located in *app -> java* and select the *New -> Activity -> Empty Activity* menu option to display the *New Android Activity* dialog as shown in Figure 52-3:

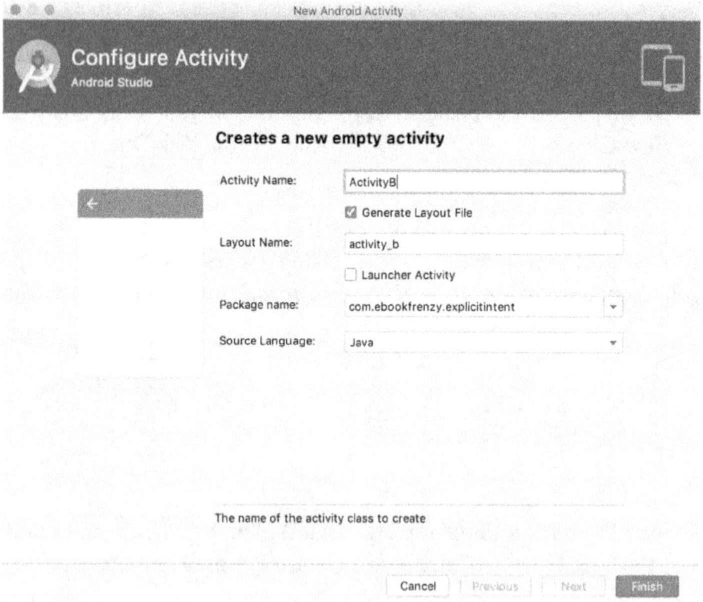

Figure 52-3

Enter *ActivityB* into the Activity Name and Title fields and name the layout file *activity_b* and change the Language menu to Java. Since this activity will not be started when the application is launched (it will instead be launched via an intent by MainActivity when the button is pressed), it is important to make sure that the *Launcher Activity* option is disabled before clicking on the Finish button.

52.4 Designing the User Interface Layout for ActivityB

The elements that are required for the user interface of the second activity are a Plain Text EditText, TextView and Button view. With these requirements in mind, load the *activity_b.xml* layout into the Layout Editor tool, and add the views.

During the design process, note that the *onClick* property on the button view has been configured to call a method named *answerQuestion*, and the TextView and EditText views have been assigned IDs *textView1* and *editText1* respectively. Once completed, the layout should resemble that illustrated in Figure 52-4. Note that the text on the button (which reads "Answer Question") has been extracted to a string resource named *answer_ question*.

With the layout complete, click on the Infer constraints toolbar button to add the necessary constraints to the layout:

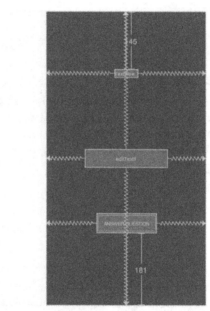

Figure 52-4

52.5 Reviewing the Application Manifest File

In order for MainActivity to be able to launch ActivityB using an intent, it is necessary that an entry for ActivityB be present in the *AndroidManifest.xml* file. Locate this file within the Project tool window (*app -> manifests*), double-click on it to load it into the editor and verify that Android Studio has automatically added an entry for the activity:

```
<?xml version="1.0" encoding="utf-8"?>
<manifest xmlns:android="http://schemas.android.com/apk/res/android"
    package="com.example.explicitintent">

    <application
```

```
            android:allowBackup="true"
            android:icon="@mipmap/ic_launcher"
            android:label="@string/app_name"
            android:roundIcon="@mipmap/ic_launcher_round"
            android:supportsRtl="true"
            android:theme="@style/AppTheme">
            <activity android:name=".ActivityB"></activity>
            <activity android:name=".MainActivity">
                <intent-filter>
                    <action android:name="android.intent.action.MAIN" />

                    <category android:name="android.intent.category.LAUNCHER" />
                </intent-filter>
            </activity>
        </application>


</manifest>
```

With the second activity created and listed in the manifest file, it is now time to write some code in the MainActivity class to issue the intent.

52.6 Creating the Intent

The objective for MainActivity is to create and start an intent when the user touches the "Ask Question" button. As part of the intent creation process, the question string entered by the user into the EditText view will be added to the intent object as a key-value pair. When the user interface layout was created for MainActivity, the button object was configured to call a method named *askQuestion()* when "clicked" by the user. This method now needs to be added to the MainActivity class *MainActivity.java* source file as follows:

```
package com.ebookfrenzy.explicitintent;

import androidx.appcompat.app.AppCompatActivity;

import android.os.Bundle;
import android.content.Intent;
import android.view.View;
import android.widget.EditText;
import android.widget.TextView;

public class MainActivity extends AppCompatActivity {

    @Override
    protected void onCreate(Bundle savedInstanceState) {
        super.onCreate(savedInstanceState);
        setContentView(R.layout.activity_a);
    }

    public void askQuestion(View view) {
```

```
Intent i = new Intent(this, ActivityB.class);

final EditText editText1 = findViewById(R.id.editText1);
String myString = editText1.getText().toString();
i.putExtra("qString", myString);
startActivity(i);
    }
}
```

The code for the *askQuestion()* method follows the techniques outlined in *"An Overview of Android Intents"*. First, a new Intent instance is created, passing through the current activity and the class name of ActivityB as arguments. Next, the text entered into the EditText object is added to the intent object as a key-value pair and the intent started via a call to *startActivity()*, passing through the intent object as an argument.

Compile and run the application and touch the "Ask Question" button to launch ActivityB and the back button (located in the toolbar along the bottom of the display) to return to MainActivity.

52.7 Extracting Intent Data

Now that ActivityB is being launched from MainActivity, the next step is to extract the String data value included in the intent and assign it to the TextView object in the ActivityB user interface. This involves adding some code to the *onCreate()* method of ActivityB in the *ActivityB.java* source file:

```
package com.ebookfrenzy.explicitintent;

import androidx.appcompat.app.AppCompatActivity;
import android.os.Bundle;
import android.content.Intent;
import android.view.View;
import android.widget.TextView;
import android.widget.EditText;

public class ActivityB extends AppCompatActivity {

    public void onCreate(Bundle savedInstanceState) {
      super.onCreate(savedInstanceState);
      setContentView(R.layout.activityb);

    Bundle extras = getIntent().getExtras();
        if (extras == null) {
                return;
        }

        String qString = extras.getString("qString");

        final TextView textView = findViewById(R.id.textView1);
        textView.setText(qString);
    }
```

}

Compile and run the application either within an emulator or on a physical Android device. Enter a question into the text box in MainActivity before touching the "Ask Question" button. The question should now appear on the TextView component in the ActivityB user interface.

52.8 Launching ActivityB as a Sub-Activity

In order for ActivityB to be able to return data to MainActivity, ActivityB must be started as a *sub-activity* of MainActivity. This means that the call to *startActivity()* in the MainActivity *askQuestion()* method needs to be replaced with a call to *startActivityForResult()*. Unlike the *startActivity()* method, which takes only the intent object as an argument, *startActivityForResult()* requires that a request code also be passed through. The request code can be any number value and is used to identify which sub-activity is associated with which set of return data. For the purposes of this example, a request code of 5 will be used, giving us a modified MainActivity class that reads as follows:

```
public class MainActivity extends AppCompatActivity {

    private static final int request_code = 5;

    @Override
    public void onCreate(Bundle savedInstanceState) {
        super.onCreate(savedInstanceState);
        setContentView(R.layout.main);
    }

    public void askQuestion(View view) {

            Intent i = new Intent(this, ActivityB.class);

            final EditText editText1 = findViewById(R.id.editText1);
            String myString = editText1.getText().toString();
            i.putExtra("qString", myString);
            startActivity(i);
            startActivityForResult(i, request_code);
        }
}
```

When the sub-activity exits, the *onActivityResult()* method of the parent activity is called and passed as arguments the request code associated with the intent, a result code indicating the success or otherwise of the sub-activity and an intent object containing any data returned by the sub-activity. Remaining within the MainActivity class source file, implement this method as follows:

```
protected void onActivityResult(int requestCode, int resultCode, Intent data) {
    if ((requestCode == request_code) &&
                (resultCode == RESULT_OK)) {

            TextView textView1 = findViewById(R.id.textView1);

            String returnString =
```

```
            data.getExtras().getString("returnData");


        textView1.setText(returnString);
    }
}
```

The code in the above method begins by checking that the request code matches the one used when the intent was issued and ensuring that the activity was successful. The return data is then extracted from the intent and displayed on the TextView object.

52.9 Returning Data from a Sub-Activity

ActivityB is now launched as a sub-activity of MainActivity, which has, in turn, been modified to handle data returned from ActivityB. All that remains is to modify *ActivityB.java* to implement the *finish()* method and to add code for the *answerQuestion()* method, which is called when the "Answer Question" button is touched. The *finish()* method is triggered when an activity exits (for example when the user selects the back button on the device):

```
public void answerQuestion(View view) {
            finish();
}


@Override
public void finish() {
        Intent data = new Intent();

        EditText editText1 = findViewById(R.id.editText1);

        String returnString = editText1.getText().toString();
        data.putExtra("returnData", returnString);

        setResult(RESULT_OK, data);
        super.finish();
}
```

All that the *finish()* method needs to do is create a new intent, add the return data as a key-value pair and then call the *setResult()* method, passing through a result code and the intent object. The *answerQuestion()* method simply calls the *finish()* method.

52.10 Testing the Application

Compile and run the application, enter a question into the text field on MainActivity and touch the "Ask Question" button. When ActivityB appears, enter the answer to the question and use either the back button or the "Submit Answer" button to return to MainActivity where the answer should appear in the text view object.

52.11 Summary

Having covered the basics of intents in the previous chapter, the goal of this chapter was to work through the creation of an application project in Android Studio designed to demonstrate the use of explicit intents together with the concepts of data transfer between a parent activity and sub-activity.

The next chapter will work through an example designed to demonstrate implicit intents in action.

53. Android Implicit Intents – A Worked Example

In this chapter, an example application will be created in Android Studio designed to demonstrate a practical implementation of implicit intents. The goal will be to create and send an intent requesting that the content of a particular web page be loaded and displayed to the user. Since the example application itself will not contain an activity capable of performing this task, an implicit intent will be issued so that the Android intent resolution algorithm can be engaged to identify and launch a suitable activity from another application. This is most likely to be an activity from the Chrome web browser bundled with the Android operating system.

Having successfully launched the built-in browser, a new project will be created that also contains an activity capable of displaying web pages. This will be installed onto the device or emulator and used to demonstrate what happens when two activities match the criteria for an implicit intent.

53.1 Creating the Android Studio Implicit Intent Example Project

Select the *Start a new Android Studio project* quick start option from the welcome screen and, within the resulting new project dialog, choose the Empty Activity template before clicking on the Next button.

Enter *ImplicitIntent* into the Name field and specify *com.ebookfrenzy.implicitintent* as the package name. Before clicking on the Finish button, change the Minimum API level setting to API 26: Android 8.0 (Oreo) and the Language menu to Java.

53.2 Designing the User Interface

The user interface for the *MainActivity* class is very simple, consisting solely of a ConstraintLayout and a Button object. Within the Project tool window, locate the *app -> res -> layout -> activity_main.xml* file and double-click on it to load it into the Layout Editor tool.

Delete the default TextView and, with Autoconnect mode enabled, position a Button widget so that it is centered within the layout. Note that the text on the button ("Show Web Page") has been extracted to a string resource named *show_web_page*.

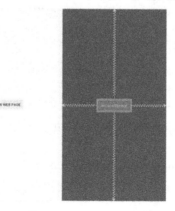

Figure 53-1

With the Button selected use the Attributes tool window to configure the *onClick* property to call a method named *showWebPage()*.

53.3 Creating the Implicit Intent

As outlined above, the implicit intent will be created and issued from within a method named *showWebPage()* which, in turn, needs to be implemented in the *MainActivity* class, the code for which resides in the *MainActivity.java* source file. Locate this file in the Project tool window and double-click on it to load it into an editing pane. Once loaded, modify the code to add the *showWebPage()* method together with a few requisite imports:

```java
package com.ebookfrenzy.implicitintent;


import androidx.appcompat.app.AppCompatActivity;
import android.os.Bundle;
import android.net.Uri;
import android.content.Intent;
import android.view.View;


public class MainActivity extends AppCompatActivity {

    @Override
    protected void onCreate(Bundle savedInstanceState) {
        super.onCreate(savedInstanceState);
        setContentView(R.layout.activity_implicit_intent);
    }

    public void showWebPage(View view) {
        Intent intent = new Intent(Intent.ACTION_VIEW,
                Uri.parse("https://www.ebookfrenzy.com"));

        startActivity(intent);
    }
}
```

The tasks performed by this method are actually very simple. First, a new intent object is created. Instead of specifying the class name of the intent, however, the code simply indicates the nature of the intent (to display something to the user) using the ACTION_VIEW option. The intent object also includes a URI containing the URL to be displayed. This indicates to the Android intent resolution system that the activity is requesting that a web page be displayed. The intent is then issued via a call to the *startActivity()* method.

Compile and run the application on either an emulator or a physical Android device and, once running, touch the *Show Web Page* button. When touched, a web browser view should appear and load the web page designated by the URL. A successful implicit intent has now been executed.

53.4 Adding a Second Matching Activity

The remainder of this chapter will be used to demonstrate the effect of the presence of more than one activity installed on the device matching the requirements for an implicit intent. To achieve this, a second application will be created and installed on the device or emulator. Begin, therefore, by creating a new project within Android Studio with the application name set to *MyWebView*, using the same SDK configuration options used when creating the ImplicitIntent project earlier in this chapter and once again selecting an Empty Activity.

53.5 Adding the Web View to the UI

The user interface for the sole activity contained within the new *MyWebView* project is going to consist of an instance of the Android WebView widget. Within the Project tool window, locate the *activity_main.xml* file, which contains the user interface description for the activity, and double-click on it to load it into the Layout Editor tool.

With the Layout Editor tool in Design mode, select the default TextView widget and remove it from the layout by using the keyboard delete key.

Drag and drop a WebView object from the *Widgets* section of the palette onto the existing ConstraintLayout view as illustrated in Figure 53-2:

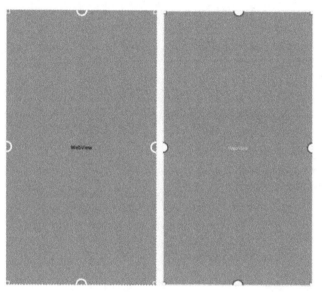

Figure 53-2

Before continuing, change the ID of the WebView instance to *webView1*.

53.6 Obtaining the Intent URL

When the implicit intent object is created to display a web browser window, the URL of the web page to be displayed will be bundled into the intent object within a Uri object. The task of the *onCreate()* method within the *MainActivity* class is to extract this Uri from the intent object, convert it into a URL string and assign it to the WebView object. To implement this functionality, modify the *MainActivity.java* file so that it reads as follows:

```
package com.ebookfrenzy.mywebview;

import androidx.appcompat.app.AppCompatActivity;
import android.os.Bundle;
import java.net.URL;
import android.net.Uri;
import android.content.Intent;
import android.webkit.WebView;

public class MainActivity extends AppCompatActivity {
```

```
    @Override
    protected void onCreate(Bundle savedInstanceState) {
        super.onCreate(savedInstanceState);
        setContentView(R.layout.activity_my_web_view);

        handleIntent();
    }

    private void handleIntent() {
        Intent intent = getIntent();

        Uri data = intent.getData();
        URL url = null;

        try {
            url = new URL(data.getScheme(),
                    data.getHost(),
                    data.getPath());
        } catch (Exception e) {
            e.printStackTrace();
        }

        WebView webView = findViewById(R.id.webView1);
        webView.loadUrl(url.toString());
    }
}
```

The new code added to the *onCreate()* method performs the following tasks:

- Obtains a reference to the intent which caused this activity to be launched

- Extracts the Uri data from the intent object

- Converts the Uri data to a URL object

- Obtains a reference to the WebView object in the user interface

- Loads the URL into the web view, converting the URL to a String in the process

The coding part of the MyWebView project is now complete. All that remains is to modify the manifest file.

53.7 Modifying the MyWebView Project Manifest File

There are a number of changes that must be made to the MyWebView manifest file before it can be tested. In the first instance, the activity will need to seek permission to access the internet (since it will be required to load a web page). This is achieved by adding the appropriate permission line to the manifest file:

```
<uses-permission android:name="android.permission.INTERNET" />
```

Further, a review of the contents of the intent filter section of the *AndroidManifest.xml* file for the MyWebView project will reveal the following settings:

```
<intent-filter>
        <action android:name="android.intent.action.MAIN" />
        <category android:name="android.intent.category.LAUNCHER" />
</intent-filter>
```

In the above XML, the *android.intent.action.MAIN* entry indicates that this activity is the point of entry for the application when it is launched without any data input. The *android.intent.category.LAUNCHER* directive, on the other hand, indicates that the activity should be listed within the application launcher screen of the device.

Since the activity is not required to be launched as the entry point to an application, cannot be run without data input (in this case a URL) and is not required to appear in the launcher, neither the MAIN nor LAUNCHER directives are required in the manifest file for this activity.

The intent filter for the *MainActivity* activity does, however, need to be modified to indicate that it is capable of handling ACTION_VIEW intent actions for http data schemes.

Android also requires that any activities capable of handling implicit intents that do not include MAIN and LAUNCHER entries, also include the so-called *browsable* and *default* categories in the intent filter. The modified intent filter section should therefore read as follows:

```
<intent-filter>
        <action android:name="android.intent.action.VIEW" />
        <category android:name="android.intent.category.BROWSABLE" />
        <category android:name="android.intent.category.DEFAULT" />
        <data android:scheme="http" />
</intent-filter>
```

Bringing these requirements together results in the following complete *AndroidManifest.xml* file:

```
<?xml version="1.0" encoding="utf-8"?>
<manifest xmlns:android="http://schemas.android.com/apk/res/android"
    package="com.ebookfrenzy.mywebview" >

    <uses-permission android:name="android.permission.INTERNET" />

    <application
        android:allowBackup="true"
        android:icon="@mipmap/ic_launcher"
        android:label="@string/app_name"
        android:theme="@style/AppTheme" >
        <activity
            android:name=".MainActivity"
            android:label="@string/app_name" >
            <intent-filter>
                <action android:name="android.intent.action.VIEW" />
                <category
                    android:name="android.intent.category.BROWSABLE" />
                <category android:name="android.intent.category.DEFAULT" />
                <data android:scheme="https" />
            </intent-filter>
```

```
        </activity>
    </application>
</manifest>
```

Load the *AndroidManifest.xml* file into the manifest editor by double-clicking on the file name in the Project tool window. Once loaded, modify the XML to match the above changes.

Having made the appropriate modifications to the manifest file, the new activity is ready to be installed on the device.

53.8 Installing the MyWebView Package on a Device

Before the MyWebView main activity can be used as the recipient of an implicit intent, it must first be installed onto the device. This is achieved by running the application in the normal manner. Because the manifest file contains neither the *android.intent.action.MAIN* nor the *android.intent.category.LAUNCHER* settings, Android Studio needs to be instructed to install, but not launch, the app. To configure this behavior, select the *app -> Edit configurations...* menu from the toolbar as illustrated in Figure 53-3:

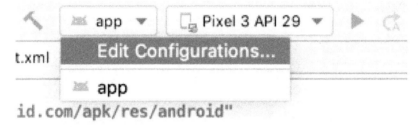

Figure 53-3

Within the Run/Debug Configurations dialog, change the Launch option located in the *Launch Options* section of the panel to *Nothing* and click on Apply followed by OK:

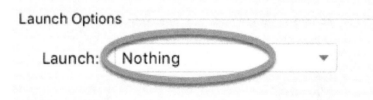

Figure 53-4

With this setting configured run the app as usual. Note that the app is installed on the device, but not launched.

53.9 Testing the Application

In order to test MyWebView, simply re-launch the *ImplicitIntent* application created earlier in this chapter and touch the *Show Web Page* button. This time, however, the intent resolution process will find two activities with intent filters matching the implicit intent. As such, the system will display a dialog (Figure 53-5) providing the user with the choice of activity to launch.

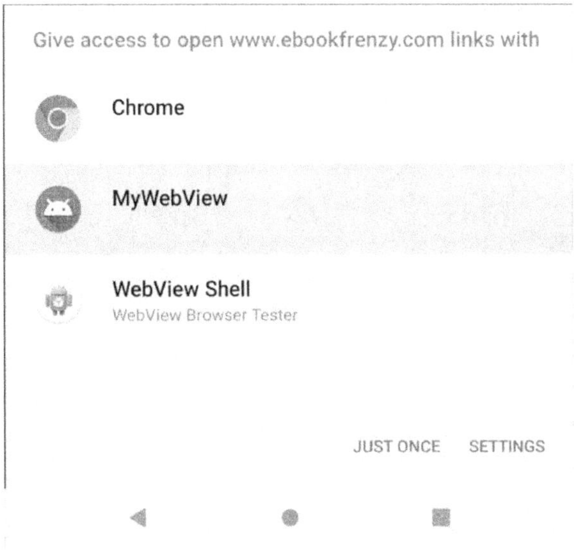

Figure 53-5

Selecting the *MyWebView* option followed by the *Just once* button should cause the intent to be handled by our new *MyWebView* main activity, which will subsequently appear and display the designated web page.

If the web page loads into the Chrome browser without the above selection dialog appearing, it may be that Chrome has been configured as the default browser on the device. This can be changed by going to *Settings -> Apps & notifications* on the device followed by *App info*. Scroll down the list of apps and select *Chrome*. On the Chrome app info screen, tap the *Open by default* option followed by the *Clear Defaults* button.

53.10 Summary

Implicit intents provide a mechanism by which one activity can request the service of another, simply by specifying an action type and, optionally, the data on which that action is to be performed. In order to be eligible as a target candidate for an implicit intent, however, an activity must be configured to extract the appropriate data from the inbound intent object and be included in a correctly configured manifest file, including appropriate permissions and intent filters. When more than one matching activity for an implicit intent is found during an intent resolution search, the user is prompted to make a choice as to which to use.

Within this chapter an example was created to demonstrate both the issuing of an implicit intent, and the creation of an example activity capable of handling such an intent.

54. Android Broadcast Intents and Broadcast Receivers

In addition to providing a mechanism for launching application activities, intents are also used as a way to broadcast system wide messages to other components on the system. This involves the implementation of Broadcast Intents and Broadcast Receivers, both of which are the topic of this chapter.

54.1 An Overview of Broadcast Intents

Broadcast intents are Intent objects that are broadcast via a call to the *sendBroadcast()*, *sendStickyBroadcast()* or *sendOrderedBroadcast()* methods of the Activity class (the latter being used when results are required from the broadcast). In addition to providing a messaging and event system between application components, broadcast intents are also used by the Android system to notify interested applications about key system events (such as the external power supply or headphones being connected or disconnected).

When a broadcast intent is created, it must include an *action string* in addition to optional data and a category string. As with standard intents, data is added to a broadcast intent using key-value pairs in conjunction with the *putExtra()* method of the intent object. The optional category string may be assigned to a broadcast intent via a call to the *addCategory()* method.

The action string, which identifies the broadcast event, must be unique and typically uses the application's package name syntax. For example, the following code fragment creates and sends a broadcast intent including a unique action string and data:

```
Intent intent = new Intent();
intent.setAction("com.example.Broadcast");
intent.putExtra("MyData", 1000);
sendBroadcast(intent);
```

The above code would successfully launch the corresponding broadcast receiver on a device running an Android version earlier than 3.0. On more recent versions of Android, however, the intent would not be received by the broadcast receiver. This is because Android 3.0 introduced a launch control security measure that prevents components of *stopped* applications from being launched via an intent. An application is considered to be in a stopped state if the application has either just been installed and not previously launched, or been manually stopped by the user using the application manager on the device. To get around this, however, a flag can be added to the intent before it is sent to indicate that the intent is to be allowed to start a component of a stopped application. This flag is FLAG_INCLUDE_STOPPED_PACKAGES and would be used as outlined in the following adaptation of the previous code fragment:

```
Intent intent = new Intent();
intent.addFlags(Intent.FLAG_INCLUDE_STOPPED_PACKAGES);
intent.setAction("com.example.Broadcast");
intent.putExtra("MyData", 1000);
sendBroadcast(intent);
```

54.2 An Overview of Broadcast Receivers

An application listens for specific broadcast intents by registering a *broadcast receiver*. Broadcast receivers are implemented by extending the Android BroadcastReceiver class and overriding the *onReceive()* method. The broadcast receiver may then be registered, either within code (for example within an activity), or within a manifest file. Part of the registration implementation involves the creation of intent filters to indicate the specific broadcast intents the receiver is required to listen for. This is achieved by referencing the *action string* of the broadcast intent. When a matching broadcast is detected, the *onReceive()* method of the broadcast receiver is called, at which point the method has 5 seconds within which to perform any necessary tasks before returning. It is important to note that a broadcast receiver does not need to be running all the time. In the event that a matching intent is detected, the Android runtime system will automatically start up the broadcast receiver before calling the *onReceive()* method.

The following code outlines a template Broadcast Receiver subclass:

```
package com.example.broadcastdetector;

import android.content.BroadcastReceiver;
import android.content.Context;
import android.content.Intent;

public class MyReceiver extends BroadcastReceiver {

    public MyReceiver() {
    }

    @Override
    public void onReceive(Context context, Intent intent) {
        // Implement code here to be performed when
        // broadcast is detected
    }
}
```

When registering a broadcast receiver within a manifest file, a *<receiver>* entry must be added for the receiver.

The following example manifest file registers the above example broadcast receiver:

```
<?xml version="1.0" encoding="utf-8"?>
<manifest xmlns:android="http://schemas.android.com/apk/res/android"
    package="com.example.broadcastdetector.broadcastdetector"
    android:versionCode="1"
    android:versionName="1.0" >

    <uses-sdk android:minSdkVersion="17" />

    <application
        android:icon="@mipmap/ic_launcher"
        android:label="@string/app_name" >
        <receiver android:name="MyReceiver" >
        </receiver>
```

```
    </application>
</manifest>
```

When running on versions of Android older than Android 8.0, the intent filters associated with a receiver can be placed within the receiver element of the manifest file as follows:

```
<receiver android:name="MyReceiver" >
    <intent-filter>
        <action android:name="com.example.Broadcast" >
        </action>
    </intent-filter>
</receiver>
```

On Android 8.0 or later, the receiver must be registered in code using the *registerReceiver()* method of the Activity class together with an appropriately configured IntentFilter object:

```
IntentFilter filter = new IntentFilter("com.example.Broadcast");

MyReceiver receiver = new MyReceiver();
registerReceiver(receiver, filter);
```

When a broadcast receiver registered in code is no longer required, it may be unregistered via a call to the *unregisterReceiver()* method of the activity class, passing through a reference to the receiver object as an argument. For example, the following code will unregister the above broadcast receiver:

```
unregisterReceiver(receiver);
```

It is important to keep in mind that some system broadcast intents can only be detected by a broadcast receiver if it is registered in code rather than in the manifest file. Check the Android Intent class documentation for a detailed overview of the system broadcast intents and corresponding requirements online at:

https://developer.android.com/reference/android/content/Intent

54.3 Obtaining Results from a Broadcast

When a broadcast intent is sent using the *sendBroadcast()* method, there is no way for the initiating activity to receive results from any broadcast receivers that pick up the broadcast. In the event that return results are required, it is necessary to use the *sendOrderedBroadcast()* method instead. When a broadcast intent is sent using this method, it is delivered in sequential order to each broadcast receiver with a registered interest.

The *sendOrderedBroadcast()* method is called with a number of arguments including a reference to another broadcast receiver (known as the *result receiver*) which is to be notified when all other broadcast receivers have handled the intent, together with a set of data references into which those receivers can place result data. When all broadcast receivers have been given the opportunity to handle the broadcast, the *onReceive()* method of the *result receiver* is called and passed the result data.

54.4 Sticky Broadcast Intents

By default, broadcast intents disappear once they have been sent and handled by any interested broadcast receivers. A broadcast intent can, however, be defined as being "sticky". A sticky intent, and the data contained therein, remains present in the system after it has completed. The data stored within a sticky broadcast intent can be obtained via the return value of a call to the *registerReceiver()* method, using the usual arguments (references to the broadcast receiver and intent filter object). Many of the Android system broadcasts are sticky, a prime example being those broadcasts relating to battery level status.

A sticky broadcast may be removed at any time via a call to the *removeStickyBroadcast()* method, passing through as an argument a reference to the broadcast intent to be removed.

54.5 The Broadcast Intent Example

The remainder of this chapter will work through the creation of an Android Studio based example of broadcast intents in action. In the first instance, a simple application will be created for the purpose of issuing a custom broadcast intent. A corresponding broadcast receiver will then be created that will display a message on the display of the Android device when the broadcast is detected. Finally, the broadcast receiver will be modified to detect notification by the system that external power has been disconnected from the device.

54.6 Creating the Example Application

Select the *Start a new Android Studio project* quick start option from the welcome screen and, within the resulting new project dialog, choose the Empty Activity template before clicking on the Next button.

Enter *SendBroadcast* into the Name field and specify *com.ebookfrenzy.sendbroadcast* as the package name. Before clicking on the Finish button, change the Minimum API level setting to API 26: Android 8.0 (Oreo) and the Language menu to Java.

Once the new project has been created, locate and load the *activity_main.xml* layout file located in the Project tool window under *app -> res -> layout* and, with the Layout Editor tool in Design mode, replace the TextView object with a Button view and set the text property so that it reads "Send Broadcast". Once the text value has been set, follow the usual steps to extract the string to a resource named *send_broadcast*.

With the button still selected in the layout, locate the *onClick* property in the Attributes panel and configure it to call a method named *broadcastIntent*.

54.7 Creating and Sending the Broadcast Intent

Having created the framework for the *SendBroadcast* application, it is now time to implement the code to send the broadcast intent. This involves implementing the *broadcastIntent()* method specified previously as the *onClick* target of the Button view in the user interface. Locate and double-click on the *MainActivity.java* file and modify it to add the code to create and send the broadcast intent. Once modified, the source code for this class should read as follows:

```
package com.ebookfrenzy.sendbroadcast;

import androidx.appcompat.app.AppCompatActivity;
import android.os.Bundle;
import android.content.Intent;
import android.view.View;

public class MainActivity extends AppCompatActivity {

    @Override
    protected void onCreate(Bundle savedInstanceState) {
        super.onCreate(savedInstanceState);
        setContentView(R.layout.activity_send_broadcast);
    }

    public void broadcastIntent(View view)
    {
        Intent intent = new Intent();
```

```
        intent.setAction("com.ebookfrenzy.sendbroadcast");
        intent.addFlags(Intent.FLAG_INCLUDE_STOPPED_PACKAGES);
        sendBroadcast(intent);
    }
}
```

Note that in this instance the action string for the intent is *com.ebookfrenzy.sendbroadcast*. When the broadcast receiver class is created in later sections of this chapter, it is essential that the intent filter declaration match this action string.

This concludes the creation of the application to send the broadcast intent. All that remains is to build a matching broadcast receiver.

54.8 Creating the Broadcast Receiver

In order to create the broadcast receiver, a new class needs to be created which subclasses the BroadcastReceiver superclass. Within the Project tool window, navigate to *app -> java* and right-click on the package name. From the resulting menu, select the *New -> Other -> Broadcast Receiver* menu option, name the class *MyReceiver* and make sure the *Exported* and *Enabled* options are selected. These settings allow the Android system to launch the receiver when needed and ensure that the class can receive messages sent by other applications on the device. With the class configured, click on *Finish*.

Once created, Android Studio will automatically load the new *MyReceiver.java* class file into the editor where it should read as follows:

```
package com.ebookfrenzy.sendbroadcast;

import android.content.BroadcastReceiver;
import android.content.Context;
import android.content.Intent;

public class MyReceiver extends BroadcastReceiver {

    @Override
    public void onReceive(Context context, Intent intent) {
        // TODO: This method is called when the BroadcastReceiver is receiving
        // an Intent broadcast.
        throw new UnsupportedOperationException("Not yet implemented");
    }
}
```

As can be seen in the code, Android Studio has generated a template for the new class and generated a stub for the *onReceive()* method. A number of changes now need to be made to the class to implement the required behavior. Remaining in the *MyReceiver.java* file, therefore, modify the code so that it reads as follows:

```
package com.ebookfrenzy.sendbroadcast;

import android.content.BroadcastReceiver;
import android.content.Context;
import android.content.Intent;
import android.widget.Toast;
```

```java
public class MyReceiver extends BroadcastReceiver {

    public MyReceiver() {
    }

    @Override
    public void onReceive(Context context, Intent intent) {
        // TODO: This method is called when the BroadcastReceiver is receiving
        // an Intent broadcast.
        throw new UnsupportedOperationException("Not yet implemented");

        Toast.makeText(context, "Broadcast Intent Detected.",
                Toast.LENGTH_LONG).show();

    }
}
```

The code for the broadcast receiver is now complete.

54.9 Registering the Broadcast Receiver

The project needs to publicize the presence of the broadcast receiver and must include an intent filter to specify the broadcast intents in which the receiver is interested. When the BroadcastReceiver class was created in the previous section, Android Studio automatically added a <receiver> element to the manifest file. All that remains, therefore, is to add code within the *MainActivity.java* file to create an intent filter and to register the receiver:

```java
package com.ebookfrenzy.sendbroadcast;
.
.
import android.content.BroadcastReceiver;
import android.content.IntentFilter;
.
.
public class MainActivity extends AppCompatActivity {

    BroadcastReceiver receiver;

    @Override
    protected void onCreate(Bundle savedInstanceState) {
        super.onCreate(savedInstanceState);
        setContentView(R.layout.activity_send_broadcast);

        configureReceiver();
    }

    private void configureReceiver() {
        IntentFilter filter = new IntentFilter();
        filter.addAction("com.ebookfrenzy.sendbroadcast");
        receiver = new MyReceiver();
```

```
    registerReceiver(receiver, filter);
  }
    .
    .
}
```

It is also important to unregister the broadcast receiver when it is no longer needed:

```
@Override
protected void onDestroy() {
    super.onDestroy();
    unregisterReceiver(receiver);
}
```

54.10 Testing the Broadcast Example

In order to test the broadcast sender and receiver, run the SendBroadcast app on a device or AVD and wait for it to appear on the display. Once running, touch the button, at which point the toast message reading "Broadcast Intent Detected." should pop up for a few seconds before fading away.

54.11 Listening for System Broadcasts

The final stage of this example is to modify the intent filter for the broadcast receiver to listen also for the system intent that is broadcast when external power is disconnected from the device. That action is *android.intent. action.ACTION_POWER_DISCONNECTED*. Modify the *onCreate()* method in the *MainActivity.java* file to add this additional filter:

```
private void configureReceiver() {
    IntentFilter filter = new IntentFilter();
    filter.addAction("com.ebookfrenzy.sendbroadcast");
    filter.addAction(
            "android.intent.action.ACTION_POWER_DISCONNECTED");

    receiver = new MyReceiver();
    registerReceiver(receiver, filter);
}
```

Since the *onReceive()* method is now going to be listening for two types of broadcast intent, it is worthwhile to modify the code so that the action string of the current intent is also displayed in the toast message. This string can be obtained via a call to the *getAction()* method of the intent object passed as an argument to the *onReceive()* method:

```
public void onReceive(Context context, Intent intent) {
    String message = "Broadcast intent detected "
                    + intent.getAction();

    Toast.makeText(context, message,
            Toast.LENGTH_LONG).show();
}
```

Test the receiver by re-installing the modified *BroadcastReceiver* package. Touching the button in the *SendBroadcast* application should now result in a new message containing the custom action string:

```
Broadcast intent detected com.ebookfrenzy.sendbroadcast
```

Next, remove the USB connector that is currently supplying power to the Android device, at which point the receiver should report the following in the toast message. If the app is running on an emulator, display the extended controls, select the *Battery* option and change the *Charger connection* setting to *None*.

```
Broadcast intent detected android.intent.action.ACTION_POWER_DISCONNECTED
```

To avoid this message appearing every time the device is disconnected from a power supply launch the Settings app on the device and select the *Apps & notifications* option. Select the BroadcastReceiver app from the resulting list and tap the *Uninstall* button.

54.12 Summary

Broadcast intents are a mechanism by which an intent can be issued for consumption by multiple components on an Android system. Broadcasts are detected by registering a Broadcast Receiver which, in turn, is configured to listen for intents that match particular action strings. In general, broadcast receivers remain dormant until woken up by the system when a matching intent is detected. Broadcast intents are also used by the Android system to issue notifications of events such as a low battery warning or the connection or disconnection of external power to the device.

In addition to providing an overview of Broadcast intents and receivers, this chapter has also worked through an example of sending broadcast intents and the implementation of a broadcast receiver to listen for both custom and system broadcast intents.

55. A Basic Overview of Threads and AsyncTasks

The next chapter will be the first in a series of chapters intended to introduce the use of Android Services to perform application tasks in the background. It is impossible, however, to understand the steps involved in implementing services without first gaining a basic understanding of the concept of threading in Android applications. Threads and the AsyncTask class are, therefore, the topic of this chapter.

55.1 An Overview of Threads

Threads are the cornerstone of any multitasking operating system and can be thought of as mini-processes running within a main process, the purpose of which is to enable at least the appearance of parallel execution paths within applications.

55.2 The Application Main Thread

When an Android application is first started, the runtime system creates a single thread in which all application components will run by default. This thread is generally referred to as the *main thread*. The primary role of the main thread is to handle the user interface in terms of event handling and interaction with views in the user interface. Any additional components that are started within the application will, by default, also run on the main thread.

Any component within an application that performs a time consuming task using the main thread will cause the entire application to appear to lock up until the task is completed. This will typically result in the operating system displaying an "Application is not responding" warning to the user. Clearly, this is far from the desired behavior for any application. This can be avoided simply by launching the task to be performed in a separate thread, allowing the main thread to continue unhindered with other tasks.

55.3 Thread Handlers

Clearly, one of the key rules of Android development is to never perform time-consuming operations on the main thread of an application. The second, equally important, rule is that the code within a separate thread must never, under any circumstances, directly update any aspect of the user interface. Any changes to the user interface must always be performed from within the main thread. The reason for this is that the Android UI toolkit is not *thread-safe*. Attempts to work with non-thread-safe code from within multiple threads will typically result in intermittent problems and unpredictable application behavior.

If a time consuming task needs to run in a background thread and also update the user interface the best approach is to implement an asynchronous task by subclassing the AsyncTask class.

55.4 A Basic AsyncTask Example

The remainder of this chapter will work through some simple examples intended to provide a basic introduction to threads and the use of the AsyncTask class. The first step will be to highlight the importance of performing time-consuming tasks in a separate thread from the main thread.

Select the *Start a new Android Studio project* quick start option from the welcome screen and, within the resulting new project dialog, choose the Empty Activity template before clicking on the Next button.

Enter *AsyncDemo* into the Name field and specify *com.ebookfrenzy.asyncdemo* as the package name. Before clicking on the Finish button, change the Minimum API level setting to API 26: Android 8.0 (Oreo) and the Language menu to Java.

Load the *activity_main.xml* file for the project into the Layout Editor tool. Select the default TextView component and change the ID for the view to *myTextView* in the Attributes tool window.

Add a Button view to the user interface, positioned directly beneath the existing TextView object as illustrated in Figure 55-1. Once the button has been added, click on the Infer Constraints button in the toolbar to add any missing constraints.

Change the text to "Press Me" and extract the string to a resource named *press_me*. With the button view still selected in the layout locate the *onClick* property and enter *buttonClick* as the method name.

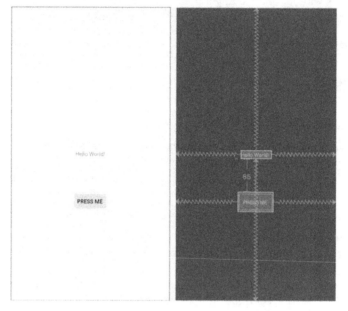

Figure 55-1

Next, load the *MainActivity.java* file into an editing panel and add code to implement the *buttonClick()* method which will be called when the Button view is touched by the user. Since the goal here is to demonstrate the problem of performing lengthy tasks on the main thread, the code will simply pause for 20 seconds before displaying different text on the TextView object:

```java
package com.ebookfrenzy.asyncdemo;

import androidx.appcompat.app.AppCompatActivity;
import android.os.Bundle;
import android.view.View;
import android.widget.TextView;

public class MainActivity extends AppCompatActivity {

    private TextView myTextView;
```

```
@Override
protected void onCreate(Bundle savedInstanceState) {
    super.onCreate(savedInstanceState);
    setContentView(R.layout.activity_thread_example);

    myTextView = findViewById(R.id.myTextView);
}


public void buttonClick(View view)
{
    int i = 0;
    while (i <= 20) {
        try {
            Thread.sleep(1000);
            i++;
        }
        catch (Exception e) {
        }
    }
    myTextView.setText("Button Pressed");
}
}
```

With the code changes complete, run the application on either a physical device or an emulator. Once the application is running, touch the Button, at which point the application will appear to freeze. It will, for example, not be possible to touch the button a second time and in some situations the operating system will, as demonstrated in Figure 55-2, report the application as being unresponsive:

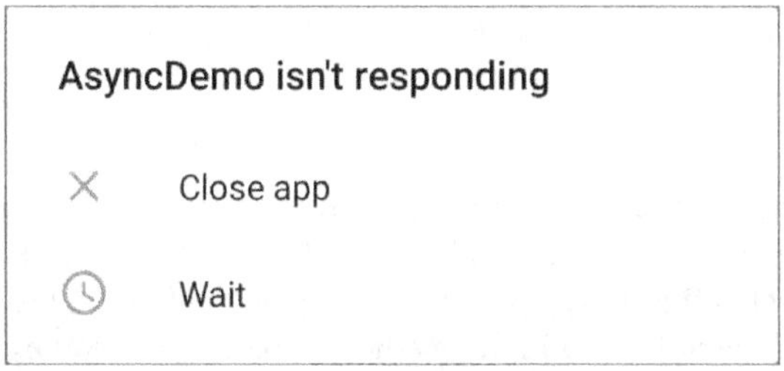

AsyncDemo isn't responding

✕   Close app

🕓   Wait

Figure 55-2

Clearly, anything that is going to take time to complete within the *buttonClick()* method needs to be performed within a separate thread.

55.5 Subclassing AsyncTask

In order to create a new thread, the code to be executed in that thread needs to be performed within an AsyncTask instance. The first step is to subclass AsyncTask in the *MainActivity.java* file as follows:

.

.

```
import android.os.AsyncTask;
```

.

```
public class MainActivity extends AppCompatActivity {


    private class MyTask extends AsyncTask<String, Void, String> {

        @Override
        protected void onPreExecute() {
        }

        @Override
        protected String doInBackground(String... params) {
        }

        @Override
        protected void onProgressUpdate(Void... values) {
        }

        @Override
        protected void onPostExecute(String result) {
        }
    }


}
```

The AsyncTask class uses three different types which are declared in the class signature line as follows:

```
private class MyTask extends AsyncTask<Type 1, Type 2, Type 3> {

```

These three types correspond to the argument types for the *doInBackground()*, *onProgressUpdate()* and *onPostExecute()* methods respectively. If a method does not expect an argument then Void is used, as is the case for the *onProgressUpdate()* in the above code. To change the argument type for a method, change the type declaration both in the class declaration and in the method signature. For this example, the *onProgressUpdate()* method will be passed an Integer, so modify the class declaration as follows:

```
private class MyTask extends AsyncTask<String, Integer, String> {


        @Override
        protected void onProgressUpdate(Integer... values) {
        }


}
```

The *onPreExecute()* method is called before the background tasks are initiated and can be used to perform initialization steps. This method runs on the main thread so may be used to update the user interface.

The code to be performed in the background on a different thread from the main thread resides in the *doInBackground()* method. This method does not have access to the main thread so cannot make user interface changes. The *onProgressUpdate()* method, however, is called each time a call is made to the *publishProgress()* method from within the *doInBackground()* method and can be used to update the user interface with progress information.

The *onPostExecute()* method is called when the tasks performed within the *doInBackground()* method complete. This method is passed the value returned by the *doInBackground()* method and runs within the main thread allowing user interface updates to be made.

Modify the code to move the timer code from the *buttonClick()* method to the *doInBackground()* method as follows:

```
@Override
protected String doInBackground(String... params) {

    int i = 0;
    while (i <= 20) {
        try {
            Thread.sleep(1000);
            i++;
        }
        catch (Exception e) {
            return(e.getLocalizedMessage());
        }
    }
    return "Button Pressed";
}
```

Next, move the TextView update code to the *onPostExecute()* method where it will display the text returned by the *doInBackground()* method:

```
@Override
protected void onPostExecute(String result) {
    myTextView.setText(result);
}
```

To provide regular updates via the *doInBackground()* method, modify the class to add a call to the *publishProgress()* method in the timer loop code (passing through the current loop counter) and to display the current count value in the *onProgressUpdate()* method:

```
@Override
protected String doInBackground(String... params) {
    int i = 0;
    while (i <= 20) {
        publishProgress(i);
        try {
            Thread.sleep(1000);
            i++;
```

```
        }
        catch (Exception e) {
            return(e.getLocalizedMessage());
        }
    }
    return "Button Pressed";


}


@Override
protected void onProgressUpdate(Integer... values) {
    myTextView.setText("Counter = " + values[0]);
}
```

Finally, modify the *buttonClicked()* method to begin the asynchronous task execution:

```
public void buttonClick(View view)
{

    AsyncTask task = new MyTask().execute();

}
```

By default, asynchronous tasks are performed serially. In other words, if an app executes more than one task, only the first task begins execution. The remaining tasks are placed in a queue and executed in sequence as each one finishes. To execute asynchronous tasks in parallel, those tasks must be executed using the AsyncTask *thread pool executor* as follows:

```
AsyncTask task = new
        MyTask().executeOnExecutor(AsyncTask.THREAD_POOL_EXECUTOR);
```

The number of tasks that can be executed in parallel using this approach is limited by the core pool size on the device which, in turn, is dictated by the number of CPU cores available. The number of CPU cores available on a device can be identified from within an app using the following code:

```
int cpu_cores = Runtime.getRuntime().availableProcessors();
```

Android uses an algorithm to calculate the default number of pool threads. The minimum number of threads is 2 while the maximum default value is equal to either 4, or the CPU core count minus 1 (whichever is smallest). The maximum possible number of threads available to the pool on any device is calculated by doubling the CPU core count and adding one.

55.6 Testing the App

When the application is now run, touching the button causes the delay to be performed in a new thread leaving the main thread to continue handling the user interface, including responding to additional button presses. During the delay, the user interface will be updated every second showing the counter value. On completion of the timeout, the TextView will display the "Button Pressed" message.

55.7 Canceling a Task

A running task may be canceled by calling the *cancel()* method of the task object passing through a Boolean value indicating whether the task can be interrupted before the in-progress task completes:

```
AsyncTask task = new MyTask().execute();

task.cancel(true);
```

55.8 Summary

This chapter has provided an overview of threading within Android applications. When an application is first launched in a process, the runtime system creates a *main thread* in which all subsequently launched application components run by default. The primary role of the main thread is to handle the user interface, so any time consuming tasks performed in that thread will give the appearance that the application has locked up. It is essential, therefore, that tasks likely to take time to complete be started in a separate thread.

Because the Android user interface toolkit is not thread-safe, changes to the user interface should not be made in any thread other than the main thread. Background tasks may be performed in a separate thread by subclassing the AsyncTask class and implementing the class methods to perform the task and update the user interface.

56. An Overview of Android Started and Bound Services

The Android Service class is designed specifically to allow applications to initiate and perform background tasks. Unlike broadcast receivers, which are intended to perform a task quickly and then exit, services are designed to perform tasks that take a long time to complete (such as downloading a file over an internet connection or streaming music to the user) but do not require a user interface.

In this chapter, an overview of the different types of services available will be covered, including *started services*, *bound services* and *intent services*. Once these basics have been covered, subsequent chapters will work through a number of examples of services in action.

56.1 Started Services

Started services are launched by other application components (such as an activity or even a broadcast receiver) and potentially run indefinitely in the background until the service is stopped, or is destroyed by the Android runtime system in order to free up resources. A service will continue to run if the application that started it is no longer in the foreground, and even in the event that the component that originally started the service is destroyed.

By default, a service will run within the same main thread as the application process from which it was launched (referred to as a *local service*). It is important, therefore, that any CPU intensive tasks be performed in a new thread within the service. Instructing a service to run within a separate process (and therefore known as a *remote service*) requires a configuration change within the manifest file.

Unless a service is specifically configured to be private (once again via a setting in the manifest file), that service can be started by other components on the same Android device. This is achieved using the Intent mechanism in the same way that one activity can launch another, as outlined in preceding chapters.

Started services are launched via a call to the *startService()* method, passing through as an argument an Intent object identifying the service to be started. When a started service has completed its tasks, it should stop itself via a call to *stopSelf()*. Alternatively, a running service may be stopped by another component via a call to the *stopService()* method, passing through as an argument the matching Intent for the service to be stopped.

Services are given a high priority by the Android system and are typically among the last to be terminated in order to free up resources.

56.2 Intent Service

As previously outlined, services run by default within the same main thread as the component from which they are launched. As such, any CPU intensive tasks that need to be performed by the service should take place within a new thread, thereby avoiding impacting the performance of the calling application.

The *IntentService* class is a convenience class (subclassed from the Service class) that sets up a worker thread for handling background tasks and handles each request in an asynchronous manner. Once the service has handled all queued requests, it simply exits. All that is required when using the IntentService class is that the *onHandleIntent()* method be implemented containing the code to be executed for each request.

For services that do not require synchronous processing of requests, IntentService is the recommended option. Services requiring synchronous handling of requests will, however, need to subclass from the Service class and manually implement and manage threading to handle any CPU intensive tasks efficiently.

56.3 Bound Service

A *bound service* is similar to a started service with the exception that a started service does not generally return results or permit interaction with the component that launched it. A bound service, on the other hand, allows the launching component to interact with, and receive results from, the service. Through the implementation of interprocess communication (IPC), this interaction can also take place across process boundaries. An activity might, for example, start a service to handle audio playback. The activity will, in all probability, include a user interface providing controls to the user for the purpose of pausing playback or skipping to the next track. Similarly, the service will quite likely need to communicate information to the calling activity to indicate that the current audio track has completed and to provide details of the next track that is about to start playing.

A component (also referred to in this context as a *client*) starts and *binds* to a bound service via a call to the *bindService()* method. Also, multiple components may bind to a service simultaneously. When the service binding is no longer required by a client, a call should be made to the *unbindService()* method. When the last bound client unbinds from a service, the service will be terminated by the Android runtime system. It is important to keep in mind that a bound service may also be started via a call to *startService()*. Once started, components may then bind to it via *bindService()* calls. When a bound service is launched via a call to *startService()* it will continue to run even after the last client unbinds from it.

A bound service must include an implementation of the *onBind()* method which is called both when the service is initially created and when other clients subsequently bind to the running service. The purpose of this method is to return to binding clients an object of type *IBinder* containing the information needed by the client to communicate with the service.

In terms of implementing the communication between a client and a bound service, the recommended technique depends on whether the client and service reside in the same or different processes and whether or not the service is private to the client. Local communication can be achieved by extending the Binder class and returning an instance from the *onBind()* method. Interprocess communication, on the other hand, requires Messenger and Handler implementation. Details of both of these approaches will be covered in later chapters.

56.4 The Anatomy of a Service

A service must, as has already been mentioned, be created as a subclass of the Android Service class (more specifically *android.app.Service*) or a sub-class thereof (such as *android.app.IntentService*). As part of the subclassing procedure, one or more of the following superclass callback methods must be overridden, depending on the exact nature of the service being created:

- **onStartCommand()** – This is the method that is called when the service is started by another component via a call to the *startService()* method. This method does not need to be implemented for bound services.

- **onBind()** – Called when a component binds to the service via a call to the *bindService()* method. When implementing a bound service, this method must return an *IBinder* object facilitating communication with the client. In the case of *started services*, this method must be implemented to return a NULL value.

- **onCreate()** – Intended as a location to perform initialization tasks, this method is called immediately before the call to either *onStartCommand()* or the *first* call to the *onBind()* method.

- **onDestroy()** – Called when the service is being destroyed.

- **onHandleIntent()** – Applies only to IntentService subclasses. This method is called to handle the processing for the service. It is executed in a separate thread from the main application.

Note that the IntentService class includes its own implementations of the *onStartCommand()* and *onBind()* callback methods so these do not need to be implemented in subclasses.

56.5 Controlling Destroyed Service Restart Options

The *onStartCommand()* callback method is required to return an integer value to define what should happen with regard to the service in the event that it is destroyed by the Android runtime system. Possible return values for these methods are as follows:

- **START_NOT_STICKY** – Indicates to the system that the service should not be restarted in the event that it is destroyed unless there are pending intents awaiting delivery.

- **START_STICKY** – Indicates that the service should be restarted as soon as possible after it has been destroyed if the destruction occurred after the *onStartCommand()* method returned. In the event that no pending intents are waiting to be delivered, the *onStartCommand()* callback method is called with a NULL intent value. The intent being processed at the time that the service was destroyed is discarded.

- **START_REDELIVER_INTENT** – Indicates that, if the service was destroyed after returning from the *onStartCommand()* callback method, the service should be restarted with the current intent redelivered to the *onStartCommand()* method followed by any pending intents.

56.6 Declaring a Service in the Manifest File

In order for a service to be useable, it must first be declared within a manifest file. This involves embedding an appropriately configured *<service>* element into an existing *<application>* entry. At a minimum, the *<service>* element must contain a property declaring the class name of the service as illustrated in the following XML fragment:

.

.

```
    <application
        android:icon="@mipmap/ic_launcher"
        android:label="@string/app_name" >
        <activity
            android:label="@string/app_name"
            android:name=".MainActivity" >
            <intent-filter>
              <action android:name="android.intent.action.MAIN" />
              <category android:name="android.intent.category.LAUNCHER" />
            </intent-filter>
        </activity>
        <service android:name="MyService>
            </service>
    </application>
</manifest>
```

By default, services are declared as public, in that they can be accessed by components outside of the application package in which they reside. In order to make a service private, the *android:exported* property must be declared as *false* within the <service> element of the manifest file. For example:

```
<service android:name="MyService"
```

```
android:exported="false">
</service>
```

As previously discussed, services run within the same process as the calling component by default. In order to force a service to run within its own process, add an *android:process* property to the <service> element, declaring a name for the process prefixed with a colon (:):

```
<service android:name="MyService"
android:exported="false"
android:process=":myprocess">
</service>
```

The colon prefix indicates that the new process is private to the local application. If the process name begins with a lower case letter instead of a colon, however, the process will be global and available for use by other components.

Finally, using the same intent filter mechanisms outlined for activities, a service may also advertise capabilities to other applications running on the device. For more details on intent filters, refer to the chapter entitled *"An Overview of Android Intents"*.

56.7 Starting a Service Running on System Startup

Given the background nature of services, it is not uncommon for a service to need to be started when an Android-based system first boots up. This can be achieved by creating a broadcast receiver with an intent filter configured to listen for the system *android.intent.action.BOOT_COMPLETED* intent. When such an intent is detected, the broadcast receiver would simply invoke the necessary service and then return. Note that, in order to function, such a broadcast receiver will need to request the *android.permission.RECEIVE_BOOT_ COMPLETED* permission.

56.8 Summary

Android services are a powerful mechanism that allows applications to perform tasks in the background. A service, once launched, will continue to run regardless of whether the calling application is the foreground task or not, and even in the event that the component that initiated the service is destroyed.

Services are subclassed from the Android Service class and fall into the category of either *started services* or *bound services*. Started services run until they are stopped or destroyed and do not inherently provide a mechanism for interaction or data exchange with other components. Bound services, on the other hand, provide a communication interface to other client components and generally run until the last client unbinds from the service.

By default, services run locally within the same process and main thread as the calling application. A new thread should, therefore, be created within the service for the purpose of handling CPU intensive tasks. Remote services may be started within a separate process by making a minor configuration change to the corresponding <service> entry in the application manifest file.

The IntentService class (itself a subclass of the Android Service class) provides a convenient mechanism for handling asynchronous service requests within a separate worker thread.

57. Implementing an Android Started Service – A Worked Example

The previous chapter covered a considerable amount of information relating to Android services and, at this point, the concept of services may seem somewhat overwhelming. In order to reinforce the information in the previous chapter, this chapter will work through an Android Studio tutorial intended to gradually introduce the concepts of started service implementation.

Within this chapter, a sample application will be created and used as the basis for implementing an Android service. In the first instance, the service will be created using the *IntentService* class. This example will subsequently be extended to demonstrate the use of the *Service* class. Finally, the steps involved in performing tasks within a separate thread when using the Service class will be implemented. Having covered started services in this chapter, the next chapter, entitled *"Android Local Bound Services – A Worked Example"*, will focus on the implementation of bound services and client-service communication.

57.1 Creating the Example Project

Select the *Start a new Android Studio project* quick start option from the welcome screen and, within the resulting new project dialog, choose the Empty Activity template before clicking on the Next button.

Enter *ServiceExample* into the Name field and specify *com.ebookfrenzy.serviceexample* as the package name. Before clicking on the Finish button, change the Minimum API level setting to API 26: Android 8.0 (Oreo) and the Language menu to Java.

57.2 Creating the Service Class

Before writing any code, the first step is to add a new class to the project to contain the service. The first type of service to be demonstrated in this tutorial is to be based on the IntentService class. As outlined in the preceding chapter (*"An Overview of Android Started and Bound Services"*), the purpose of the IntentService class is to provide the developer with a convenient mechanism for creating services that perform tasks asynchronously within a separate thread from the calling application.

Add a new class to the project by right-clicking on the *com.ebookfrenzy.serviceexample* package name located under *app -> java* in the Project tool window and selecting the *New -> Java Class* menu option. Within the resulting *Create New Class* dialog, name the new class *MyIntentService*. Finally, click on the *OK* button to create the new class.

Review the new *MyIntentService.java* file in the Android Studio editor where it should read as follows:

```
package com.ebookfrenzy.serviceexample;


public class MyIntentService {
}
```

The class needs to be modified so that it subclasses the IntentService class. When subclassing the IntentService class, there are two rules that must be followed. First, a constructor for the class must be implemented which calls the superclass constructor, passing through the class name of the service. Second, the class must override the *onHandleIntent()* method. Modify the code in the *MyIntentService.java* file, therefore, so that it reads as follows:

```java
package com.ebookfrenzy.serviceexample;

import android.app.IntentService;
import android.content.Intent;

public class MyIntentService extends IntentService {

    @Override
    protected void onHandleIntent(Intent arg0) {

    }


    public MyIntentService() {
        super("MyIntentService");
    }
}
```

All that remains at this point is to implement some code within the *onHandleIntent()* method so that the service actually does something when invoked. Ordinarily this would involve performing a task that takes some time to complete such as downloading a large file or playing audio. For the purposes of this example, however, the handler will simply output a message to the Android Studio Logcat panel:

```java
package com.ebookfrenzy.serviceexample;

import android.app.IntentService;
import android.content.Intent;
import android.util.Log;

public class MyIntentService extends IntentService {

    private static final String TAG =
                "ServiceExample";

    @Override
    protected void onHandleIntent(Intent arg0) {
        Log.i(TAG, "Intent Service started");
    }

    public MyIntentService() {
        super("MyIntentService");
    }
}
```

57.3 Adding the Service to the Manifest File

Before a service can be invoked, it must first be added to the manifest file of the application to which it belongs. At a minimum, this involves adding a <service> element together with the class name of the service.

Double-click on the *AndroidManifest.xml* file (*app -> manifests*) for the current project to load it into the editor and modify the XML to add the service element as shown in the following listing:

```xml
<?xml version="1.0" encoding="utf-8"?>
<manifest xmlns:android="http://schemas.android.com/apk/res/android"
    package="com.ebookfrenzy.serviceexample">

    <application
        android:allowBackup="true"
        android:icon="@mipmap/ic_launcher"
        android:label="@string/app_name"
        android:supportsRtl="true"
        android:theme="@style/AppTheme">
        <activity android:name=".MainActivity">
            <intent-filter>
                <action android:name="android.intent.action.MAIN" />

                <category android:name="android.intent.category.LAUNCHER" />
            </intent-filter>
        </activity>
        <service android:name=".MyIntentService" />
    </application>

</manifest>
```

57.4 Starting the Service

Now that the service has been implemented and declared in the manifest file, the next step is to add code to start the service when the application launches. As is typically the case, the ideal location for such code is the *onCreate()* callback method of the activity class (which, in this case, can be found in the *MainActivity.java* file). Locate and load this file into the editor and modify the *onCreate()* method to add the code to start the service:

```java
package com.ebookfrenzy.serviceexample;

import androidx.appcompat.app.AppCompatActivity;
import android.os.Bundle;
import android.content.Intent;

public class MainActivity extends AppCompatActivity {

    @Override
    protected void onCreate(Bundle savedInstanceState) {
        super.onCreate(savedInstanceState);
        setContentView(R.layout.activity_main);
        Intent intent = new Intent(this, MyIntentService.class);
```

```
        startService(intent);

    }

}
```

All that the added code needs to do is to create a new Intent object primed with the class name of the service to start and then use it as an argument to the *startService()* method.

57.5 Testing the IntentService Example

The example IntentService based service is now complete and ready to be tested. Since the message displayed by the service will appear in the Logcat panel, it is important that this is configured in the Android Studio environment.

Begin by displaying the Logcat tool window before clicking on the menu in the upper right-hand corner of the panel (which will probably currently read *Show only selected application*). From this menu, select the *Edit Filter Configuration* menu option.

In the *Create New Logcat Filter* dialog name the filter *ServiceExample* and, in the *by Log Tag* field, enter the TAG value declared in *MyIntentService.java* (in the above code example this was *ServiceExample*).

When the changes are complete, click on the *OK* button to create the filter and dismiss the dialog. The newly created filter should now be selected in the Android tool window.

With the filter configured, run the application on a physical device or AVD emulator session and note that the "Intent Service Started" message appears in the Logcat panel. Note that it may be necessary to change the filter menu setting back to ServiceExample after the application has launched:

```
06-29 09:05:16.887 3389-3948/com.ebookfrenzy.serviceexample I/ServiceExample:
Intent Service started
```

Had the service been tasked with a long-term activity, the service would have continued to run in the background in a separate thread until the task was completed, allowing the application to continue functioning and responding to the user. Since all our service did was log a message, it will have simply stopped upon completion.

57.6 Using the Service Class

While the IntentService class allows a service to be implemented with minimal coding, there are situations where the flexibility and synchronous nature of the Service class will be required. As will become evident in this chapter, this involves some additional programming work to implement.

In order to avoid introducing too many concepts at once, and as a demonstration of the risks inherent in performing time-consuming service tasks in the same thread as the calling application, the example service created here will not run the service task within a new thread, instead relying on the main thread of the application. Creation and management of a new thread within a service will be covered in the next phase of the tutorial.

57.7 Creating the New Service

For the purposes of this example, a new class will be added to the project that will subclass from the Service class. Right-click, therefore, on the package name listed under *app -> java* in the Project tool window and select the *New -> Service -> Service* menu option. Create a new class named *MyService* with both the *Exported* and *Enabled* options selected.

The minimal requirement in order to create an operational service is to implement the *onStartCommand()* callback method which will be called when the service is starting up. In addition, the *onBind()* method must return a null value to indicate to the Android system that this is not a bound service. For the purposes of this example, the *onStartCommand()* method will loop 3 times sleeping for 10 seconds on each loop iteration. For the sake of completeness, stub versions of the *onCreate()* and *onDestroy()* methods will also be implemented in the new *MyService.java* file as follows:

```java
package com.ebookfrenzy.serviceexample;

import android.app.Service;
import android.content.Intent;
import android.os.IBinder;
import android.util.Log;

public class MyService extends Service {

    public MyService() {
    }

    private static final String TAG =
            "ServiceExample";

    @Override
    public void onCreate() {
        Log.i(TAG, "Service onCreate");
    }

    @Override
    public int onStartCommand(Intent intent, int flags, int startId) {

        Log.i(TAG, "Service onStartCommand " + startId);

        int i = 0;
        while (i <= 3) {

            try {
                Thread.sleep(10000);
                i++;
            } catch (Exception e) {
            }
            Log.i(TAG, "Service running");
        }
        return Service.START_STICKY;
    }

    @Override
    public IBinder onBind(Intent arg0) {
        Log.i(TAG, "Service onBind");
        return null;
```

```
    }

    @Override
    public void onDestroy() {
        Log.i(TAG, "Service onDestroy");
    }
}
```

With the service implemented, load the *AndroidManifest.xml* file into the editor and verify that Android Studio has added an appropriate entry for the new service which should read as follows:

```
<service
 android:name=".MyService"
            android:enabled="true"
            android:exported="true" >
</service>
```

57.8 Modifying the User Interface

As will become evident when the application runs, failing to create a new thread for the service to perform tasks creates a serious usability problem. In order to be able to appreciate fully the magnitude of this issue, it is going to be necessary to add a Button view to the user interface of the *MainActivity* and configure it to call a method when "clicked" by the user.

Locate and load the *activity_main.xml* file in the Project tool window (*app -> res -> layout -> activity_main. xml*). Delete the TextView and add a Button view to the layout. Select the new button, change the text to read "Start Service" and extract the string to a resource named *start_service*.

With the new Button still selected, locate the *onClick* property in the Attributes panel and assign to it a method named *buttonClick*.

Next, edit the *MainActivity.java* file to add the *buttonClick()* method and remove the code from the *onCreate()* method that was previously added to launch the MyIntentService service:

```
package com.ebookfrenzy.serviceexample;

import androidx.appcompat.app.AppCompatActivity;
import android.os.Bundle;
import android.content.Intent;
import android.view.View;

public class MainActivity extends AppCompatActivity {

    @Override
    protected void onCreate(Bundle savedInstanceState) {
        super.onCreate(savedInstanceState);
        setContentView(R.layout.activity_service_example);
        Intent intent = new Intent(this, MyIntentService.class);
        startService(intent);
    }
}
```

```
public void buttonClick(View view)
{

    Intent intent = new Intent(this, MyService.class);
    startService(intent);

}
}
```

All that the *buttonClick()* method does is create an intent object for the new service and then start it running.

57.9 Running the Application

Run the application and, once loaded, touch the *Start Service* button. Within the Logcat tool window (using the *ServiceExample* filter created previously) the log messages will appear indicating that the *onCreate()* method was called and that the loop in the *onStartCommand()* method is executing.

Before the final loop message appears, attempt to touch the *Start Service* button a second time. Note that the button is unresponsive. After approximately 20 seconds, the system may display a warning dialog containing the message "ServiceExample isn't responding". The reason for this is that the main thread of the application is currently being held up by the service while it performs the looping task. Not only does this prevent the application from responding to the user, but also to the system, which eventually assumes that the application has locked up in some way.

Clearly, the code for the service needs to be modified to perform tasks in a separate thread from the main thread.

57.10 Creating an AsyncTask for Service Tasks

As outlined in *"A Basic Overview of Threads and AsyncTasks"*, when an Android application is first started, the runtime system creates a single thread in which all application components will run by default. This thread is generally referred to as the *main thread*. The primary role of the main thread is to handle the user interface in terms of event handling and interaction with views in the user interface. Any additional components that are started within the application will, by default, also run on the main thread.

As demonstrated in the previous section, any component that undertakes a time consuming operation on the main thread will cause the application to become unresponsive until that task is complete. It is not surprising, therefore, that Android provides an API that allows applications to create and use additional threads. Any tasks performed in a separate thread from the main thread are essentially performed in the background. Such threads are typically referred to as *background* or *worker* threads.

A very simple solution to this problem involves performing the service task within an AsyncTask instance. To add this support to the app, modify the *MyService.java* file to create an AsyncTask subclass containing the timer code from the *onStartCommand()* method:

```
.
.
.
import android.os.AsyncTask;
.
.
.
private class SrvTask extends AsyncTask<Integer, Integer, String> {

    @Override
    protected String doInBackground(Integer... params) {

        int startId = params[0];
```

```
        int i = 0;
        while (i <= 3) {

            publishProgress(params[0]);
            try {
                Thread.sleep(10000);
                i++;
            } catch (Exception e) {
            }
        }
        return("Service complete " + startId);
    }

    @Override
    protected void onPostExecute(String result) {
        Log.i(TAG, result);
    }

    @Override
    protected void onPreExecute() {

    }

    @Override
    protected void onProgressUpdate(Integer... values) {
        Log.i(TAG, "Service Running " + values[0]);
    }
}
```

Next, modify the *onStartCommand()* method to execute the task in the background, this time using the thread pool executor to allow multiple instances of the task to run in parallel:

```
@Override
public int onStartCommand(Intent intent, int flags, int startId) {

    AsyncTask task = new SrvTask().executeOnExecutor(
                    AsyncTask.THREAD_POOL_EXECUTOR, startId);

    return Service.START_STICKY;
}
```

When the application is now run, it should be possible to touch the *Start Service* button multiple times. When doing so, the Logcat output should indicate more than one task running simultaneously (subject to CPU core limitations):

```
I/ServiceExample: Service Running 1
I/ServiceExample: Service Running 2
I/ServiceExample: Service Running 1
I/ServiceExample: Service Running 2
```

```
I/ServiceExample: Service Running 1
I/ServiceExample: Service Running 2
I/ServiceExample: Service Running 1
I/ServiceExample: Service Running 2
I/ServiceExample: Service complete 1
I/ServiceExample: Service complete 2
```

With the service now handling requests outside of the main thread, the application remains responsive to both the user and the Android system.

57.11 Summary

This chapter has worked through an example implementation of an Android started service using the *IntentService* and *Service* classes. The example also demonstrated the use of asynchronous tasks within a service to avoid making the main thread of the application unresponsive.

58. Android Local Bound Services – A Worked Example

As outlined in some detail in the previous chapters, bound services, unlike started services, provide a mechanism for implementing communication between an Android service and one or more client components. The objective of this chapter is to build on the overview of bound services provided in *"An Overview of Android Started and Bound Services"* before embarking on an example implementation of a *local* bound service in action.

58.1 Understanding Bound Services

In common with started services, bound services are provided to allow applications to perform tasks in the background. Unlike started services, however, multiple client components may *bind* to a bound service and, once bound, interact with that service using a variety of different mechanisms.

Bound services are created as sub-classes of the Android Service class and must, at a minimum, implement the *onBind()* method. Client components bind to a service via a call to the *bindService()* method. The first bind request to a bound service will result in a call to that service's *onBind()* method (subsequent bind requests do not trigger an *onBind()* call). Clients wishing to bind to a service must also implement a ServiceConnection subclass containing *onServiceConnected()* and *onServiceDisconnected()* methods which will be called once the client-server connection has been established or disconnected, respectively. In the case of the *onServiceConnected()* method, this will be passed an IBinder object containing the information needed by the client to interact with the service.

58.2 Bound Service Interaction Options

There are two recommended mechanisms for implementing interaction between client components and a bound service. In the event that the bound service is local and private to the same application as the client component (in other words it runs within the same process and is not available to components in other applications), the recommended method is to create a subclass of the Binder class and extend it to provide an interface to the service. An instance of this Binder object is then returned by the *onBind()* method and subsequently used by the client component to directly access methods and data held within the service.

In situations where the bound service is not local to the application (in other words, it is running in a different process from the client component), interaction is best achieved using a Messenger/Handler implementation.

In the remainder of this chapter, an example will be created with the aim of demonstrating the steps involved in creating, starting and interacting with a local, private bound service.

58.3 An Android Studio Local Bound Service Example

The example application created in the remainder of this chapter will consist of a single activity and a bound service. The purpose of the bound service is to obtain the current time from the system and return that information to the activity where it will be displayed to the user. The bound service will be local and private to the same application as the activity.

Select the *Start a new Android Studio project* quick start option from the welcome screen and, within the resulting new project dialog, choose the Empty Activity template before clicking on the Next button.

Enter *LocalBound* into the Name field and specify *com.ebookfrenzy.localbound* as the package name. Before clicking on the Finish button, change the Minimum API level setting to API 26: Android 8.0 (Oreo) and the Language menu to Java.

Once the project has been created, the next step is to add a new class to act as the bound service.

58.4 Adding a Bound Service to the Project

To add a new class to the project, right-click on the package name (located under *app -> java -> com.ebookfrenzy. localbound*) within the Project tool window and select the *New -> Service -> Service* menu option. Specify *BoundService* as the class name and make sure that both the *Exported* and *Enabled* options are selected before clicking on *Finish* to create the class. By default, Android Studio will load the *BoundService.java* file into the editor where it will read as follows:

```
package com.ebookfrenzy.localbound;

import android.app.Service;
import android.content.Intent;
import android.os.IBinder;

public class BoundService extends Service {
    public BoundService() {
    }

    @Override
    public IBinder onBind(Intent intent) {
        // TODO: Return the communication channel to the service.
        throw new UnsupportedOperationException("Not yet implemented");
    }
}
```

58.5 Implementing the Binder

As previously outlined, local bound services can communicate with bound clients by passing an appropriately configured Binder object to the client. This is achieved by creating a Binder subclass within the bound service class and extending it by adding one or more new methods that can be called by the client. In most cases, this simply involves implementing a method that returns a reference to the bound service instance. With a reference to this instance, the client can then access data and call methods within the bound service directly.

For the purposes of this example, therefore, some changes are needed to the template *BoundService* class created in the preceding section. In the first instance, a Binder subclass needs to be declared. This class will contain a single method named *getService()* which will simply return a reference to the current service object instance (represented by the *this* keyword). With these requirements in mind, edit the *BoundService.java* file and modify it as follows:

```
package com.ebookfrenzy.localbound;

import android.app.Service;
import android.content.Intent;
import android.os.IBinder;
import android.os.Binder;
```

```
public class BoundService extends Service {

    private final IBinder myBinder = new MyLocalBinder();

    public BoundService() {
    }

    @Override
    public IBinder onBind(Intent intent) {
        // TODO: Return the communication channel to the service.
        throw new UnsupportedOperationException("Not yet implemented");
    }

    public class MyLocalBinder extends Binder {
        BoundService getService() {
            return BoundService.this;
        }
    }
}
```

Having made the changes to the class, it is worth taking a moment to recap the steps performed here. First, a new subclass of Binder (named *MyLocalBinder*) is declared. This class contains a single method for the sole purpose of returning a reference to the current instance of the *BoundService* class. A new instance of the *MyLocalBinder* class is created and assigned to the *myBinder* IBinder reference (since Binder is a subclass of IBinder there is no type mismatch in this assignment).

Next, the *onBind()* method needs to be modified to return a reference to the *myBinder* object and a new public method implemented to return the current time when called by any clients that bind to the service:

```
package com.ebookfrenzy.localbound;

import java.text.SimpleDateFormat;
import java.util.Date;
import java.util.Locale;

import android.app.Service;
import android.content.Intent;
import android.os.IBinder;
import android.os.Binder;

public class BoundService extends Service {

    private final IBinder myBinder = new MyLocalBinder();

    public BoundService() {
    }

    @Override
```

```
public IBinder onBind(Intent intent) {
    return myBinder;
}


public String getCurrentTime() {
    SimpleDateFormat dateformat =
            new SimpleDateFormat("HH:mm:ss MM/dd/yyyy",
                    Locale.US);
    return (dateformat.format(new Date()));
}


public class MyLocalBinder extends Binder {
    BoundService getService() {
        return BoundService.this;
    }
}


}
```

At this point, the bound service is complete and is ready to be added to the project manifest file. Locate and double-click on the *AndroidManifest.xml* file for the *LocalBound* project in the Project tool window and, once loaded into the Manifest Editor, verify that Android Studio has already added a <service> entry for the service as follows:

```
<?xml version="1.0" encoding="utf-8"?>
<manifest xmlns:android="http://schemas.android.com/apk/res/android"
    package="com.ebookfrenzy.localbound.localbound" >

    <application
        android:allowBackup="true"
        android:icon="@mipmap/ic_launcher"
        android:label="@string/app_name"
        android:theme="@style/AppTheme" >
        <service
            android:name=".BoundService"
            android:enabled="true"
            android:exported="true" >
        </service>
        <activity
            android:name=".MainActivity" >
            <intent-filter>
                <action android:name="android.intent.action.MAIN" />

                <category android:name="android.intent.category.LAUNCHER" />
            </intent-filter>
        </activity>
    </application>
```

```
</manifest>
```

The next phase is to implement the necessary code within the activity to bind to the service and call the *getCurrentTime()* method.

58.6 Binding the Client to the Service

For the purposes of this tutorial, the client is the *MainActivity* instance of the running application. As previously noted, in order to successfully bind to a service and receive the IBinder object returned by the service's *onBind()* method, it is necessary to create a ServiceConnection subclass and implement *onServiceConnected()* and *onServiceDisconnected()* callback methods. Edit the *MainActivity.java* file and modify it as follows:

```java
package com.ebookfrenzy.localbound;

import androidx.appcompat.app.AppCompatActivity;
import android.os.Bundle;
import android.os.IBinder;
import android.content.Context;
import android.content.Intent;
import android.content.ComponentName;
import android.content.ServiceConnection;
import com.ebookfrenzy.localbound.BoundService.MyLocalBinder;

public class MainActivity extends AppCompatActivity {

    BoundService myService;
    boolean isBound = false;

    @Override
    protected void onCreate(Bundle savedInstanceState) {
        super.onCreate(savedInstanceState);
        setContentView(R.layout.activity_local_bound);
    }

    private ServiceConnection myConnection = new ServiceConnection()
    {
        @Override
        public void onServiceConnected(ComponentName className,
                                        IBinder service) {
            MyLocalBinder binder = (MyLocalBinder) service;
            myService = binder.getService();
            isBound = true;
        }

        @Override
        public void onServiceDisconnected(ComponentName name) {
            isBound = false;
        }
```

```
        };
}
```

The *onServiceConnected()* method will be called when the client binds successfully to the service. The method is passed as an argument the IBinder object returned by the *onBind()* method of the service. This argument is cast to an object of type MyLocalBinder and then the *getService()* method of the binder object is called to obtain a reference to the service instance, which, in turn, is assigned to *myService*. A Boolean flag is used to indicate that the connection has been successfully established.

The *onServiceDisconnected()* method is called when the connection ends and simply sets the Boolean flag to false.

Having established the connection, the next step is to modify the activity to bind to the service. This involves the creation of an intent and a call to the *bindService()* method, which can be performed in the *onCreate()* method of the activity:

```
@Override
    public void onCreate(Bundle savedInstanceState) {
        super.onCreate(savedInstanceState);
        setContentView(R.layout.activity_local_bound);
        Intent intent = new Intent(this, BoundService.class);
        bindService(intent, myConnection, Context.BIND_AUTO_CREATE);
}
```

58.7 Completing the Example

All that remains is to implement a mechanism for calling the *getCurrentTime()* method and displaying the result to the user. As is now customary, Android Studio will have created a template *activity_main.xml* file for the activity containing only a TextView. Load this file into the Layout Editor tool and, using Design mode, select the TextView component and change the ID to *myTextView*. Add a Button view beneath the TextView and change the text on the button to read "Show Time", extracting the text to a string resource named *show_time*. On completion of these changes, the layout should resemble that illustrated in Figure 58-1. If any constraints are missing, click on the Infer Constraints button in the Layout Editor toolbar.

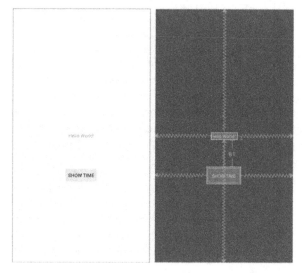

Figure 58-1

Complete the user interface design by selecting the Button and configuring the *onClick* property to call a method named *showTime*.

Finally, edit the code in the *MainActivity.java* file to implement the *showTime()* method. This method simply calls the *getCurrentTime()* method of the service (which, thanks to the *onServiceConnected()* method, is now available from within the activity via the *myService* reference) and assigns the resulting string to the TextView:

```
package com.ebookfrenzy.localbound;

import androidx.appcompat.app.AppCompatActivity;
import android.os.Bundle;
import android.os.IBinder;
import android.content.Context;
import android.content.Intent;
import android.content.ComponentName;
import android.content.ServiceConnection;
import com.ebookfrenzy.localbound.BoundService.MyLocalBinder;
import android.view.View;
import android.widget.TextView;

public class MainActivity extends AppCompatActivity {

    BoundService myService;
    boolean isBound = false;

    public void showTime(View view)
    {
        String currentTime = myService.getCurrentTime();
        TextView myTextView = findViewById(R.id.myTextView);
        myTextView.setText(currentTime);
    }
.
.
}
```

58.8 Testing the Application

With the code changes complete, perform a test run of the application. Once visible, touch the button and note that the text view changes to display the current date and time. The example has successfully started and bound to a service and then called a method of that service to cause a task to be performed and results returned to the activity.

58.9 Summary

When a bound service is local and private to an application, components within that application can interact with the service without the need to resort to inter-process communication (IPC). In general terms, the service's *onBind()* method returns an IBinder object containing a reference to the instance of the running service. The client component implements a ServiceConnection subclass containing callback methods that are called when the service is connected and disconnected. The former method is passed the IBinder object returned by the *onBind()* method allowing public methods within the service to be called.

Having covered the implementation of local bound services, the next chapter will focus on using IPC to interact with remote bound services.

59. Android Remote Bound Services – A Worked Example

In this, the final chapter dedicated to Android services, an example application will be developed to demonstrate the use of a messenger and handler configuration to facilitate interaction between a client and remote bound service.

59.1 Client to Remote Service Communication

As outlined in the previous chapter, interaction between a client and a local service can be implemented by returning to the client an IBinder object containing a reference to the service object. In the case of remote services, however, this approach does not work because the remote service is running in a different process and, as such, cannot be reached directly from the client.

In the case of remote services, a Messenger and Handler configuration must be created which allows messages to be passed across process boundaries between client and service.

Specifically, the service creates a Handler instance that will be called when a message is received from the client. In terms of initialization, it is the job of the Handler to create a Messenger object which, in turn, creates an IBinder object to be returned to the client in the *onBind()* method. This IBinder object is used by the client to create an instance of the Messenger object and, subsequently, to send messages to the service handler. Each time a message is sent by the client, the *handleMessage()* method of the handler is called, passing through the message object.

The simple example created in this chapter will consist of an activity and a bound service running in separate processes. The Messenger/Handler mechanism will be used to send a string to the service, which will then display that string in a Toast message.

59.2 Creating the Example Application

Select the *Start a new Android Studio project* quick start option from the welcome screen and, within the resulting new project dialog, choose the Empty Activity template before clicking on the Next button.

Enter *RemoteBound* into the Name field and specify *com.ebookfrenzy.remotebound* as the package name. Before clicking on the Finish button, change the Minimum API level setting to API 26: Android 8.0 (Oreo) and the Language menu to Java.

59.3 Designing the User Interface

Locate the *activity_main.xml* file in the Project tool window and double-click on it to load it into the Layout Editor tool. With the Layout Editor tool in Design mode, right-click on the default TextView instance, choose the *Convert view...* menu option and select the Button view from the resulting dialog and click Apply. Change the text property of the button to read "Send Message" and extract the string to a new resource named *send_message*.

Finally, configure the *onClick* property to call a method named *sendMessage*.

59.4 Implementing the Remote Bound Service

In order to implement the remote bound service for this example, add a new class to the project by right-clicking on the package name (located under *app -> java*) within the Project tool window and select the *New -> Service -> Service* menu option. Specify *RemoteService* as the class name and make sure that both the *Exported* and *Enabled* options are selected before clicking on *Finish* to create the class.

The next step is to implement the handler class for the new service. This is achieved by extending the Handler class and implementing the *handleMessage()* method. This method will be called when a message is received from the client. It will be passed a Message object as an argument containing any data that the client needs to pass to the service. In this instance, this will be a Bundle object containing a string to be displayed to the user. The modified class in the *RemoteService.java* file should read as follows once this has been implemented:

```java
package com.ebookfrenzy.remotebound;

import android.app.Service;
import android.content.Intent;
import android.os.IBinder;
import android.os.Bundle;
import android.os.Handler;
import android.os.Message;
import android.widget.Toast;
import android.os.Messenger;

public class RemoteService extends Service {

    public RemoteService() {
    }

    class IncomingHandler extends Handler {
        @Override
        public void handleMessage(Message msg) {

            Bundle data = msg.getData();
            String dataString = data.getString("MyString");
            Toast.makeText(getApplicationContext(),
                    dataString, Toast.LENGTH_SHORT).show();
        }
    }


    @Override
    public IBinder onBind(Intent intent) {
        // TODO: Return the communication channel to the service.
        throw new UnsupportedOperationException("Not yet implemented");
    }
}
```

With the handler implemented, the only remaining task in terms of the service code is to modify the *onBind()*

method such that it returns an IBinder object containing a Messenger object which, in turn, contains a reference to the handler:

```
final Messenger myMessenger = new Messenger(new IncomingHandler());


@Override
public IBinder onBind(Intent intent) {
        return myMessenger.getBinder();
}
```

The first line of the above code fragment creates a new instance of our handler class and passes it through to the constructor of a new Messenger object. Within the *onBind()* method, the *getBinder()* method of the messenger object is called to return the messenger's IBinder object.

59.5 Configuring a Remote Service in the Manifest File

In order to portray the communication between a client and remote service accurately, it will be necessary to configure the service to run in a separate process from the rest of the application. This is achieved by adding an *android:process* property within the <service> tag for the service in the manifest file. In order to launch a remote service it is also necessary to provide an intent filter for the service. To implement these changes, modify the *AndroidManifest.xml* file to add the required entries:

```
<?xml version="1.0" encoding="utf-8"?>
<manifest xmlns:android="http://schemas.android.com/apk/res/android"
    package="com.ebookfrenzy.remotebound" >

    <application
        android:allowBackup="true"
        android:icon="@mipmap/ic_launcher"
        android:label="@string/app_name"
        android:supportsRtl="true"
        android:theme="@style/AppTheme" >
        <service
            android:name=".RemoteService"
            android:enabled="true"
            android:exported="true"
            android:process=":my_process" >
        </service>

        <activity
            android:name=".MainActivity" >
            <intent-filter>
                <action android:name="android.intent.action.MAIN" />

                <category android:name="android.intent.category.LAUNCHER" />
            </intent-filter>
        </activity>
    </application>
```

```
</manifest>
```

59.6 Launching and Binding to the Remote Service

As with a local bound service, the client component needs to implement an instance of the ServiceConnection class with *onServiceConnected()* and *onServiceDisconnected()* methods. Also, in common with local services, the *onServiceConnected()* method will be passed the IBinder object returned by the *onBind()* method of the remote service which will be used to send messages to the server handler. In the case of this example, the client is *MainActivity*, the code for which is located in *MainActivity.java*. Load this file and modify it to add the ServiceConnection class and a variable to store a reference to the received Messenger object together with a Boolean flag to indicate whether or not the connection is established:

```
package com.ebookfrenzy.remotebound;

import androidx.appcompat.app.AppCompatActivity;
import android.os.Bundle;
import android.os.IBinder;
import android.os.Message;
import android.os.Messenger;
import android.os.RemoteException;
import android.content.ComponentName;
import android.content.Context;
import android.content.Intent;
import android.content.ServiceConnection;
import android.view.View;

public class MainActivity extends AppCompatActivity {

    Messenger myService = null;
    boolean isBound;

    @Override
    protected void onCreate(Bundle savedInstanceState) {
        super.onCreate(savedInstanceState);
        setContentView(R.layout.activity_remote_bound);
    }

    private ServiceConnection myConnection =
            new ServiceConnection() {
                public void onServiceConnected(
                        ComponentName className,
                                        IBinder service) {
                    myService = new Messenger(service);
                    isBound = true;
                }

                public void onServiceDisconnected(
                        ComponentName className) {
```

```
                mySeervice = null;
                isBound = false;
        }
    };
}
```

Next, some code needs to be added to bind to the remote service. This involves creating an intent that matches the intent filter for the service as declared in the manifest file and then making a call to the *bindService()* method, providing the intent and a reference to the ServiceConnection instance as arguments. For the purposes of this example, this code will be implemented in the activity's *onCreate()* method:

```
@Override
protected void onCreate(Bundle savedInstanceState) {
        super.onCreate(savedInstanceState);
        setContentView(R.layout.activity_remote_bound);

        Intent intent = new Intent(getApplicationContext(),
                        RemoteService.class);

        bindService(intent, myConnection, Context.BIND_AUTO_CREATE);
}
```

59.7 Sending a Message to the Remote Service

All that remains before testing the application is to implement the *sendMessage()* method in the *MainActivity* class which is configured to be called when the button in the user interface is touched by the user. This method needs to check that the service is connected, create a bundle object containing the string to be displayed by the server, add it to a Message object and send it to the server:

```
public void sendMessage(View view)
{
        if (!isBound) return;

        Message msg = Message.obtain();

        Bundle bundle = new Bundle();
        bundle.putString("MyString", "Message Received");

        msg.setData(bundle);

        try {
            myService.send(msg);
        } catch (RemoteException e) {
            e.printStackTrace();
        }
}
```

With the code changes complete, compile and run the application. Once loaded, touch the button in the user interface, at which point a Toast message should appear that reads "Message Received".

59.8 Summary

In order to implement interaction between a client and remote bound service it is necessary to implement a handler/message communication framework. The basic concepts behind this technique have been covered in this chapter together with the implementation of an example application designed to demonstrate communication between a client and a bound service, each running in a separate process.

60. An Android Notifications Tutorial

Notifications provide a way for an app to convey a message to the user when the app is either not running or is currently in the background. A messaging app might, for example, issue a notification to let the user know that a new message has arrived from a contact. Notifications can be categorized as being either local or remote. A local notification is triggered by the app itself on the device on which it is running. Remote notifications, on the other hand, are initiated by a remote server and delivered to the device for presentation to the user.

Notifications appear in the notification drawer that is pulled down from the status bar of the screen and each notification can include actions such as a button to open the app that sent the notification. Android also supports Direct Reply notifications, a feature that allows the user to type in and submit a response to a notification from within the notification panel.

The goal of this chapter is to outline and demonstrate the implementation of local notifications within an Android app. The next chapter (*"An Android Direct Reply Notification Tutorial"*) will cover the implementation of direct reply notifications.

60.1 An Overview of Notifications

When a notification is initiated on an Android device, it appears as an icon in the status bar. Figure 60-1, for example, shows a status bar with a number of notification icons:

Figure 60-1

To view the notifications, the user makes a downward swiping motion starting at the status bar to pull down the notification drawer as shown in Figure 60-2:

Figure 60-2

In devices running Android 8 or newer, performing a long press on an app launcher icon will display any pending notifications associated with that app as shown in Figure 60-3:

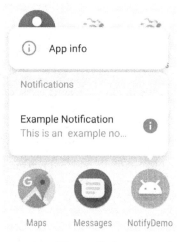

Figure 60-3

Android 8 and later also supports notification dots that appear on app launcher icons when a notification is waiting to be seen by the user.

A typical notification will simply display a message and, when tapped, launch the app responsible for issuing the notification. Notifications may also contain action buttons which perform a task specific to the corresponding app when tapped. Figure 60-4, for example, shows a notification containing two action buttons allowing the user to either delete or save an incoming message.

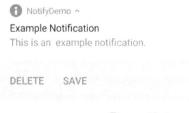

Figure 60-4

It is also possible for the user to enter an in-line text reply into the notification and send it to the app, as is the case in Figure 60-5 below. This allows the user to respond to a notification without having to launch the corresponding app into the foreground.

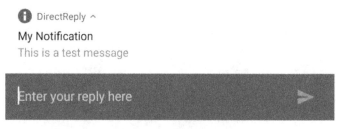

Figure 60-5

The remainder of this chapter will work through the steps involved in creating and issuing a simple notification containing actions. The topic of direct reply support will then be covered in the next chapter entitled *"An Android Direct Reply Notification Tutorial"*.

60.2 Creating the NotifyDemo Project

Select the *Start a new Android Studio project* quick start option from the welcome screen and, within the resulting new project dialog, choose the Empty Activity template before clicking on the Next button.

Enter *NotifyDemo* into the Name field and specify *com.ebookfrenzy.notifydemo* as the package name. Before clicking on the Finish button, change the Minimum API level setting to API 26: Android 8.0 (Oreo) and the Language menu to Java.

60.3 Designing the User Interface

The main activity will contain a single button, the purpose of which is to create and issue an intent. Locate and load the *activity_main.xml* file into the Layout Editor tool and delete the default TextView widget.

With Autoconnect enabled, drag and drop a Button object from the panel onto the center of the layout canvas as illustrated in Figure 60-6.

With the Button widget selected in the layout, use the Attributes panel to configure the onClick property to call a method named *sendNotification*.

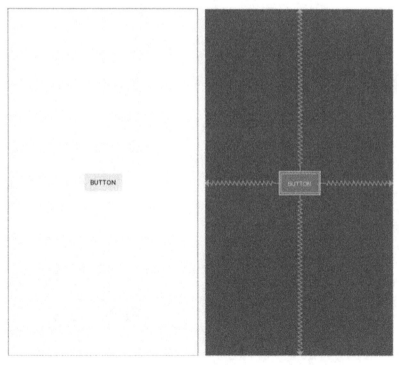

Figure 60-6

Select the Button widget, change the text property in the Attributes tool window to "Notify" and extract the property value to a string resource.

60.4 Creating the Second Activity

For the purposes of this example, the app will contain a second activity which will be launched by the user from within the notification. Add this new activity to the project by right-clicking on the *com.ebookfrenzy.notifydemo* package name located in *app -> java* and select the *New -> Activity -> Empty Activity* menu option to display the *New Android Activity* dialog.

Enter *ResultActivity* into the Activity Name field and name the layout file *activity_result*. Since this activity will not be started when the application is launched (it will instead be launched via an intent from within the notification), it is important to make sure that the *Launcher Activity* option is disabled before clicking on the Finish button.

Open the layout for the second activity (*app -> res -> layout -> activity_result.xml*) and drag and drop a TextView widget so that it is positioned in the center of the layout. Edit the text of the TextView so that it reads "Result Activity" and extract the property value to a string resource.

60.5 Creating a Notification Channel

Before an app can send a notification, it must first create a notification channel. A notification channel consists of an ID that uniquely identifies the channel within the app, a channel name and a channel description (only the latter two of which will be seen by the user). Channels are created by configuring a NotificationChannel instance and then passing that object through to the *createNotificationChannel()* method of the NotificationManager class. For this example, the app will contain a single notification channel named "NotifyDemo News". Edit the *MainActivity.java* file and implement code to create the channel when the app starts:

```
.
.
import android.app.NotificationManager;
import android.app.NotificationChannel;
import android.content.Context;
import android.graphics.Color;

public class MainActivity extends AppCompatActivity {

    NotificationManager notificationManager;

    @Override
    protected void onCreate(Bundle savedInstanceState) {
        super.onCreate(savedInstanceState);
        setContentView(R.layout.activity_main);

        notificationManager =
                (NotificationManager)
                    getSystemService(Context.NOTIFICATION_SERVICE);

        createNotificationChannel(
                "com.ebookfrenzy.notifydemo.news",
                "NotifyDemo News",
                "Example News Channel");
    }

    protected void createNotificationChannel(String id, String name,
            String description) {
```

```
        int importance = NotificationManager.IMPORTANCE_LOW;
        NotificationChannel channel =
              new NotificationChannel(id, name, importance);

        channel.setDescription(description);
        channel.enableLights(true);
        channel.setLightColor(Color.RED);
        channel.enableVibration(true);
        channel.setVibrationPattern(
           new long[]{100, 200, 300, 400, 500, 400, 300, 200, 400});
        notificationManager.createNotificationChannel(channel);
    }
    .
    .
    .
}
```

The code declares and initializes a NotificationManager instance and then creates the new channel with a low importance level (other options are high, low, max, min and none) with the name and description properties configured. A range of optional settings are also added to the channel to customize the way in which the user is alerted to the arrival of a notification. These settings apply to all notifications sent to this channel. Finally, the channel is created by passing the notification channel object through to the *createNotificationChannel()* method of the notification manager instance.

With the code changes complete, compile and run the app on a device or emulator running Android 10 or later. After the app has launched, place it into the background and open the Settings app. Within the Settings app, select the *Apps & notifications* option followed by *App info*. On the App info screen locate and select the NotifyDemo project and, on the subsequent screen, tap the *Notifications* entry. The notification screen should list the NotifyDemo News category as being active for the user:

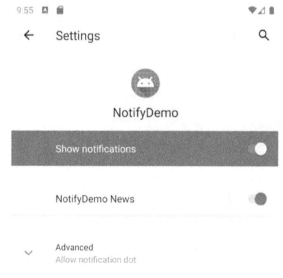

Figure 60-7

Before proceeding, check the Advanced settings to ensure that notification dots are enabled for the app.

Although not a requirement for this example, it is worth noting that a channel can be deleted from within the app via a call to the *deleteNotificationChannel()* method of the notification manager, passing through the ID of the channel to be deleted:

```
String channelID = "com.ebookfrenzy.notifydemo.news";
notificationManager.deleteNotificationChannel(channelID);
```

60.6 Creating and Issuing a Basic Notification

Notifications are created using the Notification.Builder class and must contain an icon, title and content. Open the *MainActivity.java* file and implement the *sendNotification()* method as follows to build a basic notification:

```
.
.

import android.app.Notification;
import android.view.View;

.
.

public void sendNotification(View view) {

    String channelID = "com.ebookfrenzy.notifydemo.news";

    Notification notification =
            new Notification.Builder(MainActivity.this,
                                        channelID)
        .setContentTitle("Example Notification")
        .setContentText("This is an  example notification.")
        .setSmallIcon(android.R.drawable.ic_dialog_info)
        .setChannelId(channelID)
        .build();
}
```

Once a notification has been built, it needs to be issued using the *notify()* method of the NotificationManager instance. The code to access the NotificationManager and issue the notification needs to be added to the *sendNotification()* method as follows:

```
protected void sendNotification(View view) {

    int notificationID = 101;

    String channelID = "com.ebookfrenzy.notifydemo.news";

    Notification notification =
            new Notification.Builder(MainActivity.this,
                            channelID)
        .setContentTitle("New Message")
        .setContentText("You've received new messages.")
        .setSmallIcon(android.R.drawable.ic_dialog_info)
        .setChannelId(channelID)
        .build();
```

```
notificationManager.notify(notificationID, notification);
}
```

Note that when the notification is issued, it is assigned a notification ID. This can be any integer and may be used later when updating the notification.

Compile and run the app and tap the button on the main activity. When the notification icon appears in the status bar, touch and drag down from the status bar to view the full notification:

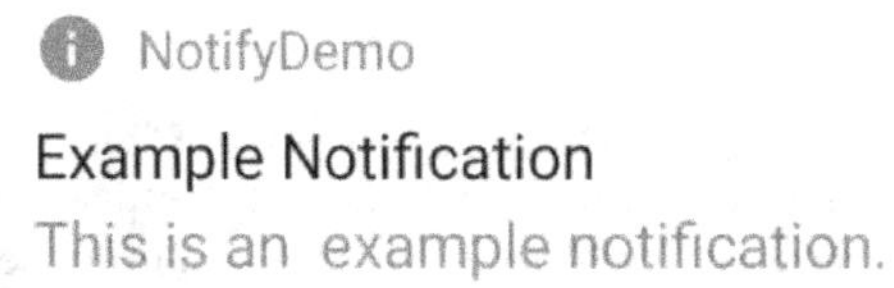

Example Notification

This is an example notification.

Figure 60-8

Click and slide right on the notification, then select the settings gear icon to view additional information about the notification:

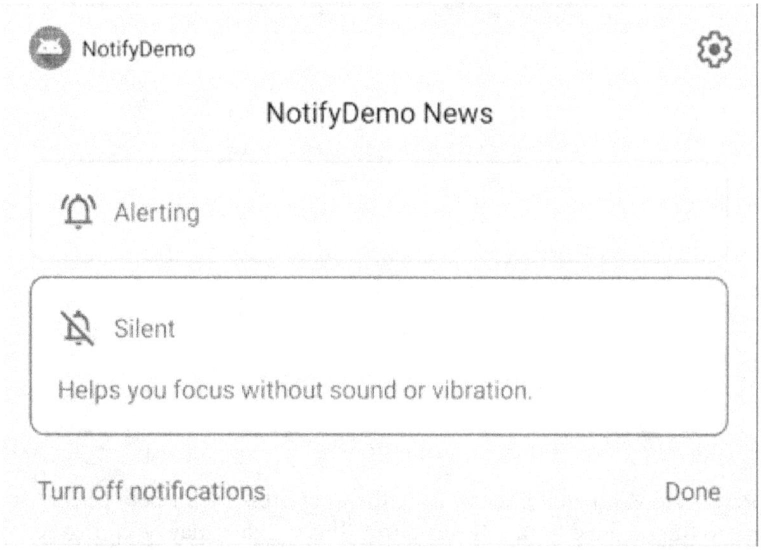

NotifyDemo   ⚙

NotifyDemo News

🔔 Alerting

🔕 Silent

Helps you focus without sound or vibration.

Turn off notifications   Done

Figure 60-9

Next, place the app in the background, navigate to the home screen displaying the launcher icons for all of the apps and note that a notification dot has appeared on the NotifyDemo launcher icon as indicated by the arrow in Figure 60-10:

Figure 60-10

If the dot is not present, check the notification options for NotifyDemo in the Settings app to confirm that notification dots are enabled as outlined earlier in the chapter. If the dot still does not appear, touch and hold over a blank area of the device home screen, select the *Home Settings* option from the resulting menu and enable the *Notification dots* option.

Performing a long press over the launcher icon will display a popup containing the notification:

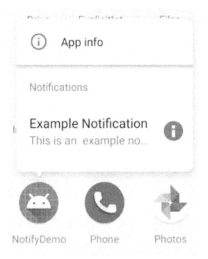

Figure 60-11

If more than one notification is pending for an app, the long press menu popup will contain a count of the number of notifications (highlighted in the above figure). This number may be configured from within the app by making a call to the *setNumber()* method when building the notification:

```
Notification notification = new Notification.Builder(MainActivity.this, CHANNEL_ID)
        .setContentTitle("Example Notification")
        .setContentText("This is an  example notification.")
        .setSmallIcon(android.R.drawable.ic_dilaog_info)
        .setChannelId(CHANNEL_ID)
        .setNumber(10)
        .build();
```

As currently implemented, tapping on the notification has no effect regardless of where it is accessed. The next step is to configure the notification to launch an activity when tapped.

60.7 Launching an Activity from a Notification

A notification should ideally allow the user to perform some form of action, such as launching the corresponding app, or taking some other form of action in response to the notification. A common requirement is to simply launch an activity belonging to the app when the user taps the notification.

This approach requires an activity to be launched and an Intent configured to launch that activity. Assuming an app that contains an activity named ResultActivity, the intent would be created as follows:

```
Intent resultIntent = new Intent(this, ResultActivity.class);
```

This intent needs to then be wrapped in a PendingIntent instance. PendingIntent objects are designed to allow an intent to be passed to other applications, essentially granting those applications permission to perform the intent at some point in the future. In this case, the PendingIntent object is being used to provide the Notification system with a way to launch the ResultActivity activity when the user taps the notification panel:

```
PendingIntent pendingIntent =
    PendingIntent.getActivity(
    this,
    0,
    resultIntent,
    PendingIntent.FLAG_UPDATE_CURRENT
);
```

All that remains is to assign the PendingIntent object during the notification build process using the *setContentIntent()* method.

Bringing these changes together results in a modified *sendNotification()* method which reads as follows:

```
.

.

import android.app.PendingIntent;
import android.content.Intent;
import android.graphics.drawable.Icon;

.

.

protected void sendNotification(View view) {

    int notificationId = 101;

    Intent resultIntent = new Intent(this, ResultActivity.class);

    PendingIntent pendingIntent =
            PendingIntent.getActivity(
                    this,
                    0,
                    resultIntent,
                    PendingIntent.FLAG_UPDATE_CURRENT
            );

    String CHANNEL_ID = "com.ebookfrenzy.notifydemo.news";
```

```
Notification notification = new Notification.Builder(MainActivity.this,
                                                       CHANNEL_ID)
            .setContentTitle("Example Notification")
            .setContentText("This is an  example notification.")
            .setSmallIcon(android.R.drawable.ic_dialog_info)
            .setChannelId(channelID)
            .setContentIntent(pendingIntent)
            .build();

    notificationManager.notify(notificationId, notification);
}
```

Compile and run the app once again, tap the button and display the notification drawer. This time, however, tapping the notification will cause the ResultActivity to launch.

60.8 Adding Actions to a Notification

Another way to add interactivity to a notification is to create actions. These appear as buttons beneath the notification message and are programmed to trigger specific intents when tapped by the user. The following code, if added to the *sendNotification()* method, will add an action button labeled "Open" which launches the referenced pending intent when selected:

```
final Icon icon = Icon.createWithResource(MainActivity.this,
              android.R.drawable.ic_dialog_info);


Notification.Action action =
        new Notification.Action.Builder(icon, "Open", pendingIntent)
                .build();


Notification notification = new Notification.Builder(MainActivity.this, CHANNEL_ID)
            .setContentTitle("Example Notification")
            .setContentText("This is an  example notification.")
            .setSmallIcon(R.drawable.ic_info_24dp)
            .setChannelId(channelID)
            .setContentIntent(pendingIntent)
            .setActions(action)
            .build();


notificationManager.notify(notificationId, notification);
```

Add the above code to the method and run the app. Issue the notification and note the appearance of the Open action within the notification (depending on the Android version it may be necessary to pull down on the notification panel to reveal the Open action):

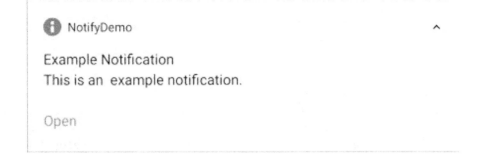

Figure 60-12

Tapping the action will trigger the pending intend and launch the ResultActivity.

60.9 Bundled Notifications

If an app has a tendency to regularly issue notifications there is a danger that those notifications will rapidly clutter both the status bar and the notification drawer providing a less than optimal experience for the user. This can be particularly true of news or messaging apps that send a notification every time there is either a breaking news story or a new message arrives from a contact. Consider, for example, the notifications in Figure 60-13:

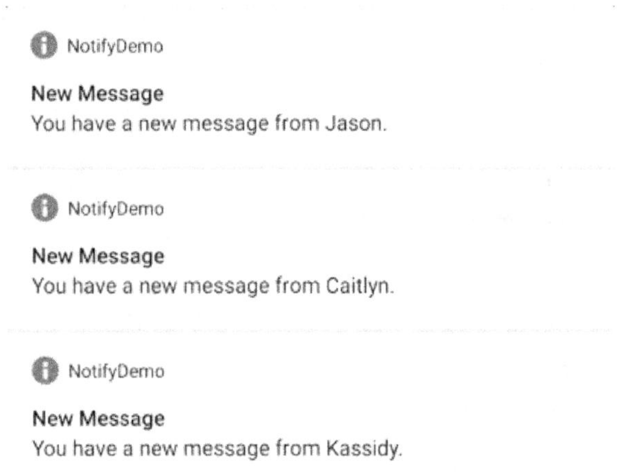

NotifyDemo

New Message
You have a new message from Jason.

NotifyDemo

New Message
You have a new message from Caitlyn.

NotifyDemo

New Message
You have a new message from Kassidy.

Figure 60-13

Now imagine if ten or even twenty new messages had arrived. To avoid this kind of problem Android allows notifications to be bundled together into groups.

To bundle notifications, each notification must be designated as belonging to the same group via the *setGroup()* method, and an additional notification must be issued and configured as being the *summary notification*. The following code, for example, creates and issues the three notifications shown in Figure 60-13 above, but bundles them into the same group. The code also issues a notification to act as the summary:

```
final String GROUP_KEY_NOTIFY = "group_key_notify";


Notification.Builder builderSummary =
        new Notification.Builder(this, channelID)
                .setSmallIcon(android.R.drawable.ic_dialog_info)
                .setContentTitle("A Bundle Example")
```

```
                    .setContentText("You have 3 new messages")
                    .setGroup(GROUP_KEY_NOTIFY)
                    .setGroupSummary(true);


Notification.Builder builder1 =
        new Notification.Builder(this, channelID)
                .setSmallIcon(android.R.drawable.ic_dialog_info)
                .setContentTitle("New Message")
                .setContentText("You have a new message from Kassidy")
                .setGroup(GROUP_KEY_NOTIFY);


Notification.Builder builder2 =
        new Notification.Builder(this, channelID)
                .setSmallIcon(android.R.drawable.ic_dialog_info)
                .setContentTitle("New Message")
                .setContentText("You have a new message from Caitlyn")
                .setGroup(GROUP_KEY_NOTIFY);


Notification.Builder builder3 =
        new Notification.Builder(this, channelID)
                .setSmallIcon(android.R.drawable.ic_dialog_info)
                .setContentTitle("New Message")
                .setContentText("You have a new message from Jason")
                .setGroup(GROUP_KEY_NOTIFY);

int notificationId0 = 100;
int notificationId1 = 101;
int notificationId2 = 102;
int notificationId3 = 103;

notificationManager.notify(notificationId1, builder1.build());
notificationManager.notify(notificationId2, builder2.build());
notificationManager.notify(notificationId3, builder3.build());
notificationManager.notify(notificationId0, builderSummary.build());
```

When the code is executed, a single notification icon will appear in the status bar even though four notifications have actually been issued by the app. Within the notification drawer, a single summary notification is displayed listing the information in each of the bundled notifications:

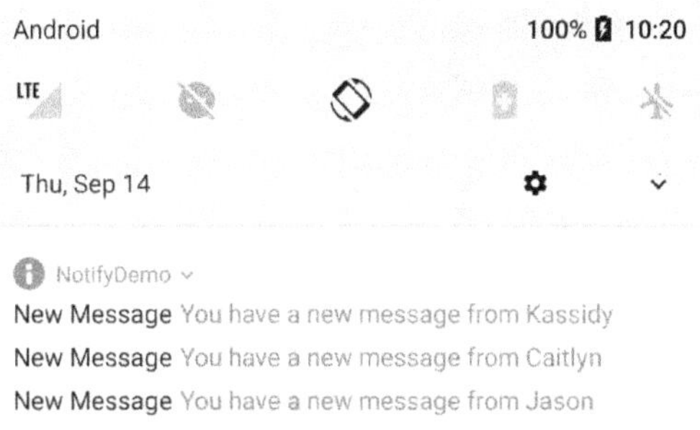

Android   100% 🔋 10:20

LTE   ⬦

Thu, Sep 14   ✿   ⌄

ℹ️ NotifyDemo ⌄
New Message You have a new message from Kassidy
New Message You have a new message from Caitlyn
New Message You have a new message from Jason

Figure 60-14

Pulling further downward on the notification entry expands the panel to show the details of each of the bundled notifications:

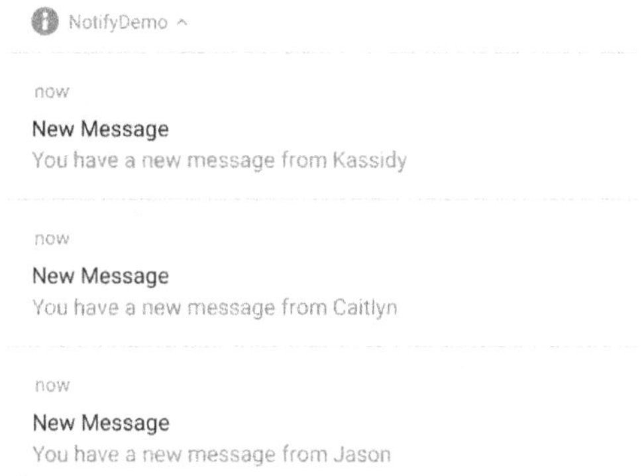

ℹ️ NotifyDemo ⌃

now

New Message
You have a new message from Kassidy

now

New Message
You have a new message from Caitlyn

now

New Message
You have a new message from Jason

Figure 60-15

60.10 Summary

Notifications provide a way for an app to deliver a message to the user when the app is not running, or is currently in the background. Notifications appear in the status bar and notification drawer. Local notifications are triggered on the device by the running app while remote notifications are initiated by a remote server and delivered to the device. Local notifications are created using the NotificationCompat.Builder class and issued using the NotificationManager service.

As demonstrated in this chapter, notifications can be configured to provide the user with options (such as launching an activity or saving a message) by making use of actions, intents and the PendingIntent class. Notification bundling provides a mechanism for grouping together notifications to provide an improved experience for apps that issue a greater number of notifications.

61. An Android Direct Reply Notification Tutorial

Direct reply is a feature introduced in Android 7 that allows the user to enter text into a notification and send it to the app associated with that notification. This allows the user to reply to a message in the notification without the need to launch an activity within the app. This chapter will build on the knowledge gained in the previous chapter to create an example app that makes use of this notification feature.

61.1 Creating the DirectReply Project

Select the *Start a new Android Studio project* quick start option from the welcome screen and, within the resulting new project dialog, choose the Empty Activity template before clicking on the Next button.

Enter *DirectReply* into the Name field and specify *com.ebookfrenzy.directreply* as the package name. Before clicking on the Finish button, change the Minimum API level setting to API 26: Android 8.0 (Oreo) and the Language menu to Java.

61.2 Designing the User Interface

Load the *activity_main.xml* layout file into the layout tool. With Autoconnect enabled, add a Button object beneath the existing "Hello World!" label. With the Button widget selected in the layout, use the Attributes tool window to set the onClick property to call a method named *sendNotification*. If necessary, use the Infer Constraints button to add any missing constraints to the layout.

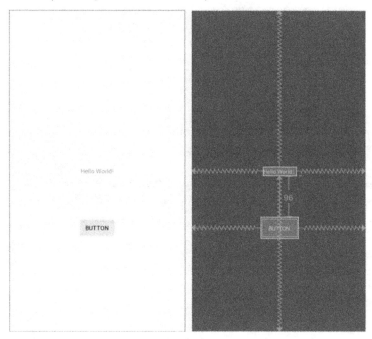

Figure 61-1

Before continuing, select the "Hello World!" TextView and change ID attribute to *textView* and modify the text on the button to read "Notify".

61.3 Creating the Notification Channel

As with the example in the previous chapter, a channel must be created before a notification can be sent. Edit the *MainActivity.java* file and add code to create a new channel as follows:

```
.
.
import android.app.NotificationChannel;
import android.app.NotificationManager;
import android.content.Context;
import android.graphics.Color;
.
.
public class MainActivity extends AppCompatActivity {

    NotificationManager notificationManager;
    private String channelID = "com.ebookfrenzy.directreply.news";

    @Override
    protected void onCreate(Bundle savedInstanceState) {
        super.onCreate(savedInstanceState);
        setContentView(R.layout.activity_direct_reply);

        notificationManager =
                (NotificationManager)
                    getSystemService(Context.NOTIFICATION_SERVICE);

        createNotificationChannel(channelID,
                "DirectReply News", "Example News Channel");
    }

    protected void createNotificationChannel(String id,
            String name, String description) {

        int importance = NotificationManager.IMPORTANCE_HIGH;
        NotificationChannel channel =
            new NotificationChannel(id, name, importance);

        channel.setDescription(description);
        channel.enableLights(true);
        channel.setLightColor(Color.RED);
        channel.enableVibration(true);
        channel.setVibrationPattern(new long[]{100, 200, 300, 400,
                        500, 400, 300, 200, 400});
```

```
        notificationManager.createNotificationChannel(channel);
    }
    .
    .
}
```

61.4 Building the RemoteInput Object

The key element that makes direct reply in-line text possible within a notification is the RemoteInput class. The previous chapters introduced the PendingIntent class and explained the way in which it allows one application to create an intent and then grant other applications or services the ability to launch that intent from outside the original app. In that chapter, entitled *"An Android Notifications Tutorial"*, a pending intent was created that allowed an activity in the original app to be launched from within a notification. The RemoteInput class allows a request for user input to be included in the PendingIntent object along with the intent. When the intent within the PendingIntent object is triggered, for example launching an activity, that activity is also passed any input provided by the user.

The first step in implementing direct reply within a notification is to create the RemoteInput object. This is achieved using the *RemoteInput.Builder()* method. To build a RemoteInput object, a key string is required that will be used to extract the input from the resulting intent. The object also needs a label string that will appear within the text input field of the notification. Edit the *MainActivity.java* file and begin implementing the *sendNotification()* method. Note also the addition of some import directives and variables that will be used later as the chapter progresses:

```
package com.ebookfrenzy.directreply;
.
.
import android.view.View;
import android.app.PendingIntent;
import android.app.RemoteInput;
import android.content.Intent;
.
.
public class MainActivity extends AppCompatActivity {

    private static int notificationId = 101;
    private static String KEY_TEXT_REPLY = "key_text_reply";
    NotificationManager notificationManager;

    private static String channelID =
                    "com.ebookfrenzy.directreply.news";
    .
    .
    .
    public void sendNotification(View view) {

        String replyLabel = "Enter your reply here";
```

```
        RemoteInput remoteInput =
            new RemoteInput.Builder(KEY_TEXT_REPLY)
                .setLabel(replyLabel)
                .build();
    }
    .
    .
    .
}
```

Now that the RemoteInput object has been created and initialized with a key and a label string it will need to be placed inside a notification action object. Before that step can be performed, however, the PendingIntent instance needs to be created.

61.5 Creating the PendingIntent

The steps to creating the PendingIntent are the same as those outlined in the *"An Android Notifications Tutorial"* chapter, with the exception that the intent will be configured to launch MainActivity. Remaining within the *MainActivity.java* file, add the code to create the PendingIntent as follows:

```
public void sendNotification(View view) {

    String replyLabel = "Enter your reply here";
    RemoteInput remoteInput =
            new RemoteInput.Builder(KEY_TEXT_REPLY)
            .setLabel(replyLabel)
            .build();


    Intent resultIntent = new Intent(this, MainActivity.class);


    PendingIntent resultPendingIntent =
            PendingIntent.getActivity(
                    this,
                    0,
                    resultIntent,
                    PendingIntent.FLAG_UPDATE_CURRENT
            );
    }
}
```

61.6 Creating the Reply Action

The in-line reply will be accessible within the notification via an action button. This action now needs to be created and configured with an icon, a label to appear on the button, the PendingIntent object and the RemoteInput object. Modify the *sendNotification()* method to add the code to create this action:

```
    .

    .

import android.graphics.drawable.Icon;
import android.app.Notification;
import android.graphics.Color;
import androidx.core.content.ContextCompat;
```

```
public void sendNotification(View view) {

    String replyLabel = "Enter your reply here";
    RemoteInput remoteInput =
            new RemoteInput.Builder(KEY_TEXT_REPLY)
            .setLabel(replyLabel)
            .build();

    Intent resultIntent = new Intent(this, MainActivity.class);

    PendingIntent resultPendingIntent =
            PendingIntent.getActivity(
                    this,
                    0,
                    resultIntent,
                    PendingIntent.FLAG_UPDATE_CURRENT
            );

    final Icon icon =
                Icon.createWithResource(MainActivity.this,
                    android.R.drawable.ic_dialog_info);

        Notification.Action replyAction =
                new Notification.Action.Builder(
                        icon,
                        "Reply", resultPendingIntent)
                        .addRemoteInput(remoteInput)
                        .build();
    }
```

At this stage in the tutorial we have the RemoteInput, PendingIntent and Notification Action objects built and ready to be used. The next stage is to build the notification and issue it:

```
public void sendNotification(View view) {

    String replyLabel = "Enter your reply here";
    RemoteInput remoteInput =
            new RemoteInput.Builder(KEY_TEXT_REPLY)
                    .setLabel(replyLabel)
                    .build();

    Intent resultIntent = new Intent(this, MainActivity.class);
```

```
PendingIntent resultPendingIntent =
        PendingIntent.getActivity(
                this,
                0,
                resultIntent,
                PendingIntent.FLAG_UPDATE_CURRENT
        );

final Icon icon =
    Icon.createWithResource(MainActivity.this,
            android.R.drawable.ic_dialog_info);

Notification.Action replyAction =
        new Notification.Action.Builder(
                icon,
                "Reply", resultPendingIntent)
                .addRemoteInput(remoteInput)
                .build();

Notification newMessageNotification =
        new Notification.Builder(this, channelID)
                .setColor(ContextCompat.getColor(this,
                        R.color.colorPrimary))
                .setSmallIcon(
                        android.R.drawable.ic_dialog_info)
                .setContentTitle("My Notification")
                .setContentText("This is a test message")
                .addAction(replyAction).build();

NotificationManager notificationManager =
        (NotificationManager)
                getSystemService(Context.NOTIFICATION_SERVICE);

notificationManager.notify(notificationId,
        newMessageNotification);
}
```

With the changes made, compile and run the app and test that tapping the button successfully issues the notification. When viewing the notification drawer, the notification should appear as shown in Figure 61-2:

DirectReply

My Notification
This is a test message

Reply

Figure 61-2

Tap the Reply action button so that the text input field appears displaying the reply label that was embedded into the RemoteInput object when it was created.

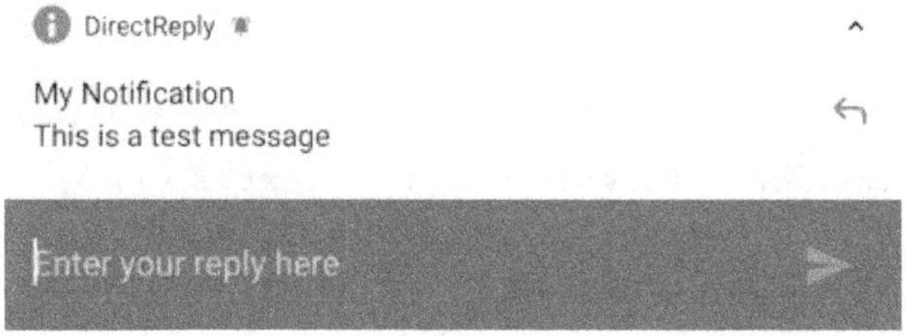

DirectReply

My Notification
This is a test message

Enter your reply here

Figure 61-3

Enter some text and tap the send arrow button located at the end of the input field.

61.7 Receiving Direct Reply Input

Now that the notification is successfully seeking input from the user, the app needs to do something with that input. The goal of this particular tutorial is to have the text entered by the user into the notification appear on the TextView widget in the activity user interface.

When the user enters text and taps the send button the MainActivity is launched via the intent contained in the PendingIntent object. Embedded in this intent is the text entered by the user via the notification. Within the *onCreate()* method of the activity, a call to the *getIntent()* method will return a copy of the intent that launched the activity. Passing this through to the *RemoteInput.getResultsFromIntent()* method will, in turn, return a Bundle object containing the reply text which can be extracted and assigned to the TextView widget. This results in a modified *onCreate()* method within the *MainActivity.java* file which reads as follows:

```
.
.
import android.widget.TextView;
.
.
@Override
protected void onCreate(Bundle savedInstanceState) {
    super.onCreate(savedInstanceState);
    setContentView(R.layout.activity_direct_reply);

    notificationManager =
            (NotificationManager)
              getSystemService(Context.NOTIFICATION_SERVICE);
```

```
createNotificationChannel(channelID, "DirectReply News",
                    Example News Channel");


    handleIntent();
}

private void handleIntent() {

    Intent intent = this.getIntent();

    Bundle remoteInput = RemoteInput.getResultsFromIntent(intent);

    if (remoteInput != null) {

        TextView myTextView = findViewById(R.id.textView);
        String inputString = remoteInput.getCharSequence(
            KEY_TEXT_REPLY).toString();

        myTextView.setText(inputString);
    }
}
.
.
```

After making these code changes build and run the app once again. Click the button to issue the notification and enter and send some text from within the notification panel. Note that the TextView widget in the MainActivity is updated to display the in-line text that was entered.

61.8 Updating the Notification

After sending the reply within the notification you may have noticed that the progress indicator continues to spin within the notification panel as highlighted in Figure 61-4:

Figure 61-4

The notification is showing this indicator because it is waiting for a response from the activity confirming receipt of the sent text. The recommended approach to performing this task is to update the notification with a new message indicating that the reply has been received and handled. Since the original notification was assigned an ID when it was issued, this can be used once again to perform an update. Add the following code to the *handleIntent()* method to perform this task:

```
private void handleIntent() {

    Intent intent = this.getIntent();

    Bundle remoteInput = RemoteInput.getResultsFromIntent(intent);

    if (remoteInput != null) {

        TextView myTextView = findViewById(R.id.textView);
        String inputString = remoteInput.getCharSequence(
                KEY_TEXT_REPLY).toString();

        myTextView.setText(inputString);

        Notification repliedNotification =
                new Notification.Builder(this, channelID)
                        .setSmallIcon(
                                android.R.drawable.ic_dialog_info)
                        .setContentText("Reply received")
                        .build();

        notificationManager.notify(notificationId,
                repliedNotification);
    }
}
```

Test the app one last time and verify that the progress indicator goes away after the in-line reply text has been sent and that a new panel appears indicating that the reply has been received:

Figure 61-5

61.9 Summary

The direct reply notification feature allows text to be entered by the user within a notification and passed via an intent to an activity of the corresponding application. Direct reply is made possible by the RemoteInput class, an instance of which can be embedded within an action and bundled with the notification. When working with direct reply notifications, it is important to let the NotificationManager service know that the reply has been received and processed. The best way to achieve this is to simply update the notification message using the notification ID provided when the notification was first issued.

62. Foldable Devices and Multi-Window Support

Foldable devices are coming whether we are ready for them or not (or, in the case of the first Samsung Galaxy Fold, perhaps even before the devices themselves are ready). In preparation for this new category of device, it is important to be aware of some additional steps that should be taken to ensure that your app performs correctly when running on a foldable device.

Fortunately, much of the behavior for supporting foldable devices already exists on Android in the form of Multi-Window support.

62.1 Foldables and Multi-Window Support

When an app is running on a foldable device there is the potential that it will end up sharing the screen with other apps and encountering significant configuration changes (such as the size of the screen changing as the user folds or unfolds the display). If your app is already designed to handle device orientation changes, it will most likely also be able to handle changes caused by screen folding, though thorough testing is recommended.

Multi-window support was originally introduced with Android 7. Unlike previous versions of Android, multi-window support in Android 7 allowed more than one activity to be displayed on the device screen at one time.

Multi-window support in Android provides three different forms of window support. Split-screen mode, available on most phone, foldable and tablet devices, provides a split screen environment where two activities appear either side by side or one above the other. A moveable divider is provided which, when dragged by the user, adjusts the percentage of the screen assigned to each of the adjacent activities:

Figure 62-1

Freeform mode provides a windowing environment on devices with larger screens and is currently enabled at the discretion of the device manufacturer. Freeform differs from split-screen mode in that it allows each activity to appear in a separate, resizable window and is not limited to two activities being displayed concurrently. Figure 62-2, for example, shows a device in freeform mode with the Calculator and a second app displayed in separate windows:

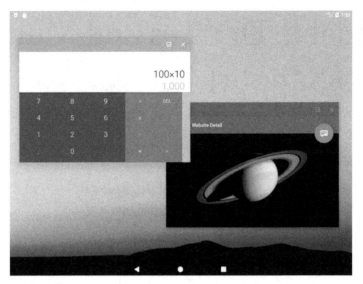

Figure 62-2

Picture-in-picture support, as the name suggests, allows video playback to continue in a smaller window while the user performs other tasks, a topic that will be covered beginning with the chapter entitled *"Android Picture-in-Picture Mode"*.

62.2 Using a Foldable Emulator

Although at time of writing there are no foldable devices on the market with which to perform app testing, foldable emulators are included with the Android SDK. To create a foldable emulator, select the Android Studio *Tools -> AVD Manager* menu option, click on the Create Virtual Device button and, from the hardware selection screen, choose one of the Foldable options as highlighted in Figure 62-3 below:

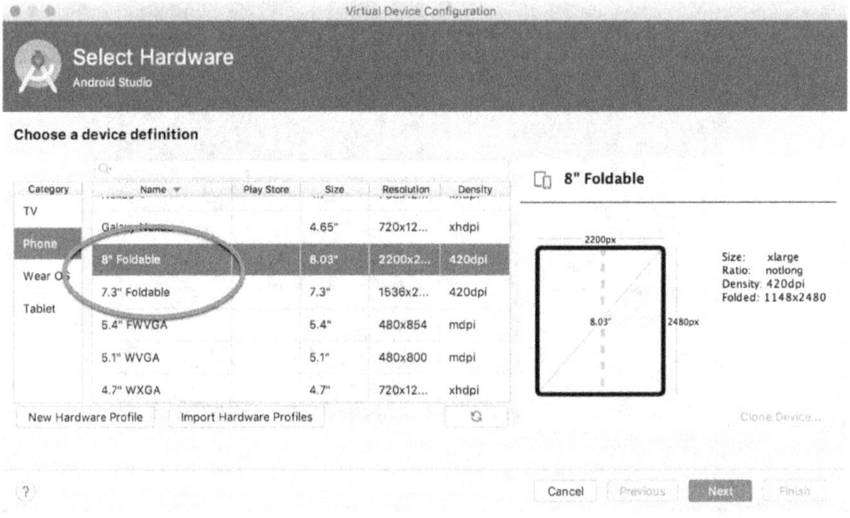

Figure 62-3

After making a foldable selection, continue through the creation process, selecting Android 10 API 29 or newer as the system image.

Once the emulator is up and running, an additional button will appear in the toolbar allowing the emulator to be switched between folded and unfolded configurations:

Figure 62-4

62.3 Entering Multi-Window Mode

Split-screen mode can be entered by displaying the Overview screen, pressing and holding the app icon in the toolbar of a listed app and selecting the Split screen menu option as indicated in Figure 62-5:

Figure 62-5

Once in split-screen mode, the Overview button will change to display two rectangles (marked A in Figure 62-6), the current activity will fill part of the screen (B) and the Overview screen will appear in the adjacent part of the screen allowing the second activity to be selected for display (C):

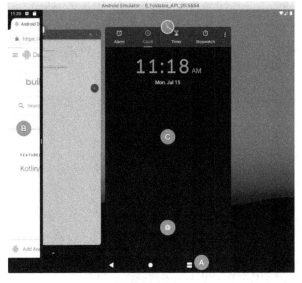

Figure 62-6

Once the second app has been selected, the screen will be split evenly as illustrated previously in Figure 62-1 above.

To exit split-screen mode, simply drag the divider separating the two activities to a far edge so that only one activity fills the screen, or press and hold the Overview button until it reverts to a single square.

62.4 Enabling and using Freeform Support

Although not officially supported on all devices, it is possible to enable freeform multi-window mode on large screen devices and emulators. To enable this mode, run the following adb command while the emulator is running, or the device is connected:

```
adb shell settings put global enable_freeform_support 1
```

After making this change, it may be necessary to reboot the device before the setting takes effect.

Once enabled, an additional option will appear within the Overview screen when performing a long press on the app icon as shown in 62.5 Checking for Freeform Support:

Figure 62-7

62.5 Checking for Freeform Support

As outlined earlier in the chapter, Google is leaving the choice of whether to enable freeform multi-window mode to the individual Android device manufacturers. Since it only makes sense to use freeform on larger devices, there is no guarantee that freeform will be available on every device on which an app is likely to run. Fortunately all of the freeform specific methods and attributes are ignored by the system if freeform mode is not available on a device, so using these will not cause the app to crash on a non-freeform device. Situations might arise, however, where it may be useful to be able to detect if a device supports freeform multi-window mode. Fortunately, this can be achieved by checking for the freeform window management feature in the package manager. The following code example checks for freeform multi-window support and returns a Boolean value based on the result of the test:

```
public Boolean checkFreeform() {
    return getPackageManager().hasSystemFeature(
            PackageManager.FEATURE_FREEFORM_WINDOW_MANAGEMENT);
}
```

62.6 Enabling Multi-Window Support in an App

The *android:resizableActivity* manifest file setting controls whether multi-window behavior is supported by an app. This setting can be made at either the application or individual activity levels. The following fragment, for example, configures the activity named MainActivity to support both split-screen and freeform multi-window modes:

```
<activity
    android:name=".MainActivity"
    android:resizeableActivity="true"
    android:label="@string/app_name"
    android:theme="@style/AppTheme.NoActionBar">
    <intent-filter>
        <action android:name="android.intent.action.MAIN" />

        <category android:name="android.intent.category.LAUNCHER" />
    </intent-filter>
</activity>
```

Setting the property to false will prevent the activity from appearing in split-screen or freeform mode and the corresponding buttons will not appear in the Overview menu for the app. Selecting an activity for which multi-window support is disabled as the second activity in a split-screen configuration will result in a message appearing indicating that the app may not support multi-window mode.

62.7 Specifying Multi-Window Attributes

A number of attributes are available as part of the <layout> element for specifying the size and placement of an activity when it is launched into a multi-window mode. The initial height, width and position of an activity when launched in freeform mode may be specified using the following attributes:

- **android:defaultWidth** – Specifies the default width of the activity.

- **android:defaultHeight** – Specifies the default height of the activity.

- **android:gravity** – Specifies the initial position of the activity (start, end, left, right, top etc.).

Note that the above attributes apply to the activity only when it is displayed in freeform mode. The following example configures an activity to appear with a specific height and width at the top of the starting edge of the screen:

```
<activity android:name=".MainActivity ">
    <layout android:defaultHeight="350dp"
            android:defaultWidth="450dp"
            android:gravity="start|end" />
</activity>
```

The following <layout> attributes may be used to specify the minimum width and height to which an activity may be reduced in either split-view or freeform modes:

- **android:minimalHeight** – Specifies the minimum height to which the activity may be reduced while in split-screen or freeform mode.

- **android:minimalWidth** - Specifies the minimum width to which the activity may be reduced while in split-screen or freeform mode.

When the user slides the split-screen divider beyond the minimal height or width boundaries, the system will stop resizing the layout of the shrinking activity and simply clip the user interface to make room for the adjacent activity.

The following manifest file fragment implements the minimal width and height attributes for an activity:

```
<activity android:name=".MainActivity ">
    <layout android:minimalHeight="400dp"
            android:minimalWidth="290dp" />
</activity>
```

62.8 Detecting Multi-Window Mode in an Activity

Situations may arise where an activity needs to detect whether it is currently being displayed to the user in multi-window mode. The current status can be obtained via a call to the *isInMultiWindowMode()* method of the Activity class. When called, this method returns a true or false value depending on whether or not the activity is currently full screen:

```
if (this.isInMultiWindowMode()) {
    // Activity is running in Multi-Window mode
} else {
    // Activity is not in Multi-Window mode
}
```

62.9 Receiving Multi-Window Notifications

An activity will receive notification that it is entering or exiting multi-window mode if it overrides the *onMultiWindowModeChanged()* callback method. The first argument passed to this method is true on entering multi-window mode, and false when the activity exits the mode. The new configuration settings are contained within the Configuration object passed as the second argument:

```
@Override
public void onMultiWindowModeChanged(boolean isInMultiWindowMode,
                                     Configuration newConfig) {
    super.onMultiWindowModeChanged(isInMultiWindowMode, newConfig);

    if (isInMultiWindowMode) {
```

```
    // Activity has entered multi-window mode
} else {
    // Activity has exited multi-window mode
}
}
```

As outlined in the chapter entitled *"Handling Android Activity State Changes"*, Android 10 and later allow multiple activities to be in the resumed state simultaneously (otherwise known as *multi-resume*). The activity with which the user most recently interacted is referred to as the topmost resumed activity. To track an activity as it gains and loses topmost resumed status, the *onTopResumedActivityChanged()* callback method may be implemented within the activity, for example:

```
@Override
public void onTopResumedActivityChanged(boolean isTopResumedActivity) {
    super.onTopResumedActivityChanged(isTopResumedActivity);

    if (isTopResumedActivity) {
        // Activity is now topmost resumed activity
    } else {
        // Activity is no longer topmost resumed activity
    }
}
```

It may also be possible to take advantage of multi-resume in an app on some devices running Android 9 by enabling the following property in the app manifest file:

```
<meta-data
android:name="android.allow_multiple_resumed_activities" android:value="true" />
```

62.10 Launching an Activity in Multi-Window Mode

In the *"Android Explicit Intents – A Worked Example"* chapter of this book, an example app was created in which an activity uses an intent to launch a second activity. By default, activities launched via an intent are considered to reside in the same *task stack* as the originating activity. An activity can, however, be launched into a new task stack by passing through the appropriate flags with the intent.

When an activity in multi-window mode launches another activity within the same task stack, the new activity replaces the originating activity within the split-screen or freeform window (the user returns to the original activity via the back button).

When launched into a new task stack in split-screen mode, however, the second activity will appear in the window adjacent to the original activity, allowing both activities to be viewed simultaneously. In the case of freeform mode, the launched activity will appear in a separate window from the original activity.

In order to launch an activity into a new task stack, the following flags must be set on the intent before it is started:

- Intent.FLAG_ACTIVITY_LAUNCH_ADJACENT
- Intent.FLAG_ACTIVITY_MULTIPLE_TASK
- Intent.FLAG_ACTIVITY_NEW_TASK

The following code, for example, configures and launches a second activity designed to appear in a separate window:

```
Intent i = new Intent(this, SecondActivity.class);

i.addFlags(Intent.FLAG_ACTIVITY_LAUNCH_ADJACENT|
        Intent.FLAG_ACTIVITY_MULTIPLE_TASK|
        Intent.FLAG_ACTIVITY_NEW_TASK);

startActivity(i);
```

62.11 Configuring Freeform Activity Size and Position

By default, an activity launched into a different task stack while in freeform mode will be positioned in the center of the screen at a size dictated by the system. The location and dimensions of this window can be controlled by passing *launch bounds* settings to the intent via the *ActivityOptions* class. The first step in this process is to create a *Rect* object configured with the left (X), top (Y), right (X) and bottom (Y) coordinates of the rectangle representing the activity window. The following code, for example, creates a Rect object in which the top-left corner is positioned at coordinate (0, 0) and the bottom-right at (100, 100):

```
Rect rect = new Rect(100, 800, 900, 700);
```

The next step is to create a basic instance of the ActivityOptions class and initialize it with the Rect settings via the *setLaunchBounds()* method:

```
ActivityOptions options = ActivityOptions.makeBasic();
ActivityOptions bounds = options.setLaunchBounds(rect);
```

Finally, the ActivityOptions instance is converted to a Bundle object and passed to the *startActivity()* method along with the Intent object:

```
startActivity(i, bounds.toBundle());
```

Combining these steps results in a code sequence that reads as follows:

```
Intent i = new Intent(this, SecondActivity.class);
i.addFlags(Intent.FLAG_ACTIVITY_LAUNCH_ADJACENT|
        Intent.FLAG_ACTIVITY_MULTIPLE_TASK|
        Intent.FLAG_ACTIVITY_NEW_TASK);

Rect rect = new Rect(100, 800, 900, 700);

ActivityOptions options = ActivityOptions.makeBasic();
ActivityOptions bounds = options.setLaunchBounds(rect);

startActivity(i, bounds.toBundle());
```

When the second activity is launched by the intent while the originating activity is in freeform mode, the new activity window will appear with the location and dimensions defined in the Rect object.

62.12 Summary

Android 7 introduced multi-window support, a system whereby more than one activity is displayed on the screen at any one time. This feature now forms the foundation of providing support for foldable devices. The three modes provided by multi-window support are split-screen, freeform and picture-in-picture. In split-screen mode, the screen is split either horizontally or vertically into two panes with an activity displayed in each pane. Freeform mode, which is only supported on certain Android devices, allows each activity to appear in a separate, movable and resizable window. As outlined in this chapter, a number of methods and property settings are available within the Android SDK to detect, respond to and control multi-window behavior within an app.

63. An Overview of Android SQLite Databases

Mobile applications that do not need to store at least some amount of persistent data are few and far between. The use of databases is an essential aspect of most applications, ranging from applications that are almost entirely data driven, to those that simply need to store small amounts of data such as the prevailing score of a game.

The importance of persistent data storage becomes even more evident when taking into consideration the somewhat transient lifecycle of the typical Android application. With the ever-present risk that the Android runtime system will terminate an application component to free up resources, a comprehensive data storage strategy to avoid data loss is a key factor in the design and implementation of any application development strategy.

This chapter will provide an overview of the SQLite database management system bundled with the Android operating system, together with an outline of the Android SDK classes that are provided to facilitate persistent SQLite based database storage from within an Android application. Before delving into the specifics of SQLite in the context of Android development, however, a brief overview of databases and SQL will be covered.

63.1 Understanding Database Tables

Database *Tables* provide the most basic level of data structure in a database. Each database can contain multiple tables and each table is designed to hold information of a specific type. For example, a database may contain a *customer* table that contains the name, address and telephone number for each of the customers of a particular business. The same database may also include a *products* table used to store the product descriptions with associated product codes for the items sold by the business.

Each table in a database is assigned a name that must be unique within that particular database. A table name, once assigned to a table in one database, may not be used for another table except within the context of another database.

63.2 Introducing Database Schema

Database Schemas define the characteristics of the data stored in a database table. For example, the table schema for a customer database table might define that the customer name is a string of no more than 20 characters in length, and that the customer phone number is a numerical data field of a certain format.

Schemas are also used to define the structure of entire databases and the relationship between the various tables contained in each database.

63.3 Columns and Data Types

It is helpful at this stage to begin to view a database table as being similar to a spreadsheet where data is stored in rows and columns.

Each column represents a data field in the corresponding table. For example, the name, address and telephone data fields of a table are all *columns*.

Each column, in turn, is defined to contain a certain type of data. A column designed to store numbers would, therefore, be defined as containing numerical data.

63.4 Database Rows

Each new record that is saved to a table is stored in a row. Each row, in turn, consists of the columns of data associated with the saved record.

Once again, consider the spreadsheet analogy described earlier in this chapter. Each entry in a customer table is equivalent to a row in a spreadsheet and each column contains the data for each customer (name, address, telephone etc). When a new customer is added to the table, a new row is created and the data for that customer stored in the corresponding columns of the new row.

Rows are also sometimes referred to as *records* or *entries* and these terms can generally be used interchangeably.

63.5 Introducing Primary Keys

Each database table should contain one or more columns that can be used to identify each row in the table uniquely. This is known in database terminology as the *Primary Key*. For example, a table may use a bank account number column as the primary key. Alternatively, a customer table may use the customer's social security number as the primary key.

Primary keys allow the database management system to identify a specific row in a table uniquely. Without a primary key it would not be possible to retrieve or delete a specific row in a table because there can be no certainty that the correct row has been selected. For example, suppose a table existed where the customer's last name had been defined as the primary key. Imagine then the problem that might arise if more than one customer named "Smith" were recorded in the database. Without some guaranteed way to identify a specific row uniquely, it would be impossible to ensure the correct data was being accessed at any given time.

Primary keys can comprise a single column or multiple columns in a table. To qualify as a single column primary key, no two rows can contain matching primary key values. When using multiple columns to construct a primary key, individual column values do not need to be unique, but all the columns' values combined together must be unique.

63.6 What is SQLite?

SQLite is an embedded, relational database management system (RDBMS). Most relational databases (Oracle, SQL Server and MySQL being prime examples) are standalone server processes that run independently, and in cooperation with, applications that require database access. SQLite is referred to as *embedded* because it is provided in the form of a library that is linked into applications. As such, there is no standalone database server running in the background. All database operations are handled internally within the application through calls to functions contained in the SQLite library.

The developers of SQLite have placed the technology into the public domain with the result that it is now a widely deployed database solution.

SQLite is written in the C programming language and as such, the Android SDK provides a Java based "wrapper" around the underlying database interface. This essentially consists of a set of classes that may be utilized within the Java or Kotlin code of an application to create and manage SQLite based databases.

For additional information about SQLite refer to *https://www.sqlite.org*.

63.7 Structured Query Language (SQL)

Data is accessed in SQLite databases using a high-level language known as Structured Query Language. This is usually abbreviated to SQL and pronounced *sequel*. SQL is a standard language used by most relational database management systems. SQLite conforms mostly to the SQL-92 standard.

SQL is essentially a very simple and easy to use language designed specifically to enable the reading and writing of database data. Because SQL contains a small set of keywords, it can be learned quickly. In addition, SQL syntax is more or less identical between most DBMS implementations, so having learned SQL for one system, it is likely that your skills will transfer to other database management systems.

While some basic SQL statements will be used within this chapter, a detailed overview of SQL is beyond the scope of this book. There are, however, many other resources that provide a far better overview of SQL than we could ever hope to provide in a single chapter here.

63.8 Trying SQLite on an Android Virtual Device (AVD)

For readers unfamiliar with databases in general and SQLite in particular, diving right into creating an Android application that uses SQLite may seem a little intimidating. Fortunately, Android is shipped with SQLite pre-installed, including an interactive environment for issuing SQL commands from within an *adb shell* session connected to a running Android AVD emulator instance. This is both a useful way to learn about SQLite and SQL, and also an invaluable tool for identifying problems with databases created by applications running in an emulator.

To launch an interactive SQLite session, begin by running an AVD session. This can be achieved from within Android Studio by launching the Android Virtual Device Manager (*Tools -> AVD Manager*), selecting a previously configured AVD and clicking on the start button.

Once the AVD is up and running, open a Terminal or Command-Prompt window and connect to the emulator using the *adb* command-line tool as follows (note that the –e flag directs the tool to look for an emulator with which to connect, rather than a physical device):

```
adb -e shell
```

Once connected, the shell environment will provide a command prompt at which commands may be entered. Begin by obtaining super user privileges using the *su* command:

```
Generic_x86:/ su
root@android:/ #
```

If a message appears indicating that super user privileges are not allowed, it is likely that the AVD instance includes Google Play support. To resolve this create a new AVD and, on the "Choose a device definition" screen, select a device that does not have a marker in the "Play Store" column.

Data stored in SQLite databases are actually stored in database files on the file system of the Android device on which the application is running. By default, the file system path for these database files is as follows:

```
/data/data/<package name>/databases/<database filename>.db
```

For example, if an application with the package name *com.example.MyDBApp* creates a database named *mydatabase.db*, the path to the file on the device would read as follows:

```
/data/data/com.example.MyDBApp/databases/mydatabase.db
```

For the purposes of this exercise, therefore, change directory to /data/data within the adb shell and create a sub-directory hierarchy suitable for some SQLite experimentation:

```
cd /data/data
mkdir com.example.dbexample
cd com.example.dbexample
mkdir databases
cd databases
```

With a suitable location created for the database file, launch the interactive SQLite tool as follows:

```
root@android:/data/data/databases # sqlite3 ./mydatabase.db
sqlite3 ./mydatabase.db
SQLite version 3.8.10.2 2015-05-20 18:17:19
Enter ".help" for usage hints.
sqlite>
```

At the *sqlite>* prompt, commands may be entered to perform tasks such as creating tables and inserting and retrieving data. For example, to create a new table in our database with fields to hold ID, name, address and phone number fields the following statement is required:

```
create table contacts (_id integer primary key autoincrement, name text, address
text, phone text);
```

Note that each row in a table should have a *primary key* that is unique to that row. In the above example, we have designated the ID field as the primary key, declared it as being of type *integer* and asked SQLite to increment the number automatically each time a row is added. This is a common way to make sure that each row has a unique primary key. On most other platforms, the choice of name for the primary key is arbitrary. In the case of Android, however, it is essential that the key be named *_id* in order for the database to be fully accessible using all of the Android database related classes. The remaining fields are each declared as being of type *text*.

To list the tables in the currently selected database, use the *.tables* statement:

```
sqlite> .tables
contacts
```

To insert records into the table:

```
sqlite> insert into contacts (name, address, phone) values ("Bill Smith", "123
Main Street, California", "123-555-2323");
sqlite> insert into contacts (name, address, phone) values ("Mike Parks", "10
Upping Street, Idaho", "444-444-1212");
```

To retrieve all rows from a table:

```
sqlite> select * from contacts;
1|Bill Smith|123 Main Street, California|123-555-2323
2|Mike Parks|10 Upping Street, Idaho|444-444-1212
```

To extract a row that meets specific criteria:

```
sqlite> select * from contacts where name="Mike Parks";
2|Mike Parks|10 Upping Street, Idaho|444-444-1212
```

To exit from the sqlite3 interactive environment:

```
sqlite> .exit
```

When running an Android application in the emulator environment, any database files will be created on the file system of the emulator using the previously discussed path convention. This has the advantage that you can connect with adb, navigate to the location of the database file, load it into the sqlite3 interactive tool and perform tasks on the data to identify possible problems occurring in the application code.

It is also important to note that, while it is possible to connect with an adb shell to a physical Android device, the shell is not granted sufficient privileges by default to create and manage SQLite databases. Debugging of database problems is, therefore, best performed using an AVD session.

63.9 The Android Room Persistence Library

SQLite is, as previously mentioned, written in the C programming language while Android applications are primarily developed using Java or Kotlin. To bridge this "language gap" in the past, the Android SDK included a set of classes that provide a layer on top of the SQLite database management system. Although still available in the SDK, use of these classes still involved writing a considerable amount of code and did not take advantage of the new architecture guidelines and features such as LiveData and lifecycle management. To address these shortcomings, the Android Jetpack Architecture Components include the Room persistent library. This library provides a high level interface on top of the SQLite database system that make it easy to store data locally on Android devices with minimal coding while also conforming to the recommendations for modern application architecture.

The next few chapters will provide an overview and tutorial of SQLite database management using the Room persistence library.

63.10 Summary

SQLite is a lightweight, embedded relational database management system that is included as part of the Android framework and provides a mechanism for implementing organized persistent data storage for Android applications. When combined with the Room persistence library, Android provides a modern way to implement data storage from within an Android app.

The goal of this chapter was to provide an overview of databases in general and SQLite in particular within the context of Android application development. The next chapters will provide an overview of the Room persistence library, after which we will work through the creation of an example application.

64. The Android Room Persistence Library

Included with the Android Architecture Components, the Room persistence library is designed specifically to make it easier to add database storage support to Android apps in a way that is consistent with the Android architecture guidelines. With the basics of SQLite databases covered in the previous chapter, this chapter will explore the basic concepts behind Room-based database management, the key elements that work together to implement Room support within an Android app and how these are implemented in terms of architecture and coding. Having covered these topics, the next two chapters will put this theory into practice in the form of an example Room database project.

64.1 Revisiting Modern App Architecture

The chapter entitled *"Modern Android App Architecture with Jetpack"* introduced the concept of modern app architecture and stressed the importance of separating different areas of responsibility within an app. The diagram illustrated in Figure 64-1 outlines the recommended architecture for a typical Android app:

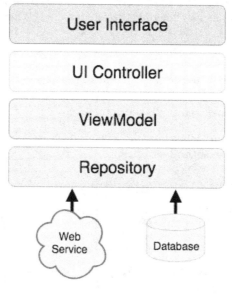

Figure 64-1

With the top three levels of this architecture covered in some detail in earlier chapters of this book, it is now time to begin exploration of the repository and database architecture levels in the context of the Room persistence library.

64.2 Key Elements of Room Database Persistence

Before going into greater detail later in the chapter, it is first worth summarizing the key elements involved in working with SQLite databases using the Room persistence library:

64.2.1 Repository

As previously discussed, the repository module contains all of the code necessary for directly handling all data sources used by the app. This avoids the need for the UI controller and ViewModel to contain code that directly accesses sources such as databases or web services.

64.2.2 Room Database

The room database object provides the interface to the underlying SQLite database. It also provides the repository with access to the Data Access Object (DAO). An app should only have one room database instance which may then be used to access multiple database tables.

64.2.3 Data Access Object (DAO)

The DAO contains the SQL statements required by the repository to insert, retrieve and delete data within the SQLite database. These SQL statements are mapped to methods which are then called from within the repository to execute the corresponding query.

64.2.4 Entities

An entity is a class that defines the schema for a table within the database and defines the table name, column names and data types, and identifies which column is to be the primary key. In addition to declaring the table schema, entity classes also contain getter and setter methods that provide access to these data fields. The data returned to the repository by the DAO in response to the SQL query method calls will take the form of instances of these entity classes. The getter methods will then be called to extract the data from the entity object. Similarly, when the repository needs to write new records to the database, it will create an entity instance, configure values on the object via setter calls, then call insert methods declared in the DAO, passing through entity instances to be saved.

64.2.5 SQLite Database

The actual SQLite database responsible for storing and providing access to the data. The app code, including the repository, should never make direct access to this underlying database. All database operations are performed using a combination of the room database, DAOs and entities.

The architecture diagram in Figure 64-2 illustrates the way in which these different elements interact to provide Room-based database storage within an Android app:

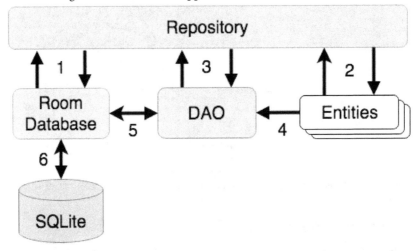

Figure 64-2

The numbered connections in the above architecture diagram can be summarized as follows:

1. The repository interacts with the Room Database to get a database instance which, in turn, is used to obtain references to DAO instances.

2. The repository creates entity instances and configures them with data before passing them to the DAO for use in search and insertion operations.

3. The repository calls methods on the DAO passing through entities to be inserted into the database and receives entity instances back in response to search queries.

4. When a DAO has results to return to the repository it packages those results into entity objects.

5. The DAO interacts with the Room Database to initiate database operations and handle results.

6. The Room Database handles all of the low level interactions with the underlying SQLite database, submitting queries and receiving results.

With a basic outline of the key elements of database access using the Room persistent library covered, it is now time to explore entities, DAOs, room databases and repositories in more detail.

64.3 Understanding Entities

Each database table will have associated with it an entity class. This class defines the schema for the table and takes the form of a standard Java class interspersed with some special Room annotations. An example Java class declaring the data to be stored within a database table might read as follows:

```
public class Customer {

    private int id;
    private String name;
    private string address;

    public Customer(String name, String address) {
        this.id = id;
        this.name = name;
        this.address = address;
    }

    public int getId() {
        return this.id;
    }
    public String getName() {
        return this.name;
    }

    public int getAddress() {
        return this.address;
    }

    public void setId(int id) {
```

```
            this.id = id;
    }


    public void setName(String name) {
        this.name = name;
    }


    public void setAddress(int quantity) {
        this.address = address;
    }

}
```

As currently implemented, the above code declares a basic Java class containing a number of variables representing database table fields and a collection of getter and setter methods. This class, however, is not yet an entity. To make this class into an entity and to make it accessible within SQL statements, some Room annotations need to be added as follows:

```
@Entity(tableName = "customers")
public class Customer {

    @PrimaryKey(autoGenerate = true)
    @NonNull
    @ColumnInfo(name = "customerId")
    private int id;

    @ColumnInfo(name = "customerName")
    private String name;

    private string address;

    public Customer(String name, String address) {
        this.id = id;
        this.name = name;
        this.address = address;
    }

    public int getId() {
        return this.id;
    }

    public String getName() {
        return this.name;
    }

    public int getAddress() {
        return this.address;
    }
```

```
public void setId(@NonNull int id) {
    this.id = id;
}

public void setName(String name) {
    this.name = name;
}

public void setAddress(int quantity) {
    this.address = address;
}
}
```

The above annotations begin by declaring that the class represents an entity and assigns a table name of "customers". This is the name by which the table will be referenced in the DAO SQL statements:

```
@Entity(tableName = "customers")
```

Every database table needs a column to act as the primary key. In this case, the customer id is declared as the primary key. Annotations have also been added to assign a column name to be referenced in SQL queries and to indicate that the field cannot be used to store null values. Finally, the id value is configured to be auto-generated. This means that the id assigned to new records will be automatically generated by the system to avoid duplicate keys.

```
@PrimaryKey(autoGenerate = true)
@NonNull
@ColumnInfo(name = "customerId")
private int id;
```

A column name is also assigned to the customer name field. Note, however, that no column name was assigned to the address field. This means that the address data will still be stored within the database, but that it is not required to be referenced in SQL statements. If a field within an entity is not required to be stored within a database, simply use the @Ignore annotation:

```
@Ignore
private String myString;
```

Finally, the setter method for the id variable is modified to prevent attempts to assign a null value:

```
public void setId(@NonNull int id) {
    this.id = id;
}
```

Annotations may also be included within an entity class to establish relationships with other entities using a relational database concept referred to as *foreign keys*. Foreign keys allow a table to reference the primary key in another table. For example, a relationship could be established between an entity named Purchase and our existing Customer entity as follows:

```
@Entity(ForeignKeys = @ForeignKey(entity = Customer.class,
                parentColumns = "id",  childColumns = "purchaseId"))

public class Purchase {
```

```
@PrimaryKey(autoGenerate = true)
@NonNull
@ColumnInfo(name = "purchaseId")
private int id;

@ColumnInfo(name = "productName")
private String name;
.
.
.
}
```

64.4 Data Access Objects

A Data Access Object provides a way to access the data stored within a SQLite database. A DAO is declared as a standard Java interface with some additional annotations that map specific SQL statements to methods that may then be called by the repository.

The first step is to create the interface and declare it as a DAO using the @Dao annotation:

```
@Dao
public interface CustomerDao {
}
```

Next, entries are added consisting of SQL statements and corresponding method names. The following declaration, for example, allows all of the rows in the customers table to be retrieved via a call to a method named *getAllCustomers()*:

```
@Dao
public interface CustomerDao {
    @Query("SELECT * FROM customers")
    LiveData<List<Customer>> getAllCustomers();
}
```

Note that the *getAllCustomers()* method returns a List object containing a Customer entity object for each record retrieved from the database table. The DAO is also making use of LiveData so that the repository is able to observe changes to the database.

Arguments may also be passed into the methods and referenced within the corresponding SQL statements. Consider the following DAO declaration which searches for database records matching a customer's name (note that the column name referenced in the WHERE condition is the name assigned to the column in the entity class):

```
@Query("SELECT * FROM customers WHERE name = :customerName")
List<Customer> findCustomer(String customerName);
```

In this example, the method is passed a string value which is, in turn, included within an SQL statement by prefixing the variable name with a colon (:).

A basic insertion operation can be declared as follows using the @Insert *convenience annotation*:

```
@Insert
void addCustomer(Customer customer);
```

This is referred to as a convenience annotation because the Room persistence library can infer that the Customer entity passed to the *addCustomer()* method is to be inserted into the database without the need for the SQL insert statement to be provided. Multiple database records may also be inserted in a single transaction as follows:

```
@Insert
public void insertCustomers(Customer... customers);
```

The following DAO declaration deletes all records matching the provided customer name:

```
@Query("DELETE FROM customers WHERE name = :name")
void deleteCustomer(String name);
```

As an alternative to using the @Query annotation to perform deletions, the @Delete convenience annotation may also be used. In the following example, all of the Customer records that match the set of entities passed to the *deleteCustomers()* method will be deleted from the database:

```
@Delete
public void deleteCustomers(Customer... customers);
```

The @Update convenience annotation provides similar behavior when updating records:

```
@Update
public void updateCustomers(Customer... customers);
```

The DAO methods for these types of database operations may also be declared to return an int value indicating the number of rows affected by the transaction, for example:

```
@Delete
public int deleteCustomers(Customer... customers);
```

64.5 The Room Database

The Room database class is created by extending the RoomDatabase class and acts as a layer on top of the actual SQLite database embedded into the Android operating system. The class is responsible for creating and returning a new room database instance and for providing access to the DAO instances associated with the database.

The Room persistence library provides a database builder for creating database instances. Each Android app should only have one room database instance, so it is best to implement defensive code within the class to prevent more than one instance being created.

An example Room Database implementation for use with the example customer table is outlined in the following code listing:

```
import android.content.Context;
import android.arch.persistence.room.Database;
import android.arch.persistence.room.Room;
import android.arch.persistence.room.RoomDatabase;


@Database(entities = {Customer.class}, version = 1)
public class CustomerRoomDatabase extends RoomDatabase {

    public abstract CustomerDao customerDao();

    private static CustomerRoomDatabase INSTANCE;

    static CustomerRoomDatabase getDatabase(final Context context) {
        if (INSTANCE == null) {
```

```
            synchronized (CustomerRoomDatabase.class) {
                if (INSTANCE == null) {
                    INSTANCE = Room.databaseBuilder(
                            context.getApplicationContext(),
                                CustomerRoomDatabase.class, "customer_database")
                                .build();
                }
            }
        }
        return INSTANCE;
    }
}
```

Important areas to note in the above example are the annotation above the class declaration declaring the entities with which the database is to work, the code to check that an instance of the class has not already been created and assignment of the name "customer_database" to the instance.

64.6 The Repository

The repository is responsible for getting a Room Database instance, using that instance to access associated DAOs and then making calls to DAO methods to perform database operations. A typical constructor for a repository designed to work with a Room Database might read as follows:

```
public class CustomerRepository {

    private CustomerDao customerDao;
    private CustomerRoomDatabase db;

    public CustomerRepository(Application application) {
        db = CustomerRoomDatabase.getDatabase(application);
        customerDao = db.customerDao();
    }
    .
    .
    .
}
```

Once the repository has access to the DAO, it can make calls to the data access methods. The following code, for example, calls the *getAllCustomers()* DAO method:

```
private LiveData<List<Customer>> allCustomers;
allCustomers = customerDao.getAllCustomers();
```

When calling DAO methods, it is important to note that unless the method returns a LiveData instance (which automatically runs queries on a separate thread), the operation cannot be performed on the app's main thread. In fact, attempting to do so will cause the app to crash with the following diagnostic output:

```
Cannot access database on the main thread since it may potentially lock the UI
for a long period of time
```

Since some database transactions may take a longer time to complete, running the operations on a separate thread avoids the app appearing to lock up. As will be demonstrated in the chapter entitled *"An Android Room Database and Repository Tutorial"*, this problem can be easily resolved by making use of the AsyncTask class (for more information or a reminder of how to use AsyncTask, refer back to the chapter entitled *"A Basic Overview of Threads and AsyncTasks").*

64.7 In-Memory Databases

The examples outlined in this chapter involved the use of a SQLite database that exists as a database file on the persistent storage of an Android device. This ensures that the data persists even after the app process is terminated.

The Room database persistence library also supports *in-memory* databases. These databases reside entirely in memory and are lost when the app terminates. The only change necessary to work with an in-memory database is to call the *Room.inMemoryDatabaseBuilder()* method of the Room Database class instead of *Room. databaseBuilder()*. The following code shows the difference between the method calls (note that the in-memory database does not require a database name):

```
// Create a file storage based database
INSTANCE = Room.databaseBuilder(context.getApplicationContext(),
                    CustomerRoomDatabase.class, "customer_database")
                    .build();

// Create an in-memory database
INSTANCE = Room.inMemoryDatabaseBuilder(context.getApplicationContext(),
                    CustomerRoomDatabase.class)
                    .build();
```

64.8 Summary

The Android Room persistence library is bundled with the Android Architecture Components and acts as an abstract layer above the lower level SQLite database. The library is designed to make it easier to work with databases while conforming to the Android architecture guidelines. This chapter has introduced the different elements that interact to build Room-based database storage into Android app projects including entities, repositories, data access objects, annotations and Room Database instances.

With the basics of SQLite and the Room architecture component covered, the next step is to create an example app that puts this theory into practice. Since the user interface for the example application will require a forms based layout, the next chapter, entitled *"An Android TableLayout and TableRow Tutorial"*, will detour slightly from the core topic by introducing the basics of the TableLayout and TableRow views.

65. An Android TableLayout and TableRow Tutorial

When the work began on the next chapter of this book (*"An Android Room Database and Repository Tutorial"*) it was originally intended that it would include the steps to design the user interface layout for the Room database example application. It quickly became evident, however, that the best way to implement the user interface was to make use of the Android TableLayout and TableRow views and that this topic area deserved a self-contained chapter. As a result, this chapter will focus solely on the user interface design of the database application to be completed in the next chapter, and in doing so, take some time to introduce the basic concepts of table layouts in Android Studio.

65.1 The TableLayout and TableRow Layout Views

The purpose of the TableLayout container view is to allow user interface elements to be organized on the screen in a table format consisting of rows and columns. Each row within a TableLayout is occupied by a TableRow instance which, in turn, is divided into cells, with each cell containing a single child view (which may itself be a container with multiple view children).

The number of columns in a table is dictated by the row with the most columns and, by default, the width of each column is defined by the widest cell in that column. Columns may be configured to be shrinkable or stretchable (or both) such that they change in size relative to the parent TableLayout. In addition, a single cell may be configured to span multiple columns.

Consider the user interface layout shown in Figure 65-1:

Figure 65-1

From the visual appearance of the layout, it is difficult to identify the TableLayout structure used to design the interface. The hierarchical tree illustrated in Figure 65-2, however, makes the structure a little easier to understand:

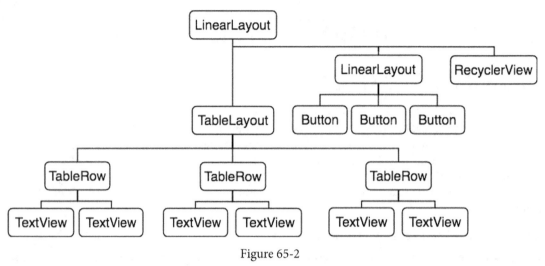

Figure 65-2

Clearly, the layout consists of a parent LinearLayout view with TableLayout, LinearLayout and RecyclerView children. The TableLayout contains three TableRow children representing three rows in the table. The TableRows contain two child views, with each child representing the contents of a table column cell. The LinearLayout child view contains three Button children.

The layout shown in Figure 65-2 is the exact layout that is required for the database example that will be completed in the next chapter. The remainder of this chapter, therefore, will be used to work step by step through the design of this user interface using the Android Studio Layout Editor tool.

65.2 Creating the Room Database Project

Select the *Start a new Android Studio project* quick start option from the welcome screen and, within the resulting new project dialog, choose the Fragment + ViewModel template before clicking on the Next button.

Enter *RoomDemo* into the Name field and specify *com.ebookfrenzy.roomdemo* as the package name. Before clicking on the Finish button, change the Minimum API level setting to API 26: Android 8.0 (Oreo) and the Language menu to Java.

65.3 Converting to a LinearLayout

Locate the *main_fragment.xml* file in the Project tool window (*app -> res -> layout*) and double-click on it to load it into the Layout Editor tool. By default, Android Studio has used a ConstraintLayout as the root layout element in the user interface. This needs to be converted to a vertically oriented LinearLayout. With the Layout Editor tool in Design mode, locate the *main* ConstraintLayout component in the Component tree and right-click on it to display the menu shown in Figure 65-3 and select the *Convert View...* option:

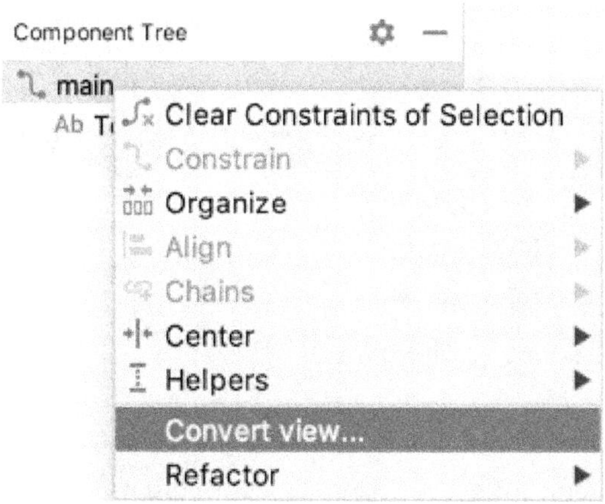

Figure 65-3

In the resulting dialog (Figure 65-4) select the option to convert to a LinearLayout before clicking on the Apply button:

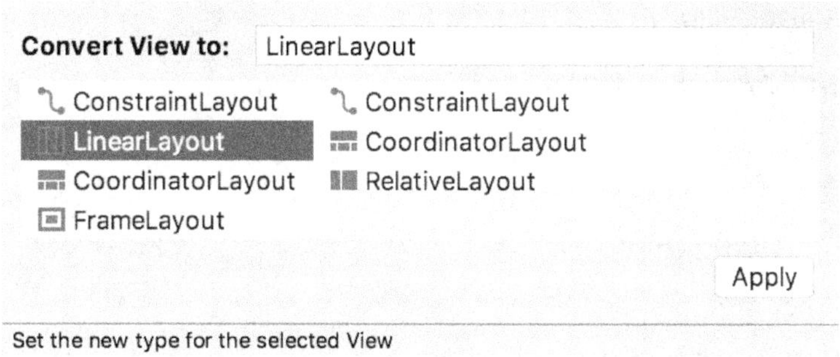

Figure 65-4

By default, the layout editor will have converted the ConstraintLayout to a horizontal LinearLayout so select the layout component in the Component Tree window, refer to the Attributes tool window and change the orientation property to *vertical*:

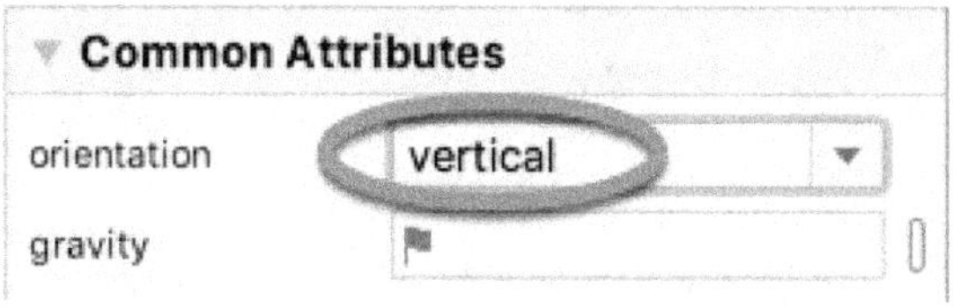

Figure 65-5

With the conversion complete, select and delete the default TextView widget from the layout.

65.4 Adding the TableLayout to the User Interface

Remaining in the *main_fragment.xml* file and referring to the Layouts category of the Palette, drag and drop a TableLayout view so that it is positioned at the top of the LinearLayout canvas area.

Once these initial steps are complete, the Component Tree for the layout should resemble that shown in Figure 65-6.

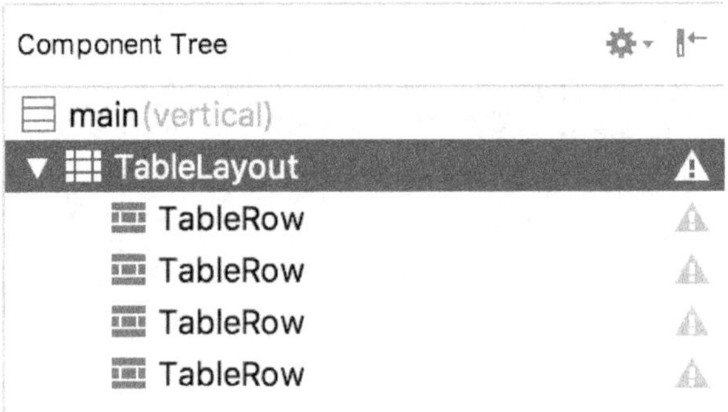

Figure 65-6

Clearly, Android Studio has automatically added four TableRow instances to the TableLayout. Since only three rows are required for this example, select and delete the fourth TableRow instance. Additional rows may be added to the TableLayout at any time by dragging the TableRow object from the palette and dropping it onto the TableLayout entry in the Component Tree tool window.

With the TableLayout selected, use the Attributes tool window to change the layout_height property to *wrap_content* and layout_width to *match_parent*.

65.5 Configuring the TableRows

From within the *Text* section of the palette, drag and drop two TextView objects onto the uppermost TableRow entry in the Component Tree (Figure 65-7):

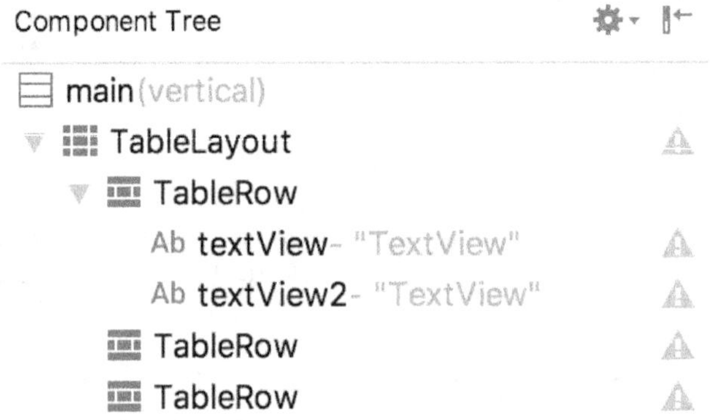

Figure 65-7

Select the left most TextView within the screen layout and, in the Attributes tool window, change the *text* property to "Product ID". Repeat this step for the right most TextView, this time changing the text to "Not assigned" and specifying an *ID* value of *productID*.

Drag and drop another TextView widget onto the second TableRow entry in the Component Tree and change the text on the view to read "Product Name". Locate the Plain Text object in the palette and drag and drop it so that it is positioned beneath the Product Name TextView within the Component Tree as outlined in Figure 65-8. With the TextView selected, change the inputType property from textPersonName to None, delete the "Name" string from the text property and set the ID to *productName*.

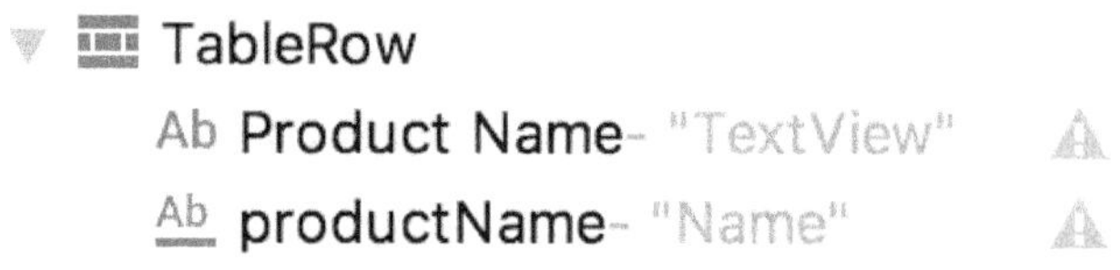

▽ ▦ **TableRow**

　　Ab **Product Name**- "TextView"　⚠

　　Ab **productName**- "Name"　⚠

Figure 65-8

Drag and drop another TextView and a Number (Decimal) Text Field onto the third TableRow so that the TextView is positioned above the Text Field in the hierarchy. Change the text on the TextView to *Product Quantity* and the ID of the Text Field object to *productQuantity*.

Shift-click to select all of the widgets in the layout as shown in Figure 65-9 below, and use the Attributes tool window to set the textSize property on all of the objects to 18sp:

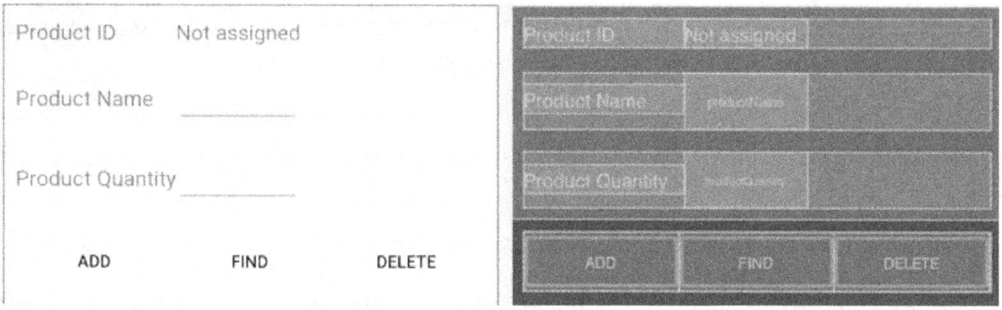

Figure 65-9

Before proceeding, be sure to extract all of the text properties added in the above steps to string resources.

65.6 Adding the Button Bar to the Layout

The next step is to add a LinearLayout (Horizontal) view to the parent LinearLayout view, positioned immediately below the TableLayout view. Begin by clicking on the small disclosure arrow to the left of the TableLayout entry in the Component Tree so that the TableRows are folded away from view. Drag a *LinearLayout (Horizontal)* instance from the *Layouts* section of the Layout Editor palette, drop it immediately beneath the TableLayout entry in the Component Tree panel and change the layout_height property to *wrap_content*:

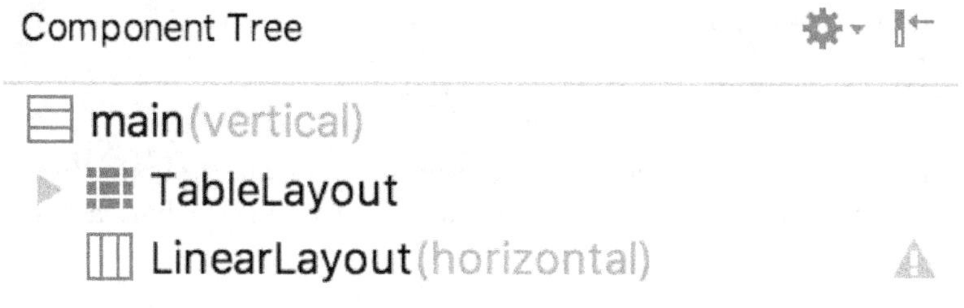

Component Tree　　　　　　　　　　　　　　⚙▾ ⊩

▤ **main**(vertical)

　▷ ▦ **TableLayout**

　　⬚ **LinearLayout**(horizontal)　　　　　⚠

Figure 65-10

Drag and drop three Button objects onto the new LinearLayout and assign string resources for each button that read "Add", "Find" and "Delete" respectively. Buttons in this type of button bar arrangement should generally be displayed with a borderless style. For each button, use the Attributes tool window to change the style setting to *Widget.AppCompat.Button.Borderless*. Change the IDs for the buttons to *addButton*, *deleteButton* and *findButton* respectively.

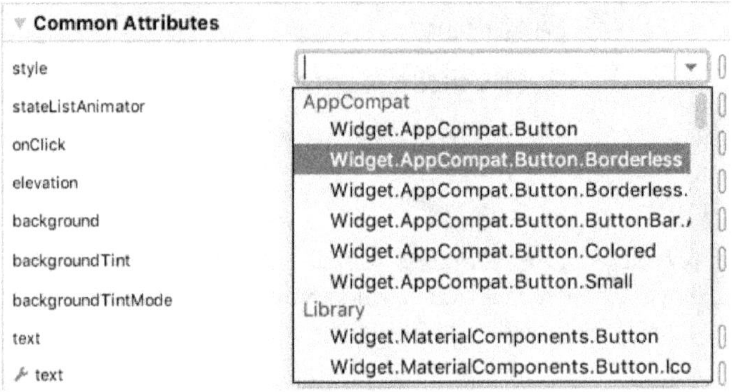

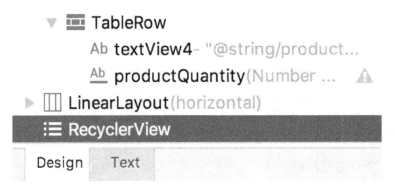

Figure 65-11

With the new horizontal LinearLayout view selected in the Component Tree change the gravity property to *center_horizontal* so that the buttons are centered horizontally within the display.

65.7 Adding the RecyclerView

In the Component Tree, click on the disclosure arrow to the right of the newly added horizontal LinearLayout entry to fold all of the children from view.

From the Containers section of the Palette, drag a RecyclerView instance and drop it onto the Component Tree so that it positioned beneath the button bar LinearLayout as shown in Figure 65-12. Take care to ensure the RecyclerView is added as a direct child of the parent vertical LinearLayout view and not as a child of the horizontal button bar LinearLayout.

Figure 65-12

When the RecyclerView is added to the layout, Android Studio may provide the option to add the corresponding library to the project build configuration as illustrated below. Click on the OK button to add this library before proceeding:

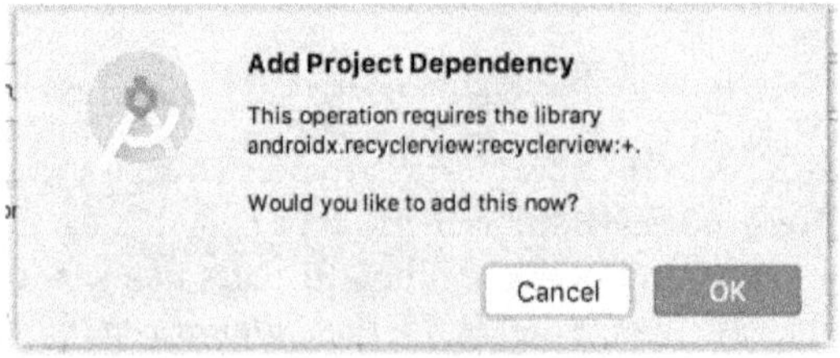

Figure 65-13

With the RecyclerView selected in the layout, change the ID of the view to *product_recycler* and set the layout_height property to *match_parent*. Before proceeding, check that the hierarchy of the layout in the Component Tree panel matches that shown in the following figure:

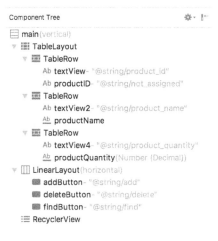

Figure 65-14

65.8 Adjusting the Layout Margins

All that remains is to adjust some of the layout settings. Begin by clicking on the first TableRow entry in the Component Tree panel so that it is selected. Hold down the Cmd/Ctrl-key on the keyboard and click in the second and third TableRows, the horizontal LinearLayout and the RecyclerView so that all five items are selected. In the Attributes panel, locate the *layout_margin* attributes category and, once located, change the value to 10dp as shown in Figure 65-15:

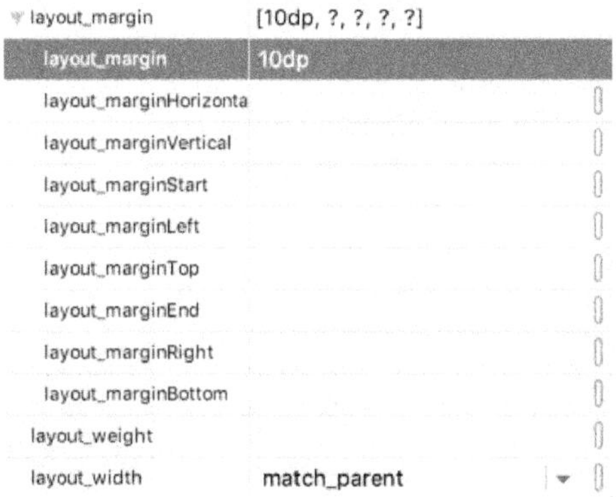

Figure 65-15

With margins set, the user interface should appear as illustrated in Figure 65-1.

65.9 Summary

The Android TableLayout container view provides a way to arrange view components in a row and column configuration. While the TableLayout view provides the overall container, each row and the cells contained therein are implemented via instances of the TableRow view. In this chapter, a user interface has been designed in Android Studio using the TableLayout and TableRow containers. The next chapter will add the functionality behind this user interface to implement the SQLite database capabilities using a repository and the Room persistence library.

66. An Android Room Database and Repository Tutorial

This chapter will combine the knowledge gained in the chapter entitled *"The Android Room Persistence Library"* with the initial project created in the previous chapter to provide a detailed tutorial demonstrating how to implement SQLite-based database storage using the Room persistence library. In keeping with the Android architectural guidelines, the project will make use of a view model and repository. The tutorial will make use of all of the elements covered in *"The Android Room Persistence Library"* including entities, a Data Access Object, a Room Databases and asynchronous database queries.

66.1 About the RoomDemo Project

The user interface layout created in the previous chapter was the first step in creating a rudimentary inventory app designed to store the names and quantities of products. When completed, the app will provide the ability to add, delete and search for database entries while also displaying a scrollable list of all products currently stored in the database. This product list will update automatically as database entries are added or deleted.

66.2 Modifying the Build Configuration

Begin by launching Android Studio and opening the RoomDemo project started in the previous chapter. Before adding any new classes to the project, the first step is to add some additional libraries to the build configuration, specifically the Room persistence library and the RecyclerView library. Locate and edit the module level *build. gradle* file (*app -> Gradle Scripts -> build.gradle (Module: app)*) and modify it as follows:

```
dependencies {
    implementation fileTree(dir: 'libs', include: ['*.jar'])
    implementation "androidx.recyclerview:recyclerview:1.0.0"
    implementation "android.arch.persistence.room:runtime:1.1.1"
    annotationProcessor "android.arch.persistence.room:compiler:1.1.1"

    .
    .
    .
}
```

66.3 Building the Entity

This project will begin by creating the entity which defines the schema for the database table. The entity will consist of an integer for the product id, a string column to hold the product name and another integer value to store the quantity. The product id column will serve as the primary key and will be auto-generated. Table 66-1 summarizes the structure of the entity:

Column	Data Type
productid	Integer / Primary Key / Auto Increment
productname	String

productquantity	Integer

Table 66-1

Add a class file for the entity by right clicking on the *app -> java -> com.ebookfrenzy.roomdemo* entry in the Project tool window and selecting the *New -> Java Class* menu option. In the Create New Class dialog, name the class *Product* and click on the OK button to generate the file.

When the *Product.java* file opens in the editor, modify it so that it reads as follows:

```
package com.ebookfrenzy.roomdemo;

public class Product {

    private int id;
    private String name;
    private int quantity;

    public Product(String name, int quantity) {
        this.id = id;
        this.name = name;
        this.quantity = quantity;
    }

    public int getId() {
        return this.id;
    }
    public String getName() {
        return this.name;
    }

    public int getQuantity() {
        return this.quantity;
    }

    public void setId(int id) {
        this.id = id;
    }

    public void setName(String name) {
        this.name = name;
    }

    public void setQuantity(int quantity) {
        this.quantity = quantity;
    }
```

}

The class now has variables for the database table columns and matching getter and setter methods. Of course this class does not become an entity until it has been annotated. With the class file still open in the editor, add annotations and corresponding import statements:

```
package com.ebookfrenzy.roomdemo;

import androidx.annotation.NonNull;
import androidx.room.ColumnInfo;
import androidx.room.Entity;
import androidx.room.PrimaryKey;

@Entity(tableName = "products")
public class Product {

    @PrimaryKey(autoGenerate = true)
    @NonNull
    @ColumnInfo(name = "productId")
    private int id;

    @ColumnInfo(name = "productName")
    private String name;
    private int quantity;

.

.

}
```

These annotations declare this as the entity for a table named *products* and assigns column names for both the *id* and *name* variables. The id column is also configured to be the primary key and auto-generated. Since a primary key can never be null, the @NonNull annotation is also applied. Since it will not be necessary to reference the quantity column in SQL queries, a column name has not been assigned to the *quantity* variable.

66.4 Creating the Data Access Object

With the product entity defined, the next step is to create the DAO interface. Referring once again to the Project tool window, right-click on the *app -> java -> com.ebookfrenzy.roomdemo* entry and select the *New -> Java Class* menu option. In the Create New Class dialog, enter *ProductDao* into the Name field and select *Interface* from the Kind menu as highlighted in Figure 66-1:

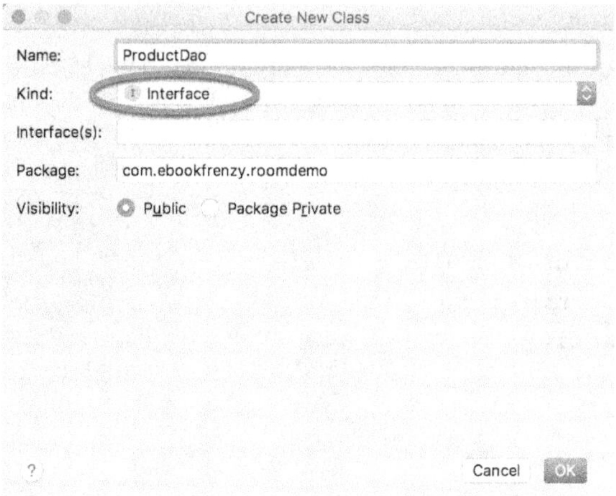

Figure 66-1

Click on OK to generate the new interface and, with the *ProductDao.java* file loaded into the code editor, make the following changes:

```
package com.ebookfrenzy.roomdemo;

import androidx.lifecycle.LiveData;
import androidx.room.Dao;
import androidx.room.Insert;
import androidx.room.Query;

import java.util.List;

@Dao
public interface ProductDao {

    @Insert
    void insertProduct(Product product);

    @Query("SELECT * FROM products WHERE productName = :name")
    List<Product> findProduct(String name);

    @Query("DELETE FROM products WHERE productName = :name")
    void deleteProduct(String name);

    @Query("SELECT * FROM products")
    LiveData<List<Product>> getAllProducts();
}
```

The DAO implements methods to insert, find and delete records from the products database. The insertion method is passed a Product entity object containing the data to be stored while the methods to find and delete records are passed a string containing the name of the product on which to perform the operation. The *getAllProducts()* method returns a LiveData object containing all of the records within the database. This method will be used to keep the RecyclerView product list in the user interface layout synchronized with the database.

66.5 Adding the Room Database

The last task before adding the repository to the project is to implement the Room Database instance. Add a new class to the project named *ProductRoomDatabase*, this time with the Kind menu set to *Class* and the *Abstract* option enabled in the Modifiers section.

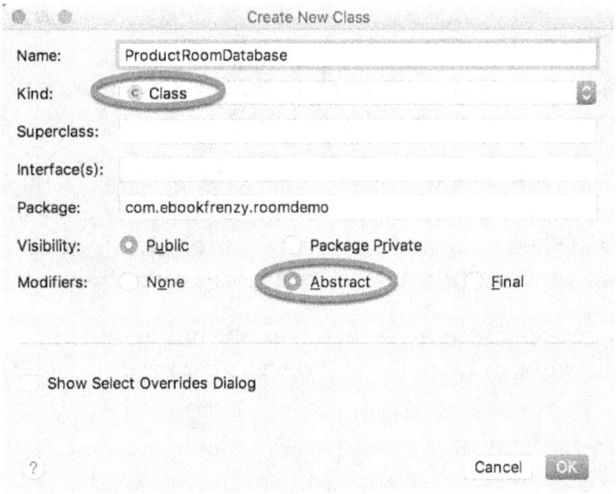

Figure 66-2

Once the file has been generated, modify it as follows using the steps outlined in the *"The Android Room Persistence Library"* chapter:

```
package com.ebookfrenzy.roomdemo;

import android.content.Context;

import androidx.room.Database;
import androidx.room.Room;
import androidx.room.RoomDatabase;

@Database(entities = {Product.class}, version = 1)
public abstract class ProductRoomDatabase extends RoomDatabase {

    public abstract ProductDao productDao();
    private static ProductRoomDatabase INSTANCE;

    static ProductRoomDatabase getDatabase(final Context context) {
        if (INSTANCE == null) {
            synchronized (ProductRoomDatabase.class) {
                if (INSTANCE == null) {
                    INSTANCE =
                        Room.databaseBuilder(context.getApplicationContext(),
                                ProductRoomDatabase.class,
                                    "product_database").build();
```

```
                }
            }
        }
        return INSTANCE;
    }
}
```

66.6 Adding the Repository

Add a new class named *ProductRepository* to the project, with the Kind menu set to *Class* and *None* enabled in the Modifiers section of the Create New Class dialog.

The repository class will be responsible for interacting with the Room database on behalf of the ViewModel and will need to provide methods that use the DAO to insert, delete and query product records. With the exception of the *getAllProducts()* DAO method (which returns a LiveData object) these database operations will need to be performed on separate threads from the main thread using the AsyncTask class.

Remaining within the *ProductRepository.java* file, add the code for the search AsyncTask. Also add a method named *asyncFinished()* which will be called by the query AsyncTask to return the search results to the repository thread:

```
package com.ebookfrenzy.roomdemo;

import android.os.AsyncTask;
import androidx.lifecycle.MutableLiveData;
import java.util.List;

public class ProductRepository {

    private MutableLiveData<List<Product>> searchResults =
            new MutableLiveData<>();

    private void asyncFinished(List<Product> results) {
        searchResults.setValue(results);
    }

    private static class QueryAsyncTask extends
            AsyncTask<String, Void, List<Product>> {

        private ProductDao asyncTaskDao;
        private ProductRepository delegate = null;

        QueryAsyncTask(ProductDao dao) {
            asyncTaskDao = dao;
        }

        @Override
        protected List<Product> doInBackground(final String... params) {
            return asyncTaskDao.findProduct(params[0]);
```

```
        }

        @Override
        protected void onPostExecute(List<Product> result) {
            delegate.asyncFinished(result);
        }
    }
}
```

The above declares a MutableLiveData variable named *searchResults* into which the results of a search operation are stored whenever an asynchronous search task completes (later in the tutorial, an observer within the ViewModel will monitor this live data object).

The AsyncTask class contains a constructor method into which must be passed a reference to the DAO object. The *doInBackground()* method is passed a String containing the product name for which the search is to be performed, passes it to the *findProduct()* method of the DAO and returns a list of matching Product entity objects which will, in turn, be passed to the *onPostExecute()* method. Finally, the *onPostExecute()* method stores the matching product list in the *searchResults* MutableLiveData object.

The repository will also need to include the following AsyncTask implementation for inserting products into the database:

```
private static class InsertAsyncTask extends AsyncTask<Product, Void, Void> {

    private ProductDao asyncTaskDao;

    InsertAsyncTask(ProductDao dao) {
        asyncTaskDao = dao;
    }

    @Override
    protected Void doInBackground(final Product... params) {
        asyncTaskDao.insertProduct(params[0]);
        return null;
    }
}
```

Once again a constructor method is passed a reference to the DAO object, though this time the *doInBackground()* method is passed an array of Product entity objects to be inserted into the database. Since the app allows only one new product to be added at a time, the method simply inserts the first Product in the array into the database via a call to the *insertProduct()* DAO method. In this case, no results need to be returned from the task.

The only remaining AsyncTask will be used when deleting products from the database and should be added beneath the insertAsyncTask declaration as follows:

```
private static class DeleteAsyncTask extends AsyncTask<String, Void, Void> {

    private ProductDao asyncTaskDao;

    DeleteAsyncTask(ProductDao dao) {
        asyncTaskDao = dao;
```

```
    }

    @Override
    protected Void doInBackground(final String... params) {
        asyncTaskDao.deleteProduct(params[0]);
        return null;
    }
}
```

With the AsyncTask classes defined, the repository class now needs to provide some methods that can be called by the ViewModel to initiate these operations. These methods will create and call appropriate AsyncTask instances and pass through a reference to the DAO. In order to be able to do this, however, the repository needs to obtain the DAO reference via a ProductRoomDatabase instance. Add a constructor method to the ProductRepository class to perform these tasks:

```
.
.
import android.app.Application;
.
.
public class ProductRepository {

    private MutableLiveData<List<Product>> searchResults =
                                          new MutableLiveData<>();
    private ProductDao productDao;

    public ProductRepository(Application application) {
        ProductRoomDatabase db;
        db = ProductRoomDatabase.getDatabase(application);
        productDao = db.productDao();
    }
.
.
```

With a reference to DAO stored, the methods are ready to be added to the class file:

```
.
.
public void insertProduct(Product newproduct) {
    InsertAsyncTask task = new InsertAsyncTask(productDao);
    task.execute(newproduct);
}

public void deleteProduct(String name) {
    DeleteAsyncTask task = new DeleteAsyncTask(productDao);
    task.execute(name);
}

public void findProduct(String name) {
```

```
QueryAsyncTask task = new QueryAsyncTask(productDao);
task.delegate = this;
task.execute(name);
}
.
.
.
```

In the cases of the insertion and deletion methods, the appropriate AsyncTask instance is created and passed the necessary arguments. In the case of the *findProduct()* method, the delegate property of the class is set to the repository instance so that the *asyncFinished()* method can be called after the search completes.

One final task remains to complete the repository class. The RecyclerView in the user interface layout will need to be able to keep up to date the current list of products stored in the database. The ProductDao class already includes a method named *getAllProducts()* which uses a SQL query to select all of the database records and return them wrapped in a LiveData object. The repository needs to call this method once on initialization and store the result within a LiveData object that can be observed by the ViewModel and, in turn, by the UI controller. Once this has been set up, each time a change occurs to the database table the UI controller observer will be notified and the RecyclerView can be updated with the latest product list. Remaining within the *ProductRepository.java* file, add a LiveData variable and call to the DAO *getAllProducts()* method within the constructor:

```
.
.
import androidx.lifecycle.LiveData;
.
.
public class ProductRepository {

    private MutableLiveData<List<Product>> searchResults =
            new MutableLiveData<>();
    private LiveData<List<Product>> allProducts;
    private ProductDao productDao;

    public ProductRepository(Application application) {
        ProductRoomDatabase db;
        db = ProductRoomDatabase.getDatabase(application);
        productDao = db.productDao();
        allProducts = productDao.getAllProducts();
    }
    .
    .
}
```

To complete the repository, add methods that the ViewModel can call to obtain references to the *allProducts* and *searchResults* live data objects:

```
public LiveData<List<Product>> getAllProducts() {
    return allProducts;
}

public MutableLiveData<List<Product>> getSearchResults() {
```

```
        return searchResults;
}
```

66.7 Modifying the ViewModel

The ViewModel is responsible for creating an instance of the repository and for providing methods and LiveData objects that can be utilized by the UI controller to keep the user interface synchronized with the underlying database. As implemented in *ProductRepository.java*, the repository constructor requires access to the application context in order to be able to get a Room Database instance. To make the application context accessible within the ViewModel so that it can be passed to the repository, the ViewModel needs to subclass AndroidViewModel instead of ViewModel. Begin, therefore, by editing the *MainViewModel.java* file (located in the Project tool window under *app -> java -> com.ebookfrenzy.roomdemo -> ui.main*) and changing the class to extend AndroidViewModel and to implement the default constructor:

```java
package com.ebookfrenzy.roomdemo.ui.main;

import android.app.Application;
import androidx.lifecycle.AndroidViewModel;
import androidx.lifecycle.LiveData;
import androidx.lifecycle.MutableLiveData;
import com.ebookfrenzy.roomdemo.Product;
import com.ebookfrenzy.roomdemo.ProductRepository;
import java.util.List;
import androidx.lifecycle.ViewModel;

public class MainViewModel extends AndroidViewModel
{
    private ProductRepository repository;
    private LiveData<List<Product>> allProducts;
    private MutableLiveData<List<Product>> searchResults;

    public MainViewModel (Application application) {
        super(application);
        repository = new ProductRepository(application);
        allProducts = repository.getAllProducts();
        searchResults = repository.getSearchResults();
    }
}
```

The constructor essentially creates a repository instance and then uses it to get references to the results and live data objects so that they can be observed by the UI controller. All that now remains within the ViewModel is to implement the methods that will be called from within the UI controller in response to button clicks and when setting up observers on the LiveData objects:

```java
MutableLiveData<List<Product>> getSearchResults() {
    return searchResults;
}

LiveData<List<Product>> getAllProducts() {
    return allProducts;
```

```
}

public void insertProduct(Product product) {
    repository.insertProduct(product);
}

public void findProduct(String name) {
    repository.findProduct(name);
}

public void deleteProduct(String name) {
    repository.deleteProduct(name);
}
```

66.8 Creating the Product Item Layout

The name of each product in the database will appear within the RecyclerView list in the main user interface. This will require a simple layout resource file containing a TextView to be used for each row in the list. Add this file now by right-clicking on the *app -> res -> layout* entry in the Project tool window and selecting the *New -> Layout resource file* menu option. Name the file *product_list_item* and change the root element to LinearLayout before clicking on OK to create the file and load it into the layout editor. With the layout editor in Design mode, drag a TextView object from the palette onto the layout where it will appear by default at the top of the layout:

Figure 66-3

With the TextView selected in the layout, use the Attributes tool window to set the ID of the view to *product_row* and the layout_height to 30dp. Select the LinearLayout entry in the Component Tree window and set the layout_height attribute to *wrap_content*.

66.9 Adding the RecyclerView Adapter

As outlined in detail in the chapter entitled *"Working with the RecyclerView and CardView Widgets"*, a RecyclerView instance requires an adapter class to provide the data to be displayed. Add this class now by right clicking on the *app -> java -> com.ebookfrenzy.roomdemo -> ui.main* entry in the Project tool window and selecting the *New -> Java Class...* menu option. In the Create New Class Dialog, name the class *ProductListAdapter*. With the resulting *ProductListAdapter.java* class loaded into the editor, implement the class as follows:

```
package com.ebookfrenzy.roomdemo.ui.main;

import android.view.LayoutInflater;
import android.view.View;
import android.view.ViewGroup;
import android.widget.TextView;
import com.ebookfrenzy.roomdemo.R;
import androidx.recyclerview.widget.RecyclerView;
import com.ebookfrenzy.roomdemo.Product;
```

```java
import java.util.List;

public class ProductListAdapter
        extends RecyclerView.Adapter<ProductListAdapter.ViewHolder> {

    private int productItemLayout;
    private List<Product> productList;

    public ProductListAdapter(int layoutId) {
        productItemLayout = layoutId;
    }

    public void setProductList(List<Product> products) {
        productList = products;
        notifyDataSetChanged();
    }

    @Override
    public int getItemCount() {
        return productList == null ? 0 : productList.size();
    }

    @Override
    public ViewHolder onCreateViewHolder(ViewGroup parent, int viewType) {
        View view = LayoutInflater.from(
                parent.getContext()).inflate(productItemLayout, parent, false);
        ViewHolder myViewHolder = new ViewHolder(view);
        return myViewHolder;
    }

    @Override
    public void onBindViewHolder(final ViewHolder holder, final int listPosition) {
        TextView item = holder.item;
        item.setText(productList.get(listPosition).getName());
    }

    static class ViewHolder extends RecyclerView.ViewHolder {
        TextView item;
        ViewHolder(View itemView) {
            super(itemView);
            item = itemView.findViewById(R.id.product_row);
        }
    }
}
```

66.10 Preparing the Main Fragment

The last remaining component to modify is the MainFragment class which needs to configure listeners on the Button views and observers on the live data objects located in the ViewModel class. Before adding this code, some preparation work needs to be performed to add some imports, variables and to obtain references to view ids. Edit the *MainFragment.java* file and modify it as follows:

```
.
.
.
import android.widget.EditText;
import android.widget.TextView;
.
.
.
public class MainFragment extends Fragment {

    private MainViewModel mViewModel;
    private ProductListAdapter adapter;

    private TextView productId;
    private EditText productName;
    private EditText productQuantity;
.
.
.
    @Override
    public void onActivityCreated(@Nullable Bundle savedInstanceState) {
        super.onActivityCreated(savedInstanceState);
        mViewModel = ViewModelProviders.of(this).get(MainViewModel.class);

        productId = getView().findViewById(R.id.productID);
        productName = getView().findViewById(R.id.productName);
        productQuantity = getView().findViewById(R.id.productQuantity);

        listenerSetup();
        observerSetup();
        recyclerSetup();
    }
.
.
.
}
```

At various stages in the code, the app will need to clear the product information displayed in the user interface. To avoid code repetition, add the following *clearFields()* convenience function:

```
private void clearFields() {
    productId.setText("");
    productName.setText("");
    productQuantity.setText("");
}
```

Before the app can be built and tested, the three setup methods called from the *onActivityCreated()* method above need to be added to the class.

66.11 Adding the Button Listeners

The user interface layout for the main fragment contains three buttons each of which needs to perform a specific task when clicked by user. Edit the *MainFragment.java* file and add the *listenerSetup()* method:

```
.
.
import com.ebookfrenzy.roomdemo.Product;
import android.widget.Button;
.
.

    private void listenerSetup() {

        Button addButton = getView().findViewById(R.id.addButton);
        Button findButton = getView().findViewById(R.id.findButton);
        Button deleteButton = getView().findViewById(R.id.deleteButton);

        addButton.setOnClickListener(new View.OnClickListener() {
            @Override
            public void onClick(View view) {

                String name = productName.getText().toString();
                String quantity = productQuantity.getText().toString();

                if (!name.equals("") && !quantity.equals("")) {
                    Product product = new Product(name,
                                        Integer.parseInt(quantity));
                    mViewModel.insertProduct(product);
                    clearFields();
                } else {
                    productId.setText("Incomplete information");
                }
            }
        });

        findButton.setOnClickListener(new View.OnClickListener() {
            @Override
            public void onClick(View view) {
                mViewModel.findProduct(productName.getText().toString());
            }
        });

        deleteButton.setOnClickListener(new View.OnClickListener() {
            @Override
```

```
        public void onClick(View view) {
            mViewModel.deleteProduct(productName.getText().toString());
            clearFields();
        }
    });
    }
    .
    .
    .
}
```

The addButton listener performs some basic validation to ensure that the user has entered both a product name and quantity and uses this data to create a new Product entity object (note that the quantity string is converted to an integer to match the entity data type). The ViewModel *insertProduct()* method is then called and passed the Product object before the fields are cleared.

The findButton and deleteButton listeners pass the product name to either the ViewModel *findProduct()* or *deleteProduct()* method.

66.12 Adding LiveData Observers

The user interface now needs to add observers to remain synchronized with the *searchResults* and *allProducts* live data objects within the ViewModel. Remaining in the *Mainfragment.java* file, implement the observer setup method as follows:

```
.
.
import androidx.lifecycle.Observer;
.
.
import java.util.List;
import java.util.Locale;
.
.

    private void observerSetup() {

        mViewModel.getAllProducts().observe(this, new Observer<List<Product>>() {
            @Override
            public void onChanged(@Nullable final List<Product> products) {
                adapter.setProductList(products);
            }
        });

        mViewModel.getSearchResults().observe(this,
                                new Observer<List<Product>>() {
            @Override
            public void onChanged(@Nullable final List<Product> products) {

                if (products.size() > 0) {
                    productId.setText(String.format(Locale.US, "%d",
```

```
                                     products.get(0).getId()));
                 productName.setText(products.get(0).getName());
                 productQuantity.setText(String.format(Locale.US, "%d",
                                     products.get(0).getQuantity()));
             } else {
                 productId.setText("No Match");
             }
          }
       });
   }

   .

   .

}
```

The "all products" observer simply passes the current list of products to the *setProductList()* method of the RecyclerAdapter where the displayed list will be updated.

The "search results" observer checks that at least one matching result has been located in the database, extracts the first matching Product entity object from the list, gets the data from the object, converts it where necessary and assigns it to the TextView and EditText views in the layout. If the product search failed, the user is notified via a message displayed on the product ID TextView.

66.13 Initializing the RecyclerView

Add the final setup method to initialize and configure the RecyclerView and adapter as follows:

```
   .

   .

import androidx.recyclerview.widget.LinearLayoutManager;
import androidx.recyclerview.widget.RecyclerView;

   .

   .

   private void recyclerSetup() {

       RecyclerView recyclerView;

       adapter = new ProductListAdapter(R.layout.product_list_item);
       recyclerView = getView().findViewById(R.id.product_recycler);
       recyclerView.setLayoutManager(new LinearLayoutManager(getContext()));
       recyclerView.setAdapter(adapter);
   }

   .

   .

}
```

66.14 Testing the RoomDemo App

Compile and run the app on a device or emulator, add some products and make sure that they appear automatically in the RecyclerView. Perform a search for an existing product and verify that the product ID and quantity fields update accordingly. Finally, enter the name for an existing product, delete it from the database and confirm that it is removed from the RecyclerView product list.

66.15 Summary

This chapter has demonstrated the use of the Room persistence library to store data in a SQLite database. The finished project made use of a repository to separate the ViewModel from all database operations and demonstrated the creation of entities, a DAO and a room database instance, including the use of asynchronous tasks when performing some database operations.

67. Accessing Cloud Storage using the Android Storage Access Framework

Recent years have seen the wide adoption of remote storage services (otherwise known as "cloud storage") to store user files and data. Driving this growth are two key factors. One is that most mobile devices now provide continuous, high speed internet connectivity, thereby making the transfer of data fast and affordable. The second factor is that, relative to traditional computer systems (such as desktops and laptops) these mobile devices are constrained in terms of internal storage resources. A high specification Android tablet today, for example, typically comes with 128Gb of storage capacity. When compared with a mid-range laptop system with a 750Gb disk drive, the need for the seamless remote storage of files is a key requirement for many mobile applications today.

In recognition of this fact, Google introduced the Storage Access Framework as part of the Android 4.4 SDK. This chapter will provide a high level overview of the storage access framework in preparation for the more detail oriented tutorial contained in the next chapter, entitled *"An Android Storage Access Framework Example"*.

67.1 The Storage Access Framework

From the perspective of the user, the Storage Access Framework provides an intuitive user interface that allows the user to browse, select, delete and create files hosted by storage services (also referred to as *document providers*) from within Android applications. Using this browsing interface (also referred to as the *picker*), users can, for example, browse through the files (such as documents, audio, images and videos) hosted by their chosen document providers. Figure 67-1, for example, shows the picker user interface displaying a collection of files hosted by a document provider service:

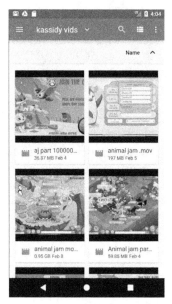

Figure 67-1

Document providers can range from cloud-based services to local document providers running on the same device as the client application. At the time of writing, the most prominent document providers compatible with the Storage Access Framework are Box and, unsurprisingly, Google Drive. It is highly likely that other cloud storage providers and application developers will soon also provide services that conform to the Android Storage Access Framework.

In addition to cloud based document providers the picker also provides access to internal storage on the device, providing a range of file storage options to the application user.

Through a set of Intents, Android application developers can incorporate these storage capabilities into applications with just a few lines of code. A particularly compelling aspect of the Storage Access Framework from the point of view of the developer is that the underlying document provider selected by the user is completely transparent to the application. Once the storage functionality has been implemented using the framework within an application, it will work with all document providers without any code modifications.

67.2 Working with the Storage Access Framework

Android includes a set of Intents designed to integrate the features of the Storage Access Framework into Android applications. These intents display the Storage Access Framework picker user interface to the user and return the results of the interaction to the application via a call to the *onActivityResult()* method of the activity that launched the intent. When the *onActivityResult()* method is called, it is passed the Uri of the selected file together with a value indicating the success or otherwise of the operation.

The Storage Access Framework intents can be summarized as follows:

- **ACTION_OPEN_DOCUMENT** – Provides the user with access to the picker user interface so that files may be selected from the document providers configured on the device. Selected files are passed back to the application in the form of Uri objects.

- **ACTION_CREATE_DOCUMENT** – Allows the user to select a document provider, a location on that provider's storage and a file name for a new file. Once selected, the file is created by the Storage Access Framework and the Uri of that file returned to the application for further processing.

67.3 Filtering Picker File Listings

The files listed within the picker user interface when an intent is started may be filtered using a variety of options. Consider, for example, the following code to start an ACTION_OPEN_DOCUMENT intent:

```
private static final int OPEN_REQUEST_CODE = 41;


Intent intent = new Intent(Intent.ACTION_OPEN_DOCUMENT);
startActivityForResult(intent, OPEN_REQUEST_CODE);
```

When executed, the above code will cause the picker user interface to be displayed, allowing the user to browse and select any files hosted by available document providers. Once a file has been selected by the user, a reference to that file will be provided to the application in the form of a Uri object. The application can then open the file using the *openFileDescriptor(Uri, String)* method. There is some risk, however, that not all files listed by a document provider can be opened in this way. The exclusion of such files within the picker can be achieved by modifying the intent using the *CATEGORY_OPENABLE* option. For example:

```
private static final int OPEN_REQUEST_CODE = 41;


Intent intent = new Intent(Intent.ACTION_OPEN_DOCUMENT);
intent.addCategory(Intent.CATEGORY_OPENABLE);
startActivityForResult(intent, OPEN_REQUEST_CODE);
```

When the picker is now displayed, files which cannot be opened using the *openFileDescriptor()* method will be listed but not selectable by the user.

Another useful approach to filtering allows the files available for selection to be restricted by file type. This involves specifying the types of the files the application is able to handle. An image editing application might, for example, only want to provide the user with the option of selecting image files from the document providers. This is achieved by configuring the intent object with the MIME types of the files that are to be selectable by the user. The following code, for example, specifies that only image files are suitable for selection in the picker:

```
intent.addCategory(Intent.CATEGORY_OPENABLE);
intent.setType("image/*");
startActivityForResult(intent, OPEN_REQUEST_CODE);
```

This could be further refined to limit selection to JPEG images:

```
intent.setType("image/jpeg");
```

Alternatively, an audio player app might only be able to handle audio files:

```
intent.setType("audio/*");
```

The audio app might be limited even further in only supporting the playback of MP4 based audio files:

```
intent.setType("audio/mp4");
```

A wide range of MIME type settings are available for use when working with the Storage Access Framework, the more common of which can be found listed online at:

https://en.wikipedia.org/wiki/Internet_media_type#List_of_common_media_types

67.4 Handling Intent Results

When an intent returns control to the application, it does so by calling the *onActivityResult()* method of the activity which started the intent. This method is passed the request code that was handed to the intent at launch time, a result code indicating whether or not the intent was successful and a result data object containing the Uri of the selected file. The following code, for example, might be used as the basis for handling the results from the ACTION_OPEN_DOCUMENT intent outlined in the previous section:

```
public void onActivityResult(int requestCode, int resultCode,
        Intent resultData) {

    Uri currentUri = null;

    if (resultCode == Activity.RESULT_OK)
    {
            if (requestCode == OPEN_REQUEST_CODE)
            {
                    if (resultData != null) {
                            currentUri = resultData.getData();
                                readFileContent(currentUri);
                    }
            }
    }
}
```

The above method verifies that the intent was successful, checks that the request code matches that for a file open request and then extracts the Uri from the intent data. The Uri can then be used to read the content of the file.

67.5 Reading the Content of a File

The exact steps required to read the content of a file hosted by a document provider will depend to a large extent on the type of the file. The steps to read lines from a text file, for example, differ from those for image or audio files.

An image file can be assigned to a Bitmap object by extracting the file descriptor from the Uri object and then decoding the image into a BitmapFactory instance. For example:

```
ParcelFileDescriptor pFileDescriptor =
            getContentResolver().openFileDescriptor(uri, "r");

FileDescriptor fileDescriptor =
            pFileDescriptor.getFileDescriptor();

Bitmap image = BitmapFactory.decodeFileDescriptor(fileDescriptor);

pFileDescriptor.close();

myImageView.setImageBitmap(image);
```

Note that the file descriptor is opened in "r" mode. This indicates that the file is to be opened for reading. Other options are "w" for write access and "rwt" for read and write access, where existing content in the file is truncated by the new content.

Reading the content of a text file requires slightly more work and the use of an InputStream object. The following code, for example, reads the lines from a text file:

```
InputStream inputStream = getContentResolver().openInputStream(uri);

BufferedReader reader = new BufferedReader(new InputStreamReader(
                        inputStream));
String readline;

while ((readline = reader.readLine()) != null) {
    // Do something with each line in the file
}
inputStream.close();
```

67.6 Writing Content to a File

Writing to an open file hosted by a document provider is similar to reading with the exception that an output stream is used instead of an input stream. The following code, for example, writes text to the output stream of the storage based file referenced by the specified Uri:

```
try{
        ParcelFileDescriptor pFileDescriptor = this.getContentResolver().
                openFileDescriptor(uri, "w");

        FileOutputStream fileOutputStream =
                new FileOutputStream(pFileDescriptor.getFileDescriptor());
```

```
        String textContent = "Some sample text";
        fileOutputStream.write(textContent.getBytes());
        fileOutputStream.close();
        pFileDescriptor.close();
} catch (FileNotFoundException e) {
        e.printStackTrace();
} catch (IOException e) {
        e.printStackTrace();
}
```

First, the file descriptor is extracted from the Uri, this time requesting write permission to the target file. The file descriptor is subsequently used to obtain a reference to the file's output stream. The content (in this example, some text) is then written to the output stream before the file descriptor and output stream are closed.

67.7 Deleting a File

Whether a file can be deleted from storage depends on whether or not the file's document provider supports deletion of the file. Assuming deletion is permitted, it may be performed on a designated Uri as follows:

```
if (DocumentsContract.deleteDocument(getContentResolver(), uri))
        // Deletion was successful
else
        // Deletion failed
```

67.8 Gaining Persistent Access to a File

When an application gains access to a file via the Storage Access Framework, the access will remain valid until the Android device on which the application is running is restarted. Persistent access to a specific file can be obtained by "taking" the necessary permissions for the Uri. The following code, for example, persists read and write permissions for the file referenced by the *fileUri* Uri instance:

```
final int takeFlags = intent.getFlags()
                & (Intent.FLAG_GRANT_READ_URI_PERMISSION
                | Intent.FLAG_GRANT_WRITE_URI_PERMISSION);


getContentResolver().takePersistableUriPermission(fileUri, takeFlags);
```

Once the permissions for the file have been taken by the application, and assuming the Uri has been saved by the application, the user should be able to continue accessing the file after a device restart without the user having to reselect the file from the picker interface.

If, at any time, the persistent permissions are no longer required, they can be released via a call to the *releasePersistableUriPermission()* method of the content resolver:

```
final int releaseFlags = intent.getFlags()
                & (Intent.FLAG_GRANT_READ_URI_PERMISSION
                | Intent.FLAG_GRANT_WRITE_URI_PERMISSION);


getContentResolver().releasePersistableUriPermission(fileUri,
                                releaseFlags);
```

67.9 Summary

It is interesting to consider how perceptions of storage have changed in recent years. Once synonymous with high capacity internal hard disk drives, the term "storage" is now just as likely to refer to storage space hosted remotely in the cloud and accessed over an internet connection. This is increasingly the case with the wide adoption of resource constrained, "always-connected" mobile devices with minimal internal storage capacity.

The Android Storage Access Framework provides a simple mechanism for both users and application developers to seamlessly gain access to files stored in the cloud. Through the use of a set of intents and a built-in user interface for selecting document providers and files, comprehensive cloud based storage can now be integrated into Android applications with a minimal amount of coding.

68. An Android Storage Access Framework Example

As previously discussed, the Storage Access Framework considerably eases the process of integrating cloud based storage access into Android applications. Consisting of a picker user interface and a set of new intents, access to files stored on document providers such as Google Drive and Box can now be built into Android applications with relative ease. With the basics of the Android Storage Access Framework covered in the preceding chapter, this chapter will work through the creation of an example application which uses the Storage Access Framework to store and manage files.

68.1 About the Storage Access Framework Example

The Android application created in this chapter will take the form of a rudimentary text editor designed to create and store text files remotely onto a cloud based storage service. In practice, the example will work with any cloud based document storage provider that is compatible with the Storage Access Framework, though for the purpose of this example the use of Google Drive is assumed.

In functional terms, the application will present the user with a multi-line text view into which text may be entered and edited, together with a set of buttons allowing storage based text files to be created, opened and saved.

68.2 Creating the Storage Access Framework Example

Select the *Start a new Android Studio project* quick start option from the welcome screen and, within the resulting new project dialog, choose the Empty Activity template before clicking on the Next button.

Enter *StorageDemo* into the Name field and specify *com.ebookfrenzy.storagedemo* as the package name. Before clicking on the Finish button, change the Minimum API level setting to API 26: Android 8.0 (Oreo) and the Language menu to Java.

68.3 Designing the User Interface

The user interface will need to be comprised of three Button views and a single EditText view. Within the Project tool window, navigate to the *activity_main.xml* layout file located in *app -> res -> layout* and double-click on it to load it into the Layout Editor tool. With the tool in Design mode, select and delete the *Hello World!* TextView object.

Drag and position a Button widget in the top left-hand corner of the layout so that both the left and top dotted margin guidelines appear before dropping the widget in place. Position a second Button such that the center and top margin guidelines appear. The third Button widget should then be placed so that the top and right-hand margin guidelines appear.

Change the text attributes on the three buttons to "New", "Open" and "Save" respectively. Next, position a Plain Text widget so that it is centered horizontally and positioned beneath the center Button so that the user interface layout matches that shown in Figure 68-1. Use the Infer Constraints button in the Layout Editor toolbar to add any missing constraints.

Select the Plain Text widget in the layout, delete the current text property setting so that the field is initially blank and set the ID to *fileText*, remembering to extract all the string attributes to resource values:

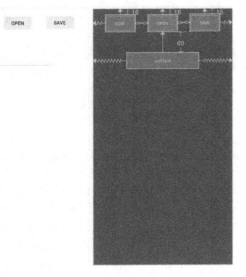

Figure 68-1

Using the Attributes tool window, configure the onClick property on the Button widgets to call methods named *newFile*, *openFile* and *saveFile* respectively.

68.4 Declaring Request Codes

Working with files in the Storage Access Framework involves triggering a variety of intents depending on the specific action to be performed. Invariably this will result in the framework displaying the storage picker user interface so that the user can specify the storage location (such as a directory on Google Drive and the name of a file). When the work of the intent is complete, the application will be notified by a call to a method named *onActivityResult()*.

Since all intents from a single activity will result in a call to the same *onActivityResult()* method, a mechanism is required to identify which intent triggered the call. This can be achieved by passing a request code through to the intent when it is launched. This code is then passed on to the *onActivityResult()* method by the intents, enabling the method to identify which action has been requested by the user. Before implementing the onClick handlers to create, save and open files, the first step is to declare some request codes for these three actions.

Locate and load the *MainActivity.java* file into the editor and declare constant values for the three actions to be performed by the application. Also, add some code to obtain a reference to the multi-line EditText object which will be referenced in later methods:

```
package com.ebookfrenzy.storagedemo;

import androidx.appcompat.app.AppCompatActivity;
import android.os.Bundle;
import android.widget.EditText;

public class MainActivity extends AppCompatActivity {

    private static EditText textView;
```

```
private static final int CREATE_REQUEST_CODE = 40;
private static final int OPEN_REQUEST_CODE = 41;
private static final int SAVE_REQUEST_CODE = 42;


@Override
protected void onCreate(Bundle savedInstanceState) {
    super.onCreate(savedInstanceState);
    setContentView(R.layout.activity_storage_demo);


    textView = findViewById(R.id.fileText);

}

}
```

68.5 Creating a New Storage File

When the New button is selected, the application will need to trigger an *ACTION_CREATE_DOCUMENT* intent configured to create a file with a plain-text MIME type. When the user interface was designed, the New button was configured to call a method named *newFile()*. It is within this method that the appropriate intent needs to be launched.

Remaining in the *MainActivity.java* file, implement this method as follows:

```
package com.ebookfrenzy.storagedemo;


import android.app.Activity;
import androidx.appcompat.app.AppCompatActivity;
import android.os.Bundle;
import android.widget.EditText;
import android.content.Intent;
import android.view.View;
import android.net.Uri;


public class MainActivity extends AppCompatActivity {

    private static EditText textView;

    private static final int CREATE_REQUEST_CODE = 40;
    private static final int OPEN_REQUEST_CODE = 41;
    private static final int SAVE_REQUEST_CODE = 42;

    .

    .

    .

    public void newFile(View view)
    {
        Intent intent = new Intent(Intent.ACTION_CREATE_DOCUMENT);

        intent.addCategory(Intent.CATEGORY_OPENABLE);
        intent.setType("text/plain");
```

```
        intent.putExtra(Intent.EXTRA_TITLE, "newfile.txt");

        startActivityForResult(intent, CREATE_REQUEST_CODE);
    }
    .
    .
}
```

This code creates a new ACTION_CREATE_INTENT Intent object. This intent is then configured so that only files that can be opened with a file descriptor are returned (via the Intent.CATEGORY_OPENABLE category setting).

Next the code specifies that the file to be opened is to have a plain text MIME type and a placeholder filename is provided (which can be changed by the user in the picker interface). Finally, the intent is started, passing through the previously declared *CREATE_REQUEST_CODE*.

When this method is executed and the intent has completed the assigned task, a call will be made to the application's *onActivityResult()* method and passed, amongst other arguments, the Uri of the newly created document and the request code that was used when the intent was started. Now is an ideal opportunity to begin to implement this method.

68.6 The onActivityResult() Method

The *onActivityResult()* method will be shared by all of the intents that will be called during the lifecycle of the application. In each case, the method will be passed a request code, a result code and a set of result data which contains the Uri of the storage file. The method will need to be implemented such that it checks for the success of the intent action, identifies the type of action performed and extracts the file Uri from the results data. At this point in the tutorial, the method only needs to handle the creation of a new file on the selected document provider, so modify the *MainActivity.java* file to add this method as follows:

```
public void onActivityResult(int requestCode, int resultCode,
        Intent resultData) {

    if (resultCode == Activity.RESULT_OK)
    {
        if (requestCode == CREATE_REQUEST_CODE)
        {
            if (resultData != null) {
                textView.setText("");
            }
        }

    }
}
```

The code in this method is largely straightforward. The result of the activity is checked and, if successful, the request code is compared to the CREATE_REQUEST_CODE value to verify that the user is creating a new file. That being the case, the edit text view is cleared of any previous text to signify the creation of a new file.

Compile and run the application and select the New button. The Storage Access Framework should subsequently display the Downloads user interface as illustrated in Figure 68-3:

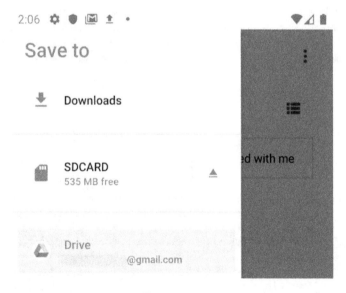

Figure 68-2

Select the menu button highlighted above and select the *Drive* option followed by *My Drive* and navigate to a suitable location on your Google Drive storage into which to save the file. In the text field at the bottom of the picker interface, change the name from "newfile.txt" to a suitable name (but keeping the *.txt* extension) before selecting the *Save* option.

Figure 68-3

Once the new file has been created, the app should return to the main activity and a notification will appear within the notifications panel which reads "1 file uploaded".

Figure 68-4

At this point, it should be possible to log into your Google Drive account in a browser window and find the newly created file in the requested location. In the event that the file is missing, make sure that the Android device on which the application is running has an active internet connection. Access to Google Drive on the device may also be verified by running the Google *Drive* app, which is installed by default on many Android devices, and available for download from the Google Play store.

68.7 Saving to a Storage File

Now that the application is able to create new storage based files, the next step is to add the ability to save any text entered by the user to a file. The user interface is configured to call the *saveFile()* method when the Save button is selected by the user. This method will be responsible for starting a new intent of type *ACTION_OPEN_DOCUMENT* which will result in the picker user interface appearing so that the user can choose the file to which the text is to be stored. Since we are only working with plain text files, the intent needs to be configured to restrict the user's selection options to existing files that match the text/plain MIME type. Having identified the actions to be performed by the *saveFile()* method, this can now be added to the *MainActivity.java* class file as follows:

```
public void saveFile(View view)
{
        Intent intent = new Intent(Intent.ACTION_OPEN_DOCUMENT);
        intent.addCategory(Intent.CATEGORY_OPENABLE);
        intent.setType("text/plain");

        startActivityForResult(intent, SAVE_REQUEST_CODE);
}
```

Since the SAVE_REQUEST_CODE was passed through to the intent, the *onActivityResult()* method must now be extended to handle save actions:

```
        public void onActivityResult(int requestCode, int resultCode,
            Intent resultData) {

            Uri currentUri = null;

            if (resultCode == Activity.RESULT_OK)
            {
                    if (requestCode == CREATE_REQUEST_CODE)
                    {
```

```
                if (resultData != null) {
                        textView.setText("");
                }
        } else if (requestCode == SAVE_REQUEST_CODE) {

                if (resultData != null) {
                    currentUri =
                            resultData.getData();
                    writeFileContent(currentUri);
                }
        }
    }
}
}
```

The method now checks for the save request code, extracts the Uri of the file selected by the user in the storage picker and calls a method named *writeFileContent()*, passing through the Uri of the file to which the text is to be written. Remaining in the *MainActivity.java* file, implement this method now so that it reads as follows:

```
package com.ebookfrenzy.storagedemo;

import java.io.FileNotFoundException;
import java.io.FileOutputStream;
import java.io.IOException;

import android.app.Activity;
import androidx.appcompat.app.AppCompatActivity;
import android.os.Bundle;
import android.widget.EditText;
import android.content.Intent;
import android.view.View;
import android.net.Uri;
import android.os.ParcelFileDescriptor;

public class MainActivity extends AppCompatActivity {

.

.

    private void writeFileContent(Uri uri)
    {
        try{
                ParcelFileDescriptor pfd =
                        this.getContentResolver().
                            openFileDescriptor(uri, "w");

                FileOutputStream fileOutputStream =
                    new FileOutputStream(
                        pfd.getFileDescriptor());
```

```
                    String textContent =
                        textView.getText().toString();

                    fileOutputStream.write(textContent.getBytes());

                    fileOutputStream.close();
                    pfd.close();
            } catch (FileNotFoundException e) {
                    e.printStackTrace();
            } catch (IOException e) {
                    e.printStackTrace();
            }
        }
.
.
.
}
```

The method begins by obtaining and opening the file descriptor from the Uri of the file selected by the user. Since the code will need to write to the file, the descriptor is opened in write mode ("w"). The file descriptor is then used as the basis for creating an output stream that will enable the application to write to the file.

The text entered by the user is extracted from the edit text object and written to the output stream before both the file descriptor and stream are closed. Code is also added to handle any IO exceptions encountered during the file writing process.

With the new method added, compile and run the application, enter some text into the text view and select the *Save* button. From the picker interface, locate the previously created file from the Google Drive storage to save the text to that file. Return to your Google Drive account in a browser window and select the text file to display the contents. The file should now contain the text entered within the StorageDemo application on the Android device.

68.8 Opening and Reading a Storage File

Having written the code to create and save text files, the final task is to add some functionality to open and read a file from the storage. This will involve writing the *openFile()* onClick event handler method and implementing it so that it starts an ACTION_OPEN_DOCUMENT intent:

```
public void openFile(View view)
{
        Intent intent = new Intent(Intent.ACTION_OPEN_DOCUMENT);
        intent.addCategory(Intent.CATEGORY_OPENABLE);
        intent.setType("text/plain");
        startActivityForResult(intent, OPEN_REQUEST_CODE);
}
```

In this code, the intent is configured to filter selection to files which can be opened by the application. When the activity is started, it is passed the open request code constant which will now need to be handled within the *onActivityResult()* method:

```
public void onActivityResult(int requestCode, int resultCode,
        Intent resultData) {
```

```
        Uri currentUri = null;

        if (resultCode == Activity.RESULT_OK)
        {

                if (requestCode == CREATE_REQUEST_CODE)
                {
                        if (resultData != null) {
                                textView.setText("");
                        }
                } else if (requestCode == SAVE_REQUEST_CODE) {

                        if (resultData != null) {
                                currentUri = resultData.getData();
                                writeFileContent(currentUri);
                        }
                } else if (requestCode == OPEN_REQUEST_CODE) {

                        if (resultData != null) {
                                currentUri = resultData.getData();

                                try {
                                    String content =
                                                readFileContent(currentUri);
                                        textView.setText(content);
                                } catch (IOException e) {
                                        // Handle error here
                                }
                        }
                }
        }
}
```

The new code added above to handle the open request obtains the Uri of the file selected by the user from the picker user interface and passes it through to a method named *readFileContent()* which is expected to return the content of the selected file in the form of a String object. The resulting string is then assigned to the text property of the edit text view. Clearly, the next task is to implement the *readFileContent()* method:

```
package com.ebookfrenzy.storagedemo;

import java.io.FileNotFoundException;
import java.io.FileOutputStream;
import java.io.IOException;
import java.io.BufferedReader;
import java.io.InputStream;
import java.io.InputStreamReader;
```

```java
import java.io.BufferedReader;
import java.io.InputStream;
import java.io.InputStreamReader;

import android.app.Activity;
import android.support.v7.app.AppCompatActivity;
import android.os.Bundle;
import android.widget.EditText;
import android.content.Intent;
import android.view.View;
import android.net.Uri;
import android.os.ParcelFileDescriptor;

public class MainActivity extends AppCompatActivity {
.
.

    private String readFileContent(Uri uri) throws IOException {

        InputStream inputStream =
                    getContentResolver().openInputStream(uri);
        BufferedReader reader =
            new BufferedReader(new InputStreamReader(
                    inputStream));
        StringBuilder stringBuilder = new StringBuilder();
        String currentline;
        while ((currentline = reader.readLine()) != null) {
            stringBuilder.append(currentline + "\n");
        }
        inputStream.close();
        return stringBuilder.toString();
    }
.
.
}
```

This method begins by extracting the file descriptor for the selected text file and opening it for reading. The input stream associated with the Uri is then opened and used as the input source for a BufferedReader instance. Each line within the file is then read and stored in a StringBuilder object. Once all the lines have been read, the input stream and file descriptor are both closed, and the file content is returned as a String object.

68.9 Testing the Storage Access Application

With the coding phase complete the application is now ready to be fully tested. Begin by launching the application on an Android device or AVD configured with your Google account identity and selecting the "New" button. Within the resulting storage picker interface, select a Google Drive location and name the text file *storagedemo. txt* before selecting the Save option located to the right of the file name field.

When control returns to your application look for the file uploading notification, then enter some text into the text area before selecting the "Save" button. Select the previously created *storagedemo.txt* file from the picker to save the content to the file. On returning to the application, delete the text and select the "Open" button, once again choosing the *storagedemo.txt* file. When control is returned to the application, the text view should have been populated with the content of the text file.

It is important to note that the Storage Access Framework will cache storage files locally in the event that the Android device lacks an active internet connection. Once connectivity is re-established, however, any cached data will be synchronized with the remote storage service. As a final test of the application, therefore, log into your Google Drive account in a browser window, navigate to the *storagedemo.txt* file and click on it to view the content which should, all being well, contain the text saved by the application.

68.10 Summary

This chapter has worked through the creation of an example Android Studio application in the form of a very rudimentary text editor designed to use cloud based storage to create, save and open files using the Android Storage Access Framework.

69. Implementing Video Playback on Android using the VideoView and MediaController Classes

One of the primary uses for smartphones and tablets is to provide access to online content. One key form of content widely used, especially in the case of tablet devices, is video.

The Android SDK includes two classes that make the implementation of video playback on Android devices extremely easy to implement when developing applications. This chapter will provide an overview of these two classes, VideoView and MediaController, before working through the creation of a simple video playback application.

69.1 Introducing the Android VideoView Class

By far the simplest way to display video within an Android application is to use the VideoView class. This is a visual component which, when added to the layout of an activity, provides a surface onto which a video may be played. Android currently supports the following video formats:

- H.263

- H.264 AVC

- H.265 HEVC

- MPEG-4 SP

- VP8

- VP9

The VideoView class has a wide range of methods that may be called in order to manage the playback of video. Some of the more commonly used methods are as follows:

- **setVideoPath(String path)** – Specifies the path (as a string) of the video media to be played. This can be either the URL of a remote video file or a video file local to the device.

- **setVideoUri(Uri uri)** – Performs the same task as the *setVideoPath()* method but takes a Uri object as an argument instead of a string.

- **start()** – Starts video playback.

- **stopPlayback()** – Stops the video playback.

- **pause()** – Pauses video playback.

- **isPlaying()** – Returns a Boolean value indicating whether a video is currently playing.

- **setOnPreparedListener(MediaPlayer.OnPreparedListener)** – Allows a callback method to be called when the video is ready to play.

- **setOnErrorListener(MediaPlayer.OnErrorListener)** - Allows a callback method to be called when an error occurs during the video playback.

- **setOnCompletionListener(MediaPlayer.OnCompletionListener)** - Allows a callback method to be called when the end of the video is reached.

- **getDuration()** – Returns the duration of the video. Will typically return -1 unless called from within the *OnPreparedListener()* callback method.

- **getCurrentPosition()** – Returns an integer value indicating the current position of playback.

- **setMediaController(MediaController)** – Designates a MediaController instance allowing playback controls to be displayed to the user.

69.2 Introducing the Android MediaController Class

If a video is simply played using the VideoView class, the user will not be given any control over the playback, which will run until the end of the video is reached. This issue can be addressed by attaching an instance of the MediaController class to the VideoView instance. The MediaController will then provide a set of controls allowing the user to manage the playback (such as pausing and seeking backwards/forwards in the video time-line).

The position of the controls is designated by anchoring the controller instance to a specific view in the user interface layout. Once attached and anchored, the controls will appear briefly when playback starts and may subsequently be restored at any point by the user tapping on the view to which the instance is anchored.

Some of the key methods of this class are as follows:

- **setAnchorView(View view)** – Designates the view to which the controller is to be anchored. This designates the location of the controls on the screen.

- **show()** – Displays the controls.

- **show(int timeout)** – Controls are displayed for the designated duration (in milliseconds).

- **hide()** – Hides the controller from the user.

- **isShowing()** – Returns a Boolean value indicating whether the controls are currently visible to the user.

69.3 Creating the Video Playback Example

The remainder of this chapter will create an example application intended to use the VideoView and MediaController classes to play a web based MPEG-4 video file.

Select the *Start a new Android Studio project* quick start option from the welcome screen and, within the resulting new project dialog, choose the Empty Activity template before clicking on the Next button.

Enter *VideoPlayer* into the Name field and specify *com.ebookfrenzy.videoplayer* as the package name. Before clicking on the Finish button, change the Minimum API level setting to API 26: Android 8.0 (Oreo) and the Language menu to Java.

69.4 Designing the VideoPlayer Layout

The user interface for the main activity will consist solely of an instance of the VideoView class. Use the Project tool window to locate the *app -> res -> layout -> activity_main.xml* file, double-click on it, switch the Layout

Editor tool to Design mode and delete the default TextView widget.

From the Widgets category of the Palette panel, drag and drop a VideoView instance onto the layout so that it fills the available canvas area as shown in Figure 69-1. Using the Attributes panel, change the layout_width and layout_height attributes to *match_constraint* and *wrap_content* respectively. Also, remove the constraint connecting the bottom of the VideoView to the bottom of the parent ConstraintLayout. Finally, change the ID of the component to *videoView1*.

Figure 69-1

69.5 Configuring the VideoView

The next step is to configure the VideoView with the path of the video to be played and then start the playback. This will be performed when the main activity has initialized, so load the *MainActivity.java* file into the editor and modify it as outlined in the following listing:

```
package com.ebookfrenzy.videoplayer;

import androidx.appcompat.app.AppCompatActivity;
import android.os.Bundle;
import android.widget.VideoView;

public class MainActivity extends AppCompatActivity {

    private VideoView videoView;

    @Override
    protected void onCreate(Bundle savedInstanceState) {
        super.onCreate(savedInstanceState);
        setContentView(R.layout.activity_video_player);
        configureVideoView();
    }
```

```
    private void configureVideoView() {

        videoView =
                findViewById(R.id.videoView1);

        videoView.setVideoPath(
                "https://www.ebookfrenzy.com/android_book/movie.mp4");

        videoView.start();
    }
}
```

All that this code does is obtain a reference to the VideoView instance in the layout, set the video path on it to point to an MPEG-4 file hosted on a web site and then start the video playing.

69.6 Adding Internet Permission

An attempt to run the application at this point would result in the application failing to launch with an error dialog appearing on the Android device that reads "Unable to Play Video. Sorry, this video cannot be played". This is not because of an error in the code or an incorrect video file format. The issue would be that the application is attempting to access a file over the internet, but has failed to request appropriate permissions to do so. To resolve this, edit the *AndroidManifest.xml* file for the project and add a line to request internet access:

```
<?xml version="1.0" encoding="utf-8"?>
<manifest xmlns:android="http://schemas.android.com/apk/res/android"
    package="com.ebookfrenzy.videoplayer" >

    <uses-permission android:name="android.permission.INTERNET" />

    <application
        android:allowBackup="true"
        android:icon="@mipmap/ic_launcher"
        android:label="@string/app_name"
        android:supportsRtl="true"
        android:theme="@style/AppTheme" >
        .
        .
        .
</manifest>
```

Test the application by running it on a physical Android device. After the application launches there may be a short delay while video content is buffered before the playback begins (Figure 69-2).

Figure 69-2

This provides an indication of how easy it can be to integrate video playback into an Android application. Everything so far in this example has been achieved using a VideoView instance and three lines of code.

69.7 Adding the MediaController to the Video View

As the VideoPlayer application currently stands, there is no way for the user to control playback. As previously outlined, this can be achieved using the MediaController class. To add a controller to the VideoView, modify the *configureVideoView()* method once again:

```
package com.ebookfrenzy.videoplayer;

import androidx.appcompat.app.AppCompatActivity;
import android.os.Bundle;
import android.widget.VideoView;
import android.widget.MediaController;

public class MainActivity extends AppCompatActivity {

    private VideoView videoView;
    private MediaController mediaController;

.
.

    private void configureVideoView() {

        final VideoView videoView =
                findViewById(R.id.videoView1);

        videoView.setVideoPath(
                "https://www.ebookfrenzy.com/android_book/movie.mp4");

        mediaController = new MediaController(this);
        mediaController.setAnchorView(videoView);
        videoView.setMediaController(mediaController);
```

```
        videoView.start();


    }
}
```

When the application is launched with these changes implemented, tapping the VideoView canvas will cause the media controls to appear over the video playback. These controls should include a seekbar together with fast forward, rewind and play/pause buttons. After the controls recede from view, they can be restored at any time by tapping on the VideoView canvas once again. With just three more lines of code, our video player application now has media controls as shown in Figure 69-3:

Figure 69-3

69.8 Setting up the onPreparedListener

As a final example of working with video based media, the activity will now be extended further to demonstrate the mechanism for configuring a listener. In this case, a listener will be implemented that is intended to output the duration of the video as a message in the Android Studio Logcat panel. The listener will also configure video playback to loop continuously:

```
package com.ebookfrenzy.videoplayer;


import android.support.v7.app.AppCompatActivity;
import android.os.Bundle;
import android.widget.VideoView;
import android.widget.MediaController;
import android.util.Log;
import android.media.MediaPlayer;


public class MainActivity extends AppCompatActivity {

    private VideoView videoView;
    private MediaController mediaController;
    String TAG = "VideoPlayer";

    private void configureVideoView() {

        final VideoView videoView =
                findViewById(R.id.videoView1);

        videoView.setVideoPath(
                "http://www.ebookfrenzy.com/android_book/movie.mp4");

        MediaController mediaController = new
```

```
        MediaController(this);
mediaController.setAnchorView(videoView);
videoView.setMediaController(mediaController);

videoView.setOnPreparedListener(new
        MediaPlayer.OnPreparedListener()  {
            @Override
            public void onPrepared(MediaPlayer mp) {
                mp.setLooping(true);
                Log.i(TAG, "Duration = " +
                        videoView.getDuration());
            }
        });
videoView.start();
    }
}
```

Now just before the video playback begins, a message will appear in the Android Studio Logcat panel that reads along the lines of the following and the video will restart after playback ends:

```
11-05 10:27:52.256 12542-12542/com.ebookfrenzy.videoplayer I/VideoPlayer:
Duration = 6874
```

69.9 Summary

Android devices make excellent platforms for the delivery of content to users, particularly in the form of video media. As outlined in this chapter, the Android SDK provides two classes, namely VideoView and MediaController, which combine to make the integration of video playback into Android applications quick and easy, often involving just a few lines of Java code.

Chapter 70

70. Android Picture-in-Picture Mode

When multi-tasking in Android was covered in earlier chapters, Picture-in-picture (PiP) mode was mentioned briefly but not covered in any detail. Intended primarily for video playback, PiP mode allows an activity screen to be reduced in size and positioned at any location on the screen. While in this state, the activity continues to run and the window remains visible regardless of any other activities running on the device. This allows the user to, for example, continue watching video playback while performing tasks such as checking email or working on a spreadsheet.

This chapter will provide an overview of Picture-in-Picture mode before Picture-in-Picture support is added to the VideoPlayer project in the next chapter.

70.1 Picture-in-Picture Features

As will be explained later in the chapter, and demonstrated in the next chapter, an activity is placed into PiP mode via an API call from within the running app. When placed into PiP mode, configuration options may be specified that control the aspect ratio of the PiP window and also to define the area of the activity screen that is to be included in the window. Figure 70-1, for example, shows a video playback activity in PiP mode:

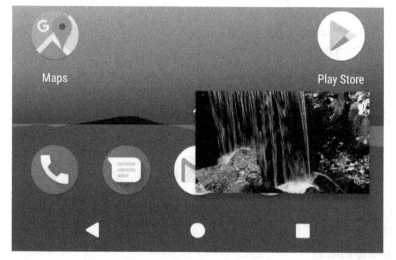

Figure 70-1

Figure 70-2 shows a PiP mode window after it has been tapped by the user. When in this mode, the window appears larger and includes a full screen action in the center which, when tapped, restores the window to full screen mode and an exit button in the top right-hand corner to close the window and place the app in the background. Any custom actions added to the PiP window will also appear on the screen when it is displayed in this mode. In the case of Figure 70-2, the PiP window includes custom play and pause action buttons:

Figure 70-2

The remainder of this chapter will outline how PiP mode is enabled and managed from within an Android app.

70.2 Enabling Picture-in-Picture Mode

PiP mode is currently only supported on devices running API 26: Android 8.0 (Oreo) or newer. The first step in implementing PiP mode is to enable it within the project's manifest file. PiP mode is configured on a per activity basis by adding the following lines to each activity element for which PiP support is required:

```
<activity android:name=".MyActivity"
    android:supportsPictureInPicture="true"
    android:configChanges=
        "screenSize|smallestScreenSize|screenLayout|orientation"
    <intent-filter>
        <action android:name="android.intent.action.MAIN" />
        <category android:name="android.intent.category.LAUNCHER" />
    </intent-filter>
</activity>
```

The *android:supportsPictureInPicture* entry enables PiP for the activity while the *android:configChanges* property notifies Android that the activity is able to handle layout configuration changes. Without this setting, each time the activity moves in and out of PiP mode the activity will be restarted resulting in playback restarting from the beginning of the video during the transition.

70.3 Configuring Picture-in-Picture Parameters

PiP behavior is defined through the use of the PictureInPictureParams class, instances of which can be created using the Builder class as follows:

```
PictureInPictureParams params =
                new PictureInPictureParams.Builder().build();
```

The above code creates a default PictureInPictureParams instance with special parameters defined. The following optional method calls may also be used to customize the parameters:

- **setActions()** – Used to define actions that can be performed from within the PiP window while the activity is in PiP mode. Actions will be covered in more detail later in this chapter.

- **setAspectRatio()** – Declares the preferred aspect ratio for appearance of the PiP window. This method takes as an argument a Rational object containing the height width / height ratio.

- **setSourceRectHint()** – Takes as an argument a Rect object defining the area of the activity screen to be displayed within the PiP window.

The following code, for example, configures aspect ratio and action parameters within a PictureInPictureParams object. In the case of the aspect ratio, this is defined using the width and height dimensions of a VideoView instance:

```
Rational rational = new Rational(videoView.getWidth(),
                                 videoView.getHeight());


PictureInPictureParams params =
        new PictureInPictureParams.Builder()
                .setAspectRatio(rational)
                .setActions(actions)
                .build();
```

Once defined, PiP parameters may be set at any time using the *setPictureInPictureParams()* method as follows:

```
setPictureInPictureParams(params);
```

Parameters may also be specified when entering PiP mode.

70.4 Entering Picture-in-Picture Mode

An activity is placed into Picture-in-Picture mode via a call to the *enterPictureInPictureMode()* method, passing through a PictureInPictureParams object:

```
enterPictureInPictureMode(params);
```

If no parameters are required, simply create a default PictureInPictureParams object as outlined in the previous section. If parameters have previously been set using the *setPictureInPictureParams()* method, these parameters are combined with those specified during the *enterPictureInPictureMode()* method call.

70.5 Detecting Picture-in-Picture Mode Changes

When an activity enters PiP mode, it is important to hide any unnecessary views so that only the video playback is visible within the PiP window. When the activity re-enters full screen mode, any hidden user interface components need to be re-instated. These and any other app specific tasks can be performed by overriding the *onPictureInPictureModeChanged()* method. When added to the activity, this method is called each time the activity transitions between PiP and full screen modes and is passed a Boolean value indicating whether the activity is currently in PiP mode:

```
@Override
public void onPictureInPictureModeChanged(
                    boolean isInPictureInPictureMode) {

    super.onPictureInPictureModeChanged(isInPictureInPictureMode);

    if (isInPictureInPictureMode) {
        // Acitivity entered Picture-in-Picture mode
    } else {
        // Activity entered full screen mode
    }
```

}

70.6 Adding Picture-in-Picture Actions

Picture-in-Picture actions appear as icons within the PiP window when it is tapped by the user. Implementation of PiP actions is a multi-step process that begins with implementing a way for the PiP window to notify the activity that an action has been selected. This is achieved by setting up a broadcast receiver within the activity, and then creating a pending intent within the PiP action which, in turn, is configured to broadcast an intent for which the broadcast receiver is listening. When the broadcast receiver is triggered by the intent, the data stored in the intent can be used to identify the action performed and to take the necessary action within the activity.

PiP actions are declared using the RemoteAction instances which are initialized with an icon, a title, a description and the PendingIntent object. Once one or more actions have been created, they are added to an ArrayList and passed through to the *setActions()* method while building a PictureInPictureParams object.

The following code fragment demonstrates the creation of the Intent, PendingIntent and RemoteAction objects together with a PictureInPictureParams instance which is then applied to the activity's PiP settings:

```
final ArrayList<RemoteAction> actions = new ArrayList<>();

Intent actionIntent = new Intent("MY_PIP_ACTION");

final PendingIntent pendingIntent =
            PendingIntent.getBroadcast(MyActivity.this,
                        REQUEST_CODE, actionIntent, 0);

final Icon icon = Icon.createWithResource(MyActivity.this,
                        R.drawable.action_icon);

RemoteAction remoteAction = new RemoteAction(icon,
                        "My Action Title",
                        "My Action Description",
                        pendingIntent);

actions.add(remoteAction);

PictureInPictureParams params =
        new PictureInPictureParams.Builder()
                .setActions(actions)
                .build();

setPictureInPictureParams(params);
```

70.7 Summary

Picture-in-Picture mode is a multitasking feature introduced with Android 8.0 designed specifically to allow video playback to continue in a small window while the user performs tasks in other apps and activities. Before PiP mode can be used, it must first be enabled within the manifest file for those activities that require PiP support.

PiP mode behavior is configured using instances of the PictureInPictureParams class and initiated via a call to the *enterPictureInPictureMode()* method from within the activity. When in PiP mode, only the video playback should be visible, requiring that any other user interface elements be hidden until full screen mode is selected. These and other mode transition related tasks can be performed by overriding the *onPictureInPictureModeChanged()* method.

PiP actions appear as icons overlaid onto the PiP window when it is tapped by the user. When selected, these actions trigger behavior within the activity. The activity is notified of an action by the PiP window using broadcast receivers and pending intents.

71. An Android Picture-in-Picture Tutorial

Following on from the previous chapters, this chapter will take the existing VideoPlayer project and enhance it to add Picture-in-Picture support, including detecting PiP mode changes and the addition of a PiP action designed to display information about the currently running video.

71.1 Adding Picture-in-Picture Support to the Manifest

The first step in adding PiP support to an Android app project is to enable it within the project Manifest file. Open the *manifests -> AndroidManifest.xml* file and modify the activity element to enable PiP support:

```
.
.
<activity android:name=".MainActivity"
 android:supportsPictureInPicture="true"
 android:configChanges="screenSize|smallestScreenSize|screenLayout|orientation">
    <intent-filter>
        <action android:name="android.intent.action.MAIN" />
        <category android:name="android.intent.category.LAUNCHER" />
    </intent-filter>
</activity>
.
.
```

71.2 Adding a Picture-in-Picture Button

As currently designed, the layout for the VideoPlayer activity consists solely of a VideoView instance. A button will now be added to the layout for the purpose of switching into PiP mode. Load the *activity_main.xml* file into the layout editor and drag a Button object from the palette onto the layout so that it is positioned as shown in Figure 71-1:

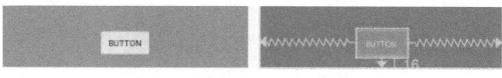

Figure 71-1

Change the text on the button so that it reads "Enter PiP Mode" and extract the string to a resource named *enter_pip_mode*. Before moving on to the next step, change the ID of the button to *pipButton* and configure the button to call a method named *enterPipMode*.

71.3 Entering Picture-in-Picture Mode

The *enterPipMode* onClick callback method now needs to be added to the *MainActivity.java* class file. Locate this file, open it in the code editor and add this method as follows:

.

.

```
import android.view.View;
import android.app.PictureInPictureParams;
import android.util.Rational;
import android.widget.Button;

.

.

public void enterPipMode(View view) {

    Button pipButton = findViewById(R.id.pipButton);

    Rational rational = new Rational(videoView.getWidth(),
            videoView.getHeight());

    PictureInPictureParams params =
            new PictureInPictureParams.Builder()
                    .setAspectRatio(rational)
                    .build();

    pipButton.setVisibility(View.INVISIBLE);
    videoView.setMediaController(null);
    enterPictureInPictureMode(params);
}
```

The method begins by obtaining a reference to the Button view, then creates a Rational object containing the width and height of the VideoView. A set of Picture-in-Picture parameters is then created using the PictureInPictureParams Builder, passing through the Rational object as the aspect ratio for the video playback. Since the button does not need to be visible while the video is in PiP mode it is made invisible. The video playback controls are also hidden from view so that the video view will be unobstructed while in PiP mode.

Compile and run the app on a device or emulator running Android version 8 or newer and wait for video playback to begin before clicking on the PiP mode button. The video playback should minimize and appear in the PiP window as shown in Figure 71-2:

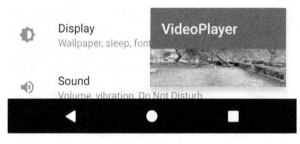

Figure 71-2

Although the video is now playing in the PiP window, much of the view is obscured by the standard Android action bar. To remove this requires a change to the application theme style of the activity. Within Android Studio, locate and edit the *app -> res -> styles.xml* file and modify the AppTheme element to use the *NoActionBar* theme:

```
<resources>
    <!-- Base application theme. -->
    <style name="AppTheme" parent="Theme.AppCompat.Light.NoActionBar">
        <!-- Customize your theme here. -->
        <item name="colorPrimary">@color/colorPrimary</item>
        <item name="colorPrimaryDark">@color/colorPrimaryDark</item>
        <item name="colorAccent">@color/colorAccent</item>
    </style>
</resources>
```

Compile and run the app, place the video playback into PiP mode and note that the action bar no longer appears in the window:

Figure 71-3

Click in the PiP window so that it increases in size, then click within the full screen mode markers that appear in the center of the window. Although the activity returns to full screen mode, note the button and media playback controls remain hidden.

Clearly some code needs to be added to the project to detect when PiP mode changes take place within the activity.

71.4 Detecting Picture-in-Picture Mode Changes

As discussed in the previous chapter, PiP mode changes are detected by overriding the *onPictureInPictureModeChanged()* method within the affected activity. In this case, the method needs to be written such that it can detect whether the activity is entering or exiting PiP mode and to take appropriate action to re-activate the PiP button and the playback controls. Remaining within the *MainActivity.java* file, add this method now:

```
@Override
public void onPictureInPictureModeChanged(boolean isInPictureInPictureMode) {
    super.onPictureInPictureModeChanged(isInPictureInPictureMode);

    Button pipButton = findViewById(R.id.pipButton);

    if (isInPictureInPictureMode) {

    } else {
        pipButton.setVisibility(View.VISIBLE);
        videoView.setMediaController(mediaController);
    }
```

```
}
```

When the method is called, it is passed a Boolean value indicating whether the activity is now in PiP mode. The code in the above method simply checks this value to decide whether to show the PiP button and to re-activate the playback controls.

71.5 Adding a Broadcast Receiver

The final step in the project is to add an action to the PiP window. The purpose of this action is to display a Toast message containing the name of the currently playing video. This will require some communication between the PiP window and the activity. One of the simplest ways to achieve this is to implement a broadcast receiver within the activity, and the use of a pending intent to broadcast a message from the PiP window to the activity. These steps will need to be performed each time the activity enters PiP mode so code will need to be added to the *onPictureInPictureModeChanged()* method. Locate this method now and begin by adding some code to create an intent filter and initialize the broadcast receiver:

```
.
.
import android.content.BroadcastReceiver;
import android.content.Context;
import android.content.Intent;
import android.content.IntentFilter;
import android.widget.Toast;
.
.
public class MainActivity extends AppCompatActivity {

    private BroadcastReceiver receiver;
    private VideoView videoView;
    private MediaController mediaController;
    String TAG = "VideoPlayer";
.
.
@Override
    public void onPictureInPictureModeChanged(
                    boolean isInPictureInPictureMode) {
        super.onPictureInPictureModeChanged(isInPictureInPictureMode);

        Button pipButton = findViewById(R.id.pipButton);

        if (isInPictureInPictureMode) {
            IntentFilter filter = new IntentFilter();
            filter.addAction(
              "com.ebookfrenzy.videoplayer.VIDEO_INFO");

            receiver = new BroadcastReceiver() {
                @Override
                public void onReceive(Context context,
                                        Intent intent) {
```

```
                Toast.makeText(context,
                  "Favorite Home Movie Clips",
                        Toast.LENGTH_LONG).show();
            }
        };


        registerReceiver(receiver, filter);


    } else {
        pipButton.setVisibility(View.VISIBLE);
        videoView.setMediaController(mediaController);

        if (receiver != null) {
            unregisterReceiver(receiver);
        }
    }
}
.
.
.
}
```

71.6 Adding the PiP Action

With the broadcast receiver implemented, the next step is to create a RemoteAction object configured with an image to represent the action within the PiP window. For the purposes of this example, an image icon file named *ic_info_24dp.xml* will be used. This file can be found in the *project_icons* folder of the source code download archive available from the following URL:

https://www.ebookfrenzy.com/retail/androidstudio35/index.php

Locate this icon file and copy and paste it into the *app -> res -> drawables* folder within the Project tool window:

Figure 71-4

The next step is to create an Intent that will be sent to the broadcast receiver. This intent then needs to be wrapped up within a PendingIntent object, allowing the intent to be triggered later when the user taps the action button in the PiP window.

Edit the *MainActivity.java* file to add a method to create the Intent and PendingIntent objects as follows:

.

```
import android.app.PendingIntent;



public class MainActivity extends AppCompatActivity {

      private static final int REQUEST_CODE = 101;



      private void createPipAction() {
         Intent actionIntent =
            new Intent("com.ebookfrenzy.videoplayer.VIDEO_INFO");

         final PendingIntent pendingIntent =
            PendingIntent.getBroadcast(MainActivity.this,
              REQUEST_CODE, actionIntent, 0);
      }


}
```

Now that both the Intent object, and the PendingIntent instance in which it is contained have been created, a RemoteAction object needs to be created containing the icon to appear in the PiP window, and the PendingIntent object. Remaining within the *createPipAction()* method, add this code as follows:

```
import android.app.RemoteAction;
import android.graphics.drawable.Icon;

import java.util.ArrayList;

private void createPipAction() {

    final ArrayList<RemoteAction> actions = new ArrayList<>();

    Intent actionIntent =
            new Intent("com.ebookfrenzy.videoplayer.VIDEO_INFO");

    final PendingIntent pendingIntent = PendingIntent.getBroadcast(
        MainActivity.this,
           REQUEST_CODE, actionIntent, 0);

    final Icon icon =
            Icon.createWithResource(MainActivity.this,
```

```
                        R.drawable.ic_info_24dp);
    RemoteAction remoteAction = new RemoteAction(icon, "Info",
                "Video Info", pendingIntent);


        actions.add(remoteAction);
}
```

Now a PictureInPictureParams object containing the action needs to be created and the parameters applied so that the action appears within the PiP window:

```
private void createPipAction() {

    final ArrayList<RemoteAction> actions = new ArrayList<>();

    Intent actionIntent =
            new Intent("com.ebookfrenzy.videoplayer.VIDEO_INFO");

    final PendingIntent pendingIntent =
        PendingIntent.getBroadcast(MainActivity.this,
            REQUEST_CODE, actionIntent, 0);

    final Icon icon =
            Icon.createWithResource(MainActivity.this,
                    R.drawable.ic_info_24dp);
    RemoteAction remoteAction = new RemoteAction(icon, "Info",
            "Video Info", pendingIntent);

    actions.add(remoteAction);

    PictureInPictureParams params =
                new PictureInPictureParams.Builder()
                        .setActions(actions)
                        .build();

    setPictureInPictureParams(params);
}
```

The final task before testing the action is to make a call to the *createPipAction()* method when the activity enters PiP mode:

```
@Override
public void onPictureInPictureModeChanged(boolean isInPictureInPictureMode) {
    super.onPictureInPictureModeChanged(isInPictureInPictureMode);
.
.
        registerReceiver(receiver, filter);
        createPipAction();
    } else {
```

```
pipButton.setVisibility(View.VISIBLE);
videoView.setMediaController(mediaController);

    .

    .

}
```

71.7 Testing the Picture-in-Picture Action

Build and run the app once again and place the activity into PiP mode. Tap on the PiP window so that the new action button appears as shown in Figure 71-5:

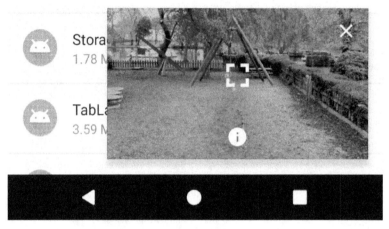

Figure 71-5

Click on the action button and wait for the Toast message to appear displaying the name of the video:

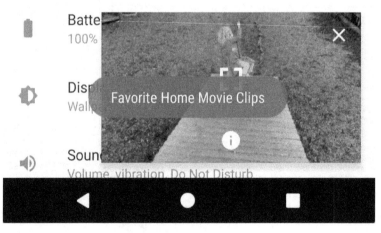

Figure 71-6

71.8 Summary

This chapter has demonstrated addition of Picture-in-Picture support to an Android Studio app project including enabling and entering PiP mode and the implementation of a PiP action. This included the use of a broadcast receiver and pending intents to implement communication between the PiP window and the activity.

72. Making Runtime Permission Requests in Android

In a number of the example projects created in preceding chapters, changes have been made to the *AndroidManifest.xml* file to request permission for the app to perform a specific task. In a couple of instances, for example, internet access permission has been requested in order to allow the app to download and display web pages. In each case up until this point, the addition of the request to the manifest was all that is required in order for the app to obtain permission from the user to perform the designated task.

There are, however, a number of permissions for which additional steps are required in order for the app to function when running on Android 6.0 or later. The first of these so-called "dangerous" permissions will be encountered in the next chapter. Before reaching that point, however, this chapter will outline the steps involved in requesting such permissions when running on the latest generations of Android.

72.1 Understanding Normal and Dangerous Permissions

Android enforces security by requiring the user to grant permission for an app to perform certain tasks. Prior to the introduction of Android 6, permission was always sought at the point that the app was installed on the device. Figure 72-1, for example, shows a typical screen seeking a variety of permissions during the installation of an app via Google Play.

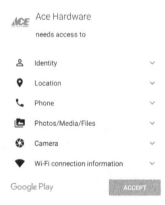

Figure 72-1

For many types of permissions this scenario still applies for apps on Android 6.0 or later. These permissions are referred to as *normal permissions* and are still required to be accepted by the user at the point of installation. A second type of permission, referred to as *dangerous permissions* must also be declared within the manifest file in the same way as a normal permission, but must also be requested from the user when the application is first launched. When such a request is made, it appears in the form of a dialog box as illustrated in Figure 72-2:

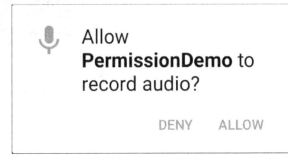

Figure 72-2

The full list of permissions that fall into the dangerous category is contained in Table 72-1:

Permission Group	Permission
Calendar	READ_CALENDAR
	WRITE_CALENDAR
Camera	CAMERA
Contacts	READ_CONTACTS
	WRITE_CONTACTS
	GET_ACCOUNTS
Location	ACCESS_FINE_LOCATION
	ACCESS_COARSE_LOCATION
Microphone	RECORD_AUDIO
Phone	READ_PHONE_STATE
	CALL_PHONE
	READ_CALL_LOG
	WRITE_CALL_LOG
	ADD_VOICEMAIL
	USE_SIP
	PROCESS_OUTGOING_CALLS
Sensors	BODY_SENSORS
SMS	SEND_SMS
	RECEIVE_SMS
	READ_SMS
	RECEIVE_WAP_PUSH
	RECEIVE_MMS

Storage	READ_EXTERNAL_STORAGE
	WRITE_EXTERNAL_STORAGE

Table 72-1

72.2 Creating the Permissions Example Project

Select the *Start a new Android Studio project* quick start option from the welcome screen and, within the resulting new project dialog, choose the Empty Activity template before clicking on the Next button.

Enter *PermissionDemo* into the Name field and specify *com.ebookfrenzy.permissiondemo* as the package name. Before clicking on the Finish button, change the Minimum API level setting to API 26: Android 8.0 (Oreo) and the Language menu to Java.

72.3 Checking for a Permission

The Android Support Library contains a number of methods that can be used to seek and manage dangerous permissions within the code of an Android app. These API calls can be made safely regardless of the version of Android on which the app is running, but will only perform meaningful tasks when executed on Android 6.0 or later.

Before an app attempts to make use of a feature that requires approval of a dangerous permission, and regardless of whether or not permission was previously granted, the code must check that the permission has been granted. This can be achieved via a call to the *checkSelfPermission()* method of the ContextCompat class, passing through as arguments a reference to the current activity and the permission being requested. The method will check whether the permission has been previously granted and return an integer value matching *PackageManager. PERMISSION_GRANTED* or *PackageManager.PERMISSION_DENIED*.

Within the *MainActivity.java* file of the example project, modify the code to check whether permission has been granted for the app to record audio:

```
package com.ebookfrenzy.permissiondemoactivity;

import androidx.appcompat.app.AppCompatActivity;
import androidx.core.content.ContextCompat;

import android.os.Bundle;
import android.Manifest;
import android.content.pm.PackageManager;
import android.util.Log;

public class MainActivity extends AppCompatActivity {

    private static String TAG = "PermissionDemo";

    @Override
    protected void onCreate(Bundle savedInstanceState) {
        super.onCreate(savedInstanceState);
        setContentView(R.layout.activity_permission_demo);

        setupPermissions();
```

```
    }

    private void setupPermissions() {
        int permission = ContextCompat.checkSelfPermission(this,
                Manifest.permission.RECORD_AUDIO);

        if (permission != PackageManager.PERMISSION_GRANTED) {
            Log.i(TAG, "Permission to record denied");
        }
    }
}
```

Run the app on a device or emulator running a version of Android that predates Android 6.0 and check the Logcat output within Android Studio. After the app has launched, the Logcat output should include the "Permission to record denied" message.

Edit the *AndroidManifest.xml* file (located in the Project tool window under *app -> manifests*) and add a line to request recording permission as follows:

```
<?xml version="1.0" encoding="utf-8"?>
<manifest xmlns:android="http://schemas.android.com/apk/res/android"
    package="com.ebookfrenzy.permissiondemoactivity" >

    <uses-permission android:name="android.permission.RECORD_AUDIO" />

    <application
        android:allowBackup="true"
        android:icon="@mipmap/ic_launcher"
        android:label="@sxtring/app_name"
        android:supportsRtl="true"
        android:theme="@style/AppTheme" >
        <activity android:name=".MainActivity" >
            <intent-filter>
                <action android:name="android.intent.action.MAIN" />

                <category
                    android:name="android.intent.category.LAUNCHER" />
            </intent-filter>
        </activity>
    </application>

</manifest>
```

Compile and run the app once again and note that this time the permission denial message does not appear. Clearly, everything that needs to be done to request this permission on older versions of Android has been done. Run the app on a device or emulator running Android 6.0 or later, however, and note that even though permission has been added to the manifest file, the check still reports that permission has been denied. This is because Android version 6 and later require that the app also request dangerous permissions at runtime.

72.4 Requesting Permission at Runtime

A permission request is made via a call to the *requestPermissions()* method of the ActivityCompat class. When this method is called, the permission request is handled asynchronously and a method named *onRequestPermissionsResult()* is called when the task is completed.

The *requestPermissions()* method takes as arguments a reference to the current activity, together with the identifier of the permission being requested and a request code. The request code can be any integer value and will be used to identify which request has triggered the call to the *onRequestPermissionsResult()* method. Modify the *MainActivity.java* file to declare a request code and request recording permission in the event that the permission check failed:

```
.
.
import androidx.core.content.ContextCompat;
.
.
public class MainActivity extends AppCompatActivity {

    private static String TAG = "PermissionDemo";
    private static final int RECORD_REQUEST_CODE = 101;
.
.
    @Override
    private void setupPermissions() {

        int permission = ContextCompat.checkSelfPermission(this,
                Manifest.permission.RECORD_AUDIO);

        if (permission != PackageManager.PERMISSION_GRANTED) {
            Log.i(TAG, "Permission to record denied");
            makeRequest();
        }
    }

    protected void makeRequest() {
        ActivityCompat.requestPermissions(this,
                new String[]{Manifest.permission.RECORD_AUDIO},
                RECORD_REQUEST_CODE);
    }
}
```

Next, implement the *onRequestPermissionsResult()* method so that it reads as follows:

```
@Override
public void onRequestPermissionsResult(int requestCode,
                                    String permissions[], int[] grantResults)
{
    switch (requestCode) {
```

```
case RECORD_REQUEST_CODE: {

    if (grantResults.length == 0
            || grantResults[0] !=
            PackageManager.PERMISSION_GRANTED) {

        Log.i(TAG, "Permission has been denied by user");
    } else {
        Log.i(TAG, "Permission has been granted by user");
    }

    }

}
```

Compile and run the app on an Android 6 or later emulator or device and note that a dialog seeking permission to record audio appears as shown in Figure 72-3:

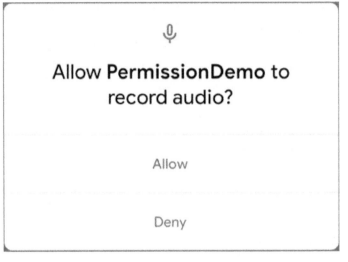

Figure 72-3

Tap the Allow button and check that the "Permission has been granted by user" message appears in the Logcat panel.

Once the user has granted the requested permission, the *checkSelfPermission()* method call will return a PERMISSION_GRANTED result on future app invocations until the user uninstalls and re-installs the app or changes the permissions for the app in Settings.

72.5 Providing a Rationale for the Permission Request

As is evident from Figure 72-3, the user has the option to deny the requested permission. In this case, the app will continue to request the permission each time that it is launched by the user unless the user selected the "Never ask again" option prior to clicking on the Deny button. Repeated denials by the user may indicate that the user doesn't understand why the permission is required by the app. The user might, therefore, be more likely to grant permission if the reason for the requirements is explained when the request is made. Unfortunately, it is not possible to change the content of the request dialog to include such an explanation.

An explanation is best included in a separate dialog which can be displayed before the request dialog is presented to the user. This raises the question as to when to display this explanation dialog. The Android documentation recommends that an explanation dialog only be shown in the event that the user has previously denied the permission and provides a method to identify when this is the case.

A call to the *shouldShowRequestPermissionRationale()* method of the ActivityCompat class will return a true result if the user has previously denied a request for the specified permission, and a false result if the request has not previously been made. In the case of a true result, the app should display a dialog containing a rationale for needing the permission and, once the dialog has been read and dismissed by the user, the permission request should be repeated.

To add this functionality to the example app, modify the *onCreate()* method so that it reads as follows:

```
.
.
import android.app.AlertDialog;
import android.content.DialogInterface;
.
.
private void setupPermissions() {

    int permission = ContextCompat.checkSelfPermission(this,
            Manifest.permission.RECORD_AUDIO);

    if (permission != PackageManager.PERMISSION_GRANTED) {
        Log.i(TAG, "Permission to record denied");

        if (ActivityCompat.shouldShowRequestPermissionRationale(this,
                Manifest.permission.RECORD_AUDIO)) {
            AlertDialog.Builder builder =
                    new AlertDialog.Builder(this);
            builder.setMessage("Permission to access the microphone is required
for this app to record audio.")
                    .setTitle("Permission required");

            builder.setPositiveButton("OK",
                    new DialogInterface.OnClickListener() {

                public void onClick(DialogInterface dialog, int id) {
                    Log.i(TAG, "Clicked");
                    makeRequest();
                }
            });

            AlertDialog dialog = builder.create();
            dialog.show();
        } else {
            makeRequest();
```

```
        }

    }

}
```

The method still checks whether or not the permission has been granted, but now also identifies whether a rationale needs to be displayed. If the user has previously denied the request, a dialog is displayed containing an explanation and an OK button on which a listener is configured to call the *makeRequest()* method when the button is tapped. In the event that the permission request has not previously been made, the code moves directly to seeking permission.

72.6 Testing the Permissions App

On the Android 6 or later device or emulator session on which testing is being performed, launch the Settings app, select the *Apps & notifications* option and scroll to and select the PermissionDemo app. On the app settings screen, tap the uninstall button to remove the app from the device.

Run the app once again and, when the permission request dialog appears, click on the Deny button. Stop and restart the app and verify that the rationale dialog appears. Tap the OK button and, when the permission request dialog appears, tap the Allow button.

Return to the Settings app, select the Apps option and select the PermissionDemo app once again from the list. Once the settings for the app are listed, verify that the Permissions section lists the *Microphone* permission:

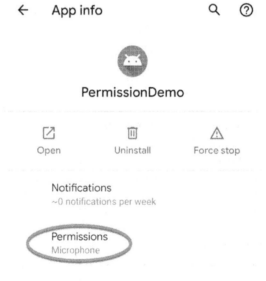

Figure 72-4

72.7 Summary

Prior to the introduction of Android 6.0 the only step necessary for an app to request permission to access certain functionality was to add an appropriate line to the application's manifest file. The user would then be prompted to approve the permission at the point that the app was installed. This is still the case for most permissions, with the exception of a set of permissions that are considered dangerous. Permissions that are considered dangerous usually have the potential to allow an app to violate the user's privacy such as allowing access to the microphone, contacts list or external storage.

As outlined in this chapter, apps based on Android 6 or later must now request dangerous permission approval from the user when the app launches in addition to including the permission request in the manifest file.

73. Android Audio Recording and Playback using MediaPlayer and MediaRecorder

This chapter will provide an overview of the MediaRecorder class and explain the basics of how this class can be used to record audio or video. The use of the MediaPlayer class to play back audio will also be covered. Having covered the basics, an example application will be created to demonstrate these techniques in action. In addition to looking at audio and video handling, this chapter will also touch on the subject of saving files to the SD card.

73.1 Playing Audio

In terms of audio playback, most implementations of Android support AAC LC/LTP, HE-AACv1 (AAC+), HE-AACv2 (enhanced AAC+), AMR-NB, AMR-WB, MP3, MIDI, Ogg Vorbis, and PCM/WAVE formats.

Audio playback can be performed using either the MediaPlayer or the AudioTrack classes. AudioTrack is a more advanced option that uses streaming audio buffers and provides greater control over the audio. The MediaPlayer class, on the other hand, provides an easier programming interface for implementing audio playback and will meet the needs of most audio requirements.

The MediaPlayer class has associated with it a range of methods that can be called by an application to perform certain tasks. A subset of some of the key methods of this class is as follows:

- **create()** – Called to create a new instance of the class, passing through the Uri of the audio to be played.

- **setDataSource()** – Sets the source from which the audio is to play.

- **prepare()** – Instructs the player to prepare to begin playback.

- **start()** – Starts the playback.

- **pause()** – Pauses the playback. Playback may be resumed via a call to the *resume()* method.

- **stop()** – Stops playback.

- **setVolume()** – Takes two floating-point arguments specifying the playback volume for the left and right channels.

- **resume()** – Resumes a previously paused playback session.

- **reset()** – Resets the state of the media player instance. Essentially sets the instance back to the uninitialized state. At a minimum, a reset player will need to have the data source set again and the *prepare()* method called.

- **release()** – To be called when the player instance is no longer needed. This method ensures that any resources held by the player are released.

In a typical implementation, an application will instantiate an instance of the MediaPlayer class, set the source of the audio to be played and then call *prepare()* followed by *start()*. For example:

```
MediaPlayer mediaPlayer = new MediaPlayer();

mediaPlayer.setDataSource("https://www.yourcompany.com/myaudio.mp3");
mediaPlayer.prepare();
mediaPlayer.start();
```

73.2 Recording Audio and Video using the MediaRecorder Class

As with audio playback, recording can be performed using a number of different techniques. One option is to use the MediaRecorder class, which, as with the MediaPlayer class, provides a number of methods that are used to record audio:

- **setAudioSource()** – Specifies the source of the audio to be recorded (typically this will be MediaRecorder.AudioSource.MIC for the device microphone).

- **setVideoSource()** – Specifies the source of the video to be recorded (for example MediaRecorder.VideoSource.CAMERA).

- **setOutputFormat()** – Specifies the format into which the recorded audio or video is to be stored (for example MediaRecorder.OutputFormat.AAC_ADTS).

- **setAudioEncoder()** – Specifies the audio encoder to be used for the recorded audio (for example MediaRecorder.AudioEncoder.AAC).

- **setOutputFile()** – Configures the path to the file into which the recorded audio or video is to be stored.

- **prepare()** – Prepares the MediaRecorder instance to begin recording.

- **start()** - Begins the recording process.

- **stop()** – Stops the recording process. Once a recorder has been stopped, it will need to be completely reconfigured and prepared before being restarted.

- **reset()** – Resets the recorder. The instance will need to be completely reconfigured and prepared before being restarted.

- **release()** – Should be called when the recorder instance is no longer needed. This method ensures all resources held by the instance are released.

A typical implementation using this class will set the source, output and encoding format and output file. Calls will then be made to the *prepare()* and *start()* methods. The *stop()* method will then be called when recording is to end, followed by the *reset()* method. When the application no longer needs the recorder instance, a call to the *release()* method is recommended:

```
MediaRecorder mediaRecorder = new MediaRecorder();

mediaRecorder.setAudioSource(MediaRecorder.AudioSource.MIC);
mediaRecorder.setOutputFormat(MediaRecorder.OutputFormat.AAC_ADTS);
mediaRecorder.setAudioEncoder(MediaRecorder.AudioEncoder.AAC);
mediaRecorder.setOutputFile(audioFilePath);

mediaRecorder.prepare();
mediaRecorder.start();
```

.

```
mediaRecorder.stop();
mediaRecorder.reset();
mediaRecorder.release();
```

In order to record audio, the manifest file for the application must include the android.permission.RECORD_ AUDIO permission:

```
<uses-permission android:name="android.permission.RECORD_AUDIO" />
```

As outlined in the chapter entitled *"Making Runtime Permission Requests in Android"*, access to the microphone falls into the category of dangerous permissions. To support Android 6, therefore, a specific request for microphone access must also be made when the application launches, the steps for which will be covered later in this chapter.

73.3 About the Example Project

The remainder of this chapter will work through the creation of an example application intended to demonstrate the use of the MediaPlayer and MediaRecorder classes to implement the recording and playback of audio on an Android device.

When developing applications that make use of specific hardware features, the microphone being a case in point, it is important to check the availability of the feature before attempting to access it in the application code. The application created in this chapter will, therefore, also include code to detect the presence of a microphone on the device.

Once completed, this application will provide a very simple interface intended to allow the user to record and playback audio. The recorded audio will need to be stored within an audio file on the device. That being the case, this tutorial will also briefly explore the mechanism for using SD Card storage.

73.4 Creating the AudioApp Project

Select the *Start a new Android Studio project* quick start option from the welcome screen and, within the resulting new project dialog, choose the Empty Activity template before clicking on the Next button.

Enter *AudioApp* into the Name field and specify *com.ebookfrenzy.audioapp* as the package name. Before clicking on the Finish button, change the Minimum API level setting to API 26: Android 8.0 (Oreo) and the Language menu to Java.

73.5 Designing the User Interface

Once the new project has been created, select the *activity_main.xml* file from the Project tool window and with the Layout Editor tool in Design mode, select the "Hello World!" TextView and delete it from the layout.

Drag and drop three Button views onto the layout. The positioning of the buttons is not of paramount importance to this example, though Figure 73-1 shows a suggested layout using a vertical chain.

Configure the buttons to display string resources that read *Play, Record* and *Stop* and give them view IDs of *playButton, recordButton,* and *stopButton* respectively.

Select the Play button and, within the Attributes panel, configure the *onClick* property to call a method named *playAudio* when selected by the user. Repeat these steps to configure the remaining buttons to call methods named *recordAudio* and *stopAudio* respectively.

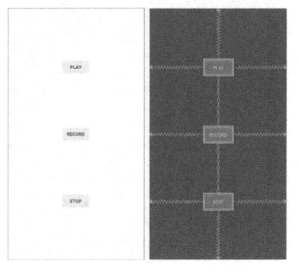

Figure 73-1

73.6 Checking for Microphone Availability

Attempting to record audio on a device without a microphone will cause the Android system to throw an exception. It is vital, therefore, that the code check for the presence of a microphone before making such an attempt. There are a number of ways of doing this, including checking for the physical presence of the device. An easier approach, and one that is more likely to work on different Android devices, is to ask the Android system if it has a package installed for a particular *feature*. This involves creating an instance of the Android PackageManager class and then making a call to the object's *hasSystemFeature()* method. *PackageManager. FEATURE_MICROPHONE* is the feature of interest in this case.

For the purposes of this example, we will create a method named *hasMicrophone()* that may be called upon to check for the presence of a microphone. Within the Project tool window, locate and double-click on the *MainActivity.java* file and modify it to add this method:

```
package com.ebookfrenzy.audioapp;

import androidx.appcompat.app.AppCompatActivity;

import android.content.pm.PackageManager;
import android.os.Bundle;

public class MainActivity extends AppCompatActivity {

    @Override
    protected void onCreate(Bundle savedInstanceState) {
        super.onCreate(savedInstanceState);
        setContentView(R.layout.activity_audio_app);
    }

    protected boolean hasMicrophone() {
        PackageManager pmanager = this.getPackageManager();
```

```
        return pmanager.hasSystemFeature(
                PackageManager.FEATURE_MICROPHONE);
    }
}
```

73.7 Performing the Activity Initialization

The next step is to modify the activity to perform a number of initialization tasks. Remaining within the *MainActivity.java* file, modify the code as follows:

```
package com.ebookfrenzy.audioapp;

import java.io.IOException;
.
.
.
import android.media.MediaRecorder;
import android.os.Environment;
import android.widget.Button;
import android.view.View;
import android.media.MediaPlayer;

public class MainActivity extends AppCompatActivity {

    private static MediaRecorder mediaRecorder;
    private static MediaPlayer mediaPlayer;

    private static String audioFilePath;
    private Button stopButton;
    private Button playButton;
    private Button recordButton;

    private boolean isRecording = false;

    @Override
    protected void onCreate(Bundle savedInstanceState) {
        super.onCreate(savedInstanceState);
        setContentView(R.layout.activity_audio_app);
        audioSetup();
    }

    private void audioSetup()
    {
        recordButton = findViewById(R.id.recordButton);
        playButton = findViewById(R.id.playButton);
        stopButton = findViewById(R.id.stopButton);

        if (!hasMicrophone())
        {
```

```
                stopButton.setEnabled(false);
                playButton.setEnabled(false);
                recordButton.setEnabled(false);
            } else {
                playButton.setEnabled(false);
                stopButton.setEnabled(false);
            }


            audioFilePath =
                    this.getExternalFilesDir(Environment.DIRECTORY_MUSIC).
                                        getAbsolutePath() + "/myaudio.3gp";

    }
    .
    .
}
```

The added code begins by obtaining references to the three button views in the user interface. Next, the previously implemented *hasMicrophone()* method is called to ascertain whether the device includes a microphone. If it does not, all the buttons are disabled, otherwise only the Stop and Play buttons are disabled.

The next line of code needs a little more explanation:

```
audioFilePath = this.getExternalFilesDir(Environment.DIRECTORY_MUSIC).
getAbsolutePath() + "/myaudio.3gp";
```

The purpose of this code is to identify the location of the external storage (which is referred to as external storage even though it is internal to the device on many Android devices) on the device and to use that to create a path to a file named *myaudio.3gp* into which the audio recording will be stored. The *getExternalFilesDir()* method takes as an argument the type of storage required (in this case we are requesting the path to the music directory, though options are also available for podcasts, audio books, movies, pictures etc).

When working with external storage it is important to be aware that such activity by an application requires permission to be requested in the application manifest file. For example:

```
<uses-permission android:name="android.permission.WRITE_EXTERNAL_STORAGE" />
```

73.8 Implementing the recordAudio() Method

When the user touches the Record button, the *recordAudio()* method will be called. This method will need to enable and disable the appropriate buttons and configure the MediaRecorder instance with information about the source of the audio, the output format and encoding, and the location of the file into which the audio is to be stored. Finally, the *prepare()* and *start()* methods of the MediaRecorder object will need to be called. Combined, these requirements result in the following method implementation in the *MainActivity.java* file:

```
public void recordAudio (View view)
{
    isRecording = true;
    stopButton.setEnabled(true);
    playButton.setEnabled(false);
    recordButton.setEnabled(false);

    try {
        mediaRecorder = new MediaRecorder();
```

```
mediaRecorder.setAudioSource(MediaRecorder.AudioSource.MIC);
mediaRecorder.setOutputFormat(
        MediaRecorder.OutputFormat.THREE_GPP);
mediaRecorder.setOutputFile(audioFilePath);
mediaRecorder.setAudioEncoder(MediaRecorder.AudioEncoder.AMR_NB);
mediaRecorder.prepare();
} catch (Exception e) {
        e.printStackTrace();
}
    mediaRecorder.start();
}
```

73.9 Implementing the stopAudio() Method

The *stopAudio()* method is responsible for enabling the Play button, disabling the Stop button and then stopping and resetting the MediaRecorder instance. The code to achieve this reads as outlined in the following listing and should be added to the *MainActivity.java* file:

```
public void stopAudio (View view)
{

        stopButton.setEnabled(false);
        playButton.setEnabled(true);

        if (isRecording)
        {
                recordButton.setEnabled(false);
                mediaRecorder.stop();
                mediaRecorder.release();
                mediaRecorder = null;
                isRecording = false;
        } else {
                mediaPlayer.release();
                 mediaPlayer = null;
                recordButton.setEnabled(true);

        }

}
```

73.10 Implementing the playAudio() method

The *playAudio()* method will simply create a new MediaPlayer instance, assign the audio file located on the SD card as the data source and then prepare and start the playback:

```
public void playAudio (View view) throws IOException
{
        playButton.setEnabled(false);
        recordButton.setEnabled(false);
        stopButton.setEnabled(true);

        mediaPlayer = new MediaPlayer();
```

```
    mediaPlayer.setDataSource(audioFilePath);
    mediaPlayer.prepare();
    mediaPlayer.start();
}
```

73.11 Configuring and Requesting Permissions

Before testing the application, it is essential that the appropriate permissions be requested within the manifest file for the application. Specifically, the application will require permission to record audio and to access the external storage (SD card). Within the Project tool window, locate and double-click on the *AndroidManifest.xml* file to load it into the editor and modify the XML to add the two permission tags:

```
<?xml version="1.0" encoding="utf-8"?>
<manifest xmlns:android="http://schemas.android.com/apk/res/android"
    package="com.ebookfrenzy.audioapp" >

    <uses-permission android:name=
                "android.permission.WRITE_EXTERNAL_STORAGE" />
    <uses-permission android:name="android.permission.RECORD_AUDIO" />

    <application
        android:allowBackup="true"
        android:icon="@mipmap/ic_launcher"
        android:label="@string/app_name"
        android:theme="@style/AppTheme" >
        <activity android:name=".MainActivity"
            android:label="@string/app_name" >
            <intent-filter>
                <action android:name="android.intent.action.MAIN" />

                <category android:name=
                        "android.intent.category.LAUNCHER" />
            </intent-filter>
        </activity>
    </application>
</manifest>
```

The above steps will be adequate to ensure that the user enables these permissions when the app is installed on devices running versions of Android pre-dating Android 6.0. Both microphone and external storage access are categorized in Android as being dangerous permissions because they give the app the potential to compromise the user's privacy. In order for the example app to function on Android 6 or later devices, therefore, code needs to be added to specifically request these two permissions at app runtime.

Edit the *MainActivity.java* file and begin by adding some additional import directives and constants to act as request identification codes for the permissions being requested:

```
.
.
import androidx.core.app.ActivityCompat;
import androidx.core.content.ContextCompat;
```

```
import android.widget.Toast;
import android.Manifest;
.
.

public class MainActivity extends AppCompatActivity {

    private static final int RECORD_REQUEST_CODE = 101;
    private static final int STORAGE_REQUEST_CODE = 102;
.
.
```

Next, a method needs to be added to the class, the purpose of which is to take as arguments the permission to be requested and the corresponding request identification code. Remaining with the *MainActivity.java* class file, implement this method as follows:

```
protected void requestPermission(String permissionType, int requestCode) {
    int permission = ContextCompat.checkSelfPermission(this,
            permissionType);

    if (permission != PackageManager.PERMISSION_GRANTED) {
        ActivityCompat.requestPermissions(this,
            new String[]{permissionType}, requestCode
        );
    }
}
```

Using the steps outlined in the *"Making Runtime Permission Requests in Android"* chapter of this book, the above method verifies that the specified permission has not already been granted before making the request, passing through the identification code as an argument.

When the request has been handled, the *onRequestPermissionsResult()* method will be called on the activity, passing through the identification code and the results of the request. The next step, therefore, is to implement this method within the *MainActivity.java* file as follows:

```
@Override
public void onRequestPermissionsResult(int requestCode,
                    String permissions[], int[] grantResults) {
    switch (requestCode) {
        case RECORD_REQUEST_CODE: {

            if (grantResults.length == 0
                || grantResults[0] !=
                    PackageManager.PERMISSION_GRANTED) {

                recordButton.setEnabled(false);

                Toast.makeText(this,
                    "Record permission required",
                        Toast.LENGTH_LONG).show();
```

```
            } else {
                requestPermission(
                    Manifest.permission.WRITE_EXTERNAL_STORAGE,
                        STORAGE_REQUEST_CODE);
            }
            return;
        }
        case STORAGE_REQUEST_CODE: {

            if (grantResults.length == 0
                    || grantResults[0] !=
                    PackageManager.PERMISSION_GRANTED) {
                recordButton.setEnabled(false);
                Toast.makeText(this,
                    "External Storage permission required",
                    Toast.LENGTH_LONG).show();
            }
        }
    }
}
```

The above code checks the request identifier code to identify which permission request has returned before checking whether or not the corresponding permission was granted. If the user grants permission to access the microphone the code then proceeds to request access to the external storage. In the event that either permission was denied, a message is displayed to the user indicating the app will not function. In both instances, the record button is also disabled.

All that remains prior to testing the app is to call the newly added *requestPermission()* method for microphone access when the app launches. Remaining in the *MainActivity.java* file, modify the *audioSetup()* method as follows:

```
private void audioSetup(){
    recordButton = findViewById(R.id.recordButton);
    playButton = findViewById(R.id.playButton);
    stopButton = findViewById(R.id.stopButton);

    if (!hasMicrophone())
    {
        stopButton.setEnabled(false);
        playButton.setEnabled(false);
        recordButton.setEnabled(false);
    } else {
        playButton.setEnabled(false);
        stopButton.setEnabled(false);
    }

    audioFilePath =
            Environment.getExternalStorageDirectory()
```

```
        .getAbsolutePath()
            + "/myaudio.3gp";

requestPermission(Manifest.permission.RECORD_AUDIO,
        RECORD_REQUEST_CODE);
}
```

73.12 Testing the Application

Compile and run the application on an Android device containing a microphone, allow the requested permissions and touch the Record button. After recording, touch Stop followed by Play, at which point the recorded audio should play back through the device speakers. If running on Android 6.0 or later, note that the app requests permission to use the external storage and to record audio when first launched.

73.13 Summary

The Android SDK provides a number of mechanisms for the implementation of audio recording and playback. This chapter has looked at two of these, in the form of the MediaPlayer and MediaRecorder classes. Having covered the theory of using these techniques, this chapter worked through the creation of an example application designed to record and then play back audio. In the course of working with audio in Android, this chapter also looked at the steps involved in ensuring that the device on which the application is running has a microphone before attempting to record audio. The use of external storage in the form of an SD card was also covered.

74. Working with the Google Maps Android API in Android Studio

When Google decided to introduce a map service many years ago, it is hard to say whether or not they ever anticipated having a version available for integration into mobile applications. When the first web based version of what would eventually be called Google Maps was introduced in 2005, the iPhone had yet to ignite the smartphone revolution and the company that was developing the Android operating system would not be acquired by Google for another six months. Whatever aspirations Google had for the future of Google Maps, it is remarkable to consider that all of the power of Google Maps can now be accessed directly via Android applications using the Google Maps Android API.

This chapter is intended to provide an overview of the Google Maps system and Google Maps Android API. The chapter will provide an overview of the different elements that make up the API, detail the steps necessary to configure a development environment to work with Google Maps and then work through some code examples demonstrating some of the basics of Google Maps Android integration.

74.1 The Elements of the Google Maps Android API

The Google Maps Android API consists of a core set of classes that combine to provide mapping capabilities in Android applications. The key elements of a map are as follows:

- **GoogleMap** – The main class of the Google Maps Android API. This class is responsible for downloading and displaying map tiles and for displaying and responding to map controls. The GoogleMap object is not created directly by the application but is instead created when MapView or MapFragment instances are created. A reference to the GoogleMap object can be obtained within application code via a call to the *getMap()* method of a MapView, MapFragment or SupportMapFragment instance.

- **MapView** - A subclass of the View class, this class provides the view canvas onto which the map is drawn by the GoogleMap object, allowing a map to be placed in the user interface layout of an activity.

- **SupportMapFragment** – A subclass of the Fragment class, this class allows a map to be placed within a Fragment in an Android layout.

- **Marker** – The purpose of the Marker class is to allow locations to be marked on a map. Markers are added to a map by obtaining a reference to the GoogleMap object associated with a map and then making a call to the *addMarker()* method of that object instance. The position of a marker is defined via Longitude and Latitude. Markers can be configured in a number of ways, including specifying a title, text and an icon. Markers may also be made to be "draggable", allowing the user to move the marker to different positions on a map.

- **Shapes** – The drawing of lines and shapes on a map is achieved through the use of the *Polyline*, *Polygon* and *Circle* classes.

- **UiSettings** – The UiSettings class provides a level of control from within an application of which user interface controls appear on a map. Using this class, for example, the application can control whether or not the zoom, current location and compass controls appear on a map. This class can also be used to configure which touch screen gestures are recognized by the map.

- **My Location Layer** – When enabled, the My Location Layer displays a button on the map which, when selected by the user, centers the map on the user's current geographical location. If the user is stationary, this location is represented on the map by a blue marker. If the user is in motion the location is represented by a chevron indicating the user's direction of travel.

The best way to gain familiarity with the Google Maps Android API is to work through an example. The remainder of this chapter will create a simple Google Maps based application while highlighting the key areas of the API.

74.2 Creating the Google Maps Project

Select the *Start a new Android Studio project* quick start option from the welcome screen and, within the resulting new project dialog, choose the Google Maps Activity template before clicking on the Next button.

Enter *MapDemo* into the Name field and specify *com.ebookfrenzy.mapdemo* as the package name. Before clicking on the Finish button, change the Minimum API level setting to API 26: Android 8.0 (Oreo) and the Language menu to Java.

74.3 Obtaining Your Developer Signature

Before an application can make use of the Google Maps Android API, it must first be registered within the Google APIs Console. Before an application can be registered, however, the developer signature (also referred to as the SHA-1 fingerprint) associated with your development environment must be identified. This is contained in a keystore file located in the *.android* subdirectory of your home directory and may be obtained using the *keytool* utility provided as part of the Java SDK as outlined below. In order to make the process easier, however, Android Studio adds some additional files to the project when the *Google Maps Activity* option is selected during the project creation process. One of these files is named *google_maps_api.xml* and is located in the *app -> res -> values* folder of the project.

Contained within the *google_maps_api.xml* file is a link to the Google Developer console. Copy and paste this link into a browser window. Once loaded, a page similar to the following will appear:

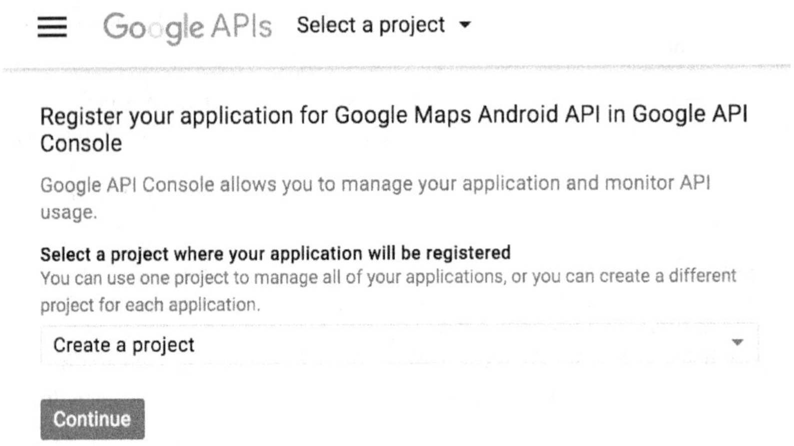

≡ Google APIs   Select a project ▾

Register your application for Google Maps Android API in Google API Console

Google API Console allows you to manage your application and monitor API usage.

Select a project where your application will be registered
You can use one project to manage all of your applications, or you can create a different project for each application.

Create a project   ▾

Continue

Figure 74-1

Verify that the menu is set to *Create a new project* before clicking on the *Continue* button. Once the API has been enabled, click on the *Create API Key* button. After a short delay, the new project will be created and a panel will appear (Figure 74-2) providing the API key for the application.

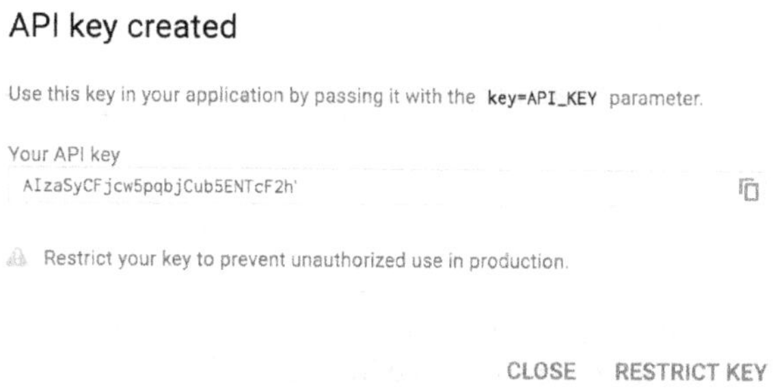

API key created

Use this key in your application by passing it with the **key=API_KEY** parameter.

Your API key
AIzaSyCFjcw5pqbjCub5ENTcF2h'

⚠ Restrict your key to prevent unauthorized use in production.

CLOSE   RESTRICT KEY

Figure 74-2

Copy this key, return to Android Studio and paste the API key into the *YOUR_KEY_HERE* section of the file:

```
<string name="google_maps_key"
templateMergeStrategy="preserve" translatable="false">YOUR_KEY_HERE</string>
```

74.4 Adding the Apache HTTP Legacy Library Requirement

Since this example project will be built for use with Android version 9.0 or later, the following declaration needs to be added within the <application> section of the *AndroidManifest.xml* file as follows:

.

.

```
<application
         android:allowBackup="true"
         android:icon="@mipmap/ic_launcher"
         android:label="@string/app_name"
         android:roundIcon="@mipmap/ic_launcher_round"
         android:supportsRtl="true"
         android:theme="@style/AppTheme">

     <uses-library
         android:name="org.apache.http.legacy"
         android:required="false" />
```

.

.

74.5 Testing the Application

Perform a test run of the application to verify that the API key is correctly configured. Assuming that the configuration is correct, the application will run and display a map on the screen.

In the event that a map is not displayed, check the following areas:

• If the application is running on an emulator, make sure that the emulator is running a version of Android that includes the Google APIs. The current operating system can be changed for an AVD configuration by selecting the *Tools -> Android -> AVD Manager* menu option, clicking on the pencil icon in the *Actions* column of the AVD followed by the *Change...* button next to the current Android version. Within the system image dialog, select a target which includes the Google APIs.

• Check the Logcat output for any areas relating to authentication problems with regard to the Google Maps

API. This usually means the API key was entered incorrectly or that the application package name does not match that specified when the API key was generated.

- Verify within the Google API Console that the *Google Maps Android API* has been enabled in the Services panel.

74.6 Understanding Geocoding and Reverse Geocoding

It is impossible to talk about maps and geographical locations without first covering the subject of Geocoding. Geocoding can best be described as the process of converting a textual based geographical location (such as a street address) into geographical coordinates expressed in terms of longitude and latitude.

Geocoding can be achieved using the Android Geocoder class. An instance of the Geocoder class can, for example, be passed a string representing a location such as a city name, street address or airport code. The Geocoder will attempt to find a match for the location and return a list of Address objects that potentially match the location string, ranked in order with the closest match at position 0 in the list. A variety of information can then be extracted from the Address objects, including the longitude and latitude of the potential matches.

The following code, for example, requests the location of the National Air and Space Museum in Washington, D.C.:

```
import java.io.IOException;
import java.util.List;

import android.location.Address;
import android.location.Geocoder;
.

.

double latitude;
double longitude;

List<Address> geocodeMatches = null;

try {
        geocodeMatches =
            new Geocoder(this).getFromLocationName(
                "600 Independence Ave SW, Washington, DC 20560", 1);
    } catch (IOException e) {
        // TODO Auto-generated catch block
        e.printStackTrace();
}

if (!geocodeMatches.isEmpty())
{
        latitude = geocodeMatches.get(0).getLatitude();
        longitude = geocodeMatches.get(0).getLongitude();
}
```

Note that the value of 1 is passed through as the second argument to the *getFromLocationName()* method. This simply tells the Geocoder to return only one result in the array. Given the specific nature of the address provided, there should only be one potential match. For more vague location names, however, it may be necessary to request more potential matches and allow the user to choose the correct one.

The above code is an example of *forward-geocoding* in that coordinates are calculated based on a text location description. *Reverse-geocoding*, as the name suggests, involves the translation of geographical coordinates into a human readable address string. Consider, for example, the following code:

```
import java.io.IOException;
import java.util.List;

import android.location.Address;
import android.location.Geocoder;
.
.
.
List<Address> geocodeMatches = null;
String Address1;
String Address2;
String State;
String Zipcode;
String Country;

try {
    geocodeMatches =
        new Geocoder(this).getFromLocation(38.8874245, -77.0200729, 1);
} catch (IOException e) {
    // TODO Auto-generated catch block
    e.printStackTrace();
}

if (!geocodeMatches.isEmpty())
{
    Address1 = geocodeMatches.get(0).getAddressLine(0);
    Address2 = geocodeMatches.get(0).getAddressLine(1);
    State = geocodeMatches.get(0).getAdminArea();
    Zipcode = geocodeMatches.get(0).getPostalCode();
    Country = geocodeMatches.get(0).getCountryName();
}
```

In this case the Geocoder object is initialized with latitude and longitude values via the *getFromLocation()* method. Once again, only a single matching result is requested. The text based address information is then extracted from the resulting Address object.

It should be noted that the geocoding is not actually performed on the Android device, but rather on a server to which the device connects when a translation is required and the results subsequently returned when the translation is complete. As such, geocoding can only take place when the device has an active internet connection.

74.7 Adding a Map to an Application

The simplest way to add a map to an application is to specify it in the user interface layout XML file for an activity. The following example layout file shows the SupportMapFragment instance added to the *activity_maps.*

xml file created by Android Studio:

```
<fragment xmlns:android="http://schemas.android.com/apk/res/android"
    xmlns:tools="http://schemas.android.com/tools"
    android:layout_width="match_parent"
    android:layout_height="match_parent"
    android:id="@+id/map"
    tools:context=".MapsActivity"
    android:name="com.google.android.gms.maps.SupportMapFragment"/>
```

74.8 Requesting Current Location Permission

As outlined in the chapter entitled *"Making Runtime Permission Requests in Android"*, certain permissions are categorized as being dangerous and require special handling for Android 6.0 or later. One such permission gives applications the ability to identify the user's current location. By default, Android Studio has placed a location permission request within the *AndroidManifest.xml* file. Locate this file located under *app -> manifests* in the Project tool window and locate the following permission line:

```
<uses-permission
        android:name="android.permission.ACCESS_FINE_LOCATION" />
```

This will ensure that the app is given the opportunity to provide permission for the app to obtain location information at the point that the app is installed on older versions of Android, but to fully support Android 6.0 or later, the app must also specifically request this permission at runtime. To achieve this, some code needs to be added to the *MapsActivity.java* file.

Begin by adding some import directives and a constant to act as the permission request code:

```
package com.ebookfrenzy.mapdemo;
.
.
import androidx.core.content.ContextCompat;
import androidx.core.app.ActivityCompat;
import android.Manifest;
import android.widget.Toast;
import android.content.pm.PackageManager;
.
.
public class MapsActivity extends FragmentActivity implements OnMapReadyCallback
{

    private static final int LOCATION_REQUEST_CODE = 101;
    private GoogleMap mMap;
.
.
}
```

Next, a method needs to be added to the class to request a specified permission from the user. Remaining within the *MapsActivity.java* class file, implement this method as follows:

```
protected void requestPermission(String permissionType,
                                 int requestCode) {
```

```
ActivityCompat.requestPermissions(this,
        new String[]{permissionType}, requestCode
);
}
```

When the user has responded to the permission request, the *onRequestPermissionsResult()* method will be called on the activity. Remaining in the *MapsActivity.java* file, implement this method now so that it reads as follows:

```
@Override
public void onRequestPermissionsResult(int requestCode,
            String permissions[], int[] grantResults) {

    switch (requestCode) {
        case LOCATION_REQUEST_CODE: {

            if (grantResults.length == 0
                    || grantResults[0] !=
                    PackageManager.PERMISSION_GRANTED) {
                Toast.makeText(this,
                    "Unable to show location - permission required",
                            Toast.LENGTH_LONG).show();
            } else {

                SupportMapFragment mapFragment =
                    (SupportMapFragment) getSupportFragmentManager()
                            .findFragmentById(R.id.map);
                mapFragment.getMapAsync(this);
            }
        }
    }
}
```

If permission has not been granted by the user, the app displays a message indicating that the current location cannot be displayed. If, on the other hand, permission was granted, the map is refreshed to provide an opportunity for the location marker to be displayed.

74.9 Displaying the User's Current Location

Once the appropriate permission has been granted, the user's current location may be displayed on the map by obtaining a reference to the GoogleMap object associated with the displayed map and calling the *setMyLocationEnabled()* method of that instance, passing through a value of *true*.

When the map is ready to display, the *onMapReady()* method of the activity is called. This method will also be called when the map is refreshed within the *onRequestPermissionsResult()* method above. By default, Android Studio has implemented this method and added some code to orient the map over Australia with a marker positioned over the city of Sidney. Locate and edit the *onMapReady()* method in the *MapsActivity.java* file to remove this template code and to add code to check the location permission has been granted before enabling display of the user's current location. If permission has not been granted, a request is made to the user via a call to the previously added *requestPermission()* method:

```
@Override
```

```
public void onMapReady(GoogleMap googleMap) {
    mMap = googleMap;

    // Add a marker in Sydney and move the camera
    LatLng sydney = new LatLng(-34, 151);
    mMap.addMarker(new MarkerOptions().position(sydney).title("Marker in
Sydney"));
    mMap.moveCamera(CameraUpdateFactory.newLatLng(sydney));

    if (mMap != null) {
        int permission = ContextCompat.checkSelfPermission(this,
                Manifest.permission.ACCESS_FINE_LOCATION);

        if (permission == PackageManager.PERMISSION_GRANTED) {
            mMap.setMyLocationEnabled(true);
        } else {
                requestPermission(
                    Manifest.permission.ACCESS_FINE_LOCATION,
                        LOCATION_REQUEST_CODE);
        }
    }
}
```

When the app is now run, the dialog shown in Figure 74-3 will appear requesting location permission. If permission is granted, a blue dot will appear on the map indicating the current location of the device.

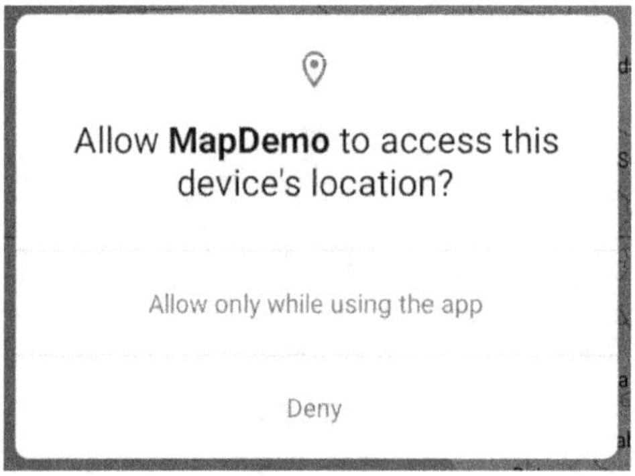

Figure 74-3

74.10 Changing the Map Type

The type of map displayed can be modified dynamically by making a call to the *setMapType()* method of the corresponding GoogleMap object, passing through one of the following values:

· **GoogleMap.MAP_TYPE_NONE** – An empty grid with no mapping tiles displayed.

· **GoogleMap.MAP_TYPE_NORMAL** – The standard view consisting of the classic road map.

· **GoogleMap.MAP_TYPE_SATELLITE** – Displays the satellite imagery of the map region.

· **GoogleMap.MAP_TYPE_HYBRID** – Displays satellite imagery with the road map superimposed.

· **GoogleMap.MAP_TYPE_TERRAIN** – Displays topographical information such as contour lines and colors.

The following code change to the *onMapReady()* method, for example, switches a map to Satellite mode:

```
.
.
if (mMap != null) {
    int permission = ContextCompat.checkSelfPermission(
            this, Manifest.permission.ACCESS_FINE_LOCATION);

    if (permission == PackageManager.PERMISSION_GRANTED) {
        mMap.setMyLocationEnabled(true);
    } else {
        requestPermission(Manifest.permission.ACCESS_FINE_LOCATION,
                LOCATION_REQUEST_CODE);
    }
    mMap.setMapType(GoogleMap.MAP_TYPE_SATELLITE);
}
.
.
```

Alternatively, the map type may be specified in the XML layout file in which the map is embedded using the *map:mapType* property together with a value of *none, normal, hybrid, satellite* or *terrain*. For example:

```
<?xml version="1.0" encoding="utf-8"?>
<fragment xmlns:android="http://schemas.android.com/apk/res/android"
        xmlns:map="http://schemas.android.com/apk/res-auto"
        android:id="@+id/map"
        android:layout_width="match_parent"
        android:layout_height="match_parent"
        map:mapType="hybrid"
        android:name="com.google.android.gms.maps.SupportMapFragment"/>
```

74.11 Displaying Map Controls to the User

The Google Maps Android API provides a number of controls that may be optionally displayed to the user consisting of zoom in and out buttons, a "my location" button and a compass.

Whether or not the zoom and compass controls are displayed may be controlled either programmatically or within the map element in XML layout resources. In order to configure the controls programmatically, a reference to the UiSettings object associated with the GoogleMap object must be obtained:

```
import com.google.android.gms.maps.UiSettings;
.
.
UiSettings mapSettings;
mapSettings = mMap.getUiSettings();
```

The zoom controls are enabled and disabled via the calls to the *setZoomControlsEnabled()* method of the UiSettings object. For example:

```
mapSettings.setZoomControlsEnabled(true);
```

Alternatively, the *map:uiZoomControls* property may be set within the map element of the XML resource file:

```
map:uiZoomControls="false"
```

The compass may be displayed either via a call to the *setCompassEnabled()* method of the UiSettings instance, or through XML resources using the *map:uiCompass* property. Note the compass icon only appears when the map camera is tilted or rotated away from the default orientation.

The "My Location" button will only appear when *My Location* mode is enabled as outlined earlier in this chapter. The button may be prevented from appearing even when in this mode via a call to the *setMyLocationButtonEnabled()* method of the UiSettings instance.

74.12 Handling Map Gesture Interaction

The Google Maps Android API is capable of responding to a number of different user interactions. These interactions can be used to change the area of the map displayed, the zoom level and even the angle of view (such that a 3D representation of the map area is displayed for certain cities).

74.12.1 Map Zooming Gestures

Support for gestures relating to zooming in and out of a map may be enabled or disabled using the *setZoomGesturesEnabled()* method of the UiSettings object associated with the GoogleMap instance. For example, the following code disables zoom gestures for our example map:

```
UiSettings mapSettings;
mapSettings = map.getUiSettings();
mapSettings.setZoomGesturesEnabled(false);
```

The same result can be achieved within an XML resource file by setting the *map:uiZoomGestures* property to true or false.

When enabled, zooming will occur when the user makes pinching gestures on the screen. Similarly, a double tap will zoom in while a two finger tap will zoom out. One finger zooming gestures, on the other hand, are performed by tapping twice but not releasing the second tap and then sliding the finger up and down on the screen to zoom in and out respectively.

74.12.2 Map Scrolling/Panning Gestures

A scrolling, or panning gesture allows the user to move around the map by dragging the map around the screen with a single finger motion. Scrolling gestures may be enabled within code via a call to the *setScrollGesturesEnabled()* method of the UiSettings instance:

```
UiSettings mapSettings;
mapSettings = mMap.getUiSettings();
mapSettings.setScrollGesturesEnabled(true);
```

Alternatively, scrolling on a map instance may be enabled in an XML resource layout file using the *map:uiScrollGestures* property.

74.12.3 Map Tilt Gestures

Tilt gestures allow the user to tilt the angle of projection of the map by placing two fingers on the screen and moving them up and down to adjust the tilt angle. Tilt gestures may be enabled or disabled via a call to the *setTiltGesturesEnabled()* method of the UiSettings instance, for example:

```
UiSettings mapSettings;
mapSettings = mMap.getUiSettings();
mapSettings.setTiltGesturesEnabled(true);
```

Tilt gestures may also be enabled and disabled using the *map:uiTiltGestures* property in an XML layout resource file.

74.12.4 Map Rotation Gestures

By placing two fingers on the screen and rotating them in a circular motion, the user may rotate the orientation of a map when map rotation gestures are enabled. This gesture support is enabled and disabled in code via a call to the *setRotateGesturesEnabled()* method of the UiSettings instance, for example:

```
UiSettings mapSettings;
mapSettings = mMap.getUiSettings();
mapSettings.setRotateGesturesEnabled(true);
```

Rotation gestures may also be enabled or disabled using the *map:uiRotateGestures* property in an XML layout resource file.

74.13 Creating Map Markers

Markers are used to notify the user of locations on a map and take the form of either a standard or custom icon. Markers may also include a title and optional text (referred to as a snippet) and may be configured such that they can be dragged to different locations on the map by the user. When tapped by the user an *info window* will appear displaying additional information about the marker location.

Markers are represented by instances of the Marker class and are added to a map via a call to the *addMarker()* method of the corresponding GoogleMap object. Passed through as an argument to this method is a MarkerOptions class instance containing the various options required for the marker such as the title and snippet text. The location of a marker is defined by specifying latitude and longitude values, also included as part of the MarkerOptions instance. For example, the following code adds a marker including a title, snippet and a position to a specific location on the map:

```
import com.google.android.gms.maps.model.Marker;
import com.google.android.gms.maps.model.LatLng;
import com.google.android.gms.maps.model.MarkerOptions;
.
.
.

LatLng position = new LatLng(38.8874245, -77.0200729);
Marker museum = mMap.addMarker(new MarkerOptions()
                    .position(position)
                    .title("Museum")
                    .snippet("National Air and Space Museum"));
```

When executed, the above code will mark the location specified which, when tapped, will display an info window containing the title and snippet as shown in Figure 74-4:

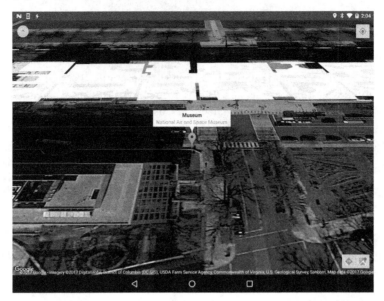

Figure 74-4

74.14 Controlling the Map Camera

Because Android device screens are flat and the world is a sphere, the Google Maps Android API uses the Mercator projection to represent the earth on a flat surface. The default view of the map is presented to the user as though through a *camera* suspended above the map and pointing directly down at the map. The Google Maps Android API allows the *target, zoom, bearing* and *tilt* of this camera to be changed in real-time from within the application:

- **Target** – The location of the center of the map within the device display specified in terms of longitude and latitude.

- **Zoom** – The zoom level of the camera specified in levels. Increasing the zoom level by 1.0 doubles the width of the amount of the map displayed.

- **Tilt** – The viewing angle of the camera specified as a position on an arc spanning directly over the center of the viewable map area measured in degrees from the top of the arc (this being the nadir of the arc where the camera points directly down to the map).

- **Bearing** – The orientation of the map in degrees measured in a clockwise direction from North.

Camera changes are made by creating an instance of the CameraUpdate class with the appropriate settings. CameraUpdate instances are created by making method calls to the *CameraUpdateFactory* class. Once a CameraUpdate instance has been created, it is applied to the map via a call to the *moveCamera()* method of the GoogleMap instance. To obtain a smooth animated effect as the camera changes, the *animateCamera()* method may be called instead of *moveCamera()*.

A summary of CameraUpdateFactory methods is as follows:

- **CameraUpdateFactory.zoomIn()** – Provides a CameraUpdate instance zoomed in by one level.

- **CameraUpdateFactory.zoomOut()** - Provides a CameraUpdate instance zoomed out by one level.

- **CameraUpdateFactory.zoomTo(float)** - Generates a CameraUpdate instance that changes the zoom level to the specified value.

- **CameraUpdateFactory.zoomBy(float)** – Provides a CameraUpdate instance with a zoom level increased or decreased by the specified amount.

- **CameraUpdateFactory.zoomBy(float, Point)** - Creates a CameraUpdate instance that increases or decreases the zoom level by the specified value.

- **CameraUpdateFactory.newLatLng(LatLng)** - Creates a CameraUpdate instance that changes the camera's target latitude and longitude.

- **CameraUpdateFactory.newLatLngZoom(LatLng, float)** - Generates a CameraUpdate instance that changes the camera's latitude, longitude and zoom.

- **CameraUpdateFactory.newCameraPosition(CameraPosition)** - Returns a CameraUpdate instance that moves the camera to the specified position. A CameraPosition instance can be obtained using CameraPosition.Builder().

The following code, for example, zooms in the camera by one level using animation:

```
mMap.animateCamera(CameraUpdateFactory.zoomIn());
```

The following code, on the other hand, moves the camera to a new location and adjusts the zoom level to 10 without animation:

```
private static final LatLng position =
        new LatLng(38.8874245, -77.0200729);


mMap.moveCamera(CameraUpdateFactory.newLatLngZoom(position, 10));
```

Finally, the next code example uses *CameraPosition.Builder()* to create a CameraPosition object with changes to the target, zoom, bearing and tilt. This change is then applied to the camera using animation:

```
import com.google.android.gms.maps.model.CameraPosition;
import com.google.android.gms.maps.CameraUpdateFactory;
.
.
.
CameraPosition cameraPosition = new CameraPosition.Builder()
    .target(position)
    .zoom(50)
    .bearing(70)
    .tilt(25)
    .build();
mMap.animateCamera(CameraUpdateFactory.newCameraPosition(
                        cameraPosition));
```

74.15 Summary

This chapter has provided an overview of the key classes and methods that make up the Google Maps Android API and outlined the steps involved in preparing both the development environment and an application project to make use of the API.

75. Printing with the Android Printing Framework

With the introduction of the Android 4.4 KitKat release, it became possible to print content from within Android applications. While subsequent chapters will explore in more detail the options for adding printing support to your own applications, this chapter will focus on the various printing options now available in Android and the steps involved in enabling those options. Having covered these initial topics, the chapter will then provide an overview of the various printing features that are available to Android developers in terms of building printing support into applications.

75.1 The Android Printing Architecture

Printing in Android is provided by the Printing framework. In basic terms, this framework consists of a Print Manager and a number of print service plugins. It is the responsibility of the Print Manager to handle the print requests from applications on the device and to interact with the print service plugins that are installed on the device, thereby ensuring that print requests are fulfilled. By default, many Android devices have print service plugins installed to enable printing using the Google Cloud Print and Google Drive services. Print Services Plugins for other printer types, if not already installed, may also be obtained from the Google Play store. Print Service Plugins are currently available for HP, Epson, Samsung and Canon printers and plugins from other printer manufactures will most likely be released in the future though the Google Cloud Print service plugin can also be used to print from an Android device to just about any printer type and model. For the purposes of this book, we will use the HP Print Services Plugin as a reference example.

75.2 The Print Service Plugins

The purpose of the Print Service plugins is to enable applications to print to compatible printers that are visible to the Android device via a local area wireless network or Bluetooth.

The presence of the Print Service Plugin on an Android device can be verified by loading the Google Play app and performing a search for "Print Service Plugin". Once the plugin is listed in the Play Store, and in the event that the plugin is not already installed, it can be installed by selecting the *Install* button. Figure 75-1, for example, shows the HP Print Service plugin within Google Play.

The Print Services plugins will automatically detect compatible printers on the network to which the Android device is currently connected and list them as options when printing from an application.

Figure 75-1

75.3 Google Cloud Print

Google Cloud Print is a service provided by Google that enables you to print content onto your own printer over the web from anywhere with internet connectivity. Google Cloud Print supports a wide range of devices and printer models in the form of both *Cloud Ready* and *Classic* printers. A Cloud Ready printer has technology built-in that enables printing via the web. Manufacturers that provide cloud ready printers include Brother, Canon, Dell, Epson, HP, Kodak and Samsung. To identify if your printer is both cloud ready and supported by Google Cloud Print, review the list of printers at the following URL:

https://www.google.com/cloudprint/learn/printers.html

In the case of classic, non-Cloud Ready printers, Google Cloud Print provides support for cloud printing through the installation of software on the computer system to which the classic printer is connected (either directly or over a home or office network).

To set up Google Cloud Print, visit the following web page and login using the same Google account ID that you use when logging in to your Android devices:

https://www.google.com/cloudprint/learn/index.html

Once printers have been added to your Google Cloud Print account, they will be listed as printer destination options when you print from within Android applications on your devices.

75.4 Printing to Google Drive

In addition to supporting physical printers, it is also possible to save printed output to your Google Drive account. When printing from a device, select the *Save to Google Drive* option in the printing panel. The content to be printed will then be converted to a PDF file and saved to the Google Drive cloud-based storage associated with the currently active Google Account ID on the device.

75.5 Save as PDF

The final printing option provided by Android allows the printed content to be saved locally as a PDF file on the Android device. Once selected, this option will request a name for the PDF file and a location on the device into which the document is to be saved.

Both the Save as PDF and Google Drive options can be invaluable in terms of saving paper when testing the printing functionality of your own Android applications.

75.6 Printing from Android Devices

Google recommends that applications which provide the ability to print content do so by placing the print option in the Overflow menu (a topic covered in some detail in the chapter entitled *"Creating and Managing Overflow Menus on Android"*). A number of applications bundled with Android now include "Print..." menu options. Figure 75-2, for example, shows the Print option accessed by selecting the "Share..." option in the Overflow menu of the Chrome browser application:

Figure 75-2

Once the print option has been selected from within an application, the standard Android print screen will appear showing a preview of the content to be printed as illustrated in Figure 75-3:

Figure 75-3

Tapping the panel along the top of the screen will display the full range of printing options:

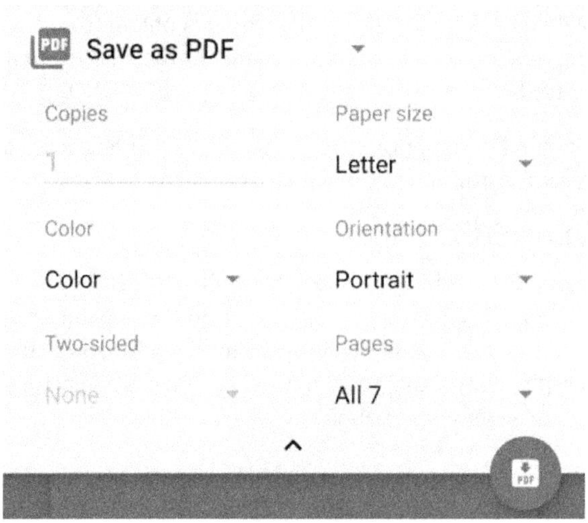

Figure 75-4

The Android print panel provides the usual printing options such as paper size, color, orientation and number of copies. Other print destination options may be accessed by tapping on the current printer or PDF output selection.

75.7 Options for Building Print Support into Android Apps

The Printing framework provides a number of options for incorporating print support into Android applications. These options can be categorized as follows:

75.7.1 Image Printing

As the name suggests, this option allows image printing to be incorporated into Android applications. When adding this feature to an application, the first step is to create a new instance of the PrintHelper class:

```
PrintHelper imagePrinter = new PrintHelper(context);
```

Next, the scale mode for the printed image may be specified via a call to the *setScaleMode()* method of the PrintHelper instance. Options are as follows:

- **SCALE_MODE_FIT** – The image will be scaled to fit within the paper size without any cropping or changes to aspect ratio. This will typically result in white space appearing in one dimension.

- **SCALE_MODE_FILL** – The image will be scaled to fill the paper size with cropping performed where necessary to avoid the appearance of white space in the printed output.

In the absence of a scale mode setting, the system will default to SCALE_MODE_FILL. The following code, for example, sets scale to fit mode on the previously declared PrintHelper instance:

```
imagePrinter.setScaleMode(PrintHelper.SCALE_MODE_FIT);
```

Similarly, the color mode may also be configured to indicate whether the print output is to be in color or black and white. This is achieved by passing one of the following options through to the *setColorMode()* method of the PrintHelper instance:

- **COLOR_MODE_COLOR** – Indicates that the image is to be printed in color.

- **COLOR_MODE_MONOCHROME** – Indicates that the image is to be printed in black and white.

The printing framework will default to color printing unless the monochrome option is specified as follows:

```
imagePrinter.setColorMode(PrintHelper.COLOR_MODE_MONOCHROME);
```

All that is required to complete the printing operation is an image to be printed and a call to the *printBitmap()* method of the PrintHelper instance, passing through a string representing the name to be assigned to the print job and a reference to the image (in the form of either a Bitmap object or a Uri reference to the image):

```
Bitmap bitmap = BitmapFactory.decodeResource(getResources(),
            R.drawable.oceanscene);
imagePrinter.printBitmap("My Test Print Job", bitmap);
```

Once the print job has been started, the Printing framework will display the print dialog and handle both the subsequent interaction with the user and the printing of the image on the user-selected print destination.

75.7.2 Creating and Printing HTML Content

The Android Printing framework also provides an easy way to print HTML based content from within an application. This content can either be in the form of HTML content referenced by the URL of a page hosted on a web site, or HTML content that is dynamically created within the application.

To enable HTML printing, the WebView class has been extended to include support for printing with minimal coding requirements.

When dynamically creating HTML content (as opposed to loading and printing an existing web page) the process involves the creation of a WebView object and associating with it a WebViewClient instance. The web view client is then configured to start a print job when the HTML has finished being loaded into the WebView. With the web view client configured, the HTML is then loaded into the WebView, at which point the print process is triggered.

Consider, for example, the following code:

```
public void printContent()
{
        WebView webView = new WebView(this);
        webView.setWebViewClient(new WebViewClient() {

                public boolean shouldOverrideUrlLoading(WebView view,
                        String url)
                {
                        return false;
                }

                @Override
                    public void onPageFinished(WebView view, String url) {
                            createWebPrintJob(view);
                            myWebView = null;
                    }
        });

        String htmlDocument =
            "<html><body><h1>Android Print Test</h1><p>"
          + "This is some sample content.</p></body></html>";
```

```
        webView.loadDataWithBaseURL(null, htmlDocument,
                "text/HTML", "UTF-8", null);


    myWebView = webView;
}
```

The code in this method begins by declaring a variable named *myWebView* in which will be stored a reference to the WebView instance created in the method. Within the *printContent()* method, an instance of the WebView class is created to which a WebViewClient instance is then assigned.

The WebViewClient assigned to the web view object is configured to indicate that loading of the HTML content is to be handled by the WebView instance (by returning *false* from the *shouldOverrideUrlLoading()*) method. More importantly, an *onPageFinished()* handler method is declared and implemented to call a method named *createWebPrintJob()*. The *onPageFinished()* callback method will be called automatically when all of the HTML content has been loaded into the web view. This ensures that the print job is not started until the content is ready, thereby ensuring that all of the content is printed.

Next, a string is created containing some HTML to serve as the content. This is then loaded into the web view. Once the HTML is loaded, the *onPageFinished()* method will trigger. Finally, the method stores a reference to the web view object. Without this vital step, there is a significant risk that the Java runtime system will assume that the application no longer needs the web view object and will discard it to free up memory (a concept referred to in Java terminology as *garbage collection*) resulting in the print job terminating prior to completion.

All that remains in this example is to implement the *createWebPrintJob()* method as follows:

```
private void createWebPrintJob(WebView webView) {

    PrintManager printManager = (PrintManager) this
            .getSystemService(Context.PRINT_SERVICE);

    PrintDocumentAdapter printAdapter =
            webView.createPrintDocumentAdapter("MyDocument");
    String jobName = getString(R.string.app_name) + " Document";

    PrintJob printJob = printManager.print(jobName, printAdapter,
            new PrintAttributes.Builder().build());
}
```

This method simply obtains a reference to the PrintManager service and instructs the web view instance to create a print adapter. A new string is created to store the name of the print job (which in this case is based on the name of the application and the word "Document").

Finally, the print job is started by calling the *print()* method of the print manager, passing through the job name, print adapter and a set of default print attributes. If required, the print attributes could be customized to specify resolution (dots per inch), margin and color options.

75.7.3 Printing a Web Page

The steps involved in printing a web page are similar to those outlined above, with the exception that the web view is passed the URL of the web page to be printed in place of the dynamically created HTML, for example:

```
myWebView.loadUrl("https://developer.android.com/google/index.html");
```

It is also important to note that the WebViewClient configuration is only necessary if a web page is to automatically print as soon as it has loaded. If the printing is to be initiated by the user selecting a menu option after the page has loaded, only the code in the *createWebPrintJob()* method outlined above need be included in the application code. The next chapter, entitled *"An Android HTML and Web Content Printing Example"*, will demonstrate just such a scenario.

75.7.4 Printing a Custom Document

While the HTML and web printing features introduced by the Printing framework provide an easy path to printing content from within an Android application, it is clear that these options will be overly simplistic for more advanced printing requirements. For more complex printing tasks, the Printing framework also provides custom document printing support. This allows content in the form of text and graphics to be drawn onto a canvas and then printed.

Unlike HTML and image printing, which can be implemented with relative ease, custom document printing is a more complex, multi-stage process which will be outlined in the *"A Guide to Android Custom Document Printing"* chapter of this book. These steps can be summarized as follows:

- Connect to the Android Print Manager

- Create a Custom Print Adapter sub-classed from the PrintDocumentAdapter class

- Create a PdfDocument instance to represent the document pages

- Obtain a reference to the pages of the PdfDocument instance, each of which has associated with it a Canvas instance

- Draw the content on the page canvases

- Notify the print framework that the document is ready to print

The custom print adapter outlined in the above steps needs to implement a number of methods which will be called upon by the Android system to perform specific tasks during the printing process. The most important of these are the *onLayout()* method which is responsible for re-arranging the document layout in response to the user changing settings such as paper size or page orientation, and the *onWrite()* method which is responsible for rendering the pages to be printed. This topic will be covered in detail in the chapter entitled *"A Guide to Android Custom Document Printing"*.

75.8 Summary

The Android SDK includes the ability to print content from within a running app. Print output can be directed to suitably configured printers, a local PDF file or to the cloud via Google Drive. From the perspective of the Android application developer, these capabilities are available for use in applications by making use of the Printing framework. By far the easiest printing options to implement are those involving content in the form of images and HTML. More advanced printing may, however, be implemented using the custom document printing features of the framework.

76. An Android HTML and Web Content Printing Example

As outlined in the previous chapter, entitled *"Printing with the Android Printing Framework"*, the Android Printing framework can be used to print both web pages and dynamically created HTML content. While there is much similarity in these two approaches to printing, there are also some subtle differences that need to be taken into consideration. This chapter will work through the creation of two example applications in order to bring some clarity to these two printing options.

76.1 Creating the HTML Printing Example Application

Select the *Start a new Android Studio project* quick start option from the welcome screen and, within the resulting new project dialog, choose the Empty Activity template before clicking on the Next button.

Enter *HTMLPrint* into the Name field and specify *com.ebookfrenzy.htmlprint* as the package name. Before clicking on the Finish button, change the Minimum API level setting to API 26: Android 8.0 (Oreo) and the Language menu to Java.

76.2 Printing Dynamic HTML Content

The first stage of this tutorial is to add code to the project to create some HTML content and send it to the Printing framework in the form of a print job.

Begin by locating the *MainActivity.java* file (located in the Project tool window under *app -> java -> com. ebookfrenzy.htmlprint*) and loading it into the editing panel. Once loaded, modify the code so that it reads as outlined in the following listing:

```
package com.ebookfrenzy.htmlprint;

import androidx.appcompat.app.AppCompatActivity;
import android.os.Bundle;
import android.webkit.WebView;
import android.webkit.WebViewClient;
import android.webkit.WebResourceRequest;
import android.print.PrintAttributes;
import android.print.PrintDocumentAdapter;
import android.print.PrintManager;
import android.content.Context;

public class MainActivity extends AppCompatActivity {

    private WebView myWebView;

    @Override
    protected void onCreate(Bundle savedInstanceState) {
```

```
        super.onCreate(savedInstanceState);
        setContentView(R.layout.activity_htmlprint);

        printWebView();
    }


    private void printWebView() {

        WebView webView = new WebView(this);
        webView.setWebViewClient(new WebViewClient() {

            public boolean shouldOverrideUrlLoading(WebView view,
                            WebResourceRequest request)
            {
                return false;
            }


            @Override
            public void onPageFinished(WebView view, String url)
            {
                createWebPrintJob(view);
                myWebView = null;
            }
        });

        String htmlDocument =
            "<html><body><h1>Android Print Test</h1><p>"
            + "This is some sample content.</p></body></html>";

        webView.loadDataWithBaseURL(null, htmlDocument,
                "text/HTML", "UTF-8", null);

        myWebView = webView;
    }
}
```

The code changes begin by declaring a variable named *myWebView* in which will be stored a reference to the WebView instance used for the printing operation. Within the *onCreate()* method, an instance of the WebView class is created to which a WebViewClient instance is then assigned.

The WebViewClient assigned to the web view object is configured to indicate that loading of the HTML content is to be handled by the WebView instance (by returning *false* from the *shouldOverrideUrlLoading()* method). More importantly, an *onPageFinished()* handler method is declared and implemented to call a method named *createWebPrintJob()*. The *onPageFinished()* method will be called automatically when all of the HTML content has been loaded into the web view. As outlined in the previous chapter, this step is necessary when printing dynamically created HTML content to ensure that the print job is not started until the content has fully loaded into the WebView.

Next, a String object is created containing some HTML to serve as the content and subsequently loaded into the web view. Once the HTML is loaded, the *onPageFinished()* callback method will trigger. Finally, the method stores a reference to the web view object in the previously declared *myWebView* variable. Without this vital step, there is a significant risk that the Java runtime system will assume that the application no longer needs the web view object and will discard it to free up memory resulting in the print job terminating before completion.

All that remains in this example is to implement the *createWebPrintJob()* method which is currently configured to be called by the *onPageFinished()* callback method. Remaining within the *MainActivity.java* file, therefore, implement this method so that it reads as follows:

```
private void createWebPrintJob(WebView webView) {

        PrintManager printManager = (PrintManager) this
                .getSystemService(Context.PRINT_SERVICE);

        PrintDocumentAdapter printAdapter =
                webView.createPrintDocumentAdapter("MyDocument");

        String jobName = getString(R.string.app_name) + " Print Test";

        printManager.print(jobName, printAdapter,
                new PrintAttributes.Builder().build());
}
```

This method obtains a reference to the PrintManager service and instructs the web view instance to create a print adapter. A new string is created to store the name of the print job (in this case based on the name of the application and the word "Print Test").

Finally, the print job is started by calling the *print()* method of the print manager, passing through the job name, print adapter and a set of default print attributes.

Compile and run the application on a device or emulator running Android 5.0 or later. Once launched, the standard Android printing page should appear as illustrated in Figure 76-1.

Figure 76-1

Print to a physical printer if you have one configured, save to Google Drive or, alternatively, select the option to save to a PDF file. Once the print job has been initiated, check the generated output on your chosen destination. Note that when using the Save to PDF option, the system will request a name and location for the PDF file. The *Downloads* folder makes a good option, the contents of which can be viewed by selecting the *Downloads* icon (renamed *Files* on Android 8) located amongst the other app icons on the device.

76.3 Creating the Web Page Printing Example

The second example application to be created in this chapter will provide the user with an Overflow menu option to print the web page currently displayed within a WebView instance.

Select the *Start a new Android Studio project* quick start option from the welcome screen and, within the resulting new project dialog, choose the Basic Activity template before clicking on the Next button.

Enter *WebPrint* into the Name field and specify *com.ebookfrenzy.webprint* as the package name. Before clicking on the Finish button, change the Minimum API level setting to API 26: Android 8.0 (Oreo) and the Language menu to Java.

76.4 Removing the Floating Action Button

Selecting the Basic Activity template provided a context menu and a floating action button. Since the floating action button is not required by the app it can be removed before proceeding. Load the *activity_main.xml* layout file into the Layout Editor, select the floating action button and tap the keyboard *Delete* key to remove the object from the layout. Edit the *MainActivity.java* file and remove the floating action button code from the onCreate method as follows:

```
@Override
protected void onCreate(Bundle savedInstanceState) {
    super.onCreate(savedInstanceState);
    setContentView(R.layout.activity_web_print);
    Toolbar toolbar = findViewById(R.id.toolbar);
    setSupportActionBar(toolbar);

    FloatingActionButton fab =
        findViewById(R.id.fab);
    fab.setOnClickListener(new View.OnClickListener() {
        @Override
        public void onClick(View view) {
            Snackbar.make(view, "Replace with your own action",
                Snackbar.LENGTH_LONG)
                .setAction("Action", null).show();
        }
    });
}
```

76.5 Designing the User Interface Layout

Load the *content_main.xml* layout resource file into the Layout Editor tool if it has not already been loaded and, in Design mode, select and delete the "Hello World!" TextView object. From the *Widgets* section of the palette, drag and drop a WebView object onto the center of the device screen layout. Using the Attributes tool window, change the layout_width and layout_height properties of the WebView to *match_constraint* so that it fills the entire layout canvas as outlined in Figure 76-2:

Figure 76-2

Select the newly added WebView instance and change the ID of the view to *myWebView*.

Before proceeding to the next step of this tutorial, an additional permission needs to be added to the project to enable the WebView object to access the internet and download a web page for printing. Add this permission by locating the *AndroidManifest.xml* file in the Project tool window and double-clicking on it to load it into the editing panel. Once loaded, edit the XML content to add the appropriate permission line as shown in the following listing:

```xml
<?xml version="1.0" encoding="utf-8"?>
<manifest xmlns:android="http://schemas.android.com/apk/res/android"
    package="com.ebookfrenzy.webprint" >

    <uses-permission android:name="android.permission.INTERNET" />

    <application
        android:allowBackup="true"
        android:icon="@mipmap/ic_launcher"
        android:label="@string/app_name"
        android:supportsRtl="true"
        android:theme="@style/AppTheme" >
        <activity
            android:name=".MainActivity"
            android:label="@string/app_name"
            android:theme="@style/AppTheme.NoActionBar" >
            <intent-filter>
                <action android:name="android.intent.action.MAIN" />

                <category android:name=
                    "android.intent.category.LAUNCHER" />
            </intent-filter>
        </activity>
    </application>

</manifest>
```

76.6 Loading the Web Page into the WebView

Before the web page can be printed, it needs to be loaded into the WebView instance. For the purposes of this tutorial, this will be performed by a call to the *loadUrl()* method of the WebView instance, which will be placed in a method named *configureWebView()* and called from within the *onCreate()* method of the MainActivity class. Edit the *MainActivity.java* file, therefore, and modify it as follows:

```java
package com.ebookfrenzy.webprint;

import android.os.Bundle;

import androidx.appcompat.app.AppCompatActivity;
import androidx.appcompat.widget.Toolbar;

import android.view.Menu;
import android.view.MenuItem;
import android.webkit.WebView;
import android.webkit.WebViewClient;
import android.webkit.WebResourceRequest;

public class MainActivity extends AppCompatActivity {

    private WebView myWebView;

    @Override
    protected void onCreate(Bundle savedInstanceState) {
        super.onCreate(savedInstanceState);
        setContentView(R.layout.activity_web_print);
        Toolbar toolbar = findViewById(R.id.toolbar);
        setSupportActionBar(toolbar);

        configureWebView();
    }

    private void configureWebView() {

        myWebView = findViewById(R.id.myWebView);
        myWebView.setWebViewClient(new WebViewClient(){
            @Override
            public boolean shouldOverrideUrlLoading(
                    WebView view, WebResourceRequest request) {
                return super.shouldOverrideUrlLoading(
                        view, request);
            }
        });
        myWebView.loadUrl(
                "https://developer.android.com/google/index.html");
```

```
        }
    .
    .
    .
}
```

76.7 Adding the Print Menu Option

The option to print the web page will now be added to the Overflow menu using the techniques outlined in the chapter entitled *"Creating and Managing Overflow Menus on Android"*.

The first requirement is a string resource with which to label the menu option. Within the Project tool window, locate the *app -> res -> values -> strings.xml* file, double-click on it to load it into the editor and modify it to add a new string resource:

```
<resources>
    <string name="app_name">WebPrint</string>
    <string name="action_settings">Settings</string>
    <string name="print_string">Print</string>
</resources>
```

Next, load the *app -> res -> menu -> menu_main.xml* file into the menu editor, switch to Text mode and replace the *Settings* menu option with the print option:

```
<menu xmlns:android="http://schemas.android.com/apk/res/android"
    xmlns:tools="http://schemas.android.com/tools"
    tools:context="com.ebookfrenzy.webprint.MainActivity" >
    <item android:id="@+id/action_settings"
            android:title="@string/action_settings"
            android:orderInCategory="100"
            app:showAsAction="never" />

    <item
        android:id="@+id/action_print"
        android:orderInCategory="100"
        app:showAsAction="never"
        android:title="@string/print_string"/>
</menu>
```

All that remains in terms of configuring the menu option is to modify the *onOptionsItemSelected()* handler method within the *MainActivity.java* file:

```
@Override
public boolean onOptionsItemSelected(MenuItem item) {
    int id = item.getItemId();
    if (id == R.id.action_print) {
        createWebPrintJob(myWebView);
        return true;
    }
    return super.onOptionsItemSelected(item);
}
```

With the *onOptionsItemSelected()* method implemented, the activity will call a method named *createWebPrintJob()*

An Android HTML and Web Content Printing Example

when the print menu option is selected from the overflow menu. The implementation of this method is identical to that used in the previous HTMLPrint project and may now be added to the *MainActivity.java* file such that it reads as follows:

```java
package com.ebookfrenzy.webprint;
.
.
.
import android.print.PrintAttributes;
import android.print.PrintDocumentAdapter;
import android.print.PrintManager;
import android.content.Context;

public class MainActivity extends AppCompatActivity {

    private WebView myWebView;
.
.

    private void createWebPrintJob(WebView webView) {

        PrintManager printManager = (PrintManager) this
                .getSystemService(Context.PRINT_SERVICE);

        PrintDocumentAdapter printAdapter =
                webView.createPrintDocumentAdapter("MyDocument");

        String jobName = getString(R.string.app_name) +
                " Print Test";

        printManager.print(jobName, printAdapter,
                new PrintAttributes.Builder().build());
    }
.
.
}
```

With the code changes complete, run the application on a physical Android device or emulator running Android version 5.0 or later. Once successfully launched, the WebView should be visible with the designated web page loaded. Once the page has loaded, select the Print option from the Overflow menu (Figure 76-3) and use the resulting print panel to print the web page to a suitable destination.

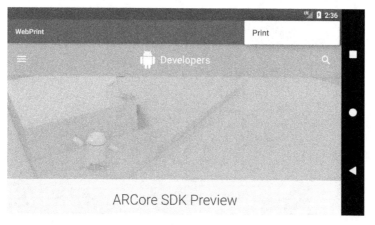

Figure 76-3

76.8 Summary

The Android Printing framework includes extensions to the WebView class that make it possible to print HTML based content from within an Android application. This content can be in the form of HTML created dynamically within the application at runtime, or a pre-existing web page loaded into a WebView instance. In the case of dynamically created HTML, it is important to use a WebViewClient instance to ensure that printing does not start until the HTML has been fully loaded into the WebView.

77. A Guide to Android Custom Document Printing

As we have seen in the preceding chapters, the Android Printing framework makes it relatively easy to build printing support into applications as long as the content is in the form of an image or HTML markup. More advanced printing requirements can be met by making use of the custom document printing feature of the Printing framework.

77.1 An Overview of Android Custom Document Printing

In simplistic terms, custom document printing uses canvases to represent the pages of the document to be printed. The application draws the content to be printed onto these canvases in the form of shapes, colors, text and images. In actual fact, the canvases are represented by instances of the Android Canvas class, thereby providing access to a rich selection of drawing options. Once all the pages have been drawn, the document is then printed.

While this sounds simple enough, there are actually a number of steps that need to be performed to make this happen, which can be summarized as follows:

- Implement a custom print adapter sub-classed from the PrintDocumentAdapter class

- Obtain a reference to the Print Manager Service

- Create an instance of the PdfDocument class in which to store the document pages

- Add pages to the PdfDocument in the form of PdfDocument.Page instances

- Obtain references to the Canvas objects associated with the document pages

- Draw content onto the canvases

- Write the PDF document to a destination output stream provided by the Printing framework

- Notify the Printing framework that the document is ready to print

In this chapter, an overview of these steps will be provided, followed by a detailed tutorial designed to demonstrate the implementation of custom document printing within Android applications.

77.1.1 Custom Print Adapters

The role of the print adapter is to provide the Printing framework with the content to be printed, and to ensure that it is formatted correctly for the user's chosen preferences (taking into consideration factors such as paper size and page orientation).

When printing HTML and images, much of this work is performed by the print adapters provided as part of the Android Printing framework and designed for these specific printing tasks. When printing a web page, for example, a print adapter is created for us when a call is made to the *createPrintDocumentAdapter()* method of an instance of the WebView class.

In the case of custom document printing, however, it is the responsibility of the application developer to design the print adapter and implement the code to draw and format the content in preparation for printing.

Custom print adapters are created by sub-classing the PrintDocumentAdapter class and overriding a set of callback methods within that class which will be called by the Printing framework at various stages in the print process. These callback methods can be summarized as follows:

· **onStart()** – This method is called when the printing process begins and is provided so that the application code has an opportunity to perform any necessary tasks in preparation for creating the print job. Implementation of this method within the PrintDocumentAdapter sub-class is optional.

· **onLayout()** – This callback method is called after the call to the *onStart()* method and then again each time the user makes changes to the print settings (such as changing the orientation, paper size or color settings). This method should adapt the content and layout where necessary to accommodate these changes. Once these changes are completed, the method must return the number of pages to be printed. Implementation of the *onLayout()* method within the PrintDocumentAdapter sub-class is mandatory.

· **onWrite()** – This method is called after each call to *onLayout()* and is responsible for rendering the content on the canvases of the pages to be printed. Amongst other arguments, this method is passed a file descriptor to which the resulting PDF document must be written once rendering is complete. A call is then made to the *onWriteFinished()* callback method passing through an argument containing information about the page ranges to be printed. Implementation of the *onWrite()* method within the PrintDocumentAdapter sub-class is mandatory.

· **onFinish()** – An optional method which, if implemented, is called once by the Printing framework when the printing process is completed, thereby providing the application the opportunity to perform any clean-up operations that may be necessary.

77.2 Preparing the Custom Document Printing Project

Select the *Start a new Android Studio project* quick start option from the welcome screen and, within the resulting new project dialog, choose the Empty Activity template before clicking on the Next button.

Enter *CustomPrint* into the Name field and specify *com.ebookfrenzy.customprint* as the package name. Before clicking on the Finish button, change the Minimum API level setting to API 26: Android 8.0 (Oreo) and the Language menu to Java.

Load the *activity_main.xml* layout file into the Layout Editor tool and, in Design mode, select and delete the "Hello World!" TextView object. Drag and drop a Button view from the Form Widgets section of the palette and position it in the center of the layout view. With the Button view selected, change the text property to "Print Document" and extract the string to a new resource. On completion, the user interface layout should match that shown in Figure 77-1:

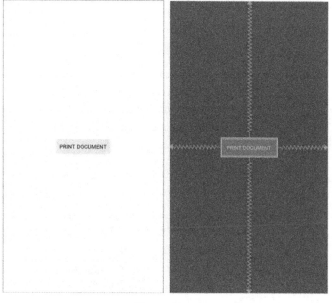

Figure 77-1

When the button is selected within the application it will be required to call a method to initiate the document printing process. Remaining within the Attributes tool window, set the *onClick* property to call a method named *printDocument*.

77.3 Creating the Custom Print Adapter

Most of the work involved in printing a custom document from within an Android application involves the implementation of the custom print adapter. This example will require a print adapter with the *onLayout()* and *onWrite()* callback methods implemented. Within the *MainActivity.java* file, add the template for this new class so that it reads as follows:

```
package com.ebookfrenzy.customprint;
.
.
import android.os.CancellationSignal;
import android.os.ParcelFileDescriptor;
import android.print.PageRange;
import android.print.PrintAttributes;
import android.print.PrintDocumentAdapter;
import android.content.Context;

public class MainActivity extends AppCompatActivity {

    public class MyPrintDocumentAdapter extends PrintDocumentAdapter
    {
        Context context;

        MyPrintDocumentAdapter(Context context)
        {
```

```
            this.context = context;
    }


    @Override
    public void onLayout(PrintAttributes oldAttributes,
                         PrintAttributes newAttributes,
                         CancellationSignal cancellationSignal,
                         LayoutResultCallback callback,
                         Bundle metadata) {

    }


    @Override
    public void onWrite(final PageRange[] pageRanges,
                        final ParcelFileDescriptor destination,
                        final CancellationSignal
                                cancellationSignal,
                        final WriteResultCallback callback) {

    }
  }
  .
  .
  .
}
```

As the new class currently stands, it contains a constructor method which will be called when a new instance of the class is created. The constructor takes as an argument the context of the calling activity which is then stored so that it can be referenced later in the two callback methods.

With the outline of the class established, the next step is to begin implementing the two callback methods, beginning with *onLayout()*.

77.4 Implementing the onLayout() Callback Method

Remaining within the *MainActivity.java* file, begin by adding some import directives that will be required by the code in the *onLayout()* method:

```
package com.ebookfrenzy.customprint;
  .
  .
import android.print.PrintDocumentInfo;
import android.print.pdf.PrintedPdfDocument;
import android.graphics.pdf.PdfDocument;

public class MainActivity extends AppCompatActivity {
  .
  .
}
```

Next, modify the MyPrintDocumentAdapter class to declare variables to be used within the *onLayout()* method:

```
public class MyPrintDocumentAdapter extends PrintDocumentAdapter
```

```
{
        Context context;
        int pageHeight;
        int pageWidth;
        PdfDocument myPdfDocument;
        int totalpages = 4;

        .

        .

        .
}
```

Note that for the purposes of this example, a four page document is going to be printed. In more complex situations, the application will most likely need to dynamically calculate the number of pages to be printed based on the quantity and layout of the content in relation to the user's paper size and page orientation selections.

With the variables declared, implement the *onLayout()* method as outlined in the following code listing:

```
@Override
public void onLayout(PrintAttributes oldAttributes,
                    PrintAttributes newAttributes,
                    CancellationSignal cancellationSignal,
                    LayoutResultCallback callback,
                    Bundle metadata) {

    myPdfDocument = new PrintedPdfDocument(context, newAttributes);

    pageHeight =
        newAttributes.getMediaSize().getHeightMils()/1000 * 72;
    pageWidth =
        newAttributes.getMediaSize().getWidthMils()/1000 * 72;

    if (cancellationSignal.isCanceled() ) {
        callback.onLayoutCancelled();
        return;
    }

    if (totalpages > 0) {
        PrintDocumentInfo.Builder builder = new PrintDocumentInfo
            .Builder("print_output.pdf").setContentType(
                PrintDocumentInfo.CONTENT_TYPE_DOCUMENT)
            .setPageCount(totalpages);

        PrintDocumentInfo info = builder.build();
        callback.onLayoutFinished(info, true);
    } else {
        callback.onLayoutFailed("Page count is zero.");
    }
}
```

Clearly this method is performing quite a few tasks, each of which requires some detailed explanation.

To begin with, a new PDF document is created in the form of a PdfDocument class instance. One of the arguments passed into the *onLayout()* method when it is called by the Printing framework is an object of type PrintAttributes containing details about the paper size, resolution and color settings selected by the user for the print output. These settings are used when creating the PDF document, along with the context of the activity previously stored for us by our constructor method:

```
myPdfDocument = new PrintedPdfDocument(context, newAttributes);
```

The method then uses the PrintAttributes object to extract the height and width values for the document pages. These dimensions are stored in the object in the form of thousandths of an inch. Since the methods that will use these values later in this example work in units of 1/72 of an inch these numbers are converted before they are stored:

```
pageHeight = newAttributes.getMediaSize().getHeightMils()/1000 * 72;
pageWidth = newAttributes.getMediaSize().getWidthMils()/1000 * 72;
```

Although this example does not make use of the user's color selection, this property can be obtained via a call to the *getColorMode()* method of the PrintAttributes object which will return a value of either COLOR_MODE_COLOR or COLOR_MODE_MONOCHROME.

When the *onLayout()* method is called, it is passed an object of type *LayoutResultCallback*. This object provides a way for the method to communicate status information back to the Printing framework via a set of methods. The *onLayout()* method, for example, will be called in the event that the user cancels the print process. The fact that the process has been cancelled is indicated via a setting within the CancellationSignal argument. In the event that a cancellation is detected, the *onLayout()* method must call the *onLayoutCancelled()* method of the *LayoutResultCallback* object to notify the Print framework that the cancellation request was received and that the layout task has been cancelled:

```
if (cancellationSignal.isCanceled() ) {
        callback.onLayoutCancelled();
        return;
}
```

When the layout work is complete, the method is required to call the *onLayoutFinished()* method of the *LayoutResultCallback* object, passing through two arguments. The first argument takes the form of a PrintDocumentInfo object containing information about the document to be printed. This information consists of the name to be used for the PDF document, the type of content (in this case a document rather than an image) and the page count. The second argument is a Boolean value indicating whether or not the layout has changed since the last call made to the *onLayout()* method:

```
if (totalpages > 0) {
        PrintDocumentInfo.Builder builder = new PrintDocumentInfo
                .Builder("print_output.pdf")
                .setContentType(
                    PrintDocumentInfo.CONTENT_TYPE_DOCUMENT)
                .setPageCount(totalpages);

        PrintDocumentInfo info = builder.build();

        callback.onLayoutFinished(info, true);
} else {
```

```
        callback.onLayoutFailed("Page count is zero.");
}
```

In the event that the page count is zero, the code reports this failure to the Printing framework via a call to the *onLayoutFailed()* method of the *LayoutResultCallback* object.

The call to the *onLayoutFinished()* method notifies the Printing framework that the layout work is complete, thereby triggering a call to the *onWrite()* method.

77.5 Implementing the onWrite() Callback Method

The *onWrite()* callback method is responsible for rendering the pages of the document and then notifying the Printing framework that the document is ready to be printed. When completed, the *onWrite()* method reads as follows:

```
package com.ebookfrenzy.customprint;

import java.io.FileOutputStream;
import java.io.IOException;
.
.
import android.graphics.pdf.PdfDocument.PageInfo;
.
.
@Override
public void onWrite(final PageRange[] pageRanges,
                final ParcelFileDescriptor destination,
                final CancellationSignal cancellationSignal,
                final WriteResultCallback callback) {

    for (int i = 0; i < totalpages; i++) {
        if (pageInRange(pageRanges, i))
        {
            PageInfo newPage = new PageInfo.Builder(pageWidth,
                pageHeight, i).create();

            PdfDocument.Page page =
                myPdfDocument.startPage(newPage);

            if (cancellationSignal.isCanceled()) {
                callback.onWriteCancelled();
                myPdfDocument.close();
                myPdfDocument = null;
                return;
            }
            drawPage(page, i);
            myPdfDocument.finishPage(page);
        }
    }
```

```
try {
        myPdfDocument.writeTo(new FileOutputStream(
                        destination.getFileDescriptor()));
} catch (IOException e) {
        callback.onWriteFailed(e.toString());
        return;
} finally {
        myPdfDocument.close();
        myPdfDocument = null;
}


        callback.onWriteFinished(pageRanges);
}
```

The *onWrite()* method starts by looping through each of the pages in the document. It is important to take into consideration, however, that the user may not have requested that all of the pages that make up the document be printed. In actual fact, the Printing framework user interface panel provides the option to specify that specific pages, or ranges of pages be printed. Figure 77-2, for example, shows the print panel configured to print pages 1-4, pages 8 and 9 and pages 11-13 of a document.

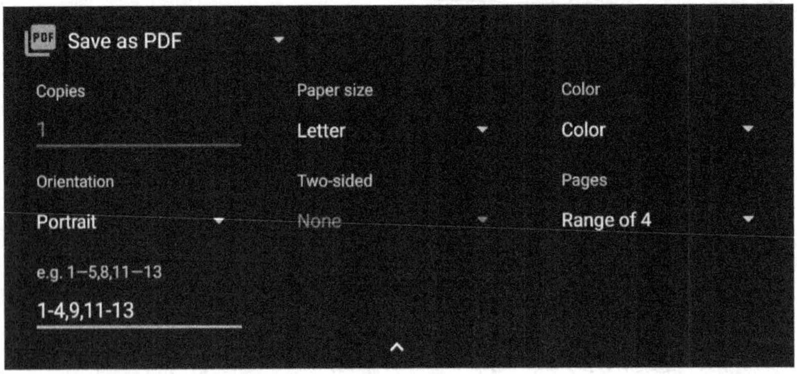

Figure 77-2

When writing the pages to the PDF document, the *onWrite()* method must take steps to ensure that only those pages specified by the user are printed. To make this possible, the Printing framework passes through as an argument an array of PageRange objects indicating the ranges of pages to be printed. In the above *onWrite()* implementation, a method named *pagesInRange()* is called for each page to verify that the page is within the specified ranges. The code for the *pagesInRange()* method will be implemented later in this chapter.

```
for (int i = 0; i < totalpages; i++) {
        if (pageInRange(pageRanges, i))
        {
```

For each page that is within any specified ranges, a new PdfDocument.Page object is created. When creating a new page, the height and width values previously stored by the *onLayout()* method are passed through as arguments so that the page size matches the print options selected by the user:

```
PageInfo newPage = new PageInfo.Builder(pageWidth, pageHeight, i).create();
```

```
PdfDocument.Page page = myPdfDocument.startPage(newPage);
```

As with the *onLayout()* method, the *onWrite()* method is required to respond to cancellation requests. In this case, the code notifies the Printing framework that the cancellation has been performed, before closing and de-referencing the myPdfDocument variable:

```
if (cancellationSignal.isCanceled()) {
        callback.onWriteCancelled();
        myPdfDocument.close();
        myPdfDocument = null;
        return;
}
```

As long as the print process has not been cancelled, the method then calls a method to draw the content on the current page before calling the *finishedPage()* method on the myPdfDocument object.

```
drawPage(page, i);
myPdfDocument.finishPage(page);
```

The *drawPage()* method is responsible for drawing the content onto the page and will be implemented once the *onWrite()* method is complete.

When the required number of pages have been added to the PDF document, the document is then written to the *destination* stream using the file descriptor which was passed through as an argument to the *onWrite()* method. If, for any reason, the write operation fails, the method notifies the framework by calling the *onWriteFailed()* method of the *WriteResultCallback* object (also passed as an argument to the *onWrite()* method).

```
try {
        myPdfDocument.writeTo(new FileOutputStream(
                destination.getFileDescriptor()));
} catch (IOException e) {
                callback.onWriteFailed(e.toString());
                return;
} finally {
                myPdfDocument.close();
                myPdfDocument = null;
}
```

Finally, the *onWriteFinish()* method of the *WriteResultsCallback* object is called to notify the Printing framework that the document is ready to be printed.

77.6 Checking a Page is in Range

As previously outlined, when the *onWrite()* method is called it is passed an array of PageRange objects indicating the ranges of pages within the document that are to be printed. The PageRange class is designed to store the start and end pages of a page range which, in turn, may be accessed via the *getStart()* and *getEnd()* methods of the class.

When the *onWrite()* method was implemented in the previous section, a call was made to a method named *pageInRange()*, which takes as arguments an array of PageRange objects and a page number. The role of the *pageInRange()* method is to identify whether the specified page number is within the ranges specified and may be implemented within the MyPrintDocumentAdapter class in the *MainActivity.java* class as follows:

```
public class MyPrintDocumentAdapter extends PrintDocumentAdapter {
.
```

```
        private boolean pageInRange(PageRange[] pageRanges, int page)
        {
                for (PageRange pageRange : pageRanges) {
                    if ((page >= pageRange.getStart()) &&
                            (page <= pageRange.getEnd()))
                        return true;
                }
                return false;
        }
}
```

77.7 Drawing the Content on the Page Canvas

We have now reached the point where some code needs to be written to draw the content on the pages so that they are ready for printing. The content that gets drawn is completely application specific and limited only by what can be achieved using the Android Canvas class. For the purposes of this example, however, some simple text and graphics will be drawn on the canvas.

The *onWrite()* method has been designed to call a method named *drawPage()* which takes as arguments the PdfDocument.Page object representing the current page and an integer representing the page number. Within the *MainActivity.java* file this method should now be implemented as follows:

```
package com.ebookfrenzy.customprint;

import android.graphics.Canvas;
import android.graphics.Color;
import android.graphics.Paint;

public class MainActivity extends AppCompatActivity {

        public class MyPrintDocumentAdapter extends
                                        PrintDocumentAdapter
        {

                private void drawPage(PdfDocument.Page page,
                                int pagenumber) {
                    Canvas canvas = page.getCanvas();

                    pagenumber++; // Make sure page numbers start at 1

                    int titleBaseLine = 72;
                    int leftMargin = 54;
```

```
            Paint paint = new Paint();
            paint.setColor(Color.BLACK);
            paint.setTextSize(40);
            canvas.drawText(
               "Test Print Document Page " + pagenumber,
                                          leftMargin,
                                          titleBaseLine,
                                          paint);


            paint.setTextSize(14);
            canvas.drawText("This is some test content to verify that
custom document printing works", leftMargin, titleBaseLine + 35, paint);


            if (pagenumber % 2 == 0)
                         paint.setColor(Color.RED);
            else
                  paint.setColor(Color.GREEN);


            PageInfo pageInfo = page.getInfo();


            canvas.drawCircle(pageInfo.getPageWidth()/2,
                            pageInfo.getPageHeight()/2,
                            150,
                            paint);
      }
 .
 .
 .
}
```

Page numbering within the code starts at 0. Since documents traditionally start at page 1, the method begins by incrementing the stored page number. A reference to the Canvas object associated with the page is then obtained and some margin and baseline values declared:

```
Canvas canvas = page.getCanvas();

pagenumber++;

int titleBaseLine = 72;
int leftMargin = 54;
```

Next, the code creates Paint and Color objects to be used for drawing, sets a text size and draws the page title text, including the current page number:

```
Paint paint = new Paint();

paint.setColor(Color.BLACK);
paint.setTextSize(40);
```

```
canvas.drawText("Test Print Document Page " + pagenumber,
                                          leftMargin,
                                          titleBaseLine,
                                          paint);
```

The text size is then reduced and some body text drawn beneath the title:

```
paint.setTextSize(14);
canvas.drawText("This is some test content to verify that custom document
printing works", leftMargin, titleBaseLine + 35, paint);
```

The last task performed by this method involves drawing a circle (red on even numbered pages and green on odd). Having ascertained whether the page is odd or even, the method obtains the height and width of the page before using this information to position the circle in the center of the page:

```
if (pagenumber % 2 == 0)
        paint.setColor(Color.RED);
else
        paint.setColor(Color.GREEN);

PageInfo pageInfo = page.getInfo();

canvas.drawCircle(pageInfo.getPageWidth()/2,
                  pageInfo.getPageHeight()/2,
                  150, paint);
```

Having drawn on the canvas, the method returns control to the *onWrite()* method.

With the completion of the *drawPage()* method, the MyPrintDocumentAdapter class is now finished.

77.8 Starting the Print Job

When the "Print Document" button is touched by the user, the *printDocument()* onClick event handler method will be called. All that now remains before testing can commence, therefore, is to add this method to the *MainActivity.java* file, taking particular care to ensure that it is placed outside of the MyPrintDocumentAdapter class:

```
package com.ebookfrenzy.customprint;
.
.
.
import android.print.PrintManager;
import android.view.View;

public class MainActivity extends AppCompatActivity {

        public void printDocument(View view)
        {
            PrintManager printManager = (PrintManager) this
                    .getSystemService(Context.PRINT_SERVICE);

            String jobName = this.getString(R.string.app_name) +
```

```
        " Document";

printManager.print(jobName, new
        MyPrintDocumentAdapter(this),
        null);
}
.
.
.
}
```

This method obtains a reference to the Print Manager service running on the device before creating a new String object to serve as the job name for the print task. Finally the *print()* method of the Print Manager is called to start the print job, passing through the job name and an instance of our custom print document adapter class.

77.9 Testing the Application

Compile and run the application on an Android device or emulator that is running Android 4.4 or later. When the application has loaded, touch the "Print Document" button to initiate the print job and select a suitable target for the output (the Save to PDF option is a useful option for avoiding wasting paper and printer ink).

Check the printed output which should consist of 4 pages including text and graphics. Figure 77-3, for example, shows the four pages of the document viewed as a PDF file ready to be saved on the device.

Experiment with other print configuration options such as changing the paper size, orientation and pages settings within the print panel. Each setting change should be reflected in the printed output, indicating that the custom print document adapter is functioning correctly.

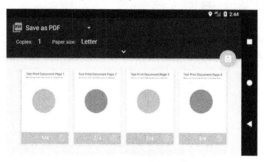

Figure 77-3

77.10 Summary

Although more complex to implement than the Android Printing framework HTML and image printing options, custom document printing provides considerable flexibility in terms of printing complex content from within an Android application. The majority of the work involved in implementing custom document printing involves the creation of a custom Print Adapter class such that it not only draws the content on the document pages, but also responds correctly as changes are made by the user to print settings such as the page size and range of pages to be printed.

78. An Introduction to Android App Links

As technology evolves, the traditional distinction between web and mobile content is beginning to blur. One area where this is particularly true is the growing popularity of progressive web apps, where web apps look and behave much like traditional mobile apps.

Another trend involves making the content within mobile apps discoverable within web search and via URL links. In the context of Android app development, the App Links feature is designed specifically to make it easier for users to both discover and access content that is stored within an Android app even if the user does not have the app installed.

78.1 An Overview of Android App Links

An app link is a standard HTTP URL intended to serve as an easy way to link directly to a particular place in your app from an external source such as a website or app. App links (also referred to as *deep links*) are used primarily to encourage users to engage with an app and to allow users to share app content.

App link implementation is a multi-step process that involves the addition of intent filters to the project manifest, the implementation of link handling code within the associated app activities and the use of digital assets files to associate app and web-based content.

These steps can either be performed manually by making changes within the project, or automatically using the Android Studio App Links Assistant.

The remainder of this chapter will outline app links implementation in terms of the changes that need to be made to a project. The next chapter (*"An Android Studio App Links Tutorial"*) will demonstrate the use of the App Links Assistant to achieve the same results.

78.2 App Link Intent Filters

An app link URL needs to be mapped to a specific activity within an app project. This is achieved by adding intent filters to the project's *AndroidManifest.xml* file designed to launch an activity in response to an *android.intent.action.VIEW* action. The intent filters are declared within the element for the activity to be launched and must contain the data outlining the scheme, host and path of the app link URL. The following manifest fragment, for example, declares an intent filter to launch an activity named MyActivity when an app link matching *http://www.example.com/welcome* is detected:

```
<activity android:name="com.ebookfrenzy.myapp.MyActivity">

    <intent-filter>
        <action android:name="android.intent.action.VIEW" />
        <category android:name="android.intent.category.DEFAULT" />
        <category android:name="android.intent.category.BROWSABLE" />

        <data
```

```
            android:scheme="http"
            android:host="www.example.com"
            android:pathPrefix="/welcome" />
    </intent-filter>
</activity>
```

The order in which ambiguous intent filters are handled can be specified using the *order* property of the intent filter tag as follows:

```
<application>
    <activity android:name=" com.ebookfrenzy.myapp.MyActivity">
        <intent-filter android:order="1">
        .
        .
```

The intent filter will cause the app link to launch the correct activity, but code still needs to be implemented within the target activity to handle the intent appropriately.

78.3 Handling App Link Intents

In most cases, the launched activity will need to gain access to the app link URL and to take specific action based on the way in which the URL is structured. Continuing from the above example, the activity will most likely display different content when launched via a URL containing a path of */welcome/newuser* than one with the path set to */welcome/existinguser*.

When the activity is launched by the link, it is passed an intent object containing data about the action which launched the activity including a Uri object containing the app link URL. Within the initialization stages of the activity, code can be added to extract this data as follows:

```
Intent appLinkIntent = getIntent();
String appLinkAction = appLinkIntent.getAction();
Uri appLinkData = appLinkIntent.getData();
```

Having obtained the Uri for the app link, the various components that make up the URL path can be used to make decisions about the actions to be performed within the activity. In the following code example, the last component of the URL is used to identify whether content should be displayed for a new or existing user:

```
String userType = appLinkData.getLastPathSegment();

if (userType.equals("newuser")) {
    // display new user content
} else {
    // display existing user content
}
```

78.4 Associating the App with a Website

By default, Android will provide the user with a range of options for handling an app link using the panel shown in Figure 78-1. This will usually consist of the Chrome browser and the target app.

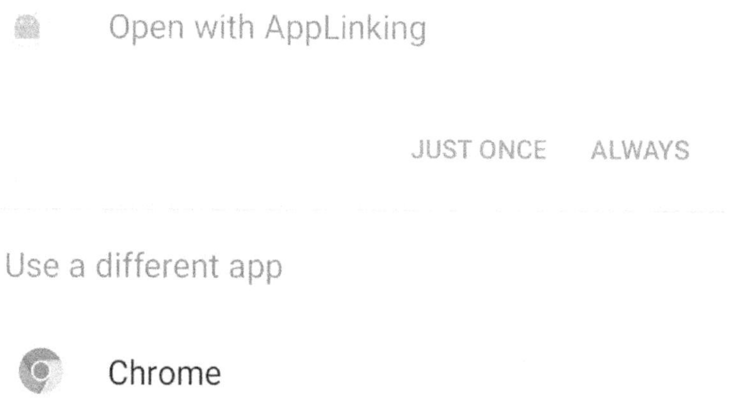

Open with AppLinking

JUST ONCE   ALWAYS

Use a different app

Chrome

Figure 78-1

To prevent this from happening the app link URL needs to be associated with the website on which the app link is based. This is achieved by creating a Digital Assets Link file named *assetlinks.json* and installing it within the website's *.well-known* folder. Note that digital asset linking is only possible for websites that are https based.

A digital asset link file comprises a *relation* statement granting permission for a target app to be launched using the web site's link URLs and a target statement declaring the companion app package name and SHA-256 certificate fingerprint for that project. A typical asset link file might, for example, read as follows:

```
[{
    "relation": ["delegate_permission/common.handle_all_urls"],
    "target" : { "namespace": "android_app",
      "package_name": "<app package name here>",
                "sha256_cert_fingerprints": ["<app certificate here>"] }
}]
```

The *assetlinks.json* file can contain multiple digital asset links, potentially allowing a single web site to be associated with more than one companion app.

78.5 Summary

Android App Links allow app activities to be launched via URL links both from external websites and other apps. App links are implemented using a combination of intent filters within the project manifest file and intent handling code within the launched activity. It is also possible, through the use of a Digital Assets Link file, to associate the domain name used in an app link with the corresponding website. Once the association has been established, Android no longer needs to ask the user to select the target app when an app link is used.

79. An Android Studio App Links Tutorial

The goal of this chapter is to provide a practical demonstration of both Android app links and the Android Studio App Link Assistant.

This chapter will add app linking support to an existing Android app, allowing an activity to be launched via an app link URL. In addition to launching the activity, the content displayed will be specified within the path of the URL.

79.1 About the Example App

The project used in this chapter is named AppLinking and is a basic app designed to allow users to find out information about landmarks in London. The app uses a SQLite database accessed through a standard Android content provider class. The app is provided with an existing database containing a set of records for some popular tourist attractions in London. In addition to the existing database entries, the app also lets the user add and delete landmark descriptions.

In its current form, the app allows the existing records to be searched and new records to be added and deleted.

The project consists of two activities named AppLinkingActivity and LandmarkActivity. AppLinkingActivity is the main activity launched at app startup. This activity allows the user to enter search criteria and to add additional records to the database. When a search locates a matching record, LandmarkActivity launches and displays the information for the related landmark.

The goal of this chapter is to enhance the app to add support for app linking so that URLs can be used to display specific landmark records within the app.

79.2 The Database Schema

The data for the example app is contained within a file named *landmarks.db* located in the *app -> assets -> databases* folder of the project hierarchy. The database contains a single table named *locations*, the structure of which is outlined in Table 79-1:

Column	Type	Description
_id	String	The primary index, this column contains string values that uniquely identify the landmarks in the database.
Title	String	The name of the landmark (e.g. London Bridge).
description	String	A description of the landmark.
personal	Boolean	Indicates whether the record is personal or public. This value is set to true for all records added by the user. Existing records provided with the database are set to false.

Table 79-1

79.3 Loading and Running the Project

The project is contained within the *AppLinking* folder of the sample source code download archive located at the following URL:

https://www.ebookfrenzy.com/retail/androidstudio35/index.php

Having located the folder, open it within Android Studio and run the app on a device or emulator. Once the app is launched, the screen illustrated in Figure 79-1 below will appear:

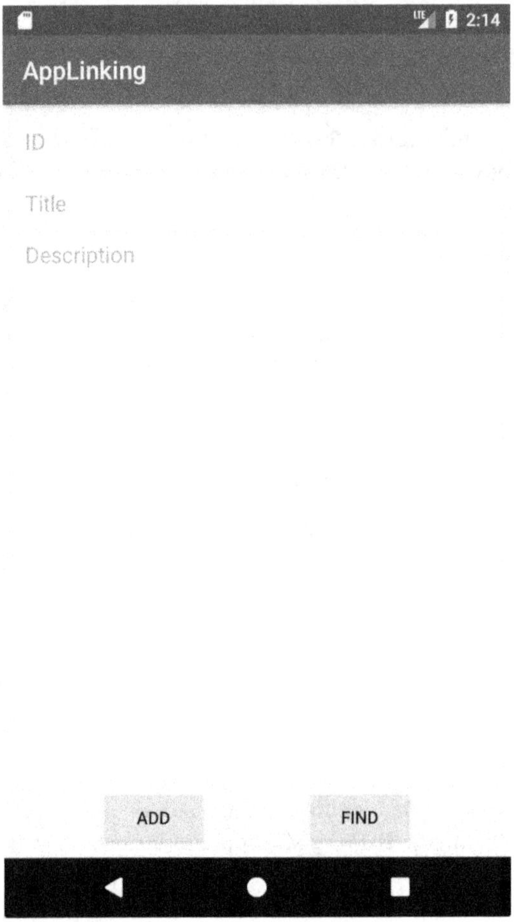

Figure 79-1

As currently implemented, landmarks are located using the ID for the location. The default database configuration currently contains two records referenced by the IDs "londonbridge" and "toweroflondon". Test the search feature by entering *londonbridge* into the ID field and clicking the *Find* button. When a matching record is found, the second activity (LandmarkActivity) is launched and passed information about the record to be displayed. This information takes the form of extra data added to the Intent object. This information is used by LandmarkActivity to extract the record from the database and display it to the user using the screen shown in Figure 79-2.

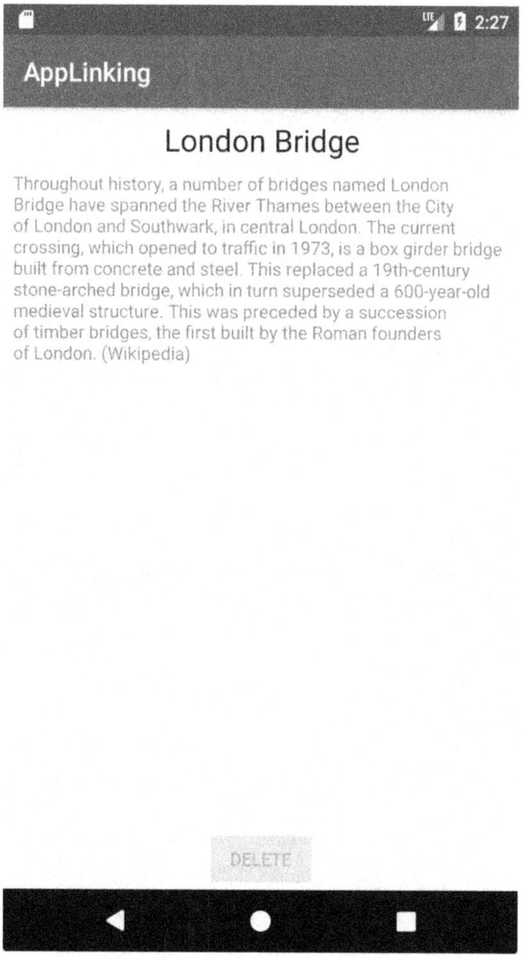

Figure 79-2

79.4 Adding the URL Mapping

Now that the app has been loaded into Android Studio and tested, the project is ready for the addition of app link support. The objective is for the LandmarkActivity screen to launch and display information in response to an app link click. This is achieved by mapping a URL to LandmarkActivity. For this example, the format of the URL will be as follows:

```
http://<website domain>/landmarks/<landmarkId>
```

When all of the steps have been completed, the following URL should, for example, cause the app to display information for the Tower of London:

```
http://www.yourdomain.com/landmarks/toweroflondon
```

To add a URL mapping to the project, begin by opening the App Links Assistant using the *Tools -> App Links Assistant* menu option. Once open, the assistant should appear as shown in Figure 79-3:

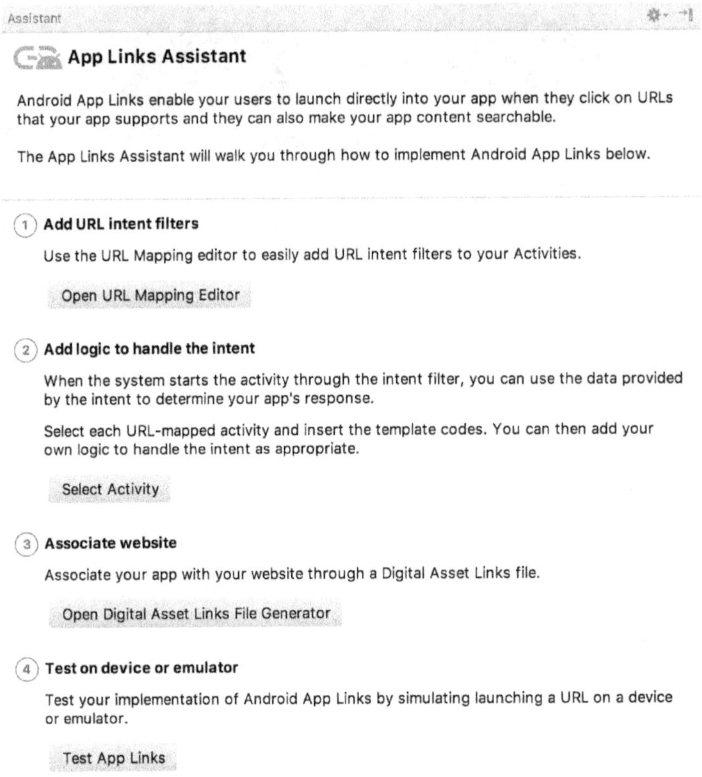

Figure 79-3

Click on the *Open URL Mapping Editor* button to begin mapping a URL to an activity. Within the mapping screen, click on the '+' button (highlighted in Figure 79-4) to add a new URL:

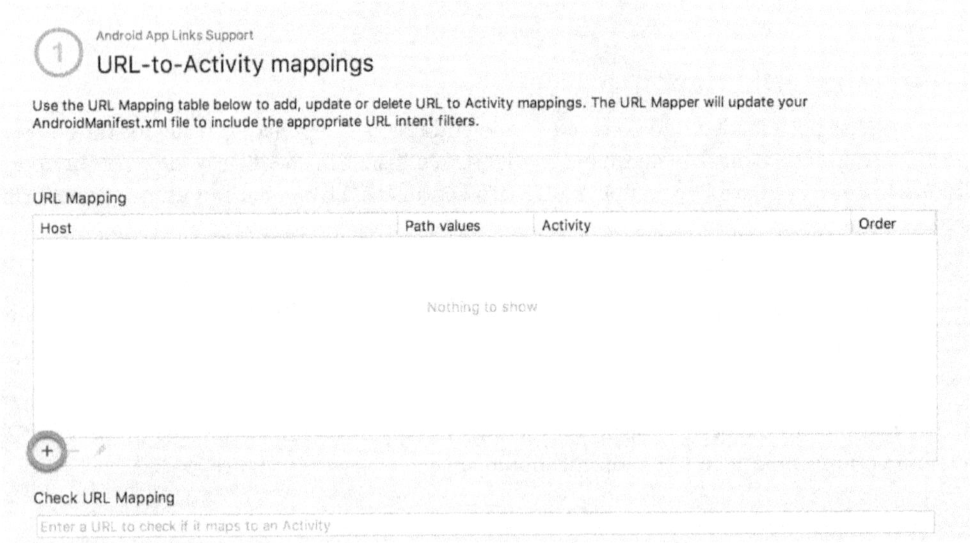

Figure 79-4

In the Host field of the *Add URL Mapping* dialog, enter either the domain name for your website or *http://www.example.com* if you do not have one.

The Path field (marked A in Figure 79-5 below) is where the path component of the URL is declared. The path must be prefixed with / so enter */landmarks* into this field.

The Path menu (B) provides the following three path matching options:

- **path** – The URL must match the path component of the URL exactly in order to launch the activity. If the path is set to /landmarks, for example, *http://www.example.com/landmarks* will be considered a match. A URL of *http://www.example.com/landmarks/londonbridge*, however, will not be considered a match.

- **pathPrefix** – The specified path is only considered as the prefix. Additional path components may be included after the */landmarks* component (for example *http://www.example.com/landmarks/londonbridge* will still be considered a match).

- **pathPattern** – Allows the path to be specified using pattern matching in the form of basic regular expressions and wildcards, for example *landmarks/*/[l-L]ondon/*

Since the path in this example is a prefix to the landmark ID component, select the *pathPrefix* menu option.

Finally, use the Activity menu (C) to select LandmarkActivity as the activity to be launched in response to the app link:

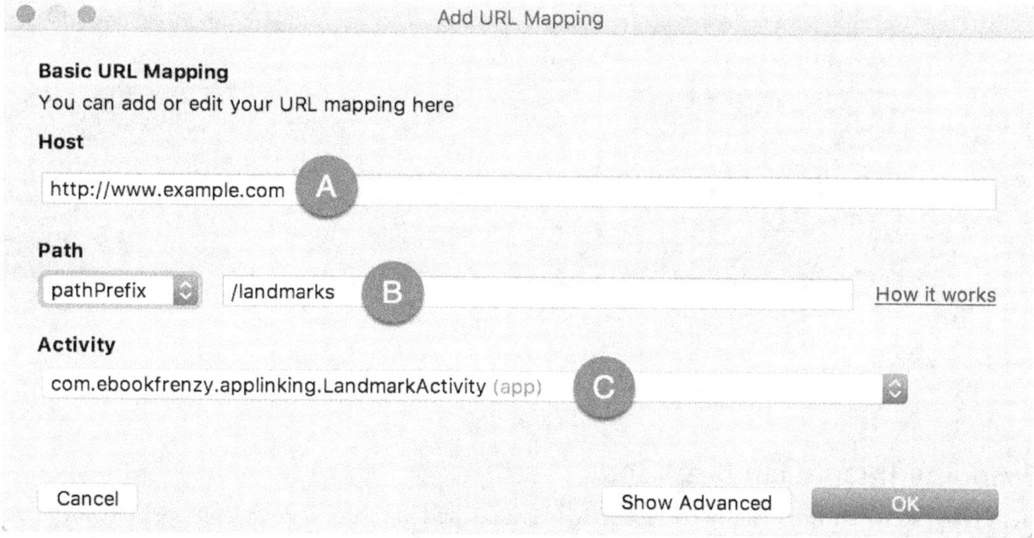

Basic URL Mapping
You can add or edit your URL mapping here

Host

http://www.example.com A

Path

pathPrefix   /landmarks B   How it works

Activity

com.ebookfrenzy.applinking.LandmarkActivity (app) C

Cancel   Show Advanced   OK

Figure 79-5

After completing the settings in the dialog, click on the *OK* button to commit the changes. Check that the URL is correctly formatted and assigned to the appropriate activity by entering the following URL into the *Check URL Mapping* field of the mapping screen (where *<your domain>* is set to the domain specified in the Host field above) :

```
http://<your domain>/landmarks/toweroflondon
```

If the mapping is configured correctly, LandmarkActivity will be listed as the mapped activity:

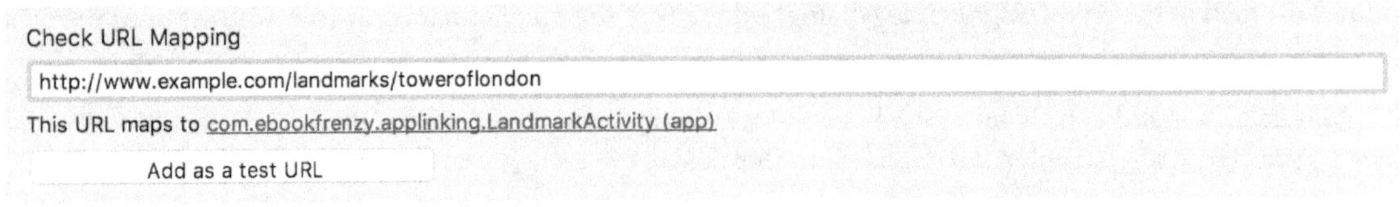

Check URL Mapping

http://www.example.com/landmarks/toweroflondon

This URL maps to com.ebookfrenzy.applinking.LandmarkActivity (app)

Add as a test URL

Figure 79-6

The latest version of Android requires that App Links be declared for both HTTP and HTTPS protocols, even if only one is being used. Before proceeding to the next step, therefore, repeat the above steps to add the HTTPS version of the URL to the list.

The next step will also be performed in the URL mapping screen of the App Links Assistant, so leave the screen selected.

79.5 Adding the Intent Filter

As explained in the previous chapter, an intent filter is needed to allow the target activity to be launched in response to an app link click. In fact, when the URL mapping was added, the intent filter was automatically added to the project manifest file. With the URL mapping selected in the App Links Assistant URL mapping list, scroll down the screen until the intent filter Preview section comes into view. The preview should contain the modified *AndroidManifest.xml* file with the newly added intent filters included:

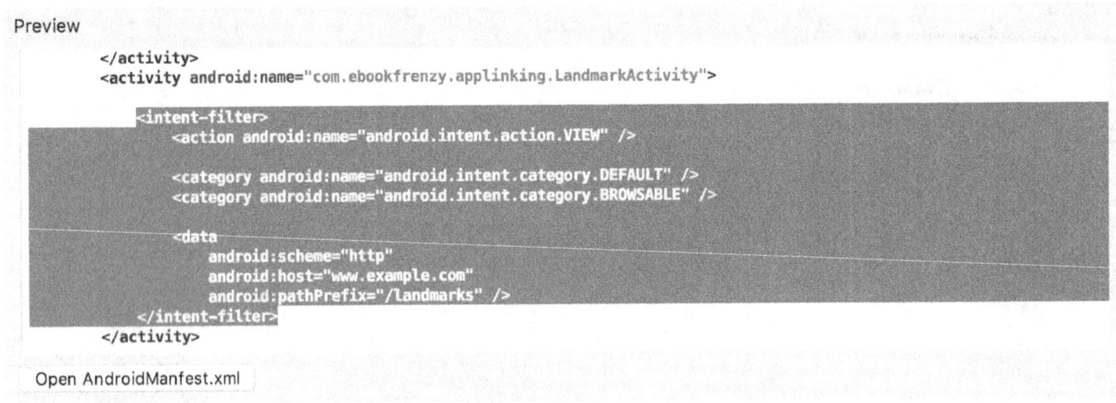

Preview

```
        </activity>
        <activity android:name="com.ebookfrenzy.applinking.LandmarkActivity">
            <intent-filter>
                <action android:name="android.intent.action.VIEW" />

                <category android:name="android.intent.category.DEFAULT" />
                <category android:name="android.intent.category.BROWSABLE" />

                <data
                    android:scheme="http"
                    android:host="www.example.com"
                    android:pathPrefix="/landmarks" />
            </intent-filter>
        </activity>
```

Open AndroidManfest.xml

Figure 79-7

79.6 Adding Intent Handling Code

The steps taken so far ensure that the correct activity is launched in response to an appropriately formatted app link URL. The next step is to handle the intent within the LandmarkActivity class so that the correct record is extracted from the database and displayed to the user. Before making any changes to the code within the *LandmarkActivity.java* file, it is worthwhile reviewing some areas of the existing code. Open the *LandmarkActivity.java* file in the code editor and locate the *onCreate()* and *handleIntent()* methods which should currently read as follows:

```
@Override
protected void onCreate(Bundle savedInstanceState) {
    super.onCreate(savedInstanceState);
    setContentView(R.layout.activity_landmark);

    titleText = findViewById(R.id.titleText);
```

```
descriptionText = findViewById(R.id.descriptionText);
deleteButton = findViewById(R.id.deleteButton);

handleIntent(getIntent());
}


private void handleIntent(Intent intent) {
    String landmarkId =
        intent.getStringExtra(AppLinkingActivity.LANDMARK_ID);
    displayLandmark(landmarkId);
}
```

In its current form, the code is expecting to find the landmark ID within the extra data of the Intent bundle. Since the activity can now also be launched by an app link, this code needs to be changed to handle both scenarios. Begin by deleting the call to *handleIntent()* in the *onCreate()* method:

```
@Override
protected void onCreate(Bundle savedInstanceState) {
    super.onCreate(savedInstanceState);
    setContentView(R.layout.activity_landmark);

    titleText = findViewById(R.id.titleText);
    descriptionText = findViewById(R.id.descriptionText);
    deleteButton = findViewById(R.id.deleteButton);

    handleIntent(getIntent());
}
```

To add the initial app link intent handling code, return to the App Links Assistant panel and click on the *Select Activity* button listed under step 2. Within the activity selection dialog, select the LandmarkActivity entry before clicking on the *Insert Code* button:

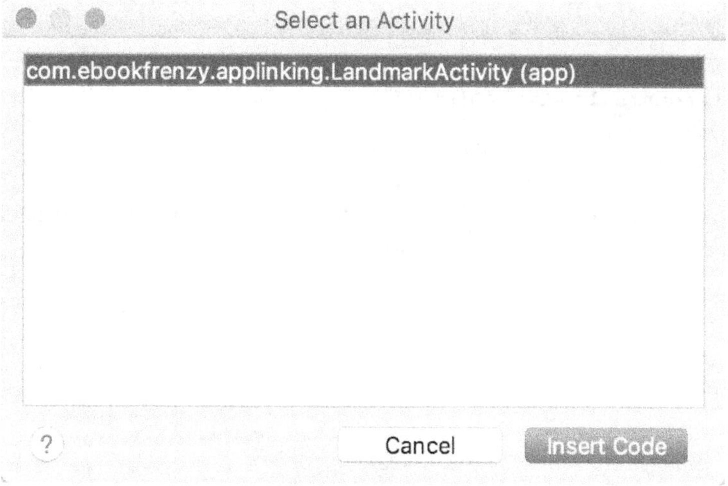

Figure 79-8

Return to the *LandmarkActivity.java* file and note that the following code has been inserted into the *onCreate()*

method (note that you can manually add this code if Android Studio is unable to complete the request):

```
// ATTENTION: This was auto-generated to handle app links.
Intent appLinkIntent = getIntent();
String appLinkAction = appLinkIntent.getAction();
Uri appLinkData = appLinkIntent.getData();
```

This code accesses the Intent object and extracts both the Action string and Uri. If the activity launch is the result of an app link, the action string will be set to *android.intent.action.VIEW* which matches the action declared in the intent filter added to the manifest file. If, on the other hand, the activity was launched by the standard intent launching code in the *findLandmark()* method of the main activity, the action string will be null. By checking the value assigned to the action string, code can be written to identify the way in which the activity was launched and take appropriate action:

```
.
.
.
import android.net.Uri;
.
.
.
@Override
protected void onCreate(Bundle savedInstanceState) {
    super.onCreate(savedInstanceState);
    setContentView(R.layout.activity_landmark);
.
.
.
    // ATTENTION: This was auto-generated to handle app links.
    Intent appLinkIntent = getIntent();
    String appLinkAction = appLinkIntent.getAction();
    Uri appLinkData = appLinkIntent.getData();

    String landmarkId = appLinkData.getLastPathSegment();

    if (landmarkId != null) {
        displayLandmark(landmarkId);
    }
}
```

All that remains is to add some additional code to the method to identify the last component in the app link URL path, and to use that as the landmark ID when querying the database:

```
@Override
protected void onCreate(Bundle savedInstanceState) {
    super.onCreate(savedInstanceState);
    setContentView(R.layout.activity_landmark);

    titleText = findViewById(R.id.titleText);
    descriptionText = findViewById(R.id.descriptionText);
    deleteButton = findViewById(R.id.deleteButton);
```

```
// ATTENTION: This was auto-generated to handle app links.
Intent appLinkIntent = getIntent();
String appLinkAction = appLinkIntent.getAction();
Uri appLinkData = appLinkIntent.getData();

if (appLinkAction != null) {

    if (appLinkAction.equals("android.intent.action.VIEW")) {
        String landmarkId = appLinkData.getLastPathSegment();

        if (landmarkId != null) {
            Log.i(TAG, "landmarkId = " + landmarkId);
            displayLandmark(landmarkId);
        }

    }
} else {
    handleIntent(appLinkIntent);
}

}
```

If the action string is not null, a check is made to verify that it is set to *android.intent.action.VIEW* before extracting the last component of the Uri path. This component is then used as the landmark ID when making the database query. If, on the other hand, the action string is null, the existing *handleIntent()* method is called to extract the ID from the intent data.

An alternative option to identifying the way in which the activity has been launched is to modify the *findLandmark()* method located in the *AppLinkingActivity.java* file so that it also triggers the launch using a View intent action:

```
public void findLandmark(View view) {

    if (!idText.getText().equals("")) {
        Landmark landmark =
                dbHandler.findLandmark(idText.getText().toString());

        if (landmark != null) {
            Uri uri = Uri.parse("http://<your_domain>/landmarks/"
                                        + landmark.getID());
            Intent intent = new Intent(Intent.ACTION_VIEW, uri);
            startActivity(intent);
        } else {
            titleText.setText("No Match");
        }

    }
}
```

This technique has the advantage that code does not need to be written to identify how the activity was launched, but also has the disadvantage that it may trigger the activity selection panel illustrated in Figure 79-10 below unless the app link is associated with a web site.

79.7 Testing the App Link

Test that the intent handling works by selecting a suitable device or emulator in the toolbar as the deployment target, returning to the App Links Assistant panel and clicking on the *Test App Links* button. When prompted for a URL to test, enter the URL (using the domain referenced in the app link mapping) for the londonbridge landmark ID before clicking on the *Run Test* button:

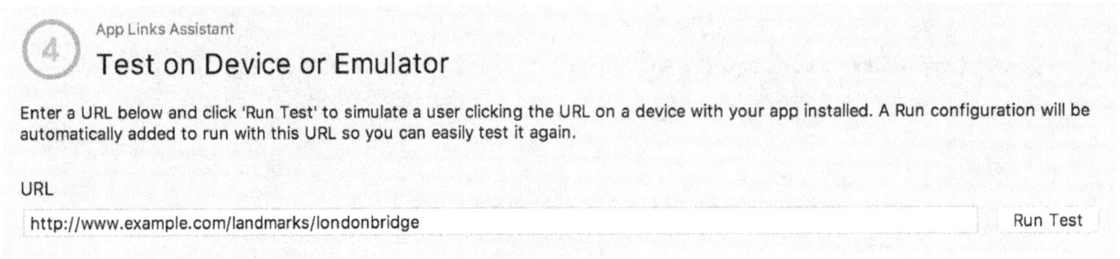

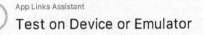

App Links Assistant

Test on Device or Emulator

Enter a URL below and click 'Run Test' to simulate a user clicking the URL on a device with your app installed. A Run configuration will be automatically added to run with this URL so you can easily test it again.

URL

http://www.example.com/landmarks/londonbridge — Run Test

Figure 79-9

Before the activity appears, it is likely that Android will display a panel (Figure 79-10) within which a choice needs to be made as to how the app link is to be handled:

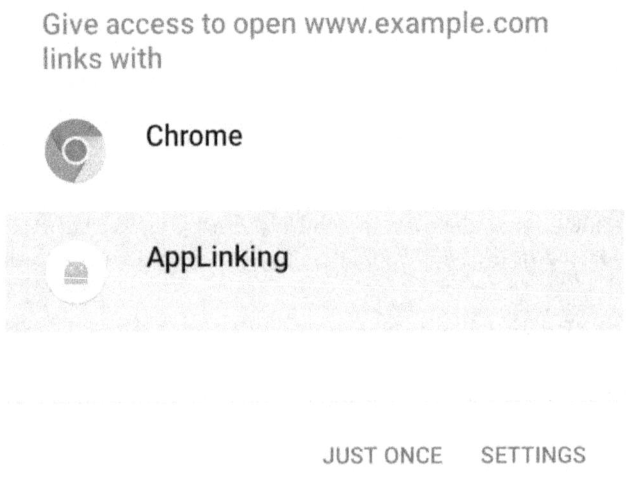

Give access to open www.example.com links with

 Chrome

 AppLinking

JUST ONCE   SETTINGS

Figure 79-10

Until the app link has been associated with a web site, Android will display this selection panel every time the activity is launched using a View intent action unless the user selects the *Always* option.

79.8 Associating an App Link with a Web Site

As outlined in the previous chapter, an app link may be associated with a web site by creating a Digital Asset Links file and installing it on the web site. Although the steps to generate this file will be covered in this chapter, it will only be possible to test these instructions using your own app (with a unique application ID) and if you have access to an https based web server onto which the assets file can be installed.

To generate the Digital Asset Links file, display the App Links Assistant and click on the *Open Digital Asset Links File Generator* button. This will display the panel shown in Figure 79-11:

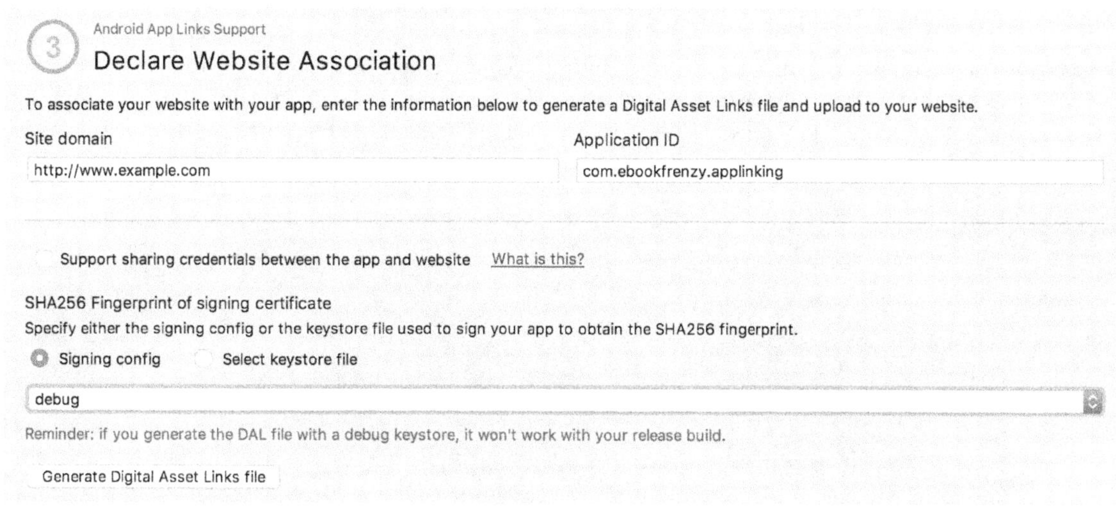

Figure 79-11

Enter the URL of the site onto which the assets file is to be uploaded and verify that the application ID matches the package name. Choose either a keystore file containing the SHA signing key for your project, or use the menu to select either the release or debug signing configuration as used by Android Studio, keeping in mind that the debug key will need to be replaced by the release key before you publish your app to the Google Play store.

If your app uses either Google Sign-In or other supported sign-in providers to authenticate users together with Google's Smart Lock feature for storing passwords, selecting the *Support sharing credentials between app and website* option will allow users to store sign-in credentials for use when signing in on both platforms.

Once the assets file has been configured, click on the *Generate Digital Asset Link File* button to preview and save the file:

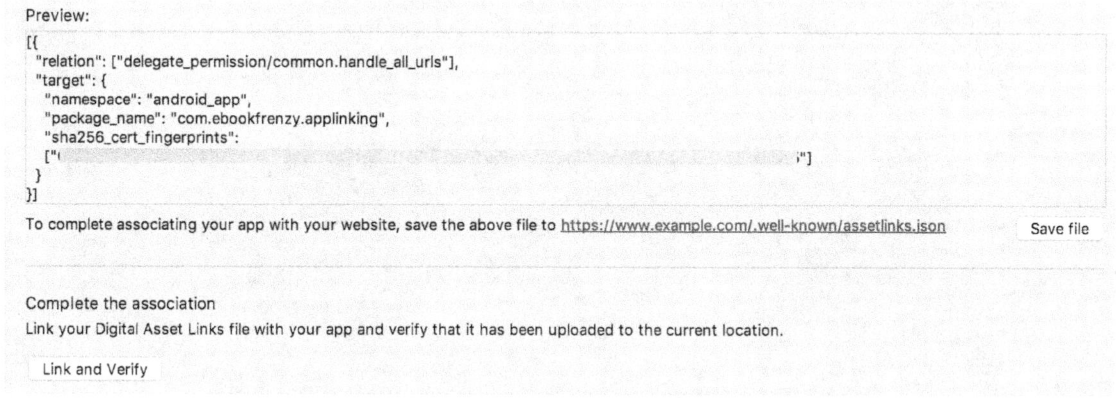

Figure 79-12

Once the file has been saved, upload it to the path specified beneath the preview panel in the above figure and click on the *Link and Verify* button to complete the process.

After the Digital Assets Link file has been linked and verified, Android should no longer display the selection panel before launching the landmark activity.

79.9 Summary

This chapter has demonstrated the steps involved in implementing App Link support within an Android app project. Areas covered in this chapter include the use of the App Link Assistant in Android Studio, App Link URL mapping, intent filters, handling website association using Digital Asset File entries and App Link testing.

80. A Guide to the Android Studio Profiler

Introduced in Android Studio 3.0, the Android Profiler provides a way to monitor CPU, networking and memory metrics of an app in realtime as it is running on a device or emulator. This serves as an invaluable tool for performing tasks such as identifying performance bottlenecks in an app, checking that the app makes appropriate use of memory resources and ensuring that the app does not use excessive networking data bandwidth. This chapter will provide a guided tour of the Android Profiler so that you can begin to use it to monitor the behavior and performance of your own apps.

80.1 Accessing the Android Profiler

The Android Profiler appears in a tool window which may be launched either using the *View -> Tool Windows -> Android Profiler* menu option or via any of the usual toolbar options available for displaying Android Studio Tool windows. Once displayed, the Profiler Tool window will appear as illustrated in Figure 80-1:

Figure 80-1

In the above figure, no processes have been detected on any connected devices or currently running emulators. To see profiling information, an app will need to be launched. Before doing that, however, it may be necessary to configure the project to enable advanced profiling information to be collected.

80.2 Enabling Advanced Profiling

If the app is built using an SDK older than API 26, it will be necessary to build the app with some additional monitoring code inserted during compilation in order to be able to monitor all of the metrics supported by the Android Profiler. To enable advanced profiling, begin by editing the build configuration settings for the build target using the menu in the Android Studio toolbar shown in Figure 80-2:

Figure 80-2

Within the Run/Debug configuration dialog, select the *Profiling* tab and enable the *Enable advanced profiling* option before clicking on the *Apply* and *OK* buttons.

80.3 The Android Profiler Tool Window

An active Profiler tool window monitoring a running app is shown in Figure 80-3.

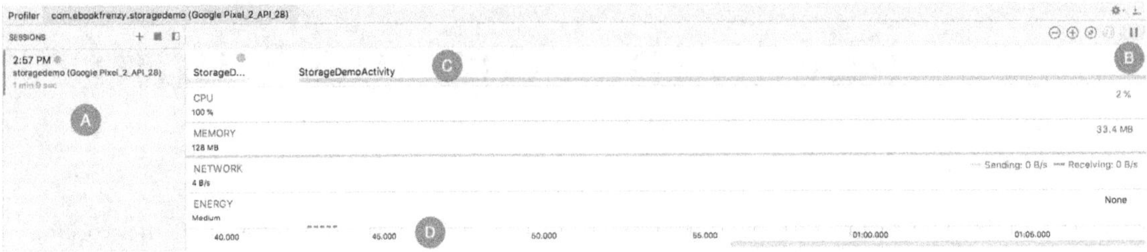

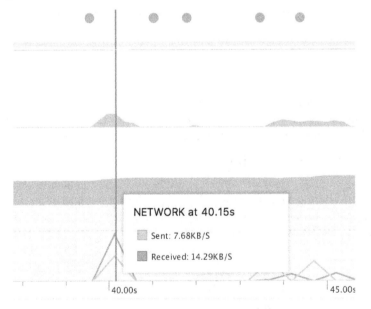

Figure 80-3

The Sessions panel (marked A) lists both the current profiling sessions and any other stored sessions performed since Android Studio was last launched. To the right of the Sessions panel is the live profiling window. The window will continue to scroll with the latest metrics unless it is paused using the *Live* button (B). Clicking on the button a second time will jump to the current time and resume scrolling. Horizontal scrolling is available for manually moving back and forth within the recorded time-line.

The top row of the window (C) is the *event time-line* and displays changes to the status of the app's activities together with other events such as the user touching the screen, typing text or changing the device orientation. The bottom time-line (D) charts the elapsed time since the app was launched.

The remaining timelines show realtime data for CPU, memory, network and energy usage. Hovering the mouse pointer over any point in the time-line (without clicking) will display additional information similar to that shown in Figure 80-4.

Figure 80-4

Clicking within the CPU, memory, networking or energy timelines will display the corresponding profiler window, each of which will be explored in the remainder of this chapter.

80.4 The Sessions Panel

When an app is running and the Profiler tool window displayed, the profiler will automatically attached to the app and begin profiling. An entry showing the app name, the device or emulator on which it is running and the start time will appear in the Sessions panel as shown in Figure 80-5. The green circle next to the time indicates a currently active profiling session. Pressing the red stop button will end the current session but the data and graphs will remain available for browsing until Android Studio exits. Additional profiling sessions can be started by clicking on the + button and selecting the device and app:

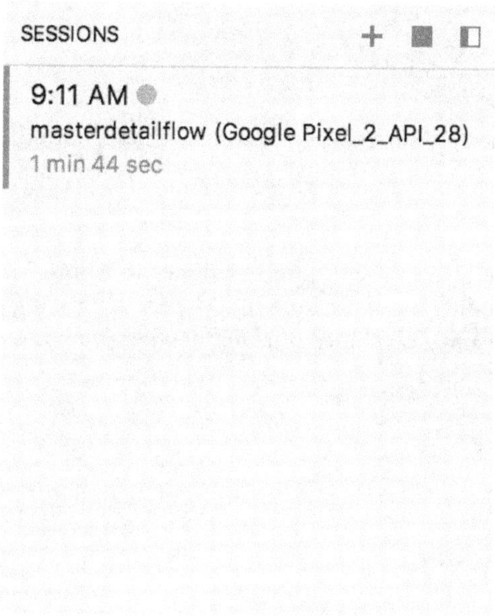

Figure 80-5

The green circle next to the time indicates a currently active profiling session. Pressing the red stop button will end the current session but the data and graphs will remain available for browsing until Android Studio exits. Additional profiling sessions can be started by clicking on the + button and selecting the device and app:

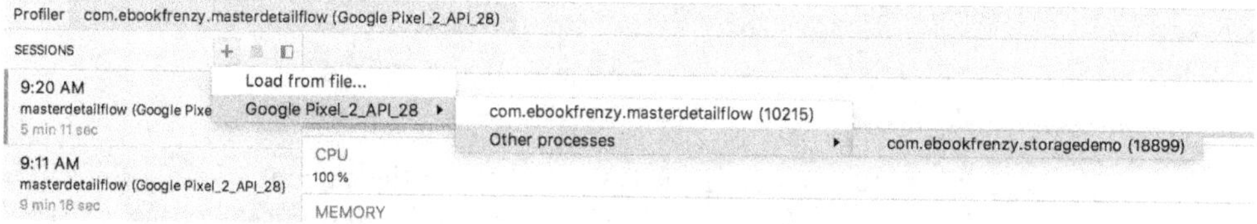

Figure 80-6

The *Load from file...* menu option allows a CPU trace previously saved from within the CPU profiler to be loaded into the Profiler for inspection.

To automatically start profiling for an app when it launches (as opposed manually starting a profiler session after the app has launched), begin by opening the *Run / Debug Configurations* dialog as outlined in Figure 80-2 above.

From within the dialog, select the Profiling screen and enable the *Start recording CPU activity startup* option:

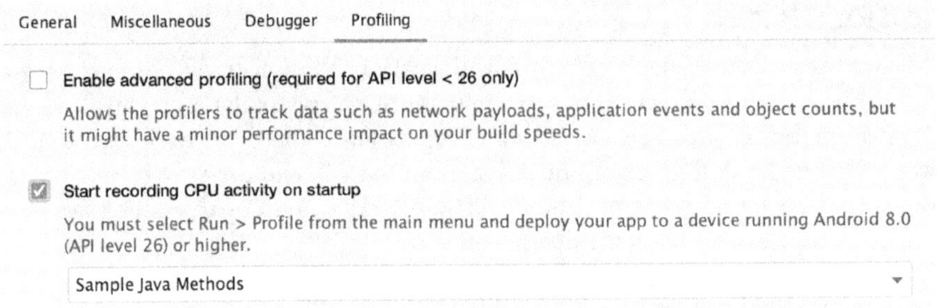

General   Miscellaneous   Debugger   **Profiling**

☐ **Enable advanced profiling (required for API level < 26 only)**

Allows the profilers to track data such as network payloads, application events and object counts, but it might have a minor performance impact on your build speeds.

☑ **Start recording CPU activity on startup**

You must select Run > Profile from the main menu and deploy your app to a device running Android 8.0 (API level 26) or higher.

Sample Java Methods   ▼

Figure 80-7

For this setting to take effect, the app must be launched using the Android Studio *Run -> Profile 'app'* menu option.

80.5 The CPU Profiler

When displayed, the CPU Profiler window will appear as shown in Figure 80-8. As with the main window, the data is displayed in realtime including the event time-line (A) and a scrolling graph showing CPU usage (B) in realtime for both the current app and a combined total for all other processes on the device:

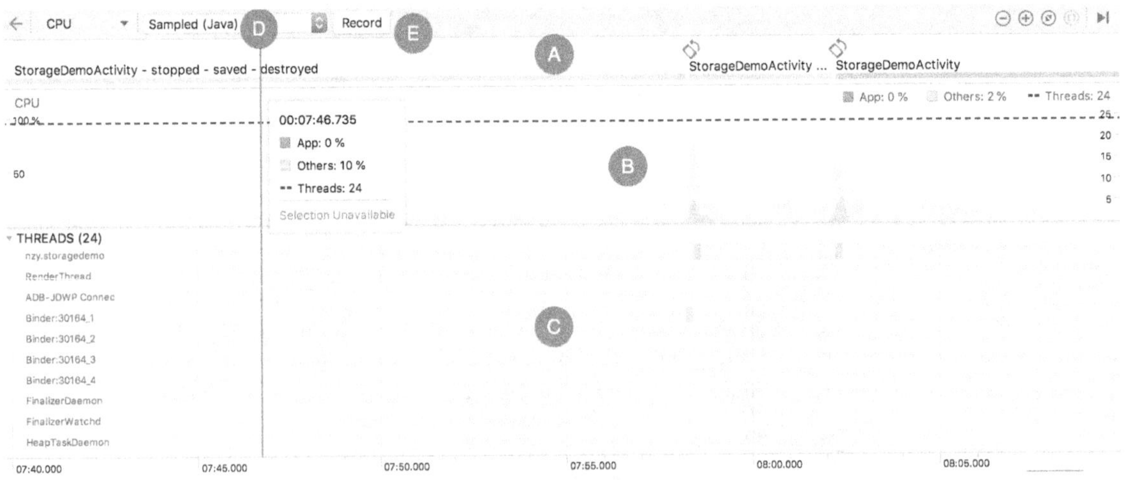

Figure 80-8

Located beneath the graph is a list of all of the threads associated with the current app (C). Referred to as the *thread activity timeline*, this also takes the form of a scrolling time-line displaying the status of each thread as represented by colored blocks (green for active, yellow for active but waiting for a disk or network I/O operation to complete or gray if the thread is currently sleeping).

The CPU Profiler supports two types of method tracing (in other words profiling individual methods within the running app). The current tracing type, either sampled or instrumented, is selected using the menu marked D. The tracing types can be summarized as follows:

- **Sampled (Java)** – Captures the method call stack at frequent intervals to collect tracing data for Java code execution. While less invasive than instrumented tracing, sampled tracing can miss method calls if they occur during the intervals between captures. Snapshot frequency may be changed by selecting the *Edit configurations...* button within the type selection menu and creating new custom trace types.

- **Instrumented (Java)** – Traces the beginning and ending of all Java method calls performed within the running app. This has the advantage that no method calls are missed during profiling, but may impact app performance due to the overhead of tracing all method calls, resulting in misleading performance data.

- **Sampled (Native)** - Captures the method call stack at frequent intervals to collect tracing data for native (for example C or C++) code execution within the app.

- **System Trace** - Profiles the system level CPU and thread activity on the device while the app is running (in other words CPU activity occurring outside the app process).

Method tracing does not begin until the record button (E) is clicked and continues until the recording is stopped. Once recording completes, the Profiler tool window will display the method trace in *call chart* format as shown in Figure 80-12 including information on execution timings for the methods. The recorded trace will also appear within the Sessions panel. Clicking on the disk icon (indicated in Figure 80-9 below) allows the trace to be saved to file for future inspection within the profiler as outlined earlier in the chapter:

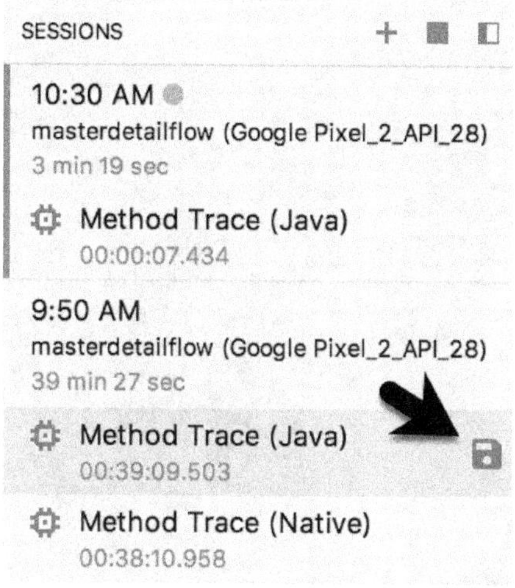

Figure 80-9

The trace results may be viewed in Top Down, Bottom Up, Call Chart and Flame Chart modes, each of which can be summarized as follows:

- **Top Down** – Displays the methods called during the trace period in a hierarchical format. Selecting a method will unfold the next level of the hierarchy and display any methods called by that method:

Figure 80-10

- **Bottom Up** – Displays an inverted hierarchical list of methods called during the trace period. Selecting a method displays the list of methods that called the selected method:

Top Down	Bottom Up	Call Chart	Flame Chart				Wall Clock Time

Name	Self (µs)	%	Children (µs)	%	Total (µs)	%
JDWP	3,498,238	99.92%	2,888	0.08%	3,501,126	100.00
dispatch() (org.apache.harmony.dalvik.ddmc.DdmServer)	1,937	0.06%	951	0.03%	2,888	0.08%
get() (java.util.HashMap)	32	0.00%	418	0.01%	450	0.01%
dispatch() (org.apache.harmony.dalvik.ddmc.DdmServer)	32	0.00%	418	0.01%	450	0.01%
getEntry() (java.util.HashMap)	120	0.00%	293	0.01%	413	0.01%
get() (java.util.HashMap)	120	0.00%	293	0.01%	413	0.01%
handleChunk() (android.ddm.DdmHandleProfiling)	36	0.00%	210	0.01%	245	0.01%
dispatch() (org.apache.harmony.dalvik.ddmc.DdmServer)	35	0.00%	210	0.01%	245	0.01%
valueOf() (java.lang.Integer)	181	0.01%	58	0.00%	239	0.01%
dispatch() (org.apache.harmony.dalvik.ddmc.DdmServer)	181	0.01%	58	0.00%	239	0.01%
equals() (java.lang.Integer)	173	0.00%	5	0.00%	178	0.01%
handleMPSS() (android.ddm.DdmHandleProfiling)	9	0.00%	119	0.00%	128	0.00%
startMethodTracingDdms() (android.os.Debug)	7	0.00%	112	0.00%	119	0.00%
startMethodTracingDdms() (dalvik.system.VMDebug)	111	0.00%	1	0.00%	112	0.00%
singleWordWangJenkinsHash() (sun.misc.Hashing)	78	0.00%	31	0.00%	109	0.00%
<init>() (java.lang.Integer)	25	0.00%	33	0.00%	58	0.00%

Figure 80-11

- **Call Chart** – Provides a graphical representation of the method trace list where the horizontal axis represents the start, end and duration of the method calls. In the vertical axis, each row represents methods called by the method above. Methods contained within the app are colored green, API methods orange and third-party methods appear in blue:

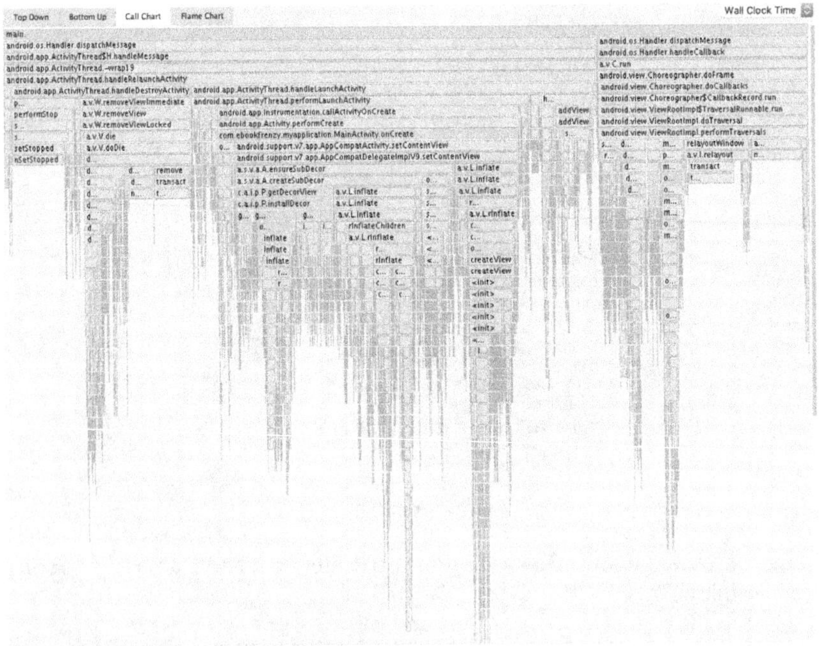

Figure 80-12

- **Flame Chart** – Provides an inverted graphical representation method trace list where each method is sized on the horizontal axis based on the amount of time the method was executing relative to other methods. Wider entries within the chart represent methods that used the most execution time relative to the other methods making it easy to identify which methods are taking the most time to complete. Note that method calls that have matching call stacks (in other words situations where the method was called repeatedly as the result of the same sequence of preceding method calls) are combined in this view to provide an overall representation of the method's performance during the trace period:

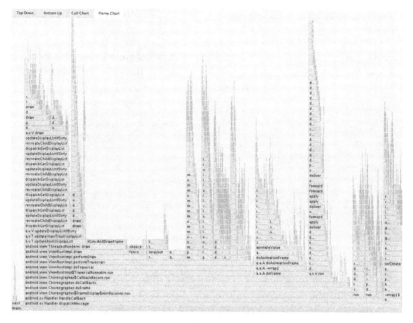

Figure 80-13

Right-clicking on a method entry in any of the above views provides the option to open the source code for the method in a code editing window.

80.6 Memory Profiler

The memory profiler is displayed when the memory time-line is clicked within the main Android Profiler Tool window and appears as shown in Figure 80-14:

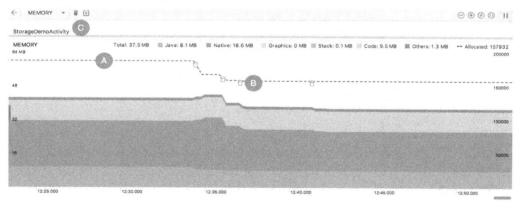

Figure 80-14

The memory time-line shows memory allocations relative to the scale on the right-hand side of the time-line for a range of different categories as indicated by the color key. The dashed line (A) represents the number of objects allocated for the app relative to the scale on the left-hand side of the time-line graph.

The trash can icons (B) indicate *garbage collection* events. A garbage collection event occurs when the Android runtime decides that an object residing in memory is no longer needed and automatically removes it to free memory.

In addition to the usual timelines, the window includes buttons (C) to force garbage collection events and to capture a heap dump.

A heap dump (Figure 80-15) lists all of the objects within the app that were using memory at the time the dump was performed showing the number of instances of the object in the heap (allocation count), the size of all instances of the object (shallow size) and the total amount of memory being held by the Android runtime system for those objects (retained size).

Class Name	Allocations	Native Size	Shallow Size	Retained Si...
app heap	9,474	112,343	686,378	2,244,844
Class (java.lang)	490	0	70,567	261,732
byte[]	1,980	0	205,510	205,510
String (java.lang)	1,677	0	25,232	80,090
Object[] (java.lang)	521	0	26,792	72,889
Editor (android.widget)	1	0	248	60,437
SelectionActionModeHelper (android.widget)	1	0	36	57,818
SelectionActionModeHelper$SelectionTracker (android.widget)	1	0	37	57,213
RuleBasedBreakIterator (android.icu.text)	2	0	114	57,183
SelectionActionModeHelper$SelectionMetricsLogger (android.widget)	1	0	25	57,163
IculteratorWrapper (java.text)	1	0	12	57,138
RBBIDataWrapper (android.icu.text)	1	0	41	55,645
char[]	15	0	46,950	46,950

Figure 80-15

Double clicking on an object in the heap list will display the Instance View panel (marked A in Figure 80-16) displaying a list of instances of the object within the app. Selecting an instance from the list will display the References panel (B) listing where the object is referenced. Figure 80-16, for example shows that a String instance has been selected and is listed as being referenced by a variable named *myString* located in the MainActivity class of the app:

Figure 80-16

Right-clicking on the reference would provide the option to go to the MainActivity class in the heap list, or jump to the source code for that class.

80.7 Network Profiler

The Network Profiler is the least complex of the tools provided by the Android Profiler. When selected the Network tool window appears as shown in Figure 80-17:

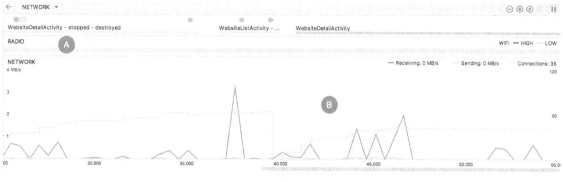

Figure 80-17

In common with the other profiler windows, the Network Profiler window includes an event time-line. The Radio time-line (marked A in Figure 80-17) shows the power status of the radio relative to the Wi-Fi connection if one is available.

The time-line graph (B) includes sent and received data and a count of the number of current connections. At time of writing, the Network Profiler is only able to monitor network activity performed as a result of HttpURLConnection and OkHttp based connections.

To view information about the files sent or received, click and drag on the time-line to select a period of time. On completing the selection, the panel labeled A in Figure 80-18 will appear listing the files. Selecting a file from the list will display the detail panel (B) from which additional information is available including response, header and call stack information:

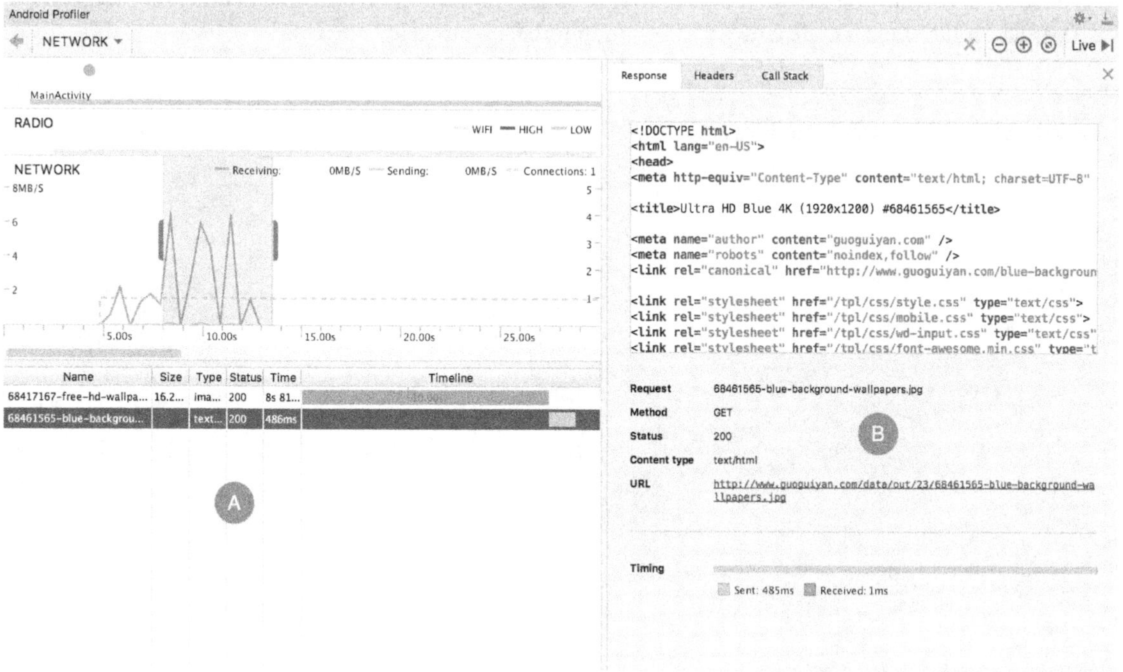

Figure 80-18

80.8 Energy Profiler

The energy profiler (Figure 80-19) provides a realtime analysis of the energy used by the currently running app categorized in terms of CPU, networking and location tracking activity.

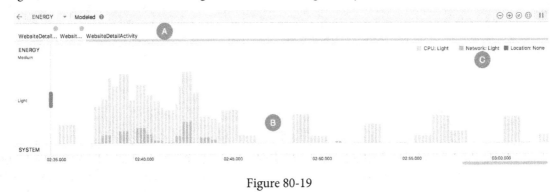

Figure 80-19

The Energy profiler includes an event timeline (A) and a graph indicating the current energy usage (B). The graph is colored based on the key (C) which also indicates the current energy usage levels of the three categories. Selecting a section of the graph will list any system processes that are contributing to excessive energy use such as alarms and jobs, location requests or wake locks.

80.9 Summary

The Android Profiler monitors the CPU, memory, network and energy resource usage of apps in realtime providing a visual environment in which to locate memory leaks, performance problems and the excessive or inefficient battery use or transmission of data over network connections. Consisting of different profiler views, the Android Profile allows detailed metrics to be monitored, recorded and analyzed.

81. An Android Biometric Authentication Tutorial

Touch sensors are now built into many Android devices to identify the user and provide access to both the device and application functionality such as in-app payment options using fingerprint recognition. Fingerprint recognition is, of course, just one of a number of different authentication methods including passwords, PIN numbers and, more recently, facial recognition.

Although only a few Android devices currently on the market provide facial recognition, it is likely that this will become more common in the near future. In recognition of this, Google has begun to transition away from what was a fingerprint-centric approach to adding authentication to apps to a less specific approach that is referred to as *biometric authentication*. In the initial release of Android 8, these biometric features only cover fingerprint authentication but this will change in future releases and updates of the Android operating system and SDK.

This chapter provides both an overview of biometric authentication and a detailed, step by step tutorial that demonstrates a practical approach to implementing biometric authentication within an Android app project.

81.1 An Overview of Biometric Authentication

The key biometric authentication component is the BiometricPrompt class. This class performs much of the work that previously had to be performed by writing code in earlier Android versions, including displaying a standard dialog to guide the user through the authentication process, performing the authentication and reporting the results to the app. The class also handles excessive failed authentication attempts and enforces a timeout before the user can try again.

The BiometricPrompt class includes a companion Builder class that can be used to configure and create BiometricPrompt instances, including defining the text that is to appear within the biometric authentication dialog and the customization of the cancel button (also referred to as the *negative button*) that appears in the dialog.

The BiometricPrompt instance is also assigned a set of authentication callbacks that will be called to provide the app with the results of an authentication operation. A CancellationSignal instance is also used to allow the app to cancel the authentication while it is in process.

With these basics covered, the remainder of this chapter will implement fingerprint-based biometric authentication within an example project.

81.2 Creating the Biometric Authentication Project

Select the *Start a new Android Studio project* quick start option from the welcome screen and, within the resulting new project dialog, choose the Empty Activity template before clicking on the Next button.

Enter *BiometricDemo* into the Name field and specify *com.ebookfrenzy.biometricdemo* as the package name. Before clicking on the Finish button, change the Minimum API level setting to API 29: Android 9.0 (Pie) and the Language menu to Java.

81.3 Configuring Device Fingerprint Authentication

Fingerprint authentication is only available on devices containing a touch sensor and on which the appropriate configuration steps have been taken to secure the device and enroll at least one fingerprint. For steps on configuring an emulator session to test fingerprint authentication, refer to the chapter entitled *"Using and Configuring the Android Studio AVD Emulator"*.

To configure fingerprint authentication on a physical device begin by opening the Settings app and selecting the *Security* option. Within the Security settings screen, select the *Fingerprint* option. On the resulting information screen click on the *Next* button to proceed to the Fingerprint setup screen. Before fingerprint security can be enabled a backup screen unlocking method (such as a PIN number) must be configured. If the lock screen is not already secured, follow the steps to configure either PIN, pattern or password security.

With the lock screen secured, proceed to the fingerprint detection screen and touch the sensor when prompted to do so (Figure 81-1), repeating the process to add additional fingerprints if required.

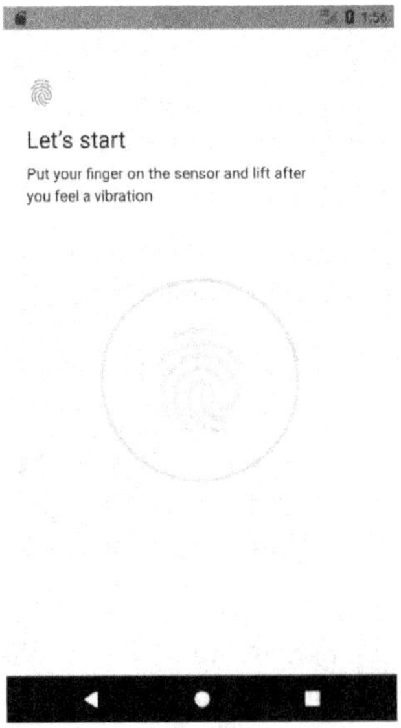

Figure 81-1

81.4 Adding the Biometric Permission to the Manifest File

Biometric authentication requires that the app request the *USE_BIOMETRIC* permission within the project manifest file. Within the Android Studio Project tool window locate and edit the *app -> manifests -> AndroidManifest.xml* file to add the permission request as follows:

```xml
<?xml version="1.0" encoding="utf-8"?>
<manifest xmlns:android="http://schemas.android.com/apk/res/android"
    package="com.ebookfrenzy.biometricdemo">

    <uses-permission
        android:name="android.permission.USE_BIOMETRIC" />
.
.
```

81.5 Designing the User Interface

In the interests of keeping the example as simple as possible, the only visual element within the user interface will be a Button view. Locate and select the *activity_main.xml* layout resource file to load it into the Layout Editor tool.

Delete the sample TextView object, drag and drop a Button object from the *Common* category of the palette and position it in the center of the layout canvas. Using the Attributes tool window, change the text property on the button to "Authenticate" and extract the string to a resource. Finally, configure the onClick property to call a method named *authenticateUser*.

On completion of the above steps the layout should match that shown in Figure 81-2:

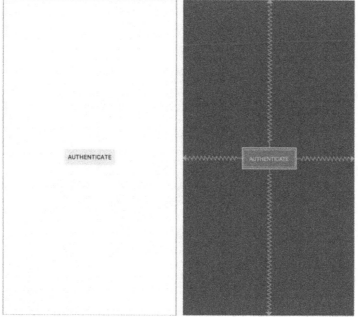

Figure 81-2

81.6 Adding a Toast Convenience Method

At various points throughout the code in this example the app will be designed to display information to the user via Toast messages. Rather than repeat the same Toast code multiple times, a convenience method named *notifyUser()* will be added to the main activity. This method will accept a single String value and display it to the user in the form of a Toast message. Edit the *MainActivity.java* file now and add this method as follows:

```
.
.
import android.widget.Toast;
.
.

    private void notifyUser(String message) {
        Toast.makeText(this,
                message,
                Toast.LENGTH_LONG).show();
```

```
        }

        ·
        ·
```

81.7 Checking the Security Settings

Earlier in this chapter steps were taken to configure the lock screen and register fingerprints on the device or emulator on which the app is going to be tested. It is important, however, to include defensive code in the app to make sure that these requirements have been met before attempting to seek fingerprint authentication. These steps will be performed within the *onCreate* method residing in the *MainActivity.java* file, making use of the Keyguard and PackageManager manager services. Note that code has also been added to verify that the USE_BIOMETRIC permission has been configured for the app:

```java
package com.ebookfrenzy.biometricdemo;

import androidx.appcompat.app.AppCompatActivity;
import androidx.core.app.ActivityCompat;

import android.widget.Toast;
import android.Manifest;
import android.content.pm.PackageManager;

import android.app.KeyguardManager;

public class MainActivity extends AppCompatActivity {

    @Override
    protected void onCreate(Bundle savedInstanceState) {
        super.onCreate(savedInstanceState);
        setContentView(R.layout.activity_biometric_demo);

        checkBiometricSupport();
    }

    private Boolean checkBiometricSupport() {

        KeyguardManager keyguardManager =
                (KeyguardManager) getSystemService(KEYGUARD_SERVICE);

        PackageManager packageManager = this.getPackageManager();

        if (!keyguardManager.isKeyguardSecure()) {
            notifyUser("Lock screen security not enabled in Settings");
            return false;
        }

        if (ActivityCompat.checkSelfPermission(this,
                Manifest.permission.USE_BIOMETRIC) !=
```

```
PackageManager.PERMISSION_GRANTED) {

    notifyUser("Fingerprint authentication permission not enabled");
    return false;
}


if (packageManager.hasSystemFeature(PackageManager.FEATURE_FINGERPRINT))
{
    return true;
}

return true;
}
.
.
.
}
```

The above code changes begin by using the Keyguard manager to verify that a backup screen unlocking method has been configured (in other words a PIN or other authentication method can be used as an alternative to fingerprint authentication to unlock the screen). In the event that the lock screen is not secured the code reports the problem to the user and returns from the method.

The method then checks that the user has biometric authentication permission enabled for the app before using the package manager to verify that fingerprint authentication is available on the device.

81.8 Configuring the Authentication Callbacks

When the biometric prompt dialog is configured, it will need to be assigned a set of authentication callback methods that can be called to notify the app of the success or failure of the authentication process. These methods need to be wrapped in a BiometricPrompt.AuthenticationCallback class instance. Remaining in the *MainActivity.java* file, add a method to create and return an instance of this class with the appropriate methods implemented:

```
.
.
.
import android.hardware.biometrics.BiometricPrompt;
.
.
.
    private BiometricPrompt.AuthenticationCallback getAuthenticationCallback() {

        return new BiometricPrompt.AuthenticationCallback() {
            @Override
            public void onAuthenticationError(int errorCode,
                                                CharSequence errString) {
                notifyUser("Authentication error: " + errString);
                super.onAuthenticationError(errorCode, errString);
            }

            @Override
```

```
            public void onAuthenticationHelp(int helpCode,
                                      CharSequence helpString) {
                super.onAuthenticationHelp(helpCode, helpString);
            }


            @Override
            public void onAuthenticationFailed() {
                super.onAuthenticationFailed();
            }


            @Override
            public void onAuthenticationSucceeded(
                        BiometricPrompt.AuthenticationResult result) {
                notifyUser("Authentication Succeeded");
                super.onAuthenticationSucceeded(result);
            }
        };
    }
.

.

.
}
```

81.9 Adding the CancellationSignal

Once initiated, the biometric authentication process is performed independently of the app. To provide the app with a way to cancel the operation, an instance of the CancellationSignal class is created and passed to the biometric authentication process. This CancellationSignal instance can then be used to cancel the process if necessary. The cancellation signal instance may be configured with a listener which will be called when the cancellation is completed. Add a new method to the activity class to configure and return a CancellationSignal object as follows:

```
.

.
import android.os.CancellationSignal;
.

.
   private CancellationSignal cancellationSignal;
.

.
    private CancellationSignal getCancellationSignal() {

        cancellationSignal = new CancellationSignal();
        cancellationSignal.setOnCancelListener(new
                        CancellationSignal.OnCancelListener() {
            @Override
            public void onCancel() {
                notifyUser("Cancelled via signal");
            }
```

```
    });
    return cancellationSignal;
}
```

.

.

81.10 Starting the Biometric Prompt

All that remains is to add code to the *authenticateUser()* method to create and configure a BiometricPrompt instance and initiate the authentication. Add the *authenticateUser()* method as follows:

.

.

```
import android.view.View;
import android.content.DialogInterface;
```

.

.

```
public void authenticateUser(View view) {
    BiometricPrompt biometricPrompt = new BiometricPrompt.Builder(this)
            .setTitle("Biometric Demo")
            .setSubtitle("Authentication is required to continue")
            .setDescription("This app uses biometric authentication to protect
your data.")
            .setNegativeButton("Cancel", this.getMainExecutor(),
                        new DialogInterface.OnClickListener() {
                @Override
                public void onClick(DialogInterface dialogInterface, int i) {
                    notifyUser("Authentication cancelled");
                }
            })
            .build();

    biometricPrompt.authenticate(getCancellationSignal(), getMainExecutor(),
                            getAuthenticationCallback());
}
```

The BiometricPrompt.Builder class is used to create a new BiometricPrompt instance configured with title, subtitle and description text to appear in the prompt dialog. The negative button is configured to display text which reads "Cancel" and a listener configured to display a message when this button is clicked. Finally, the *authenticate()* method of the BiometricPrompt instance is called and passed the AuthenticationCallback and CancellationSignal instances. The Biometric prompt also needs to know which thread to perform the authentication on. This is defined by passing through an Executor object configured for the required thread. In this case, the *getMainExecutor()* method is used to pass a main Executor object to the BiometricPrompt instance so that the authentication process takes place on the app's main thread.

81.11 Testing the Project

With the project now complete, run the app on a physical Android device or emulator session and click on the Authenticate button to display the BiometricPrompt dialog as shown in Figure 81-3:

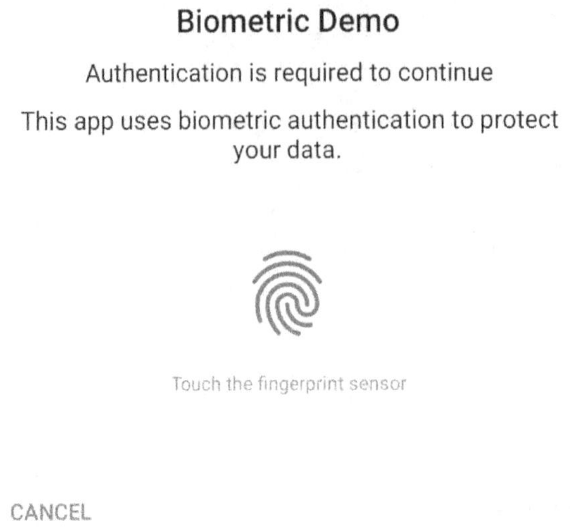

Biometric Demo

Authentication is required to continue

This app uses biometric authentication to protect
your data.

Touch the fingerprint sensor

CANCEL

Figure 81-3

Once running, either touch the fingerprint sensor or use the extended controls panel within the emulator to simulate a fingerprint touch as outlined in the chapter entitled *"Using and Configuring the Android Studio AVD Emulator"*. Assuming a registered fingerprint is detected the prompt dialog will return to the main activity where the toast message from the successful authentication callback method will appear.

Click the Authenticate button once again, this time using an unregistered fingerprint to attempt the authentication. This time the biometric prompt dialog will indicate that the fingerprint was not recognized:

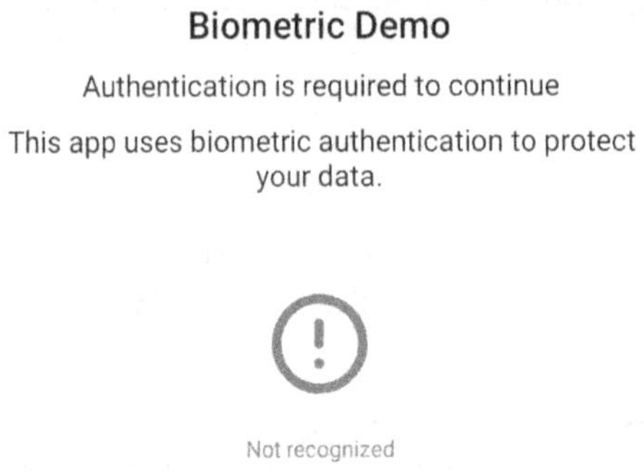

Biometric Demo

Authentication is required to continue

This app uses biometric authentication to protect
your data.

Not recognized

Figure 81-4

Verify that the error handling callback is working by clicking on the activity outside of the biometric prompt dialog. The prompt dialog will disappear and the toast message will appear with the following message:

```
Authentication error: Fingerprint operation cancelled by user.
```

Check that canceling the prompt dialog using the Cancel button triggers the "Authentication Cancelled" toast message. Finally, attempt to authenticate multiple times using an unregistered fingerprint and note that after a number of attempts the prompt dialog indicates that too many failures have occurred and that future attempts cannot be made until later.

81.12 Summary

This chapter has outlined how to integrate biometric authentication into an Android app project. This involves the use of the BiometricPrompt class which, once configured with appropriate message text and callbacks, automatically handles most of the authentication process.

82. Creating, Testing and Uploading an Android App Bundle

Once the development work on an Android application is complete and it has been tested on a wide range of Android devices, the next step is to prepare the application for submission to Google Play. Before submission can take place, however, the application must be packaged for release and signed with a private key. This chapter will work through the steps involved in obtaining a private key, preparing the Android App Bundle for the project and uploading it to Google Play.

82.1 The Release Preparation Process

Up until this point in the book, we have been building application projects in a mode suitable for testing and debugging. Building an application package for release to customers via Google Play, on the other hand, requires that some additional steps be taken. The first requirement is that the application be compiled in *release mode* instead of *debug mode*. Secondly, the application must be signed with a private key that uniquely identifies you as the application's developer. Finally, the application must be packaged into an *Android App Bundle*.

While each of these tasks can be performed outside of the Android Studio environment, the procedures can more easily be performed using the Android Studio build mechanism as outlined in the remainder of this chapter. First, however, it is important to understand a little more about Android App Bundles.

82.2 Android App Bundles

When a user installs an app from Google Play, the app is downloaded in the form of an APK file. This file contains everything needed to install and run the app on the user's device. Prior to the introduction of Android Studio 3.2, the developer would generate one or more APK files using Android Studio and upload them to Google Play. In order to support multiple device types, screen sizes and locales this would require either the creation and upload of multiple APK files customized for each target device and locale, or the generation of a large *universal APK* containing all of the different configuration resources and platform binaries within a single package.

Creating multiple APK files involved a significant amount of work that had to be repeated each time the app needed to be updated imposing a considerable time overhead to the app release process.

The universal APK option, while less of a burden to the developer, caused an entirely unexpected problem. By analyzing app installation metrics, Google discovered that the larger an installation APK file becomes (resulting in longer download times and increased storage use on the device), the less conversions the app receives. The conversion rate is calculated as a percentage of the users who completed the installation of an app after viewing that app on Google Play. In fact, Google estimates that the conversion rate for an app drops by 1% for each 6MB increase in APK file size.

Android App Bundles solve both of these problems by providing a way for the developer to create a single package from within Android Studio and have custom APK files automatically generated by Google Play for each individual supported configuration (a concept referred to as *Dynamic Delivery*).

An Android App Bundle is essentially a ZIP file containing all of the files necessary to build APK files for the devices and locales for which support has been provided within the app project. The project might, for example, include resources and images for different screen sizes. When a user installs the app, Google Play receives information about the user's device including the display, processor architecture and locale. Using this information, the appropriate pre-generated APK files are transferred onto the user's device.

An additional benefit of Dynamic Delivery is the ability to split an app into multiple modules, referred to as *dynamic feature modules,* where each module contains the code and resources for a particular area of functionality within the app. Each dynamic feature module is contained within a separate APK file from the base module and is downloaded to the device only when that feature is required by the user. Dynamic Delivery and app bundles also allow for the creation of *instant dynamic feature modules* which can be run instantly on a device without the need to install an entire app. These topics will be covered in greater detail starting with the chapter entitled *"An Overview of Android Dynamic Feature Modules".*

Although it is still possible to generate APK files from Android Studio, app bundles are now the recommended way to upload apps to Google Play.

82.3 Register for a Google Play Developer Console Account

The first step in the application submission process is to create a Google Play Developer Console account. To do so, navigate to *https://play.google.com/apps/publish/signup/* and follow the instructions to complete the registration process. Note that there is a one-time $25 fee to register. Once an application goes on sale, Google will keep 30% of all revenues associated with the application.

Once the account has been created, the next step is to gather together information about the application. In order to bring your application to market, the following information will be required:

- **Title** – The title of the application.

- **Short Description** - Up to 80 words describing the application.

- **Full Description** – Up to 4000 words describing the application.

- **Screenshots** – Up to 8 screenshots of your application running (a minimum of two is required). Google recommends submitting screenshots of the application running on a 7" or 10" tablet.

- **Language** – The language of the application (the default is US English).

- **Promotional Text** – The text that will be used when your application appears in special promotional features within the Google Play environment.

- **Application Type** – Whether your application is considered to be a *game* or an *application.*

- **Category** – The category that best describes your application (for example finance, health and fitness, education, sports, etc.).

- **Locations** – The geographical locations into which you wish your application to be made available for purchase.

- **Contact Details** – Methods by which users may contact you for support relating to the application. Options include web, email and phone.

- **Pricing & Distribution** – Information about the price of the application and the geographical locations where it is to be marketed and sold.

Having collected the above information, click on the *Create Application* button within the Google Play Console to begin the creation process.

82.4 Configuring the App in the Console

When the Create Application button is first clicked, the *Store listing* screen will appear as shown in Figure 82-1 below. The screen may also be accessed by selecting the *Store listing* option (marked A) in the navigation panel. Once all of the requirements have been met for the Store listing screen, both the *Content rating* (B) and *Pricing & distribution* (C) screens must also be completed:

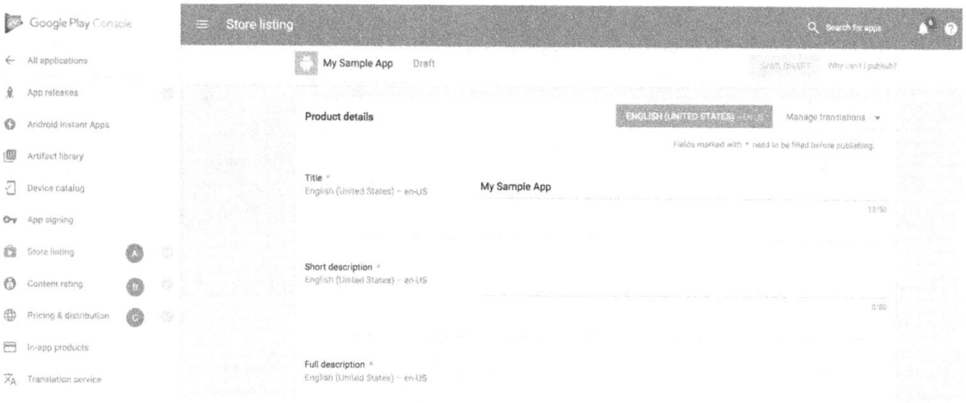

Figure 82-1

Once the app entry has been fully configured, the next step is to enable app signing and upload the app bundle.

82.5 Enabling Google Play App Signing

Up until recently, Google Play uploads were signed with a release app signing key from within Android Studio and then uploaded to the Google Play console. While this option is still available, the recommended way to upload files is to now use a process referred to as *Google Play App Signing*. For a newly created app, this involves opting in to Google Play App Signing and then generating an *upload key* that is used to sign the app bundle file within Android Studio. When the app bundle file generated by Android Studio is uploaded, the Google Play console removes the upload key and then signs the file with an app signing key that is stored securely within the Google Play servers. For existing apps, some additional steps are required to enable Google Play Signing and will be covered at the end of this chapter.

Within the Google Play console, select the newly added app entry from the dashboard and click on the *App releases* option located in the left-hand navigation panel. On the App releases screen, select the *Manage* button in the *Internal test track* section. The internal test track is particularly useful when performing tests early in the app development cycle, or when experimenting with Android App Bundles. Eventually the app will progress through Alpha and Beta testing before finally being ready for production release.

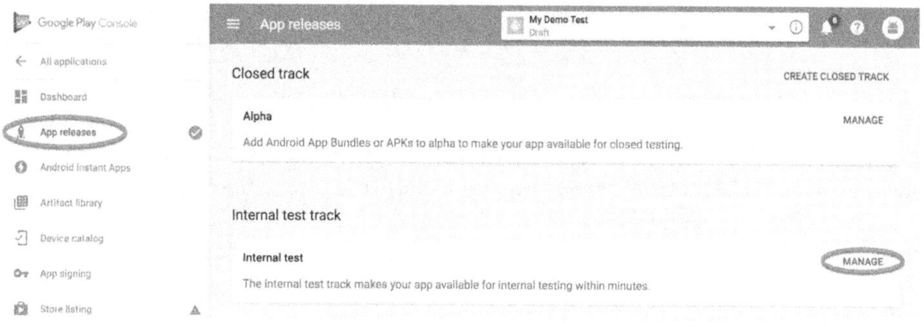

Figure 82-2

On the subsequent screen, click on the *Create Release* button to display the settings screen shown in Figure 82-3:

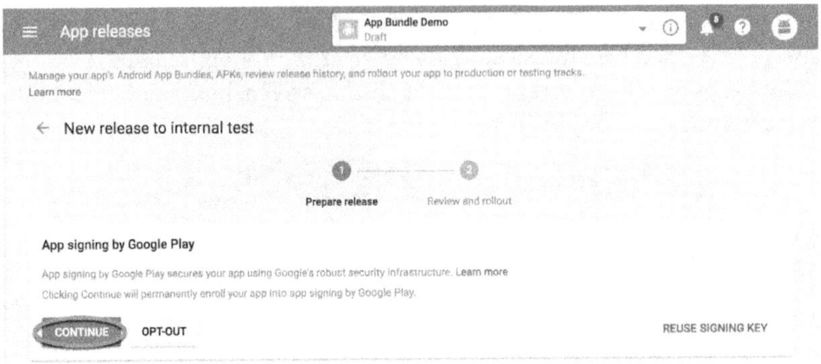

Figure 82-3

To enroll the app in Google Play App Signing, click on the *Continue* button highlighted in the above figure. This will generate an app signing certificate for the app which will be securely stored within Google Play.

The next step is to generate the *upload* key from within Android Studio. This is performed as part of the process of generating a signed app bundle.

82.6 Creating a Keystore File

To create a keystore file, select the Android Studio *Build -> Generate Signed Bundle / APK...* menu option to display the Generate Signed Bundle or APK Wizard dialog as shown in Figure 82-4:

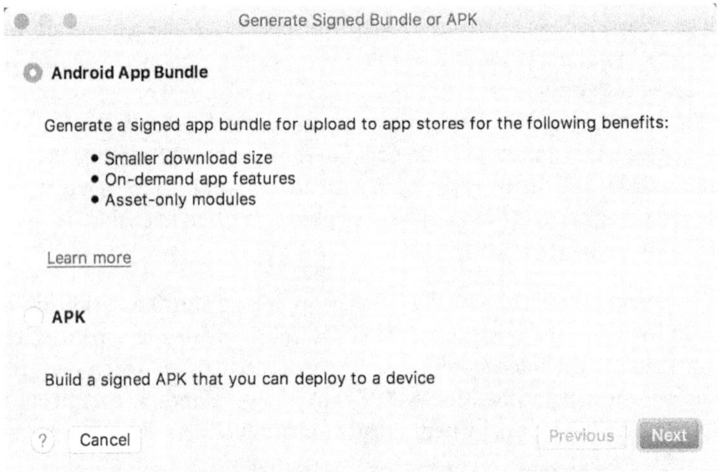

Figure 82-4

Verify that the *Android App Bundle* option is selected before clicking on the *Next* button.

In the event that you have an existing release keystore file, click on the *Choose existing...* button on the next screen and navigate to and select the file. If you have yet to create a keystore file, click on the *Create new...* button to display the *New Key Store* dialog (Figure 82-5). Click on the button to the right of the Key store path field and navigate to a suitable location on your file system, enter a name for the keystore file (for example, *release. keystore.jks*) and click on the OK button.

The New Key Store dialog is divided into two sections. The top section relates to the keystore file. In this section, enter a strong password with which to protect the keystore file into both the *Password* and *Confirm* fields. The lower section of the dialog relates to the upload key that will be stored in the key store file.

Figure 82-5

Within the *Certificate* section of the New Key Store dialog, enter the following details:

- An alias by which the key will be referenced. This can be any sequence of characters, though only the first 8 are used by the system.

- A suitably strong password to protect the key.

- The number of years for which the key is to be valid (Google recommends a duration in excess of 25 years).

In addition, information must be provided for at least one of the remaining fields (for example, your first and last name, or organization name).

Figure 82-6

Once the information has been entered, click on the *OK* button to proceed with the bundle creation.

82.7 Creating the Android App Bundle

The next step is to instruct Android Studio to build the application app bundle file in release mode and then sign it with the newly created private key. At this point the *Generate Signed Bundle or APK* dialog should still be displayed with the keystore path, passwords and key alias fields populated with information:

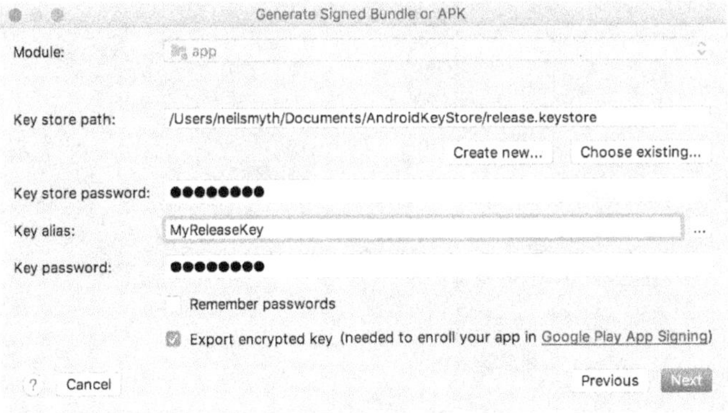

Figure 82-7

Make sure that the Export Encrypted Key option is enabled and, assuming that the other settings are correct, click on the *Next* button to proceed to the app bundle generation screen (Figure 82-8). Within this screen, review the *Destination Folder:* setting to verify that the location into which the app bundle file will be generated is acceptable. In the event that another location is preferred, click on the button to the right of the text field and navigate to the desired file system location.

Figure 82-8

Click on the *Finish* button and wait for the Gradle system to build the app bundle. Once the build is complete, a dialog will appear providing the option to open the folder containing the app bundle file in an explorer window, or to load the file into the APK Analyzer:

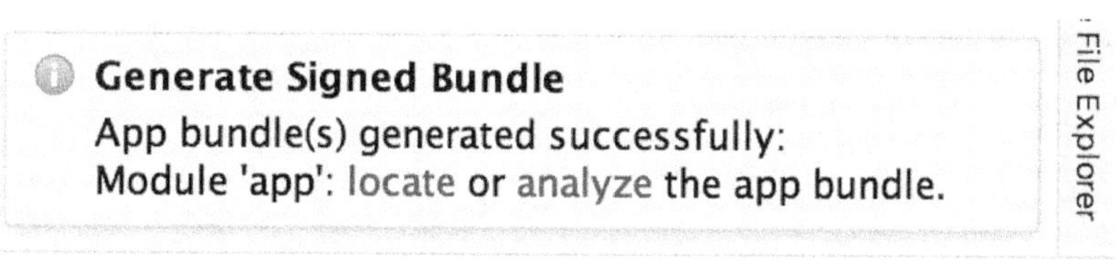

Generate Signed Bundle
App bundle(s) generated successfully:
Module 'app': locate or analyze the app bundle.

Figure 82-9

At this point the application is ready to be submitted to Google Play. Click on the *locate* link to open a filesystem browser window. The file should be named *bundle.aab* and be located in the *app/release* sub-directory of the project folder unless another location was specified.

The private key generated as part of this process should be used when signing and releasing future applications and, as such, should be kept in a safe place and securely backed up.

82.8 Generating Test APK Files

An optional step at this stage is to generate APK files from the app bundle and install and run them on devices or emulator sessions. Google provides a command-line tool called *bundletool* designed specifically for this purpose which can be downloaded from the following URL:

https://github.com/google/bundletool/releases

At time of writing, bundletool is provide as a .jar file which can be executed from the command line as follows (noting that the version number may have changed since this book was published):

```
java -jar bundletool-all-0.9.0.jar
```

Running the above command will list all of the options available within the tool. To generate the APK files from the app bundle, the *build-apks* option is used. To generate APK files that can be installed onto a device or emulator the files will also need to be signed. To achieve this include the *--ks* option specifying the path of the keystore file created earlier in the chapter, together with the *--ks-key-alias* option specifying the alias provided when the key was generated.

Finally, the *--output* flag must be used to specify the path of the file (referred to as the APK Set) into which the APK files will be generated. This file must not already exist and is required to have a *.apks* filename extension. Bringing these requirements together results in the following command-line (allowing for differences in your operating system path structure):

```
java -jar bundletool-all-0.9.0.jar build-apks --bundle=/tmp/MyApps/app/release/
bundle.aab --output=/tmp/MyApks.apks --ks=/MyKeys/release.keystore.jks --ks-key-
alias=MyReleaseKey
```

When this command is executed, a prompt will appear requesting the keystore password before the APK files are generated into the specified APK Set file. The APK Set file is simply a ZIP file containing all of the APK files generated from the app bundle.

To install the appropriate APK files onto a connected device or emulator, use a command similar to the following:

```
java -jar bundletool-all-0.9.0.jar install-apks --apks=/tmp/MyApks.apks
```

This command will instruct the tool to identify the appropriate APK files for the connected device and install them so that the app can be launched and tested.

It is also possible to extract the APK files from the APK Set for the connected device without installing them. The first step in this process is to obtain the specification of the connected device as follows:

```
java -jar bundletool-all-0.9.0.jar get-device-spec --output=/tmp/device.json
```

Creating, Testing and Uploading an Android App Bundle

The above command will generate a JSON file similar to the following:

```
{
  "supportedAbis": ["x86"],
  "supportedLocales": ["en-US"],
  "screenDensity": 420,
  "sdkVersion": 27
}
```

Next, this specification file is used to extract the matching APK files from the APK Set:

```
java -jar bundletool-all-0.9.0.jar extract-apks --apks=/tmp/MyApks.apks --output-
dir=/tmp/nexus5_apks --device-spec=/tmp/device.json
```

When executed, the directory specified via the *--output-dir* flag will contain correct APK files for the specified device configuration.

The next step in bringing an Android application to market involves submitting it to the Google Play Developer Console so that it can be made available for testing.

82.9 Uploading the App Bundle to the Google Play Developer Console

Return to the internal testing track screen within the Google Play Console and upload the app bundle by dragging and dropping it onto the designated area, or click on the button to browse for the bundle file:

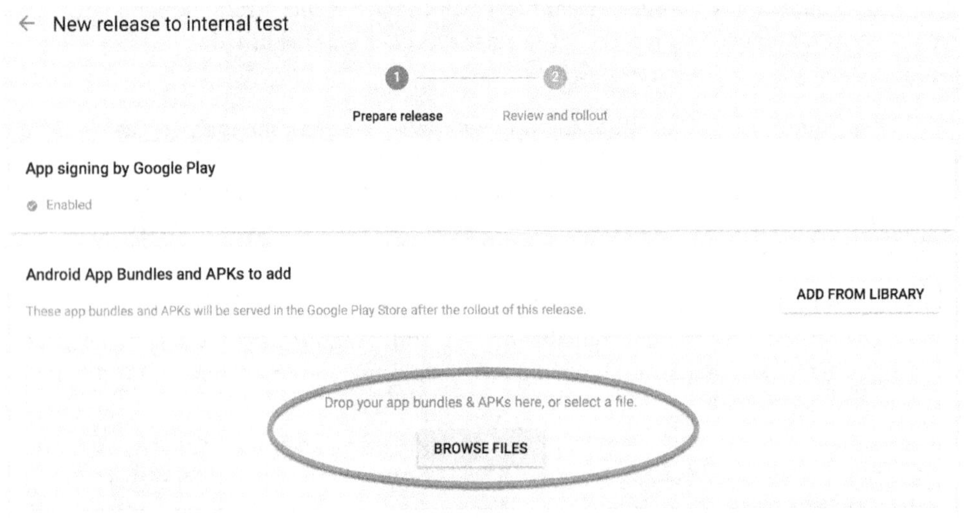

Figure 82-10

After the app bundle file has uploaded, Google Play will generate all of the necessary APK files ready for testing. Once the APK files have been generated, scroll down to the bottom of the screen and click on the *Save* button. Once the settings have been saved, click on the *Review* button.

82.10 Exploring the App Bundle

On the review screen, click on the bundle name to unfold the information about the bundle as shown in Figure 82-11:

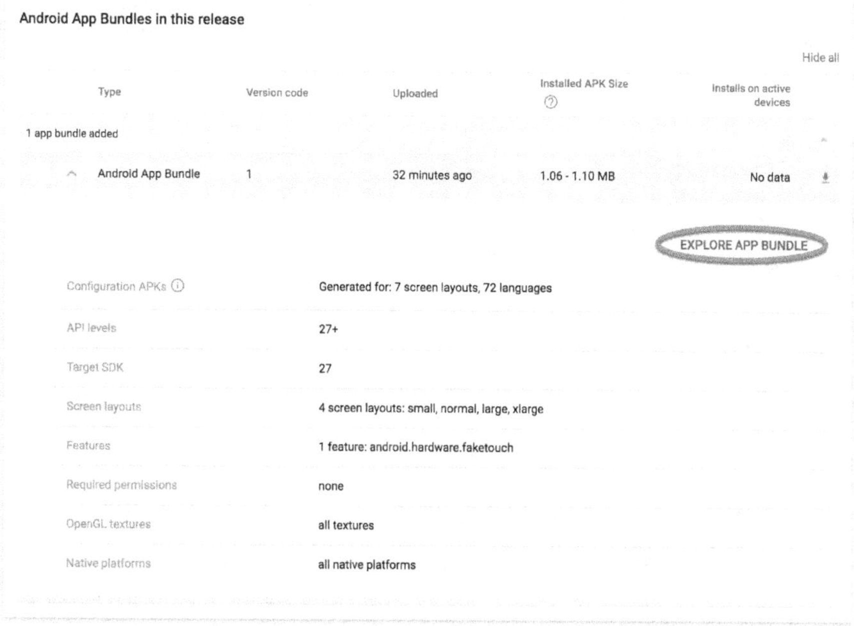
Android App Bundles in this release
Hide all
Type
Version code
Uploaded
Installed APK Size
Installs on active devices
1 app bundle added
Android App Bundle
1
32 minutes ago
1.06 - 1.10 MB
No data
EXPLORE APP BUNDLE
Configuration APKs
Generated for: 7 screen layouts, 72 languages
API levels
27+
Target SDK
27
Screen layouts
4 screen layouts: small, normal, large, xlarge
Features
1 feature: android.hardware.faketouch
Required permissions
none
OpenGL textures
all textures
Native platforms
all native platforms

Figure 82-11

This section of the screen provides summary information relating to the API levels, screen layouts and platforms supported by the app bundle. For more information, click on the *Explore App Bundle* option highlighted in the figure above. This will display information about the size savings compared to a universal APK file (marked A in Figure 82-12) and provide the option to download individual APK files for local testing purposes (B) as an alternative to using the bundletool:

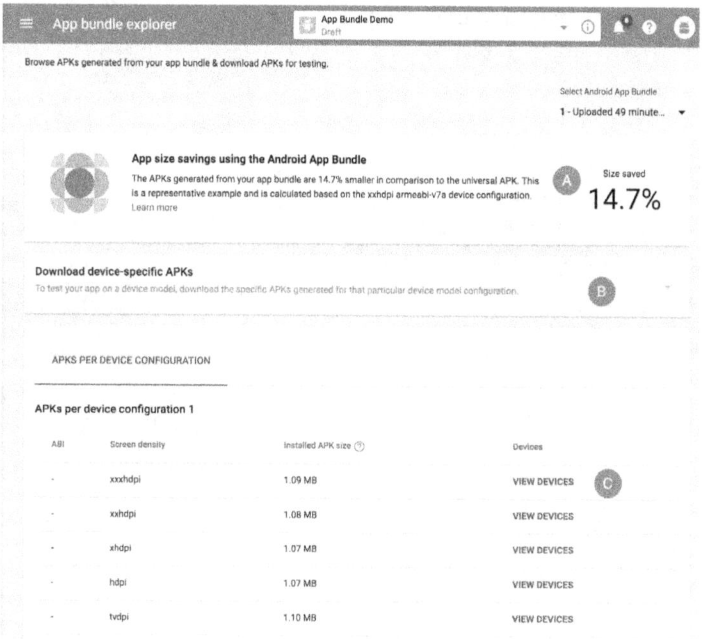
App bundle explorer
App Bundle Demo
Draft
Browse APKs generated from your app bundle & download APKs for testing.
Select Android App Bundle
1 - Uploaded 49 minute...
App size savings using the Android App Bundle
The APKs generated from your app bundle are 14.7% smaller in comparison to the universal APK. This is a representative example and is calculated based on the xxhdpi armeabi-v7a device configuration.
Learn more
A
Size saved
14.7%
Download device-specific APKs
B
APKS PER DEVICE CONFIGURATION
APKs per device configuration 1
ABI
Screen density
Installed APK size
Devices
xxxhdpi
1.09 MB
VIEW DEVICES
C
xxhdpi
1.08 MB
VIEW DEVICES
xhdpi
1.07 MB
VIEW DEVICES
hdpi
1.07 MB
VIEW DEVICES
tvdpi
1.10 MB
VIEW DEVICES

Figure 82-12

The bundle explorer also lists the supported screen densities (C) and respective install APK size. Clicking on a View Devices option for a screen density will display the devices that are supported by the APK file:

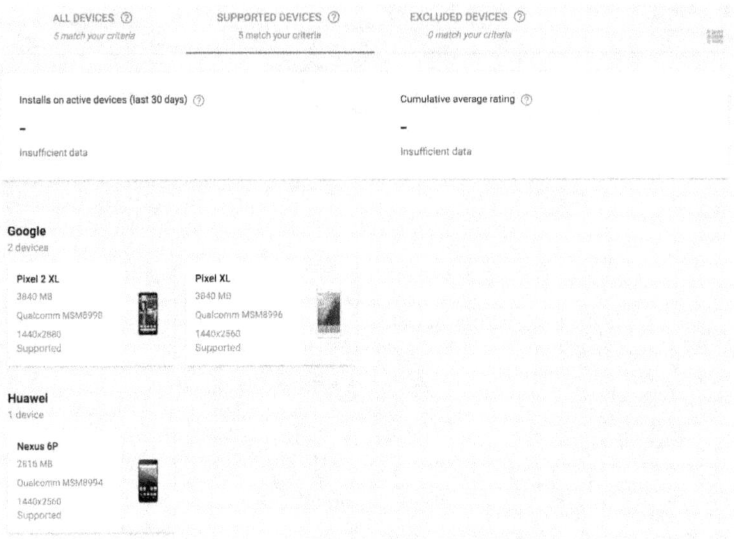

Figure 82-13

At this point, the app is ready for testing but cannot be rolled out until some testers have been set up within the console.

82.11 Managing Testers

If the app is still in the Internal, Alpha or Beta testing phase, a list of authorized testers may be specified by selecting the app from within the Google Play console, clicking on *App releases* in the navigation panel, selecting the Manage button for the release type and unfolding the *Manage testers* section of the release screen as shown in Figure 82-14:

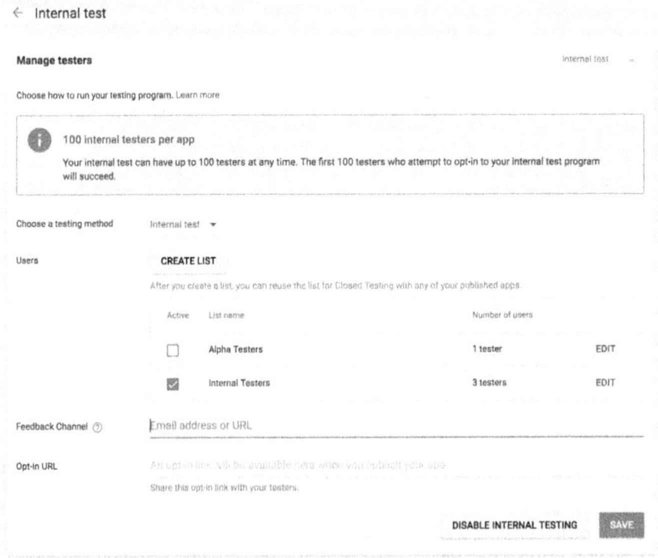

Figure 82-14

The following options are available for app testing:

- **Internal Testing** – The app is made available to up to 100 designated internal testers. This is the fastest way to get the app to a small group of known testers.

- **Closed Testing** – Testing is only available for designated users identified by email address or membership in Google Groups and Google+ communities.

- **Open Testing** – The app is made available to all users within the Google Play Store. Users are provided with a mechanism to provide feedback to you during testing. The total number of testers may also be specified (though the number cannot be less than 1000 users).

To configure testing, use the *Choose testing method* menu to select the type of testing to be performed, click on the *Create List* button and specify the email addresses for the test users either manually or by uploading a CSV file.

The opt-in URL will be displayed when the app has been rolled out for testing. Return to the Review page for the app (*App Releases -> Manage -> Edit Release -> Review*) and click on the *Start Rollout to Internal Testers* button.

The URL may now be copied from the manage testers screen (Figure 82-14 above) and provided to the test users so that they accept the testing invitation and download the app.

82.12 Uploading New App Bundle Revisions

The first app bundle file uploaded for your application will invariably have a version code of 1. If an attempt is made to upload another bundle file with the same version code number, the console will reject the file with the following error:

```
You need to use a different version code for your APK because you already have
one with version code 1.
```

To resolve this problem, the version code embedded into the bundle file needs to be increased. This is performed in the *module* level *build.gradle* file of the project, shown highlighted in Figure 82-15:

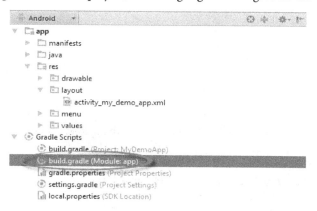

Figure 82-15

By default, this file will typically read as follows:

```
apply plugin: 'com.android.application'

android {
    compileSdkVersion 28
```

```
    defaultConfig {
        applicationId "com.example.myapplication"
        minSdkVersion 26
        targetSdkVersion 29
        versionCode 1
        versionName "1.0"
        testInstrumentationRunner "android.support.test.runner.
AndroidJUnitRunner"
    }
    buildTypes {
        release {
            minifyEnabled false
            proguardFiles getDefaultProguardFile('proguard-android-optimize.
txt'), 'proguard-rules.pro'
        }
    }
}


dependencies {
    implementation fileTree(dir: 'libs', include: ['*.jar'])
    implementation 'com.android.support:appcompat-v7:28.0.0'
    implementation 'com.android.support:support-v4:28.0.0'
    implementation 'com.android.support:design:28.0.0'
    implementation 'com.android.support.constraint:constraint-layout:1.1.3'
    testImplementation 'junit:junit:4.12'
    androidTestImplementation 'com.android.support.test:runner:1.0.2'
    androidTestImplementation 'com.android.support.test.espresso:espresso-
core:3.0.2'
}
```

To change the version code, simply change the number declared next to *versionCode*. To also change the version number displayed to users of your application, change the *versionName* string. For example:

```
versionCode 2
versionName "2.0"
```

Having made these changes, rebuild the APK file and perform the upload again.

82.13 Analyzing the App Bundle File

Android Studio provides the ability to analyze the content of an app bundle file. To analyze a bundle file, select the Android Studio *Build -> Analyze APK...* menu option and navigate to and choose the bundle file to be reviewed. Once loaded into the tool, information will be displayed about the raw and download size of the package together with a listing of the file structure of the package as illustrated in Figure 82-16:

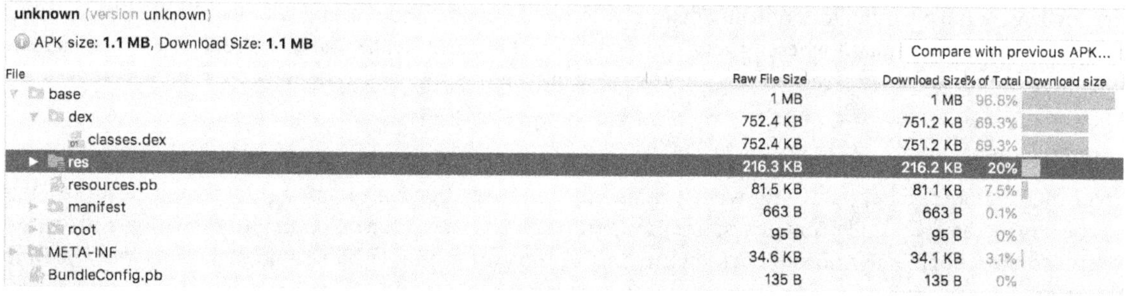

Figure 82-16

Selecting the *classes.dex* file will display the class structure of the file in the lower panel. Within this panel, details of the individual classes may be explored down to the level of the methods within a class:

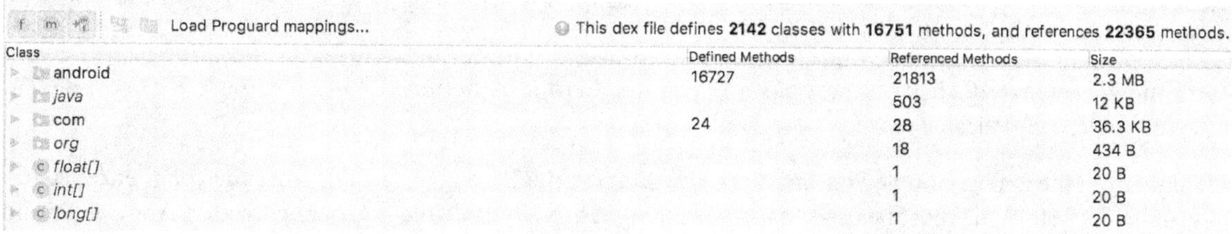

Figure 82-17

Similarly, selecting a resource or image file within the file list will display the file content within the lower panel. The size differences between two bundle files may be reviewed by clicking on the *Compare with previous APK...* button and selecting a second bundle file.

82.14 Enabling Google Play Signing for an Existing App

To enable Google Play Signing for an app already registered within the Google Play console, begin by selecting that app from the list of apps in the console dashboard. Once selected, click on the *App signing* link in the left-hand navigation panel as shown in Figure 82-18:

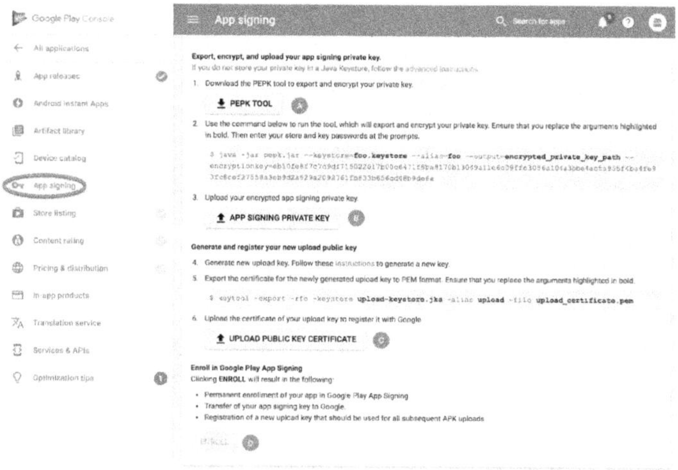

Figure 82-18

The first step is to click on the button to download the *PEPK Tool* (A) which will be used to encrypt the app signing key for the project. Once downloaded, copy it to the directory containing your existing keystore file and run the following command where (*<your app signing key file>* and *<your alias>* are replaced by the name of your keystore file and the corresponding alias key respectively):

```
java -jar pepk.jar --keystore=<your app signing key file> --alias=<your alias>
--output=encrypted_private_key_path --encryptionkey=<your app signing key>
```

Enter the keystore and key passwords when prompted, then check that a file named *encrypted_private_key_path* has been generated. This file contains your app signing key encrypted for uploading to the Google Play Store. Return to the Google Play console, click on the *App Signing Key* button (B) and upload the *encrypted_private_key_path* file.

Next, follow the steps outlined earlier in this chapter to generate the upload key and store it in a new keystore file. In a terminal or command-prompt window, change directory to the location of the upload keystore file and run the following command to convert the keystroke into a PEM certificate format file:

```
keytool -export -rfc -keystore <your upload key file> -alias <your alias> -file
upload_certificate.pem
```

With the file generated, click on the *Upload Public Key Certificate* button (C) in the Google Play console and upload the PEM certificate file.

Finally, enroll the app in Google Play Signing by clicking on the *Enroll* button (D). Once the app is enrolled, the new upload keystore file must be used whenever the signed app bundle file is generated within Android Studio.

82.15 Summary

Once an app project is either complete, or ready for user testing, it can be uploaded to the Google Play console and published for production, internal, alpha or beta testing. Before the app can be uploaded, an app entry must be created within the console including information about the app together with screenshots to be used within the Play Store. A release Android App Bundle file is then generated and signed with an upload key from within Android Studio. After the bundle file has been uploaded, Google Play removes the upload key and replaces it with the securely stored app signing key and the app is ready to be published.

The content of a bundle file can be reviewed at any time by loading it into the Android Studio APK Analyzer tool.

83. An Overview of Android Dynamic Feature Modules

As outlined in the preceding chapter, the introduction of app bundles and dynamic delivery considerably reduced the size of the application package files that need to be downloaded when a user installs an app on an Android device. Although initially intended as a way to automatically generate separate package files for each possible device configuration, another key advantage of dynamic delivery is the ability to split an app into multiple dynamic feature modules that can be installed on-demand.

In this chapter, we will begin to explore the basic concepts of dynamic feature modules in preparation for working through a detailed practical example in the next chapter.

83.1 An Overview of Dynamic Feature Modules

The primary goals of dynamic delivery are to reduce the amount of time and bandwidth it takes to install an app from the app store, while also ensuring that only the minimum storage space is occupied by the app once it is installed.

Dynamic feature modules (also referred to as *on-demand modules*) allow the different features that comprise an Android app to be packaged into separate modules that are only downloaded and installed onto the device when they are required by the user. An app might, for example, include news and discussion features. In this scenario the app might only install the news feature by default and separate the discussion feature into a dynamic feature module. When a user attempts to access the discussion feature, the app will download the feature module from the Google Play store and launch it. If the user never accesses the feature, the module will never be installed, thereby ensuring that only the absolute minimum amount of storage is used by the app.

An app that utilizes dynamic feature modules has full control over how and when modules are installed. In fact, the app could also monitor the frequency with which particular features are accessed by a user and temporarily remove any that are infrequently used.

A dynamic feature may also be designated as being an "instant" module. This replaces the Instant App concept of earlier Android releases and allows a dynamic feature module to be run on a device without having to install the app. This allows the app to appear with a "Try Now" button within the Google Play App Store, or to be instantly launched on a device by clicking on a web URL.

83.2 Dynamic Feature Module Architecture

From the outset Android was designed with modularity in mind, particularly in terms of the concepts of Intents and Activities. Dynamic features bring this philosophy to a logical conclusion by allowing an app to install only what the user needs, when the user needs it. Given the flexibility and power of this capability, the implementation of dynamic feature modules is relatively simple.

In basic terms, dynamic feature modules are built using *split APK files* which allow multiple APK files to be brought together to form a single app.

As we learned in *"Creating, Testing and Uploading an Android App Bundle"*, dynamic delivery and app bundles work by generating a custom APK file that contains only the bytecode and resources necessary to run the app on a specific device configuration. In this case, the app is still installed via a single APK file, albeit one customized for the user's device.

In contrast, dynamic feature modules work by splitting an app into multiple APK files referred to as *split APK files*.

When an app uses split APK files, only the *base module* is installed when the app is first downloaded. The base module acts as the entry point into the app via a launchable activity, and contains the bytecode and resources for the base functionality of the app together with configuration and build resources that are required by the rest of the app. The base module manifest file, for example, contains a merger of the manifest files for any dynamic feature modules bundled with the app. Also, the version number for all of the dynamic feature modules are dictated by the version code setting in the build configuration file of the base module.

The base module also includes a list of the dynamic feature modules included in the app bundle and all dynamic feature modules must list the base module as a dependency in their build configurations.

Each dynamic feature takes the from of a module containing the bytecode, manifest, resources and build configuration together with any other assets such as images or data files for that specific feature.

When a user requests the installation of an app from the app store, the store will generate the *Base APK* file for the module containing all of the bytecode and resources common to all device configurations in addition to a set of *Configuration APK* files configured specifically for the user's device. Similarly, a request to install a dynamic feature module will generate a *Dynamic Feature APK* file in addition to the corresponding Configuration APK files as illustrated in Figure 83-1 below:

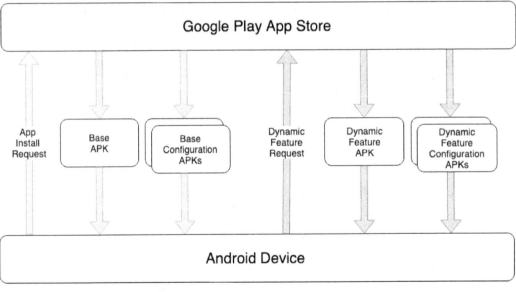

Figure 83-1

83.3 Creating a Dynamic Feature Module

A dynamic feature can be added to a project either by adding an entirely new module, or by migrating an existing module. To add a new module, simply select the Android Studio *File -> New -> New Module...* menu option. From the resulting dialog, select either the Dynamic Feature Module or Instant Dynamic Feature Module template, depending on the type of dynamic feature you are creating:

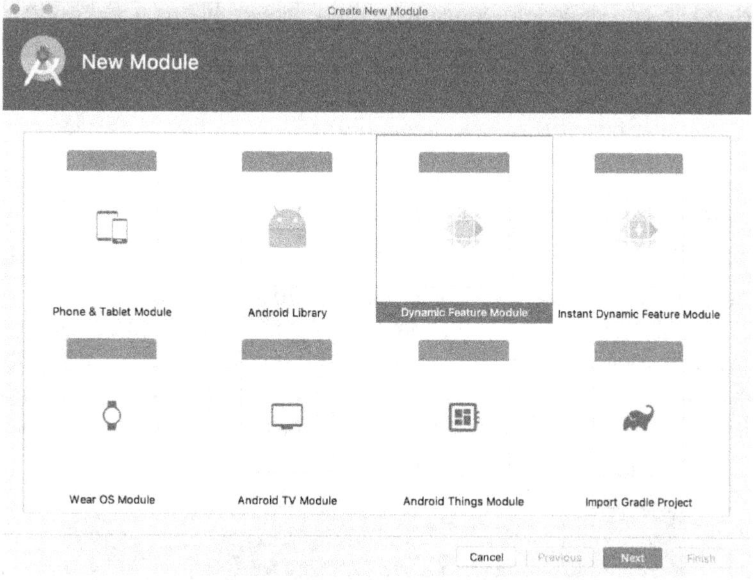

Figure 83-2

With the appropriate dynamic feature option selected, click on the *Next* button and, in the configuration screen, name the module and change the minimum API setting so that it matches the API level chosen for the base module (the project will fail to build if these versions do not match).

Click the *Next* button once more to configure the On-Demand options:

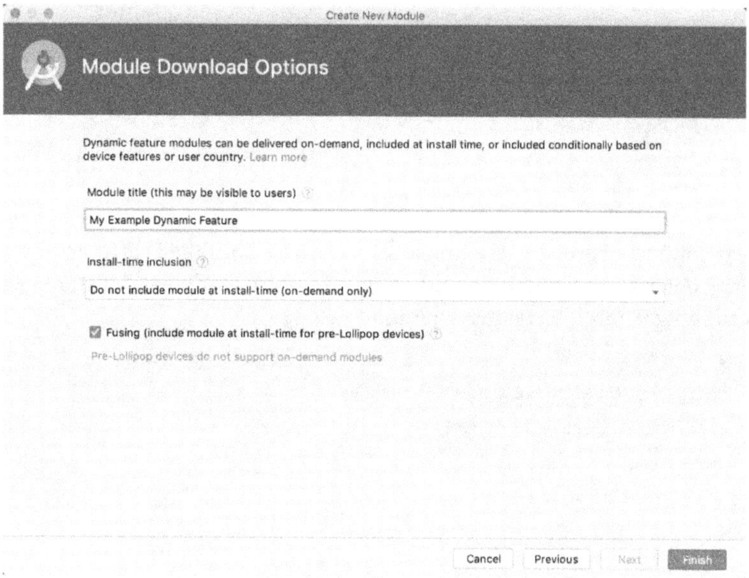

Figure 83-3

When the *Fusing* option is enabled, the module will be downloaded with the base APK on devices running older versions of Android (Android 4.4 API 20 or older) that predate the introduction of dynamic delivery. The *Module Title* string can be up to 50 characters in length and will be used by Google Play when describing the feature to users in messages and notifications.

The *Install-time inclusion* menu provides options to control the conditions under which the module will be installed on-demand as opposed to being included in the initial installation of the app on the user's device. The menu provides the following options:

- **Do not include module at install time (on-demand only)** - Regardless of device configuration and user country, the module will not be installed until it is requested by the app.

- **Include module at install time** - Disables on-demand dynamic installation for all devices and user countries. The module will be installed at the same time that the app is installed on the device.

- **Only include module at install-time for devices with specified features** - The module will be included at install time for device configurations and user countries that meet the specified criteria. All other countries and device configurations will use dynamic on-demand installation. When this option is selected, extra options will appear allowing device features to be entered. In Figure 83-4, for example, the module will be included at install time on devices with a microphone and fingerprint reader. On all other devices the module will be installed dynamically on-demand:

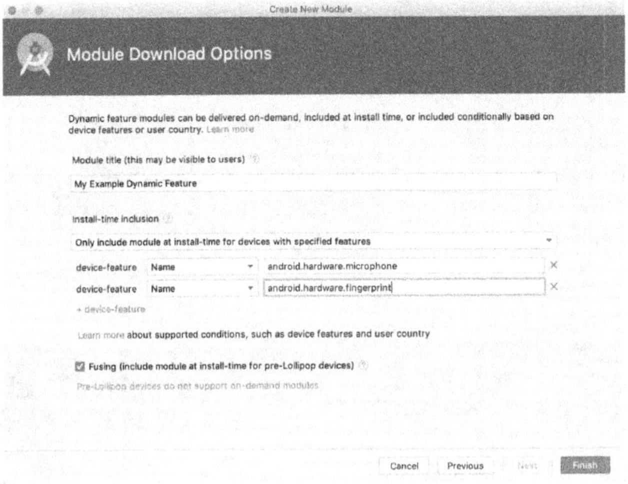

Figure 83-4

Other criteria such as countries and API level must be declared within the project manifest (*AndroidManifest.xml*) file. The following entries, for example, would disable dynamic on-demand feature installation for users in France and devices running Android versions older than API 21:

```
<dist:conditions>
  <dist:user-countries dist:exclude="true">
    <dist:country dist:code="FR"/>
  </dist:user-countries>
  <dist:min-sdk dist:value="21"/>
</dist:conditions>
```

83.4 Converting an Existing Module for Dynamic Delivery

If an app contains an existing feature that is a good candidate for dynamic delivery it can be converted to a dynamic feature with a few basic steps. Consider, for example, the following project structure:

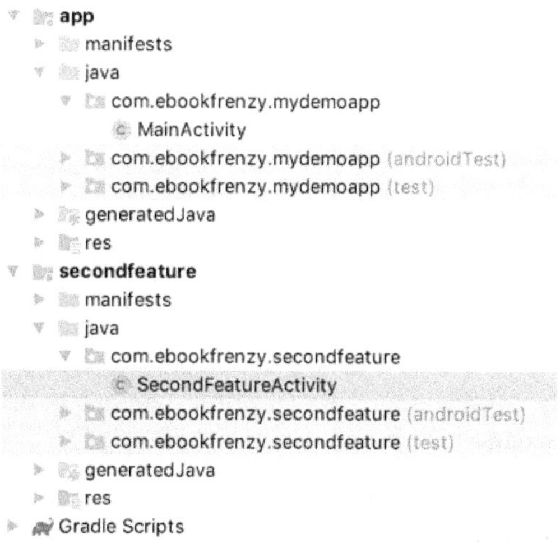

Figure 83-5

In this project, the *app* module will serve as the base module while the *secondfeature* module is an ideal candidate for conversion to a dynamic feature module.

To convert an existing module within your app to a dynamic feature module, begin by editing the module level *build.gradle* file (*Gradle Scripts -> build.gradle (Module: secondfeature)* in the above example) and modifying it to use the *com.android.dynamic-feature* instead of the *com.android.application* plugin, and changing the dependencies so that the module only depends on the base (app) module. For example:

```
apply plugin: 'com.android.application'
apply plugin: 'com.android.dynamic-feature'

.

.

dependencies {
    implementation fileTree(dir: 'libs', include: ['*.jar'])
    api 'androidx.appcompat:appcompat:1.0.2'
    api 'androidx.constraintlayout:constraintlayout:1.1.3'
    testImplementation 'junit:junit:4.12'
    androidTestImplementation 'androidx.test.ext:junit:1.1.1'
    androidTestImplementation 'androidx.test.espresso:espresso-core:3.2.0'
    implementation project(':app')
}
```

Next, edit the *AndroidManifest.xml* file for the module and modify it as follows (note in this example, that this is an on-demand module as opposed to an instant module):

```
<?xml version="1.0" encoding="utf-8"?>
<manifest xmlns:android="http://schemas.android.com/apk/res/android"
    xmlns:dist="http://schemas.android.com/apk/distribution"
    package="com.ebookfrenzy.mymodule">

    <dist:module
```

```
        dist:instant="false"
        dist:onDemand="true"
        dist:title="@string/title_my_dynamic_feature">
        <dist:fusing dist:include="true" />
    </dist:module>

    <application
        android:allowBackup="true"
.
.
```

Note the title property references a string resource which will also need to be declared in the *strings.xml* file. The use of a string resource as opposed to a hard coded string is mandatory for this property

Next, the *build.gradle* file for the base module (*build.gradle (Module: app)*) needs to be modified to reference the dynamic feature module and to add the Play Core Library as a dependency:

```
apply plugin: 'com.android.application'

android {
    compileSdkVersion 29
.

.

    }
    dynamicFeatures = [":secondfeature"]
}

dependencies {
.

.

    api 'com.google.android.play:core:1.5.0'
.

.

}
```

Finally, edit the *AndroidManifest.xml* file for the base module to declare the module as sub-classing SplitCompatApplication:

```
<?xml version="1.0" encoding="utf-8"?>
<manifest xmlns:android="http://schemas.android.com/apk/res/android"
    package="com.ebookfrenzy.mydemoapp">

    <application
        android:name=
            "com.google.android.play.core.splitcompat.SplitCompatApplication"
        android:allowBackup="true"
.

.
```

83.5 Working with Dynamic Feature Modules

Once an app project has one or more dynamic feature modules added, code will need to be written to install and manage those modules. This will involve performing tasks such as checking whether a module is already installed, installing the module, tracking installation progress and deleting an installed module that is no longer required. All of these tasks are performed using the API provided by the Play Core Library and most of these API calls involve the use of a SplitInstallManager instance which can be created as follows:

```
private SplitInstallManager manager;
manager = SplitInstallManagerFactory.create(this);
```

Usually, the first step before allowing the user to launch a dynamic feature is to check that the corresponding module has already been installed. The following code, for example, obtains a list of installed modules and checks if a specific module is installed:

```
if (manager.getInstalledModules().contains("my_dynamic_feature")) {
    // Module is installed
}
```

One or more modules may be installed by building a SplitInstallRequest object and passing it through to the *startInstall()* method of the SplitInstallManager instance:

```
.
.
private int mySessionID = 0;
.
.
SplitInstallRequest request =
        SplitInstallRequest
                .newBuilder()
                .addModule("my_dynamic_feature")
                .addModule("my_dynamic_feature2")
                .build();

manager.startInstall(request)
        .addOnSuccessListener(new OnSuccessListener<Integer>() {
            @Override
            public void onSuccess(Integer sessionId) {
                mySessionID = sessionId
            }
        })
        .addOnFailureListener(new OnFailureListener() {
            @Override
            public void onFailure(Exception exception) {
            }
        });
```

When the above code is executed, the module installation will begin immediately. Alternatively, deferred installations may be performed by passing an array of feature module names to the *deferredInstall()* method as follows:

```
manager.deferredInstall(Arrays.asList("my_dynamic_feature",
```

```
                                        "my_dynamic_feature2"));
```

Deferred downloads are performed in the background at the discretion of the operating system.

While it is not possible to track the status of deferred installations, non-deferred installations can be tracked by adding a listener to the manager:

```
SplitInstallStateUpdatedListener listener =
                    new SplitInstallStateUpdatedListener() {
    @Override
    public void onStateUpdate(SplitInstallSessionState state) {

        if (state.sessionId() == mySessionID) {
            switch (state.status()) {
                case SplitInstallSessionStatus.REQUIRES_USER_CONFIRMATION:
                    // Large module requires user permission
                    break;

                case SplitInstallSessionStatus.DOWNLOADING:
                    // The module is being downloaded
                    break;

                case SplitInstallSessionStatus.INSTALLING:
                    // The downloaded module is being installed
                    break;

                case SplitInstallSessionStatus.DOWNLOADED:
                    // The module download is complete
                    break;

                case SplitInstallSessionStatus.INSTALLED:
                    // The module has been installed successfully
                    break;

                case SplitInstallSessionStatus.CANCELED:
                    // The user cancelled the download
                    break;

                case SplitInstallSessionStatus.PENDING:
                    // The installation is deferred
                    break;

                case SplitInstallSessionStatus.FAILED:
                    // The installation failed
            }
        }
    }
}
```

```
};
```

Once the listener has been implemented, it will need to be registered with the SplitInstallManager instance and then unregistered when no longer required.

```
manager.registerListener(listener);

.


.

manager.unregisterListener(listener);
```

83.6 Handling Large Dynamic Feature Modules

The Android dynamic delivery system will not permit the download of a dynamic feature module greater than 10MB in size without first requesting permission from the user. When a request is made to download a large feature module, the listener will be called and passed a REQUIRES_USER_CONFIRMATION status. It is then the responsibility of the app to display the confirmation dialog and, optionally, implement an *onActivityResult()* handler method to identify whether the user approved or declined the download.

```
private static final int REQUEST_CODE = 101;

.


.

SplitInstallStateUpdatedListener listener =
                     new SplitInstallStateUpdatedListener() {
    @Override
    public void onStateUpdate(SplitInstallSessionState state) {

        if (state.sessionId() == mySessionID) {
            switch (state.status()) {

                case SplitInstallSessionStatus.REQUIRES_USER_CONFIRMATION:
                    try {
                        manager.startConfirmationDialogForResult(state,
                                MainActivity.this, REQUEST_CODE);
                    } catch (IntentSender.SendIntentException ex) {
                        // Request failed
                    }
                    break;

.


.
```

The above code launches an intent which, in turn, displays the built-in confirmation dialog. This intent will return a result code to the on*ActivityResult()* method which may be implemented as follows:

```
@Override
public void onActivityResult(int requestCode, int resultCode, Intent data) {
    if (requestCode == REQUEST_CODE) {
        if (resultCode == RESULT_OK) {
            // User approved installation
        } else {
            // User declined installation
        }
```

```
    }
}
```

If the user approves the request, the dynamic feature module will be downloaded and installed automatically.

83.7 Summary

Dynamic feature modules allow an Android app to be divided into separate features which are downloaded on-demand when the feature is needed by the user. Dynamic feature modules can also be configured to be instant features. Instant features can be run without installing the app on the device and can be accessed by users either via a Try Now button on the app store page, or via a web URL.

Dynamic feature implementation involves splitting an app into a base module and one or more dynamic feature modules. New dynamic feature modules can be created within Android Studio, and existing modules converted to dynamic feature modules by making a few project configuration changes.

Once dynamic feature modules have been added to an app, the download and management of those modules is handled by the app via the SplitInstall classes of the Play Core Library.

84. An Android Studio Dynamic Feature Tutorial

With the basic concepts of Android Dynamic Delivery and Dynamic Features covered in the previous chapter, this chapter will put this theory into practice in the form of an example project. The app created in this chapter will consist of two activities, the first of which will serve as the base module for the app while the second will be designated as a dynamic feature to be downloaded on demand from within the running app. This tutorial will include steps to create a dynamic module from within Android Studio, upload the app bundle to the Google Play Store for testing, and use the Play Core Library to download and manage dynamic features. The chapter will also explore the use of deferred dynamic feature installation.

84.1 Creating the DynamicFeature Project

Select the *Start a new Android Studio project* quick start option from the welcome screen and, within the resulting new project dialog, choose the Empty Activity template before clicking on the Next button.

Enter *DynamicFeature* into the Name field and specify a package name that will uniquely identify your app within the Google Play ecosystem (for example *com.<your company>.dynamicfeature)* as the package name. Before clicking on the Finish button, change the Minimum API level setting to API 26: Android 8.0 (Oreo) and the Language menu to Java.

84.2 Adding Dynamic Feature Support to the Project

Before embarking on the implementation of the app, two changes need to be made to the project to add support for dynamic features. Since the project will be making extensive use of the Play Core Library, a directive needs to be added to the build configuration to include this library. Within Android Studio, open the app level *build. gradle* file (*Gradle Scripts -> build.gradle (Module: app)*), locate the dependencies section and add the Play Core Library as follows:

```
.
.
dependencies {
    .
    .
    implementation 'com.google.android.play:core:1.6.1'
    .
    .
}
```

Once a dynamic feature module has been downloaded, it is most likely that immediate access to code and resource assets that comprise the feature will be required by the user. By default, however, newly installed feature modules are not available to the rest of the app until the app is restarted. Fortunately, this shortcoming can be avoided by enabling the SplitCompat Library within the project. By far the easiest way to achieve this is to declare the application as subclassing SplitCompatApplication in the main *AndroidManifest.xml* file (also referred to as the *base module manifest*) as follows:

```
<?xml version="1.0" encoding="utf-8"?>
```

```
<manifest xmlns:android="http://schemas.android.com/apk/res/android"
    package="com.ebookfrenzy.dynamicfeature">

<application
        android:name=
            "com.google.android.play.core.splitcompat.SplitCompatApplication"
        android:allowBackup="true"
        android:icon="@mipmap/ic_launcher"
        android:label="@string/app_name"
        android:roundIcon="@mipmap/ic_launcher_round"
```

.

.

84.3 Designing the Base Activity User Interface

At this point, the project consists of a single activity which will serve as the entry point for the base module of the app. This base module will be responsible for requesting, installing and managing the dynamic feature module.

To demonstrate the use of dynamic features, the base activity will consist of a series of buttons which will allow the dynamic feature module to be installed, launched and removed. The user interface will also include a TextView object to display status information relating to the dynamic feature module. With these requirements in mind, load the *activity_main.xml* layout file into the layout editor, delete the default TextView object, and implement the design so that it resembles Figure 84-1 below.

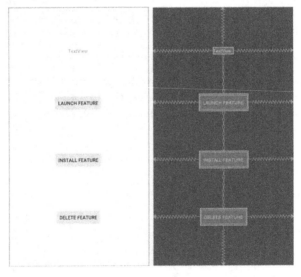

Figure 84-1

Once the objects have been positioned, select the TextView widget and use the Attributes tool window to set the id property to *status_text*. Begin applying layout constraints by selecting all of the objects within the layout, right-clicking the TextView object and choosing the *Center -> Horizontally in Parent* option from the menu, thereby constraining all four objects to the horizontal center of the screen.

With all the objects still selected, right-click on the TextView once again, this time selecting the *Chains -> Create Vertical Chain* menu option. Before continuing, extract all the button text strings to resources and configure the three buttons to call methods named *launchFeature, installFeature* and *deleteFeature* respectively.

84.4 Adding the Dynamic Feature Module

To add a dynamic feature module to the project, select the *File -> New -> New Module...* menu option and, in the resulting dialog, choose the Dynamic Feature Module option as shown in Figure 84-2:

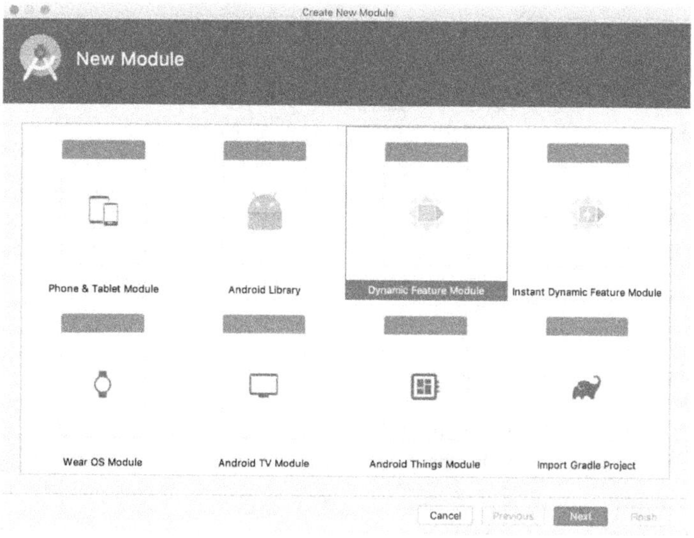

Figure 84-2

With the Dynamic Feature Module option selected, click on the *Next* button and, in the configuration screen, name the module *my_dynamic_feature* and change the minimum API setting to API 26: Android 8.0 (Oreo) so that it matches the API level chosen for the base module:

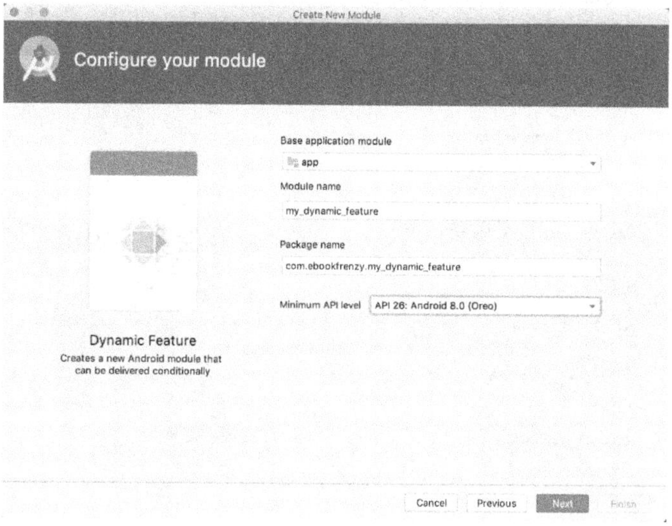

Figure 84-3

Click the *Next* button once more to configure the On-Demand options, making sure that the *Fusing* option is enabled. In the *Module Title* field, enter text which reads "My Example Dynamic Feature":

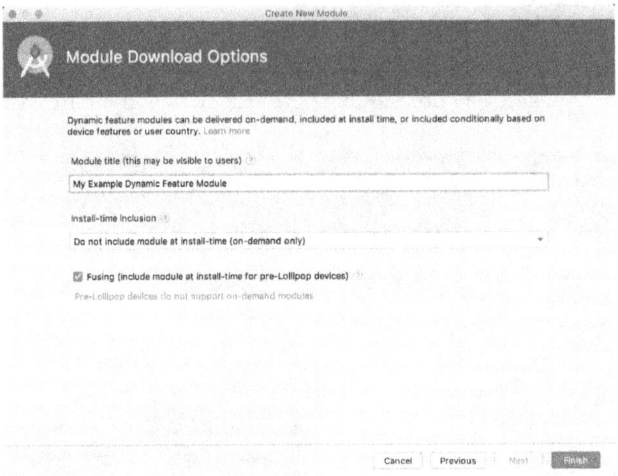

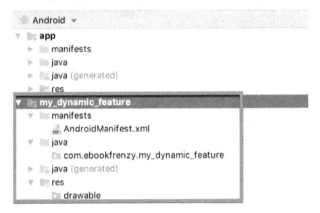

Figure 84-4

For the purposes of this example, set the *Install-time inclusion* menu to *Do not include module at install time (on-demand only)* before clicking on the *Finish* button to commit the changes and add the dynamic feature module to the project.

84.5 Reviewing the Dynamic Feature Module

Before proceeding to the next step, it is worth taking some time to review the changes that have been made to the project by Android Studio. Understanding these changes can be useful both when resolving problems and when converting existing app features to dynamic features.

Begin by referring to the Project tool window, where a new entry will have appeared representing the folder containing the new dynamic feature module:

Figure 84-5

Note that the feature has its own sub-structure including a manifest file, a package into which code and resources can be added and a *res* folder. Open and review the *AndroidManifest.xml* file which should contain the property settings that were selected during the feature creation process including the on-demand, fusing and feature title values:

```
<manifest xmlns:android="http://schemas.android.com/apk/res/android"
    xmlns:dist="http://schemas.android.com/apk/distribution"
```

```
package="com.ebookfrenzy.my_dynamic_feature">

    <dist:module
        dist:instant="false"
        dist:title="@string/title_my_dynamic_feature">
        <dist:delivery>
            <dist:on-demand />
        </dist:delivery>
        <dist:fusing dist:include="true" />
    </dist:module>
</manifest>
```

A point of particular interest is that the module title string has been stored as a string resource instead of being directly entered in the manifest file. This is a prerequisite for the title string and the resource can be found and, if necessary, modified in the *strings.xml* file (*app -> res -> values -> strings.xml*) of the base module.

The build configuration for the dynamic feature module can be found in the *Gradle Scripts -> build.gradle (Module: my_dynamic_feature)* file and should read as follows:

```
apply plugin: 'com.android.dynamic-feature'

android {
    compileSdkVersion 29

    defaultConfig {
        minSdkVersion 26
        targetSdkVersion 29
        versionCode 1
        versionName "1.0"
    }
}

dependencies {
    implementation fileTree(dir: 'libs', include: ['*.jar'])
    implementation project(':app')
}
```

The key entries in this file are the application of the *com.android.dynamic-feature* plugin which ensures that this module is treated as a dynamic feature, and the final *implementation* line indicating that this feature is dependent upon the base (app) module.

The *build.gradle* file for the base module (*Gradle Scripts -> build.gradle (Module: app)*) also contains a new entry listing the dynamic feature module:

```
apply plugin: 'com.android.application'
.

.
android {
    compileSdkVersion 29
```

```
        buildToolsVersion "29.0.0"
        defaultConfig {
            applicationId "com.ebookfrenzy.dynamicfeature"
            minSdkVersion 26
            targetSdkVersion 29
            versionCode 1
            versionName "1.0"
            testInstrumentationRunner "androidx.test.runner.AndroidJUnitRunner"
        }
        buildTypes {
            release {
                minifyEnabled false
    .


            }
        }
        dynamicFeatures = [":my_dynamic_feature"]
}

dependencies {
    .

    .
```

Any additional dynamic features added to the project will also need to be referenced here, for example:

```
dynamicFeatures = [":my_dynamic_feature", ":my_second_feature", ...]
```

84.6 Adding the Dynamic Feature Activity

From the Project tool window illustrated in Figure 84-5 above, it is clear that the dynamic feature module contains little more than a manifest file at this point. The next step is to add an activity to the module so that the feature actually does something when launched from within the base module. Within the Project tool window, right-click on the package name located under *my_dynamic_feature -> java* and select the *New -> Activity -> Empty Activity* menu option. Name the activity *MyFeatureActivity* and enable the *Generate Layout File* option but leave the *Launcher Activity* option disabled before clicking on the *Finish* button.

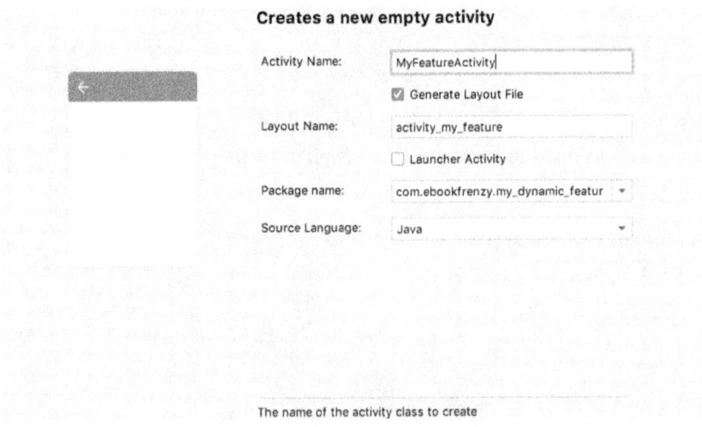

Creates a new empty activity

Activity Name:	MyFeatureActivity
	☑ Generate Layout File
Layout Name:	activity_my_feature
	☐ Launcher Activity
Package name:	com.ebookfrenzy.my_dynamic_featur ▾
Source Language:	Java ▾

The name of the activity class to create

Figure 84-6

Once the activity has been added to the module, edit the *AndroidManifest.xml* file and modify it to add an intent filter that will allow the activity to be launched by the base module (where *<com.yourcompany>* is replaced by the package name you chose in order to make your app unique on Google Play):

```xml
<?xml version="1.0" encoding="utf-8"?>
<manifest xmlns:android="http://schemas.android.com/apk/res/android"
    xmlns:dist="http://schemas.android.com/apk/distribution"
    package="com.ebookfrenzy.my_dynamic_feature">

    <dist:module
        dist:instant="false"
        dist:title="@string/title_my_dynamic_feature">
        <dist:delivery>
            <dist:on-demand />
        </dist:delivery>
        <dist:fusing dist:include="true" />
    </dist:module>

    <application>
        <activity android:name=".MyFeatureActivity">
            <intent-filter>
                <action android:name="android.intent.action.VIEW" />
                <action android:name=
                  "<com.yourcompany>.my_dynamic_feature.MyFeatureActivity" />
                <category android:name="android.intent.category.DEFAULT" />
            </intent-filter>
        </activity>
    </application>
</manifest>
```

Complete the feature by loading the *activity_my_feature.xml* file into the layout editor tool and adding a TextView object displaying text which reads "My Dynamic Feature Module":

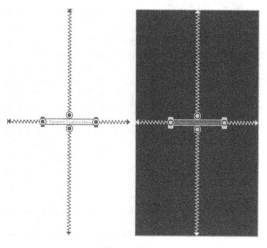

Figure 84-7

84.7 Implementing the launchIntent() Method

With the project structure and user interface designs completed it is time to use the Play Core Library to begin working with the dynamic feature module. The first step is to implement the *launchFeature()* method, the purpose of which is to use an intent to launch the dynamic feature activity. Attempting to start an activity in a dynamic feature module that has yet to be installed, however, will cause the app to crash. The *launchFeature()* method, therefore, needs to include some defensive code to ensure that the dynamic feature has been installed. To achieve this, we need to create an instance of the SplitInstallManager class and call the *getInstalledModules()* method of that object to check whether the *my_dynamic_feature* module is already installed. If it is installed, the activity contained in the module can be safely launched, otherwise a message needs to be displayed to the user on the status TextView. Within the *MainActivity.java* file, make the following changes to the class:

```java
.
.
import android.widget.TextView;
import android.view.View;
import android.content.Intent;
.
.
import com.google.android.play.core.splitinstall.SplitInstallManager;
import com.google.android.play.core.splitinstall.SplitInstallManagerFactory;
.
.
public class MainActivity extends AppCompatActivity {

    private TextView statusText;
    private SplitInstallManager manager;

    @Override
    protected void onCreate(Bundle savedInstanceState) {

        super.onCreate(savedInstanceState);
        setContentView(R.layout.activity_main);

        statusText = findViewById(R.id.status_text);
        manager = SplitInstallManagerFactory.create(this);
    }

    public void launchFeature(View view) {
        if (manager.getInstalledModules().contains("my_dynamic_feature")) {
            Intent i = new Intent(
                    "<com.yourcompany>.my_dynamic_feature.MyFeatureActivity");
            startActivity(i);
        } else {
            statusText.setText("Feature not yet installed");
        }
    }
}
```

.

.

}

84.8 Uploading the App Bundle for Testing

The project is now ready for the first phase of testing. This involves generating a release app bundle and uploading it to the Google Play Console. The steps to achieve this were outlined in the chapter entitled *"Creating, Testing and Uploading an Android App Bundle"* but can be summarized as follows:

1. Log into the Google Play Console and create a new application.

2. Work through the steps to configure the app in terms of title, descriptions, categorization and image assets (sample image assets can be found in the *image_assets* folder of the sample code download that accompanies this book) and save the draft settings.

3. Use the Android Studio *Build -> Generate Signed App Bundle / APK...* menu to generate a signed *release* app bundle.

4. In the Google Play Console, select the *App Releases* option from the left hand navigation panel, locate the *Internal test track* section in the resulting screen and click on the *Manage* button.

5. On the *Internal test* screen, click on the *Create Release* button and click *Continue* to accept the option to let Google manage key signing tasks. Drag and drop the app bundle file generated above onto the "Android App Bundles and APKs to add" box and click *Save*.

6. Complete the final configuration steps including the *Content Rating* and *Pricing & Distribution* screens.

7. Navigate within the console to the *App Releases* page and click on the *Manage* button located in the *Internal Test track* section.

8. On the *Manage testers* section add the email addresses of accounts that will be used to test the app on one or more physical devices.

9. Return to the Internal test screen and click on the *Edit Release* button. Scroll to the bottom of the page and click on the *Review* button.

10. On the confirmation screen, click on the *Start Rollout to Internal Test* button. The app will be listed as *Pending publication*. Once it has been approved by Google (a process that can take anywhere from a few minutes to a few hours), the app is ready for testing.

Once the release has been rolled out for testing and been approved, notifications will be sent out to all users on the internal testing track asking them to opt in to the test track for the app. Alternatively, copy the Opt-in URL listed on the *Manage testers* screen and send it to the test users. Once the users have opted in, a link will be provided which, when opened on a device, will launch the Play Store app and open the download page for the DynamicFeature app as shown in Figure 84-8:

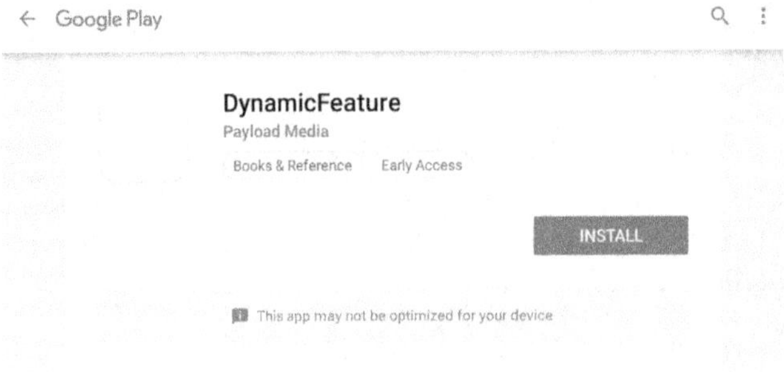

Figure 84-8

Click on the button to install the app, then open it and tap the Launch Feature button. The fact that the dynamic feature has yet to be installed should be reflected in the status text.

84.9 Implementing the installFeature() Method

The *installFeature()* method will create a SplitInstallRequest object for the *my_dynamic_feature* module, then use the SplitInstallManager instance to initiate the installation process. Listeners will also be implemented to display Toast messages indicating the status of the install request. Remaining in the *MainActivity.java* file, add the *installFeature()* method as follows:

```
.
.
import android.widget.Toast;
.
.
import com.google.android.play.core.splitinstall.SplitInstallRequest;
import com.google.android.play.core.tasks.OnFailureListener;
import com.google.android.play.core.tasks.OnSuccessListener;
.
.
    public void installFeature(View view) {

        SplitInstallRequest request =
                SplitInstallRequest
                        .newBuilder()
                        .addModule("my_dynamic_feature")
                        .build();

        manager.startInstall(request)
                .addOnSuccessListener(new OnSuccessListener<Integer>() {
                    @Override
                    public void onSuccess(Integer sessionId) {
                        Toast.makeText(MainActivity.this,
                            "Module installation started",
                                Toast.LENGTH_SHORT).show();
                    }
```

```
        })
        .addOnFailureListener(new OnFailureListener() {
            @Override
            public void onFailure(Exception exception) {
                Toast.makeText(MainActivity.this,
                    "Module installation failed" + exception.toString(),
                    Toast.LENGTH_SHORT).show();
            }
        });
    }
    .
    .
}
```

Edit the *Gradle Scripts -> build.gradle (Module: app)* file and increment the versionCode and versionName values so that the new version of the app bundle can be uploaded for testing:

```
android {
    .
    .

        versionCode 2
        versionName "2.0"
    .
    .
```

Repeat this step to declare a matching version number within the *Gradle Scripts -> build.gradle (Module: my_ dynamic_feature)* file.

Generate a new app bundle containing the changes, then return to the *Release Management -> App Releases* page for the app in the Google Play Console, click on the *Manage* button in the *Internal test track* section followed by the *Create Release* button as highlighted in Figure 84-9 below:

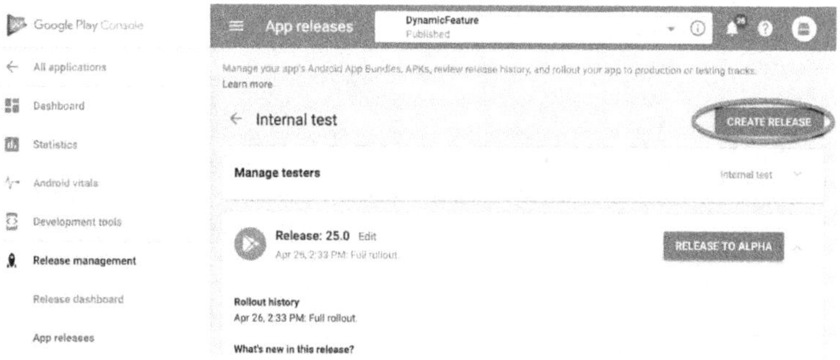

Figure 84-9

Follow the steps to upload the new app bundle and roll it out for internal testing. On the testing device, open the Google Play Store app and make sure the Install button has changed to an Update button (if it has not, close the App Store app and try again after waiting a few minutes) and update to the new release. Once the update is complete, run the app, tap the Install Feature button and check the Toast messages to ensure the installation started successfully. A download icon should briefly appear in the status bar at the top of the screen as the feature is downloaded. Once the download is complete, tap the Launch Feature button to display the second activity.

If the installation fails, or the app crashes, the cause can usually be identified from the LogCat output. To view this output, connect the device to your development computer, open a terminal or command prompt window and execute the following command:

```
adb logcat
```

This adb command will display LogCat output in real time, including any exception or diagnostic errors generated when the app encounters a problem or crashes.

84.10 Adding the Update Listener

For more detailed tracking of the installation progress of a dynamic feature module, an instance of SplitInstallStateUpdatedListener can be added to the app. Since it is possible to install multiple feature modules simultaneously, some code needs to be added to keep track of the session IDs assigned to the installation processes. Begin by adding some imports, declaring a variable in the *MainActivity.java* file to contain the current session ID and modifying the *installFeature()* method to store the session ID each time an installation is successfully started and to register the listener:

```
.
.
import com.google.android.play.core.splitinstall.SplitInstallSessionState;
import
      com.google.android.play.core.splitinstall.SplitInstallStateUpdatedListener;
import com.google.android.play.core.splitinstall.model.SplitInstallSessionStatus;
.
.
import java.util.Locale;
.
.
public class MainActivity extends AppCompatActivity {

    private TextView statusText;
    private SplitInstallManager manager;
    private int mySessionId = 0;
.
.
    public void installFeature(View view) {
.
.
        manager.registerListener(listener);

        manager.startInstall(request)
                .addOnSuccessListener(new OnSuccessListener<Integer>() {
                    @Override
                    public void onSuccess(Integer sessionId) {
                        mySessionId = sessionId;
                        Toast.makeText(MainActivity.this,
                            "Module installation started",
                                Toast.LENGTH_SHORT).show();
```

```
                }
            })
```

.

.

Next, implement the listener code so that it reads as follows:

```
SplitInstallStateUpdatedListener listener =
                        new SplitInstallStateUpdatedListener() {
    @Override
    public void onStateUpdate(SplitInstallSessionState state) {

        if (state.sessionId() == mySessionId) {
            switch (state.status()) {
                case SplitInstallSessionStatus.DOWNLOADING:
                    long size = state.totalBytesToDownload();
                    long downloaded = state.bytesDownloaded();
                    statusText.setText(String.format(Locale.getDefault(),
                        "%d of %d bytes downloaded.", downloaded, size));
                    break;

                case SplitInstallSessionStatus.INSTALLING:

                    statusText.setText("Installing feature");
                    break;

                case SplitInstallSessionStatus.DOWNLOADED:

                    statusText.setText("Download Complete");
                    break;

                case SplitInstallSessionStatus.INSTALLED:

                    statusText.setText("Installed - Feature is ready");
                    break;

                case SplitInstallSessionStatus.CANCELED:

                    statusText.setText("Installation cancelled");
                    break;

                case SplitInstallSessionStatus.PENDING:

                    statusText.setText("Installation pending");
                    break;

                case SplitInstallSessionStatus.FAILED:
```

```
                        statusText.setText("Installation Failed. Error code: " +
                                            state.errorCode());
                }
            }
        }
};
```

The listener catches many of the common installation states and updates the status text accordingly, including providing information about the size of the download and a running total of the number of bytes downloaded so far. Before proceeding, add *onPause()* and *onResume()* lifecycle methods to ensure that the listener is unregistered when the app is not active:

```
@Override
public void onResume() {
    manager.registerListener(listener);
    super.onResume();
}


@Override
public void onPause() {
    manager.unregisterListener(listener);
    super.onPause();
}
```

Test that the listener code works by incrementing the version number information in the two module level *build. gradle* files, generating and uploading a new release app bundle and rolling it out for testing. If a dynamic feature module is already installed on a device, attempts to download the module again will be ignored by the Play Core Library classes. To fully test the listener, therefore, the app must be uninstalled from within the Play Store app before installing the updated release. Of course, with the app removed there will be no Update button to let us know that the new release is ready to be installed. To find out which release the Play Store app will install, scroll down the app page to the *Read More* button, select it and check the Version field in the *App Info* section as highlighted in Figure 84-10 below:

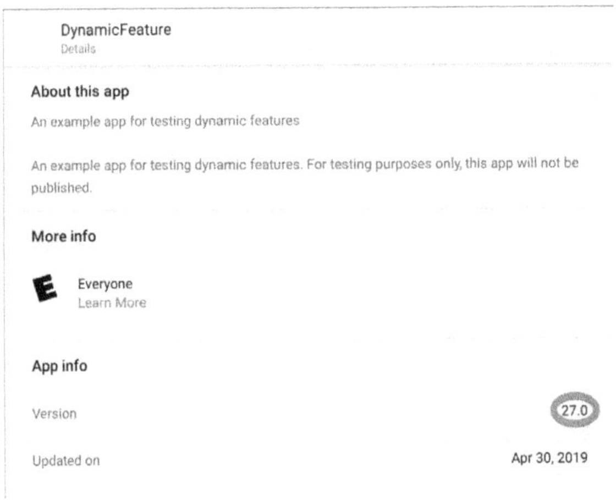

Figure 84-10

If the previous version is still listed, exit the Play app and wait a few minutes before checking again. Once the new version is listed, complete the installation, open the app and check that the status text updates appropriately when the dynamic feature module is downloaded.

84.11 Handling Large Downloads

The next task for this project is to integrate support for large feature modules by adding an additional case to the switch statement in the listener implementation as follows:

```
.

.

import android.content.IntentSender;

.

.

public class MainActivity extends AppCompatActivity {

.

.

    private static final int REQUEST_CODE = 101;

.

.

SplitInstallStateUpdatedListener listener =
                        new SplitInstallStateUpdatedListener() {
    @Override
    public void onStateUpdate(SplitInstallSessionState state) {

        if (state.sessionId() == mySessionId) {
            switch (state.status()) {

                case SplitInstallSessionStatus.REQUIRES_USER_CONFIRMATION:

                    statusText.setText(
                        "Large Feature Module. Requesting Confirmation");

                    try {
                        manager.startConfirmationDialogForResult(state,
                                MainActivity.this, REQUEST_CODE);
                    } catch (IntentSender.SendIntentException ex) {
                        statusText.setText("Confirmation Request Failed.");
                    }
                    break;

.

.
```

Also, add an *onActivityResult()* method so that the app receives notification of the user's decision:

```
@Override
public void onActivityResult(int requestCode, int resultCode, Intent data) {
    if (requestCode == REQUEST_CODE) {
        if (resultCode == RESULT_OK) {
```

```
            statusText.setText("Beginning Installation.");
        } else {
            statusText.setText("User declined installation.");
        }
    }
}
```

Before these code changes can be tested, the size of the dynamic feature module needs to be increased above the 10MB limit. To achieve this we will add a large file as an asset to the project. Begin by right-clicking on the *my_dynamic_feature* entry in the Project tool window and selecting the *New -> Folder -> Assets Folder* menu option. In the configuration dialog, change the *Target Source Set* menu to *main* before clicking on the *Finish* button.

Next, download the following asset file to a temporary location on your development system:

https://www.ebookfrenzy.com/code/LargeAsset.zip

Once downloaded, locate the file in a file system browser, copy it and then paste it into the *assets* folder in the Android Studio Project tool window, clicking OK in the confirmation dialog:

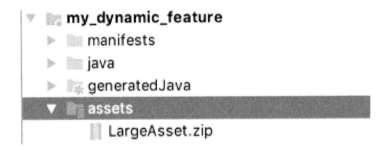

Figure 84-11

Repeat the usual steps to increment the version number, build the new app bundle, upload it to Google Play and roll out for testing. Delete the previous release from the device, install the new release and attempt to perform the feature download to test that the confirmation dialog appears as shown in Figure 84-12 below:

Figure 84-12

84.12 Using Deferred Installation

Deferred installation causes dynamic feature modules to be downloaded in the background and will be completed at the discretion of the operating system. When a deferred installation is initiated, the listener will be called with a pending status, but it is not otherwise possible to track the progress of the installation aside from checking whether or not the module has been installed.

To try deferred installation, modify the *installFeature()* method so that it reads as follows:

```
public void installFeature(View view) {
    manager.deferredInstall(Arrays.asList("my_dynamic_feature"));
}
```

Note that the *deferredInstall()* method is passed an array, allowing the installation of multiple modules to be deferred.

84.13 Removing a Dynamic Module

The final task in this project is to implement the *deleteFeature()* method as follows in the *MainActivity.java* file:

```
.
.
import java.util.Arrays;
.
.
public void deleteFeature(View view) {
    manager.deferredUninstall(Arrays.asList("my_dynamic_feature"));
}
```

The removal of the feature will be performed in the background by the operating system when additional storage space is needed. As with the *deferredInstall()* method, multiple features may be scheduled for removal in a single call.

84.14 Summary

This chapter has worked through the creation of an example app designed to demonstrate the use of dynamic feature modules within an Android app. Topics covered included the creation of a dynamic feature module and the use of the classes and methods of the Play Core Library to install and manage a dynamic feature module.

85. An Overview of Gradle in Android Studio

Up until this point it has, for the most part, been taken for granted that Android Studio will take the necessary steps to compile and run the application projects that have been created. Android Studio has been achieving this in the background using a system known as *Gradle*.

It is now time to look at how Gradle is used to compile and package together the various elements of an application project and to begin exploring how to configure this system when more advanced requirements are needed in terms of building projects in Android Studio.

85.1 An Overview of Gradle

Gradle is an automated build toolkit that allows the way in which projects are built to be configured and managed through a set of build configuration files. This includes defining how a project is to be built, what dependencies need to be fulfilled for the project to build successfully and what the end result (or results) of the build process should be.

The strength of Gradle lies in the flexibility that it provides to the developer. The Gradle system is a self-contained, command-line based environment that can be integrated into other environments through the use of plug-ins. In the case of Android Studio, Gradle integration is provided through the appropriately named Android Studio Plug-in.

Although the Android Studio Plug-in allows Gradle tasks to be initiated and managed from within Android Studio, the Gradle command-line wrapper can still be used to build Android Studio based projects, including on systems on which Android Studio is not installed.

The configuration rules to build a project are declared in Gradle build files and scripts based on the Groovy programming language.

85.2 Gradle and Android Studio

Gradle brings a number of powerful features to building Android application projects. Some of the key features are as follows:

85.2.1 Sensible Defaults

Gradle implements a concept referred to as *convention over configuration*. This simply means that Gradle has a pre-defined set of sensible default configuration settings that will be used unless they are overridden by settings in the build files. This means that builds can be performed with the minimum of configuration required by the developer. Changes to the build files are only needed when the default configuration does not meet your build needs.

85.2.2 Dependencies

Another key area of Gradle functionality is that of dependencies. Consider, for example, a module within an Android Studio project which triggers an intent to load another module in the project. The first module has, in effect, a dependency on the second module since the application will fail to build if the second module cannot be located and launched at runtime. This dependency can be declared in the Gradle build file for the first module so that the second module is included in the application build, or an error flagged in the event the second module cannot be found or built. Other examples of dependencies are libraries and JAR files on which the project depends in order to compile and run.

Gradle dependencies can be categorized as *local* or *remote*. A local dependency references an item that is present on the local file system of the computer system on which the build is being performed. A remote dependency refers to an item that is present on a remote server (typically referred to as a *repository*).

Remote dependencies are handled for Android Studio projects using another project management tool named *Maven*. If a remote dependency is declared in a Gradle build file using Maven syntax then the dependency will be downloaded automatically from the designated repository and included in the build process. The following dependency declaration, for example, causes the AppCompat library to be added to the project from the Google repository:

```
api 'androidx.appcompat:appcompat:1.0.2'
```

85.2.3 Build Variants

In addition to dependencies, Gradle also provides *build variant* support for Android Studio projects. This allows multiple variations of an application to be built from a single project. Android runs on many different devices encompassing a range of processor types and screen sizes. In order to target as wide a range of device types and sizes as possible it will often be necessary to build a number of different variants of an application (for example, one with a user interface for phones and another for tablet sized screens). Through the use of Gradle, this is now possible in Android Studio.

85.2.4 Manifest Entries

Each Android Studio project has associated with it an *AndroidManifest.xml* file containing configuration details about the application. A number of manifest entries can be specified in Gradle build files which are then auto-generated into the manifest file when the project is built. This capability is complementary to the build variants feature, allowing elements such as the application version number, application ID and SDK version information to be configured differently for each build variant.

85.2.5 APK Signing

The chapter entitled *"Creating, Testing and Uploading an Android App Bundle"* covered the creation of a signed release APK file using the Android Studio environment. It is also possible to include the signing information entered through the Android Studio user interface within a Gradle build file so that signed APK files can be generated from the command-line.

85.2.6 ProGuard Support

ProGuard is a tool included with Android Studio that optimizes, shrinks and obfuscates Java byte code to make it more efficient and harder to reverse engineer (the method by which the logic of an application can be identified by others through analysis of the compiled Java byte code). The Gradle build files provide the ability to control whether or not ProGuard is run on your application when it is built.

85.3 The Top-level Gradle Build File

A completed Android Studio project contains everything needed to build an Android application and consists of modules, libraries, manifest files and Gradle build files.

Each project contains one top-level Gradle build file. This file is listed as *build.gradle (Project: <project name>)* and can be found in the project tool window as highlighted in Figure 85-1:

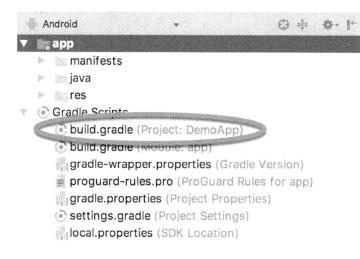

Figure 85-1

By default, the contents of the top level Gradle build file reads as follows:

```
// Top-level build file where you can add configuration options common to all sub-
projects/modules.

buildscript {
        repositories {
        google()
        jcenter()
    }
    dependencies {
        classpath 'com.android.tools.build:gradle:3.5.0-beta05'
                // NOTE: Do not place your application dependencies here; they
belong
        // in the individual module build.gradle files
    }
}

allprojects {
    repositories {
        google()
        jcenter()
    }
}

task clean(type: Delete) {
    delete rootProject.buildDir
}
```

As it stands all the file does is declare that remote libraries are to be obtained using the jcenter repository and that builds are dependent on the Android plugin for Gradle. In most situations it is not necessary to make any changes to this build file.

85.4 Module Level Gradle Build Files

An Android Studio application project is made up of one or more modules. Take, for example, a hypothetical application project named GradleDemo which contains two modules named Module1 and Module2 respectively. In this scenario, each of the modules will require its own Gradle build file. In terms of the project structure, these would be located as follows:

- Module1/build.gradle

- Module2/build.gradle

By default, the Module1 build.gradle file would resemble that of the following listing:

```
apply plugin: 'com.android.application'

android {
    compileSdkVersion 29
    buildToolsVersion "29.0.2"
    defaultConfig {
        applicationId "com.ebookfrenzy.module1"
        minSdkVersion 26
        targetSdkVersion 29
        versionCode 1
        versionName "1.0"
        testInstrumentationRunner "androidx.test.runner.AndroidJUnitRunner"
    }
    buildTypes {
        release {
            minifyEnabled false
            proguardFiles getDefaultProguardFile('proguard-android-optimize.
txt'), 'proguard-rules.pro'
        }
    }
}

dependencies {
    implementation fileTree(dir: 'libs', include: ['*.jar'])
    implementation "org.jetbrains.kotlin:kotlin-stdlib-jdk7:$kotlin_version"
    api 'androidx.appcompat:appcompat:1.0.2'
    api 'androidx.constraintlayout:constraintlayout:1.1.3'
    testImplementation 'junit:junit:4.12'
    androidTestImplementation 'androidx.test.ext:junit:1.1.1'
    androidTestImplementation 'androidx.test.espresso:espresso-core:3.2.0'
}
```

As is evident from the file content, the build file begins by declaring the use of the Gradle Android application plug-in:

```
apply plugin: 'com.android.application'
```

The *android* section of the file then states the version of the SDK to be used when building Module1.

```
android {
    compileSdkVersion 29
```

The items declared in the defaultConfig section define elements that are to be generated into the module's *AndroidManifest.xml* file during the build. These settings, which may be modified in the build file, are taken from the settings entered within Android Studio when the module was first created:

```
defaultConfig {
    applicationId "com.ebookfrenzy.module1"
    minSdkVersion 26
    targetSdkVersion 29
    versionCode 54
    versionName "54.0"
    testInstrumentationRunner "androidx.test.runner.AndroidJUnitRunner"
}
```

The buildTypes section contains instructions on whether and how to run ProGuard on the APK file when a release version of the application is built:

```
buildTypes {
    release {
        minifyEnabled false
        proguardFiles getDefaultProguardFile('proguard-android-optimize.txt'),
'proguard-rules.pro'
    }
}
```

As currently configured, ProGuard will not be run when Module1 is built. To enable ProGuard, the *minifyEnabled* entry needs to be changed from *false* to *true*. The *proguard-rules.pro* file can be found in the module directory of the project. Changes made to this file override the default settings in the *proguard-android.txt* file which is located on the Android SDK installation directory under *sdk/tools/proguard*.

Since no debug buildType is declared in this file, the defaults will be used (built without ProGuard, signed with a debug key and with debug symbols enabled).

An additional section, entitled *productFlavors* may also be included in the module build file to enable multiple build variants to be created.

Finally, the dependencies section lists any local and remote dependencies on which the module is dependent. The first dependency reads as follows:

```
implementation fileTree(dir: 'libs', include: ['*.jar'])
```

This is a standard line that tells the Gradle system that any JAR file located in the module's lib sub-directory is to be included in the project build. If, for example, a JAR file named myclasses.jar was present in the GradleDemo/Module1/lib folder of the project, that JAR file would be treated as a module dependency and included in the build process.

The last dependency lines in the above example file designate the Android libraries that need to be included from the Android Repository:

```
api 'androidx.appcompat:appcompat:1.0.2'
api 'androidx.constraintlayout:constraintlayout:1.1.3'
```

Note that the dependency declarations include version numbers to indicate which version of the library should be included.

85.5 Configuring Signing Settings in the Build File

The *"Creating, Testing and Uploading an Android App Bundle"* chapter of this book covered the steps involved in setting up keys and generating a signed release APK file using the Android Studio user interface. These settings may also be declared within a *signingSettings* section of the build.gradle file. For example:

```
apply plugin: 'com.android.application'

android {
    compileSdkVersion 28

    defaultConfig {
        .
        .
    }
    signingConfigs {
        release {
            storeFile file("keystore.release")
            storePassword "your keystore password here"
            keyAlias "your key alias here"
            keyPassword "your key password here"
        }
    }
    buildTypes {
        .
        .
        .
    }
}
```

The above example embeds the key password information directly into the build file. An alternative to this approach is to extract these values from system environment variables:

```
signingConfigs {
    release {
        storeFile file("keystore.release")
        storePassword System.getenv("KEYSTOREPASSWD")
        keyAlias "your key alias here"
        keyPassword System.getenv("KEYPASSWD")
    }
}
```

Yet another approach is to configure the build file so that Gradle prompts for the passwords to be entered during the build process:

```
signingConfigs {
    release {
        storeFile file("keystore.release")
        storePassword System.console().readLine
```

```
      ("\nEnter Keystore password: ")
    keyAlias "your key alias here"
    keyPassword System.console().readLIne("\nEnter Key password: ")
  }
}
```

85.6 Running Gradle Tasks from the Command-line

Each Android Studio project contains a Gradle wrapper tool for the purpose of allowing Gradle tasks to be invoked from the command line. This tool is located in the root directory of each project folder. While this wrapper is executable on Windows systems, it needs to have execute permission enabled on Linux and macOS before it can be used. To enable execute permission, open a terminal window, change directory to the project folder for which the wrapper is needed and execute the following command:

```
chmod +x gradlew
```

Once the file has execute permissions, the location of the file will either need to be added to your $PATH environment variable, or the name prefixed by ./ in order to run. For example:

```
./gradlew tasks
```

Gradle views project building in terms of a number of different tasks. A full listing of tasks that are available for the current project can be obtained by running the following command from within the project directory (remembering to prefix the command with a ./ if running on macOS or Linux):

```
gradlew tasks
```

To build a debug release of the project suitable for device or emulator testing, use the assembleDebug option:

```
gradlew assembleDebug
```

Alternatively, to build a release version of the application:

```
gradlew assembleRelease
```

85.7 Summary

For the most part, Android Studio performs application builds in the background without any intervention from the developer. This build process is handled using the Gradle system, an automated build toolkit designed to allow the ways in which projects are built to be configured and managed through a set of build configuration files. While the default behavior of Gradle is adequate for many basic project build requirements, the need to configure the build process is inevitable with more complex projects. This chapter has provided an overview of the Gradle build system and configuration files within the context of an Android Studio project.

Index

Symbols

<application> 445

<changeBounds> 324

<fade> 324

<fragment> 223

<fragment> element 223

<menu> 311

<receiver> 428

<service> 445, 460, 467

<transitionSet> 324

<uses-permission> 408

Code Reformatting 67

@layout/toolbar_fragment 234

.well-known folder 655

A

AbsoluteLayout 106

accelerate_decelerate_interpolator 326

accelerateDecelerateInterpolator 327

AccelerateDecelerateInterpolator 322

AccelerateDecelerateInterpolator() method 326

accelerate_interpolator 326

accelerateInterpolator 327

AccelerateInterpolator 322

AccelerateInterpolator() method 326

ACCESS_COARSE_LOCATION permission 588

ACCESS_FINE_LOCATION permission 588

ACTION_CREATE_DOCUMENT 555

ACTION_CREATE_INTENT 556

ACTION_DOWN 198

ACTION_MOVE 198

ACTION_OPEN_DOCUMENT 549

ACTION_OPEN_DOCUMENT intent 548

ACTION_POINTER_DOWN 198

ACTION_POINTER_UP 198

ACTION_UP 198

ACTION_VIEW 423

Active / Running state 80

Activity 73, 83

   adding to a project 155

   adding views in Java code 175

   class 83

   creation 14

   Entire Lifetime 88

   Foreground Lifetime 88

   lifecycle methods 86

   lifecycles 77

   returning data from 406

   state change example 91

   state changes 83

   states 80

   Visible Lifetime 88

ActivityCompat class 593

Activity Lifecycle 79

Activity Manager 72

Activity Stack 79

Actual screen pixels 166

adb

   command-line tool 53

   list devices 53

   restart server 54

ADB

   enabling on Android devices 53

   Linux configuration 56

   macOS configuration 54

   overview 53

   testing connection 56

   Windows configuration 55

addCategory() method 427

addMarker() method 617

addView() method 170

ADD_VOICEMAIL permission 588

Advanced Profiling 669

android

Index

checkableBehavior 313

commandline tool 33

exported 445

gestureColor 217

layout_behavior property 389

onClick 225

orderInCategory 312

process 467

transitionOrdering 325

uncertainGestureColor 217

android\

  onClick Resource 189

  process 446

Android

  Activity 73

  architecture 69

  events 189

  intents 74

  runtime 70

  SDK Packages 6

android.app 70

Android Architecture Components 241

android.content 70

android.content.Intent 405

android.database 70

Android Debug Bridge. *See* ADB

Android Design Support Library 343

Android Development

  System Requirements 3

Android Devices

  designing for different 105

android.graphics 70

android.hardware 70

android.intent.action 433

android.intent.action.BOOT_COMPLETED 446

android.intent.action.MAIN 423

android.intent.category.LAUNCHER 423

Android Libraries 70

AndroidManifest.xml file 156

android.media 71

Android Monitor tool window 31, 96

Android Native Development Kit 71

android.net 71

android.opengl 71

android.os 71

android.permission.RECORD_AUDIO 597

android.print 71

Android Profiler 669

Android Project

  create new 13

android.provider 71

Android SDK Location

  identifying 8

Android SDK Manager 6, 7, 9

Android SDK Packages

  version requirements 7

Android SDK Tools

  command-line access 8

  Linux 10

  macOS 10

  Windows 7 8

  Windows 8 9

Android Software Stack 69

Android Storage Access Framework 548

Android Studio

  changing theme 51

  downloading 3

  Editor Window 46

  installation 4

  Linux installation 5

  macOS installation 4

  Main Window 46

  Menu Bar 46

  Navigation Bar 46

  Project tool window 47

  setup wizard 5

  Status Bar 47

  Toolbar 46

  updating 11

  Welcome Screen 45

  Windows installation 4

android.text 71

Android tool window 49

android.util 71

android.view 71

android.view.View 108

android.view.ViewGroup 105, 108

Android Virtual Device. *See* AVD

  overview 27

Android Virtual Device Manager 27

android.webkit 71

android.widget 71

Animation framework 322

anticipate_interpolator 326

anticipateInterpolator 327

AnticipateInterpolator 322

AnticipateInterpolator() method 326

anticipate_overshoot_interpolator 326

anticipateOvershootInterpolator 327

AnticipateOvershootInterpolator 322

AnticipateOvershootInterpolator() method 326

APK analyzer 700

APK file 694

  split 704

APK File

  analyzing 700

APK Signing 732

APK Wizard dialog 692

app

  showAsAction 312

App Architecture

  modern 241

AppBar

  anatomy of 387

appbar_scrolling_view_behavior 389

App Bundles 689

  creating 694

  overview 689

  revisions 699

  uploading 696

AppCompatActivity class 85

Application

  stopping 31

Application Context 75

Application Framework 71

Application Manifest 75

Application Resources 75

App Link

  Adding Intent Filter 662

  Assistant 657

  Digital Assets Link file 655

  Intent Filter Handling 662

  Intent Filters 653

  Intent Handling 654

  Testing 666

  tutorial 657

  URL Mapping 659

  website association 666

App Link Assistant 657

App Links 653

  overview 653

Apply Changes 183

  Apply Changes and Restart Activity 183

  Apply Code Changes 183

  fallback settings 185

  options 183

  Run App 183

  tutorial 185

Architecture Components 241

ART 70

assetlinks.json 655

AsyncTask

  doInBackground() method 438

  example 435

  onPostExecute() method 438

  onPreExecute() method 438

  onProgressUpdate() method 438

  publishProgress() method 439

  subclassing 437

  thread pool executor 440

Audio

  supported formats 595

Audio Recording 595

Audo Playback 595

Autoconnect Mode 132

AutoTransition class 321, 323

AVD

  command-line creation 28, 33

Index

configuration files 34

creation 28

overview 27

renaming 34

running an application 29

starting 29

Startup size and orientation 29

B

Background Process 78

Barriers 126

adding 143

constrained views 126

Base APK file 704

Baseline Alignment 125

beginDelayedTransition

tutorial 329

beginDelayedTransition() method 321, 328

beginTransaction() method 224

Binding Expressions 265

one-way 265

two-way 266

bindService() method 444, 457, 462

Biometric Authentication 679

callbacks 683

overview 679

tutorial 679

Biometric Prompt 685

BitmapFactory 550

black activity 14

Blank template 109

Blueprint view 131

BODY_SENSORS permission 588

Bottom Up 673

bounce_interpolator 326

bounceInterpolator 327

BounceInterpolator 322

BounceInterpolator() method 326

Bound Service 443, 444, 457

adding to a project 458

Implementing the Binder 458

Interaction options 457

BoundService class 459

Broadcast Intent 427

example 430

overview 74, 427

sending 430

Sticky 429

Broadcast Receiver 427

adding to manifest file 432

creation 431

overview 74, 428

BroadcastReceiver class 428

BroadcastReceiver superclass 431

BufferedReader object 562

Build Variants 732

Build Variants tool window 49

Bundle class 100

Bundled Notifications 481

C

Calendar permissions 588

Call Chart 674

CALL_PHONE permission 588

CAMERA permission 588

Camera permissions 588

CameraUpdateFactory class

methods 618

CancellationSignal 684

Canvas class 648

Captures tool window 49

CardView

example 369

layout file 367

responding to selection of 375

CardView class 367

CATEGORY_OPENABLE 548

C/C++ Libraries 71

Chain bias 150

chain head 124

chains 124

Chains

creation of 147

Chain style

changing 149

chain styles 124

changeBounds transition 332

CharSequence 101

CheckBox 105

checkSelfPermission() method 592

Circle class 607

Code completion 62

Code Editor

  basics 59

  Code completion 62

  Code Generation 64

  Code Reformatting 67

  Document Tabs 60

  Editing area 60

  Gutter Area 60

  Splitting 61

  Statement Completion 63

  Status Bar 61

Code Generation 64

code samples

  download 1

CollapsingToolbarLayout

  example 391

  introduction 390

  parallax mode 390

  pin mode 390

  setting scrim color 393

  setting title 393

  with image 390

Color class 649

COLOR_MODE_COLOR 624, 644

COLOR_MODE_MONOCHROME 624, 644

com.android.application 707

com.android.dynamic-feature 707

Common Gestures 205

  detection 205

Component tree 17

Configuration APK file 704

Constraint Bias 123

  adjusting 137

ConstraintLayout

advantages of 128

Availability 128

Barriers 126

Baseline Alignment 125

chain bias 150

chain head 124

chains 124

chain styles 124

Constraint Bias 123

Constraints 121

conversion to 146

deleting constraints 136

guidelines 142

Guidelines 126

manual constraint manipulation 133

Margins 122, 137

Opposing Constraints 122, 139

overview of 121

Packed chain 125, 150

ratios 128, 151

Spread chain 124

Spread inside 150

Spread inside chain 124

tutorial 155

using in Android Studio 131

Weighted chain 125, 150

Widget Dimensions 126, 141

Widget Group Alignment 145

ConstraintLayout chains

  creation of 147

  in layout editor 147

ConstraintLayout Chain style

  changing 149

Constraints

  deleting 136

ConstraintSet

  addToHorizontalChain() method 172

  addToVerticalChain() method 172

  alignment constraints 171

  apply to layout 170

  applyTo() method 170

  centerHorizontally() method 171

Index

centerVertically() method 171

chains 171

clear() method 172

clone() method 171

connect() method 170

connect to parent 170

constraint bias 171

copying constraints 171

create 170

create connection 170

createHorizontalChain() method 171

createVerticalChain() method 171

guidelines 172

removeFromHorizontalChain() method 172

removeFromVerticalChain() method 172

removing constraints 172

rotation 173

scaling 172

setGuidelineBegin() method 172

setGuidelineEnd() method 172

setGuidelinePercent() method 172

setHorizonalBias() method 171

setRotationX() method 173

setRotationY() method 173

setScaleX() method 172

setScaleY() method 172

setTransformPivot() method 173

setTransformPivotX() method 173

setTransformPivotY() method 173

setVerticalBias() method 171

sizing constraints 171

tutorial 175

view IDs 177

ConstraintSet class 169, 170

ConstraintSet.PARENT_ID 170

Constraint Sets 170

Contacts permissions 588

container view 105

content layout 16

Content Provider 72

overview 75

Context class 75

CoordinatorLayout 106, 387, 389

CPU Profiler 672

createPrintDocumentAdapter() method 639

Custom Document Printing 627, 639

Custom Gesture

recognition 211

Custom Interpolator 327

Custom Print Adapter

implementation 641

Custom Print Adapters 639

cycle_interpolator 326

cycleInterpolator 327

CycleInterpolator 322

CycleInterpolator() method 326

D

dangerous permissions 587

list of 588

Dark Theme 31

enable on device 31

Data Access Object (DAO) 512

Data Access Objects (DAO) 516

Database Rows 506

Database Schema 505

Database Tables 505

Data binding

binding expressions 265

Data Binding 243

binding classes 264

enabling 271

event and listener binding 266

key components 261

overview 261

tutorial 269

with LiveData 243

DDMS 31

Debugging

enabling on device 53

decelerate_interpolator 326

decelerateInterpolator 328

DecelerateInterpolator 322

DecelerateInterpolator() method 326

Density-independent pixels 165

Density Independent Pixels

converting to pixels 180

Developer Signature 608

Device Definition

custom 118

Digital Asset Link file 667

Digital Assets Link file 655

Direct Reply Input 491

Direct Reply Notification 485

document provider 547

dp 165

Dynamic Delivery 706

Dynamic Feature APK 704

Dynamic Feature Module

architecture 703

overview 703

removal 729

tutorial 713

Dynamic Feature Modules

deferred installation 709

handling of large 711

Dynamic Feature Support

adding to project 713

Dynamic State 86

saving 99

E

Empty Process 79

Empty template 109

Emulator

battery simulation 40

cellular configuration 40

configuring fingerprints 42

creation 28

directional pad 40

extended control options 39

Extended controls 39

fingerprint 40

location configuration 39

phone settings 40

resize 39

rotate 38

Screen Record 40

Snapshots 40

starting 29

take screenshot 38

toolbar 37

toolbar options 37

Virtual Sensors 40

zoom 38

enabling ADB support 53

Energy Profiler 678

Event Handling 189

example 190

Event Listener 192

Event Listeners 190

Event Log tool window 49

Events

consuming 193

explicit

intent 74

explicit intent 405

Explicit Intent 405

Extended Control

options 39

F

Favorites tool window 49

Files

switching between 60

findPointerIndex() method 198

Fingerprint

emulation 42

Fingerprint authentication

device configuration 680

permission 680

steps to implement 679

Fingerprint Authentication

overview 679

tutorial 679

FLAG_INCLUDE_STOPPED_PACKAGES 427

Flame Chart 674

flexible space area 387

Index

floating action button 16, 17, 110, 343, 347

  changing appearance of 346

  margins 344

  overview of 343

  removing 111

  sizes 344

Foldable Devices 89

  multi-resume 89

Foldable Emulator 496

Foldables 495

Foreground Process 78

Forward-geocoding 611

Fragment

  creation 221

  event handling 225

  XML file 221, 222

FragmentActivity class 85

Fragment Communication 225

FragmentPagerAdapter class 358

Fragments 221

  adding in code 224

  duplicating 355

  example 229

  overview 221

FrameLayout 106

G

Geocoder class 610

Geocoder object 611

Geocoding 610

Gesture Builder Application 211

  building and running 212

Gesture Detector class 205

GestureDetectorCompat 209

  instance creation 209

GestureDetectorCompat class 205

GestureDetector.OnDoubleTapListener 205, 206

GestureDetector.OnGestureListener 206

GestureLibrary 211

GestureLibrary class 211

GestureOverlayView 211

  configuring color 217

  configuring multiple strokes 217

GestureOverlayView class 211

GesturePerformedListener 211

Gestures

  interception of 217

Gestures File

  creation 212

  extract from SD card 213

  loading into application 214

GET_ACCOUNTS permission 588

getAction() method 433

getFromLocation() method 611

getId() method 170

getIntent() method 406

getItemId() method 313

getPointerCount() method 198

getPointerId() method 198

getSceneForLayout() method 323, 338

getService() method 462

GNU/Linux 70

go() method 323

Google Cloud Print 622

Google Drive 548

  printing to 622

GoogleMap 607

  map types 614

GoogleMap.MAP_TYPE_HYBRID 614

GoogleMap.MAP_TYPE_NONE 614

GoogleMap.MAP_TYPE_NORMAL 614

GoogleMap.MAP_TYPE_SATELLITE 614

GoogleMap.MAP_TYPE_TERRAIN 615

Google Maps 607

Google Maps Android API 607

  Controlling the Map Camera 618

  developer signature 608

  displaying controls 615

  gesture handling 616

  Map Markers 617

  overview 607

Google Play Developer Console 690

Gradle

  APK signing settings 736

746

Build Variants 732

command line tasks 737

dependencies 731

Manifest Entries 732

overview 731

sensible defaults 731

Gradle Build File

top level 732

Gradle Build Files

module level 734

Gradle tool window 49

GridLayout 106

GridLayoutManager 365

H

Handler class 466

HP Print Services Plugin 621

HTML printing 625

HTML Printing

example 629

I

IBinder 444, 459

IBinder object 457, 465, 467

Image Printing 624

implicit

intent 74

implicit intent 405

Implicit Intent 407

Implicit Intents

example 419

in 165

In-Memory Database 519

Instant Dynamic Feature Module 704

Intent 74

explicit 74

implicit 74

Intent Availability

checking for 409

Intent.CATEGORY_OPENABLE 556

intent filters 405

Intent Filters 408

App Link 653

intent resolution 408

Intents 405

overview 405

Intent Service 443

IntentService 450

IntentService class 443, 446, 447

Intent URL 421

Internet Permission 568

Interpolator

custom 327

interpolatorElement 327

Interpolators

transition 322

transitions 326

J

Java Native Interface 71

Jetpack 241

overview 241

K

Keyboard Shortcuts 50

Keystore File

creation 692

Killed state 80

L

launcher activity 156

layout_collapseMode

parallax 392

pin 392

layout_constraintDimentionRatio 152

layout_constraintHorizontal_bias 150

layout_constraintVertical_bias 150

layout editor

ConstraintLayout chains 147

Layout Editor 17, 155

Autoconnect Mode 132

Component Tree 112

design mode 22, 112

device screen 112

Index

example project 155

Inference Mode 133

palette 112

properties panel 112

Sample Data 117

Setting Properties 115

text mode 22, 114

toolbar 112

user interface design 157

view conversion 117

Layout Editor Tool

changing orientation 17

overview 111

Layout Managers 105

LayoutResultCallback object 645

Layouts 105

layout_scrollFlags

enterAlwaysCollapsed mode 389

enterAlways mode 389

exitUntilCollapsed mode 389

scroll mode 389

libc 71

Lifecycle

awareness 279

components 244

owners 279

states and events 281

tutorial 283

Lifecycle-Aware Components 279

Lifecycle Methods 86

Lifecycle Observer 283

creating a 283

Lifecycle Owner

creating a 286

Lifecycles

modern 244

linear_interpolator 327

linearInterpolator 328

LinearInterpolator 322

LinearInterpolator() method 326

LinearLayout 106

LinearLayoutManager 365

LinearLayoutManager layout 374

Linux Kernel 70

list devices 53

ListView

adaptor 348

adding items 348

example 347

LiveData 242, 255

adding to ViewModel 255

observer 257

tutorial 255

Local Bound Service 457

example 457

Location Manager 72

Location permission 588

LogCat

enabling 96

filter configuration 96

M

Main Thread 435

Manifest File

permissions 422

Maps 607

MapView 607

adding to a layout 611

Marker class 607

Master/Detail Flow

anatomy of 397

creation 396

Object Kind 396, 397

two pane mode 395

match_parent properties 165

Material design 343

MediaController

adding to VideoView instance 569

MediaController class 566

methods 566

MediaPlayer class 595

methods 595

MediaRecorder class 595

methods 596

recording audio 596

Memory Profiler 675

Menu Editor 314

Menu Item Selections 313

Menus 311

  menu editor 314

Messenger object 467

Microphone

  checking for availability 598

Microphone permissions 588

mm 165

MotionEvent 197, 198, 219

  getActionMasked() 198

moveCamera() method 618

Multiple Touches

  handling 198

multi-resume 89

Multi-Touch

  example 198

Multi-touch Event Handling 197

Multi-Window

  attributes 499

Multi-Window Mode

  detecting 500

  entering 497

  launching activity into 501

Multi-Window Notifications 500

multi-window support 89

Multi-Window Support

  enabling 499

My Location Layer 608

N

Navigation 289

  adding destinations 301

  overview 289

  pass data with safeargs 307

  passing arguments 294

  safeargs 294

  stack 290

  tutorial 297

Navigation Action

triggering 294

Navigation Architecture Component 289

Navigation Component

  tutorial 297

Navigation Controller

  accessing 293

Navigation Graph 292, 298

  adding actions 304

  creating a 298

Navigation Host 291

  declaring 299

Network Profiler 676

non-thread-safe code 435

normal permissions 587

Notification

  adding actions 480

  direct reply 485

  Direct Reply Input 491

  issuing a basic 476

  launch activity from a 479

  PendingIntent 487

  Reply Action 488

  updating direct reply 492

Notifications 471

  bundled 481

  overview 471

Notifications Manager 72

O

Observer

  implementing a LiveData 257

onActivityResult() method 407, 416, 554, 556

onAttach() method 226

onBind() method 444, 450, 457, 465

onBindViewHolder() method 373

onClickListener 190, 192, 194

onClick() method 189

onCreateContextMenuListener 190

onCreate() method 78, 86, 444

onCreateOptionsMenu() method 312

on-demand modules 703

onDestroy() method 87, 444

Index

onDoubleTap() method 205

onDown() method 205

onFling() method 205

onFocusChangeListener 190

OnFragmentInteractionListener
  implementation 305

onGesturePerformed() method 211

onHandleIntent() method 443, 444, 448

onKeyListener 190

onLayoutFailed() method 645

onLayoutFinished() method 645

onLongClickListener 190, 193

onLongClick() method 194

onLongPress() method 205

onMapReady() method 613

onOptionsItemSelected() method 313

onOptionsItemsSelected() method 318

onPageFinished() callback 631

onPause() method 87

onReceive() method 78, 428, 429, 431

onRequestPermissionsResult() method 591, 603

onRestart() method 86

onRestoreInstanceState() method 87

onResume() method 78, 87

onSaveInstanceState() method 87

onScaleBegin() method 217

onScaleEnd() method 217

onScale() method 217

onScroll() method 205

OnSeekBarChangeListener 237

onServiceConnected() method 457, 461, 468

onServiceDisconnected() method 457, 461, 468

onShowPress() method 205

onSingleTapUp() method 205

onStartCommand() method 444, 451, 453

onStart() method 87

onStop() method 87

onTabSelectedListener 361

onTouchEvent() method 205, 217

onTouchListener 190, 197

onTouch() method 197

openFileDescriptor() method 548, 549

Overflow Menu 311
  creation 311
  displaying 312
  overview 311
  XML file 311

Overflow Menus
  Checkable Item Groups 313

overshoot_interpolator 327

overshootInterpolator 328

OvershootInterpolator 322

OvershootInterpolator() method 326

P

Package Explorer 15

Package Manager 72

PackageManager class 598

PackageManager.FEATURE_MICROPHONE 598

PackageManager.PERMISSION_DENIED 589

PackageManager.PERMISSION_GRANTED 589

Package Name 14

Packed chain 125, 150

PageRange 646, 647

Paint class 649

parent view 107

Paused state 80

PdfDocument 627

PdfDocument.Page 639, 646

PendingIntent class 487

Permission
  checking for 589

permissions
  dangerous 587
  normal 587

Persistent State 86

Phone permissions 588

picker 547

Pinch Gesture
  detection 217
  example 218

Pinch Gesture Recognition 211

Play Core Library 709, 713

Polygon class 607

Polyline class 607

PrintAttributes 644

PrintDocumentAdapter 627, 639

PrintDocumentInfo 644

Printing

   color 624

   monochrome 624

Printing framework

   architecture 621

Printing Framework 621

Print Job

   starting 650

Print Manager 621

PrintManager service 631

PROCESS_OUTGOING_CALLS permission 588

Process States 77

Profiler 669

   Bottom Up 673

   Call Chart 674

   CPU Profiler 672

   enable advanced profiling 669

   Energy Profiler 678

   Flame Chart 674

   Instrumented 673

   Memory 675

   Network 676

   Sampled 672

   Sessions Panel 671

   Top Down 673

ProgressBar 105

proguard-rules.pro file 735

ProGuard Support 732

Project Name 14

Project tool window 15, 49

pt 165

putExtra() method 405, 427

px 166

Q

Quick Documentation 67

R

RadioButton 105

ratios 151

READ_CALENDAR permission 588

READ_CALL_LOG permission 588

READ_CONTACTS permission 588

READ_EXTERNAL_STORAGE permission 589

READ_PHONE_STATE permission 588

READ_SMS permission 588

RECEIVE_MMS permission 588

RECEIVE_SMS permission 588

RECEIVE_WAP_PUSH permission 588

Recent Files Navigation 50

RECORD_AUDIO permission 588

Recording Audio

   permission 597

RecyclerView 365

   adding to layout file 366

   example 369

   GridLayoutManager 365

   initializing 374

   LinearLayoutManager 365

   StaggeredGridLayoutManager 366

RecyclerView Adapter

   creation of 371

RecyclerView.Adapter 366, 371

   getItemCount() method 366

   onBindViewHolder() method 366

   onCreateViewHolder() method 366

RecyclerView.ViewHolder

   getAdapterPosition() method 376

registerReceiver() method 429

RelativeLayout 106

release mode 689

releasePersistableUriPermission() method 551

Release Preparation 689

Remote Bound Service 465

   client communication 465

   implementation 466

   manifest file declaration 467

RemoteInput.Builder() method 487

RemoteInput Object 487

Remote Service

launching and binding 468

sending a message 469

Repository

tutorial 529

Repository Modules 244

requestPermissions() method 591

Resource

string creation 21

Resource File 22

Resource Management 77

Resource Manager 72

result receiver 429

Reverse-geocoding 611

Reverse Geocoding 610

Room

Data Access Object (DAO) 512

entities 512, 513

In-Memory Database 519

Repository 512

Room Database 512

tutorial 529

Room Database Persistence 511

Room Persistence Library 509, 511

root element 105

root view 107

Runtime Permission Requests 587

Run tool window 49

S

safeargs 294, 307

Sample Data 117, 379

tutorial 379

ScaleGestureDetector class 217

Scale-independent 166

Scenes

transition 321

Scene Transitions 322

tutorial 335

SD Card storage 597

SDK Manager 45

SDK Packages 6

SDK Settings 6

Secure Sockets Layer (SSL) 71

SeekBar 229

sendBroadcast() method 427, 429

sendOrderedBroadcast() method 427, 429

SEND_SMS permission 588

sendStickyBroadcast() method 427

Sensor permissions 588

Service

anatomy 444

launch at system start 446

manifest file entry 445

overview 74

run in separate process 446

starting 449

ServiceConnection class 468

Service Process 78

Service Restart Options 445

Service Tasks

in new thread 453

setAudioEncoder() method 596

setAudioSource() method 596

setBackgroundColor() 170

setCompassEnabled() method 616

setContentView() method 169, 175

setId() method 170

setInterpolator() method 326

setMyLocationButtonEnabled() method 616

setOnClickListener() method 189, 192

setOnDoubleTapListener() method 205, 209

setOutputFile() method 596

setOutputFormat() method 596

setResult() method 407

setRotateGesturesEnabled() method 617

setScrollGesturesEnabled() method 616

setText() method 102

setTiltGesturesEnabled() method 616

setVideoSource() method 596

setZoomControlsEnabled() method 615, 616

shouldOverrideUrlLoading() method 630

shouldShowRequestPermissionRationale() method 593

SimpleOnScaleGestureListener 217

SimpleOnScaleGestureListener class 219

SMS permissions 588

Snackbar 343, 344, 345

  adding an action item 350

  overview of 344

Snapshots

  emulator 41

sp 166

Space class 106

split APK files 704

SplitCompatApplication 708

SplitInstallManager 709

Spread chain 124

Spread inside 150

Spread inside chain 124

SQL 506

SQLite 505

  AVD command-line use 507

  Columns and Data Types 505

  overview 506

  Primary keys 506

StaggeredGridLayoutManager 366

startActivityForResult() method 407, 416

startActivity() method 405

Started Service 443

  example 447

startForeground() method 78

START_NOT_STICKY 445

START_REDELIVER_INTENT 445

startService() method 443, 450

START_STICKY 445

State

  restoring 102

State Change

  handling 81

Statement Completion 63

status bar 387

Sticky Broadcast Intents 429

Stopped state 80

stopSelf() method 443

stopService() method 443

Storage Access Framework 547

  ACTION_CREATE_DOCUMENT 548

  ACTION_OPEN_DOCUMENT 548

  deleting a file 551

  example 553

  file creation 555

  file filtering 548

  file reading 550

  file writing 550

  intents 548

  MIME Types 549

  Persistent Access 551

  picker 547

Storage permissions 589

StringBuilder object 562

strings.xml file 24

Structured Query Language 506

Structure tool window 49

SupportMapFragment class 607

Switcher 50

syncTask 435

System Broadcasts 433

system requirements 3

T

tab bar 387

TabLayout 353

  adding to layout 356

  addTab() method 360, 363

  app

    tabGravity property 362

    tabMode property 362

  example 354

  fixed mode 362

  getCount() method 353

  getItem() method 353

  onTabSelectedListener 361

  overview 353

  scrollable mode 362

  setIcon() method 363

  setting tab icons 363

  setting tab text 360

TableLayout 106, 521

TableRow 521

Index

Telephony Manager 72

Templates

  blank vs. empty 109

Terminal tool window 49

Thread Handlers 435

Threads 435

  creating 437

  overview 435

TODO tool window 49

toolbar 387

ToolbarListener 225, 226

tools

  layout 223

tool window bars 47

Tool Windows 47

Top Down 673

Touch Actions 198

Touch Event Listener

  implementation 199

Touch Events

  intercepting 197

Touch handling 197

Transition class 326

Transition File

  creating a 339

  entering 337

  loading 338

TransitionManager 331

TransitionManager class 321, 323, 324

Transitions

  custom 324

  interpolators 322

  Root Container 335

Transition Scene

  using 340

TransitionSet 321, 324

TransitionSets

  in code 324

  in XML 324

Transitions Framework 321

UiSettings class 607

unbindService() method 444

unregisterReceiver() method 429

URL Mapping 659

USB debugging

  enabling 54

USE_BIOMETRIC 680

user interface state 86

USE_SIP permission 588

V

Video Playback 565

VideoView class 565

  methods 565

  supported formats 565

View class

  setting properties 176

view conversion 117

ViewGroup 105

View Groups 105

View Hierarchy 107

ViewHolder class 366

  sample implementation 372

ViewModel

  adding LiveData 255

  data access 253

  fragment association 251

  overview 242

  tutorial 247

ViewPager 353, 357

  adapter 357

  adding to layout 356

  example 354

Views 105

  Java creation 169

View System 72

Virtual Device Configuration dialog 28

Virtual Sensors 40

Visible Process 78

W

WebViewClient 625, 630

U

WebView view 421

Weighted chain 125, 150

Widget Dimensions 126

Widget Group Alignment 145

Widgets palette 158

wrap_content properties 167

WRITE_CALENDAR permission 588

WRITE_CALL_LOG permission 588

WRITE_CONTACTS permission 588

WRITE_EXTERNAL_STORAGE permission 589

X

XML Layout File

manual creation 165

vs. Java Code 169

CPSIA information can be obtained
at www.ICGtesting.com
Printed in the USA
LVHW060333280220
648380LV00003B/64

9 781951 442019